IDENTITY'S ARCHITECT

A Biography of Erik H. Erikson

LAWRENCE J. FRIEDMAN

SCRIBNER

SCRIBNER
1230 Avenue of the Americas
New York, NY 10020

DESIGNED BY ERICH HOBBING

Set in Stempel Garamond

Manufactured in the United States of America

1   3   5   7   9   10   8   6   4   2

Library of Congress Cataloging-in-Publication Data
Friedman, Lawrence Jacob, 1940–
Identity's architect : a biography of
Erik H. Erikson / Lawrence J. Friedman.
p.   cm.
Includes bibliographical references and index.
1. Erikson, Erik H. (Erik Homburger), 1902– .
2. Psychoanalysts—United States—Biography.
3. Psychoanalysis—History. I. Title.
BF109.E7F74   1999
150.19'5'092—dc21   98-50266
[B]
CIP

ISBN 0-684-19525-9

Permission for the use of family letters and photographs
generously provided by the Erikson family.

For Sharon
with love and gratitude

Acknowledgments

This biography would not have been possible without considerable assistance from a great many people. For one, there were the archivists. Over the years, I benefited appreciably from Leslie Morris and her staff at the manuscript department of Harvard's Houghton Library, which houses the major Erikson manuscript collection. For important Erikson materials in other American collections, I owe debts to Fred Bauman at the Library of Congress Manuscript Division; Bernard Crystal at the Columbia University Manuscript Library; Thomas Rosenbaum and Darwin Stapleton at the Rockefeller Archive Center; Sharon Ochsenhirt and Marion McPherson at the Archives of the History of American Psychology (University of Akron); Peter Hirtle at the History of Medicine Division, National Library of Medicine; Judith Schiff of Yale University Manuscripts and Archives; and William Roberts at the University of California, Berkeley, campus archives. Additionally, Harriet Harvey and Frances Davidson shared their film and photographic collections, while Donald Lamm secured important data from the W. W. Norton organizational archive. Archivists abroad were exceedingly important. I owe a special debt to Ingrid Scholz-Strasser of Vienna's Sigmund Freud House, to Erica Davies and Michael Molnar at the Freud Museum in London, and to the staff of the Karlsruhe General Archives. Finn and Martha Abrahamsen's help in navigating the Danish National Archives was extraordinary.

Several in the Wellfleet group of activist scholars were crucial to my biographic formulations. Robert Lifton and Charles Strozier first suggested that I "do Erik," while biographers extraordinary Margaret Brenman-Gibson, Betty Jean Lifton, and John Mack assured me that I could accomplish the task. Gerald Holton schooled me in the Germany of Erikson's childhood. Catherine Bateson helped me connect him to her mother, Margaret Mead, and to the broader culture and personality movement. During a very early presentation at a Wellfleet gathering, Kai and Joanna Erikson encouraged me to explore all of the layers of Erik's mind and spirit and assured me that I was describing "Pop."

My mentor, Donald Meyer, initiated me to the benefits of critically evaluating a colleague's writing. For many decades now, I have been blessed with a remarkable group of colleagues who have commented extensively on early drafts of my books as I looked over their work. This sharing habit started with Ronald Takaki and then Richard King and Eliane Silverman. By the point I was ready to show the rough Erikson manuscript, the circle had come to include Bertram and Anne Wyatt-Brown, Lani and Joseph Gerson, Gerald Grob, Robert Abzug, Brewster Smith, S. P. Fullinwider, James Anderson, David Andersen, Nathan Hale, Mark McGarvie, and James Jones. Ellen Herman, Ellen Dwyer, Peter Heller, Gary Hess, Arvid Perez, Benjamin Harris, and Irving Alexander carefully evaluated troublesome chapters. Paul Roazen, an Erikson scholar himself, was exceedingly generous with insights and materials from start to finish. Indiana University colleagues helped in all sorts of ways, among them James and Jeanne Madison, John Bodnar, William Cohen, David and Esther Thelen, Wendy Gamber, James Capshew, Michael Grossberg, Nancy Cridland, and Carol Polsgrove. This is not to slight a remarkable group of Indiana doctoral students who cogently looked over my drafts as I looked over theirs: Roark Atkinson, Daphne Cunningham, Damon Freeman, Robert Grimm, Julie Plaut, Lynn Pohl, Victoria Resnick, Paul Schadewald, Steve Warren, and Cynthia Yaudes. Nor should I make light of the insights, materials, and memories provided by Erikson's own students, including Virginia and John Demos, Janice Abarbanel, Gordon Fellman, Howard Gardner, Gordon Harper, Richard Hunt, Stephen Schlein, Daniel Benveniste, John Ross, Sudhir Kakar, Richard Sennett, Peter Wood, Dorothy Zinberg, and especially Pamela Daniels.

Psychotherapists of diverse orientations enhanced my understanding of the clinical art and helped me to see why Erikson was so very good at it. Let me single out David Wilcox, Stephen Schlein, Rudolf Ekstein, Walling Mariea, Julie Bloom, Margaret Brenman-Gibson, Gerard Fromm, Ess White, and Edward Shapiro. Psychoanalyst Robert Wallerstein offered me wonderful insight about his friend Erik and gave my manuscript a very thorough reading. While she cut my hair over the years, Sue Schroeder offered some cogent clinical perspectives of her own.

In the increasingly difficult book-publishing world, I was especially fortunate. For the third time, I enjoyed the very wise counsel of Gerard McCauley, an extraordinary literary agent. Once more, I had the brilliant editing of Ellen Joseph. A decade ago, Ellen taught me how to write for a general audience and to maintain a vigorous story line. Jane Rosenman, Caroline Kim, Nan Graham, Scott Moyers, William Goldstein, and Robert Stewart all made Scribner a publishing house of choice.

In the course of a difficult decade, I came to understand and to describe Erik

Erikson. Two families—his and mine—aided substantially in the process. The warmth, encouragement, tolerance, trust, and playfulness of Joan, Jon, Sue, Kai, and Joanna were remarkable. One could not ask for more. Ruth Hirsch and Ellen Katz, Erikson's two half sisters, never ceased to share and to help. I also thank my family for putting up with my difficult days and for being there to celebrate the high moments—Sharon (to whom this book is dedicated); my very adult "kids," Beth and Brian; three Agrans—Phyllis, Larry, and Kenneth—and my always wise and vigilant mother, Lena.

"If the relation of father and son dominated the last century, then this one is concerned with the self-made man asking himself what he is making of himself."

—ERIK H. ERIKSON, 1964

Contents

Foreword

It is altogether fitting that a man who in this century did so much to help us understand ourselves psychologically and morally, and who did so much to connect psychoanalysis to the social sciences (anthropology, sociology, history), and who wrote with grace and a lucid eloquence, notwithstanding the complexity of his ideas, and who explored certain lives with memorable freshness, originality, and tact (Luther, Gandhi), thereby enriching the very nature of biographical inquiry, should now himself be the subject of a talented, conscientious historian's biography. Moreover, Erikson's life lends itself readily, even dramatically, to the old-fashioned requirements of such an effort—that the person's story, apart from what she or he accomplished, be interesting, touching, or compelling. As the reader will soon enough realize, and as the title of this book right away suggests, here was one psychoanalyst who not only constructed a powerfully suggestive, engaging theory to explain how, step by step, we build our lives (the concerns, aspirations, and worries that come and go through the years), but, more than many of us, pulled together out of the ambiguities, mysteries, confusions, of his own past a singular (and publicly as well as professionally arresting, intriguing) identity.

That last word, of course, became synonymous with Erikson. Other psychoanalysts had used it, and wisely (Allen Wheelis, most especially, in *The Quest for Identity*), but for the man whose career is described and painstakingly documented in these pages, that word had an intensely personal as well as abstract or conceptual significance. A boy named Erik, who never knew his biological father, soon enough became the adopted son of a pediatrician. Erik's mother was Jewish, his Danish father was not. Erik's stepfather was Jewish. Down the line, the young Erik Homburger, for a while a wandering artist, would almost by accident stumble into the so-called Freud circle—psychoanalysis in its early, exciting period—and gradually become part of that world (indeed, an analysand of the founding father's daughter, Anna). Soon, the German-speaking young man who was learning to be a child psychoanalyst (who had not gone to college, never mind medical school) would meet and fall in love with a Canadian woman, a dancer, who had studied sociology in America.

It was a time when Germany and Austria were about to become obsessed with the question of race and religion and nationality. Thus, this couple, married and with children, would soon be in America, for them as for millions of others, a place to start anew—and so Erik Homburger did, as Erik Homburger Erikson. His book *Childhood and Society,* published in 1950, would have an enormous impact on his adopted country—and, by indirection, that book tells us what it means to become an American (how one's psychological life is shaped by social, cultural, and economic circumstances, by where and how one spends one's time on this planet). In a sense, then, Erik H. Erikson turned his American experience into a careful, sustained investigation: What he saw and felt happening to himself (as with Freud's examination of his own dreams, memories, fantasies) became the "research" that enabled a flow of ideas, articles, books. That is, needless to say, what psychoanalysis is all about: the constant effort to learn about the mind through an examined subjectivity—the analyst's and that of his or her patient or analysand. For an artist like Erik Erikson, already attuned to intuition and its gifts, such a profession was a welcome and lucky opportunity, for sure.

Not that Erikson's personal or professional background explains in full the breadth and depth of his interests, his accomplishments. A substantial number of European psychoanalysts had to flee Hitler and his Nazi thugs as they took over one, then another, European nation. (The Eriksons were prescient in their willingness, eagerness, to leave Vienna in 1933, just as Fascism began its virulent spread.) Each of those psychoanalytic émigrés had a complex past that might well have spurred research and writing. But the sources of creativity remain obscure, as Freud noted in his famous essay on Dostoyevsky, and as any of us who work psychologically with writers or artists keep on learning. In that regard, one of the remarkable aspects of Erikson's theoretical writing is his restraint, his refusal to pin down the more elusive sides of our intellectual and emotional life with constrained (and constraining) explanatory language. He doesn't want to circumscribe and define so much as to propose tentatively and imply—a way of seeing things rather than a grand scheme of definitions. His formulations are open-ended, meant to encourage reflection rather than to declare unreservedly, to insist. He is ever the artist, shedding light amid shadows, struggling for and with form against the sure knowledge that truth (what is seen, reported) is each person's particular response to his or her surroundings.

I well remember Erikson replying to a student's question about one of his books: "Look, what you get out of it is *yours*—and may differ from what any-one else finds useful or valuable, including me." Not all writers or teachers or social or psychological theorists are so relaxed, or as willing to subscribe to Nietzsche's aphorism, "It takes two to make a truth." That aphorism applies to this book. A thoughtful, dedicated historian has spent many years trying to understand a distinguished psychoanalyst and teacher and writer, as well as his distinguished and clearheaded and knowing wife, Joan Erikson (talk about "two making a truth"!). The result is a definitive, exemplary, accessible, and thoroughly rewarding biography that will mightily instruct the many of us for whom Erik Erikson's work has been so invaluable. I can see, somewhere in this universe, those inviting, affirming smiles that could sometimes come over Erik's face, and Joan's, as they together concluded something—in this case, that Larry Friedman, to whom they, when old, entrusted the telling of their life stories, has done well, right well, by them.

—ROBERT COLES

Preface

In June of 1993, as Erik H. Erikson was on the verge of his ninety-first birthday, I was determined to bring him a special birthday gift: information to establish the identity of his father. I had been in Copenhagen with his relatives, Finn and Martha Abrahamsen, exploring historic family records, documents, and memories. I returned to the United States with a detailed family tree extending from the eighteenth century, a photograph of Erikson's mother as a young woman, and information on two potential fathers (both Danish photographers).

He sat passively in a wheelchair in the study of his home, a spacious old wood-frame structure across the street from the Cambridge Ringe and Latin School and a few blocks from the Harvard University campus. He glanced at the material I had gathered. The detailed family tree was of little interest. Likewise, the identities of two prospective fathers (both named Erik) meant little to this Erik, who, as a young man, had changed his last name to Erikson. At this point, I realized that his lifelong quest to discover the identity of his father would remain unfulfilled.

But all was not lost. Erikson picked up the photograph of his young mother, Karla Abrahamsen, and gazed at her for many minutes. "What a beauty," he remarked. Although he was very frail and nearly immobile, his eyes had come alive. A smile crossed his face. Erikson was enjoying himself amid the flow of memories of his Danish mother. He glanced at the small Danish flag on the mantel above his fireplace and back again at the photograph. After several minutes, he was ready for a nap. Even in late old age, as mind and body gave out, there could be joy, buoyancy, discovery, and even a measure of playfulness.

Erik Erikson stands out among the intellectuals, émigré scholars, and other writers of his generation. Publishing in the shadows of the Holocaust, Stalinist executions, Maoist brutality, Hiroshima, and McCarthyism, his contemporaries often described a human condition of gloom, despair, and degradation within bureaucratized, militarized mass society. Theodor Adorno and his colleagues studied the authoritarian personality, David Riesman spoke of conformist "other direction," Herbert Marcuse described the emergence of "one-dimensional man," Hannah Arendt explained the evolution of "classes into masses" and the "radical loss of self-interest," while Ralph Ellison characterized the invisibility of human beings to one another—and to themselves.

Erik Erikson was different. His words and his presence signaled hope and possibility despite the enormity of modern human tragedies. Others in his generation (sometimes referred to as postwar liberal cosmopolitan intellectuals) agreed with his embrace of human universality amid particularities, his insistence upon firm individual identity and dignity, his recognition of and respect for human diversity, and the importance of rich reciprocal relationships. However, those other intellectuals tended to regard these perspectives as vague guideposts to sanity amid pervasive global brutalities. Erikson embraced them instead as immediately attainable in modern life. They were qualities to be esteemed and pursued in the here and now.

After his arrival in America late in 1933, a passionate love affair started between the Vienna-trained child psychoanalyst and "the Americans." A federal immigration clerk in Boston smiled at the apprehensive thirty-two-year-old refugee and expressed her warm welcome to the United States. This initial introduction to the country left him ebullient. He was whistling "Yankee Doodle" as he left the immigration office, and for the next sixty years he continued to express that upbeat spirit. For him, Franklin Roosevelt's nation was more than a bulwark against a Fascist Europe gone mad. America stood for a humane attempt to reach a minimal level of economic, social, and psychological dignity for all. The United States also represented the hope of establishing a firm sense of personal identity in the context of the surrounding society. During his first several years in this country, Erikson began to forge the concept of identity and to lodge meaning in the term *identity crisis*.

A decade and a half after his arrival, however, McCarthyism gave him pause. Erikson feared that the postwar "red scare" was turning the United States against the values of trust, cooperation, and tolerance—values that had characterized FDR's America. He also became reflective about the motives behind the American destruction of Hiroshima and Nagasaki, a doubt he did not have in August of 1945.

By the late 1960s and early 1970s, Erikson's awareness of My Lai and other American atrocities in Vietnam combined with his deepening antipathy to an American foreign policy that, once again, threatened the use of atomic weapons. Although he was an old man by then, he had not lost hope.

He drew less inspiration from the tattered traditions of FDR's America and focused more on the teachings of Gandhi (at Ahmadabad during the strike of 1918) and on the sayings of Jesus during his Galilee ministry. Gandhi and Jesus became touchstones of energy, joy, and possibility.

Erikson related to the politics and culture of postwar America, then, as an intellectual who sought signs of hope. As a professor, he convinced students like Albert Gore, Jr., Carol Gilligan, and Howard Gardner to take pride in their personal and social identities, and to work to humanize society. As a clinician, he gave his patients hope. Whereas colleagues emphasized a patient's emotional deficiencies as a barrier to mental "health," Erikson underscored a patient's strengths—what he or she retained and could build upon despite traumas and abuses. His success as a therapist was not infrequent.

Erikson's life—personal and professional, conceptual and cultural—involved crossing and recrossing a variety of borders or traditional lines of demarcation, and he became increasingly adept at it. These borders concerned his disciplinary and occupational allegiances, the structure of his conceptualizations, his religious and national loyalties, his "real" and "native" languages, and even the men he could call "father." In brief, the geographic, social, disciplinary, personal, and intellectual contexts of his life were constantly changing. He was always in the process of becoming.

Known for his concept of the "identity crisis," Erikson's changing ideas and experiences required him to refashion his sense of himself again and again. He felt compelled to try, initially quite painfully but more often rather joyously, to design and modify his ideas, dispositions, and experiences. He therefore rambled over and under, between and beyond, many concepts and circumstances. "Everything is our business," he proclaimed in earnest. He was a cartographer of sorts and took joy in mapping the crossings of ideas, places, and experiences on society's broad "horizontal" plane (its social surface). As such, Erikson contrasted with Freud, a miner of sorts who thrived on "vertical" excavations into the depths of an individual's inner psyche. Although Erikson considered himself a Freudian and a depth psychologist, he preferred to dwell on the interesting and varied surface of things.

This statement of the book's theme pins down too neatly an extraordinarily complex and elusive life that was lived within layered and constantly shifting contexts. Most Erikson scholarship reduces his life to a deceptive, if alluring, clarity. It is hard to find the Erikson I knew, read, and assigned in the classroom within that body of writing.

I have experienced two conflicting allegiances in my work on Erikson. From Robert Williams, an inspiring eighth-grade teacher with the sensibility to replace *The Weekly Reader* on my desk with *The Nation,* to Donald Meyer, my brilliantly creative graduate school mentor who introduced me to Erikson's work, I have been trained to be clear, explicit, and precise. "If you can't say it so that everybody can understand you," Karl Menninger used to tell me, "you don't know what you're talking about." With that cast of instructors plus a tough-minded, reflective father who insisted on reasoned argumentation, I prized the work of precise and skillful logicians. Indeed, I thrived on it. But there was a problem. Whenever I tried to explain a life—Charles Brockden Brown's, William Lloyd Garrison's, Karl Menninger's—I found such clarity and precision reductionist. Erikson understood this as he wrote on the lives of Luther, Gandhi, Jefferson, and Jesus.

In the end, I have settled for a practice that Erikson tried to capture through a vague and perhaps unnecessary term: *disciplined subjectivity.* He advocated departure from the old Cartesian subject-object dualism that sharply distinguished the investigator from an object that was assumed to be outside his or her mind. Simultaneously, Erikson insisted that the investigator or analyst was a participant observer who shaped what he or she saw, felt, and experienced. More pointedly, Erikson recommended mixing the imperatives of clarity and logic with a flow of impressions, emotions, and aesthetic dispositions, never allowing either the imperatives or the flow to gain hegemony over the other. Two subjectivities—the investigator and the person he or she was studying—simultaneously converged and diverged through what Erikson referred to as a process of "disciplined understanding." Combining the investigator's head and heart, Erikson recommended this balancing of contrasting tendencies as a general goal or a target more than an achievable reality. I have found enormous utility in attempting to hold the two in balance.

One cold wintry night in 1992, a few years after I started to research this volume, I met with the playwright William Gibson. We had dinner in a nearly vacant restaurant in Great Barrington, Massachusetts. Because Gibson had been Erikson's close friend for decades, I expected to learn a great deal. After a dull hour had gone by, during which the mediocre food had been consumed and minor aspects of his rapport with Erikson had been volunteered, I told Gibson jokingly that he was not giving me much incentive to pay for his dinner. He laughed, called for more coffee, and recounted a little-known story concerning Neil, Joan and Erik's fourth child. Neil had suffered from Down Syndrome, Gibson explained. He was institutionalized for life and his parents rarely visited him. Erik and Joan characterized Neil as a developmental aberration and wished that he had never been born. Gibson was sure that Neil's presence had contributed significantly to Erik's work on his eight-stage model of the human life cycle—the patterns not of Neil's but of *normal* human development. This shocking account presented a very different Erikson from the upbeat, forthright clinician and intellectual with whom I was familiar.

Gibson's story provided a focus that became central to this volume: the interplay between Erikson's personal life and the concepts and texts he provided to the public. Since that unforgettable evening, I have tried to open Erikson's books and articles and diagrams to new levels of understanding through complex perspectives on his life. I have also tried to add to the comprehension of his life by pointing out some generally overlooked elements within his texts.

Erikson's texts are not easy to study. They are complicated, layered, and often difficult to pin down. His life is even more difficult to chart. It is very hard to get a sense of Erikson as an individual as well as a thinker, clinician, and writer. He had few interests and fewer passions outside of his "work." To be sure, he loved to take long walks, to swim, to eat sweets, to write out of doors, to wander through art museums, to enjoy nature, to watch well-crafted movies, to converse with bright, attractive women, to joke, and to be playful. But there was not much more that he found compelling beyond his work. An internationally renowned child psychoanalyst, he was never especially attentive to parental duties as a father or a grandfather. Appreciating the relevance of time and setting in the shaping of personality, he rarely designated the day, month, year, or location when he wrote letters, and only occasionally discussed the social circumstances.

By his late forties, writing for publication had become Erikson's all-consuming passion. Much that he thought, said, read, and did was now intertwined with his writing. Joan struggled to widen his focus. She tried to make him feel less awkward, less uncomfortable, and perhaps even less unhappy with most social situations. She urged him to dance, sing, attend musical and dramatic productions, and socialize. But she always had to be watchful of Erik's whereabouts. A solitary scholar who prized sociability in his writings, he could disappear from a dinner party or a reception that he found tedious. Usually he escaped to his study and the endless chores of writing drafts of essays and books until Joan retrieved him.

During midlife and beyond, then, Erikson prized writing and publishing—probably above all else. The breadth, diversity, and richness in the man—beyond what Joan was able to draw out—are found in the range and depth of his writing. Yet his life was not entirely lacking in diversity and variety. His intense passion for composition was not self-limiting. It evoked abundant feelings, appetites, visions, and ideas—far more than he might otherwise have experienced. He found an afternoon by the ocean at Cotuit (Cape Cod) or a ferry ride across San Francisco Bay to be enhanced, not diminished, when he could work on a chapter that required revision. With this closely focused intensity, he usually found life challenging and interesting. It produced striking results for him. If not for passions of the pen, Erikson might be known to us today as a very successful clinician, but not as identity's architect and a voice of hope amid post-Holocaust despair.

I began teaching Erikson's books and concepts as a young professor during the late 1960s and early 1970s. Indeed, I was an "Eriksonian" in the sense that I accepted his emphasis on locating an individual in an interplay between the person's inner emotions and outer social circumstances (what Erik called the psychosocial). As a young historian, I admired the way he portrayed his subjects—a Yurok medicine woman, Adolf Hitler, Martin Luther, Thomas Jefferson, and others—in their rich historical contexts while not losing sight of what was unique and idiosyncratic in each individual. Indeed, I joined the early "psychohistory" movement, becoming disenchanted after it became clear that many participants failed dismally in their historical judgments and their aesthetic sensibilities. Erikson's "psychosocial" orientation remained firm in my head and heart, however. Early in 1990, when my friends Charles Strozier and Robert Jay Lifton recommended that I prepare the first comprehensive biography of Erikson, I promptly agreed. I already admired the man's work, and a biography offered a way to discover more precisely why I found him so engaging.

Six years later I experienced a deep personal tragedy, one that profoundly influenced the final shape of this book. Someone very dear to me for over thirty years was hospitalized and walked the line between life and death for several months before gradually recovering. Spring reversed into a bleak winter as I struggled, day after day, to assure my friend's survival and help with recovery. Enormous energy was expended. Around the clock, I felt that I could never let up the pace for fear of adverse consequences.

During these impossible months, I continued to write and rewrite this biography—a few minutes here, an hour there. At a minimum, I read a few pages from it every day. This effort had a calming and reassuring effect. It seemed to ground my life, to afford an element of stability amid devastating circumstances. As the weeks progressed, I saw that the emphasis in this volume was changing. I continued with the initial goals—to explain the nuances and significance of Erikson's life and thought. But I was also trying to fathom the triumphs and tragedies of life—Erikson's, my friend's, my own. I became a romantic in the sense of cherishing, more than ever, life's extravagance and elegance, its robust, humorous, enlivening, and erotic qualities. These represented renewal. I saw them as counterpoints to the enigmas and pathos and trauma and emotional dead ends that life also presents. When I was a youngster, my mother underscored the value of "laugh-ter and the love of friends." I now see that qualities such as these represented one of the most important features of Erikson's thought. Because his descriptions of these qualities were so rich, subtle, and utterly convincing (even if he often failed to incorporate them into his own life), we must never lose touch with him.

CHAPTER ONE

Toward a New Beginning:
Infancy, Childhood, Youth

B y the late 1960s and early 1970s, Erik H. Erikson had reached the peak of his influence and popularity. Elegantly dressed in tweed jacket, blue shirt, and white moccasins, with a mane of white hair and rosy complexion, he seemed to resonate charisma and charm. He appeared on the covers of widely circulating newsmagazines as the founder of the life cycle and the identity crisis. Speaking invitations, honors, and honorary degrees abounded. Erikson enjoyed a reputation among Harvard students, graduates and undergraduates alike, as an inspirational, relevant, and profound gurulike instructor. He was sought out in advisory capacities not only by academic and psychiatric facilities but by a high official in the administration of New York's mayor John Lindsay, by members of the Kennedy family, and by Daniel Patrick Moynihan in the Nixon White House. He won a Pulitzer Prize and a National Book Award for *Gandhi's Truth*, which propounded a political ethic that could lead the world from the brink of nuclear war while addressing America's brutality in Vietnam.

Growing public acclaim seemed to have an effect upon this habitually quiet, understated man. He displayed a new buoyancy and assurance—almost a prophetlike quality. When he spoke reassuringly and approvingly to a young admirer, both regarded it as a devout and sacred ritual of mutuality. Robert Abzug, a young Danforth Graduate Fellow, would never forget a special conference in northern California where Erikson had lectured on Ingmar Bergman's classic film *Wild Strawberries*. Afterward, Abzug found himself walking along a nearby beach, saw Erikson, approached him, and offered an interpretation of a key scene in the film that Erikson had not made—Isak Borg, the main character, had never been able to wholly connect himself to his parents. Later in the conference, Erikson took Abzug aside, touched him gently on the shoulder, looked him deeply in the eye, and said that Abzug had been right in his observation on the film. This was a special moment for both. The young man sensed that he had been respected, even blessed, by a strong, unwavering prophet. Abzug gained accreditation, and Erikson felt confident that he had a devoted student of yet another generation.[1]

It is not easy to detect, from what is known of his early years, the roots of this show of confidence and inner strength in Erikson's late-life relationship. Young Erik seemed desperately to need a wise and giving adviser, such as he later became. Born out of wedlock and later adopted by his mother's second husband, he did not know who had fathered him. The problem was exacerbated by what he called the loving deceit of his mother and foster father; they had misled him for years. "Adoption was the great theme of Erikson's existence," recalled his closest childhood friend, Peter Blos. "He talked about it all the time." In an autobiographical essay written late in his life, Erikson noted that "a stepson's negative identity is that of a bastard" and provides no sense of belonging. Such a person "might use his talents to avoid belonging quite anywhere. . . ." Nonetheless, Erikson felt that deceit and illegitimacy did not set his early decades entirely on a downhill course. A "different background" also came to signify very special circumstances and a destiny that he came to accept "as a fact of life." The sense of being extraordinary was facilitated by "the pervasive love and essential stability of my childhood milieu," even with the deceptions, and by the willingness of those closest to him "to let me develop my talents and choose my own life course."[2]

Early circumstances therefore sapped and constricted young Erik. But they may also have inspired and motivated him. Despite his well-known eight-stage universal model of the human life cycle, which distributed the first two decades of life among five separate and distinct stages, he saw his own early life as a single unified stage that encompassed the entire flow of events from his birth to young adulthood. In his autobiographical essay, he characterized this stage as both broadly constrictive and energizing. Debilitating consequences were balanced by elevating ones.

Drawing upon that essay and other of Erikson's late-life reflections, it is important to determine why he regarded his infancy, childhood, youth, and young adulthood as part of a continuous and unified developmental stage—his essential beginning. Adult reflections on childhood feelings and experiences carry complex and varied agendas, to be sure, along with internal contradictions. Nevertheless, we must honor Erikson's quest to see unity in his early life by seeking out materials that lend themselves to a cohesive story even as we introduce other data that destabilize the story.

A MATTER OF PARENTAGE

Erik's mother, Karla Abrahamsen, came from a prominent Jewish family in Copenhagen that traced its genealogy back to the seventeenth century and the north of Germany. The men tended toward merchant and trade callings. There was a rabbi, a church historian, and even a Lutheran minister in the family tree, indicating some intermarriage. In addition to child-rearing duties, Abrahamsen women had maintained a tradition of embroidery and the painting of porcelain. All were "ladies" and employed housekeepers. Unlike Eastern European Jews in Copenhagen, the Abrahamsens tried to appear Danish. They spoke no Yiddish and blended the requirements of kosher food with traditional Danish dishes.[3]

Karla's father, Joseph, was a prominent dry-goods wholesaler. Her mother, Henrietta Kalckar, died when Karla was fifteen, leaving her in the care of aging Abrahamsen aunts. Joseph required the brightest of his three sons, Axel, to forsake law and join his business, now "Abrahamsen and Son." Axel went on to become a very prominent figure in the textile industry and a leader in several of the city's Jewish charities. When Joseph died in 1899, Axel largely assumed leadership over Abrahamsen family affairs. Max, Joseph's second son, worked under Axel in the family dry-goods warehouse but died at twenty-two. Two other sons, Nicholai and Einar, established their own businesses as local jewelers. Einar became a respected gemologist. Like Axel, they were active in local Jewish charities. Matilda, Axel's wife, helped run a local soup kitchen for Russian-Jewish immigrants.[4]

While Axel succeeded his father as the director of larger family affairs, his sister, Karla, emerged as the family's most remarkable member. She was the most beautiful Abrahamsen in memory, brilliant, and deeply intellectual. Indeed, she was one of the few women in the community to attend gymnasium. Unquestioning in her Judaism, she nonetheless read Kierkegaard devotedly and was taken with his culturally Danish but decidedly Christian appeal. Karla's father and brother respected and adored her. But they worried about her disposition to act on impulse and her interest in unconventional artists and craftspeople. Because Karla's mother had died when she was young, they feared that she was untutored in the sexual proprieties honored by her family and her class.[5]

In 1898, Karla, at twenty-one, married a twenty-seven-year-old Jewish stockbroker, Valdemar Isidor Salomonsen. Little is known about him. Valdemar's father, Abraham, a lawyer, was on friendly terms with the Abrahamsens. His mother, Thora, was the daughter of the well-known portrait painter David Monies. Karla's marriage to Valdemar did not last a night and was probably unconsummated. She wired Axel from her honeymoon destination in Rome to take her home. By the time Axel arrived, Valdemar had fled to either Mexico or the United States. Family lore has it that after the wedding ceremony he informed Karla of his dealings in crime, fraud, and some financial irregularities that required him to become a fugitive. He might also have beaten her and may have made her apprehensive that he had syphilis. Although Karla never saw Valdemar after the wedding night, she retained his surname for legal appearances. When Erik was born four years later, the birth certificate listed Valdemar and Karla Salomonsen as his parents. In October 1902, four months after the birth, Valdemar's father provided Karla with evidence to prove that Valdemar had died abroad that month. Erik was technically legitimate. Karla, officially a widow, was free to remarry.[6]

Since Valdemar could not have fathered Erik, who did? Karla's daughters through her second marriage, Ruth Hirsch and Ellen Katz, wish to maintain that their mother was probably a virgin until she became pregnant; she was supposedly inexperienced sexually and very proper. They suspect that Karla had too much to drink at a party hosted by her brothers and was either asleep when someone had intercourse with her or she was too drunk to recognize the man. Based upon their conversations with Karla, however, Erik and Joan Erikson assumed that she was not so innocent sexually and that she knew the real father, if only through Erik's appearance. However, she would never divulge his identity. Joan suspected that the father was one of the few Danish-speaking tourists Karla met during a vacation trip to the Isle of Capri. A persisting Abrahamsen family rumor is that Karla named Erik after the real father, and that he was a Copenhagen court photographer. Bjørn Ochsner's definitive *Fotografer i og fra Danmark til og med ar 1920* (1986) lists two from Copenhagen who were named Erik: Erik Strom and Erik Bahnsen. Strom, however, was clearly no court photographer, and evidence on Bahnsen is far too thin to make any kind of case for his paternity. In any case, it is striking that when Karla left Copenhagen for a holiday in northern Germany in 1902, she had no idea that she was pregnant. Family lore has it that she first became aware of her physical state in a bathroom shower only two months before her term was up and that she verified her pregnancy with a local physician. To avoid disgrace and scandal, the Copenhagen Abrahamsens insisted that Karla stay in Germany under the care of three aging spinster aunts. She was to give birth in Frankfurt and raise Erik Salomonsen in the small adjacent town of Buehl. The whole scandal was managed smoothly. Appearances of propriety were preserved.[7]

In Buehl, Karla raised her baby with quiet dignity. Erik felt that she "held all the confusing details together" and was most supportive. But there was also a recognition that his mother had been abandoned rather than honored, and that distressed him. A friend who worked at a Jewish hospital in the town helped Karla to secure some training as a nurse. She liked to associate with artists in the Bohemian section of town, and the men among them gave her fatherless child what he later called "my first male imprinting." Yet as the swarthy, dark-haired mother walked with the blond-haired, blue-eyed, light-skinned child asleep in his buggy, neighbors and passersby sensed that something was irregular.[8]

As an adult, Erik tried to reconstruct his infancy when he lived fatherless with Karla in Buehl. "My earliest remembrance is of the official letter arriving declaring him [Valdemar Salomonsen] dead," Erik noted. His eyes were always on Karla: "I knew she had a sadness I could not understand." When he observed much later in life how identity (the sense that "I am somebody") began with the recognition of a mother's smile, Erik was thinking of Karla. When she was not gazing at him and visually establishing a bond of trust, Erik recalled that Karla epitomized wisdom; she was "deeply involved in reading what I later found to have been such authors as Brandes, Kierkegaard, Emerson." All his life, he identified reading positively with memories of his young mother. Although living in Germany, they sometimes spoke together in Danish, which he regarded as special. At twenty-three, he sketched and carved a woodcut of Mary and the Christ child that seemed to recapitulate the trust and reciprocal engagement that he felt growing up alone with Karla. Erik felt that he knew as a very young child that Karla, sad and alone, remained deeply supportive of the specialness of her son and his potential: "I could never doubt that her ambitions for me transcended the conventions which she, nevertheless, faithfully served." The recognition, trust, and joy from looking face-to-face, eye-to-eye, at his helpful, intelligent, and beautiful mother was something that Erik dwelled on throughout his life. If the first three years of this illegitimate child's life with his mother in the north of Germany, distant from the Abrahamsens, was difficult—perhaps traumatic—it was hardly hopeless. A very special bond between mother and child had been forged.[9]

The strength of the bond between Karla and Erik was such that when she began to see a Karlsruhe pediatrician nine years her senior, small in stature with dark brown hair and a goatee, that man assumed the role of an "intruder." Erik had been a sickly child, suffering especially from gastric distress. One story has it that Karla's artist friends in Buehl recommended that she summon Theodor Homburger to examine Erik. According to another story, Karla was in transit with Erik and had stopped at the Schloss Hotel in Karlsruhe, and the hotel management called on Homburger to care for the boy. A short, staid, reserved pediatrician, and confirmed bachelor with a kindly disposition, Homburger found the problem in the milk Erik had been drinking. He changed Erik's formula and the boy recovered immediately, only to discover that his mother was very much taken by the doctor. A courting period followed, a wedding date was set, and the Karlsruhe Jewish community talked excitedly about how a leader of their larger and more "liberal" temple was about to marry a tall, dark, Danish woman who had a small, blond, blue-eyed boy. Erik recalled how it was no easy matter "to come to terms with that intruder, the bearded doctor, with his mysterious instruments." His mother seemed to be shunting him aside for Theodor. The situation was difficult for Theodor, too, for he realized that he had interrupted the very special relationship between Karla and Erik. Karla, especially, must have felt conflicted. She recognized the deep and continuing needs of her son, and that they seemed at cross purposes with the desires of her future husband. Yet she found no alternative to accommodation—to making a place for Theodor as well as for Erik in what was then a very unusual family circumstance. After all, the very conventional and intellectually limited pediatrician, who promised to move her from the artistic community in Buehl to his family home in Karlsruhe, had offered Karla a way to mitigate the sin of having given birth to an illegitimate child. Theodor was providing Karla a way to restore herself to middle-class respectability.[10]

Theodor Homburger and Karla Salomonsen became engaged in November of 1904. They married in Karlsruhe the following June 15—Erik's third birthday—and took him with them on their honeymoon. It was as if Erik was there from the start—or so they hoped. When he was a young man, Erik made a woodcut of the honeymoon boat ride to Copenhagen. It was a study of a tense, worried, and angry young boy in a sailor's suit who felt lonely and apart from his parents. They appeared on the ship's deck, seated and embracing. Erik had turned his back on them and looked up to the ship's captain on the bridge. One interpretation is that the captain was his real father and that Erik wanted to climb a ladder to join him. The ship docked in Copenhagen, where the Abrahamsens were delighted to meet Karla's new husband, a Jewish doctor who made a decent living. But they felt awkward around her illegitimate son.[11]

Clearly, the devotedly middle-class Abrahamsens were taken with Theodor Homburger. He had rescued Karla from the sin of unwed motherhood. Moreover, he was from a prominent old Karlsruhe Jewish family going back to the establishment of that city as the new capital of Baden in 1715. Indeed, the Homburger family home at 9 Scholsplatz in the town center, where Theodor would make a home with his wife and child, was built in 1722. Owing to Karlsruhe's comparatively late development, it lacked a historic Jewish ghetto. Baden, the most cosmopolitan and liberal German state, resisted Prussian monarchical pressures and cheered the triumph of reform causes in France and Belgium. Indeed, Baden granted full and complete legal emancipation to all Jews in 1862 even though it had formerly been the state capital of a Lutheran principate with a large Catholic population. By the late nineteenth century, Karlsruhe had become an industrial center producing tools, machinery, furniture, and other necessities in a rapidly industrializing nation-state. Jews gravitated toward the professions and the merchant trade. Julius Homburger had been a successful wine merchant. He and his wife, Therese Veis, had seven children. Theodor was the only one who had obtained advanced education and become a professional. He graduated from the town's Margravate Gymnasium; studied medicine in Würzburg, Munich, and Heidelberg; wrote a medical school thesis on scientific instrumentation to measure natural light in school classrooms; and opened a pediatrics practice in 1894. At the time, there were several Jewish doctors in Karlsruhe. Pediatrics was not an uncommon specialty among them.[12]

The historic Homburger family home was very large with several wings. Theodor's brothers, David and Ludwig, and his sister, Bertha Marx, lived with their families in parts of the complex, and Theodor moved his family into a three-story wing overlooking a beautiful park. His first child with Karla, Elna, was born early in 1907, but she died at two of diphtheria. This must have been a difficult time. Then, in 1909, Ruth was born; Ellen followed in 1912.[13]

When they announced their engagement late in 1904, Karla had accepted Theodor's sole request as a condition of marriage: Erik was to be told that Theodor was his biological father. Karla probably regarded this fiction as a way to bury the past and to start life afresh. As Erik observed many years later, Theodor "apparently joined her in the promise to annul the past: and they committed themselves totally to being, together, my 'real' parents." Was it "loving deceit" consistent with the perspectives of their day to protect him from an unfortunate past, as Erik once suggested, or "worse: stepfather and M decided to *keep this secret*," as he noted on another occasion. The young child must have sensed something was wrong. Even a three-year-old understood that one was not presented with a "natural" parent at that point in time; there were too "many cues" that were to the contrary, including whispers among the adults in the house concerning Erik's paternity. Thus, although Erik grew up feeling that Theodor was a caring father, he also "felt all along . . . doubt in my identity. You know, all through my childhood years." Consequently, "I was quietly convinced that I came from a different background and somewhat accepted it as a fact of life and a part of my mother's past which was not to be mentioned whether in Karlsruhe or in Copenhagen." There was a sense of specialness here, positive and negative within this retrospective portrayal.[14]

If young Erik could not quite believe that Theodor was his natural father,

Theodor had difficulty accepting Erik as his blood son. "Genes enter into it," Erik subsequently remarked ironically. An adopting father can feel that the son is not his own kind in his humor and other traits. Indeed, he can regard the son as undescended from him and can treat that son accordingly. Moreover, Theodor was almost certainly unsure of the biological father's ultimate intentions toward Erik. Under these circumstances, full commitment to Erik as a son was difficult despite Theodor's humane disposition.[15]

Even more than Karla, Theodor wanted to maintain middle-class respectability. This required that he adopt Erik immediately and have his surname legally changed from Salomonsen to Homburger. Yet no record of these proceedings appeared on their 1905 wedding certificate—the first place it could have been noted officially. Indeed, in a 1909 document naturalizing him as a German citizen, he still appeared as Erik Salomonsen. On a 1959 curriculum vitae, Erik acknowledged that the legal name change to Homburger did not occur until 1908, a few years after his parents were married. A side notation on his official Frankfurt birth certificate, dated June 1911, is especially revealing: "By decree of the Karlsruhe administration," Erik Salomonsen was officially permitted to adopt the family name of Homburger. To be sure, this change was "in administrative lieu of the Jewish congregation." Consequently, it may have been made at the Homburger's Karlsruhe synagogue beforehand—perhaps even at the time of the marriage—although that was not customary. Finally, the Registry Book of the Karlsruhe District Court for 1909 records Erik's name change from Salomonsen to Homburger while the 1911 Registry Book indicates completion of his guardianship and adoption procedure. In Karlsruhe and Frankfurt, he was not legally Theodor Homburger's son until five years after his parents' marriage.[16]

One perspective on these documents is that Theodor and Karla regarded Erik as a very young and unsuspecting child when they married. They wanted him to believe Theodor was his biological father even as they almost certainly had to acknowledge him as Theodor's adopted son at their local synagogue. Perhaps they felt no need to move legally toward German naturalization and adoption until he was nine, when he would be taking entrance examinations for admission to a local gymnasium. The problem with this interpretation for the delay is that it does not account for the enormous pressure Theodor and Karla felt to quickly bury the sins of the past. They wanted the family to appear legally—that is, within the German governmental records that they and other local Jews so highly prized—as a normal middle-class entity. That there was an extended delay on such a vital matter among people very attentive to legal formalities suggests that Theodor was ambivalent about having Erik as his son, insisting that Erik see him as his biological father while delaying the process of assuming legal paternity. Given Karla's powerful presence in the family, the delay in adoption also suggests that she may have had reservations about sharing full legal parentage with Theodor. Indeed, there was probably a complex jumble of motives on both sides. It is instructive that Theodor did not invoke full and explicit legal language to acknowledge Erik as his adopted son until 1942, when he prepared his will and testament.[17]

The awkward honeymoon trip where Erik accompanied his mother and Theodor to Copenhagen was not the last time he saw the Abrahamsens. "I made many visits there as a child," he recalled. Usually he stayed in Axel's home. Since Jewish tradition assigns the child to the religion of the mother even when the father cannot be identified, the Abrahamsens regarded Erik as a Jew, and Axel took him regularly to synagogue. He never forgot the day when the king of Denmark arrived for a service and sat next to them. But he took greatest joy in visits to his uncle Nicholai's summer house on the coastal Øresund north of Copenhagen in Skotterup Snekkersten. Roselund, Nicholai's house, was ideally located for walking in the nearby woods or for swimming and boating. Every time Erik lectured about Bergman's film *Wild Strawberries,* the vision of the Øresund depicted in the movie brought him back to his childhood and Roselund, where "I spent the sunniest summers of my early years." As a child, he recalled, "I often looked across the Sund from the Danish side" and delighted in seeing Sweden. His Scandinavian ties contributed to Erik's sense of specialness. More often than Ruth and Ellen, his Homburger half sisters, he made special trips from Karlsruhe to Copenhagen.[18]

Neither the Abrahamsens nor the Homburgers objected to young Erik's frequent visits to Copenhagen. Like other Danish and German Jews, they often crossed the border to be with one another. During World War I, the Abrahamsens sent the Homburgers of Karlsruhe what they needed most—food. In this regular interchange of families, Erik felt especially close to Henrietta, Axel's daughter. She always greeted Erik affectionately, never considering him an outsider. When Erik was twelve, he made for Henrietta a beautiful sketch of a farmhouse in winter and signed it "A remembrance from your cousin." But though the adult Abrahamsens were kind and polite to Erik, there was always an element of uneasiness in the relationship. He exaggerated this element to Peter Blos, his closest Karlsruhe friend, complaining that the Abrahamsens had cut him and his mother off. More typically, he recalled the tension in the Homburger house when the Copenhagen Abrahamsens visited, and his parents restrained them from speaking of his origins: "Like I can imagine my relatives coming down from Denmark and don't say this, don't say that. . . ."[19]

The very conditions of Erik's birth, then, created tensions in the Homburger household and among the Abrahamsens. The young child could not help but sense that something was amiss. After Karla's marriage to Homburger, Erik continued to feel as he had during his first three years living alone with his mother—that her strength and presence were his primary hope and support and the basic source for his continuing sense of specialness. Consequently, he played along with the tensions and fabrications in the Homburger household and put behind him "the period before the age of three, when mother and I had lived alone."[20]

A STEPSON'S IDENTITY

Theodor and Karla were determined to build a family of their own in Karlsruhe. When Erik was four, Elna was born. Roughly a year and a half later, the two appeared together in a photograph. Erik, dressed in a sailor's suit, sat tense and joyless. Elna leaned against him, wearing some type of sheet or diaper around her waist, although custom required fuller dress. She did not appear to be entirely normal. Within months of this photograph, Elna died of diphtheria. For Erik, the trauma of her passing was accented by the sense that he did not quite belong within the family. Ruth was born the year Elna died, and Ellen was born when he was ten. Theodor was very close to his surviving daughters. He took them for walks in the country every Sunday and talked with them about music and the novelties of nature. Although they did not learn that Erik was a half brother until they were well into their teens, they had relatively little to do with him. Erik continued to be very close to Karla and liked her artist friends in the vicinity. By the age of twelve, if not earlier, Erik was emulating them, making sketches of the local countryside, and these suggested that he had some talent. Karla encouraged a spirit of independence, he recalled, "a certain sense of choice—and the right to search." Consequently, as he grew older, he did more on his own or with young friends in town, confident that he could turn to his mother for support when he needed her.[21]

While the Homburger family featured special ties between the father and his daughters and the mother and her son, Karla ran the family's affairs. Theodor worked very long hours even though he maintained medical offices on the lower floor of the family home. He was out on house calls every morning and evening and received large numbers of office calls during the afternoon. In addition, he was a city school physician, wrote a paper on school learning conditions during wartime, and took on Karlsruhe welfare cases when he could. Beyond his medical practice and his synagogue, however, Theodor had little time and few interests. Karla maintained family finances, giving him pocket money. She also set the social and cultural agenda for the family.[22]

That agenda was congruent with the Jewish middle-class traditions of Theodor's parents and siblings. All three meals were taken together. The purposes of the various rooms in their wing of the extended multifamily complex were to be strictly observed. The children were confined to the family quarters on the second floor, though they were free to play in the arcades and the beautiful inner courtyard. Boarders lived on the third floor. Mixing of residents on all three levels occurred only during the air-raid alerts of World War I, when everybody raced into the wine cellar to seek cover from French bombers. Although Karla read a Danish newspaper daily and probably identified culturally with Denmark more than with Germany, the children were expected to use German. Indeed, Abrahamsen relatives from Copenhagen were instructed to speak German in her home. Karla was intent on maintaining a German household, not a Danish one, all the more because German was the "official" language of continental Europe. This was easier on Ruth and Ellen as the children of a German than on Erik, who was not. To his lifelong regret, he claimed that he "forgot" what Danish he had picked up during his infancy for "step-German," the language of his stepfather. Above all, Karla insisted on the strict maintenance of Jewish customs and rituals despite her abiding interest in Kierkegaard and Christian spiritual issues. There was no question, for example, that Erik was to spend years training for and to receive a traditional bar mitzvah. Karla maintained the laws of kashruth, the ceremonial celebration of Jewish festivities, and required synagogue attendance Friday evenings and on the Sabbath.[23]

The Karlsruhe synagogue that the larger Homburger family attended was extremely important in the lives of Theodor, Karla, and their children. Frequented by old, established families who had migrated to Karlsruhe in the eighteenth and nineteenth centuries, it consisted of perhaps 2,500 members and was the more "liberal" of the city's two synagogues. Unlike the smaller, more orthodox synagogue attended primarily by more recent Polish immigrants, members considered themselves assimilated into German society and culture. Nonetheless, all wore hats during services, which were prolonged during holidays, and women sat in the balcony. Theodor was a member of the synagogue's governing council for thirteen years and served five more as its president. He was a reformer, pressing for the confirmation of girls when they turned fourteen, and introducing a synagogue choir supported by an organ played by a talented Gentile. Karla regularly hosted the rabbi and his wife on Sabbath afternoons. She chaired a synagogue-based chapter of the League of Israelite Charities of Baden and supervised the "middle-class kitchen" of volunteers who fed poor and unemployed Jews, providing roughly two hundred kosher meals a day. Their synagogue activities made Theodor and Karla leaders of the Karlsruhe Jewish community.[24]

Erik stayed away from the synagogue as much as he could. Tall, blond, and blue-eyed in a congregation where many were short and dark like Theodor, he continued to sense that he was different. Owing to his physical appearance, Erik was distressed that "I acquired the nickname 'goy' in my stepfather's temple." It promoted a developing suspicion that his real father was not Jewish. He also resented the fact that Theodor thought little of his artistic interests, instead pressuring him "to become a doctor like himself." Erik claimed to remember the artistic talents and rebellious lifestyles that he had encountered living alone with his mother in Buehl. He seemed to identify with this unconventional past while Karla embraced a more somber life with Theodor. Indeed, Erik found that he could not relate very well to his stepfather, who was a product of "an intensely Jewish small-town bourgeoisie family." He resented not just the synagogue but the values that shaped family life after Karla buried her rebellious nature and married Theodor. Erik recalled that he became "intensely alienated from [the] German middle class, [from] reform Judaism, [from the] doctor role." Only much later, after his migration to America and after his identity with a rebellious young Karla had been attenuated, was Erik able to revise his portrayal of Theodor. Only then could he acknowledge that "my stepfather the pediatrician provided me, even in my rebellion, with a daily firm model of identification, centered in the concern for children and in a general Hippocratic orientation."[25]

As Erik grew older, then, he felt that his mother had acceded to Theodor's middle-class German-Jewish habits. Hugo Schiff, his rabbi, recalled that "he was aloof from everything and everybody [Jewish]." "At that point I *set out* to be different," Erik recalled. He contrasted the Karlsruhe painters' studios that he often visited with the limitations of "our house"—especially Theodor's medical office, "filled with tense and trusting mothers and children." Unlike his stepfather's home and office, the artist's studio and lifestyle offered an opportunity for the "recovery of the senses." In addition to Karla's artistic friends and his own artist acquaintances, Erik sought this visual path to recovery because he sensed that it might connect him to his biological father. Far more from romantic visions than from tangible evidence, he asserted increasingly, as he grew older, that this father was also artistic.[26]

Little beyond hope and hearsay sustained this vision of Erik's birth father. If his mother knew or strongly suspected the man's identity and conveyed it to her brothers, they passed on only very general impressions to their children. Axel's son, Svend, and his daughter-in-law, Helena, never knew the actual identity. His daughter, Henrietta, tried to find out, but without success. If Axel's brother Nicholai ever knew, Nicholai's daughter, Edith, was unable to learn despite prodigious efforts.[27]

It was no easy matter, then, for Erik to track down the man who fathered him. Much later, when he recalled his unsuccessful search, he sometimes charged that "MOTHER DECEIVED" him. This was an obvious reference to her failure to nurture and sustain him with a sense of himself and his past. At times, he underscored "how many discordant signals she must have given me as to my origins!" His quest to discover his missing father by questioning his unforthcoming mother progressed along three overlapping stages, charting Erik's increasing difficulty relating to Karla as he grew older.[28]

When Erik was three, he was told that Theodor had always been his father. This was suspicious. The fact that Theodor delayed for years changing Erik's legal name to Homburger and formally adopting him compounded the suspicion. Nor could Erik forget the day he sat under a dining table and heard the unaware adults above discuss his real father as artistic and Gentile. Between the ages of eight and fourteen, a second level of understanding emerged. As he later recounted to his friend Betty Jean Lifton, he had been walking in the Black Forest on the outskirts of Karlsruhe and came across an old peasant woman who was milking a cow. She looked up at him and asked: "Do you know who your father is?" Erik ran to Karla and demanded the truth. Karla acknowledged that Theodor had adopted him. Then she recounted how Valdemar Salomonsen, a Danish Jew and her former husband, had abandoned her while she was pregnant with Erik. This was a half truth. Salomonsen had departed years before she became pregnant, but the story left Erik assuming that Salomonsen was his biological father. Erik sensed that Karla was deeply distressed as she acknowledged her first husband; the tone of her voice and her body language told him not to press her further about issues of paternity. Consequently, he continued for some years to believe that Salomonsen fathered him, but also that Karla continued to conceal information. The suspicion deepened during adolescence and led to a third stage in his understanding. He heard new rumors and remembered others that prompted "the gradual awareness" that his father was a Danish aristocrat, with artistic talents, and probably a Christian. When Karla died in 1960, some Abrahamsen cousins of Erik's generation told him what rumors and innuendos they had learned: "They confirmed what over the years I had concluded from accidental impressions—namely, that my father was a Gentile Dane 'from a good family' and 'artistically gifted.' " When he first became attentive to the possibility of this Gentile-Danish father, however, Erik feared traveling to Copenhagen to seek him out. If his father was wealthy—possibly an aristocrat—he might conclude that Erik was only pursuing him to acquire money. Moreover, "if my father hadn't cared enough about me to want me . . . why should I look him up now?" Erik pressed for his father's identity, but only to a point.[29]

While young Erik continued to feel tied to and trusting of Karla, he became increasingly aware that she had concealed information on what was emerging as the central issue in his early life and that she wanted him to drop all inquiries. This was shocking. It did not destroy Erik's love for, need for, and dependence on Karla, but it created a barrier between them and required him to draw increasingly on his own emotional resources. He came to feel that he could hardly avoid trying "to make an identity out of being a stepson."[30]

The task of forging a stepson's identity involved more than matters of parentage. Parentage prompted Erik to explore his religion and his nationality, and to consider how he had crossed the traditional borders or limits of these designations. Was he a Jew, like his mother and his stepfather, or a Gentile, as he came to assume that his father had been? Was he a Dane like Karla, Valdemar Salomonsen, and perhaps his biological father, or a German like Theodor Homburger? He never forgot the humiliation of being referred to as a Gentile in synagogue and a Jew in school. As he became attracted to Elizabeth Goldschmidt, a Jewish girl in the synagogue, he felt conflicted because he may have been partially Gentile. At times he recalled "having been born a Dane and having had to stand the scorn of German children against a foreign-born child" (though he was actually born in Germany). Consequently, when World War I erupted and Denmark remained neutral while seeking "to steal Schleswig-Holstein" from Germany, "I developed my nationalistic German tendencies for awhile in order to convince my playmates of my loyalty." They continued to call him "Dane." In sum, Erik recalled, through a hasty notation, how strange it felt "being a *German* (born a Dane) grown up in a Jewish household." "Rabbi almost" in that notation suggested pressure to suppress a possible Gentile aspect and become more decidedly a Jew. He resisted, and these came to be years of great confusion and "FAILURE."[31]

Erik's conflicts over religion and nationality were greatest in the Homburger family home in Karlsruhe. Stepfather Theodor insisted on observance of Jewish traditions to the point where, for family vacations, he rented a house and hired maids who could adhere to strict kosher dietary requirements. Karla helped him maintain a kosher house, though her heart was not in it; Erik and his half sisters watched her eat nonkosher foods like shrimp during visits to Copenhagen. Karla also provided confusing signals when she hung up Danish and German flags in the family home and read Danish newspapers avidly while she insisted that her children speak only German and refused to teach them Danish. Erik found the family's "liberal" synagogue even more distressing, since it required ceremonies like the bar mitzvah he went through. Much of the traditional ritual had apparently been eliminated to ease his resentment, and the event took on a "theatrical character." The deepest meaning that the bar mitzvah had for him was that it fell on the day the French bombed Karlsruhe, damaged the Homburger family compound, and produced a state of unlimited war between Germany and France. A seemingly empty event like a bar mitzvah amid serious international tensions was "part of the transparent ceremonialism of a *Bürgertum* which young people yearning for relevance . . . vowed early to leave behind them with a vengeance." Indeed, Erik remembered "as an adolescent writing a long letter of disengagement to our rabbi." The letter, synagogue services, and daily family customs at home were "part of a quiet alienation from my whole childhood setting, German *and* Jewish."[32]

The young man was ready for alternatives. One was "the Christianity of the Gospels to which I early felt inescapably drawn." He recalled how "I early received from my mother a quiet and uncombative conviction that to be a Jew did not preclude a reverence for the existential aspects of Christianity." Indeed, Karla had cultivated in Erik a love for Kierkegaard's enunciation of "the core of values of Christianity." As he read Kierkegaard, walked about Karlsruhe (where "there is a crucifix on every street corner") and the nearby Black Forest, and assumed increasingly that his father was a Gentile, the young man took a "turn toward Christianity." Protestantism interested him decidedly; he assumed that a Jew in Germany could hardly be unconcerned with Luther's legacy. A crucial moment came when he spent a night at the home of a friend in a village by the upper Rhine. The next morning the friend's father, a minister, recited the Lord's Prayer in Luther's German, and Erik responded deeply: "Never having 'knowingly' heard it, I had the experience, as seldom before or after, of a wholeness captured in a few simple words, of poetry fusing the aesthetic and the moral: those who have once suddenly 'heard' the Gettysburg Address will know what I mean."[33]

This was not the full conversion experience that a well-known nineteenth-century relative in the Abrahamsen wing of Erik's family—Christian Herman Kalckar—had completed. Nor was Erik adopting German-Lutheran cultural norms to enhance his social status like some youngsters in the Karlsruhe Jewish community had done. Rather, he was speaking to a profound admiration and respect for Protestant devotion and piety, and was beginning to appropriate these aspects into his life. To be sure, they contrasted with the seemingly empty Jewish rituals of his stepfather's household and synagogue. But Erik did not feel that he was directly or consciously repudiating Judaism. Rather, he saw himself occupying a vague divide between Protestantism and Judaism.

To some extent, Erik may have been merging a decidedly Danish aspect of Christianity with his developing interest in German Lutheranism. As he later explained, a Danish mother who, through Kierkegaard, had given him his "introduction to Christianity" in an "intensively Danish" form had retained intense pride "that her family was also Jewish." She had taught him that he could cross borders, combining Judaism with "reverence for the existential aspects of Christianity" and even with aspects of Lutheran devotedness and piety. Karla had also informed him, proudly, that the Abrahamsen family included both the chief rabbi of Stockholm and a prominent church historian. Devotedness was more important than formal religious doctrines or affiliations.[34]

FROM GYMNASIUM TO *WANDERSCHAFT*

As an old man, Erik saw special significance in the fact that the Karlsruhe of his childhood was just on the German side of the Rhine. He noted that his whole childhood involved learning to navigate borders—between Judaism and Christianity; Denmark and Germany; mother, stepfather, and biological father. "I know how you could live on the line," he reminisced.[35] If Erik's earliest years centered on "living on the line" under a "stepson's identity," additional factors came into play during his adolescence and young adulthood. He became increasingly attentive to matters outside his family circle—schooling, a unique friendship, and a prolonged *Wanderschaft*.

Erik began a Karlsruhe *Vorschule* or primary school when he was six and completed it at nine. Attendance had been compulsory in all German states since the eighteenth century, well ahead of the rest of Europe. By 1900, the German literacy rate was over 91 percent. Erik did not find the drill routines of the *Vorschule* to his liking. And though Karla tutored him daily, he did not perform well.[36]

From age nine until he was eighteen, Erik attended the Karlsruhe gymnasium, emphasizing classical literature and languages. This contrasted with the German *Oberrealschule,* which focused on the natural sciences, modern languages, and mathematics, and the *Realgymnasium*—a compromise between the gymnasium and the *Oberrealschule.* Typical of the German gymnasium, Erik's school focused entirely on academics, neglecting sports, music, and extracurricular activities. At the end of nine years he took his examinations and received the *Abitur,* a certificate of graduation that gave him the right to enroll in a university. At that point, however, he had enough of formal schooling.[37]

Erik's experience in the Karlsruhe gymnasium resembled that of the fifteen-year-old Hanno in Thomas Mann's *Buddenbrooks.* Like Hanno, Erik felt that his spirit was being crushed by the strict discipline, the rote memorization, and the absence of artistic sensibilities. Nor was he pleased by being one of only two Jews in his class. Whereas almost all of the other students intended to enter professions like medicine, law, theology, and banking, Erik wrote of his desire to practice "arts and crafts." The curriculum did not accommodate that interest. He had eight years of Latin, eight of German literature, and six years of Greek. He also took several years of mathematics (algebra and geometry), physics, philosophy, French, and history (Russian, Norman, German, and the "Age of Exploration"). Much of his reading stressed battles between societies, such as Thucydides' *History of the Peloponnesian War,* and the conflicts within the self, perhaps best depicted in much of Greek tragedy.[38]

Erik often considered dropping out of the gymnasium. As a student, he walked in a stiff and awkward manner. His face was long, thin, and tight, and his ears protruded noticeably. His hair had become darker, fuller, and wavy. His eyes were deep in their sockets, and he seemed nervous, frightened, and somewhat sad. Except for Greek translation, he disliked his courses. Karla tutored him regularly and insisted that he pursue his studies through the *Abitur.* Written and oral final examinations were offered in late 1919 and early 1920, and all forty-five students who stood for them passed. A dislike of school probably explained why Erik was in the lower half of his class. On a one (excellent) to five (failure) scale, he received a cumulative grade of three. He earned threes and fours in Latin, Greek, and French, but twos in German. In mathematics, he scored a four and a two. Philosophy and physics earned him threes. History was his worst subject—three, four, and five, with a four-five on the oral part of that examination. Despite his mediocre performance and disinterest in his studies, Erik's examiners were impressed with certain personal traits. They gave him a one in conduct, a two for diligence, and a one for religious devoutness.[39]

Peter Blos, later to gain prominence in American psychoanalytic circles, was a student in Erik's graduating gymnasium class of 1920. Although he had known Erik for some time, they did not become close friends until their final year at school, when by chance they found themselves conversing enthusiastically along the streets of Karlsruhe. By dawn they had become dear friends and Erik had cultivated a lifelong love of walking. Other walks followed. There was a *Geistigkeit*—a spirituality—that drew them together in "a very special relationship to philosophy, to art, and above all, to nature. . . . We walked *in* nature and somehow nature seemed to know about it." The two were preoccupied with their own importance; the stars seemed somehow to be following them as they walked together.[40]

Some of their most pressing conversations concerned their parents. Both had Jewish mothers, but Peter's father was Gentile. Erik had increasingly become disposed to assume that his biological father was also Gentile: "We both come from families with mixed regional and religious backgrounds and we are both sons of bearded physicians, a fact which, I believe, gave us a similar professional imprinting." Neither became doctors. Erik now regarded

Theodor entirely as a stepfather; he talked constantly to Peter about possible characteristics of his birth father. Indeed, he speculated on what his life would have been if he had grown up in Copenhagen with both of his biological parents. He might have been a proud Scandinavian rather than the adopted Gentile in Theodor's Karlsruhe synagogue.[41]

Peter Blos understood that Erik was not enamored with the temple-centered life of his stepfather, nor with the man's narrow, practical range of interests. Erik was pleased that Peter "shared his father with me, a doctor both prophetic and eccentric." Edwin Blos impressed young Erik in many ways. There was his "extraordinary beard . . . with eyes that dominated the beard" and conveyed a Jesus-like appearance. Dr. Blos's "wide interests were never constricted by professional custom or tradition." He supplemented traditional medicine with emphasis on what were then revolutionary ideas—open bedroom windows in all seasons, regular exercising, and wounds left open to heal. Even more than Peter, Edwin showed Erik an "intrinsically German preoccupation with matters on the borderline between the spirit and the mind." Dr. Blos cultivated in Erik a love for great humanists like Goethe. He also coupled a "German superiority of spirit" with a profound respect for Eastern religion and philosophy. (When he was older, he wore a Buddha's gown and retreated to the Bavarian Alps.) In later life, when Erik reflected on the 1920–27 interlude between gymnasium graduation and his move to Vienna, he felt that his many conversations with Edwin Blos influenced some of his basic concepts and interests. Through Romain Rolland's *Mahatma Gandhi,* European youth became interested in India's emerging pacifist leader, whose most significant accomplishments were still ahead of him. Dr. Blos broadened Erik's knowledge of Gandhi's emerging historic significance, and thus laid some of the groundwork for the book on Gandhi that Erik later wrote. His well-known midlife essay on Gorky's childhood in central Russia also owed a debt to Blos. Even Erik's work on the polarities or conflicting pressures within each stage of the human life cycle may have begun with his conversations with Dr. Blos "*über die Polarität*" (or the polarities), which Blos had drawn from Goethe.[42]

Close and instructive contacts with Peter and Edwin Blos compensated decidedly for Erik's troubled gymnasium experience. The fact that Peter's mother was a gifted oil painter also attracted Erik to the Blos household. During one visit he became friends with Oscar Stonorov, another young Karlsruhe resident with artistic sensibilities. Through Oscar, Erik acquired a modest interest in the piano, but music never had the same attraction for him as art and humanistic ideas. Soon Erik, Peter, and Oscar would spend a significant interval together in Florence. Before that, however, Erik secured some formal art training.[43]

After Erik graduated from the Karlsruhe gymnasium, he hiked for a few months about the Black Forest. Then in 1921, he enrolled at Karlsruhe's Badische Landeskunstschule (Baden State Art School). Art was not regarded as a respectable calling within the city's Jewish community. By turning to artistic endeavors rather than university education and the professions, Erik departed from his stepfather's path. Gustav Wolf ran the small school like a studio, and students worked on sundry arts and crafts, including the hand construction of small-scale art books. Jewish and known to the Homburger family, Wolf took a liking to Erik. Although his was a facility for boys, he also allowed Erik's half sister Ellen to attend classes.[44]

The year Erik attended Badische Landeskunstschule, Wolf completed and published *Das Zeichen-Büchlein*. More a pamphlet than a book, it expounded on how pictorial sketches and letter characters were drawn and engraved (usually with wood), and how the woodcut engraving was made into a print. Black-and-white prints of sketches and characters were paired with the text. For most of the pamphlet's illustrations, Wolf's students engraved and printed works of such prominent artists as Van Gogh and Dürer. But in a few cases a student would draw his own sketch and turn it into a woodcut print. Erik's, the most striking of these, appeared at the beginning of the pamphlet. It was a full-page landscape showing a fierce sun radiating power and facing a vicious snake that was wrapped around a tree atop a mountain. Wolf voiced pride that "engravings and sentence arrangements were made together," and that the volume was a collective enterprise of teacher and student.

Das Zeichen-Büchlein propounded Wolf's philosophy of artistic creation, which he thus allowed Erik and other students to embellish and illustrate as part of their training. Erik took the effort seriously; he drew heavily upon Wolf's general perspective two years later in his personal journal. A chief premise in Wolf's pamphlet was that a truly artistic touch was inseparable from the artist's mind and spirit: "Whoever makes a mountain must himself be the mountain that he himself forms." The artist had to "be" or "become" that which he created in his work so that the creation had "meaning" deeper than mere outward appearance. In turn, the artist "stands firmly rooted in the world. . . . The power of the world streams into him: He becomes the world, space. It breaks out of him and speaks for him."[45]

For Wolf and his students, the artist's fundamental imperative was to "stand in the service of the spirit, decisive and true." The artist did this when he moved beyond concern for outer form and appearance and connected to the spirit within himself and the spirit of the society about him: "Whoever throws out decoration and elaborateness finds the spirit." True art disregards "the stroke itself" so that "his spirit only shows." In this way, the artist will "fulfill his destiny."[46]

Wolf and his students were certainly influenced by what they construed as Nietzsche's injunction "to become what one is." The process of making a woodcut engraving offered the way to fathom and advance that essence: "The engraving knife gets rid of all that is insignificant—gets down to that which is essential and basic in the subject," which is the artist's self. Through an engraved sketch that is true to what is essential, the artist "has raised himself out of his isolation and gone out into the world [and] is able to deal with the essence, the becoming, and the departing. He is not tied to present appearance, he is able to create new essence and connection." By realizing oneself in this way, the artist simultaneously realizes and expresses God and society: "The power of the Almighty flows through him, the drive of the living. The will of the earth speaks through him; he shows the likeness of the universe." Indeed, when the artist learns to express only the essence, "he is open to all that is human. His path is his end."[47]

Das Zeichen-Büchlein represented the work and thought of Gustav Wolf. But Wolf deeply respected Erik within the small student group that assisted him and engraved sketches to please him. Erik's sketch of a mountaintop scene with unusually shaped shrubs, a horse and a cow, birds overhead, and a boy sleeping by a tree amid disturbing weather conditions was especially powerful. If Erik did not subscribe fully, in 1921, to Wolf's themes of becoming one's essence and the importance of connecting the self to society, he was considering them very seriously. Wolf's book was one of the few that Erik retained from his early years until his death.

Probably at Wolf's suggestion and his own growing sense that Karlsruhe was confining, Erik left for Munich in 1922 when he was twenty. He spent a little less than two years there, and those years are sketchy. Erik enrolled in the famous Kunst-Akademie to study artistic technique. A few of his woodcuts were displayed in the Munich Glaspalast alongside Max Beckmann's paintings and Wilhelm Lehmbruck's delicate, frail statues. Yet Erik worked on his own and made most of his woodcuts outside the walls of the *Akademie*. Apparently, he had no mentor to study with as he had in Karlsruhe. He assumed that sketching "can be a good exercise in tracing impressions." Moreover, he recalled how he had "enjoyed making very large woodprints; to cut stark images of nature on this primary material conveyed an elemental sense of both art and craft." In a broad sense, to be sure, his sketches and prints represented extensions of the German naturalist and expressionist rebellion against decorative pseudoclassical style. More fundamentally, he felt that he was decidedly "impressionistic" and focused on themes of being "alone w[ith] nature like Van Gogh." His woodcuts of large fields with rocks, hills, and other objects that came alive with vibrant energy resembled Van Gogh's scenes. However, daring use of paint and color had been central to Van Gogh, and Erik bemoaned the fact that he "never learned to paint w/color." He tried to move beyond "black and white drawings and woodcuts" and felt that if he wanted a significant career as an artist, he would have to do so. But he could not develop a facility for the use of color and paint; that "was where the inhibition was," he recalled. Consequently, although his large sketches transformed into woodcut prints showed considerable energy and imagination, and commanded some recognition, Erik left Munich feeling that eventually he would have to move to some other calling. Art was not to be his vocation.[48]

Much later, Erik characterized his years at the Badische Landeskunstschule and the Kunst-Akademie as part of a prolonged, seven-year *Wanderschaft*. This interval of wandering and reflecting started with the completion of his gymnasium work. It did not end when he returned with his belongings to Karlsruhe in 1925 (he continued to take short trips), but in 1927, when Peter Blos summoned him to Freud's Vienna. While he might stay for a while at a new city or town or lake, or even stop for food and clothing in Karlsruhe, he "always again took to wandering." Erik viewed this as part of "a German cultural ritualization" that many youth went through, "a more or less artistic and reflective wandering." The *Wanderschaft* was largely (but not exclusively) a phenomenon of German adolescent boys, who went off together in postponement of adult heterosexuality. In reaction to the rigidities of German schools, with their bureaucratic regimes and rote memorization, adolescent boys hiked about aimlessly from one *Gasthaus* or camping site to another. They turned away from the pragmatic perspectives promoted by Germany's late industrialization and slow but steady urbanization, and they celebrated the laws and values of nature. Adult society recognized and accepted the wanderings of these youths with bare knees and hatless heads as they sought the spiritual and the spontaneous. It was regarded as a normal if temporary phase of life.[49]

Erik's *Wanderschaft* was longer than most. It took him from Karlsruhe through the Black Forest to a tiny village on the shore of Lake Constance, where he spent several months. From there he returned to Karlsruhe for Wolf's school and then went to Munich for two years. From Munich he headed south toward the French-Italian border where he "sat on the mountaintops" and sketched the landscape. Next he traveled into Italy. He liked Tuscany and especially Florence, with its connection to the Renaissance. There he met up with his Karlsruhe friends Peter Blos and Oscar Stonorov. He made a rather commonplace arrangement with a family in Fiesole, overlooking Florence, for room and board in exchange for sketches and woodcuts. Fiesole had long attracted writers and artists to its villas and hill dwellings amid cypress and olive trees, where they sought inspiration. But by this time, Erik had already forsaken a career as an artist. Often he sat on a bench near his Fiesole home with Blos and Stonorov, absorbing the sights and sounds of Florence and wondering together what was ahead of them. Although Stonorov had moved beyond woodcuts to painting and sculpting, and Blos had begun to write poetry, all three were experiencing what Erik later called a "psychosocial moratorium"—"we were waiting for a profession to commit ourselves to." They were concerned about "principles of artistic form and of the human measure" and therefore inattentive to the emerging political threat: "[Italian] Fascism we took in stride; it could only be a passing aberration from the classical spirit." Blos returned to Karlsruhe temporarily in 1924 and then set out for Vienna. Erik returned the following year.[50]

By this time Karlsruhe was no longer home. To be sure, Erik later applauded his mother and stepfather for "the fortitude to let me find my way unhurriedly," but he knew that Theodor was growing increasingly impatient with the wanderings of "the strange boy he brought up" and wanted Erik to settle down as another local pediatrician. The stepfather would have been even more uneasy if he had known that despite the massive German inflation of the 1920s, Karla secretly passed to Erik considerable money through a distant relative who ran a bank. Whenever he returned to Karlsruhe for short stays, Karla surreptitiously supplied him with packages of food and clothing. Theodor took no joy in his stepson's unfocused state. Erik noted years later in a general vein that "the mother openly or secretly would favor, if not envy," the adolescent son's wanderlust but "the father was considered its foe."[51]

While the mysteries of his paternity had long made the Homburger home in Karlsruhe uncomfortable for Erik, he now regarded it as an impossible place to live. His parents, especially his stepfather, considered him "almost [a] Failure" and a "drop out," although "mother believed" in him still. As long as Karla's secret financial support continued, he could escape the "*bürgerlich* [middle-class] confines" of the Homburger home and community. Like other German youth of his generation, he could hike about the south of Europe, read widely, and sketch what interested him: "This made me sturdy physically and balanced in a sensory way." And yet after Munich he knew that he would not be a professional artist. He recognized what he could not be and "did not want to be," but "I had no image of what I would be." More to the point, the wanderer's life was not very satisfying. Erik's moods seemed constantly to change and his half sisters considered him deeply disturbed. He never wrote home, which sorely tested parental tolerance. Sometimes he felt terribly driven neurotically, "bookish," and impatient with everyday life. At other moments he had romantic visions and grandiose dreams of being very special and different. Later, after he became a clinician and knew more about technical aspects of mental distress, he applied more severe diagnostic terms to these shifting moods. He had been "disturbed" to the point where he was "on the border between neurosis and psychosis" and therefore suffered from a " 'borderline' character." "I was probably close to psychosis," he recalled. Nevertheless, he cautioned that however disturbed he had been, he eventually recovered, and traditional diagnostic labels did not seem to give this sufficient attention. Consequently, he preferred, retrospectively, to call his malady simply a somewhat aggravated "identity crisis." It was not entirely abnormal to youth of his age and place, and it was less than ominous.[52]

Clearly, Erik was in a fragile state at the start of adulthood. The stepson's identity of "mixed" and confused parentage, religion, and nationality had produced a person who felt himself living precariously "on the line" and having to navigate multiple border crossings. He sought relief from the confining middle-class Homburger household in alternative lifestyles, in the values of the Blos household, and with Gustav Wolf. Yet as he moved on to Munich and Florence, artistic centers in southern Europe, he did not feel that he could master the paints and colors and techniques that were central to the painters he had hoped eventually to emulate. At this juncture, he was taken with a mid-nineteenth-century painting by Gustave Courbet ("Interior of My Studio, a Real Allegory Summing Up Seven Years of My Life as an Artist") that anticipated Impressionism. It was of a painter in his studio using color and strokes to create a landscape of trees and sky, brightness and hope. A child and a nude woman watch the painter sympathetically as he works. Erik felt that Courbet's painter was experiencing a revolution of the senses, "which all at once freed the eyes from the accustomed shades of indoor life, the imagination from moralistic repression, the body from suffocation of excess clothing, and sensuality from the shackles of convention." The landscape outside represented "an open window, a 'wide-eye,' toward the outside" of hope, beauty, and serenity. The entire painting provided "a long repressed sensual awareness of man's naked unity with observed nature." Unlike Courbet, Erik could not paint or otherwise find on a solid and lasting basis the "open window" from the repressed *Bürger*'s existence to a freer yet more hopeful and serene circumstance. His *Wanderschaft* had not carried him that far. He recalled the desperate sense that he had nowhere to go and returned to Theodor's home in Karlsruhe.[53]

"MANUSCRIPT VON ERIK"

Beginning in August of 1923, when he was twenty-one, and for the year that followed, Erik carried about a bound book of large sheets of paper intended for sketching. Instead, he filled roughly 140 pages with what he called jottings. It was his first extensive writing exercise as he pursued a new medium for sustained expression in the face of faltering efforts in art. He wrote during the last half of his *Wanderschaft* as he traveled from Munich through the mountainous terrain in the south of France and northern Italy and then into Florence. It was not a travel log. The unpaginated volume had an eerie, ungrounded quality. It did not indicate time or place, climate, the circumstances of family and friends, or political and economic issues. Little was sequential. One verse, paragraph, or note—ranging from a line or two to a full page—usually did not connect to the next. Most of Erik's passages were hasty, unmediated expressions as his hand raced over a page, often unable to keep up with his thoughts. Some sentences were grammatically flawed. Verbs were sometimes lacking and misspellings abounded. In contrast, he was extraordinarily careful with a few passages that he revised, sometimes several times, in order to express himself precisely. Some rewriting may even have occurred after he had ceased to make entries into this notebook. His handwriting was messy and sometimes very nearly illegible, rendering translation from German to English difficult and alternative translations possible.[54]

Erik dedicated the manuscript "*Ex libris*—Dr. Theodor und Karla Homburger." This seemed to suggest that he wanted his parents to learn of his thoughts. A request appended to the end of the manuscript, however, suggested that he had not necessarily given it to them to read: "Whoever finds these pages should read to the end." He characterized the volume as "a collection of notes made during a wandering" that was "not sequential. It is about how one experiences the landscape." It was not interdisciplinary but predisciplinary in the sense that it read like an adventurous exercise in expression without the imperatives of form, structure, or direction.

Although Erik wrote with obvious energy, references to personal feelings were minimal. The narrator's voice was abstract, philosophic, even impersonal and arrogant. Erik pontificated on the nature of humankind with only random notations revealing anything explicitly about himself. There were a few indications that he experienced sharply altering moods and feelings as he wrote, but he never addressed them. Emotions were subordinated to abstractions. Life was not to be considered in its tangible, day-to-day manifestations involving progression over time and place. This was a volume of abstract and random notations.

The content of several of these notations was hardly unique. Other young men who had gone through the German gymnasium curriculum had articulated similar thoughts. Erik's musings often echoed the despair, beauty, and tragedy of German adolescence and adulthood in a tradition harking back to Goethe's *The Sorrows of Young Werther*—themes that continued to be delineated in novels by Hermann Hesse and Robert von Musil in the twentieth century. Young male characters in these and similar works echoed elements of the pre–World War I German youth movement, which had interesting ties to the French Enlightenment as well as to German romanticism. These young characters critiqued the obsolete traditions of adult society, they glorified nature, they articulated idealistic goals for social change, and they embraced freedom (both abstract and erotic). Like Erik's manuscript, writings of this sort provided windows into the world of wandering European students who moved continuously about the landscape, scorned the restraints of family and school, and embraced nature, truth, and "genuine" selfhood.

While many of Erik's jottings were therefore less than unique, other notations indicated that he stood out in important ways. Perhaps more vividly than any other source, these demonstrated that he was deeply troubled. He seemed to have enormous difficulty ordering his thoughts and confronting his emotions. Decades later, he would characterize this psychological condition of adolescents and young adults as an "identity crisis." In a vague and suggestive way, the notebook also revealed several of the ideas and concepts that would transform him into a major twentieth-century intellectual. Written four years before he arrived in Vienna, he advanced certain thoughts that scholars have improperly characterized as extensions of his psychoanalytic training with Sigmund and Anna Freud. They were Erik's before he knew anything about depth psychology. With a far greater debt to German Romanticism than to Freud, Erik enunciated powerful and original thoughts of his own.

The manuscript opened with two messy and much reworked pages explaining how his diverse notations "arose out of the various experiences and landscapes" and "arranged themselves as I have recorded them here." There were apologetic qualifications over "which of my sentences, the hammer of mockery, will be directed," and how "everything that we actually know cannot be expressed." Erik acknowledged "how little I have read about all the people" that he cited in his pages. Next came the general theme—the constantly changing nature of human experience as life progressed. Childhood and youth represented a period when multiple desires arose and diverse causes were launched. Second came the more "level observation, and lofty thoughts" of middle life that were communicated to others. Finally, "death is the third and last period: the overcoming of the self in a last burst of its ethical plenitude, loving understanding, the return to the meaning of the beginning." Before he had thought much about a human life cycle, Erik announced it as the theme that united his jottings.

However, no theme or series of themes grounded the manuscript, which moved in a multiplicity of directions, and there were only scattered, limited references to life stages. Once, to be sure, he wrote cryptically of a life cycle: "The continued thread of the demonic sticks out from *the cycles of life*." At another point, he cited Goethe and Lao-tzu for his understanding of "organic development" and postulated that "it is upon intensity and total absorption in experiencing the stages that the organic succession of the next stage rests: every step is a goal." In a wholly unrelated discussion, Erik wrote of "a slow, broad, gestating in one's nature" that was "enriched and completed by the most varied experiences." Once he remarked on "the stages of character." At another point he insisted that genius involved perpetuating the style and the "sensual intensity" of one's youth "at every stage of his life." At no point did he seek to connect or amplify upon even a few of these scattered observations.

Erik was influenced heavily by German romanticism, to be sure, and by a view of development characterized by a telos or goal. Still, it is well to underscore that he was reflecting on evolving stages within the human life cycle when he was twenty-one and before he had any awareness of Freudian developmental perspective. A four-line poem intended to reference the antitheticals in life and fate was especially telling. Reflecting the influence of Hegel, Goethe, and Blake as well as his discussions with Edwin Blos "*über die Polarität*," Erik periodically juxtaposed "beauty" and "abyss," "necessity" and "freedom," the "physical" and the "spiritual," the "manly" and the "womanly," "youth" and "age," the "diamonic" and the "harmonious," "life" and "death," and other apparent antitheticals. Invoking several of these in his poem, he described the process of aging and death:

> Content dies, balanced form lives on
> (*Inhalt stirbt, Formgleichgewicht lebt*)
> Body dies, beauty lives on
> (*Körper stirbt, Schönheit lebt*)
> Actuality [fact] dies, truth lives on
> (*Tatsache stirbt, Wahrheit lebt*)
> The self [person] dies, the I [ego] lives on
> (*Person stirbt, Ich lebt*)

The concrete and the earthly (content, body, actuality, self) were succeeded by the aesthetic and the spiritual (balance, beauty, truth, the "I"). Decades later, Erik would fashion his formal model of the life cycle in a similar dialectic fashion, and with a decided shift in emphasis from the concrete to the spiritual.

The last line of Erik's verse was the most intriguing—"The self [person] dies, the I [ego] lives on." In another part of the journal, he noted how "the self is that which, living, experiences itself; for if there is no outer [world] there would not be self." Erik seemed to have meant that one experienced a distinctive sense of "self" only if one could "differentiate" oneself from others in the "outer" world. Four pages later, he noted: " 'I' is what experiences itself. The other experiences 'not self.' " The sense of "I" could emerge "passively," but it could also emerge through "an overabundant will to form a consciousness." Even allowing for the imprecisions of translation from German to English (self or person; I or ego), Erik was confused in his language and his perspectives. The "I" seemed to be somewhat fuller and more all-embracing than the "self," more intense within the individual, more enduring, and of a deeper spiritual essence. But "self" and "I" overlapped decidedly in his thinking and were tied to what he would come to call identity.

The final line in Erik's verse, plus other notebook references to "self" and "I," seemed intended to elaborate a point that had intrigued him since he became involved in Gustav Wolf's *Das Zeichen-Büchlein* two years earlier. This was the importance of Nietzsche's injunction "to become what one is"—to discover and cultivate one's essence to the utmost. Whether it was called the "self" or the "I" or the convergence of the two in ways that Erik would associate with identity, that essence was no autonomous Lockean individual. Rather, it emerged in conjunction with the other, whether the other was a lover, a leader, a parent, or God. "Self creation" came about as one looked at and "resonated together" with a much loved other, whether that other took a specific human form or was "the timeless smiling one" (i.e., God). In the years ahead, Erik would insist that strong positive identity required connection to others, even as his popularizers often misstated his perspective as a vote for atomistic individualism.

The first line in Erik's four-line poem emphasized "balanced form." His notebook housed other references to balance, harmony, centering, and equilibrium. "Harmony" comes with "a balance of the most divergent passions in productivity, in such a way that for every extreme another is at hand in the equation, as if thereby . . . there is a harmony in the relationship of the parts of the complex." One of the most important balances was between the masculine and the feminine qualities of the self. In both Goethe's writings and Leonardo da Vinci's art, Erik found "a natural yardstick of feeling reconciling 'feminine' and 'masculine' " qualities. This balancing of gendered propensities in the self would preoccupy Erik for decades to come.

There were no references to Freud anywhere in Erik's manuscript. He had mentioned to friends that the very little he knew about Freud's thought sounded absurd. Yet Erik took Nietzsche very seriously and, in this way, select elements in the notebook suggested a vague proximity to Freud. Like

Nietzsche, Erik emphasized the importance of childhood in human development. Approximating Nietzsche, Erik stressed the "I" and the "self." Most important, before Freud, Nietzsche had been deeply concerned with the dangers of repressing the instinctual urges of the body. Erik embraced this perspective. "Virtue arises from bodily need," he asserted, and true morality is impossible unless it accommodates the promptings and "feeling" within the body. Because "soul is body," the body had to be allowed to release "the intention of the ailing soul."[55]

Like many others trained in the early-twentieth-century German gymnasium tradition, Erik was thoroughly elitist and contemptuous of the "masses." The gymnasium curriculum had included study of Caesar's wars, German tragic literature, and other topics that focused on the historic importance of the great man. Hegel had hailed the hero, tied to the collective unconscious, who might promote unity and greatness. Similarly, Erik dismissed "the craze for democracy" with its "futureless values." "Leveling creates loneliness, creation of a proletariat creates division," he warned, but the great "leader's personality creates unity." Historically, the only virtue of the masses was an "instinct for leadership." The great leader displayed "strength in organization, flexible power of suggestion." He promoted "breathing space for the will [of society] to form." In what later became his characteristic manner of describing creative revolutionary leaders like Luther and Gandhi, Erik noted that such a person had the ability "to express and portray tensions and connections [in society] which cause to others a brief and hardly bearable shudder of awe." By articulating and resolving underlying tensions within society, the leader managed fundamental but well-ordered historic change.

Most of Erik's comments on the personality of a leader were general. Discussion of Moses and his leadership of the Jews represented one of his few specific, time- and culture-bound references. He emphasized that the ethics of Moses and the Jews were "boundary obliterating" and therefore inclusive of all humankind (what he would later call universal specieshood). This was admirable, for "the more worlds an individual unites in himself . . . the more inclusive he is, the truer he is." Like Goethe, Friedrich von Schiller, and Rainer Marie Rilke, Erik was holding out for a universal cosmopolitanism as his standard. But he also concluded that humankind tended to embrace exclusive races, religions, and nationalities in order "to brave the abyss of the singular." For this reason, most people invoked "jealousy of boundaries" separating their kind from others (a quality that Erik would eventually call pseudospeciation).

In other notebook jottings, however, Erik was less admiring of Moses and Judaism. Perhaps reflecting conflicting feelings over his parentage and the

Karlsruhe Jewish community, he characterized himself as "European" rather than as a Jew. He also criticized Jewish monotheism as "more a state deity than a spiritual deity" even though the Jews "in decline, covered this name with a spiritual interpretation." By asserting in one notation that Moses and the Jews were "boundary obliterating" and in another that their monotheism represented a state deity and was spiritually constrictive, Erik revealed more than a personal ambivalence. He showed his ignorance of a central element in Judaism—that it was a communitarian religion with strands of ethical socialism.

While Erik's notebook offered a multiplicity of observations and lessons for humankind, it deferred to a more primary instructor—nature—for he made more entries concerning nature than any other topic. This was congruent with the German romantic tradition on which he so heavily drew. His emphasis was also related to the fact that he jotted in his notebook as he hiked and made sketches and woodcuts of what he saw. He characterized human immersion in nature as the highest form of "actuality" (or "factuality")—interaction of a person with the conditions of the world. It was real and vital. This connection to nature was like the revelation of "Truth" that Goethe saw emerging at the point where a person's inner personal world met and mixed with external reality. "If you want to know what times you live in and what you can be in them," Erik asserted, "then encounter the open sky by the bright shining lake." One understood oneself deeply and discerned "the quiet, sublime language of the world" simply by seeing "the tree that stands sharply delineated against the blue; the stone in the glow of the sun."

Completed in the midst of his *Wanderschaft*, "Manuscript von Erik" consisted of some fascinating and unique notations even as it embraced typical concerns of the vagabond European youth. In it were the seeds of concepts he would spend a lifetime elaborating, including the human life cycle; the sense of "self," "I," and identity; the masculine balancing the feminine in the individual personality; the importance of the leader in historical transformations; and the conflict between pseudospeciation and universal specieshood. He even included what he later characterized as "integrity" in old age—"to end, in order to relish a beginning . . . to decay without becoming distorted." To be sure, Erik drew heavily from several German intellectuals, especially from the works of Nietzsche, Goethe, and Hegel, even as he formulated his most original and creative perspectives. Like Schiller, Rilke, and Goethe, he anchored his thoughts to a respect for the free individual and a displeasure with nationalism's pressures to conform. Freud, too, had drawn heavily from these same German thinkers and had embraced cosmopolitan values. This made for some compatibility between Erik and Freud. But it is well to keep in mind that in 1923 and 1924 Erik knew almost nothing about the founder of psychoanalysis as he jotted down what became some of the most significant concepts of his intellectual career.

A NEW BEGINNING

The strength and profundity found in several notations in Erik's manuscript contrasted markedly with the weak, moody, defensive, and directionless aspects of his life and personality. This distinction between life and text would be discernible at several other points in his life. He was troubled about his future as an artist. Freud had gone to Rome to see Michelangelo's work. So did Erik, and the visit augmented his sense that he could never compete with a brilliant artist. Consequently, after he finished the notebook and took up residence in Florence, he spent long periods without making any sketches or woodcuts. The inaction and despondency continued after he returned to Karlsruhe in 1925; he traveled little now. Indeed, a photograph that year of Erik sitting on a bench in Karlsruhe with his half sisters suggests that he was quite downcast. Unlike Ruth and Ellen, he appeared gaunt, tired, tense, and unable to summon a smile. As his *Wanderschaft* drew to a close and possibilities for a career in art seemed exhausted, he gave no thought to writing. "I was in many ways a nonfunctioning artist," he recalled, suffering from a serious "work disturbance," and "there were simply months when I couldn't work at all and didn't feel like putting anything on paper." Often he "did not feel like doing anything at all."[56]

Erik's depression was not entirely unique. Hermann Hesse and several others of his generation had continued to feel rudderless after the period of the *Wanderschaft*. Erik did not know where to turn. He considered emulating Gustav Wolf and becoming a local arts and crafts teacher. Peter Blos, who had gone to Vienna to study biology, was very apprehensive about his friend's emotional state. So he wrote Erik a letter early in the spring of 1927 that Erik never forgot. In fact, Erik later compared it to the way Wilhelm Fliess had rallied Freud at a difficult moment. "Nietzsche once said that a friend is the life saver who holds you above water when your divided selves threaten to drag you to the bottom," Erik recalled, and Blos had become just that lifesaver.[57]

After enrolling at the University of Vienna, Blos became the tutor to Dorothy Burlingham's four children. She was an American heiress of Tiffany wealth. Burlingham was then in analysis with Sigmund Freud and was becoming close to his daughter, Anna, who was analyzing her children. Blos lived in the Burlingham home, where he taught the children the sciences and German. Soon, though, he felt his tutoring interfered with his studies, and he resigned as the children's tutor. Burlingham and Anna Freud offered to establish him in his own school to continue teaching the four children and others (especially English and Americans) who were being analyzed or whose parents were in analysis. Blos felt that he needed a co-instructor in that venture and told Anna Freud that although Erik "knows nothing of education or teaching," he was "more gifted" than trained educators. Ms. Freud was interested. Burlingham agreed to finance Erik's trip to Vienna by commissioning him to sketch portraits of her children. Consequently, Blos wrote to Erik of the commission and the opportunity to meet with Anna Freud.[58]

In April of 1927, Robert Burlingham, Dorothy's oldest child, wrote that "a friend of Mr. Blos came and he can draw heads you know!" The Burlingham children immediately took to Erik and his sketches. At this point, Erik, not yet twenty-five, recalled how he "hardly [had] any idea who [Sigmund] Freud was" but interviewed with Freud's daughter. It was apparent during the interview that "I didn't know what I wanted. I was artistically gifted but wasn't quite sure how to employ it" and had never worked "regular hours." Anna Freud was impressed by how quickly Erik had bonded with the children and sensed a creative spark as she walked with him. Erik tutored the Burlingham children briefly that summer while Blos was away, and their mother reported favorably to Anna Freud on his potentialities. When Blos returned to Vienna, Ms. Freud told him that if he could provide the children in his school with a solid education, he could retain Erik as a co-teacher. Blos agreed, and Erik secured his first regular job teaching in a facility that was vital to the Freudian psychoanalytic circle.[59]

Interestingly, Erik Homburger chose to begin his most comprehensive autobiographical essay by describing his arrival in Vienna as "the very beginning of my career." Actually, it was a *new beginning*. Erik's life now appeared to be taking a new and solid form. The brilliant if undeveloped ideas evident in his notebook were about to be tested and amplified during a new career as a psychoanalyst. He was on his way to becoming Erik Erikson, identity's architect.[60]

CHAPTER TWO

Vienna Years:
Psychoanalysis as a Calling,
1927–33

Before Erik Homburger turned thirty-one in 1933, the Vienna Psycho-analytic Society voted to make him a member in full standing, which put him on the rolls of the International Psycho-Analytical Association and gave him global credentials as a training analyst. The vote represented a general evaluation by Vienna's senior psychoanalysts of his activities during his six-year stay in the city. Arriving in 1927, he had attended the Vienna society's important Wednesday evening meetings, had completed a training analysis with Anna Freud, and had become skilled in the new field of child analysis. He had also finished a teaching degree at the local Montessori school and had become a popular instructor at the experimental Hietzing School.[1]

His training came at a crucial time in the development of psychoanalysis in Vienna. Sigmund Freud was ailing and delegated many responsibilities for both the local and the international psychoanalytic movement to his daughter. Following the precedents of Carl Jung and Alfred Adler, a number of major psychoanalytic thinkers had left or were thinking of leaving Freud's inner circle. Moreover, until Hitler came to power, Berlin was challenging Vienna as the center for innovative theoretical and clinical work with adults. Still, Freud's ideas continued to attract global interest, while an Austrian publishing house put out a stream of psychoanalytic books, monographs, and journals. Students, patients, and interested visitors from abroad sought audiences with local psychoanalysts. Eminent figures like Heinz Hartmann, Paul Federn, and Edward Bibring continued to shape the field from Vienna, where Freud's presence was still quite inspiring. At the same time, August Aichhorn, Anna Freud, and others were turning Vienna into the pioneering center for psychoanalytic work with children and adolescents. Consequently, despite some problematic developments and the impending Fascist and Nazi threats, psychoanalysis in Vienna remained vibrant, with considerable international appeal, from 1927 to 1933.[2]

Experiencing Vienna life largely from within the psychoanalytic community and its tributaries, Erik left the city in 1933 a very different person from when he arrived. Retrospectively, he emphasized that "Anna Freud and others of the circle around him [Sigmund Freud] took me in and opened a life's work for me." He "could see Freud and Anna Freud socially" and was thus "close to the original atmosphere." It had been like "the Paulinian days of Christianity" within "a small community of special people." He felt that after a prolonged *Wanderschaft* and an abortive effort to become an artist, he had finally secured a real "vocation in the area of child psychoanalysis and education."[3]

Erik also recalled enthusiastically how this new calling of child analyst had been compatible with his strong visual and artistic impulses. He had been impressed by Sigmund Freud's "respect for form"—how the shapes and dimensions of our dreams and our arrangements of artifacts were vital in understanding both our emotions and our social circumstances. Freud's regard for the psychological meaning of artistic form allowed Erik to integrate his prior experience as an artist with his psychoanalytic clinical training. He became a "clinical artist" who studied "forms" to understand the relationship between the inner world of the maker of those forms and the outer society.[4]

In time, Erik came to refer to this way of connecting inner emotional and outer social life as his "configurational" approach, and he felt that it was central to his contribution to the psychoanalytic dialogue. To a limited extent, this approach may also have represented his way of connecting the two most important women in his life during his Vienna years. Anna Freud, his mentor, supervisor, and analyst, had been attentive to external social realities in shaping human personality. However, she was adamant in her insistence upon the orthodoxy propounded by her father (i.e., excavating the inner layers of the human psyche to the deepest level possible). In contrast, Erik's lover and wife-to-be, Joan Serson, had little patience with psychoanalytic orthodoxy. She was preoccupied with dance, crafts, and other aspects of the social world surrounding the inner self. As these two women struggled for Erik's attention and allegiance, he was primarily influenced by their conflicting emotional pull. Perhaps by invoking a configurational approach that connected inner and outer worlds theoretically, he may also, in some sense, have been accommodating their different orientations.

THE HIETZING SCHOOL

When Erik Homburger came to Vienna in the spring of 1927, he appeared to be tense and eager to break from his past. He revealed little about his Danish and German background or his interests. He tutored Dorothy Burlingham's children, accompanied the Burlinghams on summer trips with Sigmund and Anna Freud, and was "deeply impressed by his [Freud's] stoic suffering" with palate cancer. Central Europeans often assumed that men were not very good with small children, but Erik was remarkable. His "lack of training in other things didn't seem to matter much," he recalled much later, for "I had a certain sense of children's experience and that did it." When he prepared to join Peter Blos at the new school, the Freuds, Dorothy Burlingham, and their good friend Eva Rosenfeld were pleased that their plans for him were materializing.[5]

The Hietzing district, where Rosenfeld lived, was the setting for this special school, within a city that was experiencing a crucial transformation. The "Red Vienna" experiment that began in 1919 with the ascendancy of Social Democrats in city government had reached a precarious state by 1927. The Social Democrats had committed city government to an unprecedented program of social welfare, including extensive public housing, rent control, new hospitals and outpatient clinics, and branch libraries in working-class neighborhoods. Above all, the Social Democrats had committed themselves to children's programs. Under the leadership of Julius Tandler, city councilor for welfare, and school superintendent Otto Glöckel, Vienna supported a comprehensive system of children's services, including school lunches, school dental and medical examinations, after-school centers and summer camps, plus additional kindergartens, playgrounds, and wading pools in working-class districts along with special consultation clinics for troubled youngsters. Tandler ran an adoption center that found homes for orphans and those children suffering from parental neglect. Public education became more secularized and innovative programs for teacher training certification were instituted. A child-centered pedagogy emerged that deemphasized rote memorization and promoted active hands-on learning and interdisciplinary study. Though Erik was relatively apolitical, he studied briefly with Tandler at the University of Vienna and with psychologists Karl and Charlotte Bühler, who had been active in children's causes. He also thought well of Siegfried Bernfeld and Paul Federn, psychoanalysts who were committed Social Democrats. Peter Blos was even more deeply impressed by these and other social reformers of the period. Consequently, the two young men could draw upon many innovative people, ideas, and programs as they prepared an instructional program for the Hietzing School.[6]

By the late 1920s, however, they recognized that these reformers and their efforts were being critically challenged as Austrian society at large turned to the right. The rightward drift nationwide threatened Vienna policies and ideas. By 1927, a conservative Christian Social Party, devoted to monarchy and with a frightened rural Catholic constituency, had gained national leadership. Its military association, the Heimwehr, received financial support from Italy's Fascist government. Christian Social Party support markedly increased in 1929, as the international Depression struck Austria with special ferocity, with rapidly escalating unemployment, bankrupt industries, and collapse of the Rothschild banks. The ravages of the Depression were acute in Vienna, where unemployment rolls climbed sharply, a housing shortage developed, and funds to support social services began to dry up. The Vienna public educational programs and other children's services were cut significantly. Moreover, anti-Semitism raised its ugly head. The city's nearly 200,000 Jews, who dominated the legal and medical professions and comprised a large proportion of the teachers and professors, came under attack. Jewish Social Democrat activists were treated suspiciously. By the summer of 1930, torchlight parades of rightist Heimwehr youth were inescapable, and assaults on Jewish businesses, coffeehouses, and university students were increasing.[7]

The Hietzing School came into being, then, in a troubled time in a city under siege. Founders of the enterprise realized that public schools were becoming increasingly inhospitable to costly efforts at educational experimentation and social support for children. Other more specific factors were also involved in the decision to establish a school in the pleasant and modestly affluent suburban Hietzing district a few blocks from the beautiful and spacious Schönbrunn Park and Gardens. Eva Rosenfeld and her family had been close with Peter Blos's family in Karlsruhe, and she had found him the job as tutor for Dorothy Burlingham's children when he came to Vienna. Rosenfeld had been deeply distressed over the death of her daughter Mädi in a hiking accident in 1927, and volunteered the backyard of her home in Hietzing as the site of the school. It was to be a monument to Mädi and a domestic diversion from a troubled marriage to her lawyer husband: "I wanted to find comfort for my own sad heart in being with the younger ones." Rosenfeld also promised food and music for students and staff plus her considerable management skills.[8]

Anna Freud promoted the Hietzing School as part of her mission to establish child analysis as a professional calling. In her "Four Lectures on Child Analysis" (1926–27), she had advocated "a school which is organized according to psychoanalytic principles and geared to cooperation with the analyst." By thus integrating psychoanalytic work with school life, the transference relationship at the heart of analysis would be enhanced and a stronger partnership of analyst, child, and parent would be possible. By this time, Dorothy Burlingham had become a close, personal friend of Anna Freud (who had recently become her father's analysand). Indeed, Burlingham was beginning to compete with Rosenfeld for Anna Freud's attentions. She knew that her four children suffered terribly from her estranged relationship with her manic-depressive mate. Burlingham also recognized how her children felt about Blos and Erik Homburger, and calculated additional benefits if the tutorials could be enlarged into a formal alternative to the public schools. With other children and two excellent teachers, her children's personal comfort, intellectual curiosity, and pleasure in learning would continue to expand. By drawing upon her considerable wealth, Burlingham provided a level of funding necessary to build a two-story, four-room school building in Rosenfeld's large backyard, and to keep it amply furnished and supplied. Blos and Erik drew up plans for the physical structure—beautiful Norwegian timber and understated furnishings—and the Hietzing School became a reality.[9]

Initially, Burlingham's children were joined by only two or three others. During its less than five years of operation, however, the school averaged about sixteen children ranging from eight to fifteen years of age. They came from families of liberal and cultured backgrounds. Some were Americans whose parents had come for analysis and perhaps training. A few were children of prominent European analysts like August Aichhorn and Ernst Simmel. Roughly 70 percent of the children were in analysis, mostly with Anna Freud. For the most part, their parents had troubled marriages or were divorced. The situation at home was so difficult that four or five of them resided in Rosenfeld's house.[10]

Rosenfeld urged the schoolchildren to donate excess food from their sack lunches for the poorer children in the neighborhood. But this was one of the few attempts by the founders of the Hietzing School to seek to ameliorate poverty and unemployment in Vienna. Instead, they fostered a sense of mission in producing an exceptional, humanistic educational atmosphere and a strong feeling of protection from the dangerous world outside the school. Here there were no signs of the chronic anti-Semitism and poverty confronting many Viennese children. One student, Peter Heller, felt that he and his classmates might have been more resourceful in the long run without so much isolation from the "harsher social realities."[11]

Rosenfeld, Anna Freud, and Burlingham all contributed to this safe environment. Peter Blos and Erik Homburger were most responsible for the milieu. The three founders had named Blos director of the school. A strikingly handsome man at this point, he was strict, exact, and methodical. He kept full records not only of each student's educational progress, but also of parental accounts of important early habits and emotional maladies. Blos would not tolerate sloppiness or tardiness in the students, and even taught the less conventional Erik "to keep regular work hours." He tried to treat all students equally but found special support from the founders when he kept the oldest Burlingham child, Bob, in good spirits. Blos taught geography and the sciences, and emphasized "real life" conditions outside the world of psychoanalytic experiences. Dorothy Burlingham initially taught English, and various part-time teachers were brought in to cover Latin and mathematics. Erik covered the humanities, especially art, history, and German literature. Instruction, however, tended to be cross-disciplinary, as Blos introduced the Deweyite project method as it had been practiced in a model progressive school in Winnetka, Illinois. He avoided formal grades and adopted Dewey's premise that children learned best when their interests were keen and they were engaged fully in a project that unified diverse subjects. New projects pegged to specific grade levels were introduced every few weeks and each of them incorporated history, language arts, and other subjects. Blos tended to allow Erik to pick the project topics, especially for the older children. Erik often selected topics that were less than commonplace in Central European culture—such as Eskimos, Vikings, and Native Americans. The children wrote stories and poems on a topic, drew sketches, made woodcuts and paintings, and constructed tools and other artifacts of the culture.[12]

The school's yearbooks underscored Erik's influence on school life in their themes and artistry. They approximated Gustav Wolf's *Das Zeichen-Büchlein* in their heavily visual and engaging expression of teacher-student kinship. Erik urged the youngsters to use the yearbooks to describe how human lives, including their own, were influenced by culture and society. These volumes suggest that his influence approximated Blos's in promoting the school's aims. Erik was finding a vocation, a sense of place, and a capacity to make decisions at Hietzing so that when he was introduced to Joan Serson in 1929, he was no longer wandering.[13]

What sort of a teacher was Erik Homburger? His students recalled that he was nervous, self-conscious, and even idiosyncratically funny. He was tall, handsome, and well-groomed, attentive to his appearance, usually in suit and tie, and carried himself somewhat awkwardly. He seemed constantly to sip water, to hitch up his freshly pressed trousers, and to blush "ever so easily." Several students found it amusing that he "could not pass a mirror without looking at himself." Yet they all felt that he connected intuitively to their concerns.[14]

By focusing on what students found interesting (sketches, art museums, field trips, Native Americans, and the like) and what they did well, Erik eventually commanded their trust, drew them closer to their feelings, and made them better able to express to him their inner needs and fears. Already one saw signs of what came to be his characteristic clinical approach. Erik was aware of his salutary results with Hietzing students and recalled how he "immediately took to it." Anna Freud was impressed by Erik's effectiveness. On top of her duties standing in for her ailing father in the affairs of the Vienna Psychoanalytic Society, the International Psycho-Analytical Association, and other agencies of the movement he had built, she was intent on establishing the field of child analysis and suspected Erik would be successful in that calling.[15]

Yet Anna Freud also saw some problems with Erik related to her increasing apprehensions over the administration of the Hietzing School enterprise. "All they [Blos and Erik] know is compulsion or liberation from compulsion. And the latter results in chaos," she wrote to Rosenfeld in March 1929. These two teachers had chosen "liberation." Neither understood the need for sublimation as a middle ground between total freedom and total control. Neither tried to persuade the children to adhere to school requirements. Rosenfeld agreed and similarly criticized Blos and Erik. By avoiding even lesson plans, she noted, the principal instructors allowed the pupils to do whatever they wanted, leaving them undisciplined for life's tasks. For effective learning and necessary maturation, the two had to direct the children to do what they preferred to avoid. Burlingham quickly concurred that the teachers had been too permissive. By now, she would not allow Rosenfeld to outflank her in supporting Anna Freud. Retrospectively, Burlingham characterized the school as a "mistake" because of its protective milieu, which had not prepared her children for the rough-and-tumble of the outside world. Because Blos and Erik had been too lenient, her children could not have adapted well to the public schools.[16]

Although Anna Freud, Rosenfeld, and Burlingham castigated "Peter and Erik" jointly, the young men did not rebut their three patrons. Much later Blos prepared a twenty-one-page "Intimate History of the School . . ." with his version of who was to blame and what was accomplished. He deposited the manuscript in the Library of Congress and required that it be kept away from researchers until well into the twenty-first century.[17]

Erik was more forthcoming in later life, admitting that neither he nor Blos had formal training as teachers and improvised most of the time. But he insisted that Blos had been an excellent school director. While not directly rebutting Burlingham, Rosenfeld, or Anna Freud, he insisted that the school had not been "permissive" or "libertarian." European social customs and hierarchies obtained, and the children had been punctual and well mannered. He and Blos allowed "what Freud called the 'strahlend Intelligenz' (radiant intelligence) displayed by children who for some moments are permitted to function freely." But that had not made for a disorderly learning environment.[18]

It is understandable that the two principal teachers waited decades before responding to the criticism initiated by Anna Freud and elaborated by Rosenfeld and Burlingham. They were young and inexperienced at the time, and had been enmeshed in Ms. Freud's powerful circle of intimacy. Hietzing patrons, teachers, and even the students had been part of this circle. As Peter Heller, formerly a student in the school and currently its historian, has observed:

> Everybody and everything was actually interwoven with everybody and everything else. The children in analysis with Anna Freud, many living either with Eva Rosenfeld or Dorothy Burlingham, went together to the psychoanalytically oriented school run by Sigmund Freud's patients, his daughter Anna and his close friends, Dorothy Burlingham and Eva Rosenfeld. The most important teacher was Erik Homburger Erikson, in turn a patient of Anna Freud.[19]

Heller's characterization requires modest elaboration. Sigmund Freud had essentially left child analysis, which he considered a female calling, to his daughter and her colleagues. He viewed work with children as exterior to the preponderantly male leadership of the psychoanalytic movement and its focus on adult patients. Freud had also analyzed Burlingham and Rosenfeld, and had encouraged their interest in child analysis and the Hietzing School. Anna Freud never married and came to know Rosenfeld and Burlingham when their marriages were failing. Regular gift exchanges and meals together at the Freud home cemented a very strong and cordial relationship between Anna Freud and Rosenfeld. "You are me and I am you," she confided to Rosenfeld. Her relationship with Burlingham, always in conflict with her rapport with Rosenfeld, became intimate in a way that resembled a marriage. Ms. Freud began analyzing Burlingham's two older children when she arrived in Vienna without husband in 1925. Three years later, she moved with her children into an apartment a few floors above the Freuds' quarters at Berggasse 19, and the two households essentially merged. The bonds between Anna Freud and Burlingham, and the ties between Anna and Rosenfeld, gave the three women emotional space from the men central to their lives.[20]

Heller recalled how Ms. Freud's "spirit predominated and prevailed and pervaded the school," and all participants accepted the "public pronouncements of hers regarding her views on Psychoanalytic *Paedagogik.*" In some measure, she made the patrons, teachers, and students into an ersatz family of her own. She took vacations and went on outings with many of them and was solicitous of their well-being in what Heller characterized as a "well-meaning dictatorship."[21]

Consistent with Vienna child analysis generally, the Anna Freud circle of intimacy was therefore a female-dominated island in a profession that (even with exceptions like Helene Deutsch) did not regard women entirely as men's equals. Ms. Freud looked to Burlingham and Rosenfeld as partners in the Hietzing venture. In this female triumvirate, Heller detected "a tinge of hostility to masculine ways and to men." Erik regarded "that atmosphere" as strongly feminine. He recalled how, along with Blos, he had sometimes found it difficult to teach as he saw fit. This was especially true, of course, from 1929 on, when Anna Freud, Burlingham, and Rosenfeld became increasingly critical. For Erik, the problem was compounded by the fact that Anna Freud had become his training analyst; she was privy to his personal life in therapy as she controlled his professional future. This is all to say that lines of separation between female patrons of the school and young male teachers were part of a basic dynamic. The gap between the sexes replicated the larger pattern of gender relations in Sigmund Freud's Vienna. The Hietzing School closed in 1932 when hostess-manager Rosenfeld moved to Berlin and the families of the American students returned to the United States. However, disenchantment by the three patrons with Blos and Homburger did not abate.[22]

PROFESSIONAL PURSUITS

The Hietzing School offered Erik Homburger his first steady job and a place within the Vienna psychoanalytic community. It brought him into Anna Freud's circle, if on an awkward basis, and accustomed him to follow her lead. As the years passed, she exercised increasing influence over his personal and professional life. Coupled with Hietzing, he became engaged in activities and roles in other educational, psychoanalytic, psychological, and social service facilities—formal and informal networks—usually at Ms. Freud's suggestion.

Initially a schoolteacher herself, Anna Freud felt strongly about a local Montessori school that Lili Roubiczek had founded in 1922, several years before the Hietzing experiment was launched. It was called Kinderhaus and serviced primarily lower-class children under the age of six. Ms. Freud herself offered a regular seminar there for child-care providers. Perhaps because she considered Erik's teaching at the Hietzing School somewhat lacking, she urged him to pursue Montessori training and to become one of two male members of Vienna's Montessori Women's Teacher Association.[23]

Erik proudly received a Montessori diploma (in 1932) while teaching at the Hietzing School. It was the only formal degree he completed after he received his *Abitur* from the gymnasium. Few men had been so credentialed. He found Montessori training compatible with his earlier artistic experiences, for it focused on the objects that children made and arranged. Whereas his psychoanalytic training acquainted him with the "deep and symbolic meanings of childhood experience" revealed in dreams and talk, Erik recalled, Montessori training induced him to "pay attention to and to repeat with my own hands the simplest manipulation and the accompanying thought patterns which acquaint a child with the tangible world and permit him to reconstruct it in play." Like the sketches and social themes within the Hietzing special project books, Montessori training played to Erik's "visual language" as an "erstwhile artist," directing him to the external social world. Products of play became a widely applicable road map to understand how the child was navigating the social world around him.[24]

He therefore regarded Montessori training as an essential counterpoint to psychoanalytic preoccupation with inner emotional life, verbally articulated. It intensified his interest in the objects of children's play. It also pinned down the suggestions in his 1923–24 journal that a person needed "meaningful activity" in the surrounding world (what he later called actuality). At the same time, Erik realized that the Montessori method was so reality-oriented that it did not explore how children's play objects might reveal their inner fantasies. This gave him pause, for his artistic experience suggested to him that the human-made object simultaneously revealed inner feelings and outer experiences. He was moving toward what he soon would call his configurational perspective.[25]

Between 1929 and 1933, Erik periodically took courses at the University of Vienna. Although Anna Freud did not discourage this, she was not enthusiastic. She had not gone to the university herself, attending only a two-year teacher-training school. Moreover, by the late 1920s, she perceived sharp tension between the educational forums of the Vienna psychoanalytic community and those of academia. Increased anti-Semitism at the university marked by restrictive admissions and physical assaults upon Jewish students contributed to this tension, and university faculty friendly to the Freuds could not diminish the campus intolerance. Dedicated to protecting her father's psychoanalytic movement from antagonistic ideas and institutions, she favored minimal ties with the campus.[26]

There is no evidence, however, that anti-Semitism at the University of Vienna gave Erik much pause. He regarded patterns of intolerance as unfortunate political currents that were extraneous to his life. Over a period of four years, he took forty-seven semester credits. Between 1929 and 1931, he enrolled in the liberal arts curriculum on a part-time basis. At first, he simply took courses that interested him. These included classes on the geography of various European countries, on Renaissance and baroque art, a course on German sketches, and one of Karl Bühler's psychology courses. Soon he seemed to find a concentration, taking courses that satisfied requirements for a teaching credential—Methods of Teaching German, Pedagogy, Institutional Hygiene for Teachers, and Speech Theory. But before he had earned a teaching certificate or a liberal arts degree, he transferred in the fall of 1931 to the university's medical school. There he took courses from Julius Tandler, whom he had come to know during his Montessori training, in dissection and human anatomy. He also took two courses in chemistry. But he did not progress very far toward a medical degree, which his stepfather had wanted him to pursue, and he dropped out in the winter of 1933.[27]

The fact that Erik lacked a specific goal helps to explain why he failed to matriculate. Unlike contemporaries Käthe Wolfe and Else Frenkel-Brunswik, who completed psychoanalytic training while they pursued advanced degrees in psychology at the university with Karl and Charlotte Bühler, Homburger gave no thought to such a synthesis. He was not drawn to Karl Bühler's investigation of existential and introspective psychological traditions or even Charlotte Bühler's study of the developmental stages.[28]

Study at the University of Vienna proved, then, to be relatively uneventful. Erik's effort to master psychoanalysis was by far the major training venture of his Vienna residency. Anna Freud offered to take him on as a child analyst in training for the very low fee of seven dollars a month. She would conduct daily analytic sessions with him, listening to his personal revelations, and would supervise his analytic work with children. For his part, Erik "wasn't sure what that [the offer] meant," although he realized she would be exercising enormous authority over his life. He hesitated, mentioning that he "was hoping to be an artist, and I liked teaching children." Ms. Freud replied that he "could combine those interests with psychoanalysis," for such combinations were commonplace. The unstated point was that she wanted him badly as her analysand. Sensing this, Erik assented, and became a very junior member of her analytic circle. Not long after the training analysis began, he told her that he questioned whether the psychoanalytic profession was for him: "I could not see a place for my artistic inclinations in such high intellectual endeavors" that were so very "intensely verbal." Erik provided two retrospective accounts of her reply. In the first, a brief autobiographical essay prepared when he was in his seventies, he acknowledged that "to quote one's analyst is always beset with hazards of self-deception." He then stated her reply to his expression of reluctance: "You might help to make them see." In a subsequent videotaped commentary, however, Erik reported that she delayed replying to him until she was able to talk to her father: "[T]he next day she came back and she said, 'I told my father what you said, and he said tell him that he can help us to make them see,' which is such a wonderful way of saying things." Whether the advice was Anna Freud's or Sigmund's, Erik appreciated the estimation of his value as a visual and artistic psychoanalyst who could aid an emerging profession to help its patients to see. "That kind of thing can decide your identity," he later recalled. There was room for an artistic psychoanalyst.[29]

There are problems in these retrospective accounts. By late 1928 or early 1929, when the actual conversations occurred, Erik was no longer "hoping to be an artist." Nevertheless, his two versions of the "might help to make them see" remark—whether from Anna Freud or from her father—are instructive, for in the course of his analysis he often wondered whether he had assented to work with the wrong Freud.[30]

Rather than characterize his accounts of the conversation as "inaccurate" or "distorted," memories of that conversation suggest two fundamental areas of ambivalence when Erik decided to launch a psychoanalytic career—ambivalence that he needed to deal with if he was to continue his training. First, he wondered whether the profession could tolerate his visual orientation and what was left of his "artistic inclinations." Second, he suspected that his acquiescence in Anna Freud's proposal to train him as a psychoanalyst was connected with his idealized missing father. He had some sense that Sigmund Freud was not only a substitute for his stepfather, Theodor, but an embodiment of qualities that he idealized in his biological father. There was a compatibility here with Anna Freud, who suspected she had also been an unwanted child and had idealized her father to justify the sacrifices she was making as his caretaker and confidante.

As a teacher at the Hietzing School, Erik found some assurance that psychoanalysis was compatible with art and that it had a strong visual component. He felt that his sketches and woodcuts and instruction in the visual arts were central to his rapport with the children. In one of the early papers Anna Freud had encouraged him to write as part of his psychoanalytic training, "The Fate of Drives in School Compositions," he underscored how the visual aspect of his rapport with the Hietzing children helped him to discover and free their inner psychological lives.[31]

Erik was also encouraged that psychoanalysis might accommodate his "artistic inclinations" when he learned that Ernst Kris, one of his instructors at the Vienna Psychoanalytic Institute, had been a curator of the Vienna Art Museum, and that other established analysts also had backgrounds in the visual arts. This fact also underscored the connectedness among the therapeutic, the educational, and the cultural in city life. Interestingly, Erik did not exploit it fully, rarely attending exhibits of great local artists like Gustav Klimt and Egon Schiele. Instead, he was encouraged by what he sensed about the artist in Sigmund Freud, and this deepened the more he saw of the "professor." Although Freud was in fact very articulate (he won the Goethe prize for literature), Erik instead accented Freud's artistic qualities. Indeed, "I soon detected in Freud's writings vivid manifestations of an indomitable visual curiosity which sent him hurrying to Italy and through her city squares and museums whenever his work permitted." In this way, Freud was able "to see, to restore his visual impression, which he knew was difficult to maintain in that exclusively verbal field which he represented." Indeed, Erik recalled sitting in the waiting room that Sigmund and Anna Freud used jointly for their analysands and enjoying "about a hundred little statues standing around." Freud's consulting room was also "absolutely filled with little antique statues" by "artists of the archaic Mediterranean," attesting to a strong visual orientation that he felt preceded Freud's reliance on words and phrases.[32]

This characterization of Freud fit the transition into psychoanalysis that Erik was trying to make even as it misread Freud's cognitive style. He, not Freud, was coming "from art to psychoanalysis," and it was he who felt that "without that visual aspect of it, I don't think I could ever have made it." Still, there was some plausibility in his discovery, as he later related it, that Freud's "descriptions of his patients' memories and dreams also reveal that he deeply empathized with their imagery." In fact, Erik recalled that he was able to use Freud's *Interpretation of Dreams* as a model to grasp "the rich interplay of form and meaning." For Freud, Erik noted, the dream harbored "form" in its outward or "manifest expression." It revealed "meaning" when the analyst discovered what that "manifest expression" had "denied and distorted" about the inner life of the patient. Erik found that this procedure, outlined by Freud for dream analysis, beginning with the manifest aspect of the dream, was congruent with the way he regarded an artistic work. By focusing at first on the "artfulness of manifest expression" and probing beyond form for meaning, he thought that "I, as one then trained more in visual than in verbal communication," had "found a 'natural access' to such overwhelming data" of the inner psyche. Analysis of the manifest form and what it simultaneously revealed and concealed allowed Erik to connect his skills of artistic observation to Freud's procedures for dream analysis.[33]

In his capacity as a Montessori trainee and a Hietzing School teacher, Erik was working with children of various ages. The younger children could not articulate their dreams; it was not his task to discuss dreams with the older children. But if the psychoanalytic assignment was to move from the "manifest expression" of a visual form to the meaning behind what the form distorted and concealed, Erik quickly discovered that it helped to examine the way the children had arranged their play objects, had drawn pictures or shaped clay, and had even prepared compositions. He was hardly the first young analyst to emphasize these elements. Although Anna Freud herself did not use a full play therapy approach in her child analyses, and was not convinced that play had special meaning for children, she analyzed children's drawings and their daydreams. Moreover, she urged her students to explore the symbolic content behind children's behavior and feelings. Others in child analysis relied on play therapy, but Erik moved much faster and farther than most. Within a few years, he would describe the visual form of a child's play objects as a configuration that simultaneously revealed the "outer" social and material world surrounding the child and the child's "inner" emotions.[34]

Erik Homburger was very much to the point, then, when he recalled how "Freud's enormous visual talents, his genius, for example, in interpreting dreams," helped him to resolve his initial ambivalence over psychoanalytic training. It offered a potentially attractive vocation "for a young man with some [artistic] talent, but nowhere to go." Yet there was a second dimension Freud embodied that attracted Erik deeply, helping to put to rest his initial doubts about the emerging profession.[35]

Freud was very direct and personable, and these qualities encouraged Erik's receptivity to much that Freud wrote and proclaimed. Freud's appeal disposed Erik to deemphasize his increasingly authoritarian pronouncements after World War I and his secretive administration of the psychoanalytic movement. It also prompted Erik to become more attentive to Freud's increasing emphasis on the play of dramatic opposites (active vs. passive, masculine vs. feminine, love vs. hunger) and to Freud's growing concern with ways that social phenomena and collective experience influenced and were influenced by inner emotional life. Freud's new work on instinctual dualism—the primal drives of Eros and Thanatos engaged in an eternal battle within the personality—concerned him, too. Above all, there was an aspect to the founder of psychoanalysis that inclined Erik to appreciate his new stress on the growth of the ego as the locus of reason and deliberation in its tense brokerlike functions with the world external to the self, the wholly unconscious passions of the id, and the largely unconscious admonitions or rules of the guilt-inducing superego. Weak and primarily unconscious as the ego was, Freud explained how it sought to make the id tractable to pressures of the external world and of the superego while seeking to persuade the external world and the superego to comply with the needs of the id. This concern with the ego was moving Freud toward a general psychology reaching beyond issues of neurosis and addressing normal mental activity.

The most compelling aspect of Freud, which drew Erik Homburger to all of these post–World War I ideas and emphases, was Freud's personal presence. He first met Freud through the Burlinghams at a family party. Later, he went mushroom hunting with the "professor," accompanied him on an automobile trip to his doctor, saw him pass by as he talked with Freud's intellectually inclined sister-in-law, Minna Bernays, and came into direct contact with Freud on many other occasions. Owing to Erik's shyness and his apprehension over the apparent pain that talking must have caused a man with palate cancer, their relationship was more visual than verbal, cemented by Freud's writings more than through discussion. Nonetheless, Freud's name was hardly an abstraction. He knew Freud personally, and his thoughts were to be venerated.[36]

Erik reflected a great deal about Freud. He dwelled on commonalities between them. "Freud had not left his parents' household until he was twenty-seven," Erik pointed out, and, like him, Freud "had taken his time coming into his own." As a student, Freud "had been somewhat of a German nationalist within the Austro-Hungarian Empire," and Erik saw the resemblance. He had been a German nationalist in Karlsruhe during World War I so that fellow students would be less suspect of his Danish origins. Because Erik felt torn and ambivalent over his Jewish identity, it was important to discover that Freud was troubled by his as well (if not from the same circumstances or in the same way). Freud preferred "mannish intelligent women" like Marie Bonaparte, Lou Andreas-Salomé, and Minna Bernays, and Erik's own ties to Karla Homburger and Freud's daughter seemed roughly parallel. Finally, Erik learned that in *The Question of Lay Analysis,* Freud had underscored his special admiration for those who sought "to find their way into a child's mental life." And this was the path Erik was seeking to pursue.[37]

Still another important aspect of Erik's identification with Freud was that this great "mythical figure" seemed somehow to connect him, through his stepfather, Theodor, to his own much romanticized missing father: "What, in me, responded to the situation was, I think, an ambivalent identification with my stepfather, the pediatrician, mixed with a search for my own mythical father." On various occasions, Erik struggled retrospectively to enlarge on this theme. He had been quite literally a stepson in the Homburger household and felt that he did not belong there. As a young child, Erik "had maybe too much of a mother" and "needed a father" with more compelling qualities than Theodor. Owing to his unconventional artistic background, he also found in Freud's psychoanalytic community "a kind of favored stepson identity that made me take for granted that I should be accepted where I did not quite belong." Yet Freud, like Theodor, "adopted" him, and he admired both as doctors. In the end, he had accepted Anna Freud's offer to train as a child analyst, which was "as close to the role of a children's doctor as one could possibly come without going to medical school." Consequently, he was pursuing a career that seemed to mingle Freud's profession with Theodor's pediatric specialty. Erik recalled how Freud "was a doctor like my adoptive father" and seemed to awaken his quest for his artistic, biological father because of his "great interest in art." His biological father had not been around to support him, but Sigmund Freud could be; he was "the most creative person I ever met and in whose work circle I also was welcome."[38]

Erik appeared to be recalling how Freud's powerful presence had drawn him into the psychoanalytic profession and was keeping him there because he seemed to substitute for his stepfather and, more important, for his romanticized biological father. Yet Erik never advanced this connection clearly and explicitly. More typical was his recollection, decades later, of arriving in Vienna after having been estranged from Theodor's conventional middle-class Jewish household. He found in Freud: "great Jew, Mosaic stature, doctor-rebel permitting rebels to become doctor (secret identification with stepfather)." He concluded his account by stressing how: "Their love made it possible to make an identity out of being a stepson."[39]

On one level "their love" was obviously that of his mother and stepfather. But in this context, his arrival in Vienna also seemed to refer to Sigmund and Anna Freud. The stepson was essentially adopting the romanticized father of psychoanalysis as his own idealized, artistically talented father. This was central to the decision he was making to train with Freud's daughter.

AN ANALYSIS WITH ANNA FREUD

When Erik Homburger finally decided, sometime in 1929, to pursue a training analysis with Anna Freud, he became involved in her pioneering programs that extended beyond Hietzing and Montessori school connections and involved him with other figures in the psychoanalytic community. In addition to her *Kinder-seminar,* he attended her pedagogy seminar on educational techniques. Periodically, he also visited August Aichhorn's innovative seminars on adolescent psychology and juvenile delinquency. As well, Aichhorn supervised Erik in his work with delinquents. Helene Deutsch and Edward Bibring supervised his first treatment of an adult patient. Finally, Heinz Hartmann and Paul Federn joined Anna Freud and taught Erik much regarding an emerging theoretical emphasis on ego functions. Within the larger psychoanalytic community, this meant that he was heavily involved in the preponderantly female world of education and child analysis, but not exclusively so. After all, he had contact with the pioneering Aichhorn, had trained for adult treatment, and had studied with influential figures like Hartmann and Federn. This broadened his experience beyond the somewhat marginalized subcommunity where women attended to children and set Erik on the path where, by 1933, the Vienna Psychoanalytic Society voted him as a member in full standing.[40]

Still, Erik was primarily identified as Anna Freud's student and analysand, and his future was heavily in her hands. By the mid-1920s, she was part of the nucleus of what came to be known as the Vienna School of Child Analysis. As the leadership of adult analysis shifted toward Berlin, the Vienna School became the world center in child analysis during Homburger's tenure in the city. Anna Freud ran several seminars while serving actively as a training analyst. Erik found her published lectures on the technique of child analysis to be "the only safe technical statement" on the subject. As he worked with her, she prepared what became *The Ego and the Mechanisms of Defense* (1936), which furnished theoretical and practical grounding for work with children. Erik therefore regarded his contact with Anna Freud at the core of his analytic training.[41]

He profited from her pedagogy seminar—a weekly study group on psychoanalytically informed teaching techniques. In a muted form, the seminar introduced select aspects of a psychoanalytic perspective on child development into the city's school system. Specialists in each developmental stage, like Aichhorn on adolescents, made presentations. Erik recalled how the sessions enhanced his interest in human development.[42]

Anna Freud directed two other and, in some ways, more important seminars—an informal *Kinder-seminar* for younger analysts and the Vienna Training Institute's recognized child analysis seminar (Zur Technik der Kinderanalyse). The *Kinder-seminar* concentrated on theoretical and clinical issues. Heinz Hartmann, Wilhelm Reich, Jeanne Lampl-de Groot, Robert and Jenny Waelder, and Richard Sterba were among those who attended. Discussion was far-ranging and exploratory. In the institute's child analysis seminar, senior analysts sat around a table while junior analysts like Erik sat behind them or stood. This seminar was composed almost exclusively of female child analysts like Bertha Bornstein, Edith Buxbaum, and Annie Reich. Each member presented a case study of a particular child, including the child's behavior, dreams, and fantasies. Erik attended both of Anna Freud's forums and was impressed by the way she presided over them, infusing a tone of levity and an excitement that new dimensions of human experience were being discovered. There was a "*joy* which characterized our adventurous work." On the other hand, he was taken aback by the energetic professional women who overwhelmed him with their insights. "I happened to be one of the very few men of the [child analysis] seminar," he recalled, "and was sometimes astonished at the observations made by a (yes overwhelming) majority of women analysts."[43]

Between the seminars and his training analysis, Erik learned a great deal. Robert Coles, who wrote engaging books on both Anna Freud and Erikson, maintains that Erik's emphasis on the social setting for the human psyche derived heavily from Ms. Freud's teachings. After all, she maintained that the emphasis on the inner psyche in adult analysis had to be reversed in child analysis; there, the primary focus had to be on pedagogy and the external environment. Although Erik's 1923–24 notebook shows that he was quite attentive to the social setting before he met Ms. Freud, she certainly deepened his appreciation of elements in society that surrounded the specific child.[44]

For one, Anna Freud explained to Erik that a child could not develop a true transference relationship with his analyst. The child's relationship with parents and family was too concrete for the child to internalize their images and to project (transfer) those images onto the analyst. Therefore, she urged Erik and other trainees not to focus on the transference relationship between child and analyst, as in adult therapy, but to explore the symbolic meaning of the child's behavior and feelings. What was important in the context of a child's superego development was his concrete relationships and surroundings and how he acted and felt in that context.[45]

Anna Freud showed how, if the child's superego development was far more open to the influence of immediate social surroundings (the "outer world") than that of the adult, improvement of the environment would enhance the child's "inner world" or psyche. Indeed, she shared with Bernfeld and other educational reformers of the "Red Vienna" period a desire to improve the conditions of school life and to establish special child guidance centers for young children. She also lauded Aichhorn's efforts to help juvenile delinquents. Erik took specific note of these social reforms and was especially impressed by Anna's readiness to feed undernourished child patients during analytic sessions. He could never forget her humorous defense: "An expensive business, child analysis." Social and personal resources had to be available to the child, and this was costly.[46]

Finally, Anna Freud cultivated in Erik and other trainees a focus on the ego rather than the id and how the ego operated in the course of normal child development. She described how the normal ego (the "seat of observation") allowed the child to reconcile his inner drives with the demands of the world through a pattern of defenses that was, in the last analysis, the child's character. In this regard, Ms. Freud elaborated on the implications of her father's 1926 essay "Inhibitions, Symptoms, and Anxiety," which accented the importance of reality and emphasized the role of the ego in dealing with that reality (within and external to the self). Anxiety called forth ego defenses to deal with this reality, she reiterated, then proceeded to examine the wide array of ego defenses used to deal with anxieties, some far more reality-oriented and effective than others. Although Erik agreed with Hartmann that Anna Freud sometimes failed to elaborate on important ego qualities that were not defenses, and though he regarded himself less committed to her view of the ego as a rather fixed or centered entity, he still considered himself an early ego psychologist in the tradition of his training analyst. If one paid close attention to the ego, as she portrayed it, and looked beyond its defense functions, he later recalled, one saw "form and presence to each developmental step as it mediates between the id's physical nature and society's institutional variations."[47]

In the long run, Erik Homburger's most important contact with Anna Freud did not involve her seminars or her innovative and appealing psychoanalytic perspectives. It concerned her analysis of him. No "Process Notes" for his analysis have survived, but memories—proximate and distant—abound. He frequently and proudly recounted how she was willing to take him on for a personal and training analysis at a low monthly fee. He could become one of her first adult male analysands. He recalled how "she suggested I try to become a psychoanalyst who works with children." In September of 1933, however, only a few months after Erik left Vienna and migrated to Denmark, he wrote to Aichhorn about "the moment I asked Anna Freud for an analysis." Peter Blos, recollected that if Ms. Freud had even vaguely suggested an analysis, Erik jumped at the opportunity and probably pressed her to take him on. He wanted to connect to prominent figures in the analytic community, Blos recalled, and figured the training analysis was a door into Sigmund Freud's inner circle plus an opportunity to be recognized in the field.[48]

There is plausibility in Blos's suggestion that the analysis began at least out of mutual initiative, but more than ambition was involved. Erik Homburger and Anna Freud, only seven years apart, wanted to spend time together. They found emotional as well as professional benefits in an analytic relationship. At the conclusion of his analysis, Erik observed that with Ms. Freud, he repeated the "childhood which I spent with my mother alone." Like Karla Abrahamsen, Anna Freud was protective, bright, and attractive if sometimes dour, exceedingly serious, and never given to stylish clothing. In this period, Anna Freud also found herself drawn to Erik, and for more than his intelligence and teaching talents. She sensed a certain kinship with this struggling but gifted and handsome young man. Not long after he arrived in Vienna, she wrote excitedly to Eva Rosenfeld that "Erik is making a drawing of me." With short cropped hair and dull dark ankle-length dresses, she found his long, wavy hair and his colorful, stylish clothing rather alluring. Indeed, Erik appealed to her on many counts. As Sigmund Freud's caretaker, analysand, secretary, and protégée, she exalted the genius of a father whom she probably had too much of and took into analysis a young man who acknowledged that he "needed a father [and] had had maybe too much of a mother."[49]

It is difficult to determine how long Erik Homburger's analysis lasted. His estimates ranged from three to six years; three and a half to four years appears to be the most probable. It was frequently interrupted owing to Ms. Freud's travels as her father's secretary and as an increasingly influential analyst in her own right. She always accompanied the "professor" whenever he went to Berlin for medical treatment, Erik recalled, and for his vacations in the mountains. Sometimes Anna Freud asked Erik to accompany her on her travels so as not to disrupt his analysis. Usually she did not, but he did not appear to resent canceled sessions. The analysis was also disrupted temporarily, at Anna's suggestion, when Erik began courting Joan Serson.[50]

Early in his analysis, as Erik walked up the stairs in the Freud family apartment to the second-floor waiting room that separated Anna's office from her father's, he had misgivings. The room was dark and gloomy. Chairs and sofas surrounded a large table and a heavy Persian rug. When the door of either analyst opened, bright with light, one took notice. Erik was most attentive to the occasions when Freud's door opened first, and Freud summoned his next analysand. He recalled how he "would see the old 'Professor,' with a formal bow, invite that person into his study, having briefly bowed to me as well. And then Anna Freud would open her door for me." This aroused "complex feelings" within him. Usually, he felt envious of Sigmund Freud's patient. Sometimes he felt like a second-rate analysand who had been assigned to a "female track" for his analytic training. On other occasions, he felt that Anna Freud herself was second-rate and inexperienced—far inferior to her father as an analyst. Repetitions of these feelings underscored for Erik the "complications of my position." As he entered Ms. Freud's office, "I often said . . . I don't quite know really why I'm not with him [her father]." Erik had been drawn to the new "science" of the psyche largely by Freud's paternal presence and his artistic, visual qualities, but he ended up being analyzed and partially supervised by his daughter. "That was a training analysis," he once reminisced, and it should have been "with him." This put Anna Freud in an awkward position not only as Erik's analyst but as a daughter less than willing to share her father emotionally with her analysand.[51]

By the time Erik entered her office and lay down on her couch for his daily session late in the afternoon, Anna Freud had already worked with a few (mostly female) adult analysands. But she had also completed sessions with several children whom Erik taught in the Hietzing School. By March of 1929, of course, she was less than pleased with the freedoms he seemed to allow these students, and the mixing of a professional relationship with an analysis placed a heavy burden on both of them. When Anna Freud described her young patients, she sometimes tended to associate Erik with them, as when she told Rosenfeld of her "worries" concerning the foster child "Lizzie [Wellenstein] and Erik and little Peter [Heller]." On another occasion, she wrote to Rosenfeld that "I have sessions with Erik and Ernst [Freud]" and later Robert Burlingham who "has too little need of treatment" while "Erik [is] in very good shape." Erik sensed that he was sometimes being viewed in relation to his students. At least one Hietzing child, Peter Heller, also sensed the relevance of Ms. Freud analyzing him and his teacher a few hours and sometimes a few minutes apart. This timing promoted unnecessary emotional complications and even rivalries—in the children, in their teacher, and even in Anna Freud.[52]

The daily therapeutic sessions in which Ms. Freud saw both Erik Homburger and his students represented part of a more general mixture of professional with analytic relationships in the psychoanalytic community. Erik once reflected on Anna Freud's life at the time where "the personal and the official were so intertwined in an almost sacred mission." He recalled "the high condensation of personal and professional matters during my analysis" and how his hopes for professional success sometimes clashed with therapeutic expectations. Further, although "Anna Freud was my analyst . . . I still met her at meetings, and at the school or we went swimming with the children in the Danube." He added that "the relationships were so respectful and formal that they couldn't be, wouldn't be misused." At least, he hoped that they would not be.[53]

It is difficult to characterize the general atmosphere of Homburger's daily analytic sessions. Erik remembered that Ms. Freud's manner was very prim and proper and supposed that this characterized her approach with all her male analysands. She strictly observed the therapeutic admonition against touching or physical tenderness. Erik found her so "very methodical and well-organized" in her manner as he talked on the couch—"friendly listening with a silence only interrupted by her very clear interpretations." To be sure, he occasionally saw in her "a certain playfulness" and "a peacefulness and simplicity," but he usually considered her too stiff and restrained to feel entirely free and comfortable. In addition, she never quite understood his difficulty in vocalizing what he visualized. She did not appreciate how hard it was "when I, born to be a painter, tried to say in words what I saw on my inner screen in my training analysis."[54]

This is not to say that Erik's sessions were bland and perfunctory. On the contrary, they tended to be highly emotional. He was annoyed, for example, if Ms. Freud knitted during his sessions, as if she was insufficiently attentive to his needs. Yet at the end of one such session, she "smilingly handed me a small blue knitted sweater" for his first son. He also found it curious that Ms. Freud never alluded to her life with her father in the very apartment where he was being analyzed. He had no knowledge, at the time, that the "professor" had analyzed his daughter. But, reflecting Erik's competition with her for her father, he remarked decades later that "I always suspected incest!"[55]

As the analysis proceeded, Anna Freud pressed Erik on the cause of his constant "tiredness" and his frequent propensity toward "illness." The fact that he was living with and planning to marry the Canadian student of dance Joan Serson was relevant, for it meant that another woman, Erik's sexual partner, had come between him and Anna Freud. He sensed that this distressed her. Though she had balanced her intimate companionship between her father, Burlingham, and Rosenfeld, she lacked long-term intimacy with a man her own age. Erik felt that he had to ask her permission to marry and later reported to her that "you were quite right in letting me marry Joan."[56]

As might be expected, the most difficult part of the analysis concerned the most pressing topic in Erik's early life—his absent father. Again and again, he spoke of what he assumed to be his father's defining features—a tall Danish aristocrat, Gentile, with artistic talents who had betrayed his mother. Anna Freud had long been sympathetic with the emotional deprivation suffered by children during World War I and during other disasters that separated them from their fathers. According to her analysand, Esther Menaker, Anna felt that she herself was an unwanted child, and so recognized Erik's pain. She urged him to channel his uncertainties about his father in constructive directions—to sublimate and take charge or captain his ship of life so to speak. Menaker recalled Erik telling her, when they both were in analysis with Anna Freud, that this advice to take charge had called to mind a woodcut he had completed of himself as a little boy on a ship looking away from Theodor and Karla and toward the captain as if he needed to take charge of the vessel. With considerable satisfaction, Erik told Menaker that this scene was symbolic of Anna Freud's advice to transform his life, to turn a deficiency into a strength. Indeed, he may, in part, have come to see Ms. Freud as the captain. He gave the woodcut to her as a gift. But Erik also recalled another, seemingly less empathetic side of Anna Freud. Like many other European analysts of the time, she believed it was demeaning and injurious to seek out the identity of missing parents or perpetrators in family scandals. Consequently, almost every time Erik mentioned what he had pieced together about his father, she dismissed it. Adopted children fantasize about their real parents, she told him, and warned that he was transforming his father's betrayal into a life myth. Hurt and angry, Erik recalled that he once brought to an analytic session a photograph (supposedly) of a Danish aristocrat, claiming that he had found it among his mother's possessions. He insisted the man was his missing father, but Anna Freud dismissed the claim; he was fashioning a tale of a "family romance."[57]

It is difficult to comprehend how profoundly Erik Homburger was changed by his analysis. As an established American analyst in 1949, he wrote to Anna Freud that he learned to meet his adult responsibilities "only *after* my analysis, and then slowly and in an entirely new country." He added that "I felt as if to 'succeed' in the USA almost meant defeat in your eyes." Later, he became less critical of his analysis. He wrote fondly to his children in the 1960s about visiting "the room where I was analyzed," and in the early 1970s, he claimed that it was "a pretty good personal analysis." It "gave me self-awareness, led me not to fear being myself." Indeed, "the process of self-awareness, painful at times, emerged in a liberating atmosphere." He was not, of course, the best judge of the value of the analysis. The fact that following the analysis, analyst and analysand were never close is instructive. Psychologist Lois Murphy, a longtime personal friend of Erik, felt that the analysis somehow "reinforced your identity conflict and failed to make you conscious and confident." Erik's daughter, Sue Bloland, herself a clinician, suspected that he was never analyzed at a very deep level and subsequently avoided relationships (including the commonplace second analysis) that required him to be more self-exploratory.[58]

Joan Serson's arrival on the scene affected the nature of the analysis. She was a strong and independent spirit, whom he met, fell in love with, and married in the midst of his analysis, and this surely upset the balance between Erik and Anna Freud. As Joan became important in his life, Erik shared with Ms. Freud his feelings and concerns for her. Conversely, he discussed with Joan the issues that mattered most in his analysis, especially Anna Freud's tendency to dismiss his perspectives on his biological father. In a 1971 interview, Erik reminisced how he and Joan "both left our respective analyses when we met each other." They did not, in fact, do this; Erik was probably referring to an emotional rather than a physical "leaving." Joan represented a very strong tug away from Anna Freud, destabilizing if not undermining Erik's analysis. His relation with Joan even drew him away from lessons he was learning in the psychoanalytic community. When he graduated from the Vienna Psychoanalytic Society in 1933, he both embraced and questioned aspects of his training experience. In part, this reflected the competition between Anna and Joan for his allegiance.[59]

JOAN SERSON AND ERIK HOMBURGER

In June 1903, Joan Serson was born in the small town of Gananoque, Ontario, near the Thousand Island area of what is now the St. Lawrence Seaway. She avoided discussion of her early family life and destroyed her diaries of the period. Her birth name was Sarah, but she was called Sally. Her father, John, was Canadian by birth and the local Episcopal pastor. Her mother, an American, Mary MacDonald of New York City, was a devout Episcopalian from a very wealthy railroad family. Mary was extremely intelligent, but a debutante lifestyle had constricted her educational and intellectual opportunities. Her marriage was cold and distant from the start. So she often took their young children (two daughters and a son) to Europe and elsewhere. John favored his older daughter (Molly) over Joan, the youngest child. Feeling rejected by her father, Joan considered her mother remote and unstable. She could not be depended on for emotional support. When Joan was two, Mary was hospitalized, apparently for depression, and for an extended time. Joan's grandmother (nicknamed "Nama") took over the child rearing. Reverend Serson died when Joan was eight, and Mary moved to Trenton to be with friends. Joan remained with "Nama" in Gananoque, occasionally visiting and living with her mother in Trenton. Except for Nama, family life had provided scant nurturing and considerable anger at both parents. Joan was disposed to leave at the earliest opportunity.[60]

College presented the chance, and Joan enrolled at Barnard, where she obtained a bachelor's degree in education. She took a master's degree at the University of Pennsylvania in sociology. Modern dance interested her a great deal, and she taught it part-time at Columbia Teachers College and at the University of Pennsylvania while pursuing a doctorate in education at Columbia. She began a dissertation on the teaching of modern dance. When her mother left Trenton for Boston to enter an Episcopal nunnery, Joan decided to go abroad and conduct dissertation research on dance in Europe. Bold and energetic, she often made her rounds of dance studios by bicycle with a knapsack on her back. Much of her research concentrated in Germany, particularly Berlin, where she became apprehensive of the political currents. However, while there she found a more precise focus for her dissertation. She would write on the instructional programs at the dance schools that proliferated in and around Germany after World War I.[61]

In the fall of 1929, Joan, now twenty-six, traveled from Berlin to Vienna to extend the scope of her research. She took dancing lessons at the Hellerau-Laxenburg Eurythmic Ballet School, which had been moved from Dresden to Vienna. She also visited the Hietzing School, noticed Erik Homburger (one year her senior) pass by, and interviewed to teach physical education and English. Peter Heller recalled seeing this "tall, handsome Canadian woman with nobly trembling nostrils." She was a stunning woman with alert, searching eyes. Dorothy Burlingham quickly struck up a close friendship with Joan, which effectively drew her into Anna Freud's circle.[62]

Soon after her first visit to the Hietzing School, Joan was formally introduced to Erik at a masked ball celebrating Mardi Gras. The gala was held at Maria Theresa's summer palace on the outskirts of Vienna. Following local custom and accompanied by other young adults, Erik and Joan had arrived in costume. They danced together all night, then sat and talked of their future in a nearby park, arranging to meet for breakfast the next morning before returning together by train to the city. Soon Joan moved into rooms that Erik shared with Peter Blos. In the spring of 1930, Mary Serson summoned Joan to Philadelphia, where she was living and where she faced serious surgery. While caring for her mother, Joan discovered she was pregnant. Returning to Vienna, she found that Erik balked at marriage owing to his apprehension over permanent commitments and his fear that his parents would disapprove of marriage to a non-Jew. Several friends persuaded him of the propriety of matrimony—and that he must not repeat the mistake of the man who had fathered him. His child should not be born out of wedlock as he had been, and Joan should not be left alone with a newborn as Karla had been. Months later, after a long and painful delivery, their son, Kai, came into the world. The name Kai reflected Erik's Scandinavian roots and his paternity. The past intruded powerfully into the present.[63]

Once Erik agreed to marriage, three wedding ceremonies were conducted over a three-month period late in 1930—interesting interfaith exercises. Neither Erik's parents nor Joan's mother was given advance notice of these ceremonies and did not attend. To please Mary Serson, one ceremony was conducted in the Chapel of the Holy Family, a private Anglican institution, even though Anglicanism had no legal standing in Austria. Dorothy Burlingham and Joan's Philadelphia friend Frances Biddle served as witnesses. Decades later Erik recalled the ceremony rather fondly to his children. The second was a civil ceremony in the old Rathaus for which Erik designated himself as a Jew while Joan registered herself simply as a Protestant. Civil dignitaries conducted the formalities. To placate Karla and Theodor Homburger, the third was a Jewish ceremony. Valdemar Salomonsen, Karla's first husband, was listed in the registry book for this wedding as Erik's father although Erik had long known that this was untrue. Joan continued to retain her birth name of Sarah. Although an Episcopalian, she professed her conversion to Judaism to satisfy a customary requirement in both the Orthodox and Conservative Jewish marriage—yet she arrived at the synagogue from the marketplace carrying a bag of bacon and pork for the evening meal. The odor of the meat was strong, testing even Erik's tolerance for jabs at traditional Jewish customs. Dorothy Burlingham presented Joan a bouquet of red roses instead of the customary white lilies, underscoring the fact that she and Erik had lived together out of wedlock and that Joan was pregnant. Erik either forgot or neglected to bring a wedding ring.

Witness Eva Rosenfeld donated hers temporarily so the ceremony could conclude. It was at once a comedy of errors and a mockery of the middle-class Jewish propriety practiced by the Homburgers of Karlsruhe.[64]

The comedy persisted after the wedding. Ruth, the older of Erik's two half sisters, was to be married to Paul Oppenheimer shortly afterward in Karlsruhe. Erik arrived without Joan and too late to attend the ceremony. At the wedding dinner, he told Ruth, who was very devout, that he had married a non-Jew, and this news distressed her enormously. Erik had earlier informed Karla of his marriage, but there was real concern over how Theodor, a pillar in the Karlsruhe Jewish community, would accept the news. Karla persuaded Theodor to defer judgment until they visited Joan and Erik in Vienna.[65]

Erik's mother and stepfather arrived at the couple's home on a Friday evening to find Joan crocheting in defiance of the Sabbath prohibition against work. It quickly became evident that Joan had not seriously converted to Judaism and that Erik was less than observant of Jewish custom. They did not belong to a local temple or keep kosher or observe any other Jewish traditions and even disapproved of the ritual of circumcision. Nonetheless, it was obvious to Karla and Theodor that their son finally seemed happy and more stable emotionally. He was not as gaunt, his face registered less tension, and he had grown a handsome mustache. As well, he held a regular job, and his wife was strong and resourceful. Karla admired Joan from the start and could see why she was sometimes called *Die Schöne* for her remarkable beauty, with long dark hair braided in a bun and a sturdy, slim, well-proportioned body. After a few minutes with Joan, Theodor was won over by her affability, kindly disposition, beauty, and strength of character. Erik was deeply relieved to have his stepfather's approval, which signaled a thaw in their tense and often difficult relationship. Theodor began to agree with Karla that they had to help support the newlyweds financially. It was in the context of this newfound warmth and respect that Erik and Joan decided to name their firstborn Kai Theodor.[66]

About a year after their marriage, Erik Homburger made a woodcut dedicated to his wife "JH" for the top of her sewing box. In the woodcut was a picture of their tiny house on the Kueniglberg hill overlooking Vienna, and Kai on the porch reaching for an apple from a nearby tree. The family dog appeared in the background. A sense of calm and contentment pervaded the picture. The scene echoed the theme of a sketch of Joan nursing Kai that Erik had made some months earlier reflecting joy, peacefulness, and close bonding.

The woodcut and the sketch, both with strong balance in lines and proportions, reflected Erik's new sense of well-being and stability. So did a photograph of him proudly holding Kai, cheek to cheek in his arms. However, neither the woodcut, the sketch, nor the photograph fully mirrored the family's circumstances. Their house was less than adequate. A kitchen pump that froze in winter was the only source of water. So it had to be brought in from the outside. Erik was frequently ill. Kai had to accompany them to the Hietzing School because the couple could not afford day care. Indeed, the house was one of five or six low-cost rentals during their years in Vienna. The birth of Jon MacDonald (the maiden name of Mary Serson), their second son, early in 1933, compounded the child-care problem and the drain on financial resources. Joan found herself so preoccupied with domestic and child-rearing tasks, plus teaching, that she abandoned her effort to complete her dissertation. She raised her boys as Christians. Although she did not pressure Erik to relinquish Judaism, the strength of her Episcopalianism concerned him, for he found greater comfort in flexible, eclectic crossing of the lines separating different religious traditions. Erik did not share the domestic chores and continued with his psychoanalytic training unimpeded. Despite scarce income, he bought expensive editions of all of Freud's published works. A family pattern was taking shape, with Erik's career the top priority. Joan had little time for scholarly and artistic pursuits, except sporadically, along the path of Erik's professional advancement.[67]

Still, Erik and Joan's friends felt that the marriage was extremely beneficial to both. It was not a demonstrably passionate relationship. Mutual loyalty and trust were the more salient qualities. In Erik, Joan found a man who seemed to cling to her out of need and concern as her parents had not. She provided a strong and very important presence for her new family and household, a role that contrasted markedly to her younger years in the Serson household in Gananoque. If Joan found a certain young man's arrogance and *Geistigkeit* in Erik when he was with Peter Blos, he became far more pleasant when Blos was kept at a distance. Moreover, Joan sensed Erik's brilliance and profundity. He was certain to become an eminent figure in psychoanalysis. Through marriage, she would become a part of his future prominence. Joan's impact upon Erik was far more obvious than his was on her. Strong, orderly, and earthy, she augmented the disciplined, punctual manner he had to assume as a Hietzing teacher and an analyst in training. According to his half sister Ellen, Joan took a man with potentially serious emotional disorders and built a supportive social and emotional foundation for him, which stabilized his life. Ruth, Erik's older half sister, agreed. Within weeks of his marriage, Ruth recalled, Erik's life had been organized. Joan had him eating nutritious foods at set mealtimes and made him more attentive to exercise. She took charge of his daily schedule, taught him to waltz, amplified his interest in the piano, and saw to it that he met his social obligations. "He would have been nothing without Joan," Ellen concluded. Erik agreed.[68]

In her compelling historical study of marriage, *Parallel Lives,* Phyllis Rose sees those that last and thrive characterized by a certain stability where the weaker party does not feel exploited and the stronger feels amply rewarded.[69] This was the Homburger marriage. It lasted sixty-four years, with only one interval where the relationship was seriously threatened. At the beginning of the marriage, Joan felt immediately rewarded as Erik relied on her increasingly for orientation and emotional sustenance while depending less on Anna Freud.

For Joan, Erik's involvement with Ms. Freud as an analyst in training was part of his larger involvement in the Vienna psychoanalytic community, and she found that community rather insular. Her first direct experience with psychoanalysis had not gone well. When she arrived in Vienna in 1929, Joan became close to Dorothy Burlingham, went to work at the Hietzing School, came into Anna Freud's sphere of influence, and commenced a daily analysis with Ludwig Jekels, one of Freud's early disciples. An ardent socialist and a scholar, Jekels had written a psychological analysis of Napoleon and had translated some of Freud's works into Polish. Joan appreciated his warmth and his old-world charm, such as when he presented her roses in his office. At other times, he discussed local opera and theater, urging Joan to attend. Jekels was attracted to Joan's beauty and her candor, as when she replied to one of Freud's relatives who had reprimanded her for sitting on a quilt. "The hell you don't," Joan had retorted, and this delighted Jekels. But after just a few weeks in analysis, Joan developed reservations. She grew impatient when Jekels did not understand her owing to language barriers. Also the analysis was a drain on her meager financial resources, especially when Jekels charged her for sessions that she was too ill to attend. While tutoring other analysts in English, she was taken aback to learn that their apparent motive for mastering the new language was to profit from prosperous Americans coming to Vienna to be analyzed. More fundamentally, Joan never acquired an abiding interest in psychoanalysis. She did not want to become a practitioner or to enhance her self-understanding through analytic exchanges. Indeed, Joan found herself making up stories to tell Jekels, and after a few months she stopped seeing him.[70]

Not only had Joan been disenchanted with her own analysis, but, unlike Erik, she was not drawn strongly to Sigmund Freud. Although she met him on several occasions, they rarely conversed. She remembered the day Freud saw her carrying Kai on her shoulder near his summer garden in Grinzing. He remarked that Kai was very intelligent and then walked away. Joan was put off by his apparent arrogance and snobbery. She felt that many analysts put their own needs well ahead of those of their analysands. In short, Joan saw no great value in Erik's daily analytic sessions with Anna Freud and said as much. Heinz Hartmann reprimanded her for this irreverent perspective, which made Joan all the more skeptical. When Erik returned from his analysis and training seminars and his clinical supervision feeling that he was part of a major historic movement, Joan let him know she could not share in that enthusiasm. Above all, she came to loathe Anna Freud, finding her cold, preoccupied with diagnostic labels, focused like her father on excavating layers of the inner psyche, and lacking a sense of involvement in the world. Joan often laughed and touched people but felt that Ms. Freud rarely did either. Joan was also disturbed by the fact that Anna seemed aloof with her. She fretted over the effect Ms. Freud seemed to be having on her husband and freely discussed her reservations with Erik. Part of Joan's uneasiness stemmed from her devotedness; Anna Freud told Erik that religion was illusory. When Erik mentioned his desire to marry Joan, Ms. Freud warned him that "dangers lie in such analytic alliances." Joan was also distressed by Anna's disapproval of Erik's "permissive" approach to teaching. Above all, she was angry when Anna Freud dismissed Erik's account of his biological father as a family romance. She felt this reaction retarded Erik's effort to explore what he regarded as the most pressing issue in his past. Joan felt that for Erik's analysis to be effective, he needed a male analyst to help him with his missing father and related issues. Succinctly, Joan not only disliked Anna Freud, she augmented Erik's reservations about his analysis with Ms. Freud and about the general focus of orthodox psychoanalysis upon inner psychic life. As Joan's influence increased, Anna Freud had a less pronounced effect upon Erik's emotional development, his trust, and his feeling of well-being.[71]

Initially, then, analysis with Anna Freud probably helped Erik Homburger to better understand his dependence on strong, able women like his mother and his analyst and to articulate other troubling issues. But as Erik became closer to, more trusting of, and more dependent on Joan, who framed his daily life and gave full credence to his story of a betraying father, he attached less importance to his analytic sessions with Anna Freud. To be sure, he remained deeply attached to both women and their concerns, hoping in some measure to make these concerns more compatible. But judging from their emotional pulls on him, Joan was emerging as the decided winner.

PSYCHOANALYSIS WITH A DIFFERENCE

Erik Homburger's formal training in Vienna gave him a comparatively clear and coherent system of thought and an explicit theoretical framework for clinical observation. As he attended clinical seminars; mastered Freud's metapsychological papers, his *Interpretation of Dreams,* and his other works; learned to become an acute observer of children; and secured some supervision in adult treatment. Erik recalled how he suddenly realized that he had acquired a disciplined perspective: "My God, all these things mean something, they all hang together." He felt that they "hang together" because he was able to learn from "the originators and the first community that represented such new ideas." The "personal" presence of the Freuds and his other instructors made their teachings "more reliable."A bond of direct personal *trust* between trainee and mentors had been crucial. However, at the same time, he was troubled by the way certain doctrines were articulated. Though he championed what he had learned, he also found himself cautiously critical of certain lessons. This process of embracing while amplifying and subtly criticizing would become Erik Erikson's way of expressing himself before psychoanalytically informed audiences.[72]

Erik recognized that psychoanalytic theory was articulated "in terms of nineteenth-century physicalism." It was "drive-oriented," though he knew that in German usage *Trieb* stood for ennobling and upsetting forces as well as literal drives and libido. He studied how libidinal drives were repressed, how they resurfaced and were remembered, and how they were transferred from analysand to analyst. Drives introduced the issue of ego defenses (the responses through which the drives were channeled). He mastered the schema Anna Freud was developing—a progression in the types of human ego defenses ranging from very immature to the more mature ones that opened a person to inner feelings and urges. He found Ms. Freud's description of ego defenses highly "mechanistic" (though logical); this was in keeping with what was then regarded as "scientific" propriety. One of his first publications, "The Fate of Drives in School Compositions" (1931), applied drive theory quite mechanically to essays written by Hietzing children. Erik elaborated "drive enlivening inner structures" and ego defenses within those essays as any orthodox Freudian might. But he preferred to discuss ego-id interactions along lines that he would soon refer to as "verbal and visual configurations." In these pages, configurations represented forces that the patient channeled into broad and visible or audible shapes and patterns. By studying the nature of a patient's configuration, the analyst better understood what he or she "clearly suggested or flagrantly omitted" from emotional and other circumstances impinging upon his or her life. Now and again, this configurational perspective would gain hegemony over the mechanistic ego-id structural one in Erik's early writings to reveal "the very creativity of the unconscious."[73]

While he mastered the structural relationship of id and ego and periodically pinpointed the shapes and patterns that he, as identity's architect, soon would call the configurational, he scorned his teachers Anna Freud and Heinz Hartmann for their rigid distinction between the "outer world" and the "inner world." In his 1923–24 notebook, Erik had emphasized the interaction of the self with nature and the world, and though he now appreciated Anna Freud's concern about the effect of outer social forces on children, he felt that her emphasis was on analyzing the "inner world" of the unconscious psyche. In contrast, he could see that "at every step the child takes so much of the outer world into the inner world, he experiences the outer world in terms of the inner world." Thus, both worlds had to be considered on equal terms of constant interaction. It was essential to transcend Ms. Freud's and Hartmann's apparent dichotomizations, for he felt they "had completely neglected" what connected the "inner" with the "outer." Indeed, Erik challenged the very utility of the term *outer world* early in his training, pointing out that it obscured the "new closeness to social as well as inner problems"—the interrelation of the two. He felt that it was this interrelation that actually shaped all significant discussions in Anna Freud's seminars on children, even if this was rarely acknowledged. In Ms. Freud's clinical case conferences, above all, Erik recalled that study of "the patient's mutual involvement with significant persons" within a "communal unit such as the family" sometimes accounted for elements that could not be accommodated by the focus on "inner 'economics' of drive and defense" or vague reference to the "outer world" that rarely took "outer" seriously. In Joan, Erik found someone who supported his critical perspective. Indeed, Joan soon argued that real understanding of society lay "outside the analytic [view of the] social world." But Erik, less estranged from the psychoanalytic community than Joan, ambitious to succeed within it, and still in training with Anna Freud, concluded that his disagreement was more with certain of Sigmund Freud's followers than with the "professor." Freud himself had outlined a perspective that, while starting with drives and working toward ego considerations, included the crucial connection of both to society and culture. The crossings between inner psyche and outer society "seemed to me always implicit in Freud's own writings," Erik later reflected.[74]

Despite Joan's prodding, then, Erik's profound loyalty and attachment to Sigmund Freud, and no doubt his continuing training analysis with Anna Freud, kept him firmly in the psychoanalytic camp. Nonetheless, he did not feel that his work was well received, whether in Anna Freud's seminars or at the gatherings of the Vienna Psychoanalytic Society, and he worried that this could restrict his career opportunities within his new profession. When he first presented his paper based on Hietzing essays ("The Fate of Drives in School Compositions"), for example, there was no response to his allusions to visual forms (configurational elements) implicit in the essays. According to Edith Jackson, "the discussion was sluggish" and soon digressed into an argument between Anna Freud and Edith Buxbaum over whether Hietzing composition assignments were more stimulating than public school assignments. Similarly, Erik felt his paper "Psychoanalysis and the Future of Education" received an indifferent to negative response from the Vienna Psychoanalytic Society. In his estimation, his colleagues' affinity for the orthodox world of drives and restraints within a contained inner psyche was so rigid that it would not accommodate even his very limited allusions to the exchange of shapes and forms between teacher and student (a more decentered perspective). Consequently, he was apprehensive that he would "not be able to say what I really wanted to say" in order to attract support in the professional community.[75]

What Erik did not quite understand was the hesitance of some alarmist and unreflective Freudian loyalists, fearful of dissident challenges, to be open to his earliest configurational approach. His papers were attentive to the shapes children made with their toys and paintbrushes and word choices. As early as 1919, Melanie Klein, Anna Freud's intense rival among child analysts, had also attached great importance to what children did with their toys and other artifacts. It mattered little that Erik had scarcely heard of Klein, much less subscribed to her premise that the superego derived from the child's cannibalistic and sadistic impulses rooted in the deprivation of weaning. (Following Sigmund Freud, Erik assumed that the superego emerged later in development with the dissolution of the Oedipus complex.) But when Erik presented materials on his children's play constructions, a few in his Vienna audience were reminded of Klein describing the young child's shock of parental intercourse by ramming two play cars together. Although Anna Freud had no apprehension that her student was a Kleinian, other less thoughtful listeners made the suggestion privately while withholding their approval publicly. When Erik learned their response, he became quite distressed.[76]

There is another reason why Erik's initial presentations were not regarded as exemplary work of the Anna Freud school of child analysis. They departed in one very important respect from the presentations of Ms. Freud and most of her trainees and associates. In many parts of his presentations, Erik asserted quite sincerely that psychoanalytic insight could deepen the adult's understanding of the child and could facilitate the child's relationship with the adult. In other parts, however, he seemed to push psychoanalytic insight and theory aside and to view the child-adult emotional relationship with its own distinctive shades of trusting rapport and distancing disharmony. Although psychoanalytic concepts like transference and adult imposition of superego constraints on the world of the child helped him to understand this relationship, he assumed that there was a special aura to it that psychoanalysis could not quite capture. The conflicting elements were not comprehended clearly by Anna Freud or others in his audience. They sensed vaguely that something seemed "wrong" or "inconsistent" or "missing," attributing that lack to Erik's youth and inexperience, and were reserved in their response to his papers.

In these early presentations on children and parenting, Erik's allegiance to the Freudian paradigm was quite firm. He reported discussions with twelve- and thirteen-year-old boys at the Hietzing School, for example: "They spoke of aggression that is displayed and of aggression that is felt, of guilt and the desire for punishment, with an inner comprehension of which adults are hardly capable." In examining the composition of a twelve-year-old girl, Erik noted that psychoanalytic insight—knowledge of the child's Oedipal wish to destroy her mother—was indispensable. More generally, he insisted that the salient issue in healthy adult relationships with children (as teachers, analysts, and parents) concerned "which strains on the superego formation we can spare the child without weakening the strength of his conscience."[77]

Yet, while affirming the Freudian paradigm, Erik alluded to an aspect not treated by the psychoanalytic perspective, that of the concrete, specific, and personal emotional rapport between an adult and a youngster. By portraying this unique association of two generations as vital to human existence, he was connecting to entries in his 1923–24 notebook where he had underscored the importance of personal rapport between the "self" and the other, the leader and the follower, the old and the young. Interestingly, his Vienna presentations on relationships between children and adults bore little evidence of the elitist voice in the notebook.

His personal rapport with specific Hietzing School children was crucial to this less hierarchic orientation. He described how overjoyed he felt by being with Mabbie Burlingham when she sat on his knee during reading lessons: "It seemed so natural and so reassuring to her—and the teacher." He also recalled the first time he had a real and free-ranging conversation with Mickey Burlingham: "the first time I talked to a child, or rather, had him talk to me, and he had such a lovely combination of reticence and *Ausgesprochenheit*." What Mabbie and Mickey and his own children, Kai and Jon, demonstrated was "the astonishing individuality—for better and sometimes for worse—of each [child]." In his paper on "The Fate of Drives in School Compositions," he explained the remarkably full "pictures" that the children in Dorothy Burlingham's English class offered in their essays about their "interior world." Their willingness to reveal themselves originated with their rich personal relationship with their teacher. The classroom provided "the opportunity for the children to spend a few hours in contact with a person they can quickly and easily raise" to a level of trust. The key to this very personal communication was a spirit of "confidence" and trust between the teacher and her students. Erik described how "a boy with empty eyes and round face" urged the teacher to read his composition without delay, feeling she would understand: "He lays his hand on the teacher's shoulder, needy of recognition, even love—a habit well known to the teacher." Fortunately, this trusting, empathetic teacher would always "encourage the boy to approach" and to touch and exchange feelings and fears. Another paper, "Children's Picture Books," argued that both the way an adult artist drew pictures for children and the way children viewed those pictures served to register a specific rapport between the artist and the child. Indeed, this was true of all concrete adult-child emotional relationships: "Whatever behavior we adopt toward the child, it has less influence than our real impulses—whether or not we have tried to suppress them. Children (like animals) can sniff the real essence through any surface: the cruel or kind, the strong or insecure tendency." Presaging the concept of negative identity, Erik was suggesting that the child could shape him- or herself around concealed and cruel aspects of the adult as well as by positive aspects. In the end, the adult-child emotional "relationship is the crux of any effort to create a truly different environment for a child." When the adult was open, confident, genuinely respectful, and caring, the child would respond openly, respectfully, and trustingly. In most of his presentations, Erik warned that this personal relationship of trust and self-revelation occurred only if the supervising adult treated the youngster's artwork, compositions, and other representations with the same dignity that the adult expected in response to his own work. Moreover, the sketches, texts, and other work had to be regarded as serious registers of the real world as well as openings into the child's inner subjective reality. If the therapist or teacher wanted the child to trust his work and his efforts, he had to trust the reality as well as the subjectivity of the child's work.[78]

Erik's treatment of the adult-child relationship was hardly incompatible with psychoanalytic discussions of transference and countertransference. But his emphasis was different. He was specifying a very particular time in the emotional crossing of a child's life into an adult's where the adult was as open, respectful, and trusting as the child would be. Several of his sketches of Hietzing schoolchildren looking to him, the teacher-artist, with alert, trusting eyes and caring expressions, sometimes reminded him of these moments. Full adult-child reciprocity was indispensable. Implicitly, Erik was recommending equality in a very special sense that was neither legal, political, nor economic. Without using or even being quite conscious of the term *equality,* he was effectively describing it as vital for the emotional rapport between adults and children. This was not the stuff of Vienna teacher-training programs or the Anna Freud school of child analysis, much less representative of the elitist German gymnasium tradition characterized in Erik's 1923–24 notebook. Taking into account Erik's willingness to put adult (teacher or analyst) and child on an equal plane, one gets a better sense of Anna Freud's distress over his "permissive" instructional tendencies at Hietzing. Had Erik become clearer in his own mind about just what he was advocating, and had he not subordinated his message to a recitation of psychoanalytic orthodoxies, it would have provoked debate.

But even Erik Homburger did not seem to comprehend the strong egalitarian nature of his message or the degree to which emotional egalitarianism conflicted with traditional psychoanalytic and pedagogical relationships of hierarchy (between analyst and analysand, teacher and student). Indeed, he did not consider himself a rebel and was hardly ready to explore the connections between equality in the adult-child emotional relationship, his perspective on "I" and the "self," and Nietzsche's injunction "to become what one is." Formerly he had stressed that the process of becoming, or self-discovery, required one to "resonate together" with a much loved other. By urging teachers and therapists to be trustful and open with children, he was calling for such mutual "resonance." Some years later these reflections would carry him even farther afield from Anna Freud and most of her trainees and associates.

While Erik was still in Vienna and completing his psychoanalytic training, the task of amplifying the "I" necessarily engaged him with its closest equivalent—the concept of the "ego." He had listened to Anna Freud elaborate the various mature and immature defenses of the ego. When she published her formulations in the mid-1930s, he published a criticism, encouraged by Joan, that had been building for years in her seminars. Anna Freud said a great deal that was new and cogent, he claimed, about "what may limit and endanger the child's ego; it [her work] says little about the ego itself." In this sense, she replicated the failure of psychoanalysis in general to "illuminate the ego" and what about the ego allowed it to grow and enlarge—not simply to constrict and ward off drives. Erik felt that Hartmann's discussions of how the ego adapted to the environment had revealed more about the nature of ego strength, but Hartmann failed to explain the essence of the ego itself.[79]

Because he felt that Anna Freud and Hartmann did not go far enough in this regard, Erik turned to Paul Federn, a more "obscure and yet fascinating teacher." He attended several of Federn's presentations and found this very "inventive" man working to clarify his concept of "ego boundaries." As Federn struggled to elaborate what distinguished or provided boundaries or limits to the individual ego, Erik recalled that he may well have heard Federn use the term *ego identity* or something very close to it. This memory stuck in Erik's mind, for he began his book *Identity: Youth and Crisis* (1968) by recounting memories of Federn discussing ego boundaries in Vienna. He was unaware that Federn had drawn heavily on ego boundaries and identity from personal conversations with Victor Tausk, an analyst in training whose suicide represented a very sensitive issue in the Vienna psychoanalytic community. Indeed, although he had alluded to these concepts in his 1923–24 notebook, Erik did not feel ready to expound upon identity or even ego boundaries—that would happen in America. Yet he recalled that he was ready for identity, or a term close to it, because of its apparent kinship with his own interest in the sense of "I" and "selfhood"—that ego boundaries and identity represented perhaps a bridge between the "ego" and the "I."[80]

He also remembered his interest, during his Vienna training, in Ernst Kris's concept of regression in the service of the ego. As the ego regressed, Kris argued, it could find direct access to id energies for its own purposes. Kris felt that such regression in the service of the ego was especially evident when an artist made a cultural product. This helps to explain the artistic Erik's attraction to Kris's work. Like Federn's approach to identity, Kris seemed to impart deeper meaning in the nature of ego than as a mechanistic foil for the drives. So did Wilhelm Reich, whose seminar presentations Erik sometimes attended. Reich discussed various character formations, and Erik was much taken by the "armored character" who was tight and rigid as a "defensive armament" against "fluidity" and feeling. He vaguely sensed that armament and fluidity as polar opposites underscored Federn's concerns in his discussions of ego boundaries. These terms seemed to lead Erik to a fuller exploration of the identity issue. As he acknowledged frankly, the thinking of Federn, Kris, and especially Reich, became more significant a few years later in America with psychologically "fluid" young patients. Nevertheless, he was moving toward their ideas in Vienna as he sought to lodge fuller meaning in the "ego" by somehow linking it to his concern with the "I" and "selfhood."[81]

Sigmund Freud had used the term *inner identity* in a 1926 address to the Society of B'nai B'rith in Vienna; it was an aspect of his Jewishness. Naturally, Erik Homburger would have found it very helpful, during his Vienna training, if Freud had added "identity" to his conceptual arsenal. But in a larger sense, it may have been fortunate for him that Freud had not done anything of significance with the identity concept and that Federn had not carried the evolution of ego boundaries fully into a construct like identity. Erik had been drawn to ego boundaries and identity through an interest in the sense of "I" that predated his awareness of the Freudian worldview. Whether it was a quest to find meaning in the "I," the "ego," or "identity,"

Erik later recognized that he had been trying to discover meaning in his own existence all along. During his first three decades, he recalled that he never belonged "exactly to one group"—Jew or Gentile, Dane or German, artist or analyst—but had crossed the lines separating these identities. The root of the problem was that he could not know who he really was unless he knew who his father was, whose son Erik really was. According to Freud, the Oedipus complex, where the son engaged and contested the father, was fundamental to the psychoanalytic worldview. This created difficulties for Erik, whose identity was complicated by the nature of his Oedipal engagement with a father he had never known. At base, he had become preoccupied with the issue of the "I," of ego boundaries, and of identity because that pursuit, far more than the Oedipal struggle, was vital to his personal quest for self-discovery. It was an inquiry that he had to make largely on his own.[82]

PARTING REFLECTIONS

In the late winter of 1933, Erik Homburger waited outside the main meeting room of the Vienna Psychoanalytic Society while the members in full standing evaluated his record. His face was fuller and softer now, and his body stockier than when he had first arrived in Vienna. He felt greater confidence, too, and had a clearer sense of his future. He knew that despite reservations about some aspects of his work, he was regarded as a bright and talented child analyst. At the time, the requirements for membership in the society were vague and flexible. Consideration was given to an applicant's general reputation, the quality of his or her professional presentations, the strength of evaluations from more eminent members (especially Sigmund Freud and Heinz Hartmann), and the reputation and recommendation of the candidate's training analyst.

Erik had predicted that with Anna Freud's support, he would be voted to associate membership, a respectable entry level, and he could gain full membership when he became more established. After minutes that felt like hours, he was invited into the meeting room where Paul Federn, chair of the society, announced that Erik had been voted a full member. This news, from a man he deeply respected, was especially welcome. Now it was possible to become "a member of her [the society's] 'inner circle' in the professional sense." The "full" designation would allow him to practice on adult analysands as well as children. Finally, it conferred automatic membership in the International Psycho-Analytical Association; he could practice anywhere. After only modest soul searching in the weeks following the vote, Erik decided to migrate to Copenhagen, where he could begin a practice, secure

Danish citizenship, and (hopefully) get closer to his origins. Joan agreed with the decision.[83]

Actually, Erik might have left Vienna even without "regular" membership in the Vienna Society. Both he and Joan were alarmed by political events in Germany. Joan noticed signs of the drift to the right firsthand when she was in Berlin studying dance. Marriage to Erik had made her a German citizen; her two sons were as well. Erik was also very attentive to the German situation and wondered whether the political unrest could spread to Austria. When the Austrian National Assembly dissolved on March 4, 1933, and Engelbert Doll-fuss was installed as chancellor, Erik began to share Joan's mounting fear that Vienna would not escape the fate of Germany. A leader of the Christian Social Party, Dollfuss looked to Fascist Italy as a model state—an authoritarian alter-native to German and Austrian Nazi movements. But this distinction between Dollfuss and the Nazis was irrelevant to the Homburgers. Erik knew that Sán-dor Ferenczi was urging Sigmund Freud to leave the country. Freud had retorted that Austrians would not succumb to the level of brutality practiced on the German side of the border, that the Catholicism within Austro-Fascism provided protection and a barrier against invasion by Hitler. For Freud, life abroad would be very unpleasant, and he did not want to become a refugee. Freud's response became pervasive within the Vienna psychoanalytic com-munity well into the following year and, in some cases, for considerably longer. In retrospect, Erik maintained that it was an evasive posture promoted by "an intellectual concentration on the inner dynamics of the human species" while a horrid "new type of political order" triumphed. The misplaced emphasis on the "inner world" over the "outer world," which he and Joan found so troublesome, was coming home to roost.[84]

Even without the Central European political turmoil, Erik recalled that he and Joan would probably have left anyway owing to their general misgiv-ings about the Vienna psychoanalytic community. Its focus on the "inner" over the "outer" world was only a symptom of a "growing conservatism and especially a pervasive interdiction of certain [deviant] trends of thought." Freud's inner circle was turning away from its revolutionary, innovative ori-gins, Erik recalled, and promoting "a community of believers. You didn't quite know anymore whether you were getting an indoctrination or a train-ing. So it was important for me to get out of there." The "indoctrination" was especially intense among the women close to Anna Freud, "an ingrown group of hypermaternal" child analysts. "Young men didn't exactly thrive from these conditions, and I think Joan knew."[85]

Joan did know. Her desire to wrest Erik away from Anna Freud and her circle was crucial to her desire "to take us" out of the country. She felt Erik would always be an underling in Freud's Vienna, especially in the field of child analysis. She had counseled against the difficult procedure of acquiring Austrian citizenship, hoping they would not remain in Vienna very long.[86]

Admitted to full membership in the Vienna Psychoanalytic Society, Erik was ready to leave. Yet he experienced mixed feelings. "I left with a great deal of ambivalence," he recalled. "The one thing I ever learned was psychoanalysis." His aim in leaving Vienna was "not to do it [psychoanalysis] differently" but to do it "my own way." He had enjoyed "the freedom from [specialized] professionalization" in his Vienna training, but hated having "to prove that you were a faithful follower, that you did their theory." Because "my father was not a Jew but my mother was" and his wife was an Episcopal minister's daughter, he felt both part of and separate from the overwhelmingly Jewish membership of the Vienna psychoanalytic community. Six years into his training, he recalled that "my psychoanalytic identity therefore was not quite settled."[87]

Predictably, Erik felt most conflicted about leaving Vienna when discussing his plans with Anna Freud. Unusually dour and serious, she sensed her analysand's reservations and tried to counter Joan's influence. She assured him that the Nazis would never enter Austria. She was relatively apolitical and attached emotionally to the "Old Europe" that was passing away, and he disagreed with her. She also insisted that he was needed in Vienna for "the cause" of child analysis, which was central to the future of a movement that she supported with unequivocal dedication. He retorted that he hoped to advance the cause elsewhere in his own way. Above all, Erik insisted that "I needed to concentrate on helping myself . . . when so many were so irretrievably lost." They were "lost" because they followed Anna Freud's lead, he implied, and lacked the capacity to think independently. At this point, "she shrugged her shoulders and said she was sorry we were leaving." She realized that Joan's influence now exceeded her own. But she warned him not to go over to "the other side" by departing too much from the essentials of his training. The tension in the room was high and set the tone for what became a very troubled relationship. Still, Erik had one fond memory of Vienna: Sigmund Freud came to the railroad station to see his family off, urging Erik to have a kind and loving heart.[88]

In September of 1933, several months after the Homburger family had left Vienna for Copenhagen, but just before they migrated to the United States, Erik commenced an extremely revealing exchange of letters with August Aichhorn. This was curious, for his work in Vienna with Aichhorn had not been extensive.

With Siegfried Bernfeld, Aichhorn was regarded as a predecessor to Anna Freud in analytically informed work with children. She praised Aichhorn's skills and referred to him affectionately as her large, shy goy. Aichhorn had opened a child consultantship center that offered free short-term therapy, referrals, and advice to children and their parents. He had also taught periodically at the Hietzing School. Like Erik, he had been rebellious and alienated when he was young. When he supervised Erik's limited work with delinquents, Aichhorn had emphasized that the analyst had to be keenly attentive to each youth's social and economic situation and how this contributed to conflict with society's customs. Above all, the analyst had to empathize with the young delinquent and to treat him or her as an equal—an interesting and stimulating colleague of sorts—so as to promote trust.[89]

Aichhorn's focus on the "outer world" and on the somewhat egalitarian analyst-delinquent relationship separated him from pervasive perspectives in the Vienna psychoanalytic community. But Erik was receptive; Aichhorn's work seemed to bolster his own emerging egalitarian therapeutic perspective and his confidence. It allowed him to understand the limits of the traditional analytic focus on the "inner" emotional life as he reflected on one of his first analytic patients—a seventeen-year-old delinquent boy who had been shot in the head and needed both medical and social assistance. Although some in the analytic community active in the "Red Vienna" reforms were distrustful of Aichhorn as a non-Jew from an old Catholic Vienna family who was loyal to the Christian Social Party and who opposed socialism in his capacity as a minor city education official, Erik was receptive to Aichhorn's clinical orientation. In fact, he was grateful to Aichhorn for opening his "eyes to the problem of youth," some of whom had missing fathers and suffered from disorientation and despair.[90]

In his first letter from Copenhagen to Aichhorn, dated September 7, Erik focused on issues he regarded as crucial and distressing. He was upset about the state of his longtime friendship with Peter Blos, whom Aichhorn knew well. The fact that Anna Freud had offered Erik but not Blos a training analysis was crucial to the rift between them, for Blos felt that he was not only more experienced professionally, but Erik's intellectual superior. When the Hietzing School closed in 1932, Blos resumed doctoral work in biology (which he did not complete) and began an analysis. But during his short remaining time in Vienna, he felt that he had no hope of securing "regular" membership in the Vienna Psychoanalytic Society and recognized that Erik's career was outdistancing his own. Erik admitted to Aichhorn that "Peter is one shadow which I am very sad about . . . he himself (or his unfortunate education) was instrumental in making him into this shadow." Apparently, Anna Freud's refusal to supervise Blos had been central to this "shadow." Erik was disturbed by his friend's depressed mood, and remembered his own sense of despair in Karlsruhe before Blos summoned him to Vienna. Yet perhaps partially owing to Joan's discomfort with Blos, Erik did nothing now to reciprocate his friend's kind turn, and this contributed to his unease. He had jeopardized one of his longest and closest friendships; he had not helped Blos as Blos had helped him.[91]

After discussing Blos, Erik moved on to the issue that concerned him most. He told Aichhorn how "not getting closer to you [during his Vienna years] was my most serious failure, I am tempted to say defeat." Apparently, when he had first arrived in Vienna, Erik had very "promising" discussions with Aichhorn and had considered asking him for a training analysis. Ultimately, he asked Anna Freud to be his analyst instead: "With this act I followed the leaden weight of my childhood which I spent with my mother alone with my aunts, without [a] father. You will easily recognize this same fateful constellation in the Vienna aunt-ensemble in whose transmission network I was caught." For Erik, the "Vienna aunt-ensemble" was Anna Freud's circle of female child analysts, within which he had felt uncomfortable. In a hesitant and rather grudging tone, he stated that he now understood why he had repeated his childhood "aunt-ensemble." The issue "was analyzed—and successfully so, one has to say." Erik seemed to be describing rather reservedly a "successful" outcome in his analysis with Anna Freud.[92]

Erik next characterized his "spoiled" relation to Aichhorn; it was wholly his doing. He should have asked Aichhorn to be his analyst, he should have studied with him more, and he should have spent more time observing Aichhorn's clinical work. His conduct toward the senior clinician represented a betrayal, Erik insisted; it showed him to have been "so idiotic and so undependable." Fortunately, he now realized the reason for his betrayal. He had associated Aichhorn unconsciously with the "betraying father" who had left him "alone with my mother, until I was three years old." It was "my unconscious knowledge of the betraying father which made me withdraw from you, whose guidance I would have so much liked to have followed."[93]

Erik concluded his letter with the hope that the older man would "remain something like a fatherly friend" despite the geographic distance between them. He was departing for America where he now assumed his father had gone: "Naturally I always nurtured the unconscious fantasy that I would be able to find my betraying father in America, should I go there." Although Erik claimed to have gained understanding of how feelings toward his missing father interfered with his relationship with Aichhorn, he asked Aichhorn to be a "fatherly friend" as he left for the country where he fantasized that his father had gone.[94]

The letter to Aichhorn provided more than a revelation of what Erik Homburger had learned in his analysis about childhood issues, and it provided more than a narrative of opportunities lost but insights gained in Vienna. Rarely did he convey even a vague sense that he could be active, engaged, and empowered to directly shape his life. It was as if the traumas and limitations of his childhood, underlined by the story of his father's betrayal, had been augmented by a deactivating element in his analytic experience. Indeed, Erik's letter seemed to include two conflicting messages—the first rather overt and the second somewhat more indirect but begging for recognition: (1) His Vienna training and analysis helped him to understand the limitations of his childhood, thereby allowing him to move beyond those limitations in the future. (2) The emotionally upsetting and pacifying aspects of his early life had somehow asserted and reaffirmed themselves through the very psychoanalytic experience that was supposed to free his life from them. Thus, Erik regarded the Vienna world of Sigmund and Anna Freud with ambivalence; it had been both liberating and debilitating.

Not long after he received Erik's letter, Aichhorn sent a reply. Harsh and cruel, it might have been effective in an ongoing therapeutic relationship. In this context, however, it may have intensified the young man's insecurity. Aichhorn scorned Erik for using what he had learned of himself through his psychoanalytic training to "absolve" his conduct. It would be better for Erik to "consciously . . . reject its [psychoanalysis'] help and to look at life once more as others look at it." Psychoanalytic explanation had allowed Erik to deceive himself, to grant himself "absolution" for his so-called betrayal of Aichhorn. He could invoke psychoanalysis again to justify another betrayal. Instead, Erik needed to "be mistrustful of [your] own motivations." As a man with "pronounced narcissistic tendencies," Erik had "to reestablish this mistrust of himself." Aichhorn urged Erik to ask himself, in each of his new personal relationships, whether he was pursuing self-advancement and "narcissistic satisfaction" or a "true relationship" of mutual trust and sharing. By "mistrusting" his motivations, Erik would be forced "to think about the situation of the other person . . . and prevent you from having to 'betray' anybody. In this way, Aichhorn advised, Erik could eliminate his pattern of establishing personal relationships "which then you fail to fulfill."[95]

Aichhorn's reply disturbed Erik Homburger deeply. A veteran analyst whom he deeply respected had labeled him "narcissistic." Aichhorn had also accused him of using his analytic insight to excuse rather than to understand his conduct, strongly implying that Erik was overusing (indeed stylizing) the betrayal of his biological father. Worst of all, Aichhorn had responded to a young man who had equated viable selfhood and the sense of "I" with caring reciprocity with the "other." He had told that man that he had difficulty forging a "true relationship" of mutual trust owing to his self-aggrandizement. Aichhorn's charge spoke to Erik's feelings. Had he been as supportive of Peter Blos as Blos had been of him? Had he "betrayed" Anna Freud, Aichhorn's friend, by leaving Vienna and ignoring her plea to return? If he was ever to transcend the breakdown of parental trust during his childhood, he would have to build "true relationships" of mutual trust and caring in his life. Hopefully, his marriage to Joan was a start in that direction.

Wounded to the quick, Erik concluded the exchange with a short rejoinder before setting sail for America. Unlike his initial letter, it was strong and forceful though diplomatic, conveying a sense that Erik could take charge of his own life. He wholeheartedly accepted Aichhorn's advice about questioning his motives for signs of narcissism, but added: "You will know yourself that it will be hard to put into practice." In context, Erik implied that Aichhorn suffered from the same narcissistic propensity. Next, he suggested that whereas he may have invoked psychoanalytic interpretation to excuse his "betrayal" of Aichhorn, Aichhorn had also invoked psychoanalytic interpretation (while pretending not to) so as to refuse to excuse Erik. "In spite of what you say," Erik added, "you really continued my analysis, putting down my analytic zeal at the same time." If Aichhorn really meant to suggest that their letter exchange was unnecessary, Erik agreed: "Sadly I have to admit that you are right." He should not have written to Aichhorn in the first place.[96]

Erik's first and last letters to Aichhorn contrasted markedly, testifying to the ambivalent nature of his Vienna experience. The first, where he opened his past and his childhood traumas to Aichhorn, suggested that psychoanalytic training had left him with a passivity and a sense of powerlessness over conditions and events, even as it had provided new insights and methods. The last was marked by short, clever, and powerful rebuttals from a young man who seemed to regard himself as Aichhorn's equal and whose work in Vienna had apparently "added a certain inner sturdiness."[97]

In his reply to the initial letter, Aichhorn had observed that Erik Homburger had just completed one chapter of his life and was now starting a new one. Through his astute rejoinder, Erik was demonstrating precisely that to Aichhorn. The strength of the rejoinder was not lost on Aichhorn. He realized that Erik would "not have pleasant memories of me" as he began the new interval in his life. Indeed, Aichhorn wondered whether he had somewhat misjudged Erik. Several years later, he inquired of Peter Blos "how his [Erik's] life has shaped up" in America.[98]

CHAPTER THREE

"The Making of an American": From Homburger to Erikson, 1933–39

In 1901, Jacob A. Riis, a muckraking journalist-photographer and crusader against the sights and sounds of urban poverty, published *The Making of an American*. It was one of the first widely heralded autobiographies by a European immigrant to the United States. Riis described leaving his beloved town of Ribe on the north seacoast of Denmark and arriving penniless in America. He echoed the main themes of the Horatio Alger success story, explaining that his life demonstrated how just rewards resulted from hard work, perseverance, and what amounted to opportunistic striving. Depending on these and other values, plus his vivid photographs, Riis gained prominence in America as a lecturer, a social reformer, and a personal friend of President Theodore Roosevelt.

Another Danish immigrant, Erik Homburger, left Copenhagen for America in the fall of 1933. He was later to distinguish "my status as an American immigrant" from that of the intellectual "refugee émigrés" (preponderantly Jewish) from European Fascism fleeing to New York a few years later. Erik followed Riis's path, immersing himself in the language and culture of his new country. He found that effort immensely invigorating. As perhaps Boston's first child psychoanalyst, Erik found positions at Harvard and then at Yale through happenstance and opportunistic contacts. He copied the frequent immigrant practice of changing his name, and quickly became known as an effective therapist and a thoughtful intellectual. As a psychoanalyst, he discovered that there was something about the culture of this nation of immigrants that motivated him to look beyond Paul Federn's notions of ego boundaries; from this vantage point, he developed the concepts of identity and identity crisis. Identity was a phenomenon that appeared to be "naturally grounded in the experience of emigration, immigration, and Americanization." When he began to elaborate on identity as the key element in human development, his popularity in more literate segments of American society approximated what Riis's had been.[1]

Yet there was a darker side to Erik Homburger's early years in the United States. Although he was only thirty-one when he arrived, it was not the first time he had emigrated. Erik's mother, disgraced by his illegitimacy, had given birth to him on the outskirts of Frankfurt, away from her family in Copenhagen. Mother and son moved to Karlsruhe to live as German citizens with his stepfather. At twenty-five, Erik left mother, stepfather, and Germany behind and moved to Freud's Vienna, where he changed his residence nine times in six years as he acquired professional training. With a Canadian-American wife and two small children, he migrated again in 1933—to Copenhagen—and sought Danish citizenship. Unsuccessful in that effort, he traveled to America, where he continued to move about frequently, crossing the country several times. This process of constant uprooting and resettlement, even before he came to America, disposed him to "always write about the way it feels to arrive or leave, to change or to get settled." Because he "had changed nationalities before," he continued, in the United States, to pursue "one of those very important redefinitions that a man has to make who has lost his landscape and his language" and all other early "sensory and sensual impressions" upon which "conceptual images were based."[2]

This frequent uprooting was informed by Erik's predicament of not knowing his father, which left him feeling incomplete, without a sense of community or nationality, footloose, and needing constantly to move on. The relocations from Vienna to Denmark to America represented a retracing of the steps that he imagined his biological father might have taken. In the end, Erik concluded that it was "my own life history which made me marginal in regard to family, nation, religion, and profession." This desperate, sometimes depressing sense of marginality without defined personal boundaries "prepared me for feeling at home in an immigrant ideology" and was a factor in prompting him to work on the concepts of identity and identity crisis. Although he came eventually to feel comfortable in the United States, his was no Jacob Riis *Making of an American* saga, for American culture seemed to amplify the most troublesome feelings and problems of his European past. When Erik Homburger officially became Erik Erikson, American citizen, in 1939, his past continued to intrude upon his present.[3]

A DANISH INTERVAL

After the Nazis burned books by Freud and others in May of 1933, a few Jewish analysts left Germany, but the majority in Austria continued to feel secure. Erik and Joan Homburger felt otherwise. "We were convinced that the Nazis would get to Vienna . . . ," Erik recalled. They believed that Austria's fate was inseparable from Germany's, and they felt burdened by the legal technicality of being German citizens owing to Theodor Homburger's adoption of Erik and Erik's marriage to Joan. Joan did not want her children reared under either German or Austrian flags. The couple felt so pressed to leave Vienna that Erik deferred securing the analytic control cases that were required for him to become a training analyst.[4]

They did not consider migrating to Haifa, where Erik's younger half sister, Ellen, and their parents, and many other German Jews, chose to settle as the 1930s progressed. Denmark was Erik's strong preference: "I was born a Dane so I went back to Denmark," he recalled, at the same time deemphasizing his Judaism. With membership in the International Psycho-Analytical Association, he had the formal analytic credentials to assist the Greek princess Marie Bonaparte in establishing a psychoanalytic institute in Copenhagen. Although Joan preferred to bring her husband back to America, where her mother lived and where she herself had studied, she appreciated how much it meant to Erik, among other things, to learn more of his Danish past and to regain Danish citizenship. His Abrahamsen relatives in Copenhagen offered to help the young couple, and Erik was a European culturally and intellectually. America was peripheral, just then, to his thoughts and aspirations.[5]

The importance of leaving Austria and Germany behind was underscored by the Homburger family's route. Jon was a few months old and Kai was a toddler; yet the Homburgers took a long and indirect route. They rode trains through Poland and up the Polish corridor to Danzig, the children sleeping much of the way in the luggage webbing above the seats. In Danzig, they boarded an uncomfortable cattle boat for Copenhagen. A direct train ride through Germany would have been faster, cheaper, and more comfortable. But Erik and Joan both felt that because of their German citizenship papers and Erik's Jewishness, the indirect route was safer. Although associates in the Vienna psychoanalytic community called this travel venture misguided if not paranoid in its reading of the German situation, the Homburgers traveled—as Jewish immigrants would later—along a carefully planned route to circumvent the Nazis.[6]

In Copenhagen, they found that Erik's mother's generation was rapidly dwindling. Her brother Axel had died the year before, though his widow and Nicholai's widow were still alive. So was Einar, though in poor physical condition. Erik's primary rapport was with cousins of his generation—Axel's children (Henny and Svend) and Nicholai's children (Povl and Edith)—who arranged for the four to stay initially in a local boardinghouse. Pressed for income with only modest help (the equivalent of about 300 kroner monthly) from Joan's mother in America, the Homburgers moved to a small, inexpensive rental house on the southern outskirts of Copenhagen. Until Erik secured a work permit and could launch a career as a practicing analyst, his family would have to survive on sparse funds even though Kai and Jon could not make the long walk into town. The Homburgers even had problems communicating with their neighbors; Erik was unable to conduct himself in Danish, while Joan only spoke German and English.[7]

The Homburgers managed to see some of the Copenhagen sites, especially when Joan's mother visited. Marie Bonaparte introduced them to her friends and tried to make them feel at home. Erik took the opportunity to inquire about the identity of his biological father, but he learned little. His older relatives honored Theodor's request to say nothing about Erik's parentage, and they had pledged their children to silence. Even so, the cousins had no reliable information. It is significant, though, that Erik did not pressure them to reveal what they knew. Nor did he explore the meticulous Danish public records for clues. Whatever the identity of his father, Erik concluded that the man, likely artistic and of Danish nobility, had left Copenhagen years earlier for America. He seemed to find solace in this story.[8]

Nineteen thirty-three was not a good year to seek a work permit to practice psychoanalysis in Denmark. Danish analysts tended to be regarded as quacks. Sigurd Naesgaard, the leading analyst, was generally discredited by his medical colleagues, especially after he recommended psychoanalysis to cure almost any affliction. Not long after Homburger arrived in Copenhagen, he attended a public lecture on psychoanalysis by Jenö Harnik, whom Freud had characterized as a "manifest paranoiac." Harnik rambled nonstop for hours and was eventually forcefully removed from the podium and transported to the psychiatric ward of a local hospital. A few months before the Harnik episode, Marxist analyst Wilhelm Reich emigrated from Germany. In Copenhagen, he was roundly criticized when one of his first patients attempted suicide. Reich's leftist politics and his emphasis on sexual energy provoked Danish psychiatrists and the press to lobby against renewal of his temporary visa. As it happened, Erik ran into Reich at a beach, where Reich claimed to see "the same bluish light which one sees around some stars passing between couples making love." Denied permission to open a psychoanalytic clinic and refused a work permit, Reich left for Sweden late in 1933. Episodes such as these hampered Marie Bonaparte's effort to establish a Danish psychoanalytic institute despite her royalty and Freud's acclaim for her as "one of my best pupils."[9]

Erik Homburger was issued only a six-month visitor's permit, and he was not allowed to seek gainful employment. He hoped that he could extend the permit, reside in Denmark for seven years, and thereby regain the Danish citizenship lost when he was adopted by a German citizen. But most immediately, the ban on remunerative employment had to be revoked so that he could support his family. The underlying problem was that Danish authorities failed to understand the new threat from the right that was driving German Jews and other marginalized peoples into their country. To help Erik find work and salary in Copenhagen, the Abrahamsens hired C. B. Henriques, a leader of the local Jewish community and a very prominent attorney. Henriques represented Erik before the national Ministry of Justice, petitioning the ministry to issue long-term residency papers to the entire Homburger family and to provide Erik with a work permit.[10]

The papers that Henriques filed with the ministry are instructive. Axel's son, Svend, a young attorney in Henriques's office, provided him with family information. Henriques emphasized that Erik's parents, Karla Abrahamsen and Valdemar Salomonsen (who later died), were both Danish citizens. Concealing the fact that Salomonsen was not Erik's biological father, Henriques noted that Salomonsen went to America while Karla immigrated to Germany before Erik was born. As an infant, Erik was therefore a Danish citizen until Karla married Theodor and "was naturalized in Germany" as Erik Homburger. But Erik "has not had any special attachment" to Germany, Henriques emphasized. Rather, he maintained strong ties to his "propertied relatives" in Copenhagen, and they were ready to help him financially. Joan's American mother was already giving the couple money, Henriques noted, and Erik's psychoanalytic training would facilitate entry into the teaching profession. Henriques emphasized that Erik's training had been "purely scientific" and was not "politically colored."[11]

Through Svend's efforts, Henriques also submitted several reference letters from the Abrahamsens and their friends. These emphasized Erik's Danish birth and his scientific rather than his political interests. A letter from Marie Bonaparte was also included. Erik's uncle, Einar, swore a statement emphasizing the Danishness of Erik's parents. There was, however, some legal disadvantage in the surviving Danish parent being female. To compensate, Einar argued that Erik and his family should be permitted to settle in Denmark since he was a Jew and conditions for Jews in Germany and Austria were poor. Einar also detailed his own considerable wealth and underscored the willingness of all of the Abrahamsens to support the Homburgers should Erik's wages prove insufficient.[12]

Henriques and Svend Abrahamsen had fashioned a narrative and supporting documentation that characterized Erik Homburger as a Copenhagen
Abrahamsen who had lived abroad for a time but who was entitled to return
to his Danish family. Henriques's documented appeal went to the National
Board of Health, which was to advise the Ministry of Justice. The board classified the case with earlier cases of "so-called psychoanalysts," and this sealed
the fate of the Homburger family. Membership in the scandalous psychoanalytic profession outweighed belonging to a prominent and respected old
Danish family, and the board advised against accepting Henriques's appeal.
When the Ministry of Justice accepted the board's recommendation, one of
its officials suggested to Henriques that Erik Homburger's German citizenship counted against him as well as his profession. The ministry also
informed the University of Copenhagen that Homburger could not be hired
to teach in Denmark.[13]

Counting on the help of one of the most prominent and capable attor-
neys in Denmark and the support of one of its oldest and most distinguished Jewish families, Erik had expected to win the appeal. He was
shocked when the Ministry of Justice ruled against him. Indeed, he never
forgot how his hopes and dreams were dashed "because I could not get my
Danish citizenship back." Distressed and perhaps humiliated, he prepared
to leave the country.[14]

Erik and Joan needed only a day or two to decide how to respond. Anna
Freud and others invited them back to Vienna, still downplaying Hitler's intentions in Austria, but the Homburgers did not seriously consider the offer. They
had set their sights on the United States. Indeed, Erik confessed to August Aichhorn his persisting hope "that I would be able to find the betraying [biolog-
ical] father in America." A chance meeting in Vienna sometime earlier
between Erik and Hanns Sachs, a prominent member of Freud's inner circle
who was practicing in Boston, had also pointed him toward America. Sachs
had emphasized the pressing need for child analysts in Boston and promised
to help establish Erik if he settled in the United States.[15]

Joan mentioned Sachs's offer when the Danish Ministry of Justice ruled
against Erik. And she emphasized other practical considerations. Her
mother, now living in Boston, was eager to sponsor their migration to the
Massachusetts capital and to pledge financial support. Indeed, Mary Serson
had promised to work with American immigration authorities to facilitate
the relocation. The fact that Joan had lived in the United States before leaving for Europe enhanced the possibility that she would be able to bring her
husband back without a long delay. With these tangible factors supporting
her position and no alternative in sight, Joan strongly urged Erik to migrate
to America. Even in Vienna, she had preferred migrating to the United

States, and she was no more comfortable with the Danish psychoanalytic community than she had been with Freud's in Vienna. Consequently, Joan felt a certain relief when Danish authorities rejected Erik's appeal; the United States became the only sensible choice. Saddened that he could not cultivate his Danish roots, Erik recognized that Joan had "decided to take us to America" and acquiesced.[16]

AN IMMIGRANT IN AMERICA

Mary Serson procured immigration visas for the family of four. Kai was two, Jon eight months, and their parents were in their early thirties. Erik's younger half sister, Ellen, had recently migrated from Karlsruhe to Palestine but came to Copenhagen to see them off. Shortly before they were to board the SS *Scanmail* for the thirteen-day voyage to New York, an American immigration official ruled, quite mistakenly, that Erik had a serious illness and could not leave Denmark. The official was persuaded to change his ruling, but only after he had provoked much anguish among the Homburgers.[17]

Years later Erik wrote a short account of the voyage for his grandson, Per Bloland. The family boarded the *Scanmail* in Copenhagen, he noted, "where we had visited my Danish relatives." There was no mention of his distress at the failed effort to regain his Danish citizenship. The voyage was rough due to terrible storms and high waves, and the boat rocked constantly. Erik carried Kai around exploring areas of the ship. Unlike his brother and his parents, who got seasick, Jon enjoyed the constant movement of the *Scanmail* and "laughed and gurgled most of his waking hours." As the ship passed the Statue of Liberty, Erik was overwhelmed by "the tremendous size of the statue and buildings and everything. And after we landed, the automobiles! It was all a bit scary and yet inviting and encouraging."[18]

In this account of the voyage, Erik Homburger voiced his apprehension—"I knew about a hundred words of English"—about having to make a living for his family in an English-speaking country. Although he tried to read and write in the new language, he feared that he was too old to master it thoroughly and to comprehend its subtleties. But he soon discovered that he had a good ear for language. Moreover, Joan "was an enormous help: you know how well she explains things," he told his grandson. She helped him to read and speak to Americans. Fortunately, Erik recalled, Americans "were unbelievably patient with immigrants" who had not mastered their language.[19]

One such American, George Kennan, was on the *Scanmail* with his wife in the cabin next to the Homburgers. A member of the U.S. legation to Riga, Latvia, fluent in German, and destined to become a primary architect of American foreign policy, Kennan was "the first American I met." Deeply disturbed by Hitler, Erik, while still in Vienna, had apparently begun an essay analyzing the Nazi leader's appeal to German youth. Noticing Erik working on that essay on the deck of the *Scanmail,* Kennan asked to read it. He was deeply impressed by its depth and subtlety. "That should be translated" for an American audience, he told Erik. "Let's do it together." They worked on the translation for the balance of the trip, with the American diplomat essentially instructing Erik in English. They also enjoyed animated discussions about German history and culture, especially about the fear and contempt that German youth felt for their fathers. Hitler seemed to pose an appealing if dangerously "delinquent" leadership alternative to the German father. This preliminary work became one of the most important essays in *Childhood and Society.* Kennan's help and encouragement convinced Erik that he could communicate his European experience to intelligent and sophisticated Americans. The two did not make contact again until *Childhood and Society* was published in 1950, when Kennan wrote, "It is beautifully written and effectively stated." Kennan recalled "very well our passage on the boat" and was pleased that their conversations not only facilitated the Hitler essay but "helped you in the problem of understanding this new [American] milieu." Kennan was onto something. In their discussions on the *Scanmail,* he had provided Erik with some sense of America against a backdrop of German history and culture. This German context for delineating American qualities would remain crucial as Erik studied and wrote about his new national home.[20]

"I will never forget the moment when our ship first sighted the coldly competitive skyline of New York," he recalled in surprisingly stark language. "The sight more or less puts you in a mental state of survivorship, both in the sense of having to accept, without looking back too much, the fact of your survival abroad, and in the sense of being determined to survive as a family here, too." The struggle to survive in America "at first narrows your perceptiveness and, I'm afraid, your capacity to empathize with the unfortunate and the disadvantaged." Oscar Stonorov, his Karlsruhe friend, greeted the Homburgers on Ellis Island. He showed them around New York City and drove them to his home in Philadelphia, where they stayed briefly before leaving for Boston, their ultimate destination. Peter Blos greeted Erik with his early woodcuts, which Erik had left with Peter's parents. During those first honeymoon-like days in America, Erik recalled, he was very excited, hopeful, ambitious, and almost wholly blind to America's blemishes: "When you are welcome as immigrants, it is hard to look around and ask whom from abroad they are not letting in—and whom at home they are keeping down to a level below that of a newcomer."[21]

Like Otto Fenichel, Siegfried Bernfeld, and Erich Fromm, émigré psychoanalysts who had been critical of the European societies they left behind, Erik Homburger initially had only praise for his new homeland. In fact, he fell in love with Franklin Roosevelt and New Deal America. "What you call Depression here compared to Vienna was riches," he recalled. If this was true in terms of goods and housing, it was even truer spiritually. Indeed, the newly inaugurated president made everyone want to sing: "Happy days are here again, the sky is blue and clear again." A "highly playful President," if crippled from the waist down, Roosevelt conveyed a sense of *Spielraum* and motion. With support from an aide, Roosevelt "appeared always erect." His optimistic voice and his carriage were helping to elevate the mood of the country, lifting everybody's spirits. As Erik recalled the vigor and enthusiasm of the president and the early New Deal, he was euphoric.[22]

When Erik Homburger arrived in the fall of 1933, he felt that it was still possible to be an immigrant with meaningful choices about his destiny, and not a refugee from the gathering Holocaust. Danish officials had denied him these choices. He had departed from Europe at "the last moment . . . where a man with my background [Jewish] could leave voluntarily." For Erik, as for Jacob Riis decades earlier, "America still meant all of this. It meant 'Come, we'll help you, we're glad you came,' and all of this." Indeed, he frequently mentioned the clerk who greeted him at the immigration office with a very warm "Welcome." It meant, "You *wanted* to come to this country" as an immigrant and not later for sheer survival as a refugee like many Central European Jews. He was glad that he arrived in the tradition of earlier migrants like Riis before the Holocaust changed the meaning of immigration and altered the wonderfully "innocent" American "welcome."[23]

Nevertheless, Erik also harbored misgivings during his first weeks in America. He was apprehensive of a few jarring "breaks" with his European past. The sights, sounds, and rhythms of everyday life were different. Language persisted as a major concern. He missed friends and worried about his mother and stepfather, still in Karlsruhe. (Fortunately, they were able to migrate to Palestine in 1935.) Another loss was the tradition of lay analysis that Freud had sanctioned. And he worried about his employment prospects: "I am expecting nothing." Like Helene Deutsch, however, he arrived in advance of the flood of exiled European analysts. When he went to Abraham Brill's New York City office, he hoped that his analytic training would stand him in good stead. Vice president of the International Psycho-Analytical Association, Brill played a crucial role in the placement of European analysts. Erik requested help in establishing a practice in New York or, preferably, Boston, but found Brill to be condescending. Brill recommended some obscure location like St. Louis, where client prospects were bleak. Later Brill wrote to Ernest Jones, a leading British psychoanalyst, that Homburger "did not impress me much."[24]

Erik insisted that he "never took seriously" Brill's rebuff. Yet Brill's dismissal, his limited English vocabulary, and worries about family and friends abroad had a combined and telling effect. Despite the hope and good cheer of FDR's America, he sometimes felt desperate. It was the sort of uneasy feeling he would eventually designate as an "identity crisis." For an immigrant, this crisis could extend well beyond adolescence. Indeed, it seemed to correspond to immigrants' emotions as they "gave up old national identities" for "the sake of a new country." It also appeared to correspond to the national mood of uneasiness in an America confronting economic Depression at home and dangerous right-wing movements abroad. As Erik later reflected, the concept of identity crisis had almost inevitably to be elaborated on American shores.[25]

As the family shifted from the New York–Philadelphia area to Boston, Joan's mother arranged for their housing and provided financial support until Erik secured employment. He remembered Hanns Sachs's assurance that Boston desperately needed a child analyst, and Sachs's promise to facilitate his entry into the local professional community. But Sachs had not informed his colleagues that Erik was coming to Boston. Without language facility, professional degrees, or local contacts, Erik became nervous and somewhat desperate: "I had to start from scratch." He was intent on meeting important figures who might offer employment. "I was so involved in my personal needs," he recalled, that he had no overview of the Boston medical world in those early days. Sachs invited the Homburgers to a dinner, which became their first important social engagement in America. There they met the prominent reformer William Healy, head of the Judge Baker Clinic for troubled children. Recognizing what Healy could do for him but diplomatically astute, Erik made no requests. Instead, he made pleasant conversation about his Vienna training in child analysis. Before the evening was over, Healy invited Erik to discuss prospects at his clinic. A short while later, the influential Stanley Cobb of Massachusetts General Hospital invited the Homburgers to a family dinner. Here, too, Erik's charm and calculated reserve produced an invitation to visit Cobb's offices. He had become acquainted with Irmarita Putnam, daughter of American psychoanalytic pioneer James Jackson Putnam. By the end of 1933, she was informing the entire Boston psychoanalytic and medical community about the young man from Karlsruhe and Vienna. Putnam, who knew Freud well, attested to Homburger's qualifications as a very proficient analyst. Erik attributed the job opportunities that eventually materialized in Boston to Ms. Putnam's validation. Within a year, lecture invitations also arrived. For example, David Shakow, chief psychologist at Worcester State Hospital, invited Erik to present a seminar to his colleagues on the research implications of child analysis.[26]

As Erik pursued employment and lecture prospects, Joan put her professional ambitions on hold and took charge of her two young boys and the needs of her husband, making do with a paucity of income. Like many fathers of the 1930s, Erik parented in absentia. Unlike most of these absent fathers, however, he spent much of his time caring for other people's children.

The Homburger family found an apartment on Memorial Drive on the Cambridge side of the Charles River. For Joan, the neighborhood was lonely and depressing. She had to walk long distances to shop, especially to find the necessities for the healthy meals she prepared—oatmeal, wheat bread without additives, fresh vegetables for large salads (the core of the evening meal), and bowls of fresh fruit for snacks. Fish and chicken usually substituted for beef. For nicer living quarters near markets and convivial neighbors, Joan arranged to move the family to a small furnished rental house on Appian Way. To help pay the rent, she took in a boarder and arranged the downstairs living room for Erik to work with his patients. She also procured a part-time job teaching rhythmic gymnastics at the Shady Hill School, a Deweyite children's facility in Cambridge. Joan treated her children's frequent illnesses and was very attentive to Erik. He disliked shopping or cooking, liked to be served, and only grudgingly dished out leftover food from the kitchen when necessity required. In restaurants, Joan ordered for him. She knew his tastes and nutritional needs better than he did.[27]

Private analytic patients of all ages provided Erik Homburger with his first regular income. He worked out of his Appian Way home and shared another office on Boston's fashionable Marlborough Street with more established analysts. He accepted any clients who had been referred to him; most were children, adolescents, and young adults—the rich and poor of many nationalities. From the start, Erik departed from orthodox psychoanalytic emphasis on the neutrality of the therapist by visiting his patients' homes, dining with their families, and having them come to his house to meet his family. His Vienna credentials and the fact that he was one of the first child analysts in the Boston area gave some semblance of legitimacy to these practices. Indeed, through his extremely sensitive, intuitive manner, he quickly gained recognition. Sachs reported that Erik "succeeded in establishing here an extraordinarily good reputation in a relatively short time" owing to "his intuitive insight" into young people. Boston-area pediatricians, child psychologists, social workers, and others called on him for advice with difficult cases involving children and even adolescents. Felix Deutsch reported that although Erik's eclectic artistic background was deficient in "the best pre-analytic qualifications," he could "make his way here. And he has done it!"[28]

Erik's local reputation as an analyst began with his success treating the sister of John Taylor, a prominent member of the Boston Psychoanalytic Society. Because Martha Taylor was severely dyslexic as a child, her parents had kept her out of Cambridge public schools, educating her at home until she was eleven. Exceedingly bright, she graduated from Radcliffe and edited medical research reports for Harvard Medical School faculty. Emotional problems rooted in the dynamics of her family caused her to seek analysis with Otto Rank in Paris in the mid-1920s. She wanted to discover her own unique voice and to act with genuine autonomy, but this did not occur. Instead, Rank told John Taylor how pleased he was with Martha's excellence in assisting him with the completion of his book *Genetic Psychology*.[29]

Still deeply distressed late in 1933, Martha followed her brother's suggestion to look up Anna Freud's student from Vienna who had recently taken up practice in Cambridge. Erik's modest rental home contrasted with Rank's plush Paris offices, and his fees were considerably lower. He began by defying analytic convention and inviting her to dinner with his family so that she would recognize the sources of the hustle and bustle (his children) she could hear while in analysis. For over a year, she sat in his living room–home office for her daily sessions. The room was bright and cheery, scattered with toys and books and plants. Unlike Rank, Erik had no special analytic couch but an ordinary and well-worn home sofa upon which she sometimes sat and at other times reclined. Erik lacked Rank's distance and reserve, his approach more earthy and relaxed. He might excuse himself, for example, to attend to one of his crying sons when Joan was not around or to put the family cat out or to find something to eat. Taylor felt that her analysis was concrete and "homelike." Whereas Rank focused upon her specific problems, Erik prompted her to talk about her life in the context of growing family pressures and of her medical editing responsibilities. Since his command of English was poor, but also to establish collaboration between analyst and analysand, Erik sometimes asked Taylor to explain a word or a sentence more fully or to clarify an American custom. He learned language and national customs from patients like her. Often he held a random array of pictures in his hand and sometimes asked her to comment on one of them if it seemed to have bearing on her life. In this way, he detected her emotional and social strengths and worked with her to build on them. As her analysis proceeded, Martha Taylor found that she was more relaxed and more attentive to recreational outlets from family and work pressures. Most important, she felt stronger emotionally, with a voice sufficient to state her needs to relatives and professional associates. She went on to direct children's programs for the Boston Nursery Training School, for Radcliffe and Tufts, and to open her own school for children with physical-emotional handicaps.[30]

In his successful analysis of Martha Taylor, Erik seemed to be trying to help her find an identity rooted in her development and circumstances. He did not yet employ the terms *identity* and *life cycle;* they would emerge as he attempted to understand lives like hers. Word quickly spread among the members of the Boston Psychoanalytic Society that Erik's analysis had done far more for John Taylor's sister than Rank's had. This, plus the prestige that Vienna psychoanalytic training brought in those years, helped him to deal with local restrictions against lay analysts.

During its formal reorganization in 1930, the Boston Psychoanalytic Society had followed a national trend by limiting full membership to physicians who had completed their training analyses. Erik was out on both counts. Full standing in the Vienna Psychoanalytic Society, however, gave him automatic membership in the International Psycho-Analytical Association. This allowed him to escape the requirement of a medical degree that the American Psychoanalytic Association was about to impose for full membership in its ranks. But the Boston Society was a different matter. Although its influential leader, Ives Hendrick, had persuaded his colleagues to close their doors to non-physicians, he was willing to give Erik (as well as the more prominent Hanns Sachs) full membership after learning from John Taylor that his sister was helped enormously. Hendrick was also influenced by "the unusual creativity of his [Homburger's] thinking" in analytic case presentations. Indeed, he was proud that Erik went on to offer the Boston Society's first course on child analysis and to become a control analyst, so as to supervise the training of other child analysts. Hendrick was glad to refer analytic patients to Erik.[31]

Anna Freud kept current on her analysand's progress and wrote to Ernest Jones in 1934 concerning the "good news about Boston." Erik's status represented an isolated triumph for her father's position in the United States. Erik was distressed by the "medicalization" of American psychoanalysis: "In Vienna you had the feeling it was a humanistic business. It was the enlightenment. Here, psychoanalysis was a part of the medical world." American analysts "were all interested in the medical development of analysis as a medical specialty." It was therefore fortunate that Boston-area physician-analysts respected Erik's work, and the year after his arrival, the American Psychoanalytic Association named him chair of its Committee on Psychoanalysis in Childhood and Adolescence. By then, three colleagues in the Boston Psychoanalytic Society—Stanley Cobb, William Healy, and Henry Murray—had offered him employment and research opportunities. Still, he felt uneasy as perhaps the only member of the American and Boston societies who "had not completed any kind of college" education, much less medical school. Moreover, his sense of awkwardness and insecurity as a foreigner who needed to prove himself in America persisted. Every now and then, he felt "down-and-out." Overall, however, he concluded that during his first years in America, "I received only support."[32]

WIDENING PROFESSIONAL RESPONSIBILITIES

During his three years in the Boston area, Erik Homburger's responsibilities expanded. In addition to his modest practice and his work for the Boston Psychoanalytic Society, he became a consultant at the Judge Baker Clinic, a research fellow in the psychiatry department of the Harvard-affiliated Massachusetts General Hospital, a research associate at the Harvard Psychological Clinic, and even for a time a graduate student in Harvard's Department of Psychology. By 1936, his professional plate was so full that he felt sated. He began the long-standing practice of constructing his personal calendars as squares of days and weeks in various colors and with an assortment of connecting lines and arrows in colored pencils so he could see what he had to do each week and month at a glance. In *Childhood and Society,* he attributed the intense daily tugs and pulls on his time to the cultural landscape of his newly adopted country. His schedule was at once stimulating and exhausting.

William Healy had established the Judge Baker Clinic in 1917 as a model demonstration facility for emotionally disturbed children. The clinic was organized around an interdisciplinary team of psychiatrists, psychologists, and social workers who assisted each child and worked with his or her parents, teachers, and other important figures. While giving serious consideration to children's medical problems, Healy emphasized that they were social beings. Erik's case presentations and discussions at the Boston Psychoanalytic Society fascinated Healy, who thought Erik had a "special gift" as a child analyst, with unusual empathy and understanding of a child's unconscious processes. And though Erik "knows the psychoanalytic theory extremely well," he was always willing to put theory (with its emphasis on the inner life) aside and focus on actual social circumstances surrounding children. Erik liked the interdisciplinary composition of the Baker clinical teams and appreciated Healy's social and community emphasis. Healy's perspectives complemented Aichhorn's ideas in dealing with juveniles. Indeed, Erik now advocated regular preventive mental health checkups for children, and was excited when Healy invited him to take part in Judge Baker case conferences.[33]

What most impressed Healy and child-care workers throughout Boston, however, was that Erik Homburger was able to help children that his staff and other consultants characterized as hopeless. Mental health work with children was proliferating at the time, not only in Boston but in several other American cities. Rockefeller philanthropic donations had supported a variety of university research projects on children, their emotions, and their physical and cognitive capacities. Mental hygiene activists had helped to create the child guidance movement, which in turn launched child treatment facilities like Judge Baker. Interdisciplinary teams at these facilities tried to deal with troubled youngsters in ways that avoided "moral rigidities"; the teams gravitated increasingly toward psychoanalytically informed therapy and eschewed many of the behavioristic psychological assumptions of the 1920s. There was also a growing and often intersecting interest in child development, with its distinctive research and training centers, and attracting young professionals like Benjamin Spock and Lois Murphy. Mental hygienists, psychoanalysts, and Deweyite progressive educators cross-fertilized not only around guidance clinics and university research centers but in schools, summer camps, orphanages, children's home service leagues, child study groups, and other facilities for and concerning youngsters. Their optimal goal was to direct the child's impulses into the creative channels permitted by society. Yet despite this expansion of activities, plus increased federal expenditures for children's medical, social, and psychological services, success with "difficult" and "deeply troubled" children was sporadic. Social reformer Lawrence Frank had promoted foundation funding and conferences on children and would soon befriend Erik. Frank feared that American efforts failed because child-care professionals were unsympathetic to youngsters who "stuck out" from standard developmental models and aggregate research findings. Erik attracted attention precisely because he succeeded where others had failed. The Judge Baker Clinic case of six-year-old John was the first in which he made his name known among child-care professionals.

Son of a sailor, John was a downcast child with arrested emotional development and a pattern of petty delinquencies. He was often sick. When overtaken by rage and sexual excitation, he defecated in his pants and refused to communicate. Medical tests and examinations revealed no organic impediments. Psychiatrists, psychologists, and other mental health workers had no idea what troubled the boy. When he met John, Erik handed him some clay along with blocks and toys, urging him to play with the material. The boy built a grocery store with three blocks, made clay balls and put them in a toy grocery truck, then dumped the truck's contents into a corner as a grocery store delivery. He referred to one clay ball as "mother nut" and a smaller ball of the same color as "baby nut." With another color of clay, he made a long row of balls equal in size and called them "brother nuts"—"my mother's brothers." When Erik asked, "You mean uncles?" the boy became pale and rushed to the bathroom. When he returned, he noted, "This is the way I feel when I soil." Erik construed the clay nuts to represent John's family. John's bathroom panic when "brothers" became "uncles" raised Erik's suspicion that the boy harbored an unbearable secret—that the "uncles" (made of different color clay) had usurped his father's place. Erik watched the boy intently, looked again at his play construction, almost certainly reflecting on the sexual scandal and secrecy in his own early life, and finally understood. As a grocery delivery man, John had delivered the family secret to him— that John's mother had affairs with other men ("uncles") during his father's frequent absences. Clay balls became his mode of communicating a troubled family dynamic and sometimes substituted for defecation. At this point, Erik met with John's mother, who admitted warning the boy not to tell doctors or mental health workers about her affairs; she told John that "Daddy would surely kill me if he heard about it." At Erik's urging, she released John from the obligation of secrecy, which had blocked previous therapeutic efforts. Now Erik was able to make rapid progress with the boy, and words replaced the clay images. Eventually, the words became poems, first about troubling memories, then about beautiful experiences. He began sending these poems to his mother. "The eliminative impulse had found a higher level of expression," Erik concluded.[34]

As Erik wrote up this crucial Judge Baker case for the *Genetic Psychology Monographs* series, he connected it to his general research and writing on children's play arrangements. John's grocery "nuts" illustrated how "our [child] patients *act in space.*" Through such "metaphoric and symbolic use of toys," the defenses were caught off guard and "the child does what he does not dare to do in reality." Like John, the child "delivers his secret, although only in metaphoric allusion." Although John's play arrangement had a verbal element ("mother" and "baby" nut; "brother"/"uncle" nut), it was primarily a concretely visual selection and spacing of objects. The child did not need to be "verbally self-conscious" or to be articulate. The observable configuration itself gave "meaning to suffering" by connecting the child's inner emotions to his outer social circumstances. John showed both himself and Erik that what troubled and depressed him was connected to a social world where his mother had affairs and required him to hide them from his father. John's largely visual (and partially verbal) play arrangement broke through this secrecy, allowing both the therapist and his patient to understand how his emotions connected to his social circumstances. With that understanding, he was ultimately able to gain a firmer sense of his selfhood. To a significant extent, the "me" in John was "liberated" as his relationships to important others changed. Clearly, Erik was departing from an overwhelmingly individualistic notion of the subject. In this respect, he was joining contemporary American thinkers like John Dewey, W. E. B. Du Bois, and George Herbert Mead.[35]

Erik's successful analysis of Martha Taylor had shown members of the Boston Psychoanalytic Society that, even with his poor command of English, he could use Freud's talking cure sensitively and effectively. His success with John at the Judge Baker Clinic confirmed Healy's claim that Erik had a "special gift" for uncovering children's "unconscious processes." But that case also demonstrated to psychoanalysts, psychologists, social workers, and other mental health caregivers how youngsters communicated with visual arrangements (configurations) just as adults communicated with words. To be sure, Erik's view of a play arrangement as a configuration was not yet fully developed or free of problems. Indeed, he was not yet entirely comfortable with the term *configuration*. But through his work with John, Erik proved to the Boston clinical community that he was both a skillful therapist and an important conceptualizer.[36]

Healy had provided Erik Homburger with consultantships at the Judge Baker Clinic but not a job with a regular salary to put food on his table. Two others who were impressed by his initial presentations at the Boston Psychoanalytic Society, Stanley Cobb and Henry Murray, offered Erik part-time positions. Cobb headed the Department of Psychiatry at Massachusetts General Hospital (an affiliate of Harvard Medical School), while Murray directed the Psychological Clinic, an affiliate of Harvard's psychology department. As European psychoanalysts began arriving in America, their natural tendency (as Erik's had been) was to seek out psychoanalytic societies in the larger, more cosmopolitan cities. The societies facilitated income for their private analytic practices through patient referrals and psychoanalytic trainees. Recognizing that European psychoanalysts conferred prestige to American psychoanalytic societies, Cobb and Murray sought to detour the émigrés from the Boston Psychoanalytic Society to the Harvard University–Medical School complex. In this effort, they enlisted financial backing from Alan Gregg of the Rockefeller Foundation Medical Science Division, and they offered salaries and stipends to make Harvard competitive with the Boston Society. As part of this strategy, Cobb and Murray promised Anna Freud's bright and promising young analysand several part-time positions.[37]

Besides being chief of psychiatry at Massachusetts General Hospital (MGH), Cobb directed the Harvard Neurological Unit at Boston City Hospital and was professor of neuropathology at the Harvard Medical School. Like Murray, he was fascinated with psychoanalysis. Indeed, Cobb's holistic perspective on the interaction of mind, body, and environment appealed to Erik. Though the configurational perspective was "rather speculative," he enjoyed socializing with Erik. He appreciated Erik's characterization of psychoanalysis as a philosophy more than a science, and considered him "one of those natural therapists whom the Lord made" and who almost always treated "very difficult patients" successfully.[38]

Using a combination of Rockefeller funding and his own budgets, Cobb offered Erik Homburger a part-time position as research assistant in psychology at MGH and the Harvard Medical School. Lacking advanced degrees, Erik felt indebted to Cobb for his first academic appointment in America. Cobb assigned Erik to work with the noted neuropathologist Frank Fremont-Smith in his investigations of emotional factors in epilepsy, but this role was insubstantial. Limited in his English and uncomfortable with the technical world of organic medicine, Erik attended MGH staff conferences but usually remained silent. When he spoke, he was pleased that others were quite attentive, and he suspected that his Vienna credentials had something to do with this. When Cobb scheduled him to offer a six-day seminar series on child analysis at the MGH Neuropsychiatric Laboratory, attendance was strong despite the ten-dollar enrollment fee. Although his work on the MGH staff was not extensive, the staff appointment and the recognition he received represented "the beginning of a certified career" and a special "kind of homecoming" for a doctor's stepson.[39]

Henry Murray's offer in 1934 of office space and a periodic subsidy at the Harvard Psychological Clinic was also important to Erik Homburger. He did not know of the cooperative financial and strategic arrangements between Murray, Cobb, and Gregg, to be sure, but Murray's facility fostered an atmosphere of exciting and free-ranging intellectual discussion that he did not find at the Judge Baker Clinic or at MGH. The clinic offered "an intercultural and interdisciplinary encounter of a kind that had been unheard of anywhere." Through this first introduction to such "an interdisciplinary setting in America, I found the chance to develop my thinking in configurations."[40]

Morton Prince, Boston's famous neurologist, had founded the Harvard Psychological Clinic in 1927. When he took ill and died the following year, Murray, his young assistant, replaced him. Murray had been analyzed briefly by Carl Jung and credited Jung for an emotional rebirth. In the course of this rebirth, Murray evolved from a proficient physician and biochemist to an eclectic psychologist who depended heavily on Freud and Jung as well as work by others who addressed the total personality. Murray castigated experimental psychologists as "peripheralists," and went on to become one of the founders of the psychology of personality as an academic specialty. Murray's approach was dynamic and holistic, taking into account the ways people found meaning within their social setting. A charismatic leader, he assembled within the clinic diverse young psychologists (usually graduate students) comfortable with his approach, including Donald MacKinnon, Robert W. White, Saul Rosenzweig, Nevitt Sanford, and Jerome Frank. Together with a renowned guest such as Eugene O'Neill or Bertrand Russell, the group read novels and biographies as well as psychology, and they explored in seminars the recurrent themes of human nature. Owing to Murray's dismissal of much of academic psychology and his open-ended embrace of personology, neither he nor his graduate student associates were well regarded by Edwin Boring, chair of the Harvard psychology department and director of its laboratories. No friend of psychoanalytically informed personology, Harvard president James Conant brought experimentalist Karl Lashley into the psychology department in 1935. Lashley promptly joined Boring in an effort to curtail Murray and his clinic.[41]

Despite Boring and Lashley, Erik Homburger thrived at the clinic. He felt that in some ways it approximated the cosmopolitanism of his psychoanalytic training. He noted several interesting women on the clinic staff; some, like Murray's mistress Christiana Morgan, held very important positions. Murray made the clinic feel "closest to home" for Erik, especially in the library, which Murray told him to regard as an "intellectual bunk" where he could take his time mastering English-language publications. He appreciated Murray's attachment to Freud, Jung, and William James. Nonetheless, Murray and several of his male associates sometimes made Erik feel somewhat out of place as "the immigrant, the Jew." They were from upper-class, Protestant, Northeast families; enjoyed athletic competition; and sometimes carried on in their deliberations as if they were participants in an American "sports event." "Anybody who hadn't come up socially or culturally as they had," especially if he was a European Jew with artistic interests but no concern with sports, might occasionally feel uncomfortable with Murray.[42]

Between 1934 and 1936, the two years Erik was at the clinic, staff time was often occupied with a pioneering effort to integrate academic psychology and empiricism with clinical conceptions and psychoanalysis; that effort produced *Explorations in Personality*. Murray was sufficiently impressed by Erik's creative spark to put him on the Diagnostic Council, which directed the project. There, he joined experienced senior psychological researchers like William Barrett, H. Scudder Mekeel, and Christiana Morgan. After selecting fifty college-age males in the Boston area (mostly undergraduates) as their subjects, the council organized a diversity of tests and interviews to record the full life history of each. Murray's thematic apperception test and other projective tests were featured. Each subject was handed an ambiguous stimulus (like an inkblot) and encouraged to project onto it his often buried feelings, desires, and emotions (hopefully his internal unconscious processes). All testing procedures but Erik's, as he elected to run them, included heavy verbal dimensions. As part of Murray's testing, for example, he had each student write for two hours on his early life and development. Barrett sought free verbal associations from each concerning his sexual development. Mekeel relied on questionnaires and asked about the subject's memories of his family relationships during childhood and adolescence. Other staff ran similar tests and tabulated the results statistically. It was the responsibility of each researcher to prepare a chapter on the results and their implications for life history, the nature of personality, and how the self sought mastery within society.[43]

As the project progressed, Murray was often struck by Erik Homburger's inexperience in psychological testing techniques. He suggested that Erik simply use blocks and other toys to run play experiments with the college-age students not unlike his therapeutic work with children. For his contribution to *Explorations in Personality,* Erik ran a dramatic production test through which the subjects came to remember decisive moods and moments in their past as they arranged and played with children's toys. With the toys serving as stimuli to evoke feelings and emotions, the exercise was compatible with the Diagnostic Council's emphasis on projective testing. However, Erik felt that he was not conducting a formal test to elicit verbal response so much as a broad-ranging clinical exploration. His subjects made "configurational arrangements" with their toys, much as John at Judge Baker had with clay, to elucidate crucial turning points and devastating experiences of the past. As with younger children and even certain psychotics, Erik felt these students could more easily and more fully address past traumas through play than verbalization. Given his artistic background and his limited English, he also sensed that he could better understand the meaning of play configurations: "Again I could see something before I could try to understand what it meant in so many words."[44]

Published in 1938 after the Homburgers had moved from the Boston area, *Explorations in Personality* was one of several major research projects of the 1930s that sought to connect depth psychology with empiricism. It remains a classic in the history of psychology. However, Erik's chapter on the results of his dramatic production test was not well regarded. The prominent social psychologist Kurt Lewin characterized it as the weakest and most subjective part of the publication. Nevitt Sanford, a psychologist in training in Murray's clinic, agreed, determining that Erik never understood the project's goals and went off on his own tangent. Murray saw that Erik's numerical ratings of qualities of the students that he tested contrasted markedly from the ratings of other researchers. He concluded that Erik was "not scientifically minded" and was uninterested in devising experiments to test theories, nor was he able to bridge the nonverbal quality of play constructions with verbal articulateness. Thus, while Murray judged Erik's observations to be cogent, he acknowledged that Erik's chapter did little for *Explorations.* The man did not fit into a cooperative, scientific research project. In the years ahead, as Erik made his way through American universities and research centers, this would continue to be the case.[45]

The project at Murray's clinic gave Erik his first sustained contact with college-age Americans, and they fascinated him. He concluded that they "seemingly hung together in a different way" from Europeans of that age. Many remained "open and not too committed for a while," a condition Erik's Viennese colleagues would have labeled pathological. But he sensed that such a "playful, experimental" quality was not so much a deficiency as a characteristic of American cultural identity. Although "I didn't know it at the time," the young American men he tested were helping him, as an immigrant outsider, to extend Federn's concept of ego boundaries into his own perspective on the "identity crisis" of adolescents and young adults.[46]

While his work in the Harvard Psychological Clinic helped Erik to further explore the configurations people made and the issue of identity, it also had collateral benefits, such as allowing him to become involved with Henry Murray's epigenetic model of human development, which was rooted in embryology. Murray had studied chick development within the eggshell as a process of normal growth and sought to extend his observations to human, ethical, as well as biological development. This idea fascinated Erik, for it suggested that "anything that grows has a ground plan" from which each "part" has "its time of special ascendancy." He began to couple Murray's embryology based on epigenetic observations (and Murray's conflation of natural with ethical development) with Freud's concepts of psychological development in early childhood. These elements would soon become integral to his model of the human life cycle. Like Murray, he would shape his model by merging a normative view of development with a descriptive biological perspective. Much more than Freud and his Vienna circle, Murray sought to work with development in normal, healthy subjects. As Erik began work on a model of the life cycle, he grounded his research in normal development as well, and put behind him the Vienna emphasis on psychological deficiencies.[47]

Focused on personology as "the study of lives" over the whole life course, Murray and his psychological clinic therefore provided Erik with considerable intellectual stimulation. He encouraged Erik to put theory aside in order to observe "how things hang together, what they look like, what form they take, and all that." This process felt comfortable. Despite some reservations, Erik found the clinic a congenial setting. The problem was that it was affiliated with Harvard's psychology department, and the department required all of Murray's research associates to pursue psychology doctorates.[48]

Initially, Erik Homburger was not bothered by this requirement, for "everybody told me that without a degree you don't have a chance in this country." As head of the psychology department, Edwin Boring, Murray's nemesis, evaluated Erik's credentials for admission and decided that passage of the *Abitur* at a German gymnasium plus University of Vienna course work represented the equivalent of a Harvard bachelor's degree. Erik could be admitted to the psychology graduate program but was several courses short of formal doctoral candidacy. Erik had assumed that his training and studies within the Vienna Psychoanalytic Society would also be counted as relevant educational experience, but Boring ruled otherwise. Throughout 1934 and the first half of 1935, Erik took one graduate psychology course a semester. After he finished the courses, Boring judged that he was seven-eighths of a year of residency short of doctoral candidacy. Erik enrolled in Boring's own introductory-level graduate course and found it impossible. He was intimidated by the empirical experimentalist who made no room for intuition or artistry. In his nervousness, he sometimes tripped on the steps of Emerson Hall when Boring passed by. In an autobiographical essay, Erik claimed that he failed the course, although he may have done so poorly that he dropped the course to avoid failing. In either case, he left the program and never again pursued a doctorate. While his three years in the Boston area were marked by successes as a clinician and a creative thinker, he felt that "I flunked" as a graduate student. This memory of academic failure counted for much.[49]

YALE

Even in his adopted country, Erik Homburger could not stay put. Joan assumed that because he had been uprooted so often in Europe, he almost instinctively felt the need to push on after three years in Boston-Cambridge. Having located a comfortable rental house and congenial work at the Shady Hill School, Joan was reluctant to leave. Yet she realized that with his responsibilities at Judge Baker, MGH, the Harvard Psychological Clinic, and a private analytic practice, Erik was pulled in too many directions. After an uncertain start in America, he was earning a decent if modest income. Still, he felt "so involved in my personal needs" of putting together and maintaining diverse sources of income that he lacked "the overview which would help me to make a truly historical statement." He was beginning to feel a need to write, but his responsibilities were too time-consuming to make that possible.[50]

Lawrence Frank arranged an alternative in New Haven. Deeply interested in the study of childhood, especially child development, Frank felt that some sort of convergence between psychoanalysis and cultural anthropology represented the most fruitful approach to the topic. A creative promoter more than a researcher, Frank supported the early child development movement in the 1920s as a funding administrator within the Laura Spellman Rockefeller Memorial. He shifted to Rockefeller's General Education Board in 1931 and to the Josiah Macy Junior Foundation in 1936. Milton Senn called Frank "the catalyst of the surge of interest in the study of children" during the interwar period. Margaret Mead regarded him as the father of the child development movement for using foundation funds to gather "living networks of people who could learn to work together" (mainly psychoanalysts and cultural anthropologists—the major figures in the culture and personality movement). Fortunately for Erik Homburger, Frank wanted to include him in the "networks" and to facilitate a situation that made research and authorship possible.[51]

Frank lacked extensive academic training and was not put off by Erik Homburger's difficulties with Boring or his failure to complete a psychology doctorate at Harvard. The two met at an interdisciplinary gathering in New York City, where Frank was suitably impressed with Erik's hasty discussion of his configurational approach to children's work that merged libido theory with culture—the "inner" and the "outer" worlds. During an interruption in the proceedings, Frank struck Erik as "the most maternal man you ever met" in his willingness to "take care of somebody." An invitation to Frank's summer home in Holderness, New Hampshire, was soon forthcoming. With some sense of Frank's influence, Erik and Joan responded, months later, on their way south after visiting those of Joan's relatives still remaining in Ontario. They intended simply to take tea with Frank and his wife and to explore in what ways he might help Erik's career. But they stayed a week. As the days passed, Erik elaborated his configurational approach, and Frank valued it as a potentially ideal marriage between psychoanalysis and cultural anthropology. He felt that Erik needed uninterrupted time and interdisciplinary colleagues to gather more data and to write. Yale offered opportunities for cooperative interdisciplinary research and writing. With Macy Foundation money, Frank would try to arrange a regular research appointment on the campus. In the interim, he would contact Mark May, an educational psychologist and director of Yale's Institute of Human Relations, as well as Marian Putnam, an influential Yale Medical School psychiatrist, to recommend that they invite Erik to New Haven for bimonthly consultations.[52]

These bimonthly visits to Yale began at the end of 1935 and were paid for by the medical school. During the visits, Erik presented work and attended staff conferences at the Institute of Human Relations, the medical school Departments of Psychiatry and Pediatrics, and Arnold Gesell's Child Development Clinic. In short order, Putnam told May that she and her colleague Ruth Washburn wanted Erik as a research colleague: "He thinks freely but critically, and shares rather than imposes his thought on others." May was so impressed that he characterized Erik as "the leading child analyst of America." Aware that a fervor for psychoanalysis had swept academic circles in Chicago and Boston, May felt that Anna Freud's very creative student could promote that fervor in New Haven. He knew that Erik had "no medical or scientific training," but wanted him anyway as an institute research associate.[53]

Erik approved of what he saw in New Haven. At Yale, there appeared to be considerable interest in interdisciplinary ventures and interesting colleagues for "cooperative research." Frank secured a three-year Macy Foundation pledge to support him, and May sold it to high Yale administrators despite increasing anti-Semitism on campus. The institute and the medical school would bring him in as a research associate in psychoanalysis with the rank of instructor (assistant professor by 1938). He would be affiliated with the Departments of Pediatrics and Psychiatry, Gesell's Child Development Clinic, and May's institute. The Macy Foundation paid him a generous academic-year salary ($6,500 for 1936–37, $5,500 for 1937–38, $5,000 for 1938–39). Erik was permitted to earn another $1,000 a year by working with a limited number of private patients. Even with the decreasing salary scale, this level of compensation represented a substantial increase in his income and offered the promise of research and authorship. Erik was thrilled and voiced no misgivings over the anti-Semitic and nativist biases on the Yale campus, which were stronger than those at Princeton, Harvard, or Columbia. In fact, no Jew had ever received a tenured Yale faculty appointment. Outside funding (such as Erik received from Macy) was almost invariably required to bring in a Jewish immigrant on a temporary appointment. For Erik Homburger, who distinguished himself from the émigrés fleeing Hitler, and who did not practice Judaism after he married Joan, Yale's intolerance was not an overwhelming concern. Deeply ambitious and insecure as a recent immigrant, he knew that the money was good and the research potential was significant. Henry Murray advised him that it would be a mistake to decline the opportunity. Late in the summer of 1936, the Homburger family moved to New Haven.[54]

In less than a year, the move proved disappointing. For one, Erik's relationship to Arnold Gesell and his Child Development Clinic was shaky. In 1918, Gesell had literally initiated research concerning normal preschool child development. He conducted his research at his clinic and an affiliated nursery school, keeping detailed photographic as well as written records of each child's progress. Gesell firmly believed in the special individuality of each child, but he became preoccupied with age-based classification schemes and emphasized the child's genetic heritage over environmental variables. These perspectives yielded passive, lifeless descriptions of the juvenile subjects. While formally part of the Yale Medical School, Gesell's clinic was assigned in 1930 to a wing of the building that housed the Institute of Human Relations; this was to promote interdisciplinary cooperation with the institute's psychologists, psychoanalysts, anthropologists, and other scholars. Gesell balked, built a separate entrance for his staff of thirty-one, and locked connecting doors to the institute.[55]

While Gesell's pioneering work in child development and his emphasis on visual (photographic) documents appealed to Erik Homburger, he did not know much about Gesell's classificatory and genetic emphasis or his personal rigidity. On Gesell's behalf, Francis Ilg, Gesell's pleasant associate who ran the clinic's nursery, had talked with Erik before he moved to New Haven, promising him full access to the children at the clinic and their records. A greater attraction was provided by Erik's new friend Marian Putnam, who worked in the obstetrics department at Grace–New Haven Hospital. Putnam had assured him that the clinic would facilitate a wonderfully cooperative research arrangement. She had organized a special study group that included medical school child psychiatrist Edith Jackson, who had worked with Anna Freud and Dorothy Burlingham in an experimental nursery school in Vienna; Ruth Washburn, a Yale professor of child development; and sometimes Felice Begg-Emery, another Medical School psychiatrist. Erik would join the study group, which would investigate a select segment of preschool children at the clinic's nursery school and focus on the problem of incipient neuroses. All group members were sympathetic to the psychoanalytic perspective. Erik was delighted to be included. Interestingly, he was joining a circle of women again, replicating his Vienna training and his early life with his mother and Danish aunts.[56]

Shortly after Erik moved to New Haven, the study group selected six preschool children at Ilg's nursery for intensive investigation. Putnam and Jackson interviewed the children and their mothers. Washburn studied clinical records of their behaviors, administered the standard battery of psychological tests, and organized all of these materials to plot each child's developmental pattern. Erik observed and talked with the children as they played with toys. While he centered his observations on the two most troubled children, he compiled data on play arrangements of all six children plus others at the nursery. At the group's weekly meeting, he reported how children seemed to replicate the movements of adults of their gender; a girl tucked a doll into a carriage and a boy moved a toy car into a garage. This theme echoed in his 1937 *Psychoanalytic Quarterly* article "Configurations in Play." More important, he recorded the way the children arranged blocks as cylinders, triangles, rectangles, and other shapes, and observed the size of their block constructions. He distinguished boys' from girls' constructions and detected a significant statistical difference in sizes and shapes based on gender. In presenting his findings to the group, he did not postulate that girls were more inclined to make rectangles and small objects while boys seemed more disposed to triangles, cylinders, and bigger objects. His subsequent well-known correlation of girls' and boys' block constructions with the shapes of their genital organs ("Inner and Outer Space") had not been fully worked out. Yet the data he was assembling, when combined with his rather orthodox Freudian perspective on what genitals indicated about the different psychologies of the two sexes, was moving him toward that flawed formulation. The result would be a defense of psychoanalytic orthodoxy at one of its greatest points of vulnerability.[57]

When Ruth Washburn left New Haven a year later, Erik was distressed to lose the group's primary developmental researcher; he had learned much from her. He was even more upset when Gesell, unhappy over Erik's focus on the sexual implications of the children's behavior, denied him access to children's records "for administrative reasons" of confidentiality. Erik recognized the ruse. The immediate cause of the rupture had been his angry protest when Gesell suppressed photographic evidence of a little boy with an erection who was masturbating.[58]

In the days following the ban on records, Gesell became overtly hostile. His biases surfaced. He made it clear that he did not want this immigrant in his clinic. Gesell's bigotry distressed Jackson almost as much as Erik Homburger, for she was assisting European refugees in securing visas and resettling in America. Alan Gregg of the Rockefeller Medical Sciences Division was also upset. He found Gesell's developmental ideas stale and agreed with Lawrence Frank that Erik was the more innovative of the two. Underscoring his access to Rockefeller funds, Gregg asked Gesell to reverse the ban on records but could not persuade him to accept Erik as a "free colleague in his clinic." Gregg also met with Yale Medical School dean Stanhope Bayne-Jones, requesting that the Putnam-Jackson-Homburger study group function independently of Gesell. Bayne-Jones sympathized but did not see how such an arrangement was administratively possible. Moreover, Erik had written to him that there was no point in trying to "patch up the situation created by Dr. Gesell's attitude." At this point, Erik wanted no further contact with Gesell or his clinic, but simply sought assurances from Bayne-Jones that Gesell could not block publication of the research that his study group had already conducted. Lacking access to the clinical records of their six subjects, the group would simply publish on its initial findings and dissolve. After the flare-up, Bayne-Jones informed Gregg privately that there were "uncertainties and anxieties about Mr. Homburger's future" at Yale.[59]

Although his study group had to disband, Erik Homburger continued to receive full salary through his Macy Foundation grant, which supported his other major affiliation at Yale—the Institute of Human Relations. The intellectual climate at the institute was richer than at Gesell's clinic. Unlike any other department or center on the Yale campus, the institute was interested in psychoanalysis. Mark May, its energetic director, had recruited psychoanalyst Earl Zinn to teach an informal seminar in psychoanalytic theory, to administer training analyses to institute staff, and to conduct psychoanalytically informed life history interviews for institute research projects. Marian Putnam had tried to integrate child analysis with other institute research ventures. John Dollard, a very influential leader of the institute, had completed a training analysis at the Berlin Psychoanalytic Institute. He hoped the Yale institute's research on psychoanalysis would serve as the integrator of all other staff orientations. Erik was impressed with Dollard's "remarkable interdisciplinary stimulation." Likewise, Dollard was impressed with him, especially as a therapist for his five-year-old daughter. The support Erik received from intellectuals and professionals through his therapeutic success with members of their families would persist throughout his clinical career.[60]

Initially, Erik seemed to flourish at the Institute of Human Relations. He was intrigued by Dollard's exciting fusion of the "inner" and "outer" worlds in formulations connecting aggressive impulses, class, and racial caste (the basis of Dollard's classic study, *Caste and Class in a Southern Town*). More important, Erik thought well of Dollard's 1935 publication, *Criteria for the Life History*, which reinforced his own desire to broaden Freud's infancy-based and drive-oriented developmental theory. Dollard emphasized that the child's early biologic drives had to be connected to specifics in his or her social and normative life. This was to be done not only during a child's early years, but systematically through the life course. In brief, he tried to illustrate with concrete biographical material how a life history was "an account of how a new person is added to the group and becomes an adult capable of meeting the traditional expectations of his society."[61]

Dollard's *Criteria* and his encouragement helped embolden Erik to make two presentations to his institute colleagues—one elaborating upon a written outline and the other on an intricate diagram. Over the next decade, these were modified considerably and became the basis for his famous eight-stage model of the human life cycle. The outline contained a list of four developmental stages that, very close to Freud's perspective, seemed less than innovative at first glance: (1) Infancy—age birth to five (oral, anal, genital); (2) Latency period—age five to twelve; (3) Pubescent period; (4) Adult Heterosexual Adjustments. It is significant that Erik appeared eager, through this outline, to move away from Freud's emphasis on infantile development and to cover all of human life. Moreover, whereas Freud's developmental model was grounded in verbalized adult memories of childhood, Erik's was grounded in the play constructions of youngsters with whom he had worked.[62]

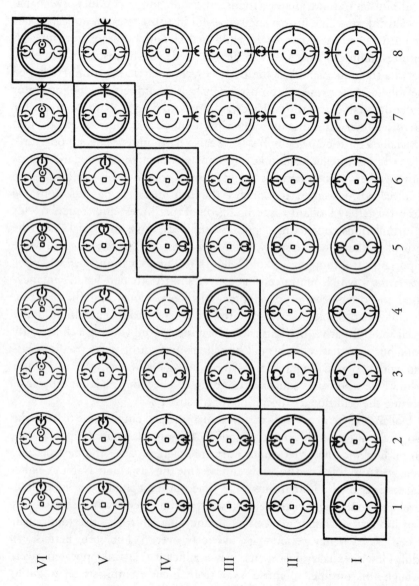

Checkerboard chart from "Configurations in Play" (1937).

Even before the move to New Haven, Erik Homburger had been working on a detailed checkerboard-like diagram that illustrated early pregenital development. When he presented his diagram (see page 132) at the institute and published it as part of a 1937 article in *Psychoanalytic Quarterly* ("Configurations in Play—Clinical Notes"), it extended over eight squares running diagonally across a checkerboard from the bottom-left corner to the top right. Each square represented the intersection of the board's vertical axis, which consisted of eight bodily "erotogenic zones," and the horizontal axis, consisting of six impulses. The zones represented intricate elaborations of diverse aspects of each of Freud's oral, anal, and genital stages (e.g., oral sucking, oral biting, anal retaining, anal expelling). Each of the eight squares represented the intersection of diverse impulse stimulations and specific body zones—"the human organism in the successive stages of emphasis." The seventh and eighth squares toward the top right of the chart illustrated the "general impulse to do something to another body or to another body's sphere of influence" as a young "social" being. Unlike his written outline of four developmental stages, his chart did not extend into adolescence or adulthood. Rather, it appeared to be an intricate visual elaboration of Freud's early developmental stages, specifying the child's precise and varied oral, anal, and genital movements in response to specific impulses. The chart carried a remarkable level of detail, originating from Erik's observations of children at play.[63]

When *Childhood and Society* appeared in 1950, it included checkerboard charts on pregenital development that seemed to be abbreviated approximations of the chart presented at the institute. It also included a chart of Erik's human life cycle model that, while closest to the four developmental stages he had outlined at the institute, included a horizontal axis incorporated from his initial checkerboard chart. Psychoanalyst Ives Hendrick attended the two presentations at the institute and considered them forerunners of Erik's eventual life cycle model. Despite the Freudian underpinnings of these presentations, Hendrick recalled Erik's interest in incorporating culture and values (the "outer world"), in talking more broadly than his materials indicated about pregenital development, and in providing significant coverage of adolescence and adulthood. Margaret Mead never attended his presentations at the institute. However, she and Erik developed an acquaintance while he lived in New Haven, and Mead found him receptive to all sorts of non-Freudian, culture-centered, anthropological, and even ethics-linked modifications of his two institute presentations. She recalled that he was especially willing to expand his checkerboard chart by exploring the general "laws of behavior in young children." If John Dollard's pioneering work on a socially connected and normative life history was not immediately discernible in the two orthodox Freudian documents Erik offered in institute talks, Hendrick and Mead recalled that he was already moving in that direction. The single most important item in *Childhood and Society*—the chart of an eight-stage bio-psycho-social life cycle—was in the process of becoming.[64]

Important as Erik Homburger's early work on the life cycle became, his institute colleagues regarded it as far less significant than the organization's major research undertaking—a large collective project headed by Clark Hull, the influential behavior psychologist. Beginning in 1936, Hull scheduled regular Monday evening meetings of institute staff to borrow their talents in a project not uncommon to American academic psychologists of the period. Hull had long worked to develop an explicitly propositional system of behavioral psychology and to test various propositional applications. For the project, he listed a number of Freud's formulations, some concerning the id's interplay with ego and superego, then asked the group to help him rework some of these into behavioral applications and to develop appropriate ways of testing them. Several sessions of the seminar were occupied with other aspects of Hull's long-term project, reflecting his behavioral concerns.[65]

Although Erik attended Hull's Monday evening seminars, he was troubled by the effort to transform psychoanalytic formulations into behavioral applications. But he was intimidated by some of the renowned researchers in the seminar and rarely commented. Once he sought to present his perspective in a disarming manner, as an "informal joke," and was distressed to learn that Hull had included it in an abstract of seminar dialogue that he intended to mail to psychology departments throughout the country. Erik canceled all his appointments that day "to re-write the summary of what I was supposed to have said at that seminar." Ambitious, a worrier, and deeply concerned with his reputation among psychological researchers, Erik subsequently found it preferable to remain silent or to choose his words very carefully.[66]

Because Hull's propositional system of behavioral psychology was a major project, it seems to have soured Homburger on the institute. He felt like a fish out of water. As Alan Gregg observed during a visit to the institute, Erik had "great difficulty getting along with the scientists" there even though "they all like him and respect him." He considered psychoanalysis primarily as an interpretive endeavor and, to a lesser extent, as a natural or objective science. Behaviorism and other forms of "objective" academic psychology remained outside his realm of interest. While Erik had hoped to benefit from the interdisciplinary potential at the institute, his view of interdisciplinarity did not involve the sort of synthesis that Hull was coordinating with May's and Dollard's support. He recognized that he could never truly "become a part of it." Even if he had approved of Hull's project, it is doubtful that he could have stayed for long at the institute. Once again, he was having difficulty with large collective research projects. He was happier working alone. Even before joining the institute staff, Erik had informed May that he wanted "to work out quietly without frequent abortions in pre-mature discussion, a small body of observations" on children and their development. He had hoped not to have to report regularly on his work to other institute colleagues and did not want to link his research to theirs.[67]

Erik grew increasingly disenchanted, but was able to find a more appeal-ing effort to connect disciplines elsewhere on the Yale campus. He discov-ered Edward Sapir. A cultural anthropologist, Sapir was as distressed as Erik over the research direction at the institute. A Jew, Sapir also sensed a subtle anti-Semitism in the social life of the institute. Erik identified with Sapir's artistic interests and his disposition to focus on the unique life of the indi-vidual. A fierce opponent of all forms of social science abstractionism, Sapir viewed anthropology, psychoanalysis, psychology, and sociology as "prelim-inary" disciplines that could facilitate data-gathering and the formulation of research problems. At the same time, it was imperative to return to specific individuals and their cultures—to examine the formation of a specific per-sonality in its concrete social matrix. Erik's contact with Sapir was limited, and he did not share the full intensity of Sapir's admonition that all explo-ration had to return to the individual. More than any of the researchers at the institute, however, Sapir introduced Erik to an interpretive and rather eclectic form of cultural anthropology. It seemed to add an important dimension to Erik's psychoanalytic perspective and to augment his interest in connecting the culture of the "outer world" to the drives and restraints of the "inner world." Sapir's was the sort of interdisciplinarity that most appealed to him.[68]

CONGENIAL INTERDISCIPLINARITY:
THE CULTURE AND PERSONALITY MOVEMENT

While Sapir was the first to introduce Erik Homburger to American cultural anthropology and its potential compatibility with psychoanalysis, other col-leagues would also push him in that direction. One of the most memorable experiences occurred in the summer of 1937. At the Harvard Psychological Clinic, Erik had become friends with H. Scudder Mekeel, a noted anthro-pologist with some psychoanalytic training, and he had successfully treated Mekeel's daughter. Sometime after Erik moved to New Haven, Mekeel invited him to a special summer institute in the heart of Oglala Sioux coun-try on the Pine Ridge reservation in South Dakota. Mekeel was aware that as a youngster, Erik had read the immensely popular novels by the German writer Karl May idealizing the Plains Indians for their noble and adventurous qualities. Without hesitation, Erik accepted Mekeel's invitation: "When I realized that Sioux is the name which we [in Germany] pronounced 'Seeux' and which for us was *the* American Indian, I could not resist." At the reservation, Mekeel introduced Erik to his long-standing Sioux informants, and their discussion focused on how Sioux children were reared "before the white man came."[69]

Erik Homburger found himself deeply impressed by traditional Sioux tribal child-rearing practices. Sioux parents invoked "an elastic tradition" that permitted the young child considerable leeway as he or she developed a communication system between self and body, self and kin. Only after the child had developed a strong body and considerable assurance did adult tribal perspectives begin to shape the child's behavior. In Erik's estimation, the Sioux had a deeply integrated culture in which children felt a sense of wholeness and contentment. Their approach contrasted starkly with childhood training in modern Western culture, where the excessively systematic regulation of bodily functions and impulses prepared youngsters for the specialized industrial and commercial tasks of adult life. This was not to say that Sioux culture was free of problems. The pursuit of the Great Plains buffalo had been basic to the Sioux economy and even to Sioux concepts of time and space. The buffalo herds were eventually decimated, while the Sioux were confined to reservations and to lives of poverty and apathy. Yet somehow the remnants of a relatively integrated culture survived in the Sioux family, promoting much trust along with elements of autonomy and initiative. For Erik, the Sioux child still enjoyed a relatively rich and spontaneous existence, certainly in comparison with the discontented lives of many white children, who were being prepared for mastery of the marketplace and the machine.[70]

This trip dramatically increased Erik's interest in the "outer world" of culture and social practice, and left him perhaps somewhat less intently preoccupied with traditional psychoanalytic considerations like dreams, free associations, and fantasies. (He wrote an article for the *Journal of Psychology* based upon his observation notes.) Indeed, the trip seemed to whet his appetite for the eclectic but heavily anthropological culture and personality movement, and his friend Lawrence Frank introduced him to several of the participants. They seemed to share with him the perspective that a "primitive society" like the Sioux possessed a wholeness and coherence lacking in modern societies.

Activists in the culture and personality movement belonged to an intellectual "class" of sorts, for their interests crossed traditional disciplines in their quest to discern the innate from the cultural in human development. Frank himself thought a lot about this issue. Erik Homburger was particularly interested in his evolving concept of "society as a patient," which drew upon psychotherapeutic techniques that had helped individual patients and used them to remedy malfunctioning social forces and institutions. Through Frank, Erik met Margaret Mead, and Frank also urged Ruth Benedict to seek Erik out. Frank felt that Kurt Lewin's work might enrich Erik's and made that introduction, too. Erik found that whatever their formal disciplinary affiliation, these professionals thought in broadly interpretive interdisciplinary terms that represented "a continuation with what I had in Vienna." Like Sapir at Yale, they talked about national character, about global questions, and about the variability of human nature in different societies. In addition, most knew and sympathized with psychoanalytic theory. Indeed, Erik later recalled that many of them helped him to formulate "the basic ideas in *Childhood and Society,* which at the time were very vague in my mind."[71]

Erik began attending seminars sponsored by those in the culture and personality movement. Caroline Zachary's seminar at Columbia University (sponsored by her Institute for the Study of Personality Development) had been active for years. Zachary had headed the Bureau of Child Guidance of the New York Board of Education, where she had been close to psychoanalysts. Her seminar drew people from all fields interested in child development, including Benjamin Spock, Lawrence Frank, and Lois Murphy. By the mid-1930s, the seminar focused on adolescent adjustment, the topic of Zachary's primary research project. Peter Blos was an active member of the seminar. When Erik presented his work on the centrality of play constructions in understanding the emotions and circumstances of children with whom he had worked, he captivated the audience. Lois Murphy remembered vividly how Erik discussed a child upset over his grandmother's death. Through blocks, the child constructed a coffin with a person in it (himself). In this "dream without words," Erik explained how the child was expressing personal guilt over the grandmother's death. Murphy felt that this and similar presentations "inspired my subsequent work on child personality" and ways to access it. Erik's approach seemed so simple yet so helpful and profound.[72]

Whereas Zachary's seminar provided Erik Homburger with his first sustained look into adolescent adjustment and offered a forum to share ideas, Abram Kardiner's required him to listen more and talk less. It began at the New York Psychoanalytic Institute, where Kardiner had been one of the most popular instructors, but shifted to Columbia University in 1936. A prominent New York City psychoanalyst who had been analyzed by Freud, Kardiner had broken with psychoanalytic orthodoxy in ways that endeared him to cultural anthropologists in his seminar like Ruth Benedict, Margaret Mead, and Cora DuBois. Indeed, Ralph Linton, the chair of Columbia's anthropology department, became Kardiner's closest intellectual associate. Kardiner was concerned with a "basic personality structure" common to members of a society and produced by shared modes of child rearing. In the course of his work, he skipped over Freud's libido theory and Freud's developmental stages; he even rejected the universality of the Oedipus complex. Nor did he accept Freud's structural theory of id-ego-superego interactions. Rather, the ego represented the "basic personality" subjectively perceived. In short, Kardiner came very close to rejecting the entire Freudian focus on the universals of human experience. He offered instead a psychological relativism compatible with the concerns of anthropologists over the values and practices specific to particular societies. When examining a specific society, Kardiner and Linton looked at "primary institutions" like the family that directly affected childhood socialization and treated "secondary institutions" like religion and folklore as consequences rather than as causes. The specific primary institutions created the basic personality structure.[73]

Erik found Kardiner's caustic manner unpleasant, and Kardiner was not impressed with him either. In the classic culture and personality debate of the period, Erik was more comfortable with Géza Róheim's allegiance to psychoanalytic universals. Still, Kardiner's and Linton's focus on time, place, and specific families and other "primary" agencies was not to be dismissed. Erik had been very attentive to these factors in his work with children. They were vital elements in the child's "outer world." Still, the Kardiner-Linton concern with primary institutions and basic personality structure was not compelling enough to keep Erik attending the seminar in the face of Kardiner's frequent barbs against him. The only reason Erik persisted was to get to know Margaret Mead and Ruth Benedict better.[74]

Mead and Benedict had been trained in cultural anthropology by Franz Boas, who had struggled rather heroically during the interwar period against scientific racism and adamantly rejected the pervasive practice of ranking races and cultural groups hierarchically. Boas made relativists of Mead and Benedict, convincing them that different historically conditioned culture systems imposed different patterns of meaning on experience. Perhaps Boas's most highly regarded students, they became close friends and colleagues. Indeed, both joined him as liberal intellectual critics of American ethnocentrism during the 1920s and 1930s.

Mead came to be known for her studies of Samoa and New Guinea and other South Pacific societies. Like Erikson with the Dakota Sioux, she praised the contented wholeness of "primitive" cultures and valued nurturing, caring customs over the more aggressive and competitive manner typical of modern societies. Mead was very attentive to gender and to the lives of women and children, and became an exponent of natural childbirth and breast feeding. However, she did not regard herself as a feminist. She emphasized the importance of adults cherishing children, and she rejected combat as a means of resolving disputes. Her mother was a successful philanthropist who thought her values exceeded to her husband's, an undistinguished professor. Mead became interested in what psychoanalysis had to say about how emotions played themselves out in families and then influenced the larger society. Always full of energy, and a very effective facilitator of cooperative research endeavors, she contacted immigrant analysts like Karen Horney and Erich Fromm, who shared her cultural concerns, and introduced them to Benedict.[75]

Of all the émigrés trained in psychoanalysis, Erik Homburger impressed Mead most. She had first met him at a conference in Cincinnati while he was struggling to make a living in Boston. Like Mead herself, he appeared to be driven by a desire for success and acceptance in the role of an educator more than as a social revolutionary. With a sixth sense, Mead immediately recognized Erik as an outsider like herself. She was also impressed that he treated bodily zones in ways Freud had not. The zones of the body that he described seemed connected to the social rituals of the Pacific cultures she observed. If the bodily zones were stimulated by impulses, Erik was also receptive to complementary social-cultural stimulation. From the bodily zones designated in Erik's initial checkerboard developmental chart, Mead discerned a social-cultural complementarity. She found that the zones were portrayed socially in the rituals of the Balinese and other societies. Soon Erik shared with Mead his interests in children's play arrangements, gender differences, and much more. She understood that he was breaking from the individualist notion of a person (the subject) that was pervasive in America; instead, Erik argued that the self was inseparable from important others within a social context. By 1939, Mead told him that "I rely more and more on your kind of thinking," and "Please, please send me everything you write. . . . I learn so much from you."[76]

By that time, Erik Homburger found himself as dependent on Mead as she was on him. Renowned by then not only for *Coming of Age in Samoa* (1928) but also for *Sex and Temperament in Three Primitive Societies* (1935), she had become a very influential figure in the culture and personality movement. Mead arranged important contacts for Erik and worked to enhance his reputation. With the intellectually engaging but physically unattractive young anthropologist, he found that he could discuss visual aspects of psychoanalytic formulations with ease and comfort—how, for example, the "psychoanalytic body image has only openings, no limbs." Yet it was relevant that the human stood upright on his limbs, posing "a special threat of disbalance, of disorientation." Homburger wrote that "every talk with you so far has cleared my ideas considerably." Mead also encouraged him to write more for publication, sometimes wielding her influence to encourage editors to accept his work. She even coached him in speaking before American audiences. Most significantly, Mead understood the import of his erratic efforts to broaden the Freudian focus on inner emotional life by examining outer social experience. She drew Ruth Benedict into their discussions even though Benedict was shy and prone to depression. Benedict's writing was coming to be highly regarded, and Mead urged Erik to study it closely.[77]

Benedict was uneasy with the universalistic portrayals of human motivation advanced by psychoanalysis—how motives transcended specific societies and cultures. She preferred Gestalt psychologists of the 1920s who had emphasized a holistic view. From fieldwork in the 1920s and early 1930s with various Native American tribes—the Zuni, Cochiti, Pima, and Apache—Benedict had formalized the term *configuration*. In a celebrated 1932 article in the *American Anthropologist,* she elaborated how a "configuration" within a particular society patterned the emotional and cognitive reactions of its members in accord with certain shared "inner necessities." For Benedict, "configurations stand to the understanding of group behavior in the relation that personality types stand to the understanding of individual behavior." A specific group or society was no biologically determined organism, as Social Darwinists claimed, but an open system with elements of order and chaos co-existing in their own particular ways.[78]

When Erik Homburger began to read Benedict's publications and discuss them with her, he was reminded of Sapir's focus on locating personality within its specific social matrix. To be sure, Sapir insisted on the uniqueness of each individual within the matrix while Benedict's view of a "configuration" subsumed the individual within the emotional and cognitive qualities of the society. Erik suspected that the individual uniqueness obvious in his clinical work co-existed with the commonalities prompted by what Benedict called a society's particular configuration. More important, he realized that he had essentially been building his own configurational approach without invoking the precise meaning that Benedict assigned to the term. While Benedict emphasized the "outer world" of a society's overtly manifested emotional and cognitive styles, she acknowledged that they were rooted in the "inner necessities" (to Erik the psychoanalytic "inner world"). Although Benedict's configurational approach emphasized the "outer world" of a collectivity while his approach stressed the "inner world" of the individual, what mattered was how "outer" and "inner" converged as a person sought to gain orientation in society. Erik discovered that even with their different emphases, he and Benedict (and other anthropologists like Mead who had worked with her) spoke:

a similar language and could speak about childhood and culture patterns in a way that eventually made dynamic sense also. Thus, I became interested in the relationship of human motivation as discovered by psychoanalysis to people's world images and economic systems: what people are hunting and where and how.

Benedict and Mead and their anthropological colleagues were moving Erik from understanding a child's "inner" and "outer" worlds through block configurations to understanding the broader styles and perceptions within specific cultures. In his mind, psychoanalysis was beginning to merge with anthropology as he crossed between the two fields with increasing facility.[79]

In 1937, Homburger published his first full professional article in the English language for *Psychoanalytic Quarterly* and titled it "Configurations in Play." The article addressed his work with children and other Americans in Boston and New Haven. He criticized psychoanalysts for too often failing to see that in children's "spatial configurations"—their toys and blocks and dolls—they communicated as valuable an array of psychological data about their lives and societies as adults communicated through language. Citing one case after another, Erik explained how children configured their playthings to communicate the shape of their inner emotions and their societies, and to secure a better sense of themselves by creatively integrating both dimensions of their lives; new play arrangements often revealed newfound success at self-integration. In describing each child's play configurations, Erik noted how he seemed to range to and fro in his clinical endeavors from the child's inner personal concerns to aspects of the child's outer world (home, parents, teachers, etc.). He was moving into children's society and, almost simultaneously, into their inner emotional lives. In that regard, he felt that he was conducting some of the fieldwork that Benedict and Mead had urged him to pursue in configurational exploration.[80]

FAMILY MATTERS IN NEW HAVEN

As Erik Homburger solidified his configurational approach through contact with Benedict, Mead, and other interdisciplinary researchers, he realized that he had something unique and important to present for professional publication. But publication in English was no small task. When Erik outlined his research agenda to his Yale Institute of Human Relations colleagues, he understood that his ideas and data would amount to little if he could not make the transition from German to precise English acceptable to scholarly forums and journals. "The greatest power that man has of self-control, self-confidence, etc.," he explained to Dollard, May, and others, "is the power to verbalize." When, in 1939, he moved from New Haven to northern California, he felt that he was in the process of acquiring this crucial "power" of command. If his English prose was not as fluid, vivid, and aesthetically attractive as it would later be in *Childhood and Society,* it was clear and readable. This was no small accomplishment for a man who was already thirty-one (an age when mastery of a new language was usually more difficult) when he arrived in America.[81]

Three factors help to account for his success. One was the trust of American patients. "The patients trusted you fully that you would understand" what they said. They "granted" him "a kind of moratorium" to make the transition to English and rarely complained over "my abysmal ignorance of the English language." If troubled patients were that tolerant, trusting that he understood them and would eventually be able to gain command of English, he could be more confident in his linguistic capabilities. Another factor was his increasing ambition to make good as a research scholar who could publish in America. Boston-area colleagues like Tracy Putnam, the Harvard Medical School neurologist, tried to explain his "scanty output of papers" since coming to America by noting his need to take all sorts of jobs to feed his family. Amply supported at Yale with Macy Foundation money, Erik had no such excuse and felt obligated to publish regularly in English-language professional journals. As Henry Murray recalled, Erik knew quite well that only by rapidly demonstrating a "taste for the language" in scholarly forums could he "move ahead." Joan Homburger's role was also very important. She thought that to make the shift from artful German to good English writing, Erik was better off unburdened by the painful and tedious grammatical rules pushed by journal editors intent on modifying his natural style. Instead, husband and wife read literature to each other in English and conversed in Erik's new language. When he first tried to write English, Joan would lovingly "guide my sentences with me." Thus, Erik quickly acquired a taste for the language. As he prepared articles for publication, Joan underscored and amplified Erik's increasingly concise, deep, yet accessible prose.[82]

Whereas a supportive wife had much to do with Erik's remarkable mastery of English, marital and family life were hardly idyllic. They rented a house in Woodbridge, a small town outside of New Haven, and the Macy Foundation grant plus private practice contributed to a respectable bank account. Joan managed that account, the family budget, and all significant expenditures. She calculated that she could afford to hire a live-in "Connecticut Yankee housekeeper" and to purchase some attractive "old New England" furniture. She did not purchase a piano, although having one might have prompted Erik to spend more time at home. Since Vienna, he enjoyed playing classical pieces and might have become quite skilled if practice time had not been limited to visits with friends who owned pianos. When Kai and Jon came of school age, Erik and Joan agreed that the expense of enrolling them in a well-regarded private institution was worthwhile; they were very ambitious for the success of the boys. But while they were less constrained by financial limitations, the Homburgers were beset with personal problems.[83]

Congruent with a pattern they had established in Vienna, Joan attended to the children and household matters while Erik traveled and worked. This division of labor was not unlike that of another scholar-clinician, Freud, who rarely saw his children. Shortly after the family moved to New Haven, Kai and Jon both came down with chicken pox, and Joan stayed home with them for several weeks. Then, during the summer while Erik was away with Mekeel on Dakota Sioux research, Kai came down with a severe case of scarlet fever. For a month and a half he had to be isolated from Jon; one boy was confined to an upstairs room and the other was kept downstairs. More serious, Jon developed a mastoid infection in the spring of 1937. Medication seemed to alleviate the problem, but it recurred the following year and was accompanied by severe pain. Surgery was required to remove the mastoid bone, resulting in an emergency blood transfusion. Then massive quantities of sulfa were administered (an experimental procedure) to guard against another infection. Jon had a very severe reaction to the sulfa, requiring rehospitalization and a long recovery period at home. During this time, Jon wanted his mother around, as she had been for his less serious illnesses. But this time Joan was herself in the hospital giving birth to Sue. To make matters worse for Jon, a massive hurricane struck while he was recovering from surgery; it upset him greatly. He was also distressed that his mother seemed so preoccupied with the baby after she returned from the hospital. The last shock occurred a few months later when he hid in his bedroom to avoid moving with the family to California. Not surprisingly, he developed a tendency to stutter soon after arriving in California, and it persisted for years. In part, Erik attributed Jon's troubles to the fact that "my wife was hindered from attending to this boy fully, because of her third pregnancy." Like many other husbands of the time, he did not suggest that the situation might have been ameliorated if he had been more attentive to Jon. Sometimes angry over Erik's lack of help with the children, Joan never demanded that he change.[84]

Amid these various crises, Joan triumphed in a pediatric reform. When Sue was born in Grace–New Haven Hospital, the staff was about to take her to a special infant nursery and return her to Joan only at specified feeding intervals. Because Joan was recovering from mumps at the time, she had been assigned to a special room. She insisted that Sue be allowed to stay with her so that she could breast-feed on demand. As it happened, Edith Jackson and Marian Putnam, Erik's research colleagues at Gesell's clinic, had appointments in the hospital's obstetrics department. Early crusaders for the benefits of breast feeding and for the right of mother and newborn to remain together in the hospital, they persuaded the staff to honor Joan's request. This became a vital precedent for the practice of "rooming in" at Grace–New Haven Hospital.[85]

Besides worries about their children, Erik and Joan were deeply concerned with the fate of Erik's family in Karlsruhe as the Nazi shadow spread across Germany. Theodor Homburger's joy at Erik's marriage to Joan prompted respectful and often cordial relationships between the Homburgers in Germany and America. Erik and Joan had urged Theodor and Karla and their daughters, Ellen and Ruth, to join them in America, but to no avail. Once Ellen, a Zionist, accepted the fact that she would not be able to pursue medical studies in Germany, she migrated to Palestine (in 1933). There she married Yaiir Katz and settled with him in Haifa, where they established a school for Jewish children who had fled Germany. When Ellen returned to Karlsruhe to visit her family in 1935, she discovered that their situation was desperate. A Nazi decree prohibited her pediatrician father from caring for his many Gentile patients. His rather substantial income was cut in half. Theodor became severely depressed. When Ellen learned that he had attempted suicide and refused to leave Germany, she instructed her mother to take him on a vacation to Italy. Unknown to Theodor, the couple was to be transported from Italy to join Ellen and her husband in Haifa. The plan worked. Had Theodor and Karla remained in Karlsruhe, they would have joined some of Theodor's siblings and several Homburger relatives in the nearby Gurs concentration camp on the French side of the border. Theodor's sister Bertha Marx died at Gurs. Years later, Erik remembered these tragedies when he wrote in *Young Man Luther* about "the bleached bones of men of my kind in Europe."[86]

The move to Haifa went smoothly. Karla and Theodor lived with Ellen and her husband, became active in a new local synagogue, and Theodor opened a small pediatrics practice. But they had lost their home, much of their money, and many personal possessions in the hurried exodus from Karlsruhe and could not make ends meet. In desperation, Karla sent all of her jewelry to her Abrahamsen relatives in Copenhagen in exchange for weekly food packages. When Erik received word in New Haven of his parents' financially troubled situation, he consulted with Joan on what they could afford to give. He sent them $100 monthly for several years, and this represented a very considerable sum. Erik acknowledged his own difficult experience as an immigrant, financially and otherwise, as he considered theirs. In

the spring of 1936 he informed Mark May that he had "assumed the responsibility of supporting my parents, in addition to my own family."[87]

While Erik assisted his parents and Ellen in Haifa, he also helped his
older half sister, Ruth, and her husband, Paul Oppenheimer. The Oppenheimers had migrated to Palestine in 1935 but could not support themselves financially, so they returned to Germany where they received an
urgent letter from Erik. He offered to make legal arrangements and to send
money for the couple to travel immediately to New Haven. They arrived in
1937 and stayed with Erik and Joan for three weeks. Erik tried to persuade
them to settle permanently in New Haven, advising against moving to New
York City, where immigrants abounded and economic opportunities might
be scarce. But the Oppenheimers went anyway. Unlike the Homburgers,
they preferred a large Jewish immigrant community over New Haven, with
its comparatively few Jews and considerable anti-Semitism. Soon, they
started a successful hotel business. Ruth was surprised by her half brother's
generosity and concern.[88]

Erik's show of concern for his parents and half sisters in the context of the
gathering Holocaust prompted an important development. If his marriage
to Joan helped to repair years of tension with his stepfather, his financial
support and solicitude from New Haven completed the task. Theodor died
in Haifa in 1944, and the provisions of his will (prepared in 1942) told
much. Erik was treated fully as the equal of Theodor's biological daughters.
For the first time in any legal document executed by Theodor, he referred to
Erik as his "adopted son." To conceal Erik's illegitimacy, however, Theodor
described him as the son "from my wife's first marriage."[89]

BECOMING ERIK ERIKSON

The Homburgers of Karlsruhe therefore split between Palestine (the parents
and the younger daughter) and America (Erik and the older daughter).
Although Ruth had seriously considered Palestine, Erik had not. After Denmark, the United States was his choice. The fact that he was the only member of his family to marry a non-Jew and a non-European affected this
decision. As well, Joan regarded America as her home and was uninterested
in migrating to Palestine.

In the fall of 1938, shortly before his family would leave New Haven for
California, Erik filed a petition for naturalization with the U.S. District
Court for the Connecticut District. For his court appearance, he wore a dark
suit, an attractive multicolored tie that Joan probably selected, and a stylish
shirt. He had gained some much needed weight over the past few years and

his face was full. He sported a well-manicured mustache. His shoulders no longer drooped. His eyes remained intense and commanded attention, but his glance had softened, and his general demeanor was confident. Erik also appeared well rested; he had become accustomed to a regular nap after lunch each day and that was probably contributory. Clearly, this was not the lean, tense, restless, downcast young man who had left Karlsruhe a decade earlier for Vienna. Although the process of acquiring citizenship was not completed until September of 1939, months after his family had moved to the San Francisco Bay area, Erik's petition was revealing. He listed his occupation as a psychologist rather than a psychoanalyst even though he had no psychology degree or certification. He noted that he was born in Germany but listed his "race" as "Scandinavian." Most important, he sought naturalized citizenship under the name *Erik Homburger Erikson.* There was no hyphen on the petition to connect Homburger with Erikson.[90]

After Erikson had become somewhat of a national celebrity in the 1970s, a controversy arose over this change in names, which appeared to reflect a transition from a Jewish name, Homburger, to a Christian name, Erikson. The conceptualizer of the "identity crisis" would be questioned over the years about the significance of this change, what it revealed about his own identity, and whether becoming an American citizen represented a repudiation of his Judaism. The controversy was distasteful, and Erik tried to deflect it by sending those who inquired one of several explanatory memoranda. He also prepared a letter to the *New York Times Book Review* with the same essential message, but decided against sending it. In his explanation for the name change, Erikson noted that "every new American is offered the option to choose another family name" and that the combination of Erik with Erikson was "quite common among Scandinavians." It was hardly a repudiation of Theodor Homburger, for "I have kept my stepfather's name as my middle name out of gratitude" and "my oldest son's middle name is my stepfather's first name, Theodor." Erikson insisted that his Jewish stepfather approved of the name change. Indeed, "the name Erikson was chosen by family and friends as befitting the descendants of an immigrant named Erik who had been born a Scandinavian."[91]

Whereas he stressed in this "official" explanation that a name change was commonplace among immigrants to the United States, he did not mention that many European immigrants of the time and their children with Jewish names elected to "Americanize" them in the face of strong anti-Semitism. Hence, Leonard Rosenberg became Tony Randall, Issur Danielovitch Demsky became Kirk Douglas, Israel Ehrenberg became Ashley Montagu, and Meyer Schkolnick became Robert Merton. While Milton Winternitz, Erikson's colleague at the Yale Medical School, decided against a name change, he disassociated himself from the New Haven Jewish community and implied that he was Gentile. Such widespread practices among European Jewish immigrants seemed to signal an intense desire to gain acceptance and work in America as the gathering Holocaust removed migratory possibilities in Europe. Name changes were particularly evident among Jewish psychologists responding to heightened anti-Semitism, which precluded employment. For example, Isadore Krechevsky, Erikson's future colleague at Berkeley, changed his name to David Krech. Psychologist Jean Walker Macfarlane, Erik's future supervisor at the University of California, wrote approvingly that "Erikson somehow fits in with your general morphology and facies better than Homburger." She meant that he did not look Jewish and the name change would help him to pass for a Christian. And she implied a course of action he eventually followed—replacing the middle name "Homburger" with the initial "H" (sometimes even eliminating it entirely). He did not correct Macfarlane's interpretation of the intent behind his name change and, while retaining a middle name or initial in his own writing, voiced no distress when she and others skipped it altogether. Writing to Macfarlane, he underscored "disconcerting experiences" himself with certain Jewish émigrés.[92]

While he acknowledged in his "official" explanation that the switch to Erikson, approved by his stepfather, was a family decision, the nature of family deliberations was reported elsewhere. According to persisting family accounts that Erik and especially Joan did much to shape, a conversation took place shortly before Erik filed his petition for naturalization. The conversation occurred due to distress over the fact that Kai and Jon had been called "Hamburgers" by teasing children at school and in the neighborhood. Erik and Joan decided that a name change was warranted to stop this harassment. Moreover, the boys were sometimes called "Hamburger" by unknowing adults, and this added to their determination. Kai was a remarkably bright and curious seven-year-old, and he probably learned from Erik about the Scandinavian custom of naming a "son" after his father. Since his father was Erik, Kai reportedly suggested that he and Jon each become "Erikson." Jon agreed, liking the sound of a proposed family name that designated him clearly as Erik's son. Erik also appeared satisfied, recognizing that paternity would be established beyond doubt for his sons. "Erik Erikson" also had a nice ring to it; the name might be helpful in literary circles for a budding author.[93]

At this point, according to family accounts of the discussion, husband and sons looked to Joan for the final decision. She carried the authority to ratify or dismiss "Erikson" as a family name. After "we decided," Erik recalled, "Joan decided" what the outcome would be, and it was hardly in doubt. Kai's memory of this point in the exchange was the same as Erik's. As an Episcopalian and a Canadian, Joan did not care to replace "Homburger" with another German-Jewish name. Also, her fear and distaste of German political culture persisted, and she had raised her sons as Protestants. She soon intended to file her own petition for naturalization and change her first name officially from Sarah to Joan. The sound of a name had always been important to Joan's sense of herself. She had invoked a string of nicknames like "Sally" and later "Aunt Sally," and when she married Erik, she came to be called Joan. She was happy with "Joan Erikson." It had a pleasant sound and seemed to separate her from her years as Sarah Serson. She consented to the name change. Kai and Jon were overjoyed.[94]

If Erik had felt uncomfortable, at this point, over the prospect of becoming Erik Erikson, Joan and the boys would almost certainly have backed off, for they were attentive to his sensitivities. In fact, Erik loved the name. As the years passed, he reflected more fully on the implications. It seemed to fit well not only with what his life was about but with what it could become.

He had always been curious about the Vikings and had introduced study of them at the Hietzing School. He knew that Erik the Red had been declared an outlaw in Norway and Iceland and had taken his family to Greenland. From there his son Leif Eriksson (who felt rootless and cut off from Norway) sailed to "Vinland" (Newfoundland). Leif was followed by his brother Thorvald Eriksson, who consolidated the initial Viking settlement in the New World. In the family romance that Erik Homburger liked to recount, his biological father was also Scandinavian, indeed, a Danish nobleman. Just as he had left Denmark for the United States, he assumed that his father had probably made that migration earlier. Although Erik never asserted that he was repeating the saga of the Viking Erikssons, the parallel was hardly lost on him.[95]

In America, Erik had admired the character of the country—a melting pot of nationalities fused into a single national identity. The "American identity was in some ways a manufactured one, a self-invented one," he later recalled, revolving around the myth of the self-made man. The myth was "fused into an idealized image of a man who almost literally made himself, created himself, manufactured himself, invented himself." America in the 1930s was experiencing what he would later call an "identity crisis" as it attempted to fuse a new national identity from its diverse immigrant descendants—people who had left the old world behind to succeed in a new land. As one who "never knew my father, for one thing, and . . . belonged to a mixed racial and religious background," Erik had to fuse the various elements in his past into a new personal identity as he sought to establish himself in America. By becoming Erikson, he could see himself as a stepson of sorts in an adoptive land.[96]

Erik recognized that his years in Boston and New Haven had been crucial to building both the national and professional qualities of his identity. He had become familiar with American universities, students, researchers, and clinical facilities, and he had not overlooked the anti-Semitism triggered by a name like Homburger among academicians and professionals generally. He also realized that he was regarded as an emerging *American* intellectual by important scholars like Henry Murray, John Dollard, and Margaret Mead; had published a few articles in American scholarly journals; and hoped to write something more substantial—perhaps a major book.

Erik assumed that an author in the New Nation, America, needed a new name, so when Kai, according to family accounts, suggested "Erikson," that resonated deeply. "The Child is the Father of the Man," Wordsworth and Laurence Sterne had asserted. Erik cited that sentence in *Gandhi's Truth* (1969): "It makes particular sense for special men: they, indeed, strive to become their own fathers." At least since he prepared his 1923–24 notebook, Erik had a sense of being special with a destiny of his own. He saw in the missing and romanticized Gentile Nordic father he pursued but never identified an important source of this specialness. In his sometimes acknowledged "fantasy" of his biological father as something of a mythic hero, he seemed to be trying to gather together various fragments in his own sense of self, and a new name could mark that effort: "I made myself Erik's son. It is better to be your own originator." With a new name, he might be born again as a whole and integrated person. The fantasy of rebirth was an element in the son's Oedipal struggle with the father that Sigmund Freud had not emphasized. Erik presumed that he could take advantage of "the freedom in America to become your own adult"—your own father.[97]

In becoming Erik Erikson, even with Homburger (reduced later to just "H") as a middle name, he had an interest in believing that he was following one of Anna Freud's suggestions when she analyzed him in Vienna. That is, he was sublimating the pressing issue of his paternity by taking charge of his own life; he was fathering himself as well as his two sons. Like Ralph Waldo Ellison and Martin Luther King, Erik invoked a new name to amplify a viable myth, augmenting his romanticized vision of his origins. Combined with other factors in his experience, the name conferred a special sense of purpose, status, vocation, and responsibility. Erik told Henry Murray's second wife, Caroline, that it had been impossible for him to remain in America as a Homburger from Karlsruhe, Germany. As a new American, with a new identity, he had to become Erik Erikson.[98]

CHAPTER FOUR

A Cross-Cultural Mosaic:
Childhood and Society

W hile essential themes and concerns of *Childhood and Society* emerged during Erik Erikson's early years in Boston and New Haven, most of the essays that became the building blocks for the book were written in the 1940s in California. The product of what he called a "conceptual itinerary" as a participant observer during that decade, the essays covered two general if overlapping topics: (1) the nature of the child and his or her development into adolescence and adulthood, and (2) the circumstances of society, culture, and history surrounding the child's growth. By 1948, Erikson had prepared a long outline for transforming these two general topics into integrating themes for a unified book. But his effort at integration fell short. Part of the problem was that one set of essays emanated from the treatment of children, their clinical problems, and their development through life. In contrast to these clinical writings, his remaining essays focused on the cultures or societies that he had investigated.

BERKELEY:
THE INSTITUTE OF CHILD WELFARE

By early 1938, Erikson realized that the great research potential Lawrence Frank had promised him at Yale had not materialized. He had not even considered undertaking a book-length study much less a series of major articles. His research and writing career had hardly been launched.[1]

At this point, Marian Putnam, his friend and research associate in an aborted project at Arnold Gesell's clinic, came up with an interesting suggestion. Robert Havighurst, the director of the Rockefeller Foundation General Education Board, had been negotiating with Jean Walker Macfarlane of the prestigious University of California Institute of Child Welfare concerning the institute's long-range study of the changing lives of select Berkeley-area children. This was the Guidance Study Macfarlane directed. Havighurst promised funds if Macfarlane could hire a child psychoanalyst interested in child development who might enhance the study. Macfarlane sought out Putnam, but she was unwilling to leave New Haven. Instead, she recommended Erikson for a five-year Rockefeller Foundation grant. As a close friend of Macfarlane and supporter of her Guidance Study, Lawrence Frank also recommended Erikson. Assistant professors on the Berkeley campus were paid roughly $3,000 annually. Macfarlane offered Erikson a "research associate" title and a salary from Rockefeller funding "to the amount you ask" (certainly more than he was earning at Yale). In addition to participation in her longitudinal Guidance Study of Berkeley children, he could work on any of his other research projects, could teach a few informal graduate seminars in the psychology department, and might augment his income through a small private psychoanalytic practice.[2]

Berkeley's Institute of Child Welfare had developed in the 1920s from an old child guidance clinic. By the 1930s, the American child guidance movement was becoming a network of often semiprivate institutions. Child guidance overlapped decidedly with an emerging child development specialty that centered its activities at the University of Michigan, the University of Chicago, and other academic institutions, but especially at Berkeley. Child guidance and child development, usually jointly but sometimes separately, established specialty areas for research and training, professional organizations, and professional journals. Somewhat more than child development, child guidance focused on redirecting the child's impulses into socially approved directions. In turn, child development addressed the parallelism of the individual child's physical, physiological, and psychobiological maturation perhaps more intently than did child guidance. Reflecting the overlap between the two movements, Macfarlane steered the Guidance Study into an investigation of child development. Widely respected and a tough academic entrepreneur who thrived on massive collections of data, she secured $13,000 annually from the Laura Spellman Rockefeller Memorial during the 1930s to support a long-term study of the development of over two hundred local eleven-, twelve-, and thirteen-year-old children. (She had monitored most of them since infancy.) In this study, Macfarlane was heavily influenced by Adolf Meyer of the Johns Hopkins Medical School in the type of data she collected on changes in the children. Viewing the youngster as a complex, balanced entity of many distinct if interrelated parts, she gathered data on their skeletal proportions, metabolisms, blood pressures, pulse and respiratory rates, and other physiological qualities. These were coupled with intelligence tests, clinical observations, and questionnaires completed by the children's parents, teachers, and peers. The children were normal physically and emotionally, and the study aimed at social application, measuring how psychological intervention might allow children to enter their adolescence as "better adjusted" teenagers. Havighurst and Gregg at Rockefeller and Frank at the Macy Foundation saw a disparity between the focus of the research (physiological and mental data) and the goal of enhanced social adjustment. It was with an eye to remedy this disparity that Havighurst had offered Macfarlane funds to hire several social scientists and a child psychoanalyst.[3]

Erikson was intrigued with Macfarlane's longitudinal project, which seemed to correspond with his emerging interest in child development. He was especially pleased that Macfarlane focused on the child as a specific individual rather than as a member of groups with shared traits. He also found the salary acceptable, while California held a certain allure for his family. Joan was especially pleased with the quality of the Berkeley public schools. Kai and Jon would not have to attend private schools as they had in New Haven. Erik warmed to Macfarlane and her piano-playing husband, Donald, a Bay Area psychoanalyst. When Erik mentioned several "disconcerting experiences" with émigré analysts, Macfarlane promised him veto power over any considered for the project. To compensate for the "loss of New England intellectualism," Macfarlane assured Erikson of an active Berkeley discussion group consisting of herself, the prominent psychologist Edward Tolman, and anthropologist Alfred Kroeber. A specialist on the Yurok of northern California, Kroeber promised Erikson fieldwork with his informants along the Klamath River. After Erikson's experience with the Dakota Sioux, the offer was enticing. But the biggest attraction of Berkeley was the chance to work with normal, healthy children at the Institute of Child Welfare over an extended period of time and to be able to help them. Unlike the often disturbed youngsters at the Judge Baker Clinic and in much of his private practice, he would not have to treat clients suffering from substantial psychological problems. Normal children could be observed to see how they drew on ego strengths as they faced life's problems. Although the focus of psychoanalysis in America, like Vienna, was on deficits, Erikson felt a pressing need to learn more about what children did well.[4]

In January of 1939, the University of California Board of Regents approved Erikson's appointment as research associate and lecturer, and the family moved from New Haven to Berkeley. They bought a modest house in the hills overlooking Berkeley where many faculty tended to reside. An unusually friendly couple, Carol and Dwight Baldwin, helped acquaint them with the vicinity. Carol was a talented photographer, Dwight an engineer. Berkeley was a beautiful city of gardens and groves of trees, highlighted by the elegance of the Greek Theater. Sather Gate, the main entrance to the university campus, was surrounded by dozens of inviting shops, restaurants, coffee counters, and bookstores. Local residents unaffiliated with the campus tended to be middle- and lower-middle-class whites, long settled in the United States; most lived in small single-family homes. But owing to jobs in shipbuilding, black and white (often immigrant) newcomers were starting to move into the East Bay area. As war orders multiplied and the number of defense-related jobs grew, the migration increased. And so did political problems. University president Robert Sproul worked to preserve university autonomy in the face of American Legion pressure to remove "reds." Sproul pressured campus student groups not to take stands on off-campus issues like war, wages, and racial discrimination. His faculty tended to be energetic teacher-scholars, regarding their freshman introductory courses as equal in significance to their research projects. The era of large federally funded research centers and prolonged research leaves had not yet transformed the campus.[5]

As the Eriksons settled in Berkeley, their family life shifted into a familiar routine. Although Erik's Rockefeller-funded salary at the Institute of Child Welfare exceeded earnings at Yale, living expenses were considerably higher in Berkeley. He now had three children to support as well as payments to his parents in Haifa. By 1942, the family car was sold to reduce expenses, and Erik sought out patients to augment his institute wages.[6]

As in New Haven, Joan was entirely in charge of child rearing and domestic life. Erik even sent the children to her when they needed permission to go to a movie and money for tickets. Always interested in crafts, Joan frequently organized craft activities for the children. A late 1939 photograph shows Erik with Sue in his arms, pointing in the direction of the camera so that she would face it. Dressed in stylish striped shirt, pants, and tie, he had just returned from work. He smiled slightly, though his posture was stiff and his grip on Sue was awkward. He rarely joined Joan in her activities with the children, although he sometimes told them bedtime stories and bought them little gifts. Sue and Jon did not recall a very congenial home life during the early 1940s, especially after their grandmother, Mary Serson, died. Joan and Mary had never gotten along, and after Mary died, Joan suffered bouts of guilt and depression, particularly after learning that her mother had willed her estate to her grandchildren and that Joan would receive nothing.[7]

According to a provision in the arrangement between the Rockefeller Foundation and the University of California, Erikson would teach a few graduate seminars in Berkeley's internationally acclaimed Department of Psychology. "A little teaching will do me good," he predicted, especially in a prestigious academic department, for he still had no academic degrees.

"Daddy, do you want to become a teacher because you talk so much?" Kai asked jokingly. Erikson's two graduate offerings were special-topics seminars—"Introduction to Psychoanalysis" and "Psychoanalysis of Childhood Problems." He distributed no syllabi, assigned little reading, and gave few writing assignments. Nor did he comment much about the emergence of psychoanalysis in Freud's Vienna as he had experienced it. Instead, he focused on a few of his clinical cases. Students like Daniel Levinson and Donald Campbell, who later became acclaimed psychologists, commented on his gentle, kind, low-keyed manner and his preference for commonsense clinical formulations over psychoanalytic jargon. Yet although they had enrolled in the seminars hoping to learn something about the life and experiences of one of Anna Freud's top students in child analysis, when the semester ended they had learned precious little on either count.[8]

When Erikson began his work on the Guidance Study at the Institute of Child Welfare, he got on well with Macfarlane and enjoyed her husband, Donald. He met regularly with the two hundred eleven- to thirteen-year-olds who comprised the study. As might be expected, he had them arrange various toys and tell him stories as they played. In England, Margaret Lowenfeld had developed the World Test—a systematic way of studying children's thoughts through their play constructions—but Erikson was unfamiliar with it. Macfarlane realized that he had no training or capacity to compile statistical profiles of what the children's toy constructions revealed, so she assigned Jane Loevinger, a psychology graduate student, to perform this task. Aware that Erikson was interested in the intersections between biological and cultural influences on child development, Macfarlane arranged for him to meet with Herbert Stoltz, who, as director of the larger institute, was heading the project in that direction. She also noticed how excited Erik was when he took weeks off to make field trips with anthropologist friends. Macfarlane tried to contour his work life so that he might find "the same dramatic possibilities" in her longitudinal Guidance Study. When she learned that Erik had brought clinical notes from New Haven for future articles unrelated to her project, she urged him to prepare them during regular work hours. At project conferences and other meetings, he began the practice of making frequent sketches and related notations on whatever he found pertinent and interesting (the beginning of a lifetime habit), and Macfarlane encouraged him. She showed great respect for his ideas, making clear to her staff that they were to do the same.[9]

At first, Erikson prized the opportunity to work on Macfarlane's longitudinal project. It was no small matter for him "to collect in regular intervals microcosmic constructions of two hundred unselected children" who were psychologically normal. Loevinger made numerical tabulations on aspects of these toy constructions and plugged her totals into the statistical composites that Macfarlane sought from all her researchers on the activities of the subjects and their physiological changes over time. Reflecting his social and cultural interests, Erikson would have preferred greater emphasis on the historical context of the children's lives, including their socioeconomic conditions and communities. Macfarlane did not discourage him from exploring these dimensions. Loevinger recalled how Erikson had his own idiosyncratic story to tell about each child he met and was intent on recounting it despite the quantitative social science methodologies of the staff. Much like Boston and New Haven, he crossed only those disciplinary boundaries that he found congenial.[10]

The many children Erikson worked with in 1939 and 1940 provided their own stories, visual and verbal. Setting an array of toys on a table, he asked each child to arrange an exciting scene from an imaginary movie, and then describe its plot. He sketched and later photographed the toy scene and tape recorded the plot description. Erikson interpreted the toy arrangement as a configuration that showed "how subjective life space in [the] child's life history was projected into play space." He was simply extending the approach he took with young John at the Judge Baker Clinic, with other children, and with the college-age students at the Harvard Psychological Clinic. The play arrangement demonstrated that the child's emotions converged with his social circumstances in an effort to establish a sense of himself. Erikson referred to this sense of self as the child's ego strength, though he would soon be speaking of how the child groped toward a sense of "identity." Consistent with his earlier work, Erikson characterized the child's configuration as a visually observable construct. Yet he seemed to attach somewhat more importance than earlier to "verbal connotations"—what children said about their play. Henry Murray's Thematic Apperception Test (TAT), which Erikson had become familiar with at the Harvard clinic, focused on the story line the subject constructed after looking at a picture. Increasing professional regard for the TAT may have contributed to Erikson's new emphasis on "verbal connotations." Within a decade, his attention to the verbal aspect would expand considerably, becoming the basis for a second type of configuration that Erikson would regard as equal in importance to the concrete, visual configuration.[11]

By late 1940, Macfarlane seemed to have a decided change of heart about Erikson as she formed a better sense of his work habits. She complained to Rockefeller Foundation officials that he was not performing up to expectation. He had written interpretive reports on less than half a dozen of the two hundred children in her project, and she felt that he didn't "function" along lines prescribed for the project unless he was strongly pressured. Macfarlane had heard that Erikson had a difficult time with collective research efforts at the Harvard Psychological Clinic and at Yale; she was distressed that the problem persisted at Berkeley. More than in the 1930s, coordinated and complex data-gathering techniques were in favor, especially in psychology and the social sciences, placing Erikson even farther out of step. He was "essentially a 'lone-wolf,' " Macfarlane reported. The man "constantly has to be given special privileges or he sulks and 'won't play ball.' " She required him to spend nineteen hours a week in his office at the Child Development Clinic. Otherwise, Macfarlane noted, he would have worked entirely at home on noninstitute projects. Above all, she scored him as "a self-seeking and destructive person who uses his intimate 'I am a fragile artist needing to be protected' technique to cover his drive against all others who stand in his way." Despite his obvious intelligence and creativity, a year of watching him had convinced her that he could not be counted on to contribute much to her longitudinal project.[12]

Erikson did not respond in kind, except to point out that it had long been his custom to work at home, to take naps after lunch, and to work at his own pace. Moreover, Macfarlane had promised to let him pursue his various writing projects. Above all, he expressed regret that Macfarlane had pressed him to apply rather rigidly some orthodox Freudian concepts such as drive theory that "were already unacceptable to me in their original form" and actually became obstacles as he sought to "explain significant trends" in the lives of the Berkeley children he met. Since his work on Macfarlane's project had become unpleasant and produced "singularly inconclusive results," he asked her to switch him to half-time employment at her institute by January of 1942. This would allow him to build up his private analytic practice and supplement his salary. Macfarlane greeted this request with "a deep personal sigh of relief." Gregg at Rockefeller approved, instructing Macfarlane that she could hire another and more proficient researcher with the half salary Erikson relinquished: "My estimate of him has proved to be wrong."[13]

With Gregg accepting Macfarlane's characterization of Erikson's work habits, his prospects for future Rockefeller funding were diminished. He worked diligently through 1942 and 1943 to build up his private analytic practice while pursuing research projects that interested him. Precious little time was spent, any longer, at the Institute of Child Welfare.

By early 1944, after the Rockefeller grant had lapsed, Erikson reported to Ruth Benedict that "I am back in full time psychoanalytic practice now" and earning over $9,000 annually. While this was modest compensation, according to national standards for the profession during the war years, it far exceeded his institute wages, and it was supplemented by periodic teaching assignments, such as a course on child development in the university's

Department of Social Welfare. With this very substantial increase in his earning power, his family's economic worries were over. Erik could spend more money for the fashionable clothes he enjoyed wearing, and he encouraged Joan to do the same (loving to see her dressed up). A family car could be purchased. It now became possible to buy a house with a swimming pool in Orinda, half an hour's drive from Berkeley, where large secluded residential lots circled a country club with a golf course. With this transition in personal and professional lifestyles, a lesson had been learned. If an institutional research project proved unpleasant, Erikson realized that he could quit and still do well financially as a private practitioner with various teaching assignments. There was no need to compromise his way of working, his research interests, or his lifestyle. The era of the apprehensive immigrant who would accept almost any job to make ends meet was over.[14]

IDENTITY AND HISTORIC CHANGE

This new confidence that he could support his family without committing himself to an institutional project helps to explain why Erikson refused employment at the prestigious Menninger Clinic in Topeka, Kansas. Instead, during the early 1940s, he frequently visited the clinic as a paid consultant, spending much of his time at Southard School (the clinic's center for emotionally disturbed children). He also gave presentations there concerning his observations of Berkeley children and discussed revisions in his checkerboard sketch of the human life cycle. Several intellectuals at the clinic, particularly Karl Menninger, David Rapaport, and Merton Gill, were impressed by the depth of Erikson's insights though not overjoyed by his tentative, unpolished English or his colorful, stylish dress amid the white coats of the Topeka staff. Karl Menninger made several overtures to Erikson, but he declined. Joan had no interest in moving to Topeka. She too much enjoyed the mild California climate and the nearby ocean. Erik also preferred Bay Area weather, although, unlike many European émigré colleagues, he did not dismiss the Great Plains or any other part of his adopted country as culturally desolate. Joan also understood Erik's preference not to subordinate his work to clinic projects. Finally, the Menninger Clinic tended to admit psychotic and deeply troubled patients, while Erikson preferred to treat less disturbed children and to observe normal youngsters at play.[15]

As Erikson's private practice prospered, he became involved in the affairs of the greater San Francisco psychoanalytic community at a time when the international center of gravity for psychoanalysis had shifted to the United States. While Soviet leaders denounced psychoanalysis as a bourgeois ideology, and Hitler subsumed it under his war against the Jews, a more receptive America became the profession's salvation. The San Francisco Psychoanalytic Society and Institute developed, during the early and mid-1940s, as a meeting place that émigré analysts like Siegfried and Suzanne Bernfeld, Bernhard Berliner, Anna Maenchen, Emanuel Windholz, and others found more congenial than university psychology departments. Early in its existence, the organization had to face the 1938 American Psychoanalytic Association ban on training lay (non-MD) members, which it enforced imperfectly and differentially. Erikson profited from the prestige of his Vienna training and his full membership in the International Psycho-Analytical and the American Psychoanalytic societies. Still, he felt gratified that the San Francisco society welcomed him. Though he lacked some prerequisites, he was appointed as a full training analyst in 1942. Young trainees eagerly sought him out. That year, he taught the society's course "Neuroses in Childhood," and in subsequent years he offered three other courses, emerging (he noted tongue in cheek) as the local "expert on dreams." Despite his profound disinterest in leadership positions, he was nominated and elected to most of the society's offices, including the presidency in 1950. But Erikson was no leader, and his record was undistinguished.[16]

Despite his role in the San Francisco Psychoanalytic Society and the hefty income provided by referrals, Erikson did not feel comfortable among Bay Area analysts. "I wish I could refer more to 'us,' meaning the psychoanalytic community," he wrote to Anna Freud, "but I have been consistently discouraged from mixing professional and social life." He characterized most of his American analytic colleagues as profit-oriented medical specialists—a far cry from the spirit of his Vienna "humanistic days." At the same time, he still was not entirely comfortable with European émigré colleagues. "The truth is," he told Anna Freud, "I do not move in any circle."[17]

The underlying difficulty was that Erikson was breaking from psychoanalytic orthodoxies at a rapid pace while retaining strong allegiance to the memory and spirit of the Vienna founders. It bothered him that his California colleagues "claim[ed] to be free" in their ideas and approach while they insisted on rigid conformity to Freudian doctrines. Some scorned him for being too accessible to his analysands; for addressing their practical, everyday problems; and for freely allowing them transference gratifications. Windholz castigated him openly in a manner that psychoanalysts found particularly insulting—that Erikson was a therapist but not an analyst. Still others took him to task for assigning a book by Anna Freud's rival, the British psychoanalyst Melanie Klein, in one of his Berkeley graduate seminars. (No champion of Klein's perspectives, he had wanted to explore alternative ideas.) But the most frequent and irritating attacks were over Erikson's increasing emphasis on the importance of society and culture in individual development. The same sort of criticism had been leveled against Erich Fromm. Further, some complained that he took too much credit as an innovator. Several linked him with "culturalists" like Margaret Mead and Ruth Benedict, who deemphasized unconscious, sexually rooted drives and the Oedipus complex for more "superficial social influences" on the psyche.[18]

In June of 1944, Erikson read the paper "Social Background and Ego Defenses" before the San Francisco Psychoanalytic Institute. It was an early version of "Ego Development and Historical Change," which appeared in 1946 in the innovative new hard-covered annual *The Psychoanalytic Study of the Child.* The paper and article provided Erikson's fullest statement to date of his posture on social and cultural forces in personality development—the relationship between "inner" and "outer" life that he had struggled with since his Vienna training. This work offered the underpinnings of much of Part Three in *Childhood and Society* ("The Growth of the Ego") and was a clear sign of the innovative psychoanalytic direction he was pursuing. It also contained evocative references to diverse cultures and cultural styles.

The overriding theme of Erikson's 1944 paper and his fuller 1946 article was that social, cultural, and historical forces contributed substantially to the ego's weaknesses and to its strengths, but that psychoanalytic ego psychology had not been sufficiently attentive to this fact. Sigmund Freud's theory that "instinctual energy is transferred, displaced, transformed in analogy to the preservation of energy in physics no longer suffices to help us manage the data which we have learned to observe." Unlike Freud's world half a century earlier, the modern analyst witnessed "the mutual complementation of ethos and ego, of group identity and ego identity," and ultimately of "ego synthesis and social organization." Even Freud in his day had some sense of the impact that history and society had upon the ego in his "habitual references to the cultural and socioeconomic coordinates of his own existence." But by stressing superego constraints upon the drives, Freud had emphasized "what social organization desires [for] the child." In contrast, Erikson's emphasis on ego strength revealed how society "keeps him alive and . . . seduces him to its particular life style." Finally, "instead of accepting the Oedipus trinity as an irreducible schema for man's irrational conduct," as Freud had done, Erikson proposed "exploring the way in which social organization predetermines the structure of the family" and the way the individual emerges from that family with a sense of ego identity. In sum, "psychoanalysis came to emphasize the individual and regressive rather than the collective and supportive"—how people broke down and were moved by irrational drives rather than how they found themselves in "the collective-supportive" culture about them. As such, Freud and his associates had emphasized "only half the story."[19]

Within the 1946 article, Erikson described the work of Anna Freud on ego defenses as an important advance over her father's focus on drives and superego constraints. But he was also quite critical of her, charging that she relegated the defenses to primitive mechanisms of adaptation to life's circumstances rather than treating them as creative processes or strategic intermediaries linking the individual ego to the surrounding society. As such, she provided a mechanized and rather impoverished version of personhood. If the modern ego craved the mechanical adaptations delineated by Anna Freud, "then we are not dealing with the nature of the ego, but with one of its historical adaptations, if not . . . dysfunctions." Indeed, Erikson mocked many "child training customs" that he felt were gaining ascendance in modern society because they emphasized adjustment or adaptation to "the exploitation of the machine and its human manipulators." This threatened "to standardize modern man."[20]

Ultimately, "Ego Development and Historical Change" was about ego identity. His configurational approach documented how inner subjective personhood interacted with society. A firm sense of ego identity obtained when the interaction provided a sense of continuity over time. There was an "awareness of the fact that there is a self-sameness and continuity to the ego's synthesizing methods and that these methods are effective in safeguarding the sameness and continuity of one's meaning for others." The ego synthesized in order "to subsume the most powerful ideal and evil prototypes (the final contestants as it were)" of good and bad, tall and small, and the like "in a simple alternative, in order to make one battle and one strategy out of a bewildering number of skirmishes." This "one battle and one strategy," resulting from ego synthesis, occurred because a firm ego identity was developed—a sense of personal sameness and historical continuity within one's own life that others could recognize.[21]

For some time, Erikson thought the "outer world" was as important as the "inner world" upon which psychoanalysis focused. Where the two worlds intersected, an individual obtained some sense of his or her pursuit of identity. The "Ego Development and Historical Change" paper grafted this perspective onto psychoanalytic ego psychology as Anna Freud, Heinz Hartmann, and others elaborated it, but then extended it considerably. Quite explicitly, Erikson emphasized the "outer world" more than any previous ego psychologist, and he underscored the "sense of identity" as the primary function of the ego. One can understand why Erikson's analytic colleagues in California were uneasy about his presentations. He critiqued the Freuds (father and daughter), offered alternative emphases, and introduced the concept of identity.

In Vienna, Erikson had worked toward a concept of ego identity as he contemplated Paul Federn's discussions of "ego boundaries," and had pursued that concept during his early years in America. His work on the concept finally gelled in the mid-1940s at the Mt. Zion Veterans Rehabilitation Clinic in San Francisco. Indeed, it was no accident that he wrote "Ego Development and Historical Change" as he worked part-time at this veterans' clinic and relied on "ego identity" and "identity crisis" as a diagnosis for many of the patients.

Psychoanalyst Jascha Kasanin established the Rehabilitation Clinic at Mt. Zion Hospital during World War II. The clinic's purpose was short-term treatment of American veterans who had been discharged for "nervous instability," "shell shock," and/or "psychoneurosis." Federal and military officials and large segments of the public had been deeply distressed by the high incidence of these mental illnesses among seemingly healthy GIs. Like many of his colleagues, Kasanin felt obligated to assist American liberal democracy during wartime as it opposed Nazi barbarism. Perhaps mindful of Freud's experience with World War I combat veterans, Kasanin appointed an orthodox Freudian analyst and physician, Czechoslovakian Emanuel Windholz, as clinical director to assist him. He also recruited other Bay Area analysts for part-time services, including Siegfried Bernfeld, Donald Macfarlane, and Jungians Joseph Henderson and Joseph Wheelwright. Early in 1943, he appointed Erikson as a consultant in psychology and child guidance. Although none of the others shared Erikson's general conceptual approach, he emerged, somewhat uncharacteristically, as a peacemaker, patching over conceptual differences between Freudians and Jungians, and urging Bernfeld (whom he had known and admired in Vienna) to be less critical of his colleagues.[22]

During staff case conferences, Erikson made a very substantial contribution. As it happened, he disagreed with pathological diagnoses for most of the veterans. If they were not "psychoneurotic" or "shell shocked" or victims of severe "nervous instability," staff associates asked, then what was their mental illness? The problem, Erikson replied, was that psychoanalysis had no diagnostic term for normal people who were experiencing difficulties, "so I guess I'll have to speak [plain] English." He noted that most of the veterans he observed had experienced dramatic historical changes as they entered adulthood. Their careers had been disrupted, they were separated from their families and loved ones, they had been transported from familiar communities to strange distant locations, and they had to deal with military procedures, including the sights and sounds of deadly combat. Reduced to its essentials, they had "lost a sense of personal sameness and historical continuity" and were experiencing "identity crises." They could not rely on ego synthesis—the intact ego's capacity to organize thousands of diverse stimuli so that the important ones could be addressed and the others ignored. Consequent to this loss of "ego identity," the veterans sensed that "their lives no longer hung together—and never would again." Their "identity crises," normal to young adults, represented the temporary absence of "a sense of what one is, of knowing where one belongs, of knowing what one wants to do."[23]

The concept of identity crisis ("a central loss of identity") therefore became "inescapably and immediately clarifying" to Erikson as he explained to his Mt. Zion colleagues that the somatic tensions and acute anxieties they observed in the veterans were not pathologic. The term and the concept "was suddenly there and seemed right for what I was observing and for what I was trying to explain at the time," he recalled. "The sense of sameness and continuity and the belief in one's social role were gone"—stolen from many of the veterans owing to specific historical circumstances. But this balance could be restored as circumstances changed. Indeed, Erikson observed that several of the veterans had learned "a certain intimacy in relation to other men" in the military that helped them feel more comfortable. They assumed "feminine chores" and behaved like cooperative families in military units. This could facilitate less constrictive gender roles in their families when they returned home. Clinicians could help the veterans in their quest to restore a sense of continuity by dropping diagnostic terms like "psychoneurotic." These labels only augmented self-doubts and feelings of inferiority. Instead, he suggested, clinicians should encourage the veterans to reestablish careers and maintain stable families. They might also counsel the returning veterans' wives so they would be more understanding of their husbands' situations. Local community leaders could help, too, by assuring the local citizenry that the veterans were simply experiencing transitory adjustments in their lives and their careers.[24]

Erikson wrote up portions of his Mt. Zion case conference remarks and reports. Some appeared in "Ego Development and Historical Change." Some were in a 1945 report he wrote for a Stanford University workshop on community leadership, "Plans for the Returning Veteran with Symptoms of Instability." Portions of these and other presentations eventually made their way into *Childhood and Society,* where they represented Erikson's clearest preliminary statement of the "sense of identity" and the identity crisis in adolescents and young adults. Much later, he speculated on why at least some of his colleagues at the Mt. Zion case conferences were swayed by his insistence that "identity crisis" fit the veterans better than traditional pathologic diagnoses. He recalled that the requests for psychotherapeutic assistance by a great many World War II veterans, who were not drastically ill, had made clinicians receptive to diagnoses and treatments for the emotionally "normal." Erik came across the concept of the identity crisis in this mid-

1940s context when he found himself empathizing with these veterans' experiences. "I identify with that to some extent"—a shattered identity owing to a sense of discontinuity in his own life history. The efforts to bridge that discontinuity had been central to the process of becoming Erik Erikson, identity's architect.[25]

Erikson neglected to mention the importance of Erich Fromm in the formation of his concept of identity. A German Jew who arrived in the United States the same year Erikson had, Fromm had received a doctorate in sociology at the University of Heidelberg and had trained at the Berlin Psychoanalytic Institute. He had been a research associate involved in the innovative work of the Frankfurt Institute for Social Research. Politically to the left of Erikson with a stronger activist bent, while less cautious professionally, he had worked at synthesizing the ideas of Freud and Marx and had been critical of the patriarchal underpinnings of Freudian theory. Fromm was especially interested in alienation and uprootedness, his primary concerns while investigating authoritarian propensities among German workers. That study led him to a deep concern with the social psychology of Fascism and that, in turn, led to *Escape from Freedom* (1941), his exceedingly important book. In this volume, Fromm discussed "the identity of our personality" and the "loss of identity" that facilitated mass conformity. Owing to the "automatization of the individual in modern society," which obliterated a sense of selfhood, Fromm thought that mass man was compelled "to conform, to seek his identity, by continuous approval and recognition of others." Man had no other recourse but to embrace a "pseudo self" and to become a "reflex of other people's expectations of him." This loss of a sense of "identity" left one "dead emotionally and mentally" and widely undifferentiated from others. Fromm's discussion of "identity" carried no farther. But his use of the term was hardly dissimilar from the way Erikson developed it at Mt. Zion in the mid-1940s. Erikson had discussed Fromm's book at a meeting of the San Francisco Psychoanalytic Society in early March of 1943. To some extent, at least, *Escape from Freedom* must have helped him to articulate a "sense of identity" and "identity crisis" when describing the war veterans at Mt. Zion.[26]

In psychoanalytic circles, Fromm had been castigated for replacing Freudian drive theory with emphasis on individuation and the formation and dissolution of selfhood or self-identity. This almost certainly explained why Erikson tended to distance himself from Fromm despite their overlapping backgrounds and interests. Remaining cautious and ambitious, and still considering himself a trained Freudian, Erikson never acknowledged Fromm's relevance to his evolving concept of "identity" as a decidedly social as well as a psychological phenomenon.

It took years before Erikson could speak publicly about an even more important (and perhaps more "heretical") influence on his life—the Jungian analyst Joseph Wheelwright. From the start, Wheelwright emerged as one of his strongest supporters at the Mt. Zion case conferences. Within days of being introduced, they struck up a friendship, and soon were bringing their wives along to dinner as they continued their intense conversations. The friendship turned out to be an enduring one. Wheelwright was able to engage Erikson's more playful, less officious side. One day, as the couples sang old jazz songs with piano accompaniment, Erikson proclaimed smilingly: "A Freudian and a Jungian meet on their lowest possible common denominator." While Wheelwright drew heavily on Freud, he brought out Erikson's undeveloped Jungian affinities. He acquainted Erikson with Jung's artistic interests, Jung's concern with collective experience, and Jung's attention to adult development. Wheelwright also noted interesting similarities between Jung's view of the self and Erikson's emerging concept of identity. Usually humorous and relaxed, Wheelwright never pressured Erikson with his discussion of Jungian perspectives. By the time Erikson published "Ego Development and Historical Change," he admitted that several of his patients communicated Jungian archetypes. He also found that Jung's perspectives on the "anima" and the "animus" seemed crucial to ego development and enhanced his understanding of gender issues.[27]

Erikson regarded Wheelwright as a breath of fresh air among the rigid Freudian analysts in northern California. He made sketches of his friend that underscored Wheelwright's irreverent, fun-loving manner and his warm, smiling face. With Wheelwright by his side, the thin-skinned Erikson could tolerate Windholz's charge, during Mt. Zion discussions, that he was not a genuine psychoanalyst. Wheelwright encouraged Erikson not only in the area of Freudian-Jungian cross-fertilization but on the need to reach beyond one's honored mentors for new ideas. Still, Erikson considered himself loyal to the psychoanalytic training that had helped to stabilize his life, even as he made fundamental modifications upon psychoanalytic perspectives.[28]

WAYWARD GERMAN YOUTH

The World War II period was important to Erikson not simply because of his progress on the nature of the "identity crisis." Within academic and governmental circles during this time, the war lent great impetus to national character studies, particularly psychologically oriented investigations. Erikson found himself in the middle of this wave of interest. As a psychoanalyst interested in the impact of culture and history on personality, he was in demand. In a world where the forces of Nazism and Fascism could emerge victorious and liberal democratic values of individual freedom and autonomy were under siege, a culturally and historically grounded concept of identity commanded widespread effort.

When war broke out in Europe in 1939, federal government agencies sought advice from many of Erikson's friends and colleagues on the cultures and personalities of the German and eventually of the Japanese adversaries. Federal officials sought ways to enhance American morale while waging war. Quick, clear policy-oriented inquiries into the character of embattled nations and their allies involved leading American social and behavioral scientists. In the fall of 1939, the Committee for National Morale (CNM) was organized as a scholarly association dedicated to investigate psychological dimensions of warfare and propaganda in ways that might benefit American morale and federal policies. Several CNM members were Erikson's friends and acquaintances, including Margaret Mead and her husband, Gregory Bateson, Ruth Benedict, Henry Murray, and Kurt Lewin. Mead and Bateson recruited CNM activists and others for another private scholarly organization, the Council on Intercultural Relations (CIR), to apply anthropological and related methods to the international crisis in ways that would facilitate Allied military efforts. A governmental agency, the Office of Strategic Services (OSS) Psychological Division, also came into being. Directed by University of California psychologist Robert Tryon, it elicited support from many who were active in the CNM and the CIR. The Psychological Division conducted surveys, polls, and interviews to enhance understanding of American, German, and other national characters and to determine the elements that shaped civilian morale. The division also called on psychologists like Murray and Donald MacKinnon to select potential American intelligence agents.[29]

Sparked by agencies like the CNM, the CIR, and the OSS, as well as military expenditures for a wide range of information and perspectives, many intellectuals and scholarly researchers throughout the nation directed their energies toward the war effort. By 1942, there were twenty-two active research seminars publishing reports and advising the federal government on everything from Hitler's personality to popular attitudes toward wardens at air-raid shelters. Psychologists screened millions of recruits to the armed forces, measured their response to stress, recommended that many be excluded from the ranks for reasons of mental instability, and summarized the patterns of their findings in reports and journal articles. Psychiatrists with similar research interests like Roy Grinker and John Spiegel studied and published on "combat exhaustion" in mentally healthy troops subjected to the stress of battle conditions such as the 1943 Tunisian campaign. Their colleague, William Menninger, transformed the army's Neuropsychiatric

Consultants Division, which became quite attentive to applied academic research and to therapeutic approaches that promised to ease GI emotional burdens. Anthropologists like Mead, Benedict, Bateson, and Geoffrey Gorer shifted their research from small so-called primitive cultures to the powerful, modern nation-states at war. Lawrence Frank's concept of "society as the patient" gained new currency, advocating the transference of psychotherapy techniques from individuals to the society at large. A considerable literature emerged from these efforts. Often hastily prepared and lacking in traditional scholarly reflection, reports and publications tended to offer sweeping generalizations without much supportive evidence. Those who wrote the materials tended, increasingly, to regard themselves as public intellectuals. They wanted to contribute significantly to policy formation and victory in the war effort, and they sought financial backing from federal and private agencies. Mead's 1942 volume *And Keep Your Powder Dry* illustrated the trend by a respected researcher who was quickly becoming a major spokesperson on pressing public concerns. More a primer for federal officials and planners on ways to engineer national unity than a reflective, documented analysis, Mead urged readers to capitalize on American traditions of anti-authoritarianism, competitiveness, and the rights of localities in meeting the totalitarian challenge.[30]

With many of Erikson's friends and associates actively involved in these investigations, his participation was inevitable. As early as November 1941, Arthur Pope, chair of the Committee for National Morale, asked him to take a three-month leave from Macfarlane's Institute of Child Welfare to work with Mead and Murray on an investigation of American attitudes and values. Later, working from the Office of War Information in Washington, Ruth Benedict commissioned Erikson to study children of foreign backgrounds in the United States to "build up a backlog of knowledge of what different civilized nations want in life and how they go after it." Throughout the war and immediately after, Mead involved Erik in a variety of projects, especially several dealing with German character and German war prisoners. She also coached him on how to secure adequate financial compensation from federal agencies for his efforts.[31]

Not stimulated by his work at the Institute of Child Welfare and never entirely engaged by his growing private practice, Erikson was thrilled by the offers to participate in the wartime studies, as they were compatible with his interest in how social and historic conditions affected personality development. There was a symbolic element, too, in his participation. Assignments as a consultant with the federal government and with agencies like the CNM and the CIR supportive of the American war effort underscored Erikson's commitment to his adopted country. FDR's America had welcomed him from Europe, and he felt passionate about helping augment his country's military effort against its enemies. Indeed, Erikson almost always accepted whatever wartime assignments came his way; he wanted to do his part. He confided to Mead and Bateson that he felt "more eagerness than ever to be disestablished [from Macfarlane's institute and from private psychoanalytic practice] for a good cause." When Benedict asked him to study Dutch childhood and wartime conditions, he replied, "I have always wanted to do some work with you," and was quite willing to take time off from his private practice. Toward the end of the war, he even proposed a new project for the CNM—to encourage European (particularly German) women to establish congresses and other agencies "to help prevent wars in the future." However, despite his enthusiasm for these wartime projects for the country that took him in, Erikson's insecurities sometimes intruded. Sensing that he "wasn't even much prepared as a psychoanalyst," he acknowledged that he did not feel on a par with a top logician with scientific training like Bateson in their collaborative work. Indeed, he confessed to "an acute case of frigidopedosis nervosa, or cold feet" over how the Office of War Information would evaluate certain of his reports.[32]

The study of Hitler's Germany was probably Erikson's most important contribution to wartime national character studies. The *Childhood and Society* chapter that came of it, "The Legend of Hitler's Childhood," was an essential backdrop to almost all the other national character culture references in the book. The essay on the country of his childhood and youth provided the organizing principle around the cross-cultural mosaic that was so conspicuous in Erikson's first book.

"The Legend of Hitler's Childhood" essay had a long gestation. As he learned of Hitler's rise to power in Germany early in 1933 and watched right-wing movements in Austria amid economic depression, Erikson began to write. Hitler seemed to be exploiting nationalistic tendencies in adolescents and young adults. As he watched from nearby Vienna while the situation in Germany deteriorated, Erik reflected on growing up in Karlsruhe as a Danish Jew who "had to stand the scorn of German children against a foreign-born child." The scorn was such that during World War I "I developed nationalistic German tendencies" in order "to convince my playmates of my loyalty." With the rise of Hitler and his movement, many of these former playmates "had turned Nazi" and they were attacking "some of my Jewish friends. They might have disposed of me if I had been there [in Germany]." During Erikson's psychoanalytic training, August Aichhorn had underscored the wayward, delinquent quality in many of Vienna's youngsters. It was not difficult to see that Hitler was appealing to the same sort of wayward youth in Germany. Erikson began writing about Hitler's appeal simply "to explain this phenomenon to myself." Aboard the *Scanmail* en route to America, he worked on the essay. Although his fellow passenger, George Kennan, had urged him to translate it and to prepare it for English publication, Erik had not.[33]

In his early years in America, Erik learned of several early psychoanalytic studies of the rise of Hitler. With precious little evidence other than *Mein Kampf*, most of these works took off from Freud's *Group Psychology and the Analysis of the Ego*. Like Freud on the leader, they characterized Hitler as a father figure appealing to the irrational needs of his followers. Some psychoanalytic revisionists like Harold Lasswell and, of course, Erich Fromm had stressed the insecure, lower-middle-class standing of these followers, but Erikson was uninterested in this perspective. Writers more attentive to emerging trends in ego psychology focused on how individual lives connected to institutions and events, and their studies especially interested Erikson. While the authors tended to be psychoanalysts without historical training, several recognized the need to avoid pure psychologizing and to incorporate social, economic, and (above all) historical data to explain the appeal of Hitler's Nazi movement. They were forerunners in the field of what Erikson later came to call psychohistory.[34]

Early in 1941, after Erikson had settled with his family in Berkeley, the CNM pressed for considerably more psychological research on Germany. In a report to William Donovan, director of the Office of Coordinator of Information (soon to be renamed the Office of Strategic Services or OSS), the CNM urgently requested an analysis of Hitler's personality. The reason for the urgency was to inform policymakers what course of action would "adversely affect Hitler's already precarious emotional stability." Donovan agreed with the CNM recommendation and commissioned several investigators to prepare reports. By 1943, Walter Langer and Henry Murray had completed theirs. Before then, however, only one commissioned report met the time deadline—Erikson's revised version of his Vienna paper. Initially titled "On Nazi Mentality," and then "Hitler's Imagery and German Youth," it was published in the November 1942 edition of *Psychiatry*. This paper, in its revised versions, was the first serious psychological analysis of Hitler and his appeal to be considered by America's war planners. This work represented Erikson's first important contact with federal policymakers and perhaps the first sign of his emergence as an important intellectual.[35]

In preparing two unpublished and one published version of this 1942 essay, Erikson did more than dust off his Vienna paper on Hitler's appeal. Through his involvement in the CNM "Canadian Project" between 1940 and 1942, he was able to add important data and observations. Margaret Mead and Gregory Bateson had included him in the project, which required interviewing German prisoners of war interned in Canada. Based on his interviews, Erikson wrote several short reports that contained the basic theme of his 1942 essay, characterizing Hitler as a gang leader who appealed to estranged German adolescents to defy their parents and respectable society, and to believe "that the adolescent is always right, that aggression is good, that conscience is an affliction, adjustment a crime." This "adolescent imagery" bonding the Führer to German youth eventually won acceptance by the "whole nation." Suspending their moral judgments, German citizens accepted Hitler's appeals to delinquency as a form of morality. In his reports for the CNM, Erikson suggested that there was only one effective counter-image: the traditional stable, loving German family of caring parents and needy children.[36]

As he prepared various versions of "Hitler's Imagery and German Youth" for government officials and for *Psychiatry*, Erikson updated his preliminary Vienna writing with the "adolescent imagery" theme that emerged during the "Canadian Project." He also studied a few speeches that Hitler delivered in 1941 and 1942, which Margaret Mead had secured from the Federal Communications Commission. But Hitler's autobiographical *Mein Kampf* was the source he relied on most.

Erikson was not troubled by gross inaccuracies in *Mein Kampf*, for he was primarily interested in how Hitler experienced and perceived his life. Indeed, he used Hitler's propaganda descriptions of his childhood to flesh out the "adolescent imagery" theme. Through *Mein Kampf*, Hitler was manufacturing a story or legend for his countrymen, Erikson asserted. The autobiography illustrated the way Hitler held himself out as a leader for wayward adolescents. Erikson focused on this psychohistorical interpretation of the gang leader quite intuitively, elaborating it with somewhat questionable documentation. This mode of presentation, almost required by acute time constraints, persisted in his writing long after the war. Erikson also demonstrated a lifelong habit of revising his writing again and again to maximize its artistic form. Sentences were recast, added, and deleted, while paragraphs were rearranged for aesthetic enhancement. As Erikson moved from preliminary drafts to the published article, he pruned extraneous material and focused on Hitler's appeal to young people more than to Germany at large. As he became more confident of Allied military victory, he gave more attention to issues of postwar reconstruction. Erik Homburger, the young artist, had made woodcut after woodcut of the same scene to enhance its aesthetic appeal and its message. Erik Erikson, the emerging wartime writer and intellectual, repeatedly polished his essay on Hitler and German culture. Indeed, he revised the final essay published in 1942 (primarily aesthetically) for *Personality in Nature, Society, and Culture*, a 1949 anthology organized by Clyde Kluckhohn and Henry Murray, and revised it again for both the first and second editions of *Childhood and Society.*[37]

Despite its numerous revisions, the 1942 published version of "Hitler's Imagery and German Youth" remains a remarkable essay. The theme of Hitler's gang leader appeal was elaborated through visual images and words communicated between leader and follower. Indeed, images and auditory "tunes" formed an organizing shape or configuration for the relation between leader and follower. Erikson described it as a "subverbal magic design." He was expanding upon the strictly visual configuration that he had delineated earlier in his work with children. The images and sounds within this expanded configuration integrated Hitler's inner emotions and outer social circumstances; they also integrated the inner and outer worlds of his youthful and heavily male adherents. Hitler offered himself as "the adolescent who never even aspired to become a father in any connotation." He bypassed German fathers and held himself out as "a gang leader who keeps 'the boys' together . . . by shrewdly involving them in crimes from which there is no way back." Unlike many other critics of the German situation, then, Erikson did not discuss Nazism in the context of a father with his children, but from the standpoint of a gang leader who encouraged his young delinquent male followers to repudiate the morals of their parents and neighbors. In this rapport between the Führer and German male youth (plus other not-so-young Germans who fell increasingly under his spell), an interesting development transpired. Each follower soon "relinquished his old self without either gaining a new self or a sustaining social recognition." Lacking a sense of self, leader and gang proclaimed to each other the validity of youthful aggression over conscience and social adjustment.[38]

Erikson did not characterize this German loss of "self" as he would later, after working with veterans in the Mt. Zion Rehabilitation Center—that is, the loss of self was not yet described as a loss of "identity," "identity confusion," or "negative identity." But he was ready for these terms. Both the Führer and his youthful following suffered sharp discontinuities in their life histories and heard common "tunes" of disconnectedness. Whereas many of the children Erikson had worked with had made configurations from blocks or toys to enhance the continuities in their lives and, thereby, their sense of viable identity, the Nazi configuration he described had undermined continuity and precluded all but the most negative identity.

Before Erikson's essay was published in 1942, Gregory Bateson emphasized to Robert Tryon, the head of the OSS Psychology Division, the revolutionary nature of Erik's finding concerning the nonpaternal delinquent bond between the Führer and young Nazi males. Bateson also underscored the obvious implication that the way to undermine the Nazi movement was to appeal "to whatever made adolescents settle down and marry." In the published essay, Erikson suggested that stronger parental models were required. Above all, German fathers needed to find greater "true inner authority" that their children could depend on in the course of their development. German mothers also needed more inner strength so that they might disrupt a pattern (not unlike that of his own mother) of generosity toward their children one moment and seeming betrayal the next.[39]

Disputing the pervasive view that Hitler was a perverse father figure, the first published version of Erikson's "Hitler's Imagery" essay contained additional contributions. Erich Fromm and several other of Erikson's predecessors had argued that the Nazis appealed most to lower-middle-class Germans. Indeed, Fromm had elaborated that theme in *Escape from Freedom* and cast it within a cultural and existential orientation that had an interesting resemblance to Erikson's. More from intuition than concrete information, Erikson felt Hitler's gang included adolescents in the entire middle class as well as the aspiring working class. Indeed, Erik did not regard class as the essential focal unit. He felt that Hitler's appeal had far more to do with the dynamics of parenting and adolescent development in the German culture at large than it pertained to economic conditions or social structure. In his Marxist underground psychoanalytic newsletter, *Rundbriefe,* Otto Fenichel attacked Erikson for ignoring the conditions of production and for slighting issues of class differentiation. Fenichel also criticized him for "using his insight and spontaneous thinking," which was considerable, instead of researching the material conditions that shaped Germany's historic evolution. Despite these charges against Erikson, the enormously complex issue of the class basis (and several other economic factors) behind Hitler's appeal remains heavily contested within academia. Some scholars of modern German history have been more disposed to Erikson's position than to Fromm's or Fenichel's.[40]

It is not surprising that Erikson's 1942 essay in *Psychiatry* also contributed to the understanding of German spatial concepts. Erik was not the first to point out that Germany's historic sense of being in a geographically "encircled and vulnerable position" in central Europe promoted Hitler's quest for lebensraum. But he was unusual in emphasizing that Hitler's territorial expansion was motivated not only from perceived geographic and political encirclement by hostile countries. Owing to a diversity of historic forces, Erikson noted, "the German mind" was unable "to crystallize, nor to assimilate economic and social evolution in gradual and logical steps." It felt "disunited" and suffered from "a deep insecurity in its basic values." Erikson added that the constant expansionism inherent in the quest for lebensraum was a call for perennial and forceful motion—militarily, economically, intellectually. In preliminary writing that resulted in *The Origins of Totalitarian-*

ism, Hannah Arendt had also stressed constant, unreflective motion in the German command at the expense of stability. But Erikson added that Hitler sometimes replaced "images of movement [with] those of stationary *endurance.*" In a speech Hitler delivered in September of 1942, for example, Erikson cited the language of Hitler's command: "We stand behind our soldiers, just as our soldiers stand in front of us." Noting Germany's greatest World War II triumph—the defeat, through blitzkrieg, of the French stationary guard on the Maginot Line—Erikson maintained that Nazism "stands and falls [psychologically] with the imagery of *Blitz* warfare." What Erikson was indicating but never quite developed was that Germans called on motion and blitzkrieg to show themselves to be a people of great merit. What they needed, instead, was a mature sense of selfhood that would have facilitated peaceful reflection—not simply "stationary endurance."[41]

Most of the essential elements of the Hitler chapter in *Childhood and Society* originated in the 1942 article. The major deficiency in his concept was the absence, until the mid-1940s, of a clear idea of identity. But he was very close to that concept and only seemed to need the term itself, plus a few descriptive phrases, to make it gel. Another concern in the 1942 essay that was remedied in *Childhood and Society* was the fullness of the discussion of the Jew in German society. The essay offered a very condensed coverage of Nazi images of the Jew as an "emasculating germ" who was "small, black, and hairy" in contrast to the tall, light, erect Aryan. Jews were treated largely as anonymous figures who appeared on the German stage. By the time the essay was transformed in *Childhood and Society* in 1950, Erikson had elaborated on the nature of Jewish identity and genius against which the Nazis tried to immunize themselves. He distinguished, for example, between dogmatic Jews, who clung to the Torah and did not allow new circumstances to alter their habits, and Jews who embraced geographic mobility and "cultural multiplicity" to the point where relativity became "the absolute." Erikson mentioned three German Jews—Marx, Freud, and Einstein—who ingeniously elaborated the relativity in human values and understanding that Hitler sought to thwart. In the 1942 essay, one might attribute the brevity and the stereotypical aspect of Erikson's discussion of the Jew to ambivalence over his own Judaism. But if this was a factor, it was hardly unique. Otto Fenichel, Ernst Simmel, Bruno Bettelheim, and several other Jewish psychoanalytic immigrants who wrote about the Nazi movement allowed their ambivalence to constrict their portrayals of anti-Semitism and the Jewish experience.[42]

The *Childhood and Society* chapter on Hitler's youth appeal had more to say about Germany's future in the postwar world than the 1942 essay. Much of the hard thinking evident in the chapter occurred as the war drew to a close. At that point, Erikson drafted reports for the CNM and the Council on Intercultural Relations, and spoke at conferences on the German situation. By then, he had been working with war veterans at the Mt. Zion clinic and his concept of identity had finally crystallized. Indeed, he spoke of the crisis of collective German "identity" in the wake of military defeat. Everyday Germans were split between paranoia, hate, and projected scapegoats (the legacy of the Nazi past) on the one hand, and "guilt feeling, insight, and love of progress" on the other. Erikson expressed optimism that most Germans (even many former Nazi Party members) could make the transition toward a positive identity. Those "who have remained potentially sensitive to civilized values [should] be given psychological support," he argued. Only those repeatedly drawn to Hitler's delinquent, adolescent imagery had to "be put out of action."[43]

In the 1942 essay for *Psychiatry*, Erikson made fleeting references to a post-Nazi Germany. These were congruent with the descriptions by Goethe that he had read as a youth. Goethe had prized a diversity or plurality of small German social-political states and independent centers. At the same time, Goethe entertained strong reservations about the value of German military power or national cultural self-sufficiency; neither signified moral strength or cultural richness. As World War II concluded, Erikson underscored Goethe's vision in an effort to undermine the militarist and culturally ethnocentric vestiges of Nazi lebensraum. "The very antithesis to Hitler's imagery is that of the *family*, the *township*, and the *region* as the basis of universal cultural life," Erikson wrote, and of Germany's local democratic cultural heritage. "As far as I can discern," he noted in 1945, "the future [for Germany] lies in cultural autonomy for regions" combined with the "economic interdependence" of all areas of the European continent. To facilitate this vision of localism, cultural diversity, and the avoidance of militarism and warfare, Erikson proposed a permanent congress of European women. "Who more than women would have the right and the duty" as child bearers, he asked, to organize for "the preservation of human resources?" Indeed, "the matter of reeducation [to combat Nazi perspectives] will logically begin with women and small children" in order to undermine practices of racial breeding. This portrait of genuine rootedness in local and regional culture, family, and women all serving to eradicate the centralized, masculinized Nazi war machine had a disconcerting aspect. Erik's characterization had a certain affinity to Nazi propaganda that abstractly romanticized community, family, child bearing, and the connection to nature. He, of course, had long been immersed in complex and contradictory strands of German ideology and culture, and his ideas sometimes carried implications that he hardly intended.[44]

Nonetheless, as he wrote of the postwar German situation, Erikson acknowledged "not having been in Germany proper since 1929." And he had no pressing desire to return. Indeed, as soon as it was safe to travel abroad, he elected to visit his mother, stepfather, and half sister in Haifa. He made subsequent visits to Haifa. After the state of Israel was mandated, he confessed that he was so impressed with the Jewish state that if he had not been an American citizen, he would almost certainly have become an Israeli. By 1951, he began to travel periodically to Germany, spoke at conferences there, and received honorary degrees. But at the time his first book was published, he hardly felt rooted in German politics or culture.[45]

When *Childhood and Society* was published in 1950, the essential theme of Hitler's appeal to the delinquent instincts of German youth was very similar to what it had been almost a decade earlier. Yet the theme was deepened considerably by the concept of identity. Indeed, by 1942, Erikson actually wrote about German fathers and sons coming "to identify with the Führer; an adolescent who never gave in." By 1945, the identity concept assumed a much fuller and richer meaning in terms of a person's feeling of connectedness and sameness or of disjunction. By 1950, one had a better sense that the word *identify* in "to identify with the *Führer*" signaled an untenable or *negative* form of identity—a feeling of being very "unnatural" and detached from one's biologic, familial, and cultural past. Hitler and his followers had experienced "identity crises" that they failed to resolve in psychologically satisfying ways when they singled out scapegoats and pursued lebensraum.[46]

The process of settling on the identity construct to account for the Hitler appeal helps to explain why Erikson maintained only "occasional contact" and no "systematic" discussion with representatives of the Frankfurt school and others who were conducting an enormously important research project eventually published as *The Authoritarian Personality.* Project researchers like R. Nevitt Sanford (a member of the San Francisco Psychoanalytic Institute and the Berkeley psychology department), the Vienna-trained émigré analyst Else Frenkel-Brunswik (who held an appointment at the Institute of Child Welfare), and their student, psychologist Daniel Levinson, sometimes worked only a few minutes' walk from Erikson. Project investigators such as these were conversant with Harold Lasswell's prewar efforts to explore the convergence between personality and political endeavors. Whereas they all shared with Erikson a strong interest in national character, they sought to delineate a rigid personality type evident in all societies that was susceptible to irrational manipulation by ruthless demagogues. Indeed, several Authoritarian Personality project staff worked to measure, precisely and quantitatively, the psychological rigidities of those susceptible to right-wing totalitarianism, characterized by blind hatreds, stereotypical thinking, vilifications, and similar qualities. Although Erikson had never been comfortable with elaborate, systematic undertakings such as this, he did not consider the investigation of authoritarian qualities to be "wrong" or even problematic. Rather, it simply was not congruent with the way he was working out the identity construct in a German context. Since he saw little immediate, tangible benefit in connecting with project investigators, Erikson never made the effort to cross the conceptual and informational borders between their inquiries and his. Hence, though *Childhood and Society* was published the same year as *The Authoritarian Personality,* Erikson referred to it in only one footnote that referenced the projection of internally distressing feelings upon an external enemy.[47]

Erikson failed to connect not only with the Authoritarian Personality project, but to much of an emerging literature on recent dictatorial regimes, especially Hitler's. For example, he was largely uninfluenced by Frankfurt School émigré Franz Newman, whose 1942 study *Behemoth* described the Third Reich as a private capitalist economy regimented by a totalitarian state. He did not appear to be familiar with Friedrich Hayek's much publicized *The Road to Serfdom* (1944)—an account of how regimentation of private economic activity, typical of Nazi rule, produced a coercive effect on all realms of life. Erikson did not cite Dwight Macdonald's sensitive essays in *Politics* (1944–49) on the warping effect of total war and totalitarian cruelty upon human personality. He was inattentive to powerful articles in this vein that Macdonald had included in *Politics* by Albert Camus, George Orwell, and Simone Weil. If Erikson was familiar with early essays by Hannah Arendt that resulted in her extraordinary account of the historic roots and essential components of Nazi and Stalinist regimes (*The Origins of Totalitarianism* [1950]), this was not indicated. Nor did he cite Bruno Bettelheim's important 1943 article "Individual and Mass Behavior in Extreme Situations." Based on observations at Buchenwald and Dachau, Bettelheim had described and explained how certain prisoners had identified with the Gestapo. Psychologically, this phenomenon was not wholly unlike the tie between Hitler and German youth that Erikson was exploring. With considerable eloquence and some proximity to Erikson's developing theory of identity, Bettelheim underscored the importance of strong autonomous selfhood in the face of Nazi pressure to conform.

Erikson's disposition toward constant revision of terms and concepts, more than systematic examination of the work of others, explained why he changed the title of his essay for the third time with the publication of *Childhood and Society.* It began as "On Nazi Mentality," shifted in late 1942 to "Hitler's Imagery and German Youth," and shifted again between 1948 and 1950 to "The Legend of Hitler's Childhood." Title changes reflected a developing psychobiographical orientation. In the 1942 version, Erikson noted how Hitler's sense of his stubborn rejection of his own father's authority was invoked and broadened as Hitler appealed to German youth to reject their fathers:

> It frequently happens in history that *an extreme and even atypical personal experience fits a universal latent conflict so well that a crisis* lifts it to a representative position. This, I feel, is the basis for the wonderment which must befall the German man who reads about Hitler's childhood as he chooses to present it.[48]

As Erikson rewrote the essay, especially in its 1950 version, he focused on how Hitler's account of his personal experience as a child (the "legend" he provided for his countrymen in *Mein Kampf*) tapped a German and even a "universal latent conflict." This focus on how the leader, by working out his own personal difficulty, found a way for members of the larger society to resolve their difficulties, would become characteristic of Erikson's subsequent work. This approach became his way of explaining widespread historical change and underscored his subsequent assessment of the revolutionary historical achievements of Luther and Gandhi. The evolution of the Hitler essay marked the beginning of Eriksonian historical psychobiography.

A few changes in phrasing in the 1950 *Childhood and Society* version of the Hitler essay reflected Erikson's personal state of mind. These changes suggested that even in his late forties, Erikson continued to wrestle with his early years in Karlsruhe as a troubled and conflicted stepson of Theodor Homburger. "During the storms of adolescence . . . when the [German] boy's identity must settle things with his father image," Erikson now observed, the father's "essential lack of true inner authority" complicated his son's rebellion. So the German son displayed a mix of "open rebellion and 'secret sin,' cynical delinquency and submissive obedience," the combination of which "is apt to break the boy's spirit, once and for all." Although Erik had certainly not been a delinquent, at times he rebelled openly and at other times he submitted to a stepfather who failed to wield an "inner authority" over him. Like the German father Erikson described in the 1950 draft of his Hitler essay, Theodor Homburger "did not oppose this rebellion, but, indeed, unconsciously fostered it" by holding himself out as Erik's biological father and insisting that Erik's mother deny her son access to his true origins. Much as the German mother in "The Legend of Hitler's Childhood" acted as a "go-between and an in-between," conveying communication between father and son, Karla was a "go-between" connecting Theodor to Erik. Both sometimes blamed Karla for what each disliked in the other. Erik's *Vorschule* and gymnasium experiences had offered little relief from this difficult situation at home. In the 1950 version of the essay, Erik recalled how " 'humanistic' education in Germany suffered from the severe split of fostering duty and discipline while glorifying the nostalgic outbreaks of poets." This was very much what young Erik felt as he completed his gymnasium work with good marks for obedience and mediocre marks in more substantive areas, as he commenced a broken *Wanderschaft,* and as he wrote a long journal that registered "nostalgic outbreaks" (sometimes in poetic verse).[49]

These are obviously loose, imprecise connections between Erikson's essay on Hitler's youth appeal and his early years in Karlsruhe. Yet the importance he attached to deficient "inner authority" on the part of German fathers must have directly linked to Theodor's own lack of "inner authority" over him. In *Young Man Luther,* Erikson's next book, the issue of deficient "inner authority" between a German father and his son became even more crucial. Although Erikson now regarded himself as an American and the son of a Dane, his German ties and the paternal dynamics of his childhood can never be discounted.

AMERICAN IDENTITY

Although "The Legend of Hitler's Childhood" was the most original and powerful essay on national culture in *Childhood and Society,* Erikson devoted considerably more space in the book to America. "Reflections on the American Identity" was intended as a counterpoint to the German essay and focused primarily on white America. Earlier in the book, Erikson included chapters on two Native American tribes—the Sioux and the Yurok. His clinical case discussions were also on Americans. Unlike a good many other European immigrant intellectuals, he was deeply curious about his adopted country.

Like the chapter on Hitler's appeal, Erikson's essays on American culture belong to a tradition growing out of the exigencies of World War II. Agencies like the OSS, the CNM, and the CIR were eager for reports on the values of wartime adversaries—what held each national culture together and what might prompt it to fragment. While Erikson was among the first to present reports and articles on Hitler's Germany, he was late in offering material on contemporary America. To be sure, he had written about the first Americans—two Indian tribes—during the late 1930s and early 1940s. But in a July 1948 outline of what would be *Childhood and Society,* he had yet to prepare the chapter on "modern America" that became "Reflections on the American Identity."[50]

Erikson's delay was not unusual. European psychoanalytic émigrés, Frankfurt School scholars, and others fleeing the old world as right-wing movements proliferated felt more confident elaborating on the deterioration in central Europe than on the situation in the United States, where they had only recently arrived. Moreover, when Erikson's close friend Margaret Mead published *And Keep Your Powder Dry* on American national culture, he was so impressed that he felt he could add little. Written the summer following the Japanese attack on Pearl Harbor, the book characterized modern Americans as philanthropic and judicious but troubled by the debilitating psychological effects of shallow materialism and single-minded economic competition. For Mead, the nuclear family was an especially troubled institution. Parents found themselves detached from and therefore untutored by their extended families. Unsure about the nature of child rearing, they pressed their children to achieve in conventional and measurable ways. Parental love was contingent on standardized successes such as the acquisition of wealth. Although Erikson felt somewhat more charitable toward FDR's America in the early 1940s, he found Mead's interpretation sobering and valid. He was especially taken by her description of the "elusive nature" of Americans—their reluctance to settle down "too early" in any regimented way. Erikson credited Mead's perspective for some years, even during the 1950s as settling down through regular dating ("going steady") and early marriage became more common.[51]

Geoffrey Gorer's *The American People* (1948) was another of the growing number of American character studies that impressed Erikson. A British anthropologist who had studied under Mead, Gorer was also very attentive to the American nuclear family. He characterized America's decision to reject King George and declare itself independent as part of a tradition characterized by the Oedipal rejection of paternal authority. This proclivity fueled hostility toward constituted government. Within the family, the tradition reduced the father's power to buddy status with his sons and elevated the mother's authority. "In few societies is the role of the father more vestigial than in the United States," Gorer wrote. The American male found "encapsulated inside him, an ethical, admonitory, censorious mother," he warned. Because "Mom" had pressured him to be a "he-man" and to assert himself at all costs, his friendships were transitory and he related more easily to machines than to people.[52]

In *Childhood and Society*, Erikson underscored the influence of the growing number of American character studies. As an immigrant, he felt compelled to master the unfamiliar customs of his new country. Consequently, he immersed himself in these materials far more than he studied the current literature on Nazi Germany and totalitarianism. A July 1948 outline for what became his "Reflections on the American Identity" chapter indicated his heavy reliance on Mead's and Gorer's conclusions about American competitiveness, the nuclear family, and the standardized, mechanized aspects of American child rearing. But the outline also revealed that his essay would focus on the more general theme of American identity. Fascinating as the concept of "American character" was in its many and varied uses at the time, he felt that it was too static to describe "an emerging American sense of identity." "To the author," he noted, "the great promise of America is that its developing identity is based on a co-existence and mutual enrichment of polar alternatives." American identity was based on "co-existent, [and] on the whole well workable opposites—the *sedentary* way of life and the *migrant* one; *individualistic* strivings and the need for rigid *standardization; competition* and cooperation, etc." Americans derived their identities "not from a decision in favor of one or the other such alternative, but rather from the conviction of having the right and chance to choose (and to change at any time) a combination of them." Next, Erikson identified the identity issues that might serve as building blocks for his chapter. He would write on American war veterans who "lost their sense of free choice, and with it their sense of identity." He would describe how the African-American struggled with "his feudal slave identity." He would show how the adolescent sought identity in a family with a strong "Mom" and a remote "Dad." And he would explain how these and other examples revealed a larger American identity. American identity could be characterized by narrow, bigoted, autocratic, and thoughtless qualities when Americans were "fearful" about themselves, but could be characterized by "fraternal, supernatural, and judicious" qualities when Americans enjoyed a fuller and more positive sense of their individual identities.[53]

Erikson's decision to title his chapter "Reflections on the American Identity" suggested a consistency with the theme of his 1948 outline. Indeed, the chapter began with the idea of identity being grounded in the choices among seeming polarities so that one "can preserve a certain element of deliberate tentativeness of autonomous choice." "To leave his choices open" and to preserve his sense of autonomy, Erikson noted, "the American, on the whole, lives with two sets of 'truths.' " One polarity that particularly struck him was how the democratic political culture embraced both "aristocracy and mobocracy (so admirably synthesized by Franklin D. Roosevelt)."[54]

More than his outline indicated would be the case, Erikson connected "American identity" in the *Childhood and Society* chapter to the myth of the self-made man who was in constant motion and was rarely reflective. In discussing the legend of John Henry, Erikson underscored how "he jumped to his feet before he had his first meal," for success required instant action considering the vast "continent before him, and the tasks required of him." John Henry insisted on choices and opportunities and "will not commit himself to any identity as predetermined by the stigmata of birth." The vastness of the American continent offered opportunities for material success or failure for the self-made man. He shed an "overdefined past" and relied on autonomy and initiative for success as well as to facilitate identity—to be "going places and doing things." These qualities were particularly evident in the westward movement, "which was crudely masculine, rudely exuberant, and, but for its women, anarchic." The potential for success by heading west was so fundamental to American identity, Erikson noted, that the travel restrictions of old age became ominous. He joked (rather soberly) that the trailer now provided older Americans with a way around even those restrictions, for it "permits them to settle down to perpetual traveling and to die on wheels."[55]

Although Erikson drew from Geoffrey Gorer's portrayal of the American "Mom" in "Reflections on the American Identity," he provided useful amplifications rooted in the success theme. As "Dads" cultivated "the role of freeborn sons" and "abdicated their dominant place in the family" in order to pursue material success, "Moms" assumed the roles of fathers and grandfathers. Agreeing with Gorer, Erikson claimed that in this role of "misplaced paternalism," the "Moms" became "the unquestioned authority in the matter of mores and morals" in the home and the community. "Mom" proved to be "egotistical in her demands, and infantile in her emotions"; she never quite reached "mature womanhood." Yet this was not entirely her fault. As long as men insisted on unfettered choices or opportunities to maximize success, "women had to become autocratic in their demands for some order." They were not encouraged to provide a more natural phenomenon, "mother love," for that was being overly "protective." A successful man had "to stand on his own feet" and "keep himself up by his own gripes." Although Erikson's portrayal of relationships between "Mom," "Dad," and their children closely paralleled Gorer's, he elaborated more on the pattern of relationships that resulted. American families did not breed love and affection, he maintained, so much as compromises over each member's interests in order to avoid undermining any member's role and thwarting his or her chances to take advantage of opportunities that presented themselves. The compromises and freewheeling conduct evident in much of American church and political life reflected this family dynamic. "Mom" could be "Mom," "Dad" could be "Dad," and institutions of family, church, and polity would not impede the free pursuit of success.[56]

Erikson's description of the modern American character comported with the myth-symbol approach to American studies and the consensus approach to American history that became fashionable (very nearly an orthodoxy) in scholarship and popular writing during the 1950s. Indeed, his apprehensions over the emotional and intellectual costs of a consensual disposition in family and society paralleled the apprehensions of historians Louis Hartz and Richard Hofstadter. Somewhat more than scholars such as these, however, Erikson addressed differences and conflicts among Americans. He found the success ethic most deeply implanted among "the stray men on the expanding frontier" who represented "the image of the man without roots, the motherless man, the womanless man." Erikson also commented on the effects of racial discrimination on African-Americans, especially children. Some embraced racial repudiation, "a whiter identity," and an "Anglo-Saxon ideal." But because discrimination left them "less Americanized," they escaped much of the puritanical "Mom" and were "often privileged in the enjoyment of a more sensual early childhood." The white children who made life difficult for African-Americans were "not really intolerant" but suffered from a "restricted vision" that caused "vague discomfort" in the presence of nonwhites. The white-black clash was therefore serious but hardly insurmountable. Erikson also discussed the children of immigrants, especially girls, who "frantically tried to emulate [American] standards of conduct which they had not learned as small children." As "the first real Americans in their family, [they] become their parents' cultural parents." In a sense, this first-generation American child, who introduced American customs to his parents, was his "own parent and master." The Homburger family gathering in 1938 comes to mind, when, according to family lore, Kai proposed changing the family name to Erikson.[57]

Erik provided a modestly positive appraisal of modern American culture. He continued to be impressed by his adopted homeland. Unlike several other European intellectuals in America, he was determined to take it on its own exciting terms rather than on European terms. So while he was critical of racial discrimination, rigid "Mom" and "Dad" dichotomies, the primacy of constant motion over reflection, and material self-seeking, he was receptive to the openness and choices in society and perhaps even the spirit of compromise in family life, church, and government. Just as *Childhood and Society* was about to be published, Erikson happened to be writing up a summary of Kenneth, a recent University of California graduate whom he had interviewed. From his perspective as an immigrant, Erikson commented on Kenneth's qualities that were "essentially American virtues":

> He is reticent in his self-expression, but honest in what he says; he is strong and essentially aggressive, but fair and protective; he is independent in his thoughts and feelings but cautious and (on the whole) polite . . . ; he is self-confident, but modest and eager to perfect himself . . . he mistrusts women, but is not intimidated by them.[58]

Erikson's profile of Kenneth and the American personality of the mid–twentieth century bears similarities to one provided by Alexis de Tocqueville more than a century earlier. In *Democracy in America,* a much cited account of the United States of the 1830s, Tocqueville had been impressed with the openness, the opportunity, and the choices available to many citizens, along with the republican participation in self-government. More than Erikson, he stressed the materialist, self-seeking spirit—how the American craved desperately to garner more wealth and status than his neighbor even as he craved social affiliations. Tocqueville had noted the moralism of "Mom" but was not as apprehensive about it as Erikson. He did, however, presage Erikson's worries about "Dad's" long and lonely pursuit of self-interest, especially "Dad" the frontiersman.

In the course of the 1940s, American and European intellectuals rediscovered *Democracy in America* and Tocqueville's other writings. Many tended to cite aspects of the French traveler's thoughts as a litmus test of sorts to validate their own observations. They tended to quote Tocqueville's critique of American individualism and the American pressure to conform, yet they did not underscore his praise for social affiliation and participational self-government. Erikson almost certainly came across these references to Tocqueville at conferences and in discussions, but there is no evidence that he read even segments of *Democracy in America* before completing his "Reflections on the American Identity" chapter. To be sure, Erikson cited Vernon Parrington's classic *Main Currents in American Thought* trilogy. It is, however, doubtful that Parrington's hasty and infrequent references to Tocqueville on the ambitious frontiersman and the nature of American democracy provided Erikson with much insight into *Democracy in America.*

Consequently, it is eerie how several of Erikson's descriptions of American tendencies toward extreme individualism would have fit so well, in phrasing and meaning, within Tocqueville's account. Erikson's description of the American quest for status (allowing for twentieth-century terms like *escalator*) parallels Tocqueville's characterization of the hard-driving "nervous American" who sought incessantly to stay socially positioned a bit above his neighbors: "Status expresses a different relativity in a more mobile society: it resembles an escalator more than a platform; it is a vehicle, rather than a goal." Tocqueville emphasized that the American man on the make, while outwardly friendly and thriving on affiliation, had to restrain communication with his neighbor for fear of divulging information that could be advantageous in the competitive chase. Similarly, Erikson wrote that despite their "jovial friendliness," too many Americans "seem to lack a certain ego tonus and a certain mutuality in social intercourse." Tocqueville lauded the civic virtue promoted by voluntary associations, characterizing the American propensity to join them as a counterpoint to the lonely quest for profits. Because voluntary associations represented a dispersal of power through diverse interest groups, Tocqueville claimed that they checked the dangers of dictators and national demagogues while enhancing republican participational self-government. Erikson, too, wrote of the diversity of American "interest groups," including "the father's occupational group, the mother's club, the adolescent's clique," and similar entities among farmers, laborers, and other constituencies. The dispersal of power among such a wide array of associations and interests sometimes made it difficult for "positive legislation" to be enacted in the republic, Erikson concluded. Yet it "not only keeps any one group from complete domination, but it also saves each group from being completely dominated."[59]

Tocqueville scholars like George Wilson Pierson, Cushing Strout, and Irving Zeitlin have documented how *Democracy in America* represented observations on America from the perspective of earth-shattering developments in Europe generally and Tocqueville's France in particular. Specifically, Tocqueville was troubled by crumbling French aristocratic traditions in the wake of the 1789 Revolution and its aftermath. Thus, he analyzed the American democratic experiment from the perspective of his fears of the European mob and of isolated individualism replacing European corporate traditions. Similarly, Erikson, the European who was born and raised in Germany, arrived at his observations on modern America partially from a European perspective—from his apprehensions over the Nazi regime captivating alienated youth, fomenting mob rule, and undermining European traditions of civility and culture upon which he had been reared. As much as Erikson tried and succeeded in observing his adopted country on its own unique terms, his viewing position was strikingly similar to Tocqueville's.[60]

Erikson did most of the writing and revising of his work on Hitler's appeal to German youth as a grateful American citizen who had lent his services to the United States war effort. In 1942, for example, he prepared an analysis of an important speech by Hitler for the Committee on National Morale. The analysis maintained that "a sweeping synthesis of America's mechanical genius, industrial spirit, and traditional personality traits (as historically based on the hatred of tyrants, the spirit of the advancing frontier, the impetus of the ranger, etc.)" was inherent in America's planned air assault on Germany. The assault "will impress the Germans" and counter Hitler's imagery of blitz warfare. When preparing an outline for *Childhood and Society* in 1948, Erik indicated that he would have chapters on America and Germany so as "to juxtapose the American Identity" with one of its "greatest opposites in recent history." When "the sons and daughters of all nations became Americans," they placed their specific old-world perspectives within the more inclusive "super identity [forged] out of all the identities imported by its constituent immigrants." In contrast, Nazi German identity obliterated specificity and difference through "an exalted existence in an unlimited spiritual *Lebensraum*."[61]

It is insufficient to attribute Erikson's and Tocqueville's overlapping appraisals of America entirely to the European backgrounds against which they wrote. After all, the French Revolution and its aftermath contrasted markedly in essentials (e.g., its moment in history, its setting, and the culture that sustained it) with Hitler's Nazi "revolution." Yet as the young Berkeley sociologist and historian Robert Nisbet recalled from his own vantage point on the same campus as Erikson during the late 1930s and early 1940s, both the French Revolution and the Nazi "revolution" seemed to involve the complicity of the masses in the rise of despotism—dictatorial "centralized, omnicompetent political power." From discussion of sources like *Democracy in America,* Nisbet remembered how many in his generation of European and American intellectuals gained greater insight into the "capture of democratic assemblies, the flattery of the masses, and military might fused with large-scale governmental paternalism"—all evident in "Nazi despotism" and its Soviet and Italian Fascist counterparts. Erikson had been part of those discussions and, though he probably had not read *Democracy in America,* he was ready for an explanation similar to Tocqueville's for the dangerous modern mass movements of the day.[62]

Whereas the America that hosted Tocqueville in the 1830s was overwhelmingly rural and agricultural, the United States of the 1940s was an urban industrial society of standardized mass production. Tocqueville was primarily disturbed by two factors threatening a sense of civic virtue: the conformity pressures of the central government and its bureaucracy, and a "tyranny of the majority" that constricted individual choices. By contrast, Erikson was upset over the pressures on Americans to emulate the efficiency and uniformity of the industrial machine.

This troublesome aspect of modern America originated with the late-nineteenth-century grandfathers of some of Erikson's patients—perhaps the blacksmith or the railroad tycoon—who "invented bigger and better machinery like gigantic playthings which were not expected to challenge the social values of the men who made them." The standardized, overadjusting, superefficiency of the machine gained increasing hegemony in modern America. A class of "Bosses" emerged (managers of the expanding national corporate economy) who "[ran] themselves like machinery" and insisted that their employees emulate the ways of the machine as well. These "Bosses" made efficient mechanical " 'functioning' itself a value above all other values" and this represented "a danger to national health." The "machine ideal of 'functioning without friction' invaded the democratic milieu," Erikson remarked. It was detectable in the way "Mom" raised her children. Erikson mocked "early bowel training and other arrangements invented to condition the child in advance of his ability to regulate himself" as a regrettable emulation of machine values. It was among the tendencies of American mothers toward "standardizing and overadjusting children." This upbringing was not restoring an individualist tradition but yielding "a mass-produced mask of individuality." If these standardized values persisted, Erikson warned, they could eradicate some of America's most endearing qualities—tolerance, affection between children and adults, and plentiful individual choices and opportunities.[63]

In a matter of time, Erikson came to consider "Bosses" and their "machines" as the primary threats to modern American culture. Indeed, his description of the emerging "machine society" with its precise, sustained productive efficiencies called to mind his description of the image of blitz warfare upon which Nazism had been psychologically predicated—precise, efficient, synchronized coordination of soldiers and machines. To be sure, Frankfurt School figures like Erich Fromm, Theodor Adorno, Herbert Marcuse, and Max Horkheimer offered broad-ranging cross-national critiques that were congruent with Erikson's when they addressed the human destructiveness of bureaucratically managed and mechanized technologies. But they did not do so with Erikson's comfort in salient aspects of American culture, with his graphic language, or with his ability to draw comparisons to the concrete everyday world of children and adolescents. Nor did any Frankfurt School intellectual juxtapose so vividly American "machine"-driven values against the values of the first Americans.

SIOUX AND YUROK: THE FIRST AMERICANS

In his outline for *Childhood and Society,* Erikson planned to discuss Native Americans (Sioux and Yurok) not only early in the book but also later as a preface to his chapter on modern American culture. Titled "The Melancholy Tribe," this prefatory essay somewhat duplicated a discussion that he planned of the Sioux. The essay was to focus on how government agents, representing the values of modern culture, provided older Sioux children with an education that contradicted traditional Sioux teachings, values, and rituals of identity. The Sioux children became disoriented and apathetic because federal Indian agents had "prejudged" them in a way that failed to sustain Sioux identity. The agents might have been better served to learn what values enabled the Sioux tribes of old to achieve a sense of wholeness and integration. Had they learned this lesson and appreciated Sioux customs and values vibrant in an earlier America, Erikson indicated, the Indian agents might have provided a contemporary American society in disarray with an important perspective.[64]

Erikson explained in the outline that he would be basing his material on the Sioux and the Yurok upon at least two very long manuscripts he had already published. "Observations on Sioux Education," fifty-five printed pages, appeared in the 1939 *Journal of Psychology*. The size of a small book, "Observations on the Yurok: Childhood and World Image" came out in the University of California's prestigious *Publications in American Archaeology and Ethnology* in 1943. These two essays were subsequently condensed and summarized as a thirty-one-page article in *The Psychoanalytic Study of the Child* in 1945 and a modest chapter three years later in the Clyde Kluckhohn and Henry Murray anthology *Personality in Nature, Society, and Culture*. For *Childhood and Society*, they were expanded modestly to consume two chapters. Yet these final essays lacked the supporting detail, clarity, precision, and immediacy of the original publications. Yale's Mark May had warned that the original essays ran the risk of being bypassed by readers because they were too long for articles and too short for books. Whether in expanded or condensed versions, the Sioux and Yurok essays did not review prior studies of "primitive" peoples or indicate how Erikson's work updated that research. Rather, he characterized his essays as products of his "clinical experience" in the field, for he had listened to American aboriginals describe what their societies once had been—"mature human living, often of a homogeneity and simple integrity which we at times might well envy." Their descriptions revealed a simpler and, in many ways, a healthier America than the modern counterpart analyzed in "Reflections on the American Identity." From this perspective, Erikson was justified in placing the Sioux and Yurok essays in one section of *Childhood and Society* (Part Two) and the chapters on modern American and German identities in another (Part Four).[65]

Like many Europeans (especially Germans), Erikson had long been fascinated by the Indians of North America. At the Hietzing School in Vienna, he had encouraged his students to learn about Native Americans. He was fascinated by Ruth Benedict's pioneering 1928 article "Psychological Types in the Culture of the Southwest" (a precursor to *Patterns of Culture*), which showed how the visual configurations constructed by Indians in their daily lives suggested rich convergence between their psychologies and their cultures. Consequently, when his friend anthropologist Scudder Mekeel invited him to Oglala Sioux country on the Pine Ridge reservation, he jumped at the opportunity. After moving to Berkeley, Erikson established a good rapport with University of California anthropologist Alfred Kroeber, a specialist on Yurok settlements along the Klamath River in northern California. Kroeber had been a practicing psychoanalyst and had applied psychoanalytic theory to his fieldwork, if in more measured fashion than Mekeel. Unfortunately, when Kroeber took Erikson along for four weeks of fieldwork with the

Yurok, the tribe was engaged in a land dispute with the federal government and did not allow them free access to their villages. Consequently, Erikson was restricted to discussions with a few of Kroeber's contacts.[66]

Erikson was not the first analyst involved in such a collaboration with cultural anthropologists. Abram Kardiner, Theodor Reik, and Géza Róheim preceded him, while Margaret Mead encouraged neo-Freudians like Karen Horney and Erich Fromm to study Native American "temperament." What made Erikson's visits to the Sioux and the Yurok special was that they did much to convert him into a lifelong student of comparative and historically grounded culture studies. He discovered that the Sioux "roamed the plains and cultivated spatial concepts of centrifugal mobility" unlike the Yurok, who "limited themselves within arbitrary borders" and clung to "an extreme localization" of meaning. But however fundamental the cultural dissimilarities between Sioux and Yurok, both represented values fundamentally different from the white Americans who expropriated most of their natural resources in the march of civilization. As Erikson came increasingly to be a student of comparative culture, he found that he could not support the assumption that civilization advanced as industrialization and the modern secular nation-state progressed. Adorno, Arendt, and Nisbet had arrived at similar conclusions, but Erikson was not conversant with their work. He became a critic of modernity, perhaps what we now might call a postcolonial critic, by reflecting on the evolution from the first Americans. As he compared them to those who dominated mid-twentieth-century American culture, both modern values and the progress of European and American empires became problematic.[67]

Sioux and Yurok cultures endured for so long, Erikson concluded, because they had an "elastic" integrative tradition that drew together "self and body and self and kin," body functions and fantasies. In a "strictly institutionalized way," this "elastic tradition" arranged the Native American's social needs, "diverting dangerous instinctual tendencies toward outer enemies, and always allowing him to project the source of possible guilt into the supernatural." Self and society blended into each other and extended into God and nature. The tools Sioux and Yurok used were simply "extensions of the human body" in this integrative life where childhood and adult culture, body and environment, all ran along a continuum. Hence, the Sioux identified themselves, their livelihood, and their culture "with the buffalo," the Yurok "with the [Klamath] river and the salmon" in the river.[68]

In contrast to this elastic, integrative Native American world, revolving around the buffalo and the river, Erikson took issue with modern Americans and Europeans who emulated the industrial machine and its segmentation. Their individual selves and their society had come to consist of distinct, separate, specialized components that did not cohere in a viable natural identity. "Machines," Erikson argued, "far from remaining an extension of the body, desire whole classes to be extensions of machinery; magic becomes secondary . . . ; and childhood, in some classes, becomes a separate segment of life with its own folklore." Indeed, modern Western child-rearing techniques generally seemed to harbor "an unconscious magic attempt to master machines by becoming more like them." This explained the "scientific accounts of children as beasts to be tamed or machines to be measured and kept in order." The close Sioux and Yurok bonds between parents and children and between members of all generations were replaced by age-segmented bifurcation where "we create isolated places" for young and old. There was a "deep estrangement between body and self and between self and parents which characterizes much of the white man's most civilized and most neurotic accomplishments." The machine and the "Bosses" who ran and emulated it created a "hierarchy of centralized bureaucracy" that subverted Jefferson's "young American democracy" after not many decades and contradicted the Native American "spirit of a hunter democracy." In this perversion of the democratic process, facilitated by "the cheerful ruthlessness of the free-enterprise system," Erikson noted that the "Indian problem loses its ancient patina and joins the problems of colored minorities, rural and urban, which are waiting for busy democratic processes to find time for them."[69]

Erikson's juxtaposition of the "elastic" and integrative quality of Sioux and Yurok life with the segmented, "machine"-driven, "unwhole" ways of modern Western culture (contemporary America in particular) represented a critical spirit toward his adopted country that he had not displayed when he first arrived. By the 1940s, he had modified his vision of a cheerful American society welcoming immigrants, rallying under the bold leadership of FDR against global economic depression and the Nazi menace. He acknowledged that he had become more sophisticated. Modern America of machinelike "Bosses" and moralistic "Moms" appeared to endanger "the remnants of tribal synthesis" that promoted integrative and positive identities "for the sake of an unknown future standard for all." To be sure, Erikson acknowledged that when the Sioux characterized a world of the plains and the buffalo as *Strong*, and the Yurok characterized a world that centered on the river as *Clean*, both were engaging in a sort of superior exclusivity (what he later called pseudospeciation). He still admired the heritage of Roosevelt's America that had welcomed him; its legacy was psychologically expansive, bringing peoples from diverse "regions, nations, continents, and classes" into a new synthesis of "more inclusive identities." However, the modern "civilization" exemplified by two military superpowers, the United States and Germany, stopped far short of universal identity and was "consolidating human gains" at a midway point between exclusivity and universality, "with race or class replacing tribe, and world domination or world revolution replacing universality." Needless to say, Hitler's Germany represented a distinctly more dangerous version of modernity than did America, where a revitalized "democratic and national education" might still lead to "a new and more universal cultural homogeneity." Indeed, Erikson still retained faith in the values and customs of his adopted country. But he felt that the United States that was at war with Germany had no claim of superiority over older Sioux and Yurok traditions.[70]

If he had offered a critical discussion of the American bombing of Hiroshima in 1945, Erikson would have been able to develop the theme of dubious progress in a more compelling way. Indeed, within *Childhood and Society,* he alluded indirectly to the federal government hiring physicists "to perfect work of the highest theoretical and most far-reaching practical significance." These physicists had developed "an inconceivable weapon." Erikson's implication was that the development of the atomic bomb was predictable in a society whose citizens lived not "in an integrated system of superstitions" but in one where "superstitions are fragmentary and individualized regressions." In the first of his 1972 Godkin Lectures at Harvard, Erikson would speak publicly of how "the American Way of Death, which means the passionless use of overkill against other species, had reached its climax in Hiroshima." He was moving toward such an appraisal of contemporary America in his first book, and his cross-cultural perspective helps explain why.[71]

What inclusion of the Sioux and the Yurok in this emerging cross-cultural perspective allows us to understand is how Erikson's "Reflections on the American Identity" essay in *Childhood and Society* moved beyond a comparison of America and Nazi Germany. Against the German example, America was an exciting society of multiple "polarities" and choices. But against the reference of "Two American Indian Tribes," America appeared to be shaped by the dangerously fragmented assembly lines of industrial machines and their standardized parts. Had Erikson organized his chapters more clearly, presenting both "The Legend of Hitler's Childhood" and the Sioux and Yurok essays as conflicting perspectives against which to evaluate modern America, readers would have grasped more fully the profundity of his evaluation and a basis for his sober appraisal of American culture. Unfortunately, he followed the Sioux and Yurok chapters with eighty-four pages on other matters before inserting his chapter on modern America, followed by the chapter on Germany. This illustrated the conceptually unstructured quality of *Childhood and Society.* Erikson often wrote brilliantly. Yet even after a decade and a half in the United States, and after considerable effort to adhere to a cohesive textual organization, he seemed to lack the ability to shape his material in a clear and logical manner. Instead of anchoring his book with a core theme, he provided a rich but rambling mosaic—perhaps a forerunner of what we have come to call postmodernism.

Nevertheless, his material on the Sioux and the Yurok should not be discounted. Fanny, an old Yurok shaman, was such a compelling figure that Erikson devoted at least one-fifth of his long 1943 essay "Observations on the Yurok" to her. That, plus a remarkable letter Erikson wrote to Alfred Kroeber from Yurok settlements along the Klamath River, suggests that Fanny had a marked effect upon him. When she was a teenager, Fanny suffered a personal tragedy. Her brother had killed her father and was, in turn, slain by a tribal elder, leaving her "in a bad state and only slowly did the pressure of communal consent make a superhuman affair of a typical hysterical experience of an adolescent girl." Fanny's mother sought to find meaning in this family tragedy, and urged Fanny to become a doctor. Perhaps some good was to be salvaged from the experience. This may have paralleled Theodor Homburger's hope that his stepson, distressed because he did not know who had fathered him, would take up medicine. In time, Fanny became a venerable shaman who "extracts 'pains' from others and gets paid" while Erikson became a psychoanalyst who was paid to "extract" distress from others. Whereas Fanny's therapeutic technique involved sucking out and swallowing the sickness within her patient, Erikson helped his patients to articulate their problems. Fanny determined what to "extract" or push out from an array of debilitating elements within her patients. She made this determination by taking "a certain inventory of sins" and correlating them with "a given number of explanations to a certain disturbance," much as modern psychiatry and psychoanalysis did. Like Erikson, Fanny realized that the patient's confession facilitated the curative process—"to confess is profitable for anybody's inner peace." He and Fanny soon "felt like colleagues," and "this feeling was based on some joint sense of the historical relativity of all psychotherapy."[72]

The similarity in their backgrounds and in their curative techniques was not the only reason for their relationship. Fanny had a charismatic quality. "There is a radiant friendliness and warmth in this very old woman," Erikson noted, and a wholeness: "It was easy to converse with this old Indian woman because usually she was merry and quite direct" with him. A sad experience would cause her smile to be "withdrawn behind the stone-carved pattern of her wrinkles," but this was a positive withdrawal for a short interval and not an "immovable sadness." His sketch of Fanny seemed to radiate strength and wholeness, kindness and warmth, amid "stone-carved" wrinkles and sad memories. Fanny had the force to insist on "the sign and privilege of a shaman, namely, her pipe" even though the pipe was "only used by men." But she was also firmly rooted in Yurok culture, with the sense that her own alimentary canal converged inextricably with the salmon-filled Klamath River that sustained the Yurok's economy and their belief system. Erikson did not feel this same connectedness to his own society and culture, and despite his collegial rapport with Fanny, "I could not claim to be her professional equal." Indeed, he felt that he had not transformed the crisis of his youth into a source of inner strength the way she almost certainly had. One day, when Erikson felt uneasy interviewing Fanny alone, without Kroeber's guidance, "the old woman laughed merrily" and reminded him: "You big man now."[73]

One reason Erikson did not feel he was a "big man" was because of the criticisms of several professional colleagues. Géza Róheim, Abram Kardiner, and others grounded in psychoanalysis tended to equate Native American "idiosyncrasies" with neurotic symptoms. Several criticized Erikson for failing to realize that Sioux and Yurok parents inflicted the same traumas on their children that they themselves had experienced. Róheim argued, for example, that Fanny and the Yurok generally had an "anal character" rooted in the oral frustration of excessively rapid weaning. Jean Walker Macfarlane felt Erikson was overemphasizing the strong cultural background of the Sioux and Yurok. John Dollard found a "speculative character" to Erikson's analysis. Although anthropologist Clyde Kluckhohn and psychoanalyst Otto Fenichel were more supportive, Erikson concluded that most of his professional colleagues found fault with his appraisal of the Sioux and the Yurok.[74]

Basically, Erikson's critics were accusing him of a romantic vision of psychological integrity in early tribal life in comparison with the modern societies that followed. They also criticized him for assuming that Fanny's strong sense of identity could survive as modernity destroyed Native American economic and cultural life. The same sort of criticism had been directed toward Margaret Mead when she portrayed "primitive" societies like those in Samoa that struggled against the fragmenting, neurotic forces of "advanced civilization." What Erikson's critics did not understand was that he was not analyzing the Sioux and Yurok in isolation from other cultures. He was also examining Hitler's Germany, modern America, and the Russia of Gorky's childhood. In the course of developing this cross-cultural mosaic, he had a large stake in equating Native Americans with a premodern psychological wholeness, even as this may have lent itself to a romantically upbeat vision. This vision anchored a historical perspective in which the "primitive" past had decided advantages over the modern industrial present. Resilient people like Fanny, moreover, made Erikson hopeful that the emotionally healthy portion of a population might somehow survive amid the American "machines" and the German blitz. In fact, they might serve as models for viable psychological and social identity—a gauge of health and possibility for citizens at large.[75]

Erikson therefore relied heavily upon his perspective of the Sioux and the Yurok. With the collapse of European colonialism in the mid–twentieth century and the emergence of independence movements in Third World countries, Western imperialist historicism was besieged. Its binary opposites of metropolis and colony, center and periphery, self and other, came under attack. As this traditional imperial or Eurocentric view or mapping of the world began to be reexamined, several disorienting and decentered perspectives gained currency. These perspectives were used to confer selfhood and positive identity to the formerly "colonized." This "decolonization" of Western thought did not become a vibrant and revolutionary intellectual movement until at least 1961, when Algerian psychiatrist Frantz Fanon published *The Wretched of the Earth*. But there were important works published before Fanon's book, including several by Jean-Paul Sartre and Louis Althusser. In a sense, Erikson's *Childhood and Society* fit in among these publications, which disputed and reversed the Western imperial engagement with the "underdeveloped other." Erikson had not characterized Fanny, the Yurok shaman, to represent a colonized or vanquished "other" but as a full, vibrant, and "whole" self whose concerns and feelings were no less legitimate than those of more "advanced" Western therapists or community leaders.

YOUNG GORKY

"The Legend of Maxim Gorky's Youth," the last substantive chapter in *Childhood and Society,* completed Erikson's cultural mosaic. Even more than Hannah Arendt's treatment of Russia in *Origins of Totalitarianism,* this discussion was a "tag on" to more pressing concerns. Within a Russian context with which Erikson was relatively unfamiliar, he reworked and amplified an earlier theme. Essentially, he explained how small and relatively undifferentiated societies like the one in which young Gorky grew up were being supplanted by modern societies where "standardization, centralization, and mechanization threaten the identities which man has inherited from primitive, agrarian, feudal, and patrician cultures."[76]

Margaret Mead had enticed Erikson into this study of Russia and Gorky. Early in 1948, her Columbia University–based Research in Contemporary Culture (RCC) project expanded through funding from the Rand Corporation. Sparked by the emergence of American-Soviet tensions that produced the Cold War, the funding was to add a whole new agenda to the RCC research program: "Studies in Soviet Culture." Abbreviated to signify the

"Russian Project," it centered in Mead's offices in the Museum of Natural History. Nathan Leites, a member of Rand's scientific research staff and husband of Mead's good friend psychoanalyst Martha Wolfenstein, administered daily operations while Mead provided general direction. Mead had Leites assemble a part-time staff of nine project workers and two consultants—all scholars but generally unseasoned in Russian studies. Sula Benet, a Warsaw-trained anthropologist interested in archaeology and history, was the staff member who most resisted psychological analysis. Anthropologist Geoffrey Gorer, heavily involved in psychoanalytically informed approaches to national character, advanced ideas that would overlap decidedly with Erikson's.[77]

In March of 1948, Mead and Leites summoned Erikson from California to New York to a Russian Project screening of a Soviet propaganda film that had been released in Moscow a decade earlier by Soyuzdet Film Production, *Detstvo Gorkogo*. This movie on Gorky's childhood was initially produced by Mark Donskoi in an attempt to boost Soviet pride. The film was completed shortly after Gorky, the eminent author, had died. The New York Museum of Modern Art had acquired a copy, and the Russian Project had borrowed it. English captions inserted in the museum's version of the film were difficult to read, so a Russian translator was hired to facilitate the screening. Mead knew that Erikson enjoyed movies and documentaries. Given his artistic background, she assumed he could offer an astute analysis of the film. Erikson was deeply affected by what he saw. "What little I know has recently been crystallized around the imagery of an outdated Russian moving picture," he observed. In this first viewing, Erikson was so involved with the film imagery that at one point he insisted that a character's gesture contradicted the translator's words. He apparently saw *Detstvo Gorkogo* a second time on his own and started immediately to write an essay about it.[78]

By July of 1948, Erikson had outlined that essay as a prospective chapter in *Childhood and Society*. Six months later, he wrote to Mead that it was his "longest chapter so far." He was treating the Soviet propaganda film as a legend of Russian childhood and "a counterpart to the imagery of Hitler's childhood" as revealed in *Mein Kampf*. By the spring of 1949, Erikson had read a draft of the chapter to the Russian Project staff at the Museum of Natural History and discussed it with colleagues at the San Francisco Psychoanalytic Institute. As the essay took shape, Erikson supplemented his impressions from the film by reading Gorky's autobiographical trilogy, Gorer's 1949 article on Russian psychological characteristics that appeared in the *American Slavic and Eastern European Review*, and a draft of *The People of Great Russia*, which Gorer was co-authoring with John Rickman. He had also managed to read Gorky's *Reminiscences of Tolstoy*, and a few lines of

Bukharin's confessional from a transcript of the famous Moscow purge trials. His research was therefore insubstantial.[79]

Erikson's narrative followed the movie from Alyosha's (young Gorky's) arrival as a child at his grandparents' home in a poor and isolated central Russian city on the Volga River to the point when Alyosha, as a young man, leaves to become an intellectual. The narrative traced Alyosha's slow turning away from the land and traditional peasant society toward notions of change, going places, and thinking systematically. But whereas film producer Mark Donskoi characterized this process as the beginning of a glorious Russian historical evolution from peasant ignorance to urbanization, industrialization, and the Bolshevik dictatorship of the proletariat, Erikson's historic interpretation was more subtle.

In the opening scenes of the film, young Alyosha, fatherless, was being taken by his mother to be raised by her parents and their larger Kashirin family. Erikson observed that the first powerful image in the movie was of Grandmother Kashirin. A large, strong woman, she "symbolized the primitive trust of the people, their ability to survive and persist," and their capacity to "endure." Further, she represented "the peace of mind of the original [central Russia] stockade, the primitive *mir* which had found some organization close to the earth." Erikson felt that this grandmother, who followed the ancient Russian folkways, was not unlike the early Native Americans. Both peoples clung to "the methods of ancient tools and of magical influence over the forces of nature" and both sought "magic" as the way to allay "evil forces." Much as young Alyosha felt protected and secure under his grandmother's vast skirts, Erikson noted that she stood for "Paradise lost": "To become or remain a party to the grandmother's strength would mean surrender to timelessness, and eternal bondage to the faith of primitive economy."[80]

Erikson characterized the second powerful image of *Detstvo Gorkogo* in the thick and readily combustible wood that characterized the housing, energy, and personality of the central Russian city where the Kashirin family resided. "Wood provided the material for the stockades as well as for the overheated ovens through the long winters," he asserted. "It was the basic material for tools." The wood caught fire easily, and when it did whole villages and surrounding forests perished. Above all, Erikson noted how the menfolk in the Kashirin clan and others in their village "are stout, square, heavy, awkward, and dull, like logs of wood; but they are highly combustible." This moody, shortsighted, wooden quality, alternating between dull sentimentality and outbursts of crude brutality, described Russian peasant culture generally, and that required explanation.[81]

Erikson found an explanation by expanding his wood imagery to include the "swaddled 'log of wood' "—the severely restricted Russian infant who could be carried about conveniently like a small wooden log. Gorer had emphasized that tight swaddling, which constricted the movements of the infant and was followed by sudden unswaddling, offered the key to Russian personality. The Russian alternated between complete restriction of his internal fear and rage on the one hand, and complete freedom, with wild bursts of pleasure and satisfaction and brutality, on the other. Erikson insisted that Gorer's swaddling hypothesis was important but reductionist.

Instead, Erikson placed Gorer's hypothesis within "the totality of a culture's configuration," pointing out that the Russian cultural configuration included "long periods of tight swaddling alternating with moments of rich interchange of joyous affection at the time of unswaddling." This constriction and release corresponded to a "compact social life" with a harsh climate in the isolated stockade of the central plains and "its periodic liberation after the spring thaws." Swaddling and unswaddling also corresponded to the "wooden endurance and apathetic serfdom" of peasant life alternating with "periodic emotional catharsis achieved by effusive soul-baring." The peasant of the Kashirins' village was therefore both "strangely imprisoned in himself" and "forever seeking other souls." The long "imprisonment" of the constrained self and the "swaddled soul" was a storehouse for emotions and motivated the quest for kindred "souls," and this was best exemplified by the film character Lyenka. This child was immobilized; he had no use of his legs. And yet he was the "most emotionally gay of all the children." Lyenka was "the child with the greatest emotion and with the most impaired motion; the child with the most vivid imagination and the greatest dependence on others." Like a restrained and swaddled "log of wood," emotions of love and hate were periodically "combusted."[82]

Alyosha and others in his juvenile circle constructed a cart with a little metal wheel to give Lyenka "locomotor liberation." Erikson pointed to this scene to illustrate the "iron and steel" imagery of the film that chronologically followed the wood imagery. The metal wheel of Lyenka's cart was no mere extension "of and prostheses for the limbs; moving within itself, it is basic for the idea of the machine, which, man-made and man-driven, yet develops a certain autonomy as a mechanized organism." Erikson insisted that the iron-and-steel image of the machine differed drastically from wood imagery. The age of wood implied human agency and human emotionality in its cycles of withdrawal and combustibility. But the machine age of iron and steel, ushered in with the Bolsheviks, obliterated this emotionality and human agency. Although steel was forged in fire, "it is not combustible" and "to master it means to triumph over the weakness of the flesh-soul and the deadness and combustibility of the wood-mind." The Bolshevik regime under Stalin (steel) and Molotov (hammer) demanded "steel-like clarity of decision, and the machine-like formness of action." The regime insisted upon an "incorruptibility of purpose, irrespective of personal feelings" in the triumph of the proletariat. The Bolsheviks replaced the Westernized Russian intellectual elite like Alyosha (Gorky) with "a planned, meticulously trained elite of political, industrial, and military engineers who believed themselves to be the aristocracy of the historical process itself. They are our cold, our dangerous adversaries today."[83]

Erikson's narration from the primitive trust of the grandmother to the containment and combustibility of the age of wood to the Bolshevik age of iron and steel was compelling. It represented a bleak vision of the evolution of Russian history, not at all what film producer Donskoi had intended. It seemed bleaker than his American narrative from the integrated wholeness of the Sioux and Yurok to the triumph of the "Boss" and his industrial machine. And yet the Bolshevik regime was not as terrible as "the regressive freak of Nazism," which entirely bypassed family and community for the totalism of the Hitler-led juvenile gang.[84]

Erikson completed *Childhood and Society* in the prevailing climate of "red fascism"—the assumption that, as a totalitarian power, Stalin's Soviet Union was virtually indistinguishable from Hitler's Germany. Various influential politicians, scholars, and journalists were insisting that just as the United States turned back the Nazis, so the country must resist the Soviet or red variation of totalitarianism. As an architect of postwar American foreign policy, George Kennan, Erikson's old acquaintance, contributed heavily to this equation. But Russian Project staff tended to reject it as a flawed comparison of the Nazi German to the Soviet Communist and a distortion of Russian history (a position Kennan did not embrace until 1956). Erikson went further than his project colleagues, providing a glimpse of the public intellectual that he would become. He argued against the emerging Cold War anticommunism that was becoming popular in his adopted country. At the same time, he emphasized the tenuous view of a "delayed Eastern protestantism" in Russia that the Bolsheviks had not been able to obliterate. This "protestantism" offered significant cultural ties between Russians and Americans that might facilitate viable co-existence.[85]

For Erikson, Alyosha, the central character in *Detstvo Gorkogo*, represented "delayed Eastern protestantism." As the son of Maxim Pyeshkov, Alyosha grew up feeling displaced within his mother's family. Alyosha's mind, senses, and experiences extended beyond Grandmother Kashirin and even beyond the "wood" society of the village. His very development illustrated "the way stations of an emergent new Russian frame of mind, a Russian individualism." This was not to be equated with Western individualist–Protestant tradition, Erikson cautioned: "No Luther, no Calvin has shown him [Alyosha] new recesses of the mind; and no [American] founding fathers and pioneers have opened up uncharted continents where he might overcome his inner and his outer serfdom." As Alyosha grew up and thought of moving to the large city in the distance, he had to develop "by himself" without these Western precedents: "He must learn to protest, and to develop—in the very protest, and to develop—in the very widest sense— a 'protestant' morality." Erikson observed that "the temptations Alyosha turns away from" as an Eastern protestant "are not dissimilar to those which the early Protestants felt emanated from Rome . . . the mystic immersion in the mass; the 'clinical' view of life as a childhood disease of the soul; and most of all, the permission 'to hide behind another's conscience.' " Like Protestants of the West who had turned from Rome, emerging Russian protestants such as Alyosha now demanded "autonomy, together with unity; and identity together with the fruits of industry."[86]

To mend the fences of time and place and encourage the Russian protestant Alyoshas, Erikson urged Americans to avoid luring them with "our new and shiny goods (so enticingly wrapped in promises of freedom)." They did not want Americans to grant them freedom from Bolshevik rule. Like Americans, they sought "the opportunity to grasp it, as equals." "We" Americans "must succeed in convincing the Alyoshas," Erikson proclaimed, that "their protestantism is ours and ours, theirs." Here Erikson was associating himself ("we") with the country of his citizenship. In the vaguest terms, he was calling on other Americans to turn back from an emerging Cold War and somehow to build bridges with the Russians over the protestant values of individualism and self-help that he felt the two nations had in common.[87]

With "The Legend of Maxim Gorky's Youth," the cultural mosaic of *Childhood and Society* was finished. Erikson connected directly and personally with Germany and America, two of the three societies evaluated in his mosaic. But he had never traveled to or read much about Russia, and he did not do much to enhance his knowledge as he prepared the Gorky essay. Rather, his interest in Russia was largely explained by his strong personal identification with Alyosha—young Maxim Gorky. Historically, Erikson's insistence that "their protestantism is ours and ours, theirs" was difficult to sustain, for the Protestantism of Luther and the West had never been a decided presence in Russia. Behind this assertion, Erikson was straining to establish a personal connection to Alyosha for the conclusion of his first book.

Similarities between Alyosha's childhood and youth and Erikson's were striking, and Erikson discussed all of them. There was the crucial matter of parentage. Alyosha's father, Maxim Pyeshkov, left the home of his in-laws, the Kashirins, and "died in a faraway region." Erikson, too, felt that his father had left Copenhagen for another "faraway region"—probably America. Alyosha's mother, Varvara, felt disgraced by her spouse's abandonment, much as Erikson's mother, pregnant with Erik, felt disgraced when she was abandoned. Varvara "finds refuge in a marriage to a petty official and moves to the city," much as Karla Abrahamsen found refuge in marriage to a respectable pediatrician, who took her to his city and adopted her son. Erikson described Varvara's decision to leave her son with the Kashirins as a "betrayal." Although Karla stayed with him, Erik thought of her marriage to Theodor Homburger as a "betrayal" of the special mother-son bond that had formed during his first three years. Alyosha felt like "a displaced Pyeshkov among the Kashirins" much as Erik felt displaced in the Homburger household, especially after his half sisters were born. Consequently, Alyosha "finds friends outside of the family" in young boys of the village like Gypsy and Lyenka while Erik became close friends with Peter Blos and Oscar Stonorov. As Alyosha moved toward adulthood, he left for the large and exciting city in the distance while Erik left on his *Wanderschaft* and then for Vienna.[88]

The similarities between the two extended further. As Alyosha grew up, Erikson wrote, he "participates rarely, but he observes eagerly, and mostly he acts by refraining from participation." Indeed, Alyosha lived and thrived through others. He "literally stalked people and situations to see [what] he could wrest from life as a homeless wanderer." Young Erik never ceased stalking his real father. Erik's many woodcuts registered sensitive observation of others, not active participation in life. His 1923–24 notebook had the tone of an observer and commentator but not of a doer in life's affairs. In Vienna, to be sure, he became a successful teacher and child analyst, a father and a husband. But despite these important new roles of self-identification, he never ceased to "stalk people and situations," to find out and "fill" much of himself through other people and circumstances. Like Alyosha, he did so as a wanderer. After Erik's prolonged *Wanderschaft*, he emigrated from Germany to Austria to Denmark to the United States. Once settled in America, he continued to move regularly—from Boston to New Haven to Berkeley and then to other places after *Childhood and Society* was published. In the end, Gorky, the writer, overcame Alyosha's troubled childhood and his existence on the sidelines of life through literary creativity. Erikson admonished that this creativity through authorship was "tangential to our discussion," but it was very much to the point as he completed his first book. As part of his new identity as a writer, Alyosha created his own name—Maxim, the first name of his missing father; Gorky meant "bitter." Similarly, Erik Salomonsen became Erik Homburger and then renamed himself Erik Erikson—Erik the son became his own father, the self-made man—on becoming an American citizen. This was a problematic and perhaps even a "bitter" resolution of the paternity issue.[89]

Erikson's close identification with Alyosha, the youngster, and with Gorky, the author, was revealing. Alyosha represented the best hope of an emerging Russian "protestantism" that might turn back the steel machine society of the Bolsheviks and forge bonds with an American Protestantism that was energized through "polarities" of choice. And yet Erikson judged Gorky, the creative "protestant" author, to be somewhat infected by Bolshevik society. After all, Gorky and others of Russia's "westernized intellectual elite" had not warned their citizenry of the real dangers of the Bolsheviks' "trained elite of political, industrial, and military engineers" who sought to rationalize "the historic process itself" to promote the values of "steel." Consequently, Erikson cautioned his readers that "there is no happy ending in this movie: no love story, no success story." Gorky did not sufficiently embrace the values of "the son of a mystic and earthy past" so as to become a viable alternative to the Bolsheviks—a humane "founding father of an industrial future." Alyosha's decision as a writer to call himself Gorky ("bitter") was a recognition of this failure.[90]

Erikson felt that there were still creative Russian "protestants" around after Gorky's death, and he held out a rather bizarre longing more than a realistic expectation that they might eventually challenge the Bolsheviks. If they did, they could co-exist with the "rebel sons" of the American Founding Fathers as joint heirs of "a [protestant] reformation, a renaissance, the emergence of nationalism and of revolutionary individualism."[91]

With these hopeful words, Erikson appeared to be laying the groundwork for his next book on the Protestant revolutionary Martin Luther more than he was discussing the possibilities within American-Soviet relations. And yet he believed that hope, however fanciful, was necessary to sustain the human condition, for the alternatives were bleak. Just as Bolshevik machine values could continue in Russia, the "Boss" and the industrial machine may have had too deep a hold on America to be overturned. The Cold War between these superpowers could persist—hardly a liberating alternative to the delinquencies of Hitler's Germany. Under that eventuality, only the Sioux and Yurok would stand for promise and hope in Erikson's cross-cultural mosaic.

CHAPTER FIVE

Lives in Cycle:
Childhood and Society II

W hile *Childhood and Society* included essays in cross-cultural exploration, it was also a book about Erik Erikson's clinical experiences. Some experiences involved work with participants in Jean Walker Macfarlane's longitudinal study at the Institute of Child Welfare. Some concerned patients at the Mt. Zion Rehabilitation Clinic, and a few involved his private patients. Three especially important clinical experiences provided the basis for special essays in *Childhood and Society*, and they were related to the human life cycle, the most striking chapter in the book. Clinical essays and work on the life cycle became intertwined with a personal crisis that allowed Erikson to connect the two conceptually.

PSYCHOANALYTIC THEORY AND CLINICAL ENDEAVOR

To prepare his clinical and life cycle material for *Childhood and Society*, Erikson felt obligated to link his clinical observations and other experiences to the theoretical perspective he had mastered in Vienna. That is, he needed to relate his own thoughts and observations to those of Sigmund Freud. In particular, Erikson was concerned that he had not found in his American patients the fundamental repressions and inhibitions of the superego that Freud had emphasized in his patients. He agreed with Freud that the superego preserved the traditions of a culture, but he insisted on emphasizing the precise nature of those traditions and the elements holding them together. Increasingly, his focus was on a horizontal plane; he addressed matters outside the patient that were on his or her cultural, historic, and geographic horizon. Freud, on the other hand, had shaped psychoanalysis to focus on psychopathology, and excavated (vertically) beneath defensive layers of the patient's inner psyche for the underlying pathologies. Not fully conscious of the contrast between his own horizontality and Freud's verticality, Erikson pointed out that most of the patients with whom he worked were more "normal" than Freud's, so they had stronger egos. Consequently, their struggles between inner drives and superego constraints were less onerous than conflicts within Freud's central European patients. Thus, his clinical observations necessarily differed from Freud's.[1]

Erikson also noted historical differences to justify the distinctions between his clinical perspective and Freud's. He characterized Freud's focus on the clash between drives and superego constraints as a replication of nineteenth-century physics—the mechanistic transformation of energy. The two world wars and vast technological innovations had moved scientists, clinicians, and patients away from that view. More succinctly: "The patient of today suffers most under the problem of what he should believe—or, indeed, might—be or become; while the patient of early psychoanalysis suffered most under inhibitions which prevented him from being what and who he thought he was." In other words, Erikson's patients typically suffered from the burden of "identity diffusion in the sense that people do not know what they stand for" or, most fundamentally, "Who am I?" In contrast, Freud's patients had been more troubled by superego constraints—from repressed (primarily sexual) impulses.[2]

Emphasizing that the perspectives emerging in his first book were congruent with Freud's, Erikson avoided citing work by psychoanalytic dissidents, including his Jungian friend Joseph Wheelwright. Erich Fromm, whose *Escape from Freedom* influenced Erikson, had offered the term *identity* within the context of horizontality—the external social forces and the culture-bound ethical traditions central to human personality development. Yet Erikson never acknowledged Fromm's influence. There were paragraphs in *Childhood and Society* in which Erikson stressed the importance of mother-child separation at weaning as a crucial moment in the emergence of the infant's sense of anxiety. Here, he was influenced decidedly by object relations theorists Melanie Klein and Michael Balint. Neither was acknowledged in the attempt to stay aligned with psychoanalytic orthodoxy.[3]

Something further was at work. As Erikson wrote the diverse clinical essays that appeared in *Childhood and Society,* he sensed that his preoccupation with how children played was moving him toward an unusual perspective. Play was far more than a particular to be considered by the analyst in order to compensate for children's verbal shortcomings. There was in fact a unique "language of play with its various cultural and age dialects." Play represented a special "sign level" that captured life's essential business. It was no mere "intermission or a vacation from urgent life." The concept of "repression" was inappropriate to the "subverbal experiences" of the play world. The conceptual baggage and the techniques that analysts customarily used with adults were not appropriate for children. The child should not be forced "to adapt himself to the verbalized and classified world." The wise analyst "enters the child's world as a polite guest and studies play as a most serious occupation."[4]

Freud characterized the study of dreams as "the royal road to the adult's unconscious." Erikson now insisted that play was the best way to understand "the infantile ego." Like adult dreams, children's play arrangements had a special "spatial grammar" and horizontality that "lies less than do words." Moreover, because play brought "into synchronization the bodily and the social processes of which one is a party" while augmenting the sense of selfhood, it was no stranger to the adult. Indeed, adults needed to play.[5]

Playfulness had become an integral part of Erikson's personality. His humorous observations and gestures and his witty jokes had become characteristic during his middle years. He also doodled extensively and dressed more casually. As his habits of playfulness and informality increased, Erikson emphasized that adults had to find ways to retain playfulness in their dealings with life: "I propose the theory that the child's play is the infantile form of the human ability to deal with experience by creating model situations and to master reality by experiment and planning." Like a child at play, the adult needed to project "past experiences into dimensions which seem manageable"—to construct a "model situation" to inform his actions. Erikson did not cite Freud or any other psychoanalyst as authority for this perspective; instead, he quoted poets. He cited Friedrich Schiller: "Man is perfectly human only when he plays." And William Blake: "The child's toys and the old man's reasons are the fruits of the two seasons." Erikson insisted that Blake intended to acknowledge not only the dignity of the child's play but "a latent infantility in mature reason." The child's successful play became the adult's efficacious reason; both reduced data "to a size and an order in which they seem manageable."[6]

The seriousness with which Erikson regarded children's play provided a conceptual elasticity that helped to free *Childhood and Society* from rigid psychoanalytic orthodoxies. It also enabled him to be an unusually effective clinician. Several essays in his book illustrated these intellectual and clinical strengths.

In an abbreviated outline for the book, Erikson emphasized that he would base all of his discussions of clinical cases upon "the relation of three co-existing processes": (1) the biological (the "process of *organismic* organization"); (2) the psychological (an individual's capacity for ego synthesis); (3) the "*social organization* of ego organisms in geographic-historical units." Through attentiveness to the three, the clinician made "everything his business." Erikson's clinical approach was based on breadth, concreteness, and specificity. Within *Childhood and Society,* he elaborated the cases of a five-year-old boy named Sam; a young (unnamed) marine; and Jean, a six-year-old girl. On the one hand, he treated each case as concrete, special, and unique; on the other, he felt compelled to cite each in order to enlarge his bio-psycho-social augmentation of psychoanalytic theory. Although his portraits of these young people were specific and tangible, he used them as a jumping-off point for building a model of identity within a developmental life cycle construct of his own making. Concrete relationships and observations facilitated theoretical psychological model building.[7]

Erikson presented the case of Sam as "our first 'specimen' of a human crisis." He detailed the family history of a young Jewish boy who had moved with his parents during the late 1930s into a predominantly Gentile town in northern California. His paternal grandmother had died one night while visiting his home. Initially, Sam's mother lied, reporting that his grandmother had left town while he was asleep and that the coffin he had seen was a box for her books. Early one morning a few days later, Sam awakened his parents with strange noises; he was having an epileptic attack. A second attack occurred a month later, shortly after Sam found a dead mole in the yard. A third came two months later, after Sam accidentally crushed a butterfly in his hand. Variations of these epileptic bouts persisted for two years, at which point Erikson became Sam's (third) therapist.[8]

Erikson quickly uncovered what eluded his predecessors. Playing dominoes with Sam, he had the boy build an oblong box out of the dominoes, with the dots all facing inward. Erikson remarked that it was necessary to be inside the box to see the dots "like a dead person in a coffin." Sam agreed. Next, he asked Sam if he was afraid that he might die because earlier the boy had hit him. Sam acknowledged this fear. Erikson assured the boy that he would not die simply because Sam struck out at him. Sam also feared his own death every time he had an epileptic attack.[9]

Soon, Erikson felt he understood essential factors behind Sam's epileptic bouts. There was a biological explanation—a brain irritation "of anatomic, toxic, or other origin." While acknowledging that the malady could "decrease the child's threshold for outer dangers," Erikson did not emphasize its causal role in the seizures: "Quite a number of individuals live with similar cerebral pathology without ever having a convulsion." Instead, he was more attentive to the psychological than the organic roots of Sam's outbreaks. When he felt endangered, Sam physically attacked, then asked questions that made others feel uneasy. Erikson labeled these behaviors as "counterphobic" defense mechanisms. Sam's defenses were characteristic of a fragile sense of ego identity that made it difficult for him to "anticipate inner as well as outer dangers . . . by integrating endowment and social opportunities." Yet Erikson concentrated less on Sam's flawed ego identity than on his social circumstances, his place in his neighborhood and his home—his cultural and geographic horizons. This focus represented an important break from the "inner world" vertical emphasis of Freud's Vienna. Yet despite his attention to Sam's "outer world," Erikson skimmed over the specific anxieties of Sam's mother that were rooted in her social situation. She had distanced herself from her Jewish origins, and this produced distress. Her desire for acceptance in a new Gentile community had provoked tensions with her husband and her mother-in-law. Her inner tumult must have had a very important effect upon the bonds of trust and mutuality between mother and child.[10]

Erikson's inattention to these sources of Sam's mother's anxieties is strange considering his perspectives on Sam's social world. He traced the boy's roots, historically, from the Jewish ghettos and pogroms of Europe. In the face of Gentile hostility and violence, Sam's ancestors had assumed "agitated attitudes" of defense and had clustered together defensively. Sam assumed these characteristics in his impulsive and pugnacious manner. Because his family "had dared the Jewish fate, by isolating itself in a Gentile town," and then pressed for Gentile respectability by insisting that Sam be a "nice boy" and curb aggressive "teaser and questioner" qualities, the boy found himself in an untenable situation. While his parents had stressed that "as a little Jew one has to be especially good in order not to be especially bad" and risk displeasing the Gentile neighbors, those very neighbors had suggested that because he was a Jew, he could not be very good. Apprehensions that his misbehavior had killed his grandmother and later had hurt his therapist both underscored Sam's sense that he was "an overwhelmingly bad boy." These social variables had disrupted his ego defenses, costing him "a sense of coherent individuation and identity."[11]

Erikson's emphasis on Sam's social world was understandable. Since adolescence, he, too, had been drifting from his European Jewish roots. He could identify with Sam's situation as a Jew who felt pressured to pass in the Gentile world. Indeed, Erikson struck a bond with the boy. He helped Sam understand his social and emotional circumstances and encouraged him to notify his parents about imminent seizures so that his pediatrician could prescribe preventive measures. Subsequently, major epileptic attacks were reduced to minor episodes. Erikson completed his account of Sam's case with a sense of confidence in his acumen as a therapist.[12]

His second key case in *Childhood and Society* involved an unnamed combat marine in his early thirties. "The presenting symptom is, again, somatic; it consists of a severe chronic headache," Erikson noted. Yet the real malady "owes its onset to one of the exigencies of social life, namely, combat in war."

The case impressed Erikson during the mid-1940s when he was on the staff of San Francisco's Mt. Zion Rehabilitation Clinic treating American veterans. In 1942, the marine (an unarmed medical soldier) found himself on a Pacific beachhead—Guadalcanal—as part of a company that was drawing heavy enemy fire during a major American military campaign. Someone put a gun in his hands, violating his personal pledge never to use such weapons. He could not remember what he did with the gun. His next memory was being in a makeshift hospital suffering from high fever, unable to move, and fearful of a surprise enemy attack. He was evacuated, and during his first meal away from the front lines, the noise of mess utensils was unbearable. He subsequently suffered from severe headaches and constant apprehension over possible metallic noises. He was one of the many psychiatric casualties at Guadalcanal.[13]

Erikson acknowledged but discounted organic factors: "The fever and toxic state had justified his first headache, but only the first one." As Erikson probed the man's childhood, the marine remembered that when he was fourteen, what remained of a thin rapport with his mother finally snapped. The drunken mother had pointed a gun at him, which he grabbed and broke. He then left home for good and pledged himself to a seemingly unrelated array of commitments—never to drink, to swear, to touch a gun, or to indulge in sex. He kept this pledge. Completely earnest, he lost any sense of play and experimentation and extravagance. Still, he was a caring individual, enlisted in the Marine Corps out of a sense of national obligation, and functioned somewhat acceptably until Guadalcanal.[14]

Erikson concluded that the marine's screening system broke down on the beachhead where he lost his capacity for ego synthesis so that he could not distinguish important from irrelevant stimuli, or separate truth from falsehood. In essence, he lost his sense of ego identity—"the ability to experience one's self as something that has continuity and sameness, and to act accordingly." When specific wartime conditions upset his ego balance, all the "infantile urges which he had rigidly held in abeyance" became unmoored, and life seemed to be in total disarray.[15]

As with Sam, Erikson indicated that specific social conditions were fundamental to the case. The marine would not have broken down "had it not been for the conditions of war and combat." His ego would have remained intact had it not been overtaxed by the panic of his immediate military superiors, group panic, and immobilization under enemy fire. These social forces, together with the high fever, undermined the organization of his ego—that is, social circumstances, more than organic factors, accounted for an acute loss of identity. This was the key to Erikson's bio-psycho-social approach; it acknowledged but deemphasized the biological.[16]

In discussing Sam and, more briefly, the marine, Erikson advanced a clinical formulation vastly different from the psychoanalytic ideas he mastered in Vienna (where "inner life" had been accented). He was continuing to develop his own unique variation of ego psychology where a horizontal surface of outer social-geographic forces (not the vertical perspective of buried inner impulses) fueled the formation of ego identity and therefore became central to a functioning personality.

Jean, Erikson's next case, provided the most striking of his three clinical narratives. When the six-year-old and her mother arrived at Erikson's home, she ran through the rooms looking at and touching objects of interest. For over a year, Erikson visited Jean's family at their home, and for some time afterward he continued to watch her progress. He came to know Jean well, yet he was circumspect in speaking of the causes of Jean's condition. Whereas previous clinicians had diagnosed her as schizophrenic, he described her malady as a form of "early ego failure." Unlike his work with Sam and the marine, he did not attempt to speak explicitly to the biological, psychological, and social factors that accounted for Jean's condition. By studying a patient with a "deficient ego," he asserted, it became possible to better understand "the functions of a healthy ego." Jean presented an opportunity for psychoanalytic-theory building. But there was also a chance for close personal rapport with a child strikingly different from any he had ever worked with.[17]

In *Childhood and Society,* Erikson began his review of his work with Jean on an evocative note. He was discomforted by the doom-and-gloom medical diagnosis of "infantile schizophrenia": "To come face to face with a 'schizophrenic' child is one of the most awe-inspiring experiences a psychotherapist can have. . . . Their facial features are often regular and pleasing, their eyes are 'soulful' and seem to express deep and desperate experience, and paired with a resignation which children should not have." With such a child, the clinician becomes convinced "that the right person and the right therapeutic regime could bring the child back on the road to coherent progress." But that was too optimistic an initial reading. To work with a child suffering from this malady was "to pioneer on this frontier of human trust" between mother, child, and clinician. Jean's case represented one of the greatest challenges in his early clinical experience.[18]

Jean first showed extreme disorientation at nine months when her mother became bedridden with tuberculosis. Mother and child were separated. In the arms of a nurse, she could see her mother only periodically from the doorway to her mother's bedroom. After four months, Jean was allowed to enter her mother's room. She avoided being touched by others and was fearful of the various objects in the room. More generally, she distrusted people and objects in her environment. "Some such maternal

estrangement may be found in every history of infantile schizophrenia,"
Erikson observed. What he did not know was whether maternal withdrawal
somehow "caused" the child's disturbance or whether "intrinsic and perhaps
constitutional reasons" were responsible. Nor did he know if such a disturbance could have been avoided by clinically guided "special dosages of well-
planned mother love."[19]

Erikson did not describe the circumstances by which he became Jean's
therapist, but he was clear about the difficulty of working with her. She suffered from a substantial "ego defect" that manifest itself in a "defective
screening system." She could not master or have perspective on "overpowering impressions as well as the disturbing impulses which intrude themselves
upon consciousness." A capacity for effectively organizing time and space
(ego synthesis) was lacking. More fundamentally, Jean lacked "the basic
grammar of two-ness." Her screening or ego synthesis was defective because
she could not "differentiate between active and passive, and between 'I' and
'you.' " Jean had no "continuous sense of identity" because she lacked the
capacity for trust and mutual engagement with her mother or anyone else.
More abstractly, Erikson felt that the child could not experience a sense of "I"
through the continuous and reliable interchange with a "you" or "thou."[20]

Known for his optimism and his success with children, Erikson set to
work. He moved Jean from a special care facility back to her family's house.
He also supervised a special program for Jean's mother designed to restore
psychological contact between mother and daughter—mutual interchange
or the "grammar of two-ness." Jean's mother was a quick learner, often inviting Jean to be near her. And she responded warmly to Jean's efforts to
express herself. The big breakthrough came with "finger play"—an
approach Erikson had rarely used. He encouraged Jean to tell stories about
each of her fingers (one finger went "to market," another finger "cried,"
etc.). In this way, Erikson theorized, "she learned to integrate time and to
establish a continuity of the various selves which had done different things
at different times." Still, Jean could not say "I did this." Her ego—her very
sense of continuous identity—remained defective. She constantly had to
retest and reintegrate what she had learned earlier. Stories about her fingers
had to be recounted in order to reestablish a "sense of the trustworthiness of
events at the time when they happened." Building on her skillful use of her
fingers and her keen auditory sense, Erikson encouraged Jean to play on a
xylophone while singing. Then Jean played the piano, Erikson's favorite
instrument, learning to play Beethoven's first sonata as if she were a gifted
musician. Unlike most of Erikson's other patients who had progressed significantly, however, Jean relapsed; she "turned against this [musical] gift."
Erikson concluded that schizophrenic children like Jean "make one believe

in the child's total progress where one is justified in believing only in isolated advances of individual faculties." Such children could learn to remember and excel, often in an artistic or musical enterprise, but "they cannot integrate it all: their ego is impotent."[21]

Work with Jean represented one of Erikson's few reported clinical failures as a child therapist. Despite his efforts, Jean developed no viable ego and lacked a firm sense of identity. Eventually she even ceased to be able to associate with children her own age. She had to be enrolled in a special school where she lost much that she had gained through her mother's and Erikson's efforts. A gifted child psychiatrist eventually took over her treatment, but the consequences were uncertain. Reflecting upon the case, Erikson was ambivalent. He hoped that mental health professionals could spot children like Jean "when they were young enough to perhaps be saved with special dosages of well-planned mother love." He assumed that "the primary deficiency in 'sending power' was in the child" and not within the mother or even the social situation in which mother and child had found themselves. In this case, he felt that nothing could prevent the ultimate breakdown of mother-child mutuality and trust. Therapy with a child with such an unstable ego and cognitive organization represented an exceedingly difficult effort on the "frontier of human trust."[22]

Jean's case humbled a hopeful clinician. Sam and the marine had more stable identities. Both had perceptions of their places in space and time and the ability to organize information. Their identities had been shattered, and primarily through specific social circumstances. Consequently, improved social conditions could help restore their identities. In contrast, if Jean had ever enjoyed an identity and intact ego functions, these assets had been lost in infancy. And though improvement in her performance was possible, at least temporarily, the underlying problem was that her ego remained "impotent" (a term Erikson had not used before in this context). An important motivation for moving to the University of California Institute of Child Welfare was to work with normal children who did not suffer from major psychological maladies. This paralleled a general shift among American mental health clinicians from a "mad" to a more "normal" patient clientele. Failure in his efforts with Jean fortified his commitment to work with clients with at least modestly intact egos. Except for Jean, there was no sustained discussion in *Childhood and Society* about people incapable of securing identities, positive or negative.

This is not to say that Erikson was uninterested in Jean and other patients who seemed constitutionally unable to repair their egos. Perhaps more than any other person described in his book, he was taken by the young girl. Working with Jean was an "awe-inspiring experience" because it concerned the unknown and the unfathomable in an era before even marginally effective psychotropic drugs were used to combat psychosis. Freud had predicted that psychoanalysis would not work with psychotics or others who could not establish transference relationships with the therapist; the experience with Jean made this painfully apparent. Erikson's configurational theoretical approach and his bio-psycho-social checklist of clinical maladies seemed only marginally more successful. Minimal success with a fascinating patient suffering from irreversible ego damage offered important lessons. He needed to amplify his theory building concerning ego identity, but to do so while working more with patients like Sam and the marine, where long-term improvement was possible. His failure with Jean paralleled his failed efforts with a developmentally impaired member of his own family, his third son, Neil.

NEIL ERIKSON

Until one gloomy day in 1944, Joan Erikson regarded herself as an exemplary mother. She delighted in recounting how she had slid down a hill one cold winter night in 1931 to deliver Kai, plump and healthy, at a Vienna hospital. Joan also boasted about refusing to part with Sue at Grace–New Haven Hospital in 1938, a refusal that had established the policy of rooming-in; mothers could now keep their newborns in their hospital rooms. Physicians often commented to Joan that she was quite healthy and did not need doctoring. She strongly preferred natural childbirth, for it enhanced a mother's control and self-esteem at the crucial moment when she first greeted her newborn. Her attitude predated the article she and Erik wrote for *Mademoiselle* espousing natural childbirth to enhance the mother's role and facilitate "The Power of the Newborn."[23]

Erik was confident when he took Joan, now forty-one, to a Berkeley hospital one evening to deliver their fourth child. Joan's obstetrician was very late in arriving at the hospital, so she had to be immobilized and drugged so that she would not deliver prior to his arrival. Weeks before the delivery, the obstetrician had recommended minor postdelivery surgery to repair damage caused by an earlier birth. Although Neil's delivery was long, difficult, and painful, he went ahead with the surgery. Consequently, Joan had to be put under additional heavy sedation. When she awoke dizzy, weak, and nauseous, she asked for her newborn. The hospital staff put her off. Finally, the obstetrician informed her that the baby had serious medical problems and was being cared for in a special facility. Joan shuddered.[24]

While Joan had been unconscious, the obstetrician and a few other doctors on the hospital staff summoned Erik to tell him that Neil was a "Mongolian idiot" (i.e., a Down Syndrome child) who had no neck muscles, would never hold up his head, and would not live more than a year or two. They recommended immediate institutionalization at a special French hospital in Berkeley. Erik may have felt some measure of responsibility for Neil. It was not uncommon among adoptees to assume that they could produce "monster" offspring. Elna, Erik's half sister who died at the age of two, may also have been abnormal at birth. Erik phoned Margaret Mead. Next to Joan, Mead was then the strong, guiding female presence in Erik's life; he had come to rely upon her in personal as well as professional matters. Mead had no doubts about the proper course for Neil. The hospital doctors were right, she told Erik. A Down Syndrome infant in the household would not benefit the children or family stability. Neil had to be institutionalized, Mead insisted, so that Joan would not form an attachment to him. Joseph Wheelwright echoed Mead's advice. Had Erik called another friend, pediatrician Benjamin Spock, or a few other pediatricians familiar with the latest research on Down Syndrome, the advice might have been different. After talking with Mead and Wheelwright, Erik signed the requisite consent forms, and Neil was transferred to the French facility.[25]

Erik waited at the hospital until Joan regained consciousness and learned that her newborn had been removed to a special facility. Then he returned home to talk with his children. Nineteen years later, he recounted to his friend Robert Lifton that he told the children that Neil had died. To "protect" them from the horrors of a Down sibling, he had lied to them, much as his mother had lied to him about the identity of his real father. She, too, had intended to "protect" him—against the knowledge of his illegitimate birth. The fact that her lies distressed Erik enormously did not prevent him, now, from misleading his children. At one point, Erik confided to Kai that Neil was alive and in an institution. Although Kai kept the confidence from his younger siblings, Jon and Sue nonetheless felt that something was amiss (much as Erik felt something was wrong when his mother had lied to him about his paternity). Thus, a family dynamic was perpetuated. In a crisis, the emotional pressures to repeat a pattern—indeed, the seeming craziness and unreality of the moment—counted for much. In turn, the vast knowledge and experience that Erik had gained as a sensitive and unusually effective child psychoanalyst seemed to be almost inoperative. He had told parents of his patients, again and again, to be open and candid with their children and never to pit one against another. But he had been untruthful to Jon and Sue and made Kai a partner to that fiction.[26]

The fact of Neil's death or disappearance affected all three children, especially Jon and Sue, who remembered feeling disoriented and apprehensive. When Joan returned home from the hospital, she did not question what

Erik told the children about Neil. Instead, she discouraged further discussion of the topic. Although bedridden, Joan insisted on being driven to the French hospital so that she could see her son. Neil was a large infant and medical tests confirmed that he had all the symptoms of Down Syndrome. When Joan arrived at the facility, he was unresponsive to her. She was devastated. Intuitively, she felt that she should bring her child home and care for him even though the doctors and her husband thought otherwise. But on another level, Joan saw validity in their perspective and, at any rate, found it difficult to summon the energy to take full charge of the situation. To be sure, she did not entirely accept the "expert" perspective that a Down child at home would be disadvantageous for her children. But Joan recognized that Neil's presence would damage the romantic image that she, even more than Erik, liked to invoke of a healthy, attractive, and vibrant family headed by a young child analyst. Appearances were not insignificant to Joan's hopes and ambitions for her family. When she regained some of her strength and was more firmly in command, she had Neil transferred from the French hospital to the home of a Berkeley woman who raised Down Syndrome children. That arrangement did not work out well and Joan carried the very "big child" to a second woman in the Berkeley hills who was more proficient with Down children. She visited Neil periodically, usually without Erik, who had become a rather passive figure in the crisis. When Neil was nearly one, doctors and other professionals recommended a more highly credentialed institutional environment—a special public hospital north of Berkeley. Still not her feisty take-charge self, Joan asked no questions and simply complied. Neil remained in that facility for the next two decades. Because Joan and Erik found themselves deeply distressed whenever they visited, trips became less frequent. Neil was almost never discussed. This pattern of silence persisted even after the younger children finally learned about Neil. It was as if two families existed, one, a normal family of five in the public eye, and the other, a less functional family of six that outsiders did not see. Erik and Joan took many photographs of their three normal children and retained family photographs of the five members of the "public family." If they ever photographed Neil, they kept no copies.[27]

An unstated factor behind Joan's decision to keep Neil institutionalized was the nature of her marital relationship. (It differed dramatically from the marriages of Margaret Mead, who seemed to take on husbands when they supported her professional growth and to divorce them when this support was lacking.) Since their wedding, Joan had assumed total responsibility for child rearing and household affairs. She had also supervised Erik's dress, diet, exercise, and social life. Indeed, he seemed to require her assent even to open or close a window. She helped with his professional writing, too, far more proficient at editing his increasing supply of prose than at producing her own. Under normal circumstances, therefore, her workday was overly full. Now, with her physical stamina depleted and depression sapping her spirits, Joan felt that she could not take care of both Erik and Neil. In some ways, Erik was like a fourth child himself, demanding more of her time and energy than Kai, Jon, or Sue. But Joan's decision to continue caring for Erik, while abandoning Neil, came at a price. Their relationship became increasingly tense. From time to time during this difficult mid-1940s interval, they contemplated divorce.[28]

The Erikson family responded to the crisis of Neil's birth in the context of what was then known about Down Syndrome, and the signals were mixed. Historian Elaine Tyler May reminds us that America's baby boom from the mid-1940s through the 1950s carried an ideological dimension. Adult fulfillment, especially for women, was considered to come primarily from successful parenting. An abundance of normal, healthy children became an important sign of proficient motherhood and good parenting. In the course of the 1950s, local, regional, and national voluntary associations for parents of retarded children proliferated, operating as mutual support groups and as publicity agencies against the stigma of retardation. They brought to light the pervasiveness of childhood retardation, demanded additional medical research and support services, and held out hope for these disadvantaged youngsters and their families. In this changing climate, celebrities like Pearl Buck, Dale Evans, and Roy Rogers acknowledged their retarded children, who were loving and special. In 1954, President Eisenhower declared the second week in November as National Retarded Children's Week. Down Syndrome children represented one of the largest groups among the severely retarded. (By 1949, it was the most frequent growth disorder among American children; 17 of every 6,650 births were Down Syndrome babies.)[29]

Joan's decision (with Erik's ready acquiescence) to hold out her household as a normal family of five was understandable. The crisis over Neil's birth had erupted before the crusade for retarded children got under way. Although Joan knew that she and Erik would not have been treated as curiosities by friends and colleagues if they had publicly supported assistance for children like Neil, supportive agencies and public figures still were not very visible in 1944. The Eriksons simply followed the pervasive response of parents of Down Syndrome children during those years—silence, shame, and profound sorrow. They became set in this pattern and did not depart from it even as public discourse became more accommodating during the 1950s.

Eschewing political activism, Joan, even more than Erik, was preoccupied with her role in Neil's care—namely, whether eventually she should raise him at home or keep him institutionalized. It was a more difficult issue in the mid-1940s, when scientific understanding of the malady was circumscribed and plagued by rumors, than in recent years after the cause of Down Syndrome was amply demonstrated (i.e., the abnormality of Chromosome 21, which often produces an extra chromosome rather than the normal pair). At the time Neil was born, prospective mothers received no genetic counseling or testing during pregnancy to determine whether they carried a healthy baby. Hospitals did not instruct parents on how to care for Down Syndrome children at home or how their conduct helped or jeopardized the child. Special adoption referral services for Down children were unavailable. At the time, the pervasive medical view was that "mongolism" was caused by congenital hypopituitarism. A damaged pituitary gland was thought to produce insufficient tropic hormones, resulting in a dysfunctional thyroid gland and abnormal metabolism and development. Other somewhat less respectable medical theories attributed Down Syndrome to an abnormally small amniotic sac, to syphilis, to alcohol consumption, and even to contraceptives. The supposed parental "deficiency" or "failing" involved in the Down birth complicated the parents' decision whether to institutionalize or to raise the child at home.[30]

The advice of Joan's obstetrician and other attending physicians represented a pervasive medical opinion at a time when doctors were widely respected. It was thought that Down Syndrome was a serious malady best managed by professionals. If taken home, the child would disrupt family life, aggravate other children in the household, and burden parents. Under pressure, to be sure, a minority of these same "authorities" acknowledged that Down Syndrome children were living longer than was often anticipated. With parental care, concern, and stimulation at home, they could learn to walk and talk, perform uncomplicated chores, and become increasingly alert. They could sometimes be kind, trusting, well behaved, and very loving. Like most parents with Down children, however, the Eriksons did not press the physicians or other professionals for these alternative perspectives. One might have expected this inaction from Erik, but Joan was uncharacteristically pliant. Given the date and the medical context, however, parental pursuit of optimistic professional advice on Neil's prospects was no guarantee of getting it.[31]

Her energy and emotional resources depleted by depression, Joan blamed herself for giving birth to a Down Syndrome child. At forty-one, she felt that she had no business bearing another child. Even the most informed medical opinion held that middle-aged women ran a significantly greater risk of giving birth to a child with Neil's handicap. What Joan did not know was that there were two types of Down Syndrome. The first usually involved younger mothers: There was an abnormality in Chromosome 21 but the total number of chromosomes remained normal (forty-six). The second generally involved older mothers: The child was born with an extra chromosome (a total of forty-seven). But in 20 percent of the cases involving this second type, the father was responsible. Genetically, Erik (who did not know his full biological history) might have been responsible for Neil's malady.[32]

To distance herself and her family from memories of Neil, Joan arranged for a move from Berkeley to nearby Orinda not long after Neil was institutionalized. Orinda was a small suburban town with large, secluded, wooded residential lots surrounding a country club and a golf course. Following the move, Joan dealt with her guilt and despair through hyperactivity. She worked long hours planting a whole hillside of healthy fruit trees. She built a room for Sue extending from the main part of the family house, doing most of the hard physical labor herself. Then Joan bought Sue a horse and arranged for a stable. She also attended to the swimming pool with its large surrounding deck. Joan became a proficient artisan, too. She learned to make beautiful jewelry and established a regional arts center. Amid this compulsive activity, Neil's existence haunted Joan, but he was never discussed. In 1951, the Erikson family moved from California to western Massachusetts because Erik wanted to leave the University of California, even if it meant working again with disturbed patients, and he accepted an offer at the Austen Riggs Center. There, Joan reinvigorated the center's patient activities program. The mentally disturbed at Riggs might find their way back to health as Joan was trying to find her way—by creating life and beauty through work and activities. Joan acknowledged later that she had done for Riggs's troubled patients what she had failed to do for her own institutionalized son.[33]

In Orinda, Neil's situation provided vital context to a pattern of fragmentation in the Erikson family. By keeping their distance from each other, the Eriksons seemed to lessen tensions. Erik spent much of his time in his studio cottage away from the house. There he spent long hours writing *Childhood and Society* and meeting with several of his patients. Sue, not yet a teenager, became an accomplished horseback rider and spent much time in her room or riding her horse. Kai and Jon, late adolescents now, busied themselves with neighborhood friends. Joan, traditional manager of household affairs, remained glum and spent much of her time with writing and crafts.[34]

For years, Neil's existence continued to painfully shape the family. When Joan and Erik left northern California, they finally told Jon and Sue of their seven-year-old brother, whom they were leaving behind. They described Neil as terribly deformed and implied that it would be pointless to visit with him. Jon recalled feeling that this brother, whom he had never seen, was being short-changed in life. Sue could never forget the fear that someday she, too, might be left behind. She remembered becoming somewhat less than trusting of her parents at this point.[35]

Roughly a year after the move to Stockbridge, Joan took a train back to California to visit Neil. She recalled that his face appeared far more normal than earlier, although he was hyperactive and tense and wore a leg brace. Neil did not recognize her. Joan wondered if other options should have been explored when Neil was younger. She feared that she had not been suffi- ciently assertive in planning his future. But she felt that it would be too painful to visit him again. Neil resurfaced a few years later when the very young adopted daughter of the Erikson's good Bay Area friends, Martha and Thomas Proctor, became pregnant. Although Joan did not oppose abortion in principle, she urged that the Proctors call off the one planned for their unmarried daughter. The Proctors refused, concluding that Joan was driven by a sense of having essentially aborted Neil and wanting to atone for it. In 1959, when Sue turned twenty-one, Neil came up again. Joan's mother had willed an inheritance to all her grandchildren (including three from Joan's older sister, Molly). The will had stipulated that no money was to be released from her estate until the youngest reached legal adulthood. No funds were dispersed in 1959, which underscored the fact that Neil, at six- teen, was the youngest grandchild. Six years later Erik and Joan were in Perugia, Italy, where Erik had taken a sabbatical leave to write. They had been entertaining the Proctors at dinner when Kai called from Georgia with a report from the Bay Area custodial facility—Neil had died. Erik took the call, relayed the news to Joan, listened to her directive, and announced that the death had been expected. Later that evening, Joan and Erik called Jon and Sue, who lived in northern California, and asked them to arrange for Neil's cremation (which had no sanction in Jewish law) and his funeral. This was a difficult task for parents to impose on their children. Erik and Joan did not return for the burial of Neil's ashes. Sue told the funeral director that despite his age, this brother she had never seen should be buried in the chil- dren's section of the cemetery; he had never grown up. Sue and Jon were saddened by the fact that Neil had been outlawed from the Erikson family. Both felt that they were not attending to the remains of a real brother so much as having to face a troublesome dream.[36]

Freud had postulated that in dreamlife what was repressed and forgotten would resurface. Rarely discussed or thought about, Neil had long remained in the shadow or dream life of the "official" Erikson family. His existence would occasionally come to the surface, however, and in disturbing ways. Shortly after arriving in Stockbridge, Joan told Riggs staff psychologist and friend Margaret Brenman-Gibson about Neil. A few years later, William Gibson, her husband, published his novel *The Cobweb,* featuring a fictitious

Nebraska mental hospital that closely resembled both Riggs (where Erik and Joan worked at the time) and the Menninger Clinic. The strong and able fictional activities therapist, Meg Reinhart, was based on Joan. In one of the scenes, the assistant clinical director spotted a copy of Dostoyevsky's *The Idiot* in the backseat of Reinhart's car. When Joan read this passage, she became very upset and deeply embarrassed. She incorrectly assumed that Brenman-Gibson had breached her confidence and that her husband had broadcast the Down child's existence to the community and the world.[37]

Though he lived thousands of miles away, Neil could not be ignored. He was fundamental not only to Erik's and Joan's personal lives but to their professional and theoretical efforts as well. Neil provided a basic negative backdrop for Erik's efforts—with Joan's help—to elaborate the nature of a "normal" life cycle.

NEIL AND THE EMERGENCE
OF A LIFE CYCLE MODEL

The eight-stage life cycle essay that appeared as a chapter in *Childhood and Society* was a shortened version of a presentation Erik gave in 1950 for the Midcentury White House Conference on Infancy and Childhood. By then the crisis over Neil's birth had eased. These two versions of this project represented Erik and Joan's closest effort to work together on a publication, even though Erik was the author and theoretical architect. The project began in earnest in the mid-1940s, perhaps a year after Neil was born, during a particularly tense time in their marriage. As the couple prepared an outline of their view of the life cycle, they reviewed Erik's various efforts since the mid-1930s to move beyond Freud's infancy-based psychosexual developmental scheme. They also reviewed some of Erik's case files to cull from them the developmental implications. Finally, with Joan taking the lead, they pondered their own and their children's developmental stages, and tried to integrate this with the other materials.

Almost half a century later, as Erik neared death in a Cape Cod nursing home, Joan talked with a guest in her home a few blocks away. She spent the full morning describing the course of the tragedy of her Down Syndrome child. Had it influenced her work with Erik at formulating the full life cycle model? She was certain that Neil's birth had contributed very decisively to the two life cycle essays of 1950: "But how it did I don't know." Exhausted by recounting the most traumatic experience of her life, Joan stated that it was not her task to come up with an explanation. She smiled over tea and seemed relieved for having described the episode. Indeed, she appeared to be discovering new energies as she talked about the wonders of winter on the Cape and attended to her houseplants. From the tape recording of the full morning, it becomes clear that Joan's narrative of the tragedy concerning Neil was also a story about the emergence of the life cycle model. She had connected the two in a compelling way, though she had not quite recognized this at the time. Indeed, Joan's narrative represents perhaps the single most powerful explanation of the connection that is available; it governs this account.[38]

Before Neil's birth in 1944, Erik seemed to have lost interest in life cycle theory. By the late 1930s, he had outlined four developmental stages—infancy (oral, anal, genital), latency, puberty, and adult heterosexual adjustment. His thinking had been close to Freud's on infantile sexual development, and he had hoped to chart the developmental process through all of human life. At the same time, he had fashioned a diagram of early pregenital development that featured eight squares running diagonally across a checkerboard from the bottom-left corner to the top right. Each square represented the intersection of a vertical axis listing bodily erotogenic zones and a horizontal axis listing impulses that activated the zones. Thinking spatially, of course, he had hoped to merge coverage of the full course of human life with a modified eight-square diagonal across a checkerboard—each square standing for a life stage. He sensed that the study of social change and culture might help in this effort, but he did not see precisely how.

In 1940, Erikson had prepared an essay for the *Cyclopedia of Medicine,* "Problems of Infancy and Early Childhood," which suggested that he continued to be stymied in his work on the life cycle, though by then he had worked with Sam and understood better how the social communities within which children grew up were crucial to their psychological development. Visits to the Sioux and, quite recently, the Yurok reinforced this understanding. Tribal social-cultural patterns seemed highly congruent with the maturational readiness of Native American children. Notwithstanding, Erikson chose not to reintroduce his checkerboard chart and rework it in the light of social considerations. He could not seem to conceptualize "how individuals change in relation to what is moving around them." Drawing on embryology, Erikson noted that each of the fetal organs went through step-by-step epigenetic development—that is, every organ in a developing life cycle came into being only at an appropriate time and bodily location, and in synchrony with every other organ. Similarly, humans developed in normal sequential steps after birth, each step occurring at the appropriate time. As the infant matured, he or she embraced, within stages, "the physical and cultural reality into which he was born." Focusing on this external reality that conditioned development, Erikson noted two circumstances in the developing child's family life—the quality of parenting and relationships with siblings. But here he got stuck. He was unable to take the checkerboard chart rooted in Freudian psychosexual stages of infancy and rewrite it based upon psychosocial development through childhood and beyond. Jane Loevinger, Erikson's research assistant at Berkeley in 1940, recalled that he was not ready to supplant Freud's early psychosexual stages with psychosocial ones covering the full life cycle. More precisely, although Erikson had made significant strides toward a developmental perspective of his own, he still lacked the words and the conceptual clarity to describe the epigenetic development of the ego in relation to social reality from birth to death.[39]

Neil's birth affected Erikson's thinking about the nature of human development less by changing the direction of his earlier conceptual work than by provoking him to continue with it, and at a brisker pace. As the crisis threw his marriage and family life into disarray, it elicited emotional, intuitive responses that, among other consequences, contributed to his thinking about human development. There is no evidence that he consciously included Joan in his developmental work as a collaborator, when the crisis erupted, to help both of them get through it. Joan recalled no remarks to that effect. Once in place, however, intellectual collaboration became a beneficial tonic. Joan became more than a critic for the major essay in *Childhood and Society*. Collaboration allowed her to work more frequently with her husband—almost as his partner in a crucial theoretical undertaking. In a climate where unmediated emotions counted for much, Erik found himself happily surprised by this consequence of spousal collaboration. Out of a horrible family tragedy, he and Joan were energized to pick up theoretically where he had left off. They worked out a final set of issues that produced an extraordinarily insightful and comprehensive developmental schema.

From the very start of their collaboration, Joan had pressed Erik to be attentive to relationships with their children. They considered intergenerational dynamics in a family with a considerable age spread and recalled how each child had behaved at earlier ages. Because Joan had observed the children at close range, she brought very essential details into the discussions as they theorized about human development. "My wife has observed with our children," he emphasized before a Menninger Clinic staff session; her information was basic to their collaborative work. Erik's clinical cases also became quite important in their developmental discussions. So was his psychoanalytic training. Always somewhat disparaging of psychoanalytic discourse, Joan emphasized that Shakespeare was richer than Freud on developmental matters because he had moved beyond the early years in his cast of characters.[40]

Husband and wife had long enjoyed reading to each other. Again and again, they read Jaques's well-known "All the world's a stage" speech in Shakespeare's play *As You Like It* on the seven ages of man. Not only was

Shakespeare discussing epigenetic development from infancy to death, he seemed to be characterizing his seven developmental stages in social and ethical far more than in sexual terms. The Eriksons recalled how exciting it was to reframe Erik's early outlines on the developmental stages and his checkerboard chart by referring to Jaques's speech. The greater age range made it possible to incorporate memorable clinical cases like Sam, Jean, and the marine, and to include their own children as well. The social-ethical focus freed them in directions Erik was moving anyway. Shakespeare's Jaques had shifted too quickly from "the infant, mewling and puking in the nurse's arms" to "the 'whining' school boy." Between early infancy and school (i.e., work), Shakespeare had missed a stage that centered on the child using play to take initiative.[41]

Having enlarged upon Shakespeare, the Eriksons sensed that something still seemed amiss as they fleshed out what they now referred to as their model for the "Stages (not ages) of Man." One day as Joan drove Erik from their home in the north Berkeley hills to a railroad depot in south San Francisco (a very long drive), they reviewed their emerging life cycle model in an attempt to fathom what had been omitted. "Hey, we left ourselves out," Joan shouted. They had characterized themselves within Shakespeare's stage of "lovers" (intimacy) without taking into account that they had moved on to a generative stage. They had generated children. In raising those children, Joan was continuing the generative process. So was Erik in his work with younger patients and the preparation of his first book. Generativity represented not only the procreativity of "lovers," it also involved intergenerational enrichment—a primary task in adult life. By the time they reached the railroad platform, the Eriksons were hoping that they were advancing beyond both Freud and Shakespeare on the developmental process. Erik's initial life cycle work was taking on creative new dimensions.[42]

Indeed, Erik recalled how "my life cycle theory" was "really ours"; this was only a modest exaggeration—Neil was also important in the intensely emotional spousal undertaking. More was involved than building a model for normal development. The Eriksons also found themselves using their collaboration as a path away from the crisis of family dysfunction rooted in Neil's birth. Their Down Syndrome infant appeared "unfinished" and "incomplete," a victim of delayed physical and mental development. He differed markedly from their children, Joan recalled, due to the low intensity of his rapport with her, his minimal attachment to Erik and others, his scant display of emotion, and even in an austere aspect to the way he played. Compared with Kai, Jon, and Sue as newborns, his temperament and personality seemed meek, shallow, and unresponsive. Neil's development—emotional and cognitive as well as physical—appeared to be stunted. Joan loved him and Erik probably did, too, although they must also have resented him. Neil required an enormous amount of attention and support from Joan and others simply to exist. There was the nagging sense that it might have been better if the child had not been born. Joan remembered how hard it was to throw off negative feelings about the way Neil's young life was progressing. Certainly, he had no place in the developmental model she and Erik were constructing.[43]

The Eriksons acknowledged they were fashioning a developmental framework for health and normalcy. To some degree, they also knew they were formulating a model for themselves and their children. After all, it was partially based on observing their own lives. At the most personal level, the model was a map that located health and normalcy and placed five Eriksons at that location. As such, it helped to assure them that they were developmentally healthy even as Neil, located elsewhere, was not. In effect, Erik and Joan had an emotional stake in placing Neil at the fringe of their map just as he remained distant from their family.

Joan's role was crucial in the mapping process, and she remembered much of it. For years, she had encouraged Erik to work with normal children. After Neil's birth, Joan's long-standing preference became Erik's as well. A life cycle framework for the development of "normal" people that comported with the lives in the "normal" Erikson family of five required Neil's disappearance—at least physically but perhaps from memory as well.

This mapping exercise would not have taken the direction it did without Erik's preliminary thoughts on human development. In "Problems of Infancy and Early Childhood"(1940), he had advanced an important observation. "The result of normal development is proper relationship of size and function among the body organs," he had noted. "If 'proper rate' and 'normal sequence' are disturbed, the outcome may be a *monstrum in excessu* or a *monstrum in defectu*." As the Eriksons looked at newborn Neil four years later, they had no doubt that both the "proper rate" and "normal sequence" were skewed. Whether in excess or insufficiency, Joan recalled how she and Erik felt numbness and disbelief that they had not created a healthy child. Then, as they learned that Neil's retardation was on the severe side within a range of Down Syndrome disabilities, they felt sorrow, disappointment, and even the sense of loss. With much pain mixed with love, Joan dwelled on how newborn Neil had seemed unusually weak and could not even raise his head. As she and Erik read prominent medical authorities on mongoloids, Joan remembered that they had emphasized departures from the proper rate and normal sequence of organ development. Those negative characterizations seemed to augment the sorrowful couple's disposition to cling to their "Eight Stages of Man" as a developmental model for normal people.[44]

Nowhere in *Childhood and Society* was Down Syndrome discussed. Yet

"Trust vs. Basic Mistrust," the first and in some ways the most fundamental stage of the Eriksons' life cycle, was treated at length. The young infant established trust in the "inner certainty" and "outer predictability" of his mother's existence and support when he could let her out of his sight without undue anxiety. He trusted that she would be constant and supportive. From this "consistency, continuity, and sameness of experience," the infant formed "a rudimentary sense of ego identity." In Jean's case, Erik had characterized infantile schizophrenia as the absence of basic trust. The primary therapeutic task was to reestablish it—a renewed sense of mutuality between child and mother such as had been possible with Sam. In the last chapter of *Childhood and Society,* Erik lauded natural childbirth—minimal medical interference with the birthing process—as an important facilitator for early mother-newborn trust. Both mother and child came into contact "less drugged and more ready to keep their eyes open." As mother and newborn regarded each other, eye to eye, they could form a trusting mutuality that made childbirth properly "woman's labor and accomplishment." Joan's first delivery had been natural, resulting in a trusting, reciprocal rapport with Kai. In contrast, considerable medical intervention and sedation had marked Neil's birth. When Joan awoke from her drugged sleep, Neil had already been taken to another facility. The relationship had not started with a meeting of the eyes. Moreover, little trust or mutuality between Joan and Neil ensued in the months that followed, although she insisted that she loved him and deeply resented people calling him an "idiot." It was in this context that Erik had reduced the trust of his other children by assuring two of them for several years that Neil had died.[45]

THE LIFE CYCLE: A HOLISTIC PRESENTATION

The birth of Neil Erikson acted, then, as a rather primitive, destructive force in the relationship between parents and children. At the same time, it drew Erik and Joan together, eventually giving them energy and incentive to tie down and complete Erik's earlier efforts at forging a creative new developmental model. In the years that followed, Neil and his gross abnormalities served as one of several pertinent factors behind this model. It underscored the relevance of family dynamics in a penetrating theoretical conceptualization.

Although Joan had been critically important to the development of the life cycle model, Erik was its author and, for the first decade at least, its major presenter, as he had been working on the model since the mid-1930s. With crucial editorial assistance from Joan, he wrote up and presented the fullest version of the model for the Midcentury White House Conference and prepared an abbreviated version for the central chapter in *Childhood and Society*. Ever since he offered these versions to the public in 1950, scholars, film producers, and popular writers have summarized, one by one, each of its eight stages in plodding, textbooklike fashion. Although Erik was often flattered by this attention, he was distressed over the stage-by-stage summaries of his writing for two reasons. To begin with, he felt that his popularizers were slighting his many significant predecessors, including Shakespeare's observations in *As You Like It* on life's seven ages, Anthony Van Dyck's painting *The Four Ages of Man*, Sándor Ferenczi's "Stages in the Development of the Sense of Reality," and the work of Erik's Berkeley colleague Else Frenkel-Brunswik on the "Course of the Life Span." Then there were Sigmund Freud's and Karl Abraham's developmental schemas. Indeed, without Freud's stage theory, Erik felt that his own work on the life cycle would never have emerged. It remained his most basic theoretical point of reference. He recognized, too, that Anna Freud had contributed significantly to developmental theory, beginning with her 1922 essay "Beating Fantasies and Daydreams." By 1945, Anna Freud was characterizing the "intactness of development" (the process of ego maturation) as inherent in the psychoanalytic focus. Although Erik himself had often incorporated the ideas of others without acknowledging them, it embarrassed him that popularizers failed to see that his own model was part of a long tradition in humanistic and scientific discourse.[46]

More significant, Erik felt that popular summaries of each of the eight stages within his developmental model betrayed a fundamental misunderstanding of what he had written. He had charted his stages diagonally rather than vertically to show that all of the eight stages, which recorded conflict between polarized opposites, were "present at the beginning of life and remain ever present." What was important was not the time sequence, one stage following another in a progression of moral virtues (a polemic tradition evident even in Benjamin Franklin's list of thirteen virtues that had gradually to be acquired to achieve "moral perfection"). What mattered was how each stage was similar to and overlapped with the others. All of "the later stages are present in the earlier ones" and each concerned the same fundamental problem of mutuality—that is, each involved struggles to move beyond oneself and to become engaged with others. Erik was perhaps even more distressed by the fact that those who summarized him had generally been more precise and exact than he had been. This "search for measurable definitions" through mechanistic stage-by-stage descriptions precluded the sense of constant flow among all eight stages. Erik might have conveyed this sense of flow and connectedness more clearly by replacing "stages" with "trends" or "segments" or "tendencies" or some other term that conveyed a better sense of their constant movement and inseparability. Essentially, he felt that he was only beginning to get a sense of the vast complexity of the human life cycle, and he was irritated by popularizers who cast it in overly finite form.[47]

Perhaps the most objectionable aspect of this popularization was that it overlooked the relationship between various generations within a family. Especially owing to Joan's decisive influence, Erik recognized that he was not discussing the psychological growth of the individual so much as the relationship between children and parents. In large measure, the Eriksonian life cycle concerned the bonds of trust and sharing between parents and their children that facilitated adolescent identity (stage five) and old-age integrity (stage eight). Neither formal psychoanalytic theory nor elaborate attentiveness to life cycle modeling spoke directly or fully to these personal bonds.

The life cycle presentation that Erik wrote up began with "trust vs. mistrust" and was followed by "autonomy vs. shame, doubt." These signaled the emergence not so much of selfhood but of a sense of self; this sense was inseparable from recognition by others. The parallel to Jacques Lacan's "mirror stage" was striking. Consciousness of selfhood began as the baby and others (usually mother or father) smiled at each other in mutual recognition. At that moment, "he recognizes that he represents something to a significant person." This initial "object relation" (the beginning of human development) was therefore intergenerational—a connectedness between infant and parent(s). When the mother "combines sensitive care of the baby's individual needs and a firm sense of personal trustworthiness within the trusted framework of their community's life style," she imparted to her child a trust and confidence in his environment that was the basis for his subsequent "sense of identity." Confident in himself, the child sought to take confident possession or knowledge of his environment. With a firm pregenital attachment to his parents that promoted trust and then autonomy, the child began "the slow process of becoming a parent, a carrier of tradition." At some point in this process, one discerned "the beginning of adulthood in the child; it is the taking over of the moral self-regulation." One could gauge how "the child's superego is developing by the way he treats younger children as if he were already an adult." Thus, early childhood concerned the formation of the child's trust and autonomy through parental response that provoked an emulative quality in the child. He came to learn to parent.[48]

While the early stages of the Erikson life cycle were rooted in parenting, the seventh and longest stage of adulthood was based on the quality of care for children. Unlike earlier points in life, where Freudian stage theory was a constant guide, Freud's abbreviated discussion of adult genitality was not of overriding importance. As Erik and Joan sought to formulate the meaning of this stage within the context of their mixed performances as parents, they rejected characterizing it as "productivity" or "creativity." They wanted to

A Stages	B Criteria of the Healthy Personality								C Social Radius
I "Oral" and "Sensory"	Trust vs. Mistrust								"Existence," mother
II "Muscular" and "Anal"		Autonomy vs. Shame, Doubt							Mother, father etc.
III "Locomotor" and "Infantile-genital"			Initiative vs. Guilt						Parents siblings playgroups, etc.
IV "Latency"				Industry vs. Inferiority					Schoolmasters teachers etc.
V "Puberty" and "Adolescence"					Identity vs. Diffusion				Cliques social prototypes two sexes, etc.
VI "Young Adulthood"						Intimacy vs. Isolation			
VII "Adulthood"							Generativity vs. Self-Absorption		
VIII "Maturity"								Integrity vs. Disgust, Dispair	

For Midcentury White House Conference on Infancy and Childhood (1950)

	1	2	3	4	5	6	7	8
ORAL SENSORY	TRUST VS. MISTRUST							
MUSCULAR-ANAL		AUTONOMY VS. SHAME, DOUBT						
LOCOMOTOR-GENITAL			INITIATIVE VS. GUILT					
LATENCY				INDUSTRY VS. INFERIORITY				
PUBERTY AND ADOLESCENCE					IDENTITY VS. ROLE CONFUSION			
YOUNG ADULTHOOD						INTIMACY VS. ISOLATION		
ADULTHOOD							GENERATIVITY VS. STAGNATION	
MATURITY								INTEGRITY VS. DISGUST, DESPAIR

"Eight Ages of Man" in *Childhood and Society* (1950)

capture "a *generative* tendency, and beyond this a tendency to take care of what was generated." This stage involved more than giving birth to and raising offspring—"anything that one produced or created." The stage focused on "guiding the next generation" and assuming toward society generally "a parental kind of responsibility." Where this generativity was lacking, adults clung to one another in "pseudo-intimacy" but felt "stagnation and interpersonal impoverishment." A parent in that state acted as if life "still owed him something which he in turn cannot give to the child unless life first gives [it] to him." Such adults failed to see that "the pleasure that they could get out of life at this stage was derived from giving and not from receiving." Essentially, the primary task of adult life was to parent children in a way that promoted childhood trust and autonomy. For Erik, this signified that "the individual life stages are 'interliving,' cogwheeling with the stages of others which move him along as he moves them." In Erik's view, this intergenerational connectedness distinguished his model from the orthodox Freudian "reconstruction of the infant's beginnings." With Joan, Erik wrote about the connectedness of parents with their children from the pride of parenting Kai, Jon, and Sue, and from the enervating sense of having failed to parent Neil. With only the uninspiring memory of how Theodor Homburger fathered, Erik Erikson, the son of himself, was doing the best he could to avoid behaving as if he was his "own one and only child."[49]

"Identity," the fifth and most central stage in the life cycle, emerged from the intergenerational mutuality between children in their early stages and parents at the generative stage. Erikson first invoked the term in working with the combat marine and others like him; he elaborated on it in *Childhood and Society* and at the White House conference. There was a decided tentativeness to his elaborations. Identity as the central outcome of the intergenerational relationship would, indeed, preoccupy Erikson for years to come. He recalled Anna Freud's description of adolescence in *The Ego and the Mechanisms of Defense* (1936) as a unique period when youths often refused to accept compromises between conflicting drives and sought new ideals opposing those of their parents. And he remembered Paul Federn's discussion of "ego boundaries" between self and others. But neither colleague had spoken to the question of identity as a product of intergenerational dynamics. Erikson felt that he was very much on his own.[50]

Unlike popularizers of his identity concept, Erikson refused to describe it as a fixed, definite entity or quality. "Identity" was not a thing but a process that motivated a person in a certain direction. As the child was drawn to respond to his parents' generative behavior, he formed "fragmentary identifications." These "fragmentary" or "tentative" identities represented mergers of "what one feels one is" and what one's particular culture expected of the person. The two converged and were integrated into a total identity as part of the passage from childhood to adulthood. When this occurred, one acquired a firm sense of "the inner sameness and continuity" within one's own life and an "accrued confidence" in "the sameness and continuity of one's meaning for others, as evidenced in the tangible promise of a 'career.' " The opposite propensity, "identity diffusion," represented a "breakdown of the sense that there is continuity and sameness and meaning to one's life history." (This was the situation of the marine at Guadalcanal.) Translated into more traditional psychoanalytic terms, identity took hold at the end of adolescence when the mature ego "integrates the infantile ego stages and neutralizes the autocracy of the infantile superego." Where this integration was lacking, the superego aligned permanently with "remnants of latent infantile rage." For Erikson, there were two frequent signs of the youthful struggle between identity and identity diffusion, and they revealed the heavily Western aspect of his identity construct, for youth in several other parts of the globe did not share them. The first sign was when a young person felt strong ambivalence in settling on an occupation. The other sign was the youth projecting self-images on another in the process of falling in love. When the images were reflected in the loved other, Erikson felt they were then sometimes clarified. Because the struggle to consolidate a firm sense of identity was often prolonged and intense, there were moments of failure or "passing identity diffusion." Showing the upbeat and obviously Americanized aspect of his identity construct, Erikson cautioned clinicians against reading deep pathogenic significance into those intervals of failure.[51]

What made his description of identity as a developmental stage especially troublesome was that, despite his intentions, it seemed to convey a very cohesive and sequential view of the full life cycle. After all, the four stages that preceded it seemed clearly to have involved working toward identity, while the subsequent three stages appeared to be governed by identity consolidation. The problem with this progressive, linear neatness was that if identity concerned the place of an individual in his culture and his historical moment (as Erikson insisted), it was constantly being reworked throughout a person's life. The pursuit of a sense of continuity and sameness in time and place was jagged and unending. The pursuit was especially intense in certain national cultures like America's, Erikson acknowledged. In such a society, well-being was contingent on constant adjustment and readjustment to an unending pace of change. As an immigrant to America who never felt entirely settled, he knew this well. A person had "to derive a sense of identity out of change itself, out of the ability to choose change as the basic element of life." At all points in one's life within such a society, one had to be "ready to grasp many chances and ready to adjust to changing necessities of booms and busts, of peace and war, of migration and determined sedentary life." In a culture like America's, with its "dominant idea of progress, change is part of your cultural identity." Identity was both a discrete stage and the entire life cycle. In the United States, it called for decidedly protean qualities.[52]

The propensity for Erikson's eight-stage life cycle model to become rigid in the hands of popularizers was a major difficulty. The problem may have been of his own making, for it seemed connected to his amplification of natural biological development along moral and ethical lines.

The problem was evident in Erikson's treatment of old age, the last stage of life, which was highlighted by a sense of integrity—"the individual's ability to accept his personal life cycle as meaningful within the segment of history within which he lives." If he or she cultivated, early on, a sense of trust and mutuality, forged a viable identity, and cultivated a generative relationship with the younger generations—all in "accord with the moral and aesthetic realization" of his community—the older person reached a confident "style of integrity." Moving along a life cycle valued and sustained by his or her community and culture, he or she felt "the seal of his moral paternity of himself" so that "death loses its sting." Integrity approximated "what Jung means by integration" of personality: "You now become your own parent, as it were," having "overcome the sense of dependency, as well as the sense of mistrust." An adult who moved successfully through generativity toward this sense of integrity, without apprehensions of death, had the wherewithal to cultivate trust in his children. Those children "will not fear life if their parents have integrity enough not to fear death." There may have been a modicum of glibness here as Erikson elevated integrity over the constant and realistic apprehension of a great many people toward the finality of death. In juxtaposition to late-life integrity (an ethical good), Erikson postulated that when a parent's life cycle was characterized by the dystonic— identity confusion over identity, self-absorption over generativity, and finally despair and disgust overcoming integrity—he or she mobilized old infantile fears in himself (ethical failings) and conveyed them to his children. These fears underscored his "contempt for himself," often hidden behind professions of displeasure and contempt for others. This drift of the aging adult toward despair thwarted the propensity of younger people with whom he or she associated to acquire the ethically useful qualities of trust, mutuality, and identity.[53]

Even with his ethical translation of a biological developmental perspective, Erikson preferred that his 1950 presentations on the life cycle be construed in a circular manner more than in a progressive linear fashion. Almost in defiance of his formal life cycle charts, he described life stages as circling back on themselves and adults connecting in their development to children in theirs.

Reflecting the nature of his attentiveness to key patients like Sam and Jean, Erikson also stressed the social and cultural backdrop to individual development. Indeed, the diagram he prepared for his White House conference paper included a column listing the "social radius" of each developmental stage. This horizontal emphasis (i.e., the broad milieu surrounding the self) pushed Erikson significantly afield from Freud's vertical or "depth" focus in charting psychosexual development (i.e., piercing layers of the self). The initial stage of life, Erikson felt, included mother and newborn. In subsequent stages the "social radius" enlarged to include the father and other significant persons, play groups, school staff, and cliques. In *Childhood and Society,* Erikson suggested (in an overly tidy and rather arbitrary fashion) that each stage was integrally related to the social institutions of the person's historical era; the trust of infancy was linked to "the institution of religion, the problem of autonomy as reflected in basic political organization and that initiative in the economic order." He added that "industry is related to technology, identity to social stratification, intimacy to relation patterns, generativity to education, art, and science; and integrity finally to philosophy." In time, he hoped to reformulate all eight developmental stages "as a series of *encounters* such as only human life institutionalizes." Each stage represented an "intensive encounter with particular educative measures" in the society at a particular historical moment. Through this reformulation, Erikson hoped better to advise parents how they could "represent to the child a deep, and almost somatic conviction" in the social meaning of the child's actions. This representation from parent to child of "societal meaning" was the best way to ward off neurosis and to facilitate healthy development.[54]

Perhaps to somewhat destabilize the rigid ethical progression inherent in his life cycle model, perhaps also for modest leeway from the patriarchal gender assumptions of Freud's Vienna, Erikson emphasized the ways in which all human perspectives were relative to their specific historical moments and their social settings. However, his developmental discussions in both *Childhood and Society* and the White House conference paper echoed some of the relatively orthodox Freudian gender perspectives presented in his earlier writings. At the White House gathering, Ives Hendrick, Erikson's onetime colleague at the Boston Psychoanalytic Society, criticized him for presenting a chart of the life cycle that failed to make "any distinction in the development of the male and the female." Like Freud, Hendrick charged, Erikson was implying that male development was normative. Hendrick's critique was not entirely correct. In textual commentary concerning his 1950 charts, Erikson distinguished male from female developmental qualities. But essentially he followed Freud's lead, assigning to women different and lesser qualities. In discussing his third stage, characterized by child initiative versus guilt, for example, Erikson noted that while girls had the same locomotor, mental, and social development as boys, "they lack one item: the penis. While the boy has this visible, erectable, and comprehensive organ to which he can attach dreams of adult bigness, the girl's clitoris only poorly sustains dreams of sexual equality." Hence, while the boy sought "'making' by head-on-attack, . . . the girl . . . sooner or later changes to 'making' by making herself attractive and endearing." Following the inward contours of her genital organ, the girl was disposed "to modes of 'catching' the attention of others and sometimes of 'snatching' and 'bitchy' possessive-ness." Erikson was probably conveying a more negative perspective on female development than he intended. In several respects, his attitude approximated what Betty Friedan would soon deride as the "feminine mys-tique." In some measure, his closeness to Freudian gender orthodoxy con-tradicted his very abbreviated portrayal of female inner space as vital to human connectedness. With the emergence of strong currents of European and American feminism, Erikson would be publicly attacked for reinforcing dominant sexist and patriarchal perspectives in Western culture.[55]

COMPLETING *CHILDHOOD AND SOCIETY*

Although the birth of his Down Syndrome child energized Erikson to pick up and rework his earlier views of human development so that he clearly went beyond Freud's psychosexual model, there were no plans for a life cycle chapter in his detailed July 1948 outline for *Childhood and Society*. An invi-tation to participate in the 1950 White House conference on children—a largely ceremonial event staged every decade since Theodore Roosevelt's presidency to convey national concern for youth—prompted him to trans-form his diverse notes and conversations on the life cycle into a full, coher-ent essay. His condensed and better-written version of this essay became the most innovative chapter in *Childhood and Society*, contributing significantly to the book's enduring importance.

Beginning in 1946, the pattern of Erikson's professional writing changed. In the next four years, he published only one article ("Ego Development and Historical Change") plus a short tribute to Ruth Benedict. A full-time psychoanalytic practice, including services as a training analyst, and peri-odic teaching duties at the University of California left little time for writ-ing. Even more than amplifying his life cycle perspective, Erikson felt he needed whatever spare time he could find to transform the overcondensed papers that he had written since coming to America into a volume united by a thematic structure.[56]

Perhaps more than at any other time in his life, Erikson seemed driven to find the thematic unity in his written work. He felt handicapped because "I still do not know how to handle a typewriter" and required the costly services of a stenographer. More important, he was having difficulty reworking seven published articles. By 1948, he had decided to include six more essays that were unpublished. The problem was that there was "too little time in which to say too much." In July of 1948, he was still at the stage of reoutlining and reorganizing the thirteen essays but had not rewritten any of them: "I am just about to write a book." If he could put aside his duties as a training analyst "just for a month or two," he predicted that he could have all thirteen essays rewritten by the fall. By June of 1949, he had a rough first draft of the book and hoped to complete a total rewrite during his vacation in July. He had just been advanced from lecturer status to a regular professor at Berkeley, and he felt that professors were required to publish books.[57]

Feeling pressured, Erikson organized his time as he never had before. There were no free minutes for piano playing even though the family now owned one. One day a week, he retreated to the empty beach house of a friend for uninterrupted writing. In his cottage by the family home, he wrote several hours each day before and after seeing patients. When the weather permitted, he wrote on a picnic table surrounded by trees and shrubs. Once a week, Erikson and Joseph Wheelwright met at a restaurant, and were joined by others in the local psychoanalytic community, but only on the condition that they listen to Erik read passages from his manuscript. When he took a few hours off to go to the beach, he always brought the draft of a chapter with him to work over. Joan insisted that he needed a real break. Tuesdays were set aside for family, neighbors, and friends. This day of recreation on the large deck of the Erikson swimming pool was highlighted by his special and tasty iced tea beverages and by his growing store of jokes.[58]

Detailed outline in hand by mid-1948, Erikson began to seek a publisher. He was naive about commercial publishing. "Do publishers ever advance money?" he asked sociologist David Riesman. If they did, he might use the advance to reduce clinical duties "and to concentrate entirely on the book." A former lawyer and onetime clerk to Supreme Court Justice Louis Brandeis, who had launched a second career as a University of Chicago sociologist, Riesman was emerging as a major postwar social scientist and intellectual. In 1950, he would publish *The Lonely Crowd*, a monumental study of social conformity. After Erikson successfully treated Riesman's daughter, their friendship had flourished. Beginning with *Childhood and Society*, Riesman would guide Erikson on professional and publication decisions for years to come. Advance or no advance, Erikson recounted to Riesman, publishers were very reluctant to issue him a contract. The editorial offices at

Harper and Knopf had both rejected the proposed volume outright on the ground that the essays he was preparing would not add up to a coherent book. Harvard psychiatrist Carl Binger and muckraking journalist Carey McWilliams were impressed by the innovative quality of those essays, and they recommended the project to the house of W. W. Norton. Priding itself on acquiring enduring books like Freud's *New Introductory Lectures* and Franz Alexander's *The Medical Value of Psychoanalysis,* Norton was interested. Binger's recommendation proved to be fortuitous, as he was a friend of Storer Lunt, president of the company.[59]

Lunt examined Erikson's outline and his first draft and shared the reservations of his counterparts at Harper and Knopf. A book of essays would command limited sales. Yet Binger's appraisal was important to Lunt, and he consulted with Katherine Barnard, an editor charged with enhancing Norton's psychology list. A Smith College graduate who was more attentive to her professional career than her marriage prospects, Barnard's wit and grace distinguished her from the image of the austere New England spinster. She was won over by the depth and profundity of Erikson's writing. Lobbying assiduously, she persuaded Lunt to issue him a contract based on a second draft. Neither Barnard nor Lunt expected sales to exceed a few thousand copies. To limit expenses and thereby reduce Norton's financial gamble, Lunt insisted that Erikson cut nearly 20,000 words from his text. Erikson had prepared beautiful multicolored charts and sketches to illustrate the life cycle, children's play constructions, and other items that he wanted readers to *see.* Lunt ruled that colored illustrations were too expensive and should be replaced by black-and-white ones with broken lines or some other easily reproducible format. Desperate for a book contract, Erikson agreed to these changes. Lunt offered the standard royalty scale—10 percent of the $4.75 list price for the first 5,000 copies, 12.5 percent for the next 5–10,000 if sales ever reached that level, and 15 percent beyond 10,000. Initially, no advance was provided. In May of 1950, Erikson wrote to Lunt: "I need money. It is not easy in one year to write a book, to turn professor, and to pay taxes on past (and spent) income." Lunt sent him $500—the extent of his advance for what eventually became one of the most important volumes in Norton's publishing history.[60]

As they read drafts of *Childhood and Society,* Lunt and Barnard were impressed by Erikson's engaging and colorful style, knowing that English was not his first language. He had forgotten whatever Danish he had picked up during his earliest years, and felt that he "never had a mother tongue really" (even with his proficiency in German). Barnard noted the "occasional wrong choice of [a] word . . . or of the phrasing of a whole sentence." Lunt was impressed that a European immigrant, nearly fifty, had found such a "remarkable" facility with English. Yet he wanted the entire manuscript to go through a close sentence-by-sentence review to correct occasional confused or obscure phrasing. "Is this something Mrs. Erikson can handle," Lunt asked Erik, "or something that we should take on ourselves?" Erik had no problem deciding: "I expect to have certain details of style taken care of by my wife, before I consider the M.S. finished." Joan had edited every article Erik had ever written, and she was careful not to curb his idiosyncratic style or the unique voice behind that style. Above all, she had been intent on safeguarding his meaning and the sometimes long, rambling sentences that he often felt were necessary to express himself. With Joan as the major editor of *Childhood and Society,* Erik felt that something wonderful occurred akin to Alva Myrdal sitting at a desk facing her husband, Gunnar, and drawing out his style and meaning for *An American Dilemma.* Joan understood the free-ranging, artistic quality of Erik's temperament and could help him channel that quality into an engaging first book. "It was the transfer of an artistic imagination to writing," Erik recalled, that Joan had facilitated. Writing breaks—long walks together in Orinda, and especially strolls in view of San Francisco Bay—were joyous ventures that seemed to help with this transfer. In time, Joan would identify her role with that of Pietho, the Greek goddess of persuasion, who enriched and strengthened the messages of Prometheus, Orpheus, and Socrates.[61]

Joan's work as her husband's principal editor involved more than style and clarity. She helped Erik find his audience. Joan had always been less than enamored with psychoanalytic jargon or by the factional struggles and ambitions of Freud's followers. She wanted Erik to move "beyond" the analysts, to reach a general audience of readers. Erik felt that Freud himself had achieved just that through broad-ranging and jargon-free texts. The clearest example of this concern with a wider audience was a decision to delete a particular essay included in his 1948 outline. This essay was a reexamination of Freud's famous discussion of his own Irma Dream in his magnum opus, *The Interpretation of Dreams.* In the outline, Erik proposed a different interpretation of the dream, showing that it revealed not only Freud's unconscious drives but also the ego's efforts at synthesizing or incorporating the society and culture of the day. Feeling that it was of interest only to psychoanalysts, Joan urged Erik to delete the essay. She also feared that it would accentuate his differences with Freud, and so would not enhance his career. David Riesman disagreed. Because Erikson would demonstrate how Freud's use of dream analysis reflected his own life and society, Riesman felt the essay would illustrate how Freud's psychoanalytic perspectives were culturebound. Erikson considered Riesman's advice. In the end, he agreed with Joan, but subsequently published the essay in a psychoanalytic journal. At roughly the same time, the Eriksons decided to include an abbreviated version of their White House conference paper on the life cycle as the seventh chapter ("Eight Ages of Man") in *Childhood and Society.* Chapter seven was, of course, Freud's famous elaborative chapter that made *The Interpretation of Dreams* a coherent and enduring classic. Erikson never indicated that he was contesting Freud's preeminent position by designating the major essay of his book as the seventh chapter. This placement may have been prompted more by a sense of aesthetics and syncretism than out of a calculated desire to outflank Freud.[62]

Deciding against limiting himself to a psychoanalytic audience, Erikson thought of a broader, educated, if still somewhat limited public consisting of psychiatrists, psychologists, social workers, and physicians. He also assumed that his audience would be primarily American. He had no idea that the book would eventually go into multiple foreign as well as American printings and become required reading in colleges and graduate schools. In addition to considering his audience, Erikson reflected on the unifying theme of his book. He remained determined to produce more than a loose collection of essays. Despite his initial reservations about the disparate essays, Storer Lunt found the second draft "a little scattered in its organization" but now felt that it "does hold together nicely." Yet Lunt could not specify a theme that held the material together.[63]

Erikson was a harsher critic of his thematic mission than Lunt. He told the Norton staff, for example, that a proposal for a picture of an Native American baby on the dust jacket was "too specific"—this was more than a book about Native Americans or even about children in general. But what were the contours of the wider unity? Erikson advanced one theme after another. In his 1948 outline, the theme was that "living historical ideas are created and survive not primarily in and through words and ideas consciously transmitted from adult to adult, but . . . through pre-verbal and emotional conditioning in childhood." Closer to completion, he realized that this important thematic statement pertained only to parts of his manuscript. Consequently, he broadened the theme. In a promotional blurb Erikson prepared for Norton, he described *Childhood and Society* as a book on "the relationship between childhood training and cultural accomplishment, and between childhood fear and social anxiety." But he felt that this blurb was too general. Thus, in the final draft of the manuscript, he wrote that the "main chapters" concerned efforts to understand and remedy "anxiety in young children, apathy in American Indians, confusion in veterans of war, arrogance in young Nazis." But then, perhaps realizing that this theme did not cover his analysis of the life cycle, American character, Gorky's childhood, or clinical patients, he asserted that his essays were assembled in four sections—the biological basis of psychoanalytic theory, pressing social issues, the ways of the ego, and adolescence. In the years after publication, Erikson made still other assertions of his unifying theme. As he became conscious of his reputation as identity's architect, for example, he remarked that "identity held them [the essays] together."[64]

In part, Erikson may have shifted between overly constrictive and vague, expansive thesis statements because parts of his book involved particular people and issues while other parts coupled broad assertions with sparse data. He had very particular, detailed field observations for his essays on the Sioux and the Yurok, for example, and lengthy clinical notes for his discussions of individual patients. On the other hand, he lacked solid and specific detail for his chapters on national character and his essay on the life cycle. In the end, Erikson acknowledged that *Childhood and Society* was "a subjective book, a conceptual itinerary" that reflected his highly varied experiences and readings.[65]

One of the more general thematic statements Erikson offered in the first edition of *Childhood and Society* was that it was "a psychoanalytic book on the relation of the ego to society" or "the ego's roots in social organization"—that is, the ego sought to integrate instinct, ideals, and other elements of a person's inner life with the external conditions in the society about him or her. In a sense, Erikson offered to embrace and bridge the old Cartesian dualism between the inner subject and the outer object of inquiry. Two years after his book was published, he prepared notes for a seminar presentation that amplified this perspective. He conveyed in a single paragraph what he thought he had argued in *Childhood and Society,* but in clearer and fuller terms than before or since:[66]

> The functioning society, through the agencies of tradition (family, school) takes the individual in trust and (through its child training methods) tries to give consistent meaning to the emerging drive fragments and growing capacities. Where the individual and the environment succeed in establishing a certain mutuality of purpose and a certain sameness and continuity in growth and development, a series of positive basic attitudes are fostered which enrich both society and individual.

In thus describing the relation of ego to self and society, Erikson was not offering a single unifying theme for his book. Many of his most important observations and discussions connected only tangentially to this relationship. Yet if one had to specify the most enduring general element in *Childhood and Society,* this was probably it.[66]

Toward the end of *Childhood and Society,* Erikson noted that "I have nothing to offer except a way of looking at things." In all that he had written before his first book, this "way" involved an observable configurational perspective. He had studied a concrete arrangement of artifacts to see how inner emotion and outer social circumstance converged in the life of the person. He had often deployed this approach in his work with children and had studied their play arrangements at the Judge Baker Clinic, at Yale, and at the Berkeley Institute of Child Welfare. When he dealt with adults like the combat marine at the VA clinic, he had broadened his "way of looking" to include the shapes and forms of objects in dreams and the shapes resident within verbal and written discourse.[67]

By the time he outlined *Childhood and Society* in 1948, Erikson hoped he could draw many of his essays together by calling "on the residues within one of my pre-psychological occupations, namely art: I shall try to make the reader see as well as think." Having completed the book, he felt that a "configurational level" of analysis had emerged where he had been able to focus on the bridge between "the obvious, manifest behavior, and the latent, hidden meaning" of a person's concrete expressions—the outer social and inner emotional worlds. Through the configurational perspective that pervaded the volume, his clinical and artistic "sides come to some kind of agreement." By showing how the ego synthesized inner life and outer social organization, the configurational approach had reconciled his visual-artistic interests with his psychoanalytic and clinical activities. Because he had revealed this "way of looking at things" in one essay after another, Erikson hoped that he had not only made *Childhood and Society* a book but shown himself to be an author of some capacity and promise.[68]

The centrality of the configurational approach to emphasize the tie of self to society also suggested that Erikson, the émigré, had become an American author. In her important article on national cultural expressions in psychoanalytic psychology, Suzanne Kirschner presents compelling evidence to the effect that this link of inner self (a suspiciously vague construct) to outer society has been most uniquely American. Certainly, it has had little currency in Japan. In France and in Latin cultures, one's inner self has been regarded as fixed at birth, having no connection with an outer self resident in society. Despite the fact that England's strong traditions of radical Protestantism crossed the ocean to America, expression of inner selfhood in daily social life has never been as popular as in the United States. Rupert Wilkinson arrives at a perspective approximating Kirschner's in his definitive volume on American national character studies since the 1940s. The complex connection in America between the individual and the community has long been a central theme for students of American national character, occupying such distinguished Erikson contemporaries and collaborators as Margaret Mead and Geoffrey Gorer.[69]

Completion of *Childhood and Society,* therefore, helped Erikson to define himself in terms of profession and nationality and to fuse his artistic with his clinical talents through a unique configurational "way of looking at things." Indeed, authorship seemed to draw together the sedentary calling of a psychoanalyst and the mobility of an anthropological field worker. It also appeared to link the introspection of a therapist with the social scientist's attentiveness to cultural context. Authorship had even rejuvenated his relationship with his wife after the crisis following Neil's birth. With Joan's considerable help, he felt that he had become "a writing psychoanalyst, if again, in a language which had not been my own," and he was beginning "to repay my debt to the Freuds too, only in my currency."[70]

In addition to reconciling and unifying his diverse vocations and interests, Erikson felt that completion of the book helped him organize his future work. The book completed "the first phase of one worker's itinerary." Most of the essays in *Childhood and Society* concerned childhood. Erikson wrote to David Riesman that he had pretty fully expressed his thoughts on early life and was now ready to "leave childhood behind me and to join people like you in 'more adult' research." Specifically, he could study adolescents and adulthood—the latter stages of the life cycle. He was also eager to address the life cycle as an integrated totality and felt that he would soon be ready to proceed. Completion of *Childhood and Society* also prompted Erikson to investigate religious experience. As he had amplified his thoughts on basic trust in human development, he had found a perspective on religious feeling and belief that partially prompted him to start his next book on Martin Luther. But there was still another transitional point. Erikson felt that "my first book was written during the Roosevelt era, when the whole American enterprise, foreign and domestic," seemed to be so promising in its "anti-totalitarian and anti-racist direction." However, that hopeful era seemed to be receding. Indeed, in the chapter on American character, he was already beginning to voice serious reservations about his newly adopted country. Those reservations would proliferate in the years to come, eventually prompting Erikson to investigate a South Asian spokesman from the third world as a model for progressive change.[71]

Shortly before *Childhood and Society* was to be published, Erikson wrote to Katherine Barnard at Norton: "You were very kind," he told her, "in taking care of the needs of a wayfarer." The process of finishing the book made him less of a "wayfarer," and set him on a course to explore themes and personalities far from home. In the decades ahead, he would find comfort and orientation in his writing. The pen became crucial to the ongoing process of becoming Erik Erikson, identity's architect.[72]

ERIKSON'S AUDIENCE

Because Erikson made the necessary cuts in length and omitted colored illustrations, Norton was able to price *Childhood and Society* under five dollars a copy. First-year sales were mediocre—roughly 1,500 cloth copies. Norton sent promotional material to professionals in organizations in which Erikson had been a member, including the American Psychoanalytic Association, the American Orthopsychiatric Association, the Society for Research in Child Development, the American Psychological Association, and the Society for Applied Anthropology. The first show of interest came from political scientists, sociologists, and anthropologists. Only after some years passed did psychoanalysts in significant numbers begin reading the book. Social workers were more attentive than psychologists, while readership among psychiatrists, theologians, and historians remained minimal. By January 1955, sales exceeded 16,000, nearly one-third from college and university course adoptions—primarily from research campuses like Harvard, Michigan, Indiana, Johns Hopkins, and Berkeley. This figure exceeded Norton's expectations. Several foreign editions also went into print. Yet while hardback sales totaled a very respectable 50,000 by November 1961, they did not surge until 1963, when, to take advantage of course adoptions, Norton produced a revised paperback edition at a college textbook price of $3.45.[73]

Initially, Erikson was apprehensive about the sales and general reception of his first book. He told Lunt that he had "no idea how many copies of my book you printed and how well they sold," and he demanded an accounting. "I don't know what lies ahead," he informed Barnard. "People seem to take their time in reading the book and are slow in telling me anything about it." Erikson often demanded advances on his royalty checks to help pay his taxes, to cover the cost of airfare for seminars abroad, and for other expenses. The frequency and nature of these demands suggested that his living expenses were exceeding his appreciable clinical income. Costs involving Neil's care contributed to the shortfall. Because Erikson had hoped that *Childhood and Society* would significantly augment his income, he was deeply disappointed by sales figures for the first several years. The *New York Times* delayed a review until the spring of 1951, and Erikson told Barnard how agitated he was when it finally came out: "It is the most incompetent review among the few there are." He was even more distressed by comments in the psychoanalytic community to the effect that the book represented a "deviation" from Freud's perspective. "I was simply saying in my own words what I had learned" from the founder.[74]

Judging from most of the early book reviews and letters from friends, Erikson might have been less apprehensive. There was widespread recognition that he had written a very important volume. Riesman assured him that his "relationship to Freud has a generativity and intimacy. And you handle English in a way that reminds me of no one so much as Joseph Conrad." Riesman added that Erikson "succeeded in bringing the biological, the social, and the historical together, in a way that no one has done." A social critic, he appreciated Erikson's reservations about American pressures to conform; they matched his own, articulated in *The Lonely Crowd.* Finally, Riesman found striking similarity between his antidote to such pressures—individual autonomy—and Erikson's antidote, a strong sense of identity. David Rapaport, the very scholarly, brilliant, and demanding Hungarian émigré psychologist and psychoanalytic theorist, criticized Erikson for failing to amplify the life cycle chapter with specific case illustrations and to describe the concrete experiences that helped him build the model. He nevertheless characterized the volume as "a thing of beauty" and a courageous venture into unexplored terrain. Psychologist Robert Holt, Rapaport's promising junior colleague, felt Erikson had proven "that 'orthodox' psychoanalysis can absorb the best that the other sciences of man have to offer, and that it is *not* necessary to found a splinter group of post-Freudians in order to keep one's scientific integrity." Joseph Wheelwright found *Childhood and Society* wholly compatible with his Jungian theoretical perspective and lauded it as "a real *magnum opus*—an important book." The German émigré psychoanalyst Martin Grotjahn insisted that anyone in his profession "who misses the study of these pages is almost negligent of his obligation to inform himself about progress in the field." Predictably, psychiatrists supportive of the actively reformist and socially oriented postwar Group for the Advancement of Psychiatry appreciated Erikson's social emphasis. Robert Knight, a GAP leader, praised Erikson for "having thought your way far out of the consulting room into the societal matrix where people live and are shaped." Walter Bromberg, director of the Mendicino State Hospital, characterized the book as a crucial "modal point in the convergence of clinical psychologic sciences with the social and political sciences in our psychologic century."[75]

Erikson wanted *Childhood and Society* to be absorbed emotionally as well as intellectually. It "is and must be a subjective book." In his review, psychologist Robert W. White felt that it had achieved that end. Not a text with a systematic treatise or even a wholly new theory, it had "a certain power to promote ego development in the reader" because Erikson was a "man of . . . great wisdom." For White, who specialized in the study of personality, Erikson wrote in a decidedly clinical voice and encouraged readers to seek their own inner integrity. Garn Kern, a professor of Russian literature at the University of Rochester, observed that he had spent much of his life trying to understand how his German father and American mother had shaped his personal life. Kern finally understood the "effect of this combination" after reading Erikson's national character chapters, and felt a new mastery over himself. Erikson's former boss at the Harvard Psychological Clinic, Henry Murray, advised him that he and several other faculty in Harvard's Department of Social Relations had assigned *Childhood and Society*, and the book had encouraged their students to explore critical issues in their personal lives in illuminating and profoundly insightful ways. Karl Menninger detected a similar propensity among the residents he was teaching at the Menninger School of Psychiatry.[76]

This is not to say that readers and reviewers were unanimous in praising the book. Erikson was hurt but not entirely surprised upon learning that Anna Freud did not care for the volume. The relationship between them had been cool since he left Vienna in 1933. Wanting greater intellectual independence at that time, he had questioned the preoccupation of orthodox psychoanalysis with inner psychic life at the expense of social context. As well, Anna Freud had never forgotten the distressing circumstances of his departure. Privately, she now characterized *Childhood and Society* as mere "sociology" and not psychoanalysis. Another of his former Vienna teachers, Ernst Kris, lumped it with Erich Fromm's works as polemical and far removed from the essentials of psychoanalytic thought. Erikson was displeased when analyst-anthropologist Géza Róheim accused him of softening Freud's critical terminology and of encouraging individual conformity to society's demands. While Anna Freud, Kris, and Róheim criticized him for deviating from Freud's work, Mable Blake Cohen argued the opposite: His social analysis was "overweighed by the psychoanalytic theory of child development." Barrington Moore, the formidable political and social theorist, claimed that Erikson was insufficiently attentive to "the massive structural changes in modern society." Brandeis sociologist Beatrice Whiting, a prominent culture and personality researcher, criticized him for arbitrariness in selecting specific cultures to study and for addressing certain aspects of adult personality while ignoring others. He had not mastered the sampling methods of social science.[77]

Whether favorable or critical, reviews and letters fell short during the years that followed publication in some essentials. For one, there was no questioning whether Erikson really needed an abstract and implicitly moralistic developmental model of the life cycle for his major chapter. Although the issue concerned Rapaport, he never addressed the matter in public. Nobody critiqued Erikson's moralistic developmental model by assuming a Kantian perspective and asking whether the highest morality was to go against what was natural in a developmental sense. In addition, no commentator located

Childhood and Society within an obvious tradition of social criticism. Beginning with Max Weber's *The Protestant Ethic and the Spirit of Capitalism* (finished in 1905), this tradition became quite discernible with Erich Fromm's *Escape from Freedom* (1941). Like Weber, Fromm, and even his friend Riesman, Erikson explored in exciting and profound ways how a modern society predicated upon industrialization, bureaucratization, and advanced technology could undermine a sense of individual selfhood. Nor did reviewers connect Erikson's book with monumental studies almost simultaneous with his, like the multiauthored *The Authoritarian Personality* (1950) and Hannah Arendt's *The Origins of Totalitarianism* (1951). When *Childhood and Society* was published, the world was operating in the recent shadows of Nazi death camps and Stalinist exterminations, as well as the devastating American bombings at Hiroshima and Nagasaki. Along with the work by many of his contemporaries, Erikson's book was informed by these tragedies of "advanced" industrial, bureaucratized societies. Yet commentators failed to place his book in this exceedingly important intellectual context.

As well, those who commented on Erikson's volume did not, at first, appreciate its methodological contribution. Although some saw it delineating the ego's roots in social organization, they failed to wrestle seriously with the fact that Erikson had illuminated this psychoanalytic perspective through his configurational approach. By studying concrete artifacts and texts to see how a person's inner emotions converged with his or her outer social circumstances in an attempt to fathom one's identity, Erikson had advanced a fresh and remarkably open-ended process for gathering and interpreting evidence. He at once embraced and sought to transcend Cartesian subject-object dualism as he explored, through configurations, how individuality and society interfaced. Yet not a single reviewer of the early and mid-1950s suggested that such an interface served as a foundation for most of the essays in *Childhood and Society.* Only considerably later would favorable critics like David Elkind and Robert Rubenstein, and harsher commentators like Abram Kardiner, take adequate note of this innovation.[78]

The delayed appreciation of this innovative contribution was matched by a delay in Erikson's emergence as a cultural celebrity. Although *Childhood and Society* was the most profound and prominent of all his books, it did not become a widely selling or discussed volume in college and professional circles for some time. To be sure, translations came out during the 1950s through publishers in Japan, Sweden, Germany, Egypt, Spain, and France, while the Imago Publishing Company in London printed a special British edition. The book increasingly appeared during its first decade, moreover, on reading lists for American psychiatric residency programs. However, not until Norton brought out a revised paperback edition in 1963, with college textbook discounts, did sales soar. The book became required reading in a great many American college courses in sociology, social work, and psychology, and found itself a space in some history, philosophy, theology, and anthropology classes. Sales tripled. Norman Rockwell had predicted this would be the case—that American students would enjoy the book—and made a comic sketch of Tom Sawyer totally immersed in *Childhood and Society*. During the 1950s, Erikson had received many letters from faculty to the effect that college students found deep, personal meaning in his volume. This correspondence increased appreciably by the late 1960s and early 1970s, as he became a hero to many campus student activists. By then Robert Coles reported that student activists generally, especially those involved in civil rights, seemed to intuit Erikson's themes better than their more reflective professors. Much idolized herself by this 1960s generation of students, Margaret Mead used the *American Scholar* to nominate *Childhood and Society* as the most important book of the past quarter century. This delayed but substantial response, which finally came in the 1960s, had also characterized the reception of Riesman's *The Lonely Crowd*, Robert Nisbet's *The Quest for Community*, Ralph Ellison's *Invisible Man*, and several other books of the early 1950s concerned with maintaining viable selfhood in a hostile culture. With the publication of the revised paperback edition, "Eriksonian" became almost a household term on many campuses.[79]

Between publication of *Childhood and Society* in 1950 and the emergence of his status as a culture hero a decade later, Erikson underwent a struggle to find his own voice and to articulate the nature of "speaking out" in McCarthyite America. This searing experience provided a crucial context in explaining the resonance of his voice and texts. In a sense, it represented one of the "seeds of the 1960s."

CHAPTER SIX

Voice and Authenticity:
The 1950s

E rik Erikson wrote to Henry Murray that he had recently spoken in
Frankfurt, the city of his birth, at a celebration of the hundredth
anniversary of Freud's birth (1856). He had heard himself "speak
German before the microphones and the German president," and it had
gone well. Erikson also recounted how he had just written a book about the
exceedingly German Martin Luther. In the book, he had tried to capture
"the voice of young Luther," who had resolved an acute personal crisis by
learning "to speak to God, directly, and without embarrassment." For Erikson himself, voice became a sign of personal power, agency, and authenticity
in the course of the 1950s. Voice also assumed these dimensions for Erikson's Luther as Luther readied himself for the Reformation.[1]

THE LOYALTY OATH CRISIS

Erikson's abiding interest in voice was discernible shortly after he received a
professorship at Berkeley in 1949. That year, the University of California
was the largest higher education system in the United States. The Berkeley
campus alone was one of the most prominent research centers in the world,
with a large endowment, acclaimed libraries, and one of the six most productive faculties in the country.

Berkeley's psychology department enhanced this reputation. Chaired by
Edward Tolman (internationally recognized as an experimental psychologist
and a forerunner of cognitive psychology), it grew during the 1940s from a
modest department of eleven faculty to a sizable unit of twenty-five specialists. Several were behaviorists. Like Clark Hull at Yale, Tolman had hopes of
integrating behaviorism with psychoanalysis. He had recruited European
émigré Else Frenkel-Brunswik and American Nevitt Sanford to give psycho-

analysis a higher profile. Tolman also had his eye on Erikson, who had occasionally taught graduate courses in his department.[2]

The Institute for Personality Assessment and Research (IPAR) opened in 1949 as an important affiliate of the Berkeley Department of Psychology. It grew out of an OSS Officers Selection Service Program that had conducted psychological evaluations of potential American military officers and intelligence agents during World War II. Henry Murray, the OSS program head, had modeled it on the psychological clinic he directed at Harvard. Murray recruited his former Harvard doctoral student Donald MacKinnon (who had studied with Carl Jung in Zurich and with Kurt Lewin in Berlin) to run a large selection station in Fairfax, Virginia. MacKinnon had set up the station's officer assessment program to identify the ideal personality characteristics for American overseas operatives. After the war, Tolman (supported by Sanford) invited MacKinnon to join the Berkeley psychology department and to establish IPAR, which would revise the wartime assessment program to deal with the concerns of civilian society. MacKinnon then persuaded Sanford to help him set up a personality assessment project at IPAR. The project used as subjects various advanced graduate students from sixteen Berkeley academic departments. In addition to subjects, MacKinnon needed a research staff. He had known Erikson from a stint at Murray's Harvard clinic in the mid-1930s and wanted to hire him as a project staff investigator—hopefully with regular faculty status. Assisted by Sanford, he enlisted Tolman's support for the hire despite almost certain opposition within the psychology department from Jean Walker Macfarlane owing to her difficult experience with Erikson at the Institute for Child Welfare. By endorsing Erikson for the IPAR staff, Tolman knew that he was very nearly welcoming him to faculty status in his own department, which encompassed IPAR.[3]

Prodded by Tolman and MacKinnon, the dean of the College of Arts and Sciences appointed an interdepartmental faculty committee to consider Erikson. The committee recommended a tenured faculty appointment that would straddle the psychology department and IPAR (60 percent) and the psychiatry division of the medical school (40 percent). As might be expected, the committee was concerned about Erikson's unwillingness to master scientific methodologies in a disciplined and scholarly way. But it did not want Yale, which had offered Erikson an associate professorship in pediatrics and psychiatry, to get him. The University Budget Committee opposed the recommendation to hire because Erikson lacked "scientific responsibility" and did not support his conclusions with "adequate" data. Initially both the dean and the university president, Robert Sproul, agreed with the budget committee. However, strong endorsement of Erikson's work by Rockefeller Foundation officials and the persistence of Tolman and

MacKinnon led to a reversal. Erikson was offered a full professorship in psychology and a lecturer position in psychiatry. This was quite a promotion over his previous lecturer and research appointments, which were supported by soft money, especially from grant income. He would be salaried at $4,320, with permission to augment his income as he saw fit through his private psychoanalytic practice.[4]

Erikson recognized that he lacked the customary academic credentials of a professor with tenure, and that his Jewish lineage counted against him in academia. He was flattered beyond belief by the various offers and knew that he was professionally surpassing Freud, who had never secured an appointment as "a full, active professor." Although the Menninger Foundation subsequently outbid Berkeley on salary, it could not offer him a professorship. His choice was between Berkeley and Yale. He turned to Margaret Mead, who recommended Berkeley, where the combination of an academic salary plus private practice would exceed his Yale salary. Aware of Erikson's disposition, as a footloose immigrant, to move at frequent intervals, she felt that a continued stay in the Bay Area might mitigate against this tendency. Impressed by the higher professorial rank at Berkeley, Erikson was also pleased that Tolman and his psychology colleagues "know my weaknesses" but were still willing "to let me work in my own way." He told Anna Freud that he felt increasingly uncomfortable with "the medical mechanization of the psychoanalytic institutes" in northern California; faculty status at Berkeley afforded greater independence. Erikson formally assumed his new position in July 1949.[5]

At the time, McCarthyism was spreading. The Cold War had intensified in the late 1940s, particularly with the fall of Chiang Kai-shek's regime to the Chinese Communists, the Soviet detonation of an atomic bomb, and the efforts by ambitious politicians like Richard Nixon to test the electoral appeal of domestic anticommunism. The foremost public issue for American educators—whether Communists or Communist "sympathizers" should be allowed to teach—was troublesome. Throughout the country at all levels of education, loyalty oaths emerged as the primary weapon against Communist "subversion" in the classroom. Early in 1949, California state legislator Jack Tenny proposed enactment of such an oath to ensure faculty loyalty at the University of California (UC). For generations UC faculty had signed an oath of allegiance to the federal and California constitutions. To head off the Tenny bill, which threatened UC autonomy, and to underscore the university's policy against employing Communists, President Sproul proposed an alternative oath, which his Board of Regents adopted. All UC employees had to sign a pledge that they neither belonged to nor supported "any party or organization that believes in, advocates, or teaches the overthrow of the United States government by force or violence." A champion of professorial freedom up to this point, Sproul excepted Communists and claimed that their party membership precluded objective scholarship. Faculty objections prompted a slight revision in Sproul's policy. In early 1950, his regents placed the essential terms of the oath in the annual contract that UC employees signed. If an employee did not sign this contract, he or she could testify before a faculty Committee on Privilege and Tenure to establish loyalty. That committee would recommend either termination or retention to Sproul and the regents.[6]

Faculty response to the oath was varied and complex. Initially, roughly ninety members of the UC academic senate refused to sign and some were suspended. At one point, forty-eight courses were dropped for want of qualified instructors. Most UC undergraduates and even some segments of the faculty were indifferent. Most faculty who opposed the oath adopted a "sign, stay, and fight" posture; they signed the document so they could stay at UC and fight the oath. The ranks of nonsigners shrunk weekly. In the end, the final holdouts consisted mostly of internationally distinguished scholars like Ernst Kantorowicz and Ludwig Edelstein, who could readily find academic employment elsewhere.[7]

At Berkeley, the psychology department and its IPAR affiliate became the center of opposition to the loyalty oath. Shortly after the oath requirement was instituted, Tolman proclaimed that he would not sign. He headed the Group for Academic Freedom, which provided financial and moral support to nonsigners. Several others in psychology and IPAR followed Tolman's lead. In their testimony before the Committee on Privilege and Tenure, some nonsigners indicated that they were not Communists, and the committee usually recommended they be allowed to stay. But others, like Tolman and Sanford, refused to state whether they were Communists, claiming this was not the committee's business. They invoked the legal and ethical standard of "privacy" and were dismissed from the university. Tolman and Sanford cautioned younger colleagues, faculty who lacked independent sources of income, and all naturalized American citizens, that it would not be immoral if they signed the oath or testified to the committee that they were non-Communists. They emphasized practical considerations of retaining employment and citizenship as well as the dangers of a nativist political climate. What they considered significant was to actively oppose the principle of a loyalty requirement even if one signed the oath. Tolman and Sanford were pleased with MacKinnon, for example, when he articulated his contempt for the loyalty principle while putting his pen to an oath document.[8]

Teaching in the psychology department and interviewing graduate students for the IPAR assessments, Erikson was therefore in the eye of the storm. He watched as Tolman and Sanford, who had championed his controversial professorship, mobilized the opposition. Friends in other departments, such as Alexander Meiklejohn, were also outspoken opponents. Like Sanford, Erikson could maintain a steady income simply by enlarging his private practice if refusal to sign the oath cost him his job. He was less than comfortable, anyway, with the disciplined, methodology-oriented research procedures at both IPAR and the psychology department. On the other hand, he enjoyed teaching graduate psychology seminars and was exceedingly proud of having secured a professorship. The professorship required public speaking obligations, including forums beyond the classroom. Erikson found speaking in academic forums to be exceedingly stimulating. Lecturing and presenting to interested new audiences was most gratifying and seemed to affirm his sense of himself. He acknowledged that "academic life has become somewhat of a necessity for me, as a balance to clinical life, and as a mode of intellectual exchange." Still, there were free speech issues at hand, and "the time has passed (if there ever was one) when we must hold on to professorships at all costs."[9]

Erik sought guidance from his family. The Eriksons had put considerable money and labor into their home in Orinda, and signing would allow them to stay. They also feared that because Erik (like others on staff at the Mt. Zion Rehabilitation Center) had offered a course at the politically leftist California Labor School, he might be charged as a Communist sympathizer. In his "Legend of Gorky's Youth" essay (which had been circulated and discussed enthusiastically even before publication), he appealed for bridge-building between Western and Russian "protestants." That might have "validated" charges of subversion. On the other hand, Erik and Joan continued to feel that they had not been sufficiently open and honorable in their handling of Neil's birth, and failure to be forthright had carried a cost. Moreover, they were pleased with their other sons' responses. Jon prepared a high school essay insisting that no conscientious American citizen could sign the oath, while Kai chaired a college committee that strenuously opposed it. With *Childhood and Society* in the works, a moderately lucrative private practice, and several good job prospects at out-of-state clinics and universities, the Eriksons also knew that an ethical stand would cost relatively little. As the months went by, therefore, Joan began to urge Erik not to sign the oath.[10]

While Erikson was obviously influenced by his wife and family circumstances, he also pondered the theoretical and ethical dimensions of his posture on the loyalty oath. His immigrant status played a role in his consideration. Erikson believed he was indebted to the country that had taken him in; he had happily pledged his loyalty to its government and laws when he became an American citizen. He would now seem ungrateful if he spoke out against a pledge of loyalty. Erikson also feared that he did not adequately understand the meaning of an oath in American political culture. Unlike, say, Herbert Marcuse, an immigrant intellectual with a surer sense of himself, Erikson was reluctant to criticize his new homeland. However, he also felt that the oath violated "the psychological spirit of the [federal] Constitution." Disregarding James Madison's hard-nosed skepticism, the Constitution was for Erik a document promoting trust and mutuality, and the oath contradicted that spirit. Because the oath became "a test of my American identity," he had to oppose it. Endangered American troops in Korea had pledged themselves to this spirit of the Constitution (or so he assumed), and he wanted to support them. Most important, being keenly aware of "what had happened in Europe [the rise of Nazism and Fascism]," he could project "what the McCarthy period might lead to."[11]

Other European immigrant colleagues at Berkeley also sensed that a loyalty oath was painfully similar to Nazi German demands for unquestioning obedience. Ernst Kantorowicz, the distinguished medieval historian, compared the UC oath to the University of Frankfurt oath of allegiance to Hitler that he had refused to sign. Two of Erikson's psychology colleagues, Else Frenkel-Brunswik and Nevitt Sanford, had taken active roles in the distinguished *Authoritarian Personality* project, which had been designed to determine the psychological qualities that attracted people to totalitarianism. Perhaps too loose with language and conceptualization, both psychologists characterized the UC oath as "unmistakably totalitarian." In his graduate seminars, Erikson periodically compared their formulations on totalitarian attractions with his findings on Hitler's youth appeal; the California oath was not lost in his discussion. While he was apprehensive of the personal consequences of going on record against the loyalty oath, he felt that history demonstrated that it was even more dangerous not to speak out.[12]

In the end, Erikson refused to sign. During the spring of 1950, he testified before the UC Committee on Privilege and Tenure to explain why. He arrived at the hearing with a carefully crafted statement and read it aloud. He also sent the statement to the president of the American Psychoanalytic Association. It was read to those attending the APA annual meeting the following winter. A major professional journal, *Psychiatry*, published the statement in 1951. While only two printed pages long, it represented Erikson's first experience at speaking out on a political issue in a planned and public way before academic and psychoanalytic forums.

Erikson began by disavowing Communist affiliations "inside 'the party' or outside, in this country or abroad." That provided a technical basis for the faculty committee to recommend continuation of his employment—for the moment but not necessarily on a long-term basis. The balance of Erikson's statement was more principled and forthright.[13]

For one, he characterized his refusal to sign the oath as an act of solidarity with a younger generation, providing an appropriate example to his students. Were he to sign the oath, his students would be instructed by his example to "suspect themselves and one another," to abdicate human trust. They would also see his hypocrisy if he confessed to his political beliefs and values as if they were "objective truth." In contrast, by refusing to acknowledge the "official truth" of the loyalty oath, he encouraged in his students "those deep and often radical doubts which are the necessary condition for the development of thought." Erikson's statement did not mention the junior faculty who had not signed the oath and had been dismissed. But elsewhere he made clear that this was another reason he could never assent to the oath. To sign was to betray the courageous ethical actions of junior colleagues. He would remain in solidarity with this generation and was prepared to resign his professorship to maintain it.[14]

Erikson's statement to the Committee on Privilege and Tenure enunciated a second principle: "My field includes the study of 'hysteria,' private and public, in 'personality' and 'culture,' " he announced. The nation was in the grips of such a hysteria, " 'bunching together' of all that seems undeniably dangerous; spies, bums, Communists, liberals, and 'professors.' " Universities were obligated to resist this and to launch "the countermove of enlightenment." Instead of signing the oaths, professors should show "a conviction born of judiciousness" and teach about "the tremendous waste in human energy which proceeds from irrational fear and from the irrational gestures which are part of what we call 'history.' " Because he taught students about the dangers of mass hysteria, Erikson concluded that he could not participate in the current wave of hysteria: "My conscience did not permit me to sign the [UC employment] contract after having sworn that I would do my job to the best of my ability."[15]

The Committee on Privilege and Tenure recommended Erikson's retention: He was no Communist. His statement indicated that, unlike Communists, he was capable of impartial scholarship. For a diffident intellectual who now seemed to have found inner strength and the capacity to speak out, this exoneration was insufficient. Faculty personnel records indicate that he resigned his professorship effective June 30, 1950, three months before *Childhood and Society* was published. Erikson's public explanation was that he could not continue his professorship while other, largely junior, faculty who had not been exonerated by the committee were dismissed.[16]

Six weeks after Erikson resigned, IPAR director MacKinnon wrote a long letter to Alan Gregg of the Rockefeller Foundation, detailing the devastating effects of the UC loyalty oath upon his staff and requesting financial support to repair some of the damage. MacKinnon reported that Erikson was "fed up with conditions which have obtained during the past year" and was not continuing on the faculty. He noted, however, that Erikson was *"willing to sign the new form of contract in order to continue his work in the Institute as research associate or consultant."* By then, the regents had replaced the initial loyalty oath with a provision in staff contracts that echoed the language of the oath. Through the "new form of contract," as it was called, an employee pledged "that I am not a member of the Communist Party or any other organization which advocates the overthrow of the Government by force or violence and that I have no commitments in conflict with my responsibilities with respect to impartial scholarship and free pursuit of truth." In his statement to the Committee on Privilege and Tenure, Erikson objected not only to the language of the original oath but to this pledge as well. To be sure, many faculty viewed the earlier oath as more invidious than the new contractual provision. Calling the revision a moral victory, they signed the "new form of contract." Most IPAR staff, however, regarded the "new form" as a ruse.[17]

Nothing in the UC archives or personnel records proves conclusively that Erikson signed the "new form of contract" (which he was required to do in order to remain on the IPAR staff). Psychologist Donald Brown, his IPAR colleague and friend, vividly recalls that Erikson continued to work with him on IPAR assessments through the 1950–51 academic year. Erikson's name did not appear in records of IPAR proceedings for that interval, but that is no proof that Brown was mistaken. Just before the 1950–51 academic year began, MacKinnon told Alan Gregg of Rockefeller that he needed special funding for two IPAR staff members who had been dismissed by the university, but that Erikson would be able "to continue his work" uninterrupted (presumably because he had signed the "new form of contract"). In two subsequent vitae that he prepared, Erikson designated himself as a UC employee well into 1951 (a good while after he officially resigned his professorship). It was not until the fall of 1951 that he left Berkeley and joined the staff of the Austen Riggs Center.[18]

It is almost certain that Erikson signed the "new form of contract" containing the very loyalty oath language that he publicly opposed. There was simply no other way he could have continued at IPAR as a UC employee after he resigned his professorship. To be sure, he gained little favor from administrators and others favoring compliance with the oath by signing the "new form of contract." However, it is inconceivable that he did not sense the inconsistency of his posture—that he had refused to sign and publicly attacked a loyalty oath that he had signed in a different form. This contradiction had to produce unease. Erikson felt very uncomfortable with "the kind of high-visibility public stand that other non-signers were taking," IPAR colleague Harrison Gough recalled. Sanford was more familiar with

Erikson and had a more cogent appraisal. He insisted that Erikson had taken as strong a stand as he could for one who was schooled in the apolitical traditions of "Old Vienna" intellectual culture, who was deeply grateful that he had been given American citizenship, and who knew all too well that he labored at a major university with no advanced degree. Erikson's posture was stronger than at any other time in the fifteen years that Sanford had known him. Indeed, Erikson had been rather brave. Sanford, however, also pointed out that he and Tolman had felt Erikson's backing "almost not at all" as they led the fight against the oath.[19]

Having fired thirty-one faculty by October of 1951, the UC regents deleted the oath provision from the "new form of contract." They did so because the California legislature had enacted the Levering Oath that all state employees were required to sign. Consequently, when the California Supreme Court declared both forms of the UC loyalty oath invalid in *Tolman* vs. *Underhill* (1952), it was on the grounds that, through the Levering Oath, the state had preempted the Board of Regents. The university could not require its employees to sign anything if the state assumed that authority. Those who had been fired could return to the university with back pay, but they would still have to sign the Levering Oath. The California court did not address the issue of whether the university oath provision or the Levering Oath was valid under state police powers or whether they violated the right of free speech guaranteed in the federal Constitution. As such, the Tolman decision did not undermine the pervasive McCarthyite climate.[20]

Among many American intellectuals and professionals, however, Tolman and Sanford were regarded as heroes fighting the red scare. Most assumed that Erikson had taken a similar, uncompromising stand. Karl Menninger lauded Erikson for his courage and required Menninger School of Psychiatry residents to study his statement to the Committee on Privilege and Tenure. David Riesman praised Erikson for refusing to be "lured by the many convincing rationalizations for signing" the UC oath and promised to assist him in finding another academic position. Storer Lunt of W. W. Norton congratulated Erikson for his "undeniably correct statement" to the committee and urged him to write a sequel to *Childhood and Society* incorporating his recent experience: "You have commanding and telling things to say." A public persona was being constructed more heroic and powerful than Erikson himself.[21]

Erikson appreciated the show of support, but he never characterized his posture on the oath (refusing to sign its most invidious form but signing the "new form of contract") as a great moment of conscience. Indeed, he rarely talked about the experience at all. "It was a bitter business," he confided to Riesman. He hoped to understand better his role in the oath dispute and, more generally, how American culture promoted conformity by reading Riesman's *The Lonely Crowd.* He instructed Katherine Barnard to delete all references to his UC professorship in publicity for *Childhood and Society* since he had relinquished the position and planned to leave the university. He was putting this conflict behind him—or so he hoped.[22]

In 1953, with the oath controversy behind him but McCarthyism still very much alive, Erikson delivered a paper at a conference on totalitarianism sponsored by the American Academy of Arts and Sciences. His presentation on "Wholeness and Totality" spoke explicitly to the totalistic solutions of German Nazis and Soviet Stalinists. But he also addressed McCarthyism in America. People generally, and above all youth, needed to feel "wholeness," Erikson explained in less-than-exacting language. "Wholeness" came with "a sense of continuity and sameness which gradually united the inner and outer worlds"—the inner emotions and the outer social circumstances— leaving one with a clear identity and strong confidence. Unlike "wholeness" (the psychological "boundaries of which are open and fluent"), its opposite of "totality" always "evokes a *Gestalt* in which an absolute boundary is emphasized" so that "nothing that belongs inside must be left outside, nothing that must be outside can be tolerated inside." When people, especially the young, felt fragmented and endangered, they were disposed to seek "a synthetic identity (extreme nationalism, racism, or class consciousness)" and to castigate "a totally stereotyped enemy of the new identity." This rigid separation of the world into a virtuous "we" and a villainous "they" represented the "totalitarian conditions . . . for organized terror and for the establishment of major industries of extermination." America had the potential to follow that totalitarian road to Auschwitz, Erikson feared. But he held out hope that a nation of immigrants would pursue "wider and firmer identities . . . to meet all the diversities, dissonances, and relativities which emerge" as Americans "evolve a new world-image—an image which encompasses all of mankind." This was an image of "wholeness." (Later, Erikson would refer to "universal specieshood"—the unity of all humankind despite superficial distinctions.) He sensed that his adopted country, which he hoped would soon reject McCarthyism, was headed toward wholeness. He felt that he was headed there, too, as he sought to recover more of what he started vaguely to conceive of as his authentic voice. Such a voice could enhance his sense of unity and convey wholeness by pushing him closer to his "genuine" inner self. At least, that is what he wanted to believe. Erikson seemed to be embracing an odd mix of the German romanticism so conspicuous in his late adolescent journal and an emerging postwar American cult of authenticity that postulated the potential for the emergence a "true" self.[23]

STOCKBRIDGE

By 1951, Erik, Joan, and Sue Erikson were on the move again—back to the northeast from which they had migrated in 1939. Jon remained in Orinda with the family of a friend so he could finish his senior year of high school, while Kai was already off to college. Vienna-trained, experienced in conducting training analyses, proficient in English, and author of a broad-ranging and significant book, Erik enjoyed bountiful job prospects. Yale continued to want him on its faculty. The Denver Mental Hygiene Clinic, a prominent child guidance facility affiliated with the University of Colorado Medical Center, also sought him. The Western Psychiatric Institute at the University of Pittsburgh Medical School extended an attractive offer, and so did the Menninger Foundation in Topeka, Kansas.[24]

Since early 1947, Robert Knight, chief of staff at Menninger, had his eye on Erikson. As it happened, Knight left Topeka later that year, dejected that he had no future at the top level of management despite his skills, experience, and reputation. The Menninger Foundation was a family organization, he recognized; the founding brothers would always retain control, and he would never have more status than as an adopted son or stepson. This recognition seemed to bond him to Erikson (literally an adopted son) from the start. Knight accepted an offer to direct the Austen Riggs Center in the small Berkshire town of Stockbridge in western Massachusetts. By 1948, he had brought with him the creative core of Menninger's clinical psychology department and its research staff, including David Rapaport, Roy Schafer, Margaret Brenman-Gibson, and Merton Gill. When Erikson had visited Topeka to consult and to lecture, this "Stockbridge exodus" group, or so it was called, had been his most appreciative audience. Knight had offered Erikson a job in Topeka and renewed the offer for Riggs even before he had assumed his directorship there. Although Erikson rejected both offers, Knight persisted during the late 1940s and early 1950s. When Brenman-Gibson and Rapaport learned that Erikson had refused to sign the UC loyalty oath, they suggested to Knight that it was time to tender another offer. He telephoned Erikson, pledging an attractive salary plus large blocks of time free of clinical duties for travel and writing. Knight also promised to allow Erikson to work for a few days every other week with Benjamin Spock at the Arsenal Nursery School of the Western Psychiatric Institute, an affiliate of the University of Pittsburgh. Erikson would be designated formally as a professor on the Pittsburgh faculty.[25]

Knight had been shrewd in helping to arrange this professorship. Erikson was deeply distressed over losing his faculty position at Berkeley and the prospect of another academic title was important. But other factors besides salary, free time, and a title induced Erikson to accept Knight's offer this time. Location was relevant. The Austen Riggs Center was in a very small, beautiful New England town that had been founded in 1734 as a mission station and school for local Mohicans. Jonathan Edwards had come here after his controversial Northampton ministry. Over the decades, prominent theologians, intellectuals, and artists, including Reinhold Niebuhr, Thornton Wilder, and Norman Rockwell, settled in the town. A Rockwell depiction for *McCall's* had turned Stockbridge into a beloved icon of a small-town America untarnished by shopping malls and traffic. Tanglewood, the summer home of the Boston Symphony Orchestra, was nearby, the Red Lion Inn offered elegant dining, the Berkshire Playhouse staged exciting performances, and St. Paul's Church, a captivating Norman-style nineteenth-century building, added to the quiet dignity of the setting.

The Riggs Center was vital to the Stockbridge economy. It operated in a well-organized open-hospital setting. There were no locked wards, and patients were free to walk into town. The openness yet protectiveness of the place appealed to Erikson: "My introversion calls for a place like Stockbridge, with cautious field trips into the metropolitan jungles." After the crises prompted by the loyalty oath and a Down Syndrome child, he and Joan appreciated a calmer, more supportive environment. Conscious of his Jewish upbringing, Erikson had inquired about anti-Semitism in the historic stronghold for Congregationalism. Fortunately, it was not a problem in the town and certainly not on the Riggs campus. The possibility of owning a large house in the country, with plenty of bedrooms and studies, plus a barn and acres of hilly and wooded land at an affordable price, represented another decided plus. The prospect of regular contact with David Rapaport, a brilliant émigré intellectual with expertise in psychoanalytic metapsychology, was also important. Finally, there was the ease of working under Knight after his unfortunate experiences with Arnold Gesell and Jean Walker Macfarlane, who could not tolerate his free-ranging and seemingly undisciplined work habits. Knight understood that Erikson was intuitive and aesthetic and needed his space and freedom to pursue his own concerns without pressure to join group research projects and formal scientific investigations. For Erikson, Knight embodied a *beseelte Sachlichkeit,* or lively matter-of-factness, that mixed decisiveness with warmth, efficiency with loyalty. Knight was tall, handsome, Protestant, and gregarious—admirable American qualities as far as Erikson was concerned. Knight may also have had the Christian and Nordic features that Erikson had long imagined as those of his missing Danish father. When Knight told Erikson that he and Rapaport were "just bursting at the prospect of your joining us," Erikson knew that he would be coming. He told David Riesman of his decision, but added that he would "make excursions from Stockbridge" periodically to pursue other possible university affiliations.[26]

The relocation from Berkeley to Stockbridge carried tangible benefits. By the mid-1950s, Erikson was earning over $20,000 annually between his Austen Riggs salary (which exceeded others on staff) and his bimonthly Arsenal Nursery School consultantship. This was not insubstantial for a clinical psychologist. Other professional income, namely *Childhood and Society* royalties plus honoraria for speaking engagements, added three or four thousand dollars. Though not wealthy, Erikson was very comfortable financially. Knight asked him to attend three staff meetings weekly, to oversee therapy for two or three patients, and to conduct a few training analyses. By staff standards, this was a very light load. Erikson had considerable time for what was becoming his first love—writing.[27]

He wrote in a large and tastefully furnished farmhouse on the outskirts of Stockbridge from which he could see the barn that his wife had turned into a crafts shop. A stream, trees, and hills were in full view. Joan managed household needs and arranged for social visits and parties while Knight attended to Erik's professional needs. "I'm an immigrant and to me there are just a few, very few places where I feel at home," he remarked. Stockbridge was one. Whenever he left town, he could remember comforting local scenes "the way the immigrant[s] would remember what they saw in Europe." Long walks with Knight and Rapaport discussing psychoanalytic theory or clinical work provided some of the pleasant memories. The excursions mixed Knight's "American jokes" with Rapaport's "inexhaustible Jewish collection, brought over from Hungary. And nothing can reconcile reality and conscience better than humor." There were also other intellectuals in the area to whom Erikson might turn for stimulating discussions. Almost always he transformed conversations with them into ways of testing the appeal of what he was writing. Playwright William Gibson lived down a dirt road, while Reinhold and Ursula Niebuhr were a few minutes away. David and Evelyn Riesman maintained a vacation house in Bennington, Vermont, and regularly exchanged visits with the Eriksons. Friendships such as these were sometimes enhanced by Erikson's considerable skill as a therapist. He could care better than most clinicians for the friend's needy relatives and even for the friend's children.[28]

In California, the crisis over Neil had strained Erik's relationships with his other children. He hoped for less stressful days in Stockbridge, with Sue living at home and the boys spending vacations and summers with their parents. From western Massachusetts, Neil, three thousand miles away, could be "forgotten" more easily. As Erik sought better relations with his children, he saw an advantage in averting another troublesome matter from the past—his Jewish upbringing. Long ago, he had acquiesced in Joan's rearing the three as less-than-devout Christians.

Erik felt most comfortable with Kai, who pursued the sort of intellectual and scholarly path Erik found increasingly congenial. At Reed College in Oregon, Kai had done well in his studies. After graduation, he worked with delinquent boys in the Berkshires. Then he entered the sociology graduate program at the University of Chicago, completing a master's degree in 1955 and a doctorate in 1963. Riesman, the eminent sociologist, helped to guide Kai through professional circles where academics too often asked (insensitively) whether he was Erik Erikson's son. Father and son co-authored a paper in the *Chicago Review* on juvenile delinquency that showed a sympathetic, nonpunitive approach toward wayward youth along the lines that Erik had learned from August Aichhorn in Vienna. The paper reflected Erik's interest in negative and positive psychological identities. But Kai added to this an emphasis on social structure. The essay revealed the ways in which juvenile courts, jails, and other punitive social institutions worked to confirm many delinquents in their deviant antisocial identities. The co-authorship was important for both father and son, marking the beginning of gratifying lifelong intellectual exchanges. Erik confided to a professional acquaintance that he "would like to work with him [Kai], but, of course, must let him go his way." Kai quickly became an important scholar in his own right. By 1960, he was teaching sociology at the University of Pittsburgh Medical School with a joint appointment in the Department of Sociology. Prestigious academic appointments at Emory in 1963 and Yale in 1966 would follow. All of Kai's publications revealed him as an innovative scholar in his own right, although he continued to be attentive to his father's ideas.[29]

Erik's relationship with Jon, who, at eighteen, elected to remain in the Bay Area after his parents moved to Stockbridge, was more troubled. Jon appeared to replicate the wandering, artist-bohemian aspect of Erik's early life, much as Kai's life resembled Erik's more orderly and respectable middle years. Although Erik realized this, he never went out of his way to share his *Wanderschaft* memories with Jon in order to build a deeper rapport with him. Indeed, not until Jon reached middle age did Erik show him the woodcuts he made during his vagabond years. Much like Theodor Homburger, who had pressured Erik to become a professional, Erik pushed Jon to follow Kai's lead—to attend college and study for a profession. Jon, however, was no scholar. He strung out his college years studying agricultural engineering while taking off for travel and other interests. He was drafted into the army, which became a significant departure from his studies. After Jon finally completed a bachelor's degree at Berkeley in 1958, he attended the Los Angeles County Art Institute for a semester. Then he found employment in

California movie studios as a laborer, and for years alternated between this work and his first love, international travel. Erik fretted over Jon's erratic work life, and tried to help him to locate a speech therapy program that might cure a long-standing stuttering problem. In order to avoid stuttering, Jon talked as little as possible. Apprehensive that Jon was allowing himself "too little leeway" in the use of his voice—that he was not speaking enough to serve his needs—Erik sought out one speech therapist after another. If he could find a good speech clinic, it might set Jon's life in better order and perhaps facilitate the kind of rapport he enjoyed with Kai.[30]

Even though Sue was the only child who moved to Stockbridge with her parents, she sometimes sensed that her father was closer emotionally to her brothers and did not feel that her mother's attentions compensated. A 1953 family photograph shows Erik bunched together with Kai and Jon, a tree trunk separating the three from Sue and Joan. As she slimmed out and became more attractive physically, Erik became somewhat more comfortable with Sue and complimented her on her appearance. Joan, however, remained deeply critical of her daughter. Sue found an academic and social niche in the private Stockbridge School. In some ways, the school was more comfortable than home, and Sue's teachers felt she was doing so well that she skipped eighth grade and completed ninth grade with ease. Not quite understanding what Stockbridge School meant to Sue, Joan and Erik transferred her to the prestigious Putney School in Vermont. This distressed Sue enormously, and the upset was compounded when the Putney School director assigned her back to ninth grade. Erik recommended that Sue be given a chance to do tenth-grade work but failed to understand the more fundamental upheaval of an adolescent who was forced to leave a facility she loved and where she had thrived. Sue felt much more comfortable by the late 1950s, after she had enrolled in Oberlin College. She majored in philosophy but was reluctant to read *Childhood and Society* as her classmates had. Erik's relationship with his only daughter remained uneven and communication was often difficult. In a life of sons, fathers, and fatherless sons, Erik seemed ill-prepared to raise a daughter.[31]

After Erik's difficult years with Joan following Neil's birth, the move to Stockbridge was a welcome relief. Here Joan found an important calling, a vocation far more her own than editing Erik's publications. In 1951, when a rather traditional Riggs activities therapist resigned, Joan took over and revolutionized the program. The activities area had been primarily an adjunct of the psychotherapy program. Clinicians assigned various activities randomly as potentially healthy outlets for their patients' pent-up impulses. Joan moved all activities work to a building in the Stockbridge business district away from the Riggs campus. She dropped formal references to therapeutic regimes and even to "patients." A "patient" was somebody with a deficiency; she geared her program to what a person did well. He or she became a craftsperson, an artist, a dramatist, a carpenter, or a doer of any other activity that augmented a sense of competence and worth. Viewing themselves from positive identities, the "workers" in Joan's activities program never harmed themselves or others (however severe their psychiatric diagnoses) as they worked on projects in town.[32]

Gradually, Joan enlarged her activities program to involve the local citizenry. Her craftspeople from the Riggs patient wards organized a public film series, staged plays, discussed seminal books, produced a newsletter, and put on numerous exhibits of their sculpture and painting. Most important, Joan helped her craftspeople to organize a nursery school for the children of the Stockbridge community. The enterprise became a great success, involving the children in a rich array of arts and crafts while their instructor-patients grew considerably more confident and content. Several instructors were able to remember troubled aspects of their own early years that they had repressed but that the children had brought to mind. Consistent with Erik and Joan's life cycle model, the nursery school was a striking illustration of the fruits of intergenerational enrichment. Remarking that Joan's activities program was designed to encourage the patients' talents and produced striking results, Knight encouraged Riggs clinicians to build on their patients' ego *strengths* in their formal therapy sessions. This emphasis seemed to produce better results than the standard medical-psychiatric model, which addressed the patient's problems or *deficiencies*. Riggs clinicians also became aware that they had to concern themselves with more than the verbal exchange between therapist and patient. There was a salutary effect to creating new forms and shapes out of cloth, clay, wood, and other materials. He or she found a new sense of competence and worth that therapeutic discourse at its optimal best did not always produce. A few months after her activities program had been launched, Joan watched as several of her "craftspeople," psychiatric patients for years, demonstrated such a level of energy, purpose, and confidence that they could leave protected Stockbridge for the comparative anonymity of large cities and suburbs.[33]

Not surprisingly, Erik became the strongest advocate of Joan's program. By regarding himself as a local craftsperson, the patient secured "true communal recognition," Erik observed. Theoretically, he noted that Joan's efforts were promoting "the ego's activated adaptability and heightened sense of reality, to the mobilized condition of the whole person." The program was also facilitating social support—"the mutual actualization of individuals on which all community depends." Above all, Joan's program "helped me to understand the curative as well as the creative role of work."

What she had taught was helping him to understand why young Martin Luther (the subject of his next book) attached so much importance to the benefits of work when it involved good "works."[34]

In part, Erik's advocacy of Joan's program was to be expected, as it drew heavily on the theoretical life cycle framework they had formulated together in California. The goals of Joan's program were the essential traits of positive human development—trust, a firm sense of identity, and intergenerational assistance or mutuality. Erik also sensed—and probably understood—why Joan was committed to the Riggs activities program; it compensated for her failure to work with her own child, Neil, thousands of miles away. While she had not helped to enhance Neil's life, she could at least work to enrich the existence of her emotionally handicapped "craftspeople." Joan appreciated Erik's empathy and support, and their life as a couple grew richer. Photographs for the period show them walking and smiling, arm in arm, through the Stockbridge village. They entered waltz contests at staff parties and (drawing upon their Vienna experience) often won awards—perhaps as much for their elegance as a couple as for their skills on the dance floor. Erik ceased to poke fun at the Sunday morning church service that meant so much to Joan, became deeply interested in liberal Christian theology and neoorthodoxy (encouraged by teas with Reinhold and Ursula Niebuhr), and talked with Joan a good deal about the "Ultimate Other." After Joan underwent major throat surgery early in 1957 for a tumor that proved benign, he fretted because her voice was not immediately back to normal. Jon still stuttered. Two members of the household with flawed voices may have been especially troubling to a clinician who, since the loyalty oath crisis, was keenly attentive to the importance of speaking out.[35]

Erik enjoyed a much improved relationship with Joan and Kai, then, after the move to Stockbridge, and perhaps a marginally enhanced relationship with Jon and Sue. But age was beginning to take a toll as health problems arose. Early in 1954, for example, his right eye temporarily ceased to focus properly. Major surgery later that year arrested the protrusion of part of his stomach into his chest cavity. Often walking across the Riggs campus in a blue blazer, a colorfully patterned tie, white buckskin shoes, a ruddy complexion, a cordial countenance, and stunning long wavy white hair, he showed more flare than others on the medical staff. He took new joy in ice cream, chocolate-covered coffee beans, a glass of cognac, and long walks to West Stockbridge or Lee. Usually, he seemed confident and outgoing, and he enjoyed humor. When young Riggs clinician Margaret Brenman-Gibson noticed him climbing out of her pool (as was customary) without swimming trunks, he covered himself and blushed as she insisted that it was not a big deal. Laughingly, he corrected her: "It is not modesty, but that I have so little to hide." He thrived on jokes by polished humorists like Rapaport and Knight, tried not to miss the televised comedy shows of Sid Caesar and George Gobel, and made his own contributions. At a 1958 meeting with other mental health consultants on Cape Cod, for example, he told the story of a tomcat he had known who had been sexually active every night but had recently been fixed. Other cats had asked Tom what he was doing out so late in view of his neutered state. "I'm a consultant (for my colleagues)," Erik announced, mimicking the sounds of a tomcat. The audience was in stitches. In his own somewhat understated and rather cerebral way, he was developing a taste for "hearty laughter" and the capacity to cultivate it through a repertory of jokes.[36]

CLINICAL PRACTICE:
TRACKING *YOUNG MAN LUTHER*

Erikson thrived in Stockbridge and the Riggs Center. A year after he arrived, he explicitly compared Riggs to the safe sanitarium in the Alps that Thomas Mann had characterized in *The Magic Mountain.* Yet he found it refreshing at times to "escape our magic mountain here for a little while and to see some productive dust and fertile dirt of which Pittsburgh has plenty." Erikson was overstating the contrast between Riggs and his bimonthly consulting duties at the Arsenal Nursery School and periodically at two cooperative institutions—the parent Western Psychiatric Institute and the local psychoanalytic society—all affiliated with the University of Pittsburgh and the city of Pittsburgh. The nursery was on the grounds of a Civil War arsenal. Under the leadership of the renowned pediatrician Benjamin Spock, it cared for children of the city's working class, many of whom were jobless. The larger Arsenal Health Center was a therapeutic and counseling facility for the parents, the older children, and relatives. A fair proportion of the nursery pupils and their families were black. Most, however, were from Polish, Czech, and German immigrant families who lived in Lawrenceville, an older part of the city. Erikson had not worked with such ethnically diverse, low-income children before. He described the Nursery Center as "a place I am very fond of." He was excited by "the vitality of large immigrant families" and the industrial setting that less than adequately supported them. He found the study of urban ethnicity compelling. There was a strength and resilience in the children of central European immigrants at Arsenal, he noted, despite economic hardship. Periodically, Erikson identified his own immigrant experience with them. But he did not find such vigor in many of the black children at the nursery. He began to think more seriously about issues of race and became increasingly appreciative of African-American novelists like Richard Wright, Ralph Ellison, and James Baldwin. He was especially moved by a story related to him by a staff colleague concerning a four-year-old African-American girl who tried to scrub the color out of her skin and later painted a paper white. The story awakened in Erikson a sense of the identity dilemma of black Americans "who are made to feel so inexorably 'different' that legal desegregation can only be the beginning of a long and painful inner re-identification."[37]

Benjamin Spock had summoned Erikson to Pittsburgh early in the 1950s to consult at the Arsenal Nursery and to participate in case conferences in the larger Health Center. The two had been introduced to each other in the early 1940s by psychologist Caroline Zachary. Erikson appreciated both Spock's very flexible psychoanalytic orientation and his commitment to reforming the social conditions in which children were reared. He was reminded of August Aichhorn's work in Vienna. Erikson had not elected to talk with the author of *The Common Sense Book of Baby and Child Care* at the time of Neil's birth, despite Spock's access to the latest medical literature on Down Syndrome. At that point, they were not yet close friends.

Their friendship developed at the Midcentury White House Conference, when Erikson presented a model of the life cycle that Spock found to be deeply appealing. Like Erikson, he was primarily concerned with developmental and other issues that involved normal children. When Spock read *Childhood and Society*, he discovered that they shared a larger social vision. Both admired seemingly less complex, more cooperative cultures of old like the Sioux, where children were free to follow flexible natural schedules. Youngsters fared better under those conditions, both felt, than under the "ambitious striving" and "boundless discontent" of modern complex societies. Spock and Erikson agreed that modern economic institutions were too competitive while modern social institutions were insufficiently grounded in history and tradition. As a result of these instabilities, youngsters tended to be excessively fearful, frustrated, and insecure. Both men hoped that the situation might be mitigated through loving, flexible, comforting, yet consistent parenting. This kind of parenting flourished in families that were democratic and participational, and where children naturally assumed new developmental tasks as they matured. When Erikson commenced his trips to Pittsburgh and participated in Arsenal Health Center case conferences, Spock saw him for the first time not only as an intellectual and a developmental theorist but as a brilliant clinician. Fred Rogers, a young staff associate at Arsenal before launching his well-known television program for children, agreed. According to Spock, Erikson usually "knew more about the patient than the staff members treating him." He saw Erikson as "a tonic to the entire staff," offering penetrating perspectives on seemingly obscure issues. In addition to Spock and Rogers, Erikson met a bright, lively, and attractive staff member at the Western Psychiatric Institute who would become quite accomplished in the study of early child development and would come to date his son, Kai. Joanna Slivka walked with Erik through Pittsburgh's immigrant neighborhoods and industrial sites. Erik was fascinated. Indeed, both found these jaunts to be stimulating learning experiences. In time, Erik, the son without the father, wondered what it might be like to become a father-in-law.[38]

In short, Pittsburgh provided an important change of pace. Indeed, the city intrigued Erikson for the rest of his life. But his main work consisted of clinical duties at Austen Riggs. During the 1950s, the Riggs patient population changed significantly, and the median age dropped from thirty-six in 1948 to twenty-one by the late 1950s. Diagnoses ranged from severe psychoneuroses to character disorders (including depression) and early schizophrenia. A good many patients were classified by the clinical term *borderline*—that is, they were more troubled than those with severe neuroses but not "malignantly" ill like those diagnosed as schizophrenic. Most were young adults who experienced major troubles in college, in their vocations, or in their marital lives. Many matched Erikson's characterization of "identity crisis" or "identity diffusion," and he pointed this out, again and again, in clinical case conferences. The traditional Riggs approach of regimenting patient lives through schedules, rules, and activities was proving difficult with these young patients, who tended to be scornful of social regulation. Consequently, the facility began to evolve into an open residential center where patients were allowed increasing amounts of freedom. Demanding rules were phased out, replaced by patient responsibilities. Patients could work within committees to help plan activities and set up rules of governance. As the center's atmosphere became more liberal, severe cases requiring extensive medical and psychiatric attention were referred elsewhere for treatment. With a monthly charge of about $1,800 per patient and only modest concessions to financial need, considerable family wealth was required to cover the average patient stay of three to six months.[39]

Arriving at Riggs as a senior psychoanalyst and distinguished author, Erikson spent much of his time supervising younger clinicians and analyzing a few on staff as part of their preparation to become psychoanalysts. Writing also became an increasingly important part of his life. Yet he found himself intrigued by the patients, for they provided the clinical data he needed to flesh out a life cycle model that he and Joan realized they had presented in 1950 in only a very preliminary way. The fifth stage involving adolescence— the young-adult tug between identity and role confusion—had been the anchor of that model. In their work with Riggs patients, Erik and Joan found themselves increasingly preoccupied with this identity crisis period. Indeed, as the 1950s progressed, they often found themselves discarding the traditional psychiatric labels like "borderline," "psychosis," and "malignant pathology." Instead, they insisted that the patients were experiencing an "aggravated developmental crisis"—an extreme form of what was character- istic of people of their age and culture. The crisis would pass with time, empathy, and understanding. The essential therapeutic task, the Eriksons insisted, was to build on the strengths of youths in crisis. The therapeutic goal, Erik argued, was "to find out what a good work experience would be or what a satisfactory adjustment would be and to try to make these satisfactory experiences recur again in the larger world." Reduced to its essence, the way out of even an acute "identity crisis" was to build on the patient's strengths. This was a dramatic reversal of the traditional psychiatric focus on deficien- cies, even at prestigious and caring institutions like the Menninger Founda- tion. Although the gifted British child analyst and theoretician Donald Winnicott did not know Erikson well despite their remarkable theoretical similarities, he recalled very generally how Erikson's propensity to work with a patient's strengths had strongly influenced his own clinical work.[40]

During his ten years at Riggs, Erikson was the principal therapist for eight or nine patients (an incredibly small caseload). Through staff case con- ferences, however, he observed and commented on many other patients. Robert Knight presided over those conferences, directing patients in and out, questioning supervising clinicians, and chairing the staff discussion. Colleagues felt that Knight's concluding summary always contained wis- dom, experience, and eminent fairness. David Rapaport often reported the psychological test results, underscoring their theoretical and diagnostic implications with precision and logic. He questioned supervising clinicians sharply, supported cogent staff insights, and castigated sloppy thinking. Erikson rarely spoke, but he seemed to observe everything. Artistic doodling concerning the patient and his therapist often represented Erikson's "notes" to sustain his conference commentaries. Once he sketched a staff physician who, overintellectualizing with his patient, remarked to the patient with dismay: "You don't care to have an Oedipus complex?" He labeled another sketch "Parents of the Patient," caricaturing the parents with long, twisted necks and intrusive heads, refusing to give their youngster sufficient emo- tional space. On the rare occasions when he spoke, always in a soft voice and with a pronounced German accent, everyone listened. Even when he dis- agreed with the supervising clinician, Erikson emphasized what he liked about that clinician's presentation. This matched his general clinical approach—to build on personal assets. He slowly fleshed out the more fragmentary and mechanical perspectives of other staff, ending with a vivid and concrete portrait of the patient, often capturing qualities that were not reflected in the psychological tests or organic work-ups. Because he preferred "identity crisis" to more ominous pathological labels, Knight once asked whether the conference might start using the term as the formal diagnosis of a patient. Erikson did not want it to be used in this way until other mental health facilities adopted the term *identity crisis* and (more important) the thinking behind the term. He knew that this was not likely to happen. After Erikson's comments, the staff tended to be quiet and reflective. At these moments, a few thought of Erikson as "the professor" (a more than oblique connection to Freud). Rapaport frequently broke the magical silence by agreeing with Erikson's insights, and Knight's conference summary usually accented Erikson's comments. Indeed, Knight sometimes wrote "identity crisis" or "identity confusion" in the official diagnosis.[41]

Several recurrent themes characterized Erikson's case conference commentaries. Even with the most troublesome and desperate patients, he would almost always find cause for hope. When a twenty-five-year-old male patient had been diagnosed as "borderline schizophrenic," for example, Erikson felt his problem was less ominous. The young man "feels somebody has to help him" but wards off assistance because he feels "he has to help himself." The staff simply had to be patient, because "he needs a lot of time to accept help." In another case involving a very troubled woman in her late fifties, Erikson recommended against a traditional analysis because it would underscore her deficiencies and miss the fact that she had "a great deal of integrity" and a rather "whole life in her relationships." As the 1950s progressed, he tended increasingly to couple his optimism with jokes and humorous gestures, perhaps reflecting his deepening clinical confidence. For instance, to lighten the mood of staff members treating a middle-aged Jewish male patient with a hypochondriac preoccupation with everything he ate, Erikson gravely recounted the story of an elderly Jewish man who vomited each morning. When a worried physician questioned the patient and verified that he did indeed vomit as soon as he awoke, the patient looked bewildered and replied: "Doesn't everybody?" As the staff laughed and relaxed, Erik smiled and completed the thought: "So this man is worried about his health. Sure. Isn't everybody?"[42]

Besides optimism and humor, Erikson's conference commentaries accented the visual. He offered very precise observations on how a patient walked into and out of the conference room, the patient's facial contours, physical beauty, energy level, and general well-being. When a colleague claimed that a patient had a cowboylike personality, Erikson disputed the characterization by minutely describing the patient's walk, insisting that working cowboys would make fun of such a gait. Erikson persistently noted the ways in which social-cultural habits shaped personal life. In a case concerning a white southern woman, for example, he discussed the regional rape complex—the projection of violent white male sexual imposition upon black women onto the black male. In another case, he remarked jokingly about "a New England conscience here, reaching borderline proportions" and discussed the importance of the seventeenth-century Puritan legacy on New England life. In a case involving an executive at an advertising firm, Erikson explained how the man's choice of vocation matched "a whole life style of self-advertising." This patient felt "a certain emptiness" internally that the American advertising industry sought to fill by promoting consumption. Erikson also relied on his social-cultural emphasis to dismiss disparaging staff remarks about a boastful and arrogant physician turned patient who was somewhat sadistic. That was the culture of the American medical profession, Erikson charged: "This man is a rather normal man as our culture at the moment goes."[43]

Although there was not much material in *Childhood and Society* about religion or faith, Erikson's Riggs case conference remarks emphasized this dimension, revealing his growing interest in religion. Unlike Freud, he was neither disparaging nor negative about religious experience. Faith and theology could sometimes "exteriorize" pathological thinking and allow a person to function well "for quite a while." From experience with Catholic patients and from what he knew of religion in the Middle Ages, Erikson displayed a respect for that faith's deep-seated sense of tradition. When asked, at case conferences and in other clinical situations, if he was Jewish, he tended to reply that he was "partly so" (showing ambivalence about that aspect of his identity). Yet he did not feel that it was efficacious for a Jew— patient or staff member—to reaffirm the faith unless it connected "with positive and absolute values." One should not assert one's Judaism simply to ward off anti-Semitism. Erikson spoke of Jewish patients whose sense of their religion provided real strength in their lives. But he wondered, at the same time, whether a certain depressive state was also endemic to members of that long-suffering faith.[44]

Finally, Erikson emphasized the patient's voice in his case conference remarks, describing it as masculine or feminine, powerful or frail, convinced or confused. In part, this underscored his growing concern with speaking out since the loyalty oath crisis and since helping Jon find treatment for his stuttering. But his attentiveness to voice also related to the fact that some of his patients were public intellectuals. If they could be helped to voice their thoughts vigorously, Erikson seemed to suggest, they could both help themselves emotionally and provide better guidance to society at large. In this sense, Erikson was moving toward a principal theme of his second book on one of the most important public intellectuals in world history.[45]

Young Man Luther did not begin as a psychological biography but as an account of several young-adult patients at Riggs. Initially, the book was titled *Varieties of Identity Diffusion* and was to focus on five specific patients, all late adolescents and young adults with emotional crises. One interested Erikson most and moved him, more than any other clinical experience, toward a close study of the breakdown of young Martin Luther. In his early twenties, this patient had been a student in a theology seminary and was training for missionary work in Asia. He suffered a serious breakdown, and after attempts to help him through individual therapy failed, he ended up at Austen Riggs.[46]

The Riggs staff characterized the patient's breakdown as a borderline psychotic episode. The episode had been preceded by severe depression, hyperactivity, suicidal impulses, and obsessive-compulsive behaviors. His father, for whom he felt little warmth, was a successful physician. The seminarian felt closer to his mother, and also to her father—an old horse-and-buggy country doctor. Admitted to Riggs in the early 1950s, the seminarian was examined by a young staff psychiatrist who officially diagnosed the man as obsessive-compulsive with borderline psychotic features. The psychiatrist sensed that the young man's troubles were rooted in his relationship with his mother, whom he felt had always tried to dominate and emotionally castrate him. The psychiatrist recommended that an experienced psychoanalytic therapist take over the case. At a staff conference, Erikson's term was on everybody's tongue, for the patient seemed to suffer from "identity diffusion." As identity's conceptual architect, he became the therapist of choice. Erikson worked with the seminarian on an inpatient basis for a year and for two more years as an outpatient.[47]

After six months of psychotherapy, the seminarian recounted a striking dream to Erikson: it was of "a big face sitting in a buggy of the horse-and-buggy days. The face was completely empty, and there was horrible, slimy, snaky hair all around it. I am sure it wasn't my mother." All subsequent work with the seminarian centered on this dream, and Erikson was eventually able to understand its multiple meanings. The buggy, obviously his grandfather's, represented a long-standing image that the patient had of stability and firm identity. Erikson felt that the patient's shifting interests in Congregationalism, Episcopalianism, and even Catholicism bespoke an identity confusion common to many Riggs patients. He also recalled the many biblical images of God's face that the seminarian had recounted to him. In these, God made "his face shine upon" man or turned his face away from man. Erikson sensed that the dream, seen in the context of the seminarian's religious scruples and family history, concerned "a wish to break through to a provider of identity." The provider had something to do with the minister he was studying to become. It also concerned his grandfather and his father, both doctors, who promoted health. Erikson felt that when he discovered the meaning of the empty face, he would understand not so much why the young man was diagnosed clinically as a "borderline psychotic" but, less ominously, why he was undergoing an identity crisis.[48]

Erikson felt that the "hair" around the face in the dream was, in part, his own facial hair, and that the seminarian had felt abandoned while Erikson had been away for abdominal surgery. But he was not satisfied with this interpretation of simple transference; there was more. The grandfather's buggy supporting the face suggested the patient's efforts to acquire substitute mothering, Erikson decided. At this point, the void in the face made sense on multiple levels. The seminarian insisted that "it wasn't my mother" because it definitely was. Erikson recalled how Freud had construed the Medusa of classical antiquity with her angry face, snake hair, and open mouth to symbolize the masculine fear of femininity. Freud also interpreted facelessness as an inner void and symbolic castration. The young man had been engaged in a long, mortal struggle with his mother, who threatened to swallow him up or cut him off. And then Erikson realized the all too obvious meaning in the empty face: "a danger to the continuous existence of individual identity." The seminarian had never established a trusting relationship with his mother; he saw in her face the denial of his own—his very identity. The empty face represented the quality of "identity diffusion" that Erikson had been planning to write his book about. The seminarian was trying to differentiate himself (his own face) from his mother.[49]

Having unlocked this "Medusa dream" (as he came to call it), Erikson realized that the case of the seminarian was the most important of the five he planned to build his book around. Although the young man eventually abandoned his religious training, entered the "provider" profession of medicine, and ceased to be his patient, the case left a deep and lasting impression on Erikson. In a 1957 public lecture, Erikson indicated his decision to use his other four cases simply as contextual background. The seminarian's case would serve as a springboard for the new book, which would focus on the identity crisis of Martin Luther, another young seminarian. The case of the "Medusa dream" deepened Erikson's interest in the psychology of religious experience and silenced his residual doubts that by treating religion seriously, he was being disloyal to Freud. The seminarian had revealed his personal quest for identity through prayer and missionary work; Erikson understood that religious expression was hardly antithetical to psychoanalytic insight.[50]

This case also required Erikson to probe more deeply the nature of clinical endeavor. He had begun work with the seminarian with some trepidation because of his limited experience with psychotic or even borderline patients, because of his failure with Jean, and because of his doubt about what course to follow if the seminarian became fully psychotic. But as he made progress into the "Medusa dream," he grew more confident of his clinical skills. One day Erikson discovered that when the seminarian played a jazz saxophone melody, he was essentially representing his mother's loving voice combined with his own noisy infantile voice. Preoccupied as he had been with voice since the loyalty oath crisis, Erikson found that his personal experience and concern had helped him to understand the seminarian.[51]

The seminarian was successfully discharged in 1957 after four years of intermittent treatment. At this point, Erikson felt he could articulate his concept of "disciplined subjectivity" as the essence of successful clinical work. He discussed the case later that year for a Massachusetts Institute of Technology lecture titled "The Nature of Clinical Evidence." In his presentation, he argued that "disciplined subjectivity" emerged in clinical work when the therapist and patient enriched each other, when "the two subjectivities join the kind of disciplined understanding and shared insight which we think are operative in a cure." Unlike scientists who sought objective knowledge by "finding out what they can do" by acting upon things, the clinician learned about his patient "in the attempt to do something *for* and *with* him." In successful therapy, "the communication between therapist and patient 'keeps moving,' leading to new and surprising insights and to the patient's greater assumption of responsibility for himself." That is how Erikson and the seminarian achieved a viable rapport, he explained, each acknowledging his own inner apprehensions and subjectivities and together unlocking "the image of a Medusa—a Gorgon which, neither of us being a hero, we could yet slay together." The young man, who had never established a bond of trust or mutuality with his mother, had established one between himself and his elegant if enigmatic therapist. In turn, Erikson found new confidence and insight from this case, and that confidence carried over into his work with other adolescents and young adults at Riggs suffering from "borderline" psychoses and other maladies. The case also prompted Erikson to investigate another young seminarian—a project that would turn him into a historian.[52]

YOUNG MAN LUTHER

The process of replacing a book project based on several cases with a study of young Martin Luther was not difficult. Initially, Erikson had planned a short essay on Luther as an epilogue to a series of essays on Riggs patients.

Gradually, the Luther piece expanded while even the proposed essay on the seminarian patient faded into the background, for Erikson felt that Luther represented "a historic borderline case of great dimensions" and threw "much light on such religious and ideological scruples as some of our patients had." Like the seminarian and many other Riggs patients, Luther was young, gifted, and troubled emotionally. Yet because Luther was a distant historical figure, Riggs patients and other young readers would not see a book on him revealing intimate and troublesome details about themselves.[53]

Erikson felt that even with his limited clinical duties, he needed a year away from Stockbridge to complete the book. Since Riggs was a clinical institution, sabbatical leaves were rarely granted. He needed to procure financial support elsewhere. The Foundations Fund for Research in Psychiatry provided a year off by covering his Riggs salary. Erikson felt that this arrangement obligated him to return to Stockbridge, and he refused to pursue several university possibilities—at least for a while—even though the sabbatical policy and writing time offered by research universities was increasingly appealing.[54]

Initially, Erik and Joan rented a summer beach house in southern California. Within a few short weeks, they found that the recreational atmosphere and the absence of community feeling among beach residents was less than conducive to serious writing. Erik needed to be situated in a place with a more traditional Catholic culture than a burgeoning California beach development. He set his sights on rural Mexico, where the Catholic Church represented a conspicuous and unifying physical and spiritual presence as it had in Luther's day. The craving to separate himself (at least to some extent) from contemporary America while writing was reinforced by his sense that Luther's life and work had German and universal implications. Like Lionel Trilling, David Riesman, Reinhold Niebuhr, and Sidney Hook, he felt some kinship with a postwar intelligentsia (disproportionately Jewish) with loyalties to universal cosmopolitan values. Like them, Erik was coming to believe that this universalism clashed with the increasing nativism and ethnic particularism in modern American life.[55]

Early in 1957, the Eriksons settled in the small, quiet, and relatively inexpensive fishing village of Ajijic on Lake Chapala. It was part of the state of Jalisco and not far from Guadalajara. Artists and literary figures from the United States and Europe (most notably D. H. Lawrence) had completed some of their most productive work in this quiet, protected setting. The area was another "magic mountain." Due to the five-thousand-foot altitude and dry climate, Joan was free of sinus troubles for the first time in years. She easily made friends among area craftspeople and constructed jewelry again. The Eriksons rented a pleasant house surrounded by high walls and beautiful trees. Joan sometimes worked mornings in the garden. Erik found that he could usually write outside "in the open air which I like best." For breaks, the couple swam and walked through town. Erik was amused by the tradition of sexual promiscuity among American and European residents of the village. In a letter to his Riggs colleagues, he joked that "a few years ago, we heard, an American had spent a night with his own wife and the scandal has never been forgotten." In *Young Man Luther,* he insisted that despite the dominant mood of a historical period, "there are always islands of self-sufficient order . . . where sensible people manage to live relatively lusty and decent lives." Ajijic appeared to be one such island, providing a setting in which he could complete a rich and complex book in less than a year.[56]

In some measure, Erikson wrote rapidly because he was less than assiduous about research. This trait contrasted with his meticulous concern for detail in almost all of his clinical endeavors. Realizing that he had not read deeply or widely about Luther, Margaret Mead prepared a bibliography consisting of printed Luther sources in English, including full citations to facilitate interlibrary loan requests from the larger Mexican libraries, as there was no library in Jalisco with interlibrary privileges. Erikson never traveled to the larger libraries nearby. Unlike *Childhood and Society,* which he completed after extensive discussion with scholars, clinicians, and intellectuals, Erik conversed almost exclusively with Joan during the writing process. To be sure, he had already read widely and generally in German sources about medieval and Reformation Europe. Moreover, he sometimes felt obligated to translate from Latin: "I had to be thoroughly historical just once," he jested. If the search for evidence did not slow Erikson significantly, neither did theoretical considerations. He acknowledged to David Rapaport that he simply could not bother to explore "all the theoretical implications of what I am doing."[57]

Erikson restricted his task in still another way. While providing glimpses of Luther's childhood and his later life, he focused on seven years in Luther's mid- to late twenties. The interval began with Luther's entrance into a monastery at Erfurt in 1505 and concluded in 1512 when Luther gave his first lectures on the Psalms at the University of Wittenberg. Erikson felt that these were the years in which Luther experienced an "identity crisis" that was characterized by his need to discover the "Meaning of 'Meaning It.' " The event that most significantly illustrated this crisis of identity was a "fit" that Luther experienced in the choir of the Erfurt monastery in 1507. This "fit" set into motion Luther's pained exploration of the meaning of what Erikson vaguely characterized as a type of personal authenticity. The exploration culminated in 1512 when Luther experienced a "revelation in the tower" while lecturing on the Psalms. Erikson's longtime friend and sometimes mentor Henry Murray had invoked the term *metabiography* for the study of crucially important life events that formed a person's understanding of his existence. The event was a turning point from which all subsequent events and behavior derived (a strongly reductionist premise). For Murray, the subject interpreted important events according to a "unity thema" that gave wholeness to his life. Influenced by Murray, Erikson constructed Luther's narrative for the 1505–12 period from "represented events" like the "fit in the choir" and the "revelation in the tower." Erikson found Luther's "unity thema" in his quest for personal identity and a uniquely Protestant sense of being "real" or "authentic."[58]

Electing not to produce a comprehensive biography, Erikson intended nevertheless to write more than the clinician's traditional "case history" or "life history"—the essential emotional and medical events of a patient's life. He would write "a study in psychoanalysis and history" that connected Luther's personal "identity crisis" to the larger crisis of Christianity in late medieval Europe. With considerable discomfort, he referred to this interdisciplinary approach as "psycho-history," framing the term with quotation marks and hyphenating it to emphasize its provisional nature. Clinicians and historians both were beginning to integrate specific case histories with larger historical developments, Erikson noted. As this trend continued, the term *psychohistory* could be discarded. He saw no need for a specialty historical subfield.[59]

Uninterested in leading or participating in a psychohistory movement, Erikson concentrated on his subject, wanting historians and psychoanalysts to appreciate how "Luther was the herald of the age which was in the making and is—or was—still our age: the age of literacy and enlightenment, of constitutional representation, and of the freely chosen contract." This "age of the printed word" had persistently "tried to say what it meant and to mean what it said, and provided identity through its very effort." Young Luther had inaugurated this modern struggle for identity. Erikson criticized his psychoanalytic colleagues for their inattention to Luther's legacy. They failed to perceive the relativity of time and place—and history. But professional historians should not have overlooked young Luther's historical accomplishments. Erikson felt historians had shortchanged Luther because they were reticent to work with sparse and often problematic data on childhood and adolescence. Like the clinician treating a patient when all the factors in the patient's illness were not yet known, the historian had to learn "to sift even questionable sources in such a way that a coherent predictive hypothesis emerges." Mocking those historians who restricted themselves to "objective" data, Erikson noted how they "blithely go on writing whole world histories without any women and children in them." Historians had to give up their preoccupation with the "objective study" of hard data in order to assure a deeper "historical accuracy." They needed to make broad predictive hypotheses from limited and imperfect sources if they were to address the pressing historical issues of their time. Erikson was insufficiently involved with historians to realize that he was contributing to a general destabilization of the objectivity standard that had grounded professional historical scholarship since the late nineteenth century.[60]

He was not unmindful, however, that many academic historians would find fault with *Young Man Luther*. Since the book was intended to focus on Luther's intense struggle to fathom his identity, Erikson felt that he had to make something of Luther's "fit in the choir" at the Erfurt monastery. Erikson reported that Luther had this fit as a twenty-three-year-old priest plagued by self-doubt while celebrating his first Mass. The fit was followed by prolonged and painful introspection, and then by "revelation" and a new sense of himself. Erikson emphasized how Luther, consequent to the fit, reached a state of "utter integrity in reporting the steps which marked the emergence of his identity as a genuine *homo religious*." The profundity and authenticity of Luther's "reporting" represented "a decisive step in human awareness and responsibility."[61]

There was a problem here, and it concerned Erikson's scholarship. Luther himself never alluded to having a fit in the choir. Moreover, the three contemporaries who reported the fit were unreliable sources. Nonetheless, Erikson assumed that it "could well have happened" because Luther had several comparable "extreme mental states" that led "to weeping, sweating, and fainting" (i.e., how he was reported to have behaved in the choir). Erikson acknowledged that Luther's fit may, in part, have been legend. However, it needed to be acknowledged in historical scholarship because it had "a ring of truth; and yields a meaning consistent with psychological theory." Whether true, partially true, or legend, the "fit in the choir" helped one read "the balance sheet of his [Luther's] victories and defeats" as he struggled to find a sense of authentic selfhood.[62]

Young Man Luther did far more than describe Luther's "revelation." Erikson advanced a bold perspective concerning Luther's historical relevance. He felt that Luther (along with Michelangelo and Donatello) had helped to facilitate "the victory of the Renaissance spirit over Medieval construction." Luther had heralded the birth of modern humanism, enlightenment, and individual self-affirmation. The Reformation that Luther sparked, Erikson argued, "is continuing in many lands, in the form of manifold revolutions, and in the personalities of protestants of varied vocations." Indeed, Erikson postulated that "in contemporary history the basic trend of the Reformation is still alive." He informed David Riesman (no fan of Luther) that his participation in current protests against nuclear weapons would be unthinkable without the tradition of dissidence started by Luther. Erikson wanted to portray Luther, the young protestant, as the beginning of a modern temperament where individuals made choices and took stands sustained by abundant ego strength. To some degree, this position represented an uncritical embrace of the emergence of a tradition of Western individualism. Erikson bypassed considerable evidence indicating that even in his (purportedly) vibrant younger years, Luther viewed man as a failed figure lacking in free will or the capacity to achieve anything by his own merit.[63]

Erikson had incentives to make light of this evidence, insisting instead that Luther had introduced a life-affirming, humanistic spirit into Western culture. He placed Luther in the context of a German historic experience that centered upon "embattled borderlines dividing ideologies and world images such as the Catholic and the Protestant religions, the Eastern and the Western worlds, and . . . the worlds of capitalism and communism." There were other borders or splits in German identity: "the provincial and the national, the intellectual and the soldierly, the sentimental and the sadistic, the romantic and the organizational, the humble and the overbearing." Erikson felt an aesthetic and emotional compulsion to split Luther's life between creative Renaissance youth and dictatorial (Hitler-like) older age. When he spoke at Frankfurt and Heidelberg in 1956, Erikson had recognized "the rubble of the cities" and "the bleached bones of men of my kind in Europe"—the Jewish Homburger family, several of whom had been transported by the Nazis to the Gurs concentration camp. (Some may have been moved from there to Auschwitz.) He acknowledged this aspect of his German past in *Young Man Luther*. In the next sentence, however, he recounted a very different event from his early life. At a friend's home in a small village by the Upper Rhine, the friend's father, a Protestant pastor, had delivered the Lord's Prayer in Luther's German. Erikson never forgot this experience, which seemed to permeate his innermost being. Basically, Erikson had come to regard life-affirming young Luther on one side of the nation's "embattled borderlines" countering Hitler and an older Luther on the other side. He hoped, of course, that the spiritual force behind the legacy of the former would overcome the crude authoritarianism of the latter. Neither in the mid-1950s, when he wrote *Young Man Luther*, nor later in his life, could Erikson be shaken by German or Reformation historians from his hopeful portrait of the younger Luther. Erich Fromm, whose *Escape from Freedom* and certain other writings had emphasized Luther's authoritarianism and anti-Semitism, could not sway Erikson either. During their visits together in Mexico, as Erikson wrote his second book, he would not engage Fromm in critical discussion. When he went with Joan to visit Fromm in Cuernavaca, for example, he was more attentive to the bright pink bedroom and the peacocks in the yard than to Fromm's unflattering characterizations of Luther. Erikson appeared to require hopefulness in his view of young Luther and of his own German past as a counterpoint to the gloom and tyranny of Hitler and an older Luther.[64]

While Erikson experienced considerable difficulty relating to academic historians and their methodologies as he prepared *Young Man Luther,* he left them with a very important approach to historical change. To some extent, this approach had been anticipated during the 1940s in his writing concerning Hitler's dynamic appeal to German youth. Briefly, Erikson used Luther to demonstrate that an innovative leader could render major historical change for the society at large. He explained that Luther shared the deepest apprehensions of his contemporaries—"*fears* aroused by new discoveries and inventions" and "*anxieties* aggravated by the decay of dominant institutions," plus worries over radically changing perspectives on time and geographic space, and (above all) "*dread* of an existential vacuum." In response to these pervasive apprehensions, which racked his own life, the leader struggled to resolve and to rise above them. Like Luther, the leader courted "sickness, failure, or insanity, in order to test the alternative [of] whether the established world will crush him, or whether he will disestablish a sector of this world's overworn fundaments and make a place for a new one." Like Luther posting his ninety-five theses at Wittenberg, the leader will "convincingly claim to have an answer." This answer will be "an excessive restatement" of some preexisting ideas in a way that "sharpens our perception of our own frontiers."[65]

In brief, Erikson's study of Luther illustrated how, through the personality of the leader, "the resources of tradition fuse with new inner resources to create something potentially new: a new person; and . . . a new generation, and with that, a new era." By resolving his anxieties, the leader showed members of the larger society how to resolve theirs. Erikson had predecessors in this perspective on historical change. In *Moses and Monotheism,* Freud described how a great leader like Moses transformed his contemporaries, "through his personality and through the idea for which he stands." In *Blick ins Chaos,* Hermann Hesse characterized a prophet as a man capable of interpreting his own problems in terms of universal significance for a community or for an age. Similarly, Harold Lasswell had portrayed politics as the displacement of private affects (usually by the leader) upon public objects. Erikson had read all three. In *Young Man Luther,* he did not present his view of leadership as the key to historical change with the theoretical precision and rigor of Lasswell or Freud, and perhaps not even as elegantly as Hesse. Yet he exhibited a quality prized by professional historians: a capacity for vivid descriptive narrative. Erikson's rich psychological and historical story of young Luther's transformation was at the heart of his book and perhaps the most engaging of all efforts at psychologically informed history.[66]

LUTHER TRANSFORMED
AND *YOUNG MAN LUTHER* COMPLETED

Erikson understood young Luther's developmental crisis to be rooted in identity diffusion. Like the seminarian and other of Erikson's patients, Luther lacked "inner repose." At twenty-two, when he vowed during a thunderstorm to enter the monastery at Erfurt and to become a priest, Luther felt "exposed to anarchic manifestations of his drives" and seemed to require "oversystematized thoughts and overvalued words to give a semblance of order to his inner world." For Erikson, Luther was victimized by "that alliance of erotic irritability and hypersensitivity of conscience which brings identity diffusion to a head." Like the seminarian, Luther at twenty-two suffered "a borderline psychotic" state as a result of "prolonged adolescence and reawakened infantile conflict." But Erikson also detected in Luther an inner core of strength. This strength proved insufficient because, like many other young adults, Luther "half-realizes that he is fatally overcommitted to what he is not." The young man was struggling to "become well enough to make the 'environment' adapt to him." William James had referred to a "growth crisis" that was designed to "convert" a young person's "center of . . . personal energy." Erikson described it as the beginnings of an "identity crisis."[67]

Luther's overriding concern, Erikson explained, was to search for and find a fatherly image of strength and wisdom with which he could connect his own life. Of course, this was also one of Erikson's own pursuits. He postulated that a father could be a guardian "of the child's autonomous existence. Something passes from the man's bodily presence into the child's budding self." Erikson acknowledged that personally he "never felt thus generated, 'grown,' as an individual by his father" whom he never knew; sometimes he felt "half annihilated." Nor did young Luther feel properly connected to Hans, his father. Hans had clear plans for the young man in the prosperous merchant class of his community and demanded total submission to his will. Luther tried to figure out a way to submit to Hans "without being emasculated, or rebel without emasculating" his father. In the process, he became less "Martin than Luther," less "son than man," less "follower than leader." He asked Hans for permission to join an Augustinian order at the Erfurt monastery. Hans opposed it but later consented in a moment of weakness as he grieved over the deaths of two of his sons. Yet Luther realized that his "father did not mean it"; this moved him toward embracing "creedal explicitness" and what came in the course of the 1950s to be called "authenticity." Approximately three years after Hans consented, Luther came under the influence of Dr. Staupitz, a vicar general who sponsored him at an Augustinian monastery at Wittenberg. Staupitz became a "good father" and therapist, allowing the troubled young man to talk end-lessly of his guilt and apprehensions. Staupitz enjoyed "fathering something truly religious in Luther." Like a skilled clinician, he restored a sense of trust in Luther that had existed in infancy but had long been lost. With this trust restored, Luther was on the road to fathoming his identity, "to experiment with ideas like those he was soon to find deep in himself." He had found new ego strength and was on the way to becoming what Erikson called a "liberated craftsman" by finding the capacity to sublimate libidinal and aggressive strivings and to act creatively. He could take on the pope and, as Nietzsche put it, could learn "to speak to God, directly and without embar-rassment." Protestantism was about to be born.[68]

Luther's identity crisis and its resolution centered almost exclusively on male-male relationships to which Erikson could relate. In addition to the obvious father-son connection, the mentoring relationship between Staupitz and Luther replicated the supportive nurturing Erikson received from his clinical director, Robert Knight. Yet what of women? Erikson was almost apologetic about the fact that "Luther provided new elements for the West-ern male's identity . . . but he contributed only one new feminine identity—the parson's wife." There was almost no data on Luther's mother, Erikson complained, and yet he was certain "that nobody could speak and sing as Luther later did if his mother's voice had not sung to him of some heaven." Indeed, Erikson felt that as Luther was becoming a great revolutionary char-acterized by strong activity, he also cultivated a feminine "passivity" that per-mitted him to let "the data of his competency speak to him." Luther found this feminine passivity in the biblical image of a mother with "a generosity to which he could open himself, and which he could pass on to others, at last a mother's son." Hardly a Jungian, Erikson approximated the Jungian world-view by emphasizing the need for "a metabolism of passivity and activity."[69]

Freud, too, had elaborated on feminine qualities in conjunction with maleness. But Erikson's emphasis on mothering and the feminine was heav-ily autobiographical. So was his entire narrative of Luther's transformation. His description of Luther's "sad isolation" rooted in his mother and the ditty she sang to him overlapped decidedly with his descriptions of his first three years alone with Karla near Frankfurt. She, too, was sad in her isolation, but her constant smiles of recognition and her habit of reading conveyed to Erik the "sense that I am somebody." Later, as a child in Karlsruhe, Erikson acknowledged that he felt a strong affinity to young Luther, especially after the night at the friend's house where he heard the Lord's Prayer in Luther's German and experienced "wholeness." This experience had been accompa-nied by "alienation from everything my bourgeois (Homburger) family stood for"; like young Luther, "I wanted to be different." But Erikson was not quite characterizing his own conversion to Protestantism, since he described, almost simultaneously, "the bleached bones" of European Jews of the Holocaust like those of his Homburger family ("my kind"). Erikson was essentially recalling a crossing and recrossing of the Jew-Christian divide. He acknowledged, on the one hand, that *Young Man Luther* suggested "my turn toward Christianity" and that he felt "inescapably drawn" to "the Christianity of the Gospels." On the other hand, like Leslie Fiedler, Alfred Kazin, and several other Jewish intellectuals of his generation, the Holocaust almost mandated that he embrace his Jewish heritage. Indeed, he often felt drawn to Israel, where his mother and younger half sister lived.[70]

What captivated Erikson most about young Luther was his discovery of "The Meaning of 'Meaning It.' " To "Mean It" was to know and trust one's thoughts while simultaneously trusting God. It was to regain the basic trust of one's infancy, to rediscover "the guiding voice of infantile parent images." To know and to trust oneself with the guidance of parental images was to rejuvenate one's essential beliefs or ideology, to regain a sense of authenticity. Essentially, one secured a firm sense of identity. Luther had learned to "Mean It" when he developed the inner trust and confidence that allowed him to "let himself go." Once Luther had summoned this capacity, he was able to move on and to face "the problems of *human existence* in the most forward terms of his era." Drawing on the work of William of Occam, Luther had been able to champion unmediated individual faith in God. He attacked earthly hierarchies and ceremonies, the building of cathedrals, and other vanities that obscured the vision of God. Whether Luther ever actually said "Here I stand" at any special moment, his "emphasis on individual conscience" became a departure point for all subsequent concepts of individual liberty.[71]

As Erikson narrated Luther's transformation from identity confusion to self-mastery, he was impressed by the young man's strong, self-assured voice and language. Luther's resolution of his identity crisis centered on the discovery of his unique voice. This resolution was facilitated when Luther spoke in a language that was decidedly his own. Erikson characterized Luther as a "servant of the Word" who, like certain others, "never know what they are thinking until they hear themselves say it." "The theme of Voice and the Word," Erikson insisted, was "intertwined with the theme of Luther's identity and with his influence on the ideology of his time." Here Erikson was embracing a romantic view of individual voice as a form of self-authenticity and intertwining it with a romance of early Protestantism. He was not the first intellectual to do so.[72]

For young Luther to find his voice, Erikson warned, there had to be a language within which he could resonate—"*his* language." The Latin schools he attended had barred German. But as he rebelled against the limitations of the monastery at Erfurt, the Roman church, and the pope, Luther "created a living language by translating it." His translation of the Bible into German, to be sure, was not the first such translation. But it was the most artistic and the most emotive—the most liberating of the self. Luther's sermons (spoken in German), his table talk, and his theological writings were also in the German language. As he translated, composed, and spoke in German, he discovered an "immense gift for language: his receptivity for the written word; his memory for the significant phrase; and his range of verbal expression (lyrical, biblical, satirical, and vulgar) which in English is paralleled only by Shakespeare." In the end, Luther created "a language not intended as poetry for the few, but as inspiration in the life of the people." Succinctly, "language was the means by which Luther became a historical force" and a "moral energy." Erikson deeply respected Luther's rejuvenation of the German language. Through it, he found a direct personal connection between his early years in Karlsruhe and Luther's early years—"of all things German certainly the language had become most part of me."[73]

Having created "his language," Luther's most singular achievement was to broadcast it. Erikson noted that both Luther's father and the schools Luther attended had suppressed all spontaneous and creative speech. Consequently, when he began to learn to speak up, he released "a highly compressed store of defiance." He found the courage to say "what he had been unable to say to his father and to his teachers; and in due time he said it all with a vengeance to the Pope." In the process of speaking out, Luther learned to trust his thoughts and to trust God. He discovered "that a thing said less elegantly and meant more truly is better work." Indeed, "the voice that means it, the voice that really communicates in person, became a new kind of sacrament." To find and use this authentic voice was inseparable from discovering "The Meaning of 'Meaning It.'" It at once facilitated and affirmed a liberated "craftsmanship," a person who had found and was living out his true identity.[74]

Erikson once confided to his Stockbridge neighbor Helmut Wohl that *Young Man Luther* was regarded by most readers as a case study of a youth's identity crisis, which it was. More fundamentally, though, he told Wohl, it was about a youth finding his voice. Words and language, enunciated through voice, was the key to Luther's newfound identity. Erikson was gratified that he had discovered "the voice of young Luther." In a sense, this discovery culminated Erikson's romantic preoccupation with voice and "Meaning It" and a resultant sense of what he regarded as authenticity or wholeness.[75]

Erikson's intense concern with voice from 1950 to the publication of *Young Man Luther* in 1958 suggested that he was expanding his configurational approach. As he took on adult patients, his emphasis began to shift from interpreting configurations implicit in children's play arrangements and other material artifacts to configurations rendered through written and spoken words. More fully than before, *Young Man Luther* represented Erikson's analysis of words as the building blocks for this second type of configuration, which had the same bridge effect as the first, connecting inner psyche to outer social circumstance. Words, like the concerns that a child expressed when arranging toys, came from within the self and were directed at objects in the external world. Indeed, Erikson embraced words architecturally, searching for the underlying shapes and designs behind them much as he had looked for the underlying patterns that children had made with their toys. In a portion of the Luther book manuscript that he deleted prior to publication, Erikson discussed the two types of configurations when he described the work of the southern Renaissance, which centered on art and the visual, and compared it with the work of the northern Renaissance. The latter had involved voice and a musicality; it had been initiated by Luther's "liberation of the German word" and "crowned by Bach."[76]

Throughout *Young Man Luther,* but especially at the end of the book, Erikson connected the young German revolutionary of the early sixteenth century to Freud, an early-twentieth-century revolutionary with strong German affinities. Both did "the dirty work of their respective ages: for each kept human conscience in focus in an era of material and scientific expansion." Both sought "to increase the margin of man's inner freedom by introspective means applied to the very center of his conflicts." Luther's "soul-searching prayer" was not unlike Freud's self-analysis, for both were devices to help man become whole. More explicitly, as Erikson explained to Henry Murray, "Luther worked through what it really means to mean something with one's whole collected being; Freud, what it means not to be able to mean it because of split off meanings" or unconscious self-deceptions. As Luther struggled to "Mean It" and Freud to expose "unconscious deals with morality and reality," both men worked within the context of "the father complex."[77]

By connecting young Luther to Freud in this way, Erikson implied a compatibility between what was essentially liberal Protestantism and psychoanalysis. His problem, of course, was that Freud had characterized religion as a hopeless regression antithetical to enlightenment. Erikson agreed with Freud that religion often involved regression to an infantile state, but he questioned the inherent pathology of such a movement. He pointed out that "we regress in our dreams, too. . . . Yet dreaming itself is a healthy activity, and a necessary one." Indeed, religions tended to "use mechanisms analogous to dream life, reinforced at times by a collective genius of poetry and artistry, to offer creative ceremonial dreams of great recuperative value." Religions "at their creative best" were compatible with enlightenment, Erikson insisted, for they reached "back to the earliest individual sources of trust" and kept "alive the common symbols of integrity distilled by the generations." A regression to be sure, such religious experience retraced "firmly established path ways, [and] returns to the present amplified and clarified." In this sense, religion was compatible with Freud's science of the psyche.[78]

Erikson did not view himself as a neo-Freudian but as an independent, questioning sort of champion of mainline psychoanalysis. The Freuds (Sigmund and Anna) had been his mentors. Yet his discovery of a creative, probing young Luther meant a great deal to him. It offered the insight that Protestantism in its origins must have been as bold and rigorously honest as psychoanalysis was when Freud formulated its basic tenets. In laying out an intellectual road from Luther to Freud, Erikson was staking a claim quite foreign to traditional psychoanalysis. By postulating a human need for heroes and legends as he discussed Luther and Freud, Erikson was also overlooking Freud's negativity toward illusions.

Signs of a rift with Freudianism manifested itself in other ways as Erikson completed *Young Man Luther*. Two friends, sociologist David Riesman and psychologist Gardner Murphy, detected some of these as they read drafts of the manuscript. Riesman charged that Erikson, still quite visually oriented, was expressing strong reservations about Freud's prescribed method for conducting analyses (i.e., the analyst was to sit behind the patient and not to face him). Riesman felt that Erikson essentially argued for visual contact between analyst and patient, like that between Staupitz and Luther, to establish therapeutic trust. Indeed, he knew that this was how Erikson conducted several of his analyses. Riesman therefore urged Erikson to openly attack "Freudian rationalizations" for the traditional therapeutic arrangement that precluded eye contact. Murphy went farther. He felt that Erikson was fundamentally interested in "the cognitive problem of the self and its relation to its context." Yet Freud's concept of the self was "very primitive" and would not permit Erikson to pursue his interest to any degree. The Luther manuscript indicated both this limitation and the importance of moving beyond Freud. Consequently, Erikson simply had to acknowledge that he was probing beyond psychoanalytic orthodoxy.[79]

Interestingly, neither Riesman nor Murphy pointed out Erikson's most glaring breach with orthodoxy in a manuscript dealing heavily with fathers and sons. Freud had postulated an Oedipal tension (rooted in fantasy) between father and son for the attentions of the wife/mother. In contrast, Erikson (and Erikson's Luther) had the son seeking to relate to a more concrete and real father—present or missing—as part of a wider dialogue with God the father. A female presence was not central to this dynamic. "King Oedipus" was a pompous royal figure with a crown whom Erikson liked to sketch during Riggs case conferences to quietly mock the psychoanalytic orthodoxy of some of his colleagues. He was making the same point much more obviously in *Young Man Luther.* But as he pushed beyond the Oedipal construct, Erikson was leaving largely unexplored the female presence in Luther's life. Preoccupied with the connections between fathers and sons, Erikson appeared less than willing to explore tensions with mothers, wives, and daughters, important as those tensions had been in his own life.

These issues aside, Erikson had broken new ground, conceptually and experientially. As he completed a book that championed the earnest voice without temporizing, he was addressing his growing reservations about psychoanalytic orthodoxy. As he described Luther reaching a new level of authenticity and forcefulness, he could have been referring to himself.

After half a year in Jalisco where *Young Man Luther* was largely completed, Erik and Joan spent two months in another artistic community—Taos, New Mexico. There he put the finishing touches on the manuscript after Joan critiqued it and Harvard Divinity School professor James Luther Adams combed through it (privately and anonymously) for errors in scholarship. Then copies were sent to Margaret Mead, Reinhold Niebuhr, Robert Knight, David Rapaport, Lois and Gardner Murphy, David Riesman, and others, hoping they might uncover any remaining problems. In contrast, chapters for *Childhood and Society* had been critiqued by associates years before Erikson ever had a sense of the overall shape of the book. He felt that he had secured some needed "quiet time" and "got a lot off my chest" by writing *Young Man Luther* through to completion before anyone other than Joan could evaluate it. It was almost as if he needed a moratorium in a Mexican village comparable to Luther at the monastery at Erfurt from which he could emerge, cross the border into the United States, and broadcast an "authentic" voice of Protestantism to the American intellectual, theological, psychoanalytic, and historical communities.[80]

Young Man Luther arrived at the editorial offices of W. W. Norton as a substantially finished manuscript. Erikson had already made revisions suggested by some of his friends, and Joan read the chapters one last time for style and organization. Storer Lunt was delighted with the work: "even more profound and exciting" than *Childhood and Society.* But while assigning a very bright and talented editor, George Brockway, to the manuscript, Lunt issued no more than the standard author's contract that he had provided for Erikson's first book. His staff at Norton made no extraordinary effort at promotion and seemed unable to decide which academic and scholarly fields it would appeal to, nor were they able to persuade the *New York Times* to review the book. Only at Erikson's prompting did review copies go to the *International Journal of Psycho-Analysis* and the *Journal of the American Psychoanalytic Association. Childhood and Society* had been a Basic Book Club selection, and this had enhanced early distribution. However, the club did not take *Young Man Luther*. Only the much smaller Mid-Century Book Society did. The Harvard Coop and many other bookstores placed it in the less-than-popular theology section much as Erikson had feared. No paperback edition was issued until 1962, and even then Norton never sent copies to campus bookstore managers with a college textbook discount to stimulate sales. By the 1964–65 academic year, when sales for the paperback of *Childhood and Society* approximated 28,000 copies, the *Young Man Luther* paperback sold 9,900. Erikson was hurt and angry: "Can review editors, booksellers, and [the] buying public be expected to know what to make of a book," he asked Brockway, "if the publisher himself does not show any eagerness to tell them what kind of a book it is?" He wondered whether he should ever publish with Norton again.[81]

To be sure, *Young Man Luther* attracted some of the same broadly interdisciplinary readers as had *Childhood and Society*, and a few of their reviews were perceptive. Charles Rycroft wrote in the *Observer* (London) that Erikson was a sort of "artist *manqué* who is not altogether at home in the American psychoanalytic movement." Talcott Parsons agreed and pointed out that unlike most analysts, Erikson did not dwell on inner emotional life but used social structure and culture to explain Luther's "fatal creativity as a religious leader." John Osborne may have been too appreciative. He converted Erikson's book into a play on young Luther without acknowledging his source and drew substantial London audiences.[82]

Perhaps because Erikson was regarded as a psychoanalyst or a psychologist, historians initially paid little attention to *Young Man Luther*. Boyd Shafer, the editor of the *American Historical Review*, did not regard it as professional history and would not send it out for review. G. R. Elton, the prominent English historian, glibly dismissed the book for failing to "contribute anything of value to an understanding of Luther or his age." William Langer, however, stepping down as president of the American Historical Association, found the galley proofs replete with "interesting insights." More important, *History and Theory* published a brilliant review by the young scholar Donald Meyer. A profoundly gifted member of the UCLA history department, Meyer understood and applauded Erikson's essential themes and methodological accomplishments. He presented the book as a model for his colleagues. *Young Man Luther* offered a creative new way in which history could organize its narratives and bridge the gap between the individual and society, Meyer asserted. He described the volume as "phenomenally fascinating" and chided fellow historians for their single-minded preoccupation with the discovery of evidence: "Erikson's book is based, not on fresh data, but upon data refreshed, rescued from suppression, from invention, and from reduction." While Erikson was not well read on his topic, Meyer concluded, he read deeply and innovatively. Richard Hofstadter (perhaps the most influential postwar American historian) was also appreciative of Erikson's accomplishment and substantially concurred with Meyer's remarks. During the 1960s and early 1970s, *Young Man Luther* caught on with a wide variety of historians. James Stayer recalled that history graduate students were excited about *Young Man Luther*. A few decided to read *Childhood and Society* as well. John Demos and Fawn Brodie studied Erikson's work very closely and made measured uses of his approach. Others used him incautiously, falling flat in their efforts to produce "psychohistory" and "psychobiography." Erikson considered most of these studies unfortunate "excesses." As historians became more conscious of psychological life, he hoped that the "psychohistory" label would disappear.[83]

Neither historians nor other socially oriented reviewers explained that the emphasis in *Young Man Luther* on finding an inner sense of selfhood and authenticity ("Meaning It") in the context of the surrounding society was an integral part of the literature in America during the 1950s. Novels like Sloan Wilson's *The Man in the Gray Flannel Suit* and Ralph Ellison's *Invisible Man* were joined by social commentaries such as Robert Nisbet's *The Quest for Community* and William Whyte's *The Organization Man*. Several books and articles of the period by David Riesman and C. Wright Mills also echoed Erikson's concerns. In diverse settings and contexts, these works spoke to the decline of individual autonomy in an urban industrial society that was shifting from production consciousness to an ethos of consumerism. Perhaps more than the transformation of Luther's Europe, Erikson had addressed these contemporary conditions. He had predecessors, of course. As T. Jackson Lears's *No Place of Grace* (1981) reminds us, Henry Adams, Frank Norris, Vida Dutton Scudder, and other turn-of-the-century social and cultural critics had participated in a similar quest for authenticity and autonomy outside the realm of Victorian respectability and emerging consumer capitalism.

Most theologians and scholars of religious studies had been inattentive to Erikson's first book. But they were deeply concerned about *Young Man Luther*. Mirroring their distaste for psychoanalysis and its preoccupation with sexuality, several voiced outrage at the volume. However, Erikson's Stockbridge neighbor and occasional patient Reinhold Niebuhr found it "one of the most interesting things I have ever read" and drafted a flattering blurb for the dust jacket. The Reverend Richard Boeke of Flushing concurred and reported that pastors of the Missouri Synod [Lutheran] in the New York City area came together weekly to discuss how they could apply the book to their work. However, the Titus Street Professor of Ecclesiastical

History at Yale, Reformation specialist Roland Bainton, set the tone for the attack. Erikson had made only a passing reference to Bainton's widely heralded *Here I Stand: A Life of Martin Luther* (1950) and had chided Bainton for "no attempt at psychological thinking." In his review of *Young Man Luther*, Bainton emphasized that Erikson was decidedly on the short side with his data, and had attempted to depict the young Luther from the table talk of an older Luther that had been preserved by inaccurate student note-takers. Erikson had attributed a theology of humility to Luther, Bainton charged, against overwhelming evidence that Luther had simply followed Staupitz, his teacher-confessor. If, as Erikson claimed, Luther's attitude toward death was rooted in his relationship with his father, why did Erasmus (with a very different paternal background) share that attitude? More generally, Bainton insisted that many elements typical of German life and thought at the time could not have been personal to young Luther. Erikson was therefore a weak researcher and a poor historian.[84]

Erikson drafted replies to his more damaging critics, but most responses were sent only to friends and private correspondents. His letter to the editor of *Contemporary Psychology* was intended for the general public, but he decided not to mail it. Erikson's refusal to publicly respond precluded a sustained and open intellectual and scholarly dialogue over *Young Man Luther*. But it is less than helpful to attribute his refusal to a residual insecurity, for Erikson was going through a transition. His willingness to defend his book privately suggested a measure of inner strength that had not been evident earlier in his life. He singled out Roland Bainton. "Notes on Bainton's Review," a short essay Erikson distributed to friends, characterized this eminent Luther scholar as "totally unenlightened" about a psychoanalytic approach. More important, Bainton failed to appreciate one of his major points: that Luther verbalized in a very personal way the outstanding problems of his day. Luther did not merely typify the problems of his society (Bainton's perspective). By grappling with these problems on a personal level, Luther helped his society address them. Erikson attacked another reviewer for failing to realize that his book concerned the vicissitudes of postadolescent identity in relationship to ideology. He criticized still another, the chancellor of St. Paul's Cathedral, for being just plain antipsychiatric. Erikson also complained to a rabbi friend, Arnold Wolf, about "some Jews" in his reading audience who continued to dismiss Luther as an anti-Semite; they refused to recognize Luther's "unique role in the history of spirituality."[85]

Erikson's biggest complaint about most of his readers, whether associates or even favorable reviewers, was their failure to understand that *Young Man Luther* was only secondarily a study of Luther, his identity crisis, and the coming of the Reformation. Primarily, the book represented his continuing effort (now focusing on words and voice) to elaborate the life cycle. "I was more interested in the human life cycle than in biography as such," he recalled to a minister friend. Identity was simply one of eight developmental stages in that cycle. Ever since his work with Joan preparing a paper for the White House conference of 1950, "the human life cycle, and the relation of the whole to its parts, has become my dominant interest."[86]

Erikson may not have been entirely fair to his readers. Troubled youth and the identity crisis had been his preoccupations since arriving at the Austen Riggs Center. Six of eight chapters in *Young Man Luther* focused on the theoretical, biographical, and historical dimensions of Luther's identity crisis. As Erikson's narrative progressed from Luther as a young adult to Luther in midlife and beyond, his discussion became hurried and undeveloped. Indeed, he acknowledged that it would require another book to flesh out the psychological and social nature of adulthood—the next point on the life cycle. As it happened, he would write another book in the next decade on a middle-aged revolutionary.

Nevertheless, Erikson completed his second book feeling the urgency to offer general statements on the nature of the entire life cycle. He ended *Young Man Luther* with accounts of trips, during his stay in Mexico, to Lake Pátzcuaro near Guanajuato. An island in the lake was dominated by a large statue depicting José Morelos, the Mexican revolutionary, "his right arm raised in a gesture much like Luther's when he spoke at Worms." It was a gesture of "stubborn puritanism" revolting against the recurrent global problem of human exploitation. There would be less need of the services of revolutionaries like Morelos and Luther, Erikson insisted, if humans learned "to raise truly less exploitable men—men who are first of all masters of the human life cycle." Mastery of the life cycle would occur when man understood its essence—"the cycle of generations in man's own lifespace"—how his own life and growth connected inextricably to the younger and the older people in his daily life. By caring for them, man augmented his inner strength and made himself "less exploitable." The overwhelming reference here to "man" and "men" indicated Erikson's acceptance of the gender orientation of his generation.[87]

As the reviews of *Young Man Luther* were published, Erikson wrote to Julian Huxley, whom he had come to know while attending a World Health Organization Study Group. Huxley had been receptive to a rapprochement between evolutionary biology and psychoanalysis. Erikson sensed that Huxley's work on ritualizations among animals might connect to his work on the life cycle. He explained to Huxley that he needed to consider the stages of human development, intergenerational features and all, as they related to " 'eternal' values." He had to figure out how "such values as faith, will, truth, reason, etc.," corresponded with or attended each of his eight developmental stages. His first major venture into the psychology of religious experience had convinced him that these values needed to be freed "*from* a disturbing moralistic weight" so that they could help to amplify each of the eight "stages of life." By the early and mid-1960s, he was preparing important essays that expanded his life cycle model along this line.[88]

A PARALLEL TRACK:
CONTESTING "FREUD'S FIELD"

Erikson subtitled the Luther book "A Study in Psychoanalysis and History." While he had few compunctions about crossing disciplinary boundaries, he continued to identify himself as a psychoanalyst. Yet very few psychoanalysts were interested in the agenda on eternal values he had proposed to Huxley. Freud's disparagement of religious experience continued to influence psychoanalysts despite the compelling case Erikson made for young Luther. Moreover, few psychoanalysts were willing to explore the psychology of middle and late life; the profession's preoccupation remained with infancy and childhood. Clearly, Erikson's emerging interests and concerns were not those of most practitioners in his field, and few bothered to read his book. To make matters worse, Anna Freud voiced her distaste for *Young Man Luther* and the future work that it implied concerning the life cycle. Erikson observed that she had "not taken cognizance of the book which I sent to her" despite his homage to "Sigmund Freud's monumental work" and Anna's innovative theoretical contribution to ego development. Her criticism bothered him, for he had always been very solicitous of the opinions of strong intellectual women, and his former analyst was no exception. Photographs of Erikson with Anna Freud during this interval suggested tension and sadness; neither made eye contact with the other. However, one respected figure in the profession, David Rapaport, appreciated Erikson's book. The Luther study "fills me with real excitement," Rapaport wrote to him. What Rapaport did not say but knew was that Erikson had been pursuing his own agenda for some time now. Erikson had been experimenting with expressing his own separate and unique voice as an analyst while remaining a loyal Freudian. Rapaport sensed that this divergence from Freud was perhaps the most exciting (and frightening) aspect of *Young Man Luther*.[89]

Erikson's friendship with Rapaport began just as *Childhood and Society* was completed and he was trying to deal with the loyalty oath crisis at Berkeley. Like Erikson, Rapaport was a central European émigré and one of the few men to earn a Montessori degree in kindergarten teaching. He had completed a doctorate in psychology at Budapest's Royal Hungarian University and a personal analysis with Theodor Rajka. With Robert Knight, he moved from the Menninger Clinic to Austen Riggs, where he assumed a role in institutional policy making, particularly on Riggs's relationship with the psychoanalytic profession. When he read the galleys of *Childhood and Society,* Rapaport was deeply impressed by Erikson's intuitive insights and by the way he drew cultural considerations into psychoanalytic formulations. Specifically, Rapaport was taken by the way Erikson connected inner emotions with outer social circumstances. Comfortable with leftist politics and Marxist dialectical materialism, he had applauded Erikson's public stand against the loyalty oath. "Dear Erik," he had written when the Eriksons considered moving to Riggs, "I wish nothing more than to have an opportunity to mix my systematic sterility with your unsystematic intuitive grasp." Rapaport became Erikson's closest friend at Riggs. They chatted together regularly, often during long walks. When Erikson went to Mexico to write *Young Man Luther,* Rapaport confided that his absence "made me feel empty and sad."[90]

Erikson and Rapaport complemented each other. Erikson was the more experienced and sensitive clinician. Rapaport admired how he intuited a patient's particular concerns that others on staff missed. Rapaport was especially appreciative that Erikson assisted his daughters with their social and emotional problems. It was customary for Erik to offer professional help in the process of fortifying a friendship. He helped, too, in some measure in drawing Rapaport away from the ponderousness of the Germanic scholarly tradition and from a habitual use of overly sharp conceptual dichotomizations. In his writing, Rapaport became somewhat more playful.[91]

Rapaport tried to remedy perhaps Erikson's primary intellectual deficiency—a conceptual and theoretical vagueness and imprecision that was probably inherent in his artistic, nonlinear manner of expressing himself. Erikson joked that Rapaport always nagged him "about making order of all my terms" and especially about distinguishing (which he rarely did) between identity, ego-identity, and self-identity. In theoretical discussions, Erikson recalled, "David always put me in my place." "You know, he tells me what I said," Erikson often remarked (only half-jokingly). As the years passed, he referred to Rapaport as "my conceptual grandfather" who made "passionate demands for a certain rigorous fidelity to the grand theory" enunciated in Freud's writings. Indeed, Rapaport's influence may help to explain why *Young Man Luther* was Erikson's most closely written and tightly organized book, thematically united under Luther's quest to find "The Meaning of 'Meaning It.'" But Erikson also found that Rapaport's "single-mindedness and intensity can, at times, be . . . too much." He would not track down sources with Rapaport's meticulousness or transform himself into a Talmudic expert in psychoanalytic metapsychology. He would not even skim many of the books and articles that Rapaport recommended; his preference was simply to learn verbally from Rapaport what the publications argued.[92]

It is interesting to chart the deepening of this friendship. Rapaport worried constantly that Erikson's propensity toward incomplete research and incautious writing could provoke charges of psychoanalytic deviancy or neo-Freudianism. He invoked his reputation within psychoanalytic circles for theoretical acumen to protect Erikson from the more orthodox within the profession. Indeed, Rapaport considered Erikson a solid Freudian. Rapaport, however, found it increasingly difficult to protect his friend. In the course of the 1950s, Erikson published three articles and a volume of essays that provoked extreme distress among some orthodox Freudians. They generally regarded Young Man Luther as peripheral to mainline psychoanalytic endeavor since it was "only history." But the articles and essays were written for analysts like themselves and contested their assumptions.

None was more controversial than the first, "The Dream Specimen of Psychoanalysis." Freud's The Interpretation of Dreams (1900) had been the most formidable contribution to his conceptual edifice. Freud's analysis of a personal dream concerning one of his female patients (Irma) was an anchoring chapter in the book, concretizing the new "science" of dream analysis. Erikson regarded Freud's discussion of his Irma Dream as vital to the origins, the therapeutic technique, and the theoretical structure of psychoanalysis. He planned an essay on Freud's crucial chapter for Childhood and Society, but ultimately did not include it. Instead, he presented the material in a series of lectures before the San Francisco Psychoanalytic Society in 1949. The reception was favorable.[93]

Now, Erikson reworked the essay and submitted it to the International Journal of Psycho-Analysis (London) in mid-1952. The prestigious journal was edited by his old friend Willi Hoffer, and Erikson had been on the editorial board the previous year. Problems arose when Hoffer forwarded the essay for evaluation to the powerful British psychoanalyst Ernest Jones, author of a eulogistic, if comprehensive, biography of Freud. Jones objected to Erikson's persistent "guesses" concerning Freud's personal psychology (especially his potentially lustful attraction to Irma) at the time Freud wrote up his dream about Irma. The founder and his movement were too important to be dealt with in such a personal, inferential, and potentially damaging manner. Hoffer reported Jones's reaction to Erikson and recommended that he "not publish this paper at all," because his reputation among psychoanalysts could be badly damaged. Erikson rejected the recommendation and asked Hoffer to have the full editorial board evaluate the essay for pub-

Karla Abrahamsen in Copenhagen, circa 1895.

Erik's woodcut (circa 1925) of himself (foreground) on the 1905 honeymoon cruise of Karla and Theodor Homburger (background) to Copenhagen.

Erik and Karla Abrahamsen Homburger,
Karlsruhe, circa 1906.

Erik and his first half sister, Elna Homburger,
Karlsruhe, 1907–8.

Erik with half sisters Ellen (left) and Ruth (right) in Karlsruhe in 1925,
soon after his long *Wanderschaft* period had concluded.

Erik as Hietzing School teacher with his students in a Christmas skit, Vienna, circa 1930.

Joan Homburger with Kai,
her first born, Vienna, 1931.

Erik, Joan, Kai, and Jon Homburger in
Scituate, Massachusetts, 1934, shortly
after their arrival in America.

Erik and Sue Erikson in Berkeley, late 1939.

The Erikson family (Jon, Kai, Erik, Sue, and Joan) in Stockbridge, 1953.

(Image Photos/Clemens Kalischer)

Erik with his mother,
Karla Homburger,
in Stockbridge 1953.
(Image Photos/Clemens Kalischer)

Erik and Joan, Tiburon, late 1950s.

Erik Erikson and Anna Freud, circa 1970.

Erik's seminar with Austen Riggs students and staff, circa 1980.

(Image Photos/Clemens Kalischer)

Erik and Joan dancing
at the wedding of Amy
Wallerstein, Sausalito,
California, 1986.

Erik at ninety in Cambridge, Massachusetts, 1992.

lication. Erikson's uncharacteristic show of determination may have been bolstered by a personal communication on the essay from the eminent Heinz Hartmann, at least Jones's equal in the hierarchy of the psychoanalytic movement. Hartmann saw genuine utility in Erikson's general approach to dream analysis, and this counted for much. Erikson insisted to Hoffer that "my paper gives significantly more weight to the representative and legitimate issues involved in this historic dream than to questionable particulars of Freud's life." If Jones or others had suggestions for rewriting his "tentative auxiliary interpretations" that concerned Freud's personal life, those were welcome. The editorial board of the *International* sided with Jones and rejected the essay. Although Anna Freud was not a member of the board at the time, Hoffer was her friend and confidant. He relayed to her the main points in the essay, almost certainly allowed her to read it, and probably gave her veto rights over publication. She agreed with Jones's evaluation. The vehemence behind her opposition to publication seemed to lend greater credence to Erikson's qualified and reflective suggestion that Freud had perhaps lusted for Irma. (Indeed, it fueled the long-standing speculation among some Freud scholars, psychoanalysts, and others that Anna Freud's father was, in fact, deeply attracted sexually to Irma at the precise time when his wife was about to give birth to their daughter.) After his article was rejected by the *International,* Erikson confided to Rapaport that he was hurt by the opposition to his essay but "found little to change." Erikson was the only nonphysician on the board of editors of the *Journal of the American Psychoanalytic Association,* and he sensed that his associates there would be fairer. Also, Robert Knight exerted influence over editorial decisions. Early in 1954, the *American* published his essay in substantially unrevised form. Knight republished it later that year in an Austen Riggs volume of clinical and theoretical papers.[94]

After the *American* published Erikson's article, Anna Freud made her objections known to the psychoanalytic community. When Erikson learned about her criticism, he became quite disturbed, feeling as if he was "cutting off all connection with my roots" in the psychoanalytic field "to Anna Freud and through Anna Freud to her father." Rapaport tried to assure him that his Freudian roots remained firm. That helped. Indeed, Erikson continued to feel that his essay spoke directly to Sigmund Freud on fundamental issues in the psychoanalytic enterprise. He would not recant. He seemed to exhibit a reservoir of inner strength, such as Luther possessed centuries earlier; he was showing his analytic colleagues that he "Meant It."[95]

The central point in Erikson's controversial article received considerably less attention than his remarks on Freud's personal life and passions. Erik's basic intention was to examine Freud's distinction between the manifest or surface part of a dream and the latent dream containing the deeper emotional issues that concerned the dreamer. Erikson criticized "many in his [Freud's] field" for equating the manifest dream with superficiality. Because the manifest part of a dream consisted largely of forms and shapes, it was exceedingly important: "Like good surveyors, we must be at home on the geological surface as well as in the descending shafts." These comments succinctly contrasted his "horizontal" orientation with Freud's overwhelming "verticality." The manifest dream was "by no means a mere shell to the kernel, the latent dream" because it reflected a person's orientation toward time and space and the way one's ego operated—"the frame of reference for all its defenses, compromises, and achievements." To fortify the point, Erikson insisted that observation of the forms and shapes in children's play and in tests like the Rorschach and thematic apperception all demonstrated that "psychoanalysis has given new depth to the surface." The surface or manifest part of a dream involved a variety of dimensions—verbal, sensory, spatial, temporal, somatic, interpersonal, and affective. While these dimensions revealed much about the dreamer's external social world, they were also vital to his inner emotional world. Through the manifest dream, one comprehended how the dreamer "takes the outer world into the inner one." As Freud's dream of Irma illustrated, latent or depth wishes and fantasies were "imbedded in a manifest dream structure which on every level reflects significant trends in the dreamer's total situation." Erikson was arguing for "a complicated continuum of more manifest or more latent items" often discernible in the manifest dream. This was a revolutionary approach to dream analysis.[96]

His view of a continuum suggested what a preponderance of Freudians were unwilling to acknowledge: the central interconnection between "inner" emotional and "outer" social existence. Freud had bought heavily into English physician John Hughlings Jackson's higher-lower doctrine, which had juxtaposed highly rational processing of sensory input against primitive and chaotic lower levels of processing. Freud postulated that analysis could permeate vertically downward beyond the "manifest" dream into those lower levels. Erikson's embrace of "horizontality" militated against Freud's hydraulic perspective with its depth excavation. One could detect the convergence between "outer" and "inner" life, Erikson insisted, by taking the manifest dream no less seriously than the latent dream. This contention was not appreciated by analysts in Britain like Jones, who influenced policy at the *International Journal*, for they were deeply committed to excavating "inner life." Knight and other American analysts who shaped the *American* had been more flexible on this point. Most assuredly, Erikson was speaking out earnestly for an alternative to strict Freudian "verticality" and "Meant It." He was voicing a "truth" that he had been cultivating since his days as an itinerant artist.

As he discussed Freud's account of his Irma Dream, especially its manifest content, Erikson recognized Freud's quest to acquire a sense of "ego identity." Freud used the term "*innere Identität* in a peripheral pronouncement" to describe this sense of sameness and continuity over the life course. His dream revealed that he was struggling to achieve that sense. At the same time, Erikson insisted that Freud's dream signaled a quest for generativity. At the time of the dream, Freud and his wife were creating life—she was pregnant with their daughter. He was also experiencing a "growing sense of harboring a discovery apt to *generate new thought*"—he was creating dream analysis, the most formidable tool in his psychoanalytic arsenal. Freud's generativity, therefore, signaled "a drive to create and secure personal children" and "to *generate* new thought" for his own and a younger generation.[97]

There was considerably more of a technical sort in Erikson's "Dream Specimen of Psychoanalysis" article. He was seeking to stake out an independent position in psychoanalytic discourse by treating identity, generativity, the configurational, the "horizontal," and other perspectives that he valued. Both Ernest Jones and Anna Freud had badly misread the essay. Erikson was not out to explore Freud's life psychologically so much as to present his own voice, sharp, clear, and "authentically" in a psychoanalytic discourse that elaborated and extended Freud's foundations. He did not regard himself as a neo-Freudian or a deviant "culturalist." But he would not be an unreflective echo of the founder.

Rapaport understood and appreciated this. Still, he worried about the substantial controversy that Erikson's article had fostered. If Erikson intended to prepare additional essays for psychoanalytic audiences, he recommended that they be more precise, cautious, and politically sensitive. To some degree, Erikson followed Rapaport's advice, for he felt that the editorial board of the *International Journal of Psycho-Analysis* had rejected his article out of an "objection to my way of dealing with data for Freud's life." In 1955, the board apparently allowed Erikson to "rehabilitate" himself, asking him to review a volume of Freud–Wilhelm Fliess correspondence and notes covering the 1887–1902 period. The volume had appeared in German a few years earlier. Erikson was to review the new English translation, titled *The Origins of Psycho-Analysis*. He considered the title problematic because the correspondence underscored Freud's struggle to articulate his basic psychoanalytic premises through personal exchanges with his closest intellectual associate. In the main, the volume housed Freud's side of the correspondence. (In his later years, Freud destroyed the letters Fliess had written to him.) Erikson noted that the letters revealed much about Freud's "levels of mood, selected confessions, and habitual admissions." However, he would focus on the formal and public aspects of what was essentially private mate-

rial, for Freud's passions and "intellectual intimacy" with Fliess were characteristic of the era—"familiar features of intellectual correspondence of the
past century."[98]

Consistent with this purpose, Erikson was attentive to details of the
English translation. He was interested in the technical product. While "the
translation, on the whole, is readable and accurate," he observed, it did not
always capture "the manly abundance and tender strength of expression, the
courage of precision, the play of literary allusions, colloquialisms, and neol-
ogisms, which made up Freud's German." Erikson cited several examples of
flawed translation that avoided "all the nuances of Freud's surprisingly personal style" and he cautioned readers who sought these nuances to consult
the original German. In an acclaimed *New Yorker* article twenty-seven years
later, Bruno Bettelheim elaborated this essential point.[99]

For Erikson, the most obvious lesson of the Freud-Fliess correspondence
was that the science of psychoanalysis had not "issued from Freud's head as did
Athene from Zeus'." Rather, it derived from his neuroses, his emotions, his
intellect, his creativity, and his psychological development. At thirty-one, Erikson explained, Freud needed Fliess's friendship and support to help him bridge
a major psychological crisis as he shifted from the "academic monastery" to the
"medical parsonage." Once again, Erikson was underscoring his profound interest in the private as public and in problems of finding and sustaining identity
within the life cycle. He reported how Freud worried that he would die pre-
maturely, how he had longed to see Rome, how he felt lonely at times,
sensed his failings at some intervals, and had visions of glory at other times.
In the end, Erikson concluded, the Freud-Fliess exchange revealed that
Freud's intellectual and conceptual gifts were tied "to his inner motivations."
The letters also indicated that Freud's thoughts were connected "to the main
currents of his time." Erikson was articulating the same issues and concerns
that filled the pages of *Young Man Luther.* Surely desirous of earning the good
graces of the *International Journal of Psycho-Analysis* and Anna Freud, he
nonetheless could not contain or suppress his primary concerns. He had cultivated a stronger voice and a fuller general presence than those who had known
him a few years earlier were accustomed.[100]

After publishing two articles on Freud and psychoanalysis in successive years,
Erikson received one of the greatest honors a psychoanalyst could receive.
Through the prompting of Alexander Mitscherlich, prominent psychoanalyst
and director of a psychosomatic clinic at the University of Heidelberg, he was
invited to lecture in 1956—to honor the hundredth anniversary of Freud's
birth. The anniversary was to be sponsored by the Frankfurt Institute for Social
Research and Heidelberg University. Erikson was included with three of the
world's great analysts—Franz Alexander, Heinz Hartmann, and René Spitz—

in the city "of my childhood." Hartmann suggested that the celebration would mark a critical point in post-Holocaust German self-examination. Erik sensed that he would "complete the immigrant's cycle" by returning to Frankfurt and honoring the founder of his profession.[101]

Although Erikson was very appreciative of the invitation, he also felt burdened. He had visited Germany four years earlier and was distressed by the "violence of political party strife," military rearmament, and the cynicism of German youth. The ghost of Hitler hovered over the country. He also confided to Mitscherlich that "public lectures are difficult for me"; speaking in German within a few miles of his own birthplace on the birthday of a man who had been forced to flee the Nazi war machine was problematic. Would he minimize Germany's brutality? Would he betray Freud and harm Mitscherlich's effort to reestablish a viable psychoanalytic movement in central Europe?[102]

At the close of a Mendelssohn rendition, Erikson was introduced by the president of the West German Republic. He began his lecture speaking of Freud and psychoanalysis as "a student of Rapaport's." He went on to identify himself as an unabashed "Freudian" who "knew Freud when he was very old, and I was very young." Erikson recalled that he felt a special kinship with Freud, "a man who had unearthed mankind's demoniac inner world" while retaining a special appreciation for artistry and form. Erikson detailed Freud's discoveries: the power of the unconscious; the nature of transference and countertransference; the role of dreams, traumas, and fantasies; and much more. But he also emphasized that Freud was mortal, plagued by doubts and misgivings—matters of personal identity—as his contact with Fliess amply demonstrated. Like any astute investigator in old Vienna or the present, Freud experienced conflict between "emotional participation" in what he observed and a "methodological rigor required to advance his field and human welfare." Essentially, Erikson concluded, Freud was like Moses, a "supreme law-giver." In the process of "finding a method of healing himself," he gave to his society a brilliant new "psychological rationale for man's laws." A hero who understood and cured himself, he gave society a cure—the laws of psychoanalysis.[103]

With the preeminent psychoanalysts flanking him on the stage, Erikson felt he had represented his profession well. He had emphasized Freud's talents and depth to such a degree that none could accuse him of being a "culturalist" or a neo-Freudian. At the same time, he had not ignored the human Freud—a fallible man beset by personal struggles. While Erikson's speech lacked the profundity and complexity of his "Dream Specimen" article, he finished feeling that he had finally found his psychoanalytic voice. "I all of a sudden heard myself speak German before the microphones," he told Henry Murray, and he spoke with a forcefulness and with what he described as an authenticity. "We haven't heard this kind [of German] for more than two decades," an excited and grateful listener told him, and "I felt good." He had connected to the spoken German of his earlier years, bypassing the coarse "emendations" of the Nazi period. In some ways, his lecture seemed to be connecting him to "the voice of young Luther." Erikson felt that he was no mere conduit of psychoanalytic dogmas; his voice was as Protestant as it was affirmational.[104]

Rapaport remained in Stockbridge while Erikson lectured in Frankfurt, but he was very happy for his friend. If Erikson's centenary speech did not emphasize his fealty to the psychoanalytic community and his acceptance of its values, Rapaport was now busy "demonstrating" those precise points with his impeccable command of the evolution of psychoanalytic theory. In lectures, seminar presentations, and a scholarly essay that he was preparing, Rapaport strived to put Erikson's contribution "into the terms of the standard psychoanalytic metapsychology" since it still remained "grossly underestimated." He was particularly disturbed, Rapaport told Erikson, by Ernst Kris's "deliberate disregard of what you have been doing." Specifically, Rapaport noted that his paper would develop, fully and precisely, the rich theoretical connections among Freud, Hartmann, and Erikson.[105]

In 1959, Rapaport used his paper to introduce the first issue of *Psychological Issues,* a journal concerned with general psychoanalytic theory and research. Published by International Universities Press, which specialized in psychoanalytic topics, the journal was intended to accommodate book-length monographs or a series of related essays by the same author. Rapaport introduced three previously published Erikson essays. Two, "Ego Development and Historical Change" (1946) and "Growth and Crisis of the Healthy Personality" (the 1950 White House Conference paper on the life cycle), had made their way into *Childhood and Society* in abbreviated and modified forms. In the third essay, "The Problem of Ego Identity" (1956), Erikson had applied his concept of identity to young George Bernard Shaw. The essay represented a trial run, of sorts, for his more significant study of Luther. More important, it presaged Erikson's large-scale revision, during the early and middle 1960s, of his entire life cycle model.

Erikson wrote a short introductory statement for the special volume of *Psychological Issues* to justify republication of the three essays under a unifying title: "Identity and the Life Cycle." All three were very much in demand from "different professional quarters," he explained, and they addressed a common psychological issue. That issue was "the unity of the human life cycle and the specific dynamics of each of its stages, as prescribed by the laws of individual development and of social organization." This psychosocial approach to the life cycle had been his abiding interest since he had included a chapter on it in *Childhood and Society* and had focused *Young Man Luther* on identity (the stage that he found most compelling). For a decade now, he especially wanted psychoanalytic colleagues to be attentive to his thoughts on the topic. Ever the artist who had constantly to retouch and rework, feeling he had never actually finalized a sketch or an essay, Erikson acknowledged that the three articles were augmented by some new footnotes and italics. He also justified the "repetitiousness" of publishing articles already in print with the specious claim that "direct oral and social communication across disciplines and continents is to a large extent replacing the solitary and detailed study of books." He seemed to be seeking justification for a recurrent pattern—publishing distinctive papers as articles and then gathering those articles together, slightly revised, as books. *Childhood and Society* had been that sort of volume. With the exception of *Young Man Luther,* Erikson was essentially an essayist. *Gandhi's Truth,* his next major volume, returned to this loose essay mode despite a unifying subject—the Mahatma.[106]

Erikson thanked Rapaport for opening "Identity and the Life Cycle" by offering "a comprehensive paper" that took his three "less systematic papers" and anchored them "in the history of psychoanalytic theory and in the work of my teachers." Essentially, Erikson was suggesting that Rapaport had assumed for him the task of building metapsychological links between his works and two principal leaders of his profession—Sigmund Freud and Heinz Hartmann. Rapaport's task was impossible. Freud and Hartmann had assumed that the ego's prime referent was the inner or intrapsychic world. While Erikson was quite attentive to this intrapsychic world, he characterized outer society as an equally fundamental point of orientation for the ego. Far more than Freud and Hartmann, Erikson grounded his work on the ego's adaptive fit—indeed the whole self's fit—with society. In the very process of positioning himself, he had taken a sharp turn from the traditional psychoanalytic domain.[107]

Rapaport's essay, "A Historical Survey of Psychoanalytic Ego Psychology," deemphasized Erikson's departure in a valiant effort to promote a place for his friend in the psychoanalytic mainstream. He did this by stretching Freud's and Hartmann's perspectives so that they appeared to be closer to Erikson's. Freud's ego psychology implied a certain area of ego autonomy, Rapaport argued. Hartmann's concept of a "conflict-free sphere" within the ego (unbattered by instinctual pressures) had owed a debt to Freud. So had Erikson in his work on ego identity. Essentially, Rapaport was implying that Hartmann's "conflict-free sphere" overlapped with Erikson on ego identity, that somehow both extended Freud's concession to ego autonomy. More pointedly, Rapaport struggled to connect Erikson's effort to locate individual identity in society with Freud and Hartmann. He charged that Freud had implied a place for a theory of "interpersonal (psychosocial) relationships" and that Hartmann's theory of ego adaptation represented an early shift in that direction. While Rapaport acknowledged that Hartmann regarded the ego as an inner psychic structure containing its own energies, he nonetheless portrayed Hartmann's view of ego adaptation as a forerunner of Erikson's view that ego identity was achieved when inner psychic structures connected to external social circumstances. Rapaport argued that Hartmann, followed by Erikson, had amplified Freud's doctrine. Freud's torch had essentially passed to Hartmann and then to Erikson.[108]

Having postulated through general assertions that Hartmann and Erikson were Freud's leading students—the principal architects of psychoanalytic ego psychology—Rapaport then doubled back, trying to demonstrate more convincingly that Hartmann and Erikson were "consistent with and complementary to each other." In this effort, he found it unfortunate that neither Hartmann nor Erikson had tried to connect theoretically with the other. Rapaport, however, did point out that Hartmann's view of autonomous ego development and adaptation had generalized Freud's view on the development of anxiety. While Hartmann conceded a role for social relations in this development, he did "not provide a specific and differentiated psychosocial theory." Rapaport insisted that Erikson's psychosocial developmental theory "particularizes Hartmann's theory of reality relations, in that it dealt with the [internal] ego aspect and the social aspect of object relations." Hartmann had assumed "an inborn coordination to an average expectable environment," Rapaport pointed out. Erikson had pinned this down by showing how "the crucial coordination is between the developing individual and his human (social) environment."[109]

Rapaport had explained Erikson's configurational approach, connecting inner emotions and outer social circumstances, using language and references that psychoanalysts could understand. By slighting the primacy that Freud and Hartmann (unlike Erikson) had placed on inner psychic life and deemphasizing Erikson's horizontal social orientation, he was able to represent Erikson building on a mainline Freud-Hartmann tradition in ego psychology. This did not displease Erikson. In some measure, he continued to regard himself as a student of these two giants even as he departed from them.

Rapaport acknowledged to the analytic community that Erikson was a vague and undisciplined theoretician, ranging "over phenomenological, specifically clinical psychoanalytic psychological propositions without systematically differentiating among them." He asked his psychoanalytic colleagues to help systematize and clarify Erikson's theoretical work. But Rapaport almost certainly recognized that his friend would fare better if they did not, for that would emphasize Erikson's departure from orthodoxy.

As psychoanalyst John Gedo wisely notes, those who made the attempt in later years effectively turned Erikson into a less-than-central figure in psychoanalytic ego psychology by showing that his focus was not primarily on a person's inner psychic life.[110]

From another perspective, however, Rapaport was right to place Erikson in the mainstream. As Suzanne Kirschner has shown in her brilliant multinational comparative essay, the whole direction of Anglo-American psychoanalytic theory in the past quarter century has been on ego development over the life course, the nature of autonomous selfhood, and the capacity for mature relations. Correspondingly, traditional issues of inner emotional life like instinctual renunciation and Oedipal conflict have received considerably less emphasis. That would place Erikson's work, with its emphasis on the life cycle, identity, and mutuality on a horizontal social plane more in the mainstream than the periphery of what is assuredly a post-Freudian perspective. In this sense, he contested Freud, lost among orthodox Freudians, but won a conspicuous place among many for whom Freud's cardinal assumptions had lost their currency.[111]

CONTESTING KARLA ABRAHAMSEN HOMBURGER

Because Erikson's articles comprised a whole volume of *Psychological Issues* and were introduced by perhaps the most reflective psychoanalytic theoretician in the United States, his voice was broadcast quite directly to the psychoanalytic community. Through *Young Man Luther*, it was also being broadcast to theologians, social critics, historians, and other humanistic scholars. His works were part of a gradual migration of Freudian and post-Freudian thought from psychoanalytic institutes to academia and the discourse of public intellectuals.

As Erikson worked to fashion what he thought to be an authentic and largely public voice, he often found himself reflecting upon and taking stock of his own life history. In the fall of 1953, for example, he traveled with Jon, his artistically inclined and self-searching younger son, to Fiesole, overlooking Florence. Decades earlier Erik Homburger had stayed there; he had been trying to gain a sense of himself by working to fashion a life as an artist. As father and son sat on the bench where Erik had spent many hours gazing at the sights of Florence and pondering his fate, the father sensed that he "could formulate much of what in my artist days had remained vague—very vague indeed." At an Austen Riggs case conference a few years later, he recalled his first arrival in Boston, apprehensive about how the local medical establishment would receive an immigrant who lacked academic and medical degrees. Well into midlife, Erikson seemed attentive to the turning points of his past.[112]

His most intense personal memories during the 1950s concerned parentage and adoption, reflecting his continuing concern with his missing father. In *Young Man Luther,* Erikson had explored Luther's relationship to his father; he wrote of troublesome "doubts about our biological origin" and how young children suffered without "parental sponsorship." Surrogate fathers could never "guard the beginnings of their identities." At Riggs case conferences, he showed particular concern for patients who, as children, did not know much about their biological fathers and experienced difficult adoptions much as he had. He fretted that one who had never seen his father suffered most acutely because "he had no father to contend with or identify with or to be supported by." An "adopted child never stops looking" for his real parent.[113]

The concern with missing parentage (primarily paternal) intensified in January of 1960 when Erikson's mother, Karla, died in Haifa. She was eighty-four. She had survived Erik's stepfather by eleven years and was the only person he knew who, presumably, could reveal the identity of his father. Her silence on the question over the decades increased the possibility that she had been seduced or raped by a stranger. Having decided that "her time had come," Karla had concealed her prescribed medications and had "let her heart run out." Haifa had been her home since 1935. She had lived there with her younger daughter, Ellen, and had watched over Ellen's children. With an active interest in public affairs, Karla had witnessed the creation of Israel as an independent Jewish state. She had regularly visited her two other children, Ruth and Erik, in America and enjoyed being with their children. Karla was pleased that Erik had become a prominent psychoanalyst, intellectual, and author, and she had tried to master all of his writings. "She is an admirable woman, but of a very penetrating personality, hard on a son," Erik had once confided to Anna Freud.[114]

Erik had been proud of Karla's struggle, beginning with his stepfather's death in 1949, to recover compensation from Germany for the family's financial loss when they fled Nazi Germany. The Generallandesarchiv Karlsruhe holds a thick restitution file of Karla's persistent efforts to satisfy insensitive German bureaucrats and gain compensation. They demanded proof of her husband's exact monthly income between 1930 and 1935 as a Karlsruhe pediatrician. She provided it, demonstrating precisely how anti-Jewish boycotts had halved his earnings. When German authorities ruled that they would pay only for Theodor Homburger's financial loss before he moved to Haifa, Karla had the decision reversed. She also filed documents to require Karlsruhe authorities to pay off on two of her husband's German life insurance policies. Karla did not garner substantial assets from this decade-long struggle, but she exceeded the paltry sums most German-Jewish émigrés received and showed German officials that she was a remarkably strong and persistent old woman who spoke her mind.[115]

Erik was different. While he could identify with the force and authenticity of young Luther and could even contest Freud, he was no match for a powerful and articulate woman like his mother. Since his early years, the identity of his biological father had been at least as important to him as compensation for Nazi wrongs had been to Karla. He had written *Young Man Luther,* which had stressed the importance of a relationship between a son, a father, and God the father. But he felt powerless to ask Karla to tell him about his father. Decades earlier, Karla had informed him that Valdemar Salomonsen (her first husband) was his actual father and that he was never to pursue the issue further with her. He had complied, but at a cost. Like his seminarian patient at Riggs who struggled to differentiate himself from the overpowering presence of his mother, Erik realized by the late 1950s that he had to advance beyond where Karla had drawn the line. Indeed, despite his growing facility at speaking out and "Meaning It," he had never found a way to open up to Karla concerning his sense of disability because he had not come to grips with his paternity. He had not even broached with Karla his memories of how she had seemed to shunt him aside when she met his stepfather. His seminarian patient had dreamed of an empty face; he had worked with Erik to understand how this had signaled an inner emptiness and an inability to push away from his mother. With understanding, the seminarian had gained control of his problem, and was able to discuss it openly. In some measure, the seminarian had bypassed his therapist.

After Karla died, Abrahamsen cousins from Copenhagen wrote to Erikson about the little they knew concerning his paternity. Their parents (Karla's brothers) had told them that Valdemar Salomonsen was not his father and had abandoned Karla years before Erik was born. Erik also learned from his cousins that "I was the illegitimate outcome of a love affair with a Dane of good family (not Jewish) and artistically gifted." Various stories he had heard over the years, many of which had apparently passed through generations of Abrahamsens, now seemed validated; they helped to explain "my struggle for identity." Excitedly, Erik showed Joan the letters from Copenhagen. Then he relayed to Sue, Kai, and Jon the supposed fact that his biological father was artistically talented and of Danish royalty. A story steeped in folklore of distinguished paternity that passed from generation to generation now passed from Erik, the father, to his sons and daughter. To be sure, it had all the makings of a family romance. Yet it animated and conveyed hope to a man who had not found the full meaning of "Meaning It" even as he contested psychoanalytic orthodoxy.[116]

Aided by the information from his Abrahamsen cousins, Erikson might have made substantial progress in discovering the identity of his father. He might have asked his relatives for pertinent documents that had belonged to their parents and grandparents. In fact, he could have taken a research trip to Copenhagen to peruse the meticulous records of the Danish National Archives. Coincidentally, a movement for the rights of adoptees to learn about their biological parents had commenced in the United States, and several pioneers of that movement would almost certainly have assisted him in his research efforts abroad. Initially, however, Erikson did nothing, honoring his mother's prohibition against inquiry. He mentioned to Kenneth Keniston, a young friend and scholar, that her death was such a large and "overshadowing" event, it seemed to leave him incapable of doing much of anything.[117]

Less than two years after Karla's death, Erikson turned to one of her relatives, Herman Kalckar, a professor of biochemistry at Harvard Medical School. He was six years younger than Erik. Born in Denmark, he had migrated to the United States after World War II, spoke Danish fluently, and frequently traveled to Copenhagen. He knew that Karla's mother had been a Kalckar from his extensive work on Kalckar-Abrahamsen family genealogy. Erikson, who asserted that he "spoke Danish as a small child and forgot it for step-German," enlisted Kalckar's assistance. Kalckar urged Erikson to accompany him on a trip to Copenhagen to pursue the investigation, but he declined. If Kalckar discovered the identity of Erik's biological father or the children of his father during that trip, he explained, his presence might be considered intrusive or it might seem as if he were seeking remuneration by tagging along. Indeed, he had no desire to embarrass an eminent Danish family with stories of an extramarital scandal. Kalckar would speak for him.[118]

When Kalckar arrived in Copenhagen, he asked Edith Abrahamsen, one of Erik's cousins, what she knew about the identity of Erik's father. Based on family rumors, Edith suspected the father might have been a local photographer. Kalckar tried to locate a suitable candidate in source books on turn-of-the-century Danish photographers but was unsuccessful. Edith told Kalckar that her cousin, Svend Abrahamsen, probably knew more than she did. The son of Axel Abrahamsen, Svend acted as the family historian and archivist for pertinent family documents. Over the years, Axel had passed a great many family stories on to Svend. Kalckar was unable to meet with Svend, however, because of the urgency of his own business dealings and Svend's ill health. He returned home and reported to Erikson what he had learned. Erikson was calm and did not press him with questions or concerns.[119]

A few years elapsed. Svend's health continued to fail, so Erikson decided to try again. This time, he designated a strong and intelligent female envoy, his half sister Ellen, who traveled from Haifa to Copenhagen to see what she could uncover. Svend died after Ellen arrived in Copenhagen but before she could meet with him. She decided there was nothing more she could do. Ellen reported to Erik, much as Karla might have done, that with Svend's death, the identity of his father would never be known. Further inquiries were inappropriate. This advice from a sister with whom he had been close and whose judgment he had respected concluded his inquiries. He never contacted Svend's son, Finn, to explore the many family documents and memories passed on to him or to explore a number of leads that Finn might have offered.[120]

The way Erikson dealt with the issue of his paternity after Karla's death resembled his response to the loyalty oath crisis a decade earlier. When she died, his desire to learn the identity of his biological father intensified as it had not in years. But he could not summon the strength to visit his Danish relatives and pursue their leads until he learned who had fathered him. A decade earlier, Erikson had issued a statement to the Berkeley faculty Committee on Privilege and Tenure contemptuous of an opinion-silencing loyalty oath. For him, this was a demonstration of "Meaning It." Not long after, however, he almost certainly signed a document with the language of the original oath.

The disparity between a desire and a capacity to fulfill that desire can be overemphasized, however, especially in a person with profoundly reflective and aesthetic sensibilities who lacked an activist bent. Between the oath crisis and the death of Karla, moreover, he had become intensely concerned with voice and the salutary effects of speaking out. His Riggs patients enhanced their lives when they found their unique voices. As he discovered how a capacity to speak out and "Mean It" had given Luther strength and orientation, Erikson seemed to find new power and capacity in himself. Before psychoanalytic audiences globally, he strongly asserted his own mixed perspectives on "Freud's field."

During this decade, Erikson had come a long way in discovering and using what he considered to be an authentic voice—one that embodied the essence of a unique sense of selfhood. This quest for the authentic—the "real" and the "meaningful"—was compatible with a growing trend in American popular and intellectual culture, and it would provide him a very important platform in the public discourse of the 1960s as a Harvard professor. In some measure, Erikson's capacity to articulate the nature of an authentic voice was helping him to exhibit one. As his friend David Riesman wrote to McGeorge Bundy in 1959, Erikson's old "diffidence" had receded decidedly; he had found "a greater confidence in his own powers" to articulate and persuade.[121]

Erikson's developing voice and sense of authenticity related primarily to men—sons and fathers. Although he had characterized a young Luther who spoke out against his father and for God the father, and had advanced his "horizontal" perspective against Sigmund Freud's "verticality," he was unwilling to contest the strong, intelligent, nurturing women in his life— Anna Freud, Karla Abrahamsen, Ellen Katz, Margaret Mead, or his wife, Joan. Voice and authenticity operated within a world of men and was not a resource when Karla prohibited him from inquiring about the most important issue in his life.

CHAPTER SEVEN

Professor and Public Intellectual: The 1960s

"The sixties" is often tagged to represent a complex and multifaceted social, cultural, and political phenomenon. Naturally, it has signified different qualities to different commentators. Some of the more discerning have characterized it as a series of interrelated developments that took hold in America at some point in the 1950s and continued for roughly two decades. Social critic Dwight Macdonald found the spirit of the 1960s in the spontaneity and idealism of civil rights and student activists, and in their romantic notions of protest and community. African-American historian Lawrence Reddick argued that the spirit of the sixties was represented most clearly by the Montgomery bus boycott of 1955–56. For Reddick, Martin Luther King's leadership during that protest illustrated how "the philosophy of Thoreau and Gandhi can triumph." Cultural historian W. T. Lhamon, Jr., felt the dynamics behind developments of the 1960s evolved in the 1950s. For him, "the sixties" was a label for a pervasive sense of depersonalization, the loss of individuality in the corporate workplace and in other institutions, the erosion of family and community ties, and a more general apprehension over the incapacity of the self to cope with modern existence.[1]

Hundreds of publications on the "self under siege" and the necessity of fundamental change influenced discourse from the middle 1950s until at least the early 1970s. Evocative and broad-ranging books like David Riesman's *The Lonely Crowd* (1950), Robert Nisbet's *The Quest for Community* (1953), and Erik Erikson's *Childhood and Society* (1950) became conspicuous in college bookstores and undergraduate classrooms during this time. This was due, in part, to the paperback revolution in the publishing industry that enabled the mass distribution of low-cost editions. Reflecting the decided overlap and interplay between the 1950s and the 1960s, Margaret Mead discussed these books in general, and *Childhood and Society* in particular, in 1955. She insisted that "a new concept is clamoring for acceptance—the concept of identity." It was about to become one of the most "burning problems of the present age." Mead predicted that Erikson, the architect of a powerful perspective on identity that connected self to society and community, would soon become a central public figure.[2]

Mead predicted accurately. By the late 1960s and the early 1970s, a significant number of Americans would find selfhood, meaning, and identity to be in conflict with the difficult, bureaucratized conditions that seemed to be gaining hegemony over modern life. Identity, especially, would become a useful way to frame the pervasive sense that one's beliefs and values seemed temporary, contingent, and socially situated. The identity construct did not frame an "Age of Erikson," but several of Erikson's basic concerns—the "identity crisis," for example, and relationships between generations—resonated widely during these years, especially among the young and the college educated. A professor during much of this period, he spoke and wrote most engagingly to this segment of the population.

There was also, among those in this segment, a developing quest for personal authenticity, often characterized by visions of a free, playful, adventurous self that lived "deeply." Theodore Roszak's *The Making of a Counter Culture* (itself an important artifact of the sixties) described counterculture as both a search for authenticity and an attack on the myth that people, like machines, could be made objective and efficient, unobstructed by magic, spirituality, or playfulness. This critical perspective found abundant support in Erikson's presentations and publications.[3]

Finally, the distinction between public and private life eroded markedly during these years, as evident in the popular slogan that "the personal is the political." Psychoanalytic ego psychology became a theoretical vehicle to connect the public and the private self, for it concerned negotiations between the deepest inner aspect of personality (the id) and external social constraints (the superego). Erikson's books and articles were almost certainly the most popular and accessible of the works by ego psychologists, speaking vividly and compellingly of the links between self and society. He emerged as a major intellectual and public figure of the period.

HARVARD NEGOTIATIONS

Erikson better engaged the emerging cultures and ideas in American society by moving in 1960 from the isolated Austen Riggs Center to academia and the metropolis. He had hardly tested the university setting at Berkeley in 1950 when the loyalty oath controversy cost him his prized professorship.

Even as he signed on at Riggs, Erikson had been attentive to future university positions. He trusted his friend David Riesman, viewed *The Lonely Crowd* (which was heavily influenced by Erich Fromm) as a companion volume to *Childhood and Society,* and knew that Riesman would alert him to academic possibilities. By 1956, he confided to Riesman a pressing need for "extra-clinical colleagues and students." Riesman moved from the University of Chicago to Harvard the following year and arranged for his friend to spend some time with undergraduates who resided on campus at Winthrop House. Erikson found the experience very gratifying and hoped for a permanent position. To be sure, he had some concern because McGeorge Bundy, dean of Harvard College, had not always protected faculty rights during the McCarthy period. But that era had passed even though some loyalty hearings persisted. By the late 1950s, Harvard influenced large areas of American intellectual life, garnered nearly $30 million in federal grants, and exerted a substantial influence upon national public policy discussions. The campus consisted of an expanding and exciting network of research specialties, educational experiments, social services, and consultantships that were not far removed from the highest centers of national power. Erikson's alternatives were clear: "stay at Riggs forever, comfortable and well-protected, or face academic life" at Harvard, with all its challenges, uncertainties, and potential for a teacher and an intellectual.[4]

If the comfort and protection of Riggs had been important to Erikson after the vexing California loyalty oath crisis, they became less so as time passed. Although he had been unusually proficient and often brilliant in clinical endeavors during the 1950s, clinical life had been losing much of its allure. He had needed to leave Riggs's clinical atmosphere in order to write *Young Man Luther,* and authorship was emerging as his first professional love. Work in Stockbridge with "borderline cases, like that [earlier] with children, gets to be more strenuous as one grows older," he confided to Anna Freud. He had "further developmental and historical studies" on his writing agenda, Erikson explained to Robert Knight, and that agenda could best be served by the free time academia offered plus the "closeness to scholars in other fields." David Rapaport had been the only broad-ranging scholar who had engaged him at Riggs, and his premature death from a heart attack in 1960 left a great gap in Erikson's life. While the Riggs activities program that Joan had developed had given her important roots in the community, she was deeply attentive to Erik's need to write, to teach, and to associate with scholars. Moreover, Joan had always placed his career ahead of her own, and she recognized Erik's keen interest in returning to a university setting. "It was Erik's move," Joan recalled.[5]

Erikson made the move in his characteristically cautious way. While giving friends at Harvard like Riesman and Talcott Parsons the go-ahead in 1958 to start exploratory discussions on his behalf, he accepted a part-time visiting professorship at the Massachusetts Institute of Technology to see if he would enjoy teaching in the Boston area. Once a week, he drove from Stockbridge to Cambridge to conduct an MIT graduate seminar open to scholars in the vicinity. With *Young Man Luther* as a model, each participant investigated the life history of a revolutionary innovator—among them Simón Bolívar, Woodrow Wilson, and Mahatma Gandhi. Erikson conducted the seminar like a Riggs patient case conference and was pleased to see that the format appealed to young scholars with no formal psychological training. Like the instructor, they were discovering an affinity for a broad-ranging interdisciplinary study centering on biography, history, and psychoanalysis.[6]

It was no small accomplishment for Erikson's friends in the professorate to secure him a senior tenured faculty position at the most prestigious university in the country. After all, he had no academic degree and did not really fit within a single academic department. Harvard's Department of Social Relations was less adverse to a faculty line for Erikson than other academic units. Created in 1946, it combined clinical and social psychology, sociology, and cultural anthropology. Erikson knew the department chair, psychologist Robert W. White, from his days at Henry Murray's Harvard Psychological Clinic. Cooperating with Riesman and Parsons, White engineered formal departmental endorsement of Erikson's appointment but then ran into strong reservations among several colleagues on the grounds of deficient academic credentials. Consequently, he asked Dean Bundy to approve an independent, nondepartmental appointment.[7]

David Riesman's 1957 appointment as Henry Ford II Professor of Social Sciences was a model for Erikson's. It was the first of several independent, nondepartmental professorships that Bundy created with private funding. These professorships went to preeminent scholars and carried comparatively high salaries plus reduced teaching loads. In some measure, they signaled a modest effort by the Office of the Dean to assert an influence over traditional academic departments concerning fields of scholarship. Bundy believed firmly in interdisciplinary study and innovative instruction, fought for them against entrenched campus programs, and viewed the special professorships as part of his campaign to shift faculty positions from departments to creative interdisciplinary centers. Michael Maccoby, a young doctoral candidate in clinical psychology with considerable influence as a well-liked assistant to the dean, had been instrumental in Riesman's appointment. As well, he admired Erikson's work and was responsive to Riesman's and Parsons's prompting on Erikson's behalf. Maccoby approached Marshall Field and other potential donors to request roughly

$250,000 for a special professorship "to support Erikson until retirement." But Bundy was already won over to Erikson's strengths and told Maccoby he would make up any fund-raising deficit out of college funds. He therefore awaited the considerable debate and reports from diverse college committees and faculty before formalizing the appointment.[8]

The faculty was polarized. Erikson's lack of academic credentials rankled many. Several mocked him as a psychoanalyst. "Why not Christian Science?" one senior psychologist queried. The influential political theorist Barrington Moore lobbied for Herbert Marcuse as a more viable alternative. He considered Marcuse a more substantial thinker and the sort of profound political radical that Harvard needed. David McClelland dismissed Erikson as a glamor appointment; for the same money, Harvard could recruit more systematic researchers who could help to establish the details of human personality. Erikson's friends on the faculty defended him against these and other attacks. Clyde Kluckhohn, who had helped him with his Yurok research years earlier, insisted that undergraduates would love Erikson and that his ideas would percolate throughout the campus. Henry Murray characterized Erikson as "the most distinguished psychoanalyst in America" and a remarkable oddity: "part scientist, part artist." Talcott Parsons, perhaps at the height of his influence as a social theorist, noted that Erikson was one of a few exceedingly competent analysts who could enrich Harvard. Parsons insisted that Erikson treated human personality not only psychoanalytically, but with an eye to the social and historical context. Riesman's support was strongest of all—and most elaborate. He noted that Erikson wrote "like Conrad in an alien tongue." There was a "tentativeness that marks all his writing and talking" and that was important in areas of academia "where sureness is often a sign of repressed fear or ignorance." Although Erikson was a quiet man who worked alone, Riesman added that he would function as "an intellectual switchboard," drawing together "people in a great many fields of intellectual endeavor."[9]

If most Harvard faculty who voiced opinions were less than enthusiastic about this faculty position, some of the most prominent were exceedingly positive, and they gave Bundy the support to proceed with an appointment that he was determined to make and that he knew President Nathan Pusey would accept. Bundy offered Erikson a special professorship outside any academic department and a $20,000 salary for the 1960–61 academic year (with regular annual raises to follow). This was at the top end of the Harvard faculty pay scale. The Austen Riggs retirement plan provided only $750 annually if he retired at age seventy. Bundy understood that this was no basis for a comfortable retirement and guaranteed a more substantial contribution to Erikson's retirement benefits. The university would contribute 7.5 percent of

Erikson's annual salary (uncharacteristically high); another 7.5 percent would be deducted from his annual wages. The university would also provide a comfortable house it owned near the campus at a nominal rent and would permit Erikson to supplement his income with a private clinical practice. Also, book royalties garnered additional revenue. Consequently, Erikson would be very comfortable financially if he accepted a professorship at America's most prestigious university. Bundy had gone overboard to move him to Cambridge.[10]

Riesman predicted that Erikson would accept. He wrote to Bundy that his friend from Stockbridge continued to feel somewhat unsure about his capabilities outside the clinical setting. Riesman, however, felt that in recent years Erikson had assumed "a greater confidence in his own powers as a teacher and colleague and fellow researcher." His discovery of the strength of voice and language—Luther's, his Riggs patients', and his own—were important sources of this new confidence. He thought of himself increasingly as a writer and intellectual as well as a psychoanalyst. He also considered the university, more than the clinic or the psychoanalytic institute, as the emerging setting for serious Freudian discourse. On Bundy's behalf, Michael Maccoby invited Erikson to speak to a small select group of undergraduates so that he could determine whether teaching these young adults appealed to him. It did, decidedly so. As an instructor for "these bright and searching young people," Erikson wrote to Margaret Mead, he could "bridge the gap between the clinical and the educational." Moreover, he could test ideas in the classroom for his writing projects as he had not been able to do during his previous stints in academia, where he had been obligated to concentrate on research and writing within systematic research projects headed by others. By communicating regularly with young people at Harvard in his own way, he could "develop some kind of teachable *and* sound framework for our insights."[11]

According to Bundy, Erikson asked to be designated officially as "Professor of Human Development." Much as he had named himself on becoming an American citizen, he had identified his professional title. With the approval of the medical school dean, Bundy also gave him a lectureship in the school's Department of Psychiatry. As chair of the social relations department, Robert White gave Erikson a sort of unofficial departmental membership despite reservations from several of his colleagues. Bundy had told Paul Buck, the director of the Widener Library, that Erikson was "a man of very great distinction" and merited a faculty study where he could work and meet with his students. Buck obliged and assigned Erikson a study that had originally belonged to Charles Eliot Norton and, more recently, to Edmund Wilson. It was spacious, with new desks and chairs and abundant bookshelves. With Bundy's intervention, Erikson also received use of a small conference room in Prince House to conduct his weekly graduate seminar, to

meet with students, and to see a few private patients. Finally, Bundy allowed
Erikson to take the spring semester and summer off his first year at Harvard
under a Ford Foundation grant so that he would have free time to write.
Erikson was grateful for all that Bundy had done for him and was happy to
regard the Harvard College dean as his boss and mentor. He showed Bundy
a paper he was writing for his undergraduate course, for example, along with
a detailed course outline. Bundy praised the paper but told Erikson that it
was improper for a dean to review a faculty member's teaching plans. While
appreciative of his special status at Harvard, Erikson did not yet understand
how a senior faculty member was to conduct himself.[12]

A PROFESSORIAL VENTURE

Lacking academic degrees and experienced only in small psychoanalytic
seminar courses during his brief stint as a Berkeley professor, Erikson experienced trepidations over Social Science 139, his primary teaching assignment at Harvard. Social Science 139 was a large undergraduate general
education course featuring a one-hour lecture twice a week plus four small
one-hour discussion sections, each supervised by a teaching assistant. The
life cycle, centering on the fifth or identity stage, still preoccupied Erikson,
and that became the framework for the course. But how did one talk to 150
or more students lacking psychoanalytic or clinical backgrounds? More fundamentally, how did a clinician experienced in treating disturbed young
adults go about teaching normal students of roughly the same age? His children had grown up and left home, he explained to Anna Freud, and he
seemed ready for another nonclinical assignment with the younger generation: "Maybe, having learned to cure *some* young people, I felt that there
must be something I can teach many of them."[13]

Understanding Erikson's apprehensions over the transition, Riesman
offered to assist. He could sympathize with Erik, for he had arrived at Harvard with a law degree but no doctorate and not much formal disciplinary
training in his field of sociology. Riesman showed Erikson the syllabus for
Social Science 136, his course on "Character and Social Structure in America," and discussed the nature of his reading and writing assignments and
the way in which he supervised his teaching assistants. He also arranged for
Kenneth Keniston, his own head teaching assistant ("chief section man"),
who would publish important works on 1960s student activism, to help
with book and film orders, lecture schedules, and the hiring of teaching
assistants. Keniston promised to spend some time with Erikson to organize
the new interdisciplinary course the summer before the semester began.

Riesman understood that Erikson's view of interdisciplinary study was rooted in the culture and personality movement of the 1930s and 1940s, which had drawn heavily on fusions between cultural anthropology and psychoanalysis. The closest equivalent at Harvard in 1960 was the social relations department, which had a few culture and personality carryovers on its faculty. Riesman tried to interest Erikson in this social relations agenda but was less than successful. He therefore offered advice and support as Erikson fashioned his own course with his own interdisciplinary materials. Riesman also attended Erikson's lectures from time to time to provide reassurance.[14]

After some weeks preparing for SS 139 with Keniston in his Stockbridge home, and following regular doses of Riesman's coaching, Erikson appeared on the Harvard campus to start the fall semester. From the start, he made a vivid impression. Eschewing the conservative dark suit and tie worn by many faculty members, he often wore a blue shirt, a tweed jacket with a striking check design, and white moccasins. With a well-combed mane of white hair that seemed to glow, a distinguished gray and white mustache, and a reddish face, he was pleased that students considered him suave and elegant, for physical appearance still meant much to him. Although the hearing aid in his left ear was visible, he appeared tanned, confident, and robust. He was "breathtaking and mesmerizing," one undergraduate recalled. Women of all ages were taken by him and several found him sexually attractive. Erikson lectured in clear English with a decided German accent in a gentle and courtly manner. He relied on his considerable reservoir of jokes to ease tense situations. "Children can be obscene [seen] but not absurd [heard]," he jested in class. In an obvious attempt to connect the clinical to the academic realm for his students, he recounted the story of the rabbi who counseled a disgruntled wife with complaints about her husband. "You're absolutely right," he told her. Then the rabbi also agreed with similar complaints by her husband. When the rabbi's wife confronted him with the contradiction of agreeing with both spouses, he told her, "You're absolutely right." Erikson was out to please and to ease as he began his new professorial assignment—not to confront during a decade that was already marked by tense confrontations on college campuses.[15]

Because Erikson did not belong to any department, he felt a bit uneasy over being excluded from faculty meetings. But before long, he had his share of campus affiliations and responsibilities. He became Harvard faculty representative to the Radcliffe Board of Trustees; the education of young women interested him considerably. Members of the century-old Cambridge Scientific Club voted unanimously to invite him into their proceedings. He enjoyed monthly dinners with the university president, Nathan Pusey, and internationally acclaimed humanities scholars like Samuel Eliot Morison and Crane Brinton to discuss topics of intellectual and cultural concern. But the daily routines of Social Science 139 represented his most pressing engagement.[16]

At the beginning of the academic year in September 1960, Erikson distributed a well-organized course syllabus to roughly two hundred undergraduates. With Keniston's help, he had fashioned a comprehensive document, and it did not change much over the years. It did not impose great demands upon the preponderantly senior-level students, requiring them to write several short papers and a long final essay on any subject that seemed pertinent. Replacing formal examinations, written assignments did not call for precise definitions or logical, closely argued positions. Like their teacher, students were free to be impressionistic and artistic, "to visualize and empathize." The linear logic endemic to the college classroom was conspicuously absent. Indeed, after a few weeks of lecturing, Erikson implored the undergraduates to put away their pens and notepads so he could communicate with them face-to-face: "When you write, you put your heads down. And when I can't see your eyes, it is as if I were talking only to myself." Reading assignments were light: "The student is expected to read well rather than much." The basic assignments were from Erikson's own books and articles. Like the artist he once had been, he was holding up his own work for public viewing. Students might come to "visit" his writings as they "visited" artistic showings. Erikson's publications were supplemented by regular films; selections from classics like those of William James, Freud, and Piaget; and essays by Erikson's friends like Mead, Kluckhohn, and Riesman.[17]

The syllabus outlined the primary agenda for this class on the nature and course of the human life, with special attention to "the *borderlines of humanness*" and dangerous acts of inhumanity. Erikson's eight-stage life cycle would structure the course, beginning with infancy, ending with old age, and attentive to the "mutual dependencies" of people at different stages. Ethical as well as intellectual and physical development was relevant, as was the connection between "the *sequence* of life stages and the *institutions* of the social order." Erikson acknowledged that this orientation to the life cycle originated in "clinical necessity"—that is, in his treatment of patients at various life stages. This " 'clinical' vantage point" would therefore be central to the class. But rather than begin the course with a Riggs case conference approach to the development of a patient, Erikson instead showed and discussed Ingmar Bergman's *Wild Strawberries*. Bergman's film was a study of "the acute integrity crisis of an old man at the height of his career—a crisis which brings back to him, in the span of one fateful day, the critical way stations of his life." In the course of a day-long automobile trip with his daughter-in-law, Isak Borg recalled how he had negotiated his prior seven life stages with people of different generations and values. *Wild Strawberries* represented a very effective preview of SS 139 and helped to establish an emotional rapport between the fifty-nine-year-old instructor and students younger than his children. Isak Borg captured his past through memories, fantasies, and dreams, and Erikson discussed them in a free-ranging and emotional way. Rationality and logic were present in his comments on the film, but only very modestly. Erikson was pushing the undergraduates into a closer rapport with their hidden feelings through discussions that resembled a stream of consciousness. Many of the students had never experienced this approach before.[18]

At times in his introductory lecture, Erikson announced his primary purpose to be an increase in empathy with other peoples in other cultures and other times. Sometimes he seemed to call for the acquisition of what Michael Polanyi called tacit knowledge—a type of understanding of otherness that came from experience but could not be verbalized. At other moments, Erikson emphasized a fusion of the empathy inherent in the clinical setting with cross-cultural and historical scholarship. This was a very large goal, which he recognized the student could not accomplish entirely on his or her own. For assistance, Erikson drew upon a variety of prominent specialists whom he had gotten to know (some were good friends) as guest lecturers. They ranged from pediatrician Benjamin Spock and anthropologist Margaret Mead to Beat poet Allen Ginsberg and physicist Gerald Holton. But the work of a remarkable staff of teaching assistants (usually eight) was probably even more important to the undergraduates. In discussion groups of twenty-five, students met for an hour a week with Robert Coles, Pamela Daniels, Carol Gilligan, Richard Sennett, Stephan Thernstrom, Mary Catherine Bateson, or others. Many were to become important intellectuals and public figures.[19]

Christopher Jencks and David Riesman's classic study of American higher education in the 1960s characterized a buffer role for graduate student teaching assistants in research universities between the undergraduates and the faculty, handling not only grading and discussion sections but student complaints of every sort. While Erikson's graduate assistants were very important to the undergraduates, they hardly filled buffer roles. Especially during the early 1960s, they often guided him through the teaching process.[20]

At the recommendation of faculty friends whom he trusted, Erikson regularly hired a "chief section man." This "man" (often a woman) hired the other teaching assistants and oriented them to their assignments. Keniston initially performed this function. Trained as a psychologist, he had worked at the Harvard Psychological Clinic and helped Erikson draw clinical data from his Riggs patient files for use in his lectures. Doctoral student Gordon Fellman, a sociologist in the social relations department, succeeded Keniston. He, too, had taught in Riesman's interdisciplinary course, already provided indications of the master-teacher at Brandeis that he would become, and was especially interested in the culture and politics of modern India. Like Keniston, Fellman found that while Riesman had explicitly informed the section head and other teaching assistants about his goals and what they had to do to help him meet them, Erikson was far less authoritative. Indeed, he often asked the head section man and other assistants to advise him on these matters. To some degree, they were to take care of him as he took care of the course.[21]

For short intervals during the early 1960s, a few other section heads followed Keniston and Fellman until Pamela Daniels assumed the post on a regular basis. A doctoral student in political science, Daniels was put off by the quantitative emphasis and theoretical abstraction within the Harvard department. Susanne Rudolph, an untenured member of that department and a specialist on India who had worked briefly in SS 139, became her mentor in political science but suggested that Erikson might help her with her biographical and historical interests in Indian nationalism. Eight months pregnant, Daniels met with Erikson in the spring of 1963. He had begun his research on Gandhi and they discussed Indian nationalist leadership, but conversation focused on Erikson's increasingly pressing interest in intergenerational contact and support. He, Daniels, and her baby represented just such a connectedness. "Far from disqualifying me," Daniels recalled, "motherhood somehow enhanced my qualifications to teach in that course." Within a few years, she became his commanding "chief section man" and much more, satisfying Erikson's long-standing reliance on a strong, intelligent, female presence. While managing her own section and directing other teaching assistants, Daniels mastered Erikson's writings in minute detail and with considerable subtlety, arranging and rearranging them at points on the syllabus to maximize their appeal. She designed and redesigned student paper assignments with the hope that students might learn to rely on Erikson's configurational psychosocial approach. Daniels made sure all course grades were turned in on time. She even prepared reference letters requested by undergraduates, handing them to Erikson to sign. Soon, Daniels joined Joan Erikson as a major editorial assistant, checking over early drafts of many of Erik's professional writings much as Joan had done for decades. With considerable propriety, Erikson referred to SS 139 as "our course." He was ecstatic about Daniels's "rare combination of conceptual understanding, vivid expression, and direct application of the theory we taught" and her always proficient "follow-up contact with the students." Without Daniels, Erikson acknowledged, he simply could not have gone on teaching "that large class of seniors."[22]

Meanwhile, Daniels's own career goals were neglected. While attending to Erikson's needs, she made little progress toward the completion of her doctoral work, and that was telling about his mentorship. Although he had no formal departmental affiliation and could not officially chair dissertation committees, many of his teaching assistants regarded him as their de facto mentor. Yet Erikson never really supervised or appreciably facilitated the work even of those with whom he felt closest. There were excuses: He lacked academic credentials, he felt unlearned in the nuances of academic politics, and he was unsure of himself in the role of mentor. More to the point, he felt that he did not have sufficient time. Although the generativity stage of his life cycle model described adult assistance to youth, Erikson was far more preoccupied with his own writing and classroom teaching than the progress of his graduate students. Unlike David Riesman, who had put his doctoral students on closely supervised research and writing schedules and sought employment prospects to advance their careers, Erikson simply wished his students well. Although Fellman taught and provided research materials for Erikson and not for Alex Inkeles, for example, it was Inkeles who found him a job in the Brandeis sociology department. Similarly, when Susanne Rudolph and her husband, Lloyd, came up for tenure in political science, Erikson prepared a favorable but hasty and less than glowingly detailed letter of support. It did not cross his mind that an unambiguously favorable and detailed letter was mandatory at a university that customarily discharged most junior faculty.[23]

It was also apparent that Erikson lacked a commanding presence at the weekly staff meetings that he convened, beginning in the fall of 1960, for his teaching assistants. They met over lunch or in his faculty study in the Widener Library. Erikson rarely took charge of these gatherings but instead engaged in enjoyable banter. The "chief section man" brought up administrative details. Sometimes Erikson sought reassurance that his recent lectures had been successful with the undergraduates. Teaching assistants commented on developments in their discussion sections. Not infrequently, one of them ran a section very nearly as a separate, autonomous course. One section focused on fairy tales, for example, while another concerned the nature of "individual freedom." A prominent and experienced psychiatrist and social activist, Robert Coles pursued his interests in literature and civil rights within his section. Soon to become a major feminist intellectual, Carol Gilligan and her students often dealt with issues of gender and family. Erikson never complained that these pursuits might detract from the syllabus and the main lines of his lectures. Nor did he respond to the more general problem of grade inflation in the discussion sections. Although he disapproved of overly generous grades, he did not instruct or pressure teaching assistants to be more rigorous.[24]

Most of Erikson's meetings with his teaching assistants, then, were relaxed and nonconfrontational. These were gatherings in intergenerational borrowing. When they first met in his Widener Library study, however, a crucifix on the wall preoccupied them. None had anticipated this from any of their contacts with him. Had he become a Christian? some asked themselves. A few recalled his description of something like a conversion experience in the preface to *Young Man Luther*. Indeed, had there been a Christian, even Protestant, tone to his Social Science 139 lectures all along? He was not a practicing Christian, they knew. Indeed, he rarely attended Cambridge's Memorial Church with Joan, despite her prompting. When Gordon Fellman summoned the courage to refer to the crucifix, he asked if Erikson considered himself and his orientation Jewish or Christian. "If you are anti-Semitic, I'm a Jew," Erikson retorted, essentially halting the inquiry.[25]

Especially during his first few years in the classroom, Erikson visited all discussion sections at least once every semester and listened closely as the undergraduates conversed. He cared about their feelings and concerns, recognizing all the while that he was learning much about American youth and their identity needs that he could incorporate in his writing. Unlike the traditional professor at the research university who essentially counted on graduate students to do the real teaching, Erikson placed great value upon a solid rapport with the undergraduates (up from 150 to 250 each semester by the mid-1960s and primarily seniors). They crammed his lecture room twice a week. Fire marshals were sometimes required to clear aisles and exits. During one lecture, Erikson openly castigated professorial colleagues for being overly concerned with enhancing their professional status and overlooking the most indispensable psychological task of adulthood: caring for the next generation—their students. Perhaps somewhat seductively, he proclaimed this nurturing and support of students to be his essential task as their professor.[26]

Roughly one-quarter of all Harvard seniors took Erikson's undergraduate course, which fulfilled the upper-level general education requirement in the social sciences. Many were serious about the ethical and public issues that he discussed. The majority majored in the humanities, and several wrote for the Harvard *Crimson*. Far more women enrolled than in the typical senior offering. Unlike several of his colleagues, Erikson never denigrated them; he seemed especially interested and appreciative of their insights. Foreign students were pleased by Erikson's strong cross-cultural emphasis and his obvious interest in and respect for their customs and beliefs.[27]

Erikson was not an impromptu lecturer. Going into his first week of classes in 1960, he maintained full sets of lecture notes and reworked them assiduously. Jon recalls car rides where his father sat in the backseat revising his notes. These notes were more "map" than text—bold handwriting in different sizes with connecting lines and circled items all differentiated by red, green, and black ink. Comparison of a few tape-recorded lectures with the corresponding lecture "maps" suggests that Erikson roamed freely from the extensive preparatory notes. He circled around topics rather than approach them directly, logically, or sequentially. Some students, like law student and future reform mayor of Irvine, California, Larry Agran, were more comfortable with precise formulations and tight logic. They tended to find Erikson's manner confusing. Others, like Peter Wood, who would become an eminent American historian, found it a welcome relief from Henry Kissinger and other Harvard social science faculty, who were preoccupied with power and authority in their manner as well as in their subject matter. Erikson spoke softly, more in a flat, conversational style than in a formal manner. He took special pleasure when students interrupted him to ask questions. By rewording a question to fit his artistic, ethical, or configurational concerns of the moment, Erikson seemed to give the inquiry a special import and relevance that encouraged other students to question, too. Above all, he opened the lecture platform to aspects of his own life and emotions. He urged the students to think about and feel their own experiences and concerns in a similar way as they reflected on course topics. One left an Erikson lecture grateful that one would not have to take an examination, because it was often less than clear what his themes were. Again and again, students recalled how Erikson essentially encouraged them to open themselves to the seemingly random, chaotic world of unconscious process. They were participating in a deeply emotional, introspective, revealing *event* more than a traditional academic lecture. It resembled the festive, chanting parade of inquiry and introspection, propounded by Allen Ginsberg, that actively involved everyone. Some characterized it as a clinical encounter. Others described it as a religious experience.[28]

In the course of this clinical-religious happening that passed itself off as SS 139, students found in Erikson a person who was grounded and profoundly ethical. To some extent, this was captured in the story he recounted in class at least once every semester about the little boy who asked his mother where people went when they died. "Well," she told him, "your body goes into the ground and your soul goes up to heaven." To this, the boy matter-of-factly replied: "I'd just as soon keep all my stuff together." Despite unsettling experiences in his personal life, Erikson at a podium symbolized "keeping all one's stuff together," physically, emotionally, and spiritually. As he told his students how he simply wished "to teach, to learn, to be taught by you," many thought of their own idealized, absent, or deceased fathers. "I felt that I needed the ideas and words of 'father' Erikson to validate my conclusions, to 'protect me,'" future Thoreau scholar Richard Lebeaux recalled. Student activist Mark Gerzon characterized Erikson as "a moral as well as psychological compass" to the self, a "grandparent" to Gerzon's generation. To Ned Towle, an unusually reflective senior, Erikson "transcended the academic categories" but was a genuine "human being" and a very wise man. For Janice Abarbanel, a Radcliffe undergraduate who would become a clinician, he was a deeply spiritual counselor who filled in for her absent father. Such bonds continued outside the classroom. When Erikson once gently touched him on the forearm, Peter Wood recalled, it was like the "laying on the hands," a profoundly spiritual experience where manner and inner sense mattered far more than words and academic context. When several students who had taken his undergraduate course saw Erikson join others on the podium at a Harvard commencement, they broke into a loud if inappropriate ovation.[29]

The strength of this resonance between the students and their ruminating professor was obviously rooted in the fact that Erikson helped his undergraduates explore and gain a firmer sense of their own personal and social identities. From the first day of class in 1960, SS 139 on the life cycle was deliberately grounded in the fifth stage—identity. That was a point in time in which almost all of the undergraduates situated themselves. The syllabus moved toward and centered itself on adolescence and young adulthood; then it covered midlife and old age in a very summary fashion. In his initial course syllabus, Erikson acknowledged that the identity crisis of the fifth stage was "being experienced in some form by the students themselves. One may wish, therefore, to present this crisis in a magnified manner" yet with due recognition to "its relative place within the sequence of life crises and in the history of social thought." To attain familiarity with the general fifth stage of Identity vs. Identity Confusion revolving around the identity crisis, Erikson required students to read his 1956 article, "The Problem of Ego Identity." They were also to read about "the classical identity drama of the Sons of Kings" (Shakespeare's *Hamlet*) and then to explore "the religious crisis of one who tried to be the Son of the Church, but decided for the Son of God" (Erikson's *Young Man Luther*). He suggested that his students might also consult Joyce's *Portrait of the Artist as a Young Man* for a modern author's "account of his second birth as the Child of Genius." Pertinent classics by Willa Cather, Mary McCarthy, Alfred Kazin, and others were also recommended.[30]

Given the age of the students and the emphasis of the course, it was not surprising that most wrote their major semester paper on topics connected with the fifth stage. The identity crises of Eugene O'Neill, August Strindberg, Hermann Hesse, Richard Wright, and even Mozart represented typical topics. Others sought to personalize their learning through even more familiar subjects that bore on their identities. For example, Albert Gore, Jr., wrote on his father, the U.S. senator from Tennessee, while a classmate wrote on "Ritual, Sex, Sin, Catholicism and Me." If SS 139 students wrote no examinations and often took no lecture notes, they nonetheless demonstrated a capacity to apply Erikson's concept of identity to topics that engaged their interest.[31]

Although Erikson maintained an outward calm, during the early 1960s he was especially concerned about the way undergraduates grasped and used his identity conceptualization. Like most representatives of the mass media, many students saw it as a variant of individualism and overlooked the emphasis Erikson placed on human connectedness. This disturbed him. Richard Hunt, one of his teaching assistants, estimated that perhaps only one in four of the undergraduates ever arrived at a sophisticated understanding of Erikson's identity concept. Erikson was at first amused but eventually distressed when undergraduates approached him in Harvard Yard professing to be in the middle of identity crises. After first ascertaining that the student was not suffering from an emotional malady, Erikson responded to him or her with humor rather than anger: "Are you bragging or complaining?" The student usually had no idea of the more essential developmental question for young adulthood: "What do I want to make of myself—and what do I have to work with?" Erikson was also dismayed to realize that some of his undergraduates defined their identities—positive and negative—by using his teaching assistants as role models.[32]

Seeing that most students could not grasp the rich subtleties of the crucial fifth stage of identity versus identity confusion as he had delineated it in his books and articles, Erikson began, by the fall of 1963, to use more direct and evocative language in his syllabus and lectures. For example, he described how identity was achieved when one felt most active and alive, when everything "hangs together." One did not properly seek identity consciousness by asking "Who am I?" but found it when "a voice inside speaks and says 'This is the real me.' " That is, it was necessary to trust "one's inner voice whenever it speaks strongly and makes one act with a sense" of deep feeling. That was identity achieved.[33]

More helpful even than these blunt descriptions, Erikson enhanced his students' perspectives on identity by having them watch Karel Reisz's 1960 British film *Saturday Night and Sunday Morning*. Based upon Alan Sillitoe's 1958 novel, the movie focused on Albert Finney in the role of a young adult factory worker in a drab English industrial town. Erikson described him as an extraordinary person in an ordinary setting where other workers became as dull and lifeless as the factory machinery. "Don't let the bastards grind you down" became Finney's slogan. Erikson described how Finney struggled under these circumstances to be intense, active, and alive without the aid of surrounding ideologies or social movements. He acknowledged to his students that this was not unlike his own struggle as a youth in industrial Karlsruhe, although he could draw on some romantic German ideologies, youth protest traditions, and the *Wanderschaft.* The Finney character's father did not provide relief from the pressures to conform that pervaded his social environment. Erikson compared this father to his own stepfather in Karlsruhe in this regard. Yet Finney's brother was sympathetic to his rebellion as Peter Blos had been to Erikson's. In the end, Erikson noted that Finney learned to draw from the strengths inherent in his family and community and in his innermost self. He summoned the strength to choose more freely where he would play, when he would work, and what he would believe. Finney also found elements of his own voice. He expressed himself better by trying to engage his father, by voicing distaste for his foreman, and by finding validation in an elderly female abortionist. He was also willing to move into a wider social and economic world in order to test his talents and his individuality. While Finney had not yet secured a firm sense of identity, Erikson explained, he was moving decidedly in that direction.[34]

Almost every former SS 139 student interviewed on Erikson insisted that his comments on *Saturday Night and Sunday Morning* provided the essential feel for the nature of an identity crisis and its resolution, much as his discussion of *Wild Strawberries* afforded for the entire life cycle. If they forgot other lectures and texts, Erikson's insights on these films remained with them decades later. Students claimed they had not secured from his course a sophisticated theoretical understanding of identity in the life cycle. Rather, they found in "identity" over the life course a general if firm perspective to hang on to in the face of acute inner anxieties. Their uncertainties and perplexities were legitimated and became all the more normal and tolerable. Unlike Freud, Mark Gerzon recalled, Erikson gave his students hope that their lives "were not predestined to be a mechanical repetition of patterns imprinted on us in childhood." While their parents and their other professors "spoke of 'career ladders' and sound [financial] investments," Gerzon recalled, "here was a man who reminded us that one of the responsibilities of adult theory was *to continue to grow.*" He reaffirmed their hopes and idealism, understood their sense of disorientation, and assured them that they would eventually find themselves.[35]

While SS 139 was Erikson's major Harvard teaching assignment, he also offered SR 224, a graduate seminar sponsored by the Department of Social Relations. He interviewed and admitted or rejected those who applied for the seminar—often faculty colleagues or their spouses as well as graduate students. To take SR 224, especially during the first years it was offered, one had to be engaged in a biographical investigation. Expertise about the subject was not, however, central. Erikson admitted entering graduate student David Winter, for example, simply because Winter had traveled to India. For a course title, Erikson came up with "Life History and History." Students were expected to concentrate on the psychological development and wider historical context of their subject. *Young Man Luther* modeled Erikson's expectations for these biographical exercises even though he permitted seminar participants to take any approach to life history that suited them. Early in his important career as a clinician and intellectual (whose activities in southern civil rights fascinated Erikson), Robert Coles wrote about a young black child he had encountered. Soon to become leading American historians, John Demos wrote on William Lloyd Garrison and Richard Bushman prepared his paper on Jonathan Edwards. Margaret Mead's daughter, Mary Catherine Bateson, chose Saint Teresa as her subject. Others searched for issues of identity and progression along the life cycle in, among others, Marx, Helen Keller, and Charles de Gaulle. These represented early versions of Eriksonian psychobiographies, which became conspicuous among a number of young historians from the middle 1960s to the early 1970s.[36]

Erikson organized SR 224 much like the Austen Riggs clinical case conferences. Each seminar participant was expected to bring photographs or other visual material of his subject as well as a rich array of detail on the subject's life and times. As a student reported, Erikson often pondered photographs, maps, and diagrams, frequently regarding these as considerably more important than textual illustrations. As to a patient at a medical conference, he wanted to connect to Garrison or Edwards or de Gaulle or Keller. If he lacked background or training in bibliographic and archival research, he seemed intuitively to have a sense of additional information that the researcher could seek out. But Erikson advanced these suggestions only after others in the seminar had commented extensively on the presentation or irritated him sufficiently by misstating how his psychological concepts applied to a biographical subject. When he finally entered the discussion, his remarks were usually short though pertinent. Unlike in the SS 139 classroom, he seemed, at least during the early 1960s, to take the remarks of female students somewhat less seriously than those of the male students. Often he spoke to an aspect of a specific life history (one that either he or a student had worked on) as if the setting had been a clinical case conference.[37]

Erikson acknowledged "that I have little experience in graduate training" and had no real idea of the proper role of an instructor. All he knew how to do, he admitted, was to offer an interpretive summation to a student's presentation much as Robert Knight had done after a therapist had presented on a patient and the staff discussed the presentation. Knight never himself presented on a patient with whom he was especially familiar and Erikson never offered a formal presentation of what would become his principal bio-graphical subject beginning in 1964—Gandhi. Nevertheless, he com-mented on Gandhi even before he began to research *Gandhi's Truth*. At one seminar session, for example, Erikson returned again and again to Gandhi, but hardly in a sequential or logical fashion. He compared "confessions" on the analytic couch to "propagandistic" autobiographies like Gandhi's. He also alluded to the Oedipus complex and how sons grew up to replace fathers. He referred to the generativity stage of the life cycle and how Gandhi took care of his enemies. Erikson noted that Gandhi had "let down his children" and that Gandhi's son went to a Bombay brothel the year his father was assassinated. Toward the end of this seminar, he invoked Freud's ego-superego-id structural theory for inner conflict and how one's inner voice could provide the solution of conflict. By the close of the seminar, it was apparent that Erikson was operating on a somewhat unconscious level, more concerned with voicing an insight here and an observation there—the process of understanding—than in offering his students a coherent picture of his or their work. The unconscious was to become only semiconscious in this clinical-academic venture called a graduate seminar. Those who could tolerate the "disorder" and the "clutter" of random observations felt they profited enormously. Others dropped out after one or two sessions.[38]

STUDENT UNREST

The protests that swept college campuses, beginning very early in the 1960s, influenced Erikson. He recalled insisting, not long after arriving at Harvard, that "teaching can advocate too," even when the professor did not march with his students or sign their petitions.[39]

While Erikson eschewed a public role in high-level national policy dis-cussions early in the decade, he was not silent as the protests gathered momentum. David Riesman recalled that, from the start, Erikson was far more sympathetic to all sorts of student protest traditions and eclectic man-ifestations of counterculture than he had been. Undergraduate Randall Kehler listened to Erikson's lectures and felt Erikson gave off a special aura of "integrity." Erikson's message and spirit emboldened him to stand up for his principles while embracing unpopular political causes. Erikson encour-aged white South African student Pamela Reynolds to return home, despite her opposition to her country's white ruling elite, to teach and become involved in the ways South African children learned. Todd Gitlin and Judith Herman, two unusually articulate student political activists, appreciated Erikson's unwillingness to dismiss student protests as Oedipal issues; he found substance in their pleas for civil rights and against the developing American presence in Vietnam. Unlike many of his faculty colleagues, Erikson even sympathized with hippies, for they displayed an ethic of naturalness and spontaneity that contrasted favorably with those who pursued financial "success and conformity" in "this era of mechanization." They also called to mind his lifestyle as a young man.[40]

However sympathetic he was, though, Erikson refused to sign almost any protest petition. Riesman and Norbert Mintz (one of Erikson's graduate teaching assistants) were active in the local Committee on Correspondence effort in 1960 to circulate petitions for nuclear disarmament and against the American policy of nuclear deterrence. No sympathizer with the premises behind Cold War containment policy, Erikson quibbled with the way the committee worded its petitions. He claimed the petitions were vague and arrogant, and that his traumatic experience with the California loyalty oath made him cautious about imprecise language. In contrast, when Gordon Fellman asked him to sign a petition protesting the American attempt to invade Cuba at the Bay of Pigs in 1961, Erikson did not cite the loyalty oath crisis. Instead, he insisted that as a refugee, he was reluctant to be overly critical of the United States. Finally, even with his very early and unambiguous opposition to American intervention in Vietnam, Erikson refused to sign antiwar petitions—usually on the ground that he did not "know enough."[41]

As protest movements grew more vocal, Erikson's sympathy sometimes waned. He resented the "storming of administration buildings as if they were [tsarist] Winter Palaces" and the "faking of pregenital freedom" through love-ins. Erikson was particularly distraught while attending a Timothy Leary lecture in William James Hall during which Leary urged students to "tune in, turn on, and drop out" with LSD. Quite uncharacteristically, the soft-spoken Erikson stood up before the question period began and told Leary and the audience of roughly 150 that he was "tuning out." He left alone. Silence pervaded the auditorium for several minutes.[42]

Erikson's conduct was not entirely dissimilar to some on the Harvard senior faculty who gave lip service to liberal views initially but eventually felt uncomfortable with various aspects of student protest. Yet there was a more pertinent level of explanation. Like many other aspects of Erikson's life, he shifted between a favorable disposition toward political activism and personal withdrawal, never resting for long on one side of the line or the other. A number of factors disposed him toward inaction or withdrawal. Similar to many immigrant intellectuals from central Europe, he had some sense of the pre-Nazi "Old Europe," where political engagement was not demanded or even viewed as very essential. Erikson was also grateful to the United States for welcoming him during a difficult time in his life and for making him feel at home as an American citizen. He felt that it would appear ungrateful if he then went on record criticizing national policies. Moreover, even in the early 1960s, he continued to respect traditional authorities—governmental, familial, and academic. Finally, Erikson sincerely believed that his professorial duties required that he spend more time teaching students and less time on activist matters. Temperamentally, too, Erikson continued to be at least modestly reluctant to advance his agenda publicly.[43]

On the other hand, perhaps the primary factor that prompted Erikson toward periodic and sometimes bold defense of student activism was intergenerational, the sense of connectedness he felt with his students. Amid campus controversies, Erikson's relationship with students focused on elucidating and connecting their lives to the ethical, social, and psychological imperatives of his eight-stage life cycle. A professor at the generative stage, who needed to parent and support, had connected to younger people at the identity stage immersed in self-discovery and ethical assertion. Even though the connection usually took the form of classroom remarks linked to assignments from his publications and not close personal rapport, the relationship was very real nevertheless to many of his students.

OUTSIDE CAMBRIDGE

As committed as Erikson was to his Harvard students, he was less than enamored by Cambridge. When he and Joan arrived from Stockbridge, they took a Harvard-owned house on Fernald Drive near Radcliffe College, perhaps a twenty-minute walk from Harvard Yard. The couple found the house comfortable but hardly comparable to their house in Stockbridge. The neighborhood was pleasant, but the streets were always crowded with parked cars, sidewalks were not always shoveled after winter snowfalls, and the Eriksons sometimes had to travel the ice-glazed streets. The easy stroll to the post office in small, uncrowded Stockbridge could not be matched in Cambridge. A bout with angina symptoms (fortunately quite temporary) made Erik a bit anxious about physical overexertion despite assurance that his heart was sound. The long walks that he had grown to love were compromised further by his local celebrity status. Constant stares on the Cambridge streets made him uncomfortable and overly self-conscious.[44]

Nor did Erikson take especially well to academic life when he arrived at Harvard. Despite his tenured full professorship, he continued to feel insecure, the outsider. He attributed his discomfort to the fact that he had no academic degrees, although this was a bit of a simplification. Erikson felt uneasy when the social relations department did not invite him to its meetings after he had joined the faculty. Still very much a European culturally, he sought to have a couch moved into his Widener Library study for afternoon naps. Library staff did not understand its importance, and Erikson assumed the staff did not want him. He asked McGeorge Bundy to secure permission for him to have a couch. When Bundy left Harvard in 1961 to join the Kennedy administration, Erikson hoped that Nathan Pusey would afford similar forms of assistance, but Pusey had no appreciation of what Erikson was about. After he refused to admit Pusey's wife into his graduate seminar, the president became wholly unwilling to accommodate him.[45]

Joan was even more displeased with life in Cambridge. She had taken great pride in creating Riggs's innovative and successful activities therapy program. Now she felt comparatively isolated and lacked significant work. Joan found what she interpreted to be the role of a Harvard faculty wife (to be attentive to the latest literary and culinary fashions and to help facilitate the academic ambitions of one's husband) excessively limiting. Soon, however, she became close friends with Nina Holton, who made jewelry and shared Joan's interest in crafts. She also took special joy in getting to know Herman and Agnete Kalckar, two of Erik's Danish relatives. Joan began some weavings of the eight-stage human life cycle at this time, with colors and columns and intersecting threads conveying much of the dynamism and complexity of the flow between developmental stages and chronological ages. She was beginning to assert an implicit proprietary claim on one of the few theoretical projects where husband and wife had been partners. Still, Joan continued to miss her many friends in Stockbridge and did not replace them with very many new friends in Cambridge.[46]

The Eriksons left Cambridge as often as Erik could get away. By this point in his life, he looked upon himself not so much as a professor or a clinician but as "a writer" who spoke to a general audience of the curious, the intelligent, and the broadly interdisciplinary. In his late fifties with only two books published when he joined the Harvard faculty, he felt driven to complete a number of writing projects and was apprehensive of death before many books came to fruition. With hundreds of undergraduates to teach, teaching assistants to supervise, graduate seminars to conduct, faculty service functions to perform, and all too many invitations to local dinners, receptions, and lectures, Erikson felt more and more that he had to get away. He had to be able to focus more fully on his writing than Harvard obligations permitted.

A "real" writing day consisted of rising very early and composing for a few hours, breaking briefly for breakfast, and then writing until afternoon when he would take a nap and a swim before completing the final stretch of composition. Days such as this were difficult to come by in Cambridge.

After his first and very exhausting semester at Harvard, he took a leave of absence to catch up on his writing under Ford Foundation funding in an isolated cabin in the south of France. "Solitude is a rare privilege, even more keenly felt in these times," he explained to President Pusey, "but it does help to get writing done." He took off two semesters during his decade at Harvard to write at Stanford's Center for Advanced Studies in the Behavioral Sciences. He also enjoyed one-semester sabbaticals roughly every two years, while other faculty waited six years. After teaching for only a couple of years, he took off on a yearlong grant. He declined an opportunity to head a new Center for the Psychological Study of Lives on the grounds that managerial functions would interfere with his writing, and he rejected the Boston Psychoanalytic Institute's offer to become a training analyst for the same reason—he wanted to devote more time to his writing.[47]

Periodically, Erikson also returned to Stockbridge to earn extra money through Riggs consultation arrangements. He maintained a house in town. He gave workshops for the staff, participated in some clinical case conferences, and discussed his writing projects in staff seminars. Sometimes he invited young psychologists, psychiatrists, and social workers in training into his study. Often these sessions served to clarify issues in his writing.[48]

THE BEGINNING OF AN INDIAN VENTURE

In his early years at Harvard, the farthest Erikson managed to travel beyond Cambridge was not France but India. Since his adolescence in Karlsruhe, he had revered Gandhi. Later in life he characterized this reverence as a transference reaction rooted in his "adolescent search for a spiritual fatherhood." Like others of his age and education in central Europe, he had read French pacifist Romain Rolland's popular *Mahatma Gandhi* and had been impressed by "that pervasive presence" that derived from a life of "total commitment." He had been fascinated by Gandhi's trial by the British in Ahmadabad and compared it to the trial of Socrates. Even more, Erikson had been preoccupied by a 1918 textile strike in that city involving the Sarabhai family, which became the basis for *Gandhi's Truth*. The strike pitted Ambalal Sarabhai, who owned a large textile mill, against his sister, Anasuya, who aided the striking workers, and Gandhi, who led them. Young Erik had made notes about this event during his *Wanderschaft* and rediscovered the notes decades later.[49]

Despite his early interest in Gandhi, Erikson's knowledge of Indian history and culture was minimal. Gardner and Lois Murphy, old friends and prominent psychologists, had become experts. Both had visited India in the aftermath of Indian independence, Gardner on a UNESCO research project and Lois to investigate childhood and child-rearing patterns. Guatam Sarabhai, son of Ambalal, helped to facilitate Lois Murphy's research. In turn, both Murphys persuaded Guatam and his wife, Kamalina, to study psychoanalysis and not to be neglectful of Erikson's contributions. Soon, the whole Sarabhai family became fascinated with *Childhood and Society.* Guatam's younger brother, physicist Vikram Sarabhai, and his wife, Renalane, were especially impressed, even more so after meeting the Eriksons in Cambridge not long after Erik and Joan moved to town. Kamla Chowdhry, Vikram's acknowledged mistress and a follower and admirer of Ambalal's sister, Anasuya, worked as a social psychologist at the Indian Institute of Management. She met the Eriksons while teaching temporarily at the Harvard Business School. Vikram and Kamla invited the Eriksons to visit Ahmadabad and to stay in the Sarabhai family compound. A special seminar on the life cycle would be convened in their honor. With little hesitation, the Eriksons accepted. They arrived for a three-month stay in November 1962 in the city where, forty-four years earlier, Gandhi had launched his first major effort to mobilize the Indian masses.[50]

Initially, Erik considered the visit simply as a respite from teaching duties and Cambridge winters, hoping to complete some of his writing projects while abroad. But he found himself captivated by India from the moment his airplane landed in New Delhi. To be sure, he never cared for the food and was less than enamored of Indian music, but the visual experience was arresting: the bright and varied colors, the historic shrines, the costumes, and the appearance of the women. Unlike America and Germany, he detected what he felt was a profoundly female quality to the nation—sensual and welcoming, intricate and alluring. The culture seemed less linear, less logic-driven, and less aggressive than the culture of Western nations. The people of this long-colonized country interested him far more than the values and perspectives of the British colonizers. Shortly after he arrived, Erik learned of the incarceration of two prominent Indian political leaders, and this alerted him to the sometimes explosive quality of Indian civil society.[51]

When the Eriksons visited the Sarabhais in Ahmadabad, Erik found himself awestruck by the industrial city of avenues, bridges, mills, and roughly 1,250,000 people. Ahmadabad reminded him of Pittsburgh, with its large industrial workforce and considerable ethnic diversity. At the Sarabhai family compound, Ambalal "led me to one of his terraces which overlook a sea of trees, and offered it to me as a study." Ambalal emphasized that the great writer-poet Rabindranath Tagore had also used the facility. Anasuya resided a hundred yards away, and Erik paid "the saintly yet simple old woman" his respects. Within days, he referred to India as his "adoptive country," although it contrasted markedly with Theodor Homburger's Germany.

Soon, the reading that Erikson had done on "the Event" (the 1918 strike) when he had been young " 'came back to me' almost sensually," and with that memory "the powerful presence" of Gandhi himself. Walking by the local prison where Gandhi had been incarcerated, Erikson realized that several key participants in the strike were still alive. He was not yet ready to interview them or to write about "the Event," but almost immediately upon returning to the United States he prepared an application to the American Institute of Indian Studies for funding to return. He hoped to investigate the "dramatic core" episode of 1918 through "psychological and cultural as well as economic and historical terms." By his second trip to India in 1964, he had determined to write a book about the Ahmadabad strike and what it revealed about Gandhi. The main focus of the book would be on Gandhi's pursuit of *Satyagraha,* a term that translates from Sanskrit as a tenacious, stubborn, and demanding mode of truth-grasping or truth-seizing. Erikson defined it as Truth Force: an active "perseverance in truth" and the "leverage of truth." He would concentrate on Gandhi's "ascent to national leadership" at Ahmadabad by pursuing this Truth Force. An occurrence "which I had dimly read about when I was young" became a story that a man in his early sixties wanted to tell.[52]

Some weeks after Erikson first arrived in Ahmadabad, he made a presentation to the seminar that had been convened for him. Those attending had been assigned a paper on Tagore's childhood. Erikson (still knowing precious little about Indian society or culture) had prepared a short typed comment on the paper and read it aloud. The comment presaged vital issues he pursued in his investigation of the Mahatma and pointed to a preexisting agenda, however tentative.

For Erikson, biographical studies of the beloved Tagore, Gandhi's friend, had wrongly assumed "that psychological insight would undermine the magic of a man's image." The task at hand was to pursue the "progressive unification of themes which clarifies the process of how he *became himself* as he *became his public image,* i.e., how he came to feel most himself where he meant most to his people" and then connected to much of humanity. From extremely fragmentary evidence, Erikson located the unification of early themes in the "basic 'geography' of Tagore's childhood." The boy had been "imprisoned on the fringe of the big house" or family estate between the "inner world" of his mother's elaborate quarters and the "great outer world" beyond the mansion that commanded his father's attention. Situated with young Tagore between "inner" and "outer" worlds were "the people"—the house servants, the teachers employed by the family, and a "minor" relative or two. Here Erikson invoked a distinction he had made since the early 1940s—in his work with Jean Walker Macfarlane's longitudinal research project—distinguishing between female psychological "inner space" and male "outer space." Tagore sought to unify in himself both his mother's "mysterious *inner sanctum*" and his father's "great *outer world*." This became Tagore's "unity theme." In order to become a great poet and national spokesman, Tagore eventually succeeded in restoring "his sense of unification" and giving it a universal meaning to Indians at large—"the people."[53]

For Erikson, Tagore as great national poet and essayist was therefore "born through a gradual integration of the masculine and the feminine in him." In his poems and through his presence, "he combined feminine shyness with a tall, masculine body. His beard was patriarchal, but his robes veiled some mysterious pregnant body." Gandhi understood how, against "the masculinity of the British beefeater . . . Tagore reasserted the traditional inclusion of the Indian identity of the feminine and the maternal, the sensual and the experimental, the receptive and the transcendental in human life." Gandhi had exuded a similar presence, Erikson insisted, conveying to outsiders "something superior" and awe-inspiring as Gandhi pursued Indian identity and independence against the less sympathetically portrayed British colonial regime. Like Freud and other "great men," Erikson concluded, Tagore had the same impulses, strengths, and weaknesses as his many Indian admirers. Unlike them, however, Tagore enjoyed a special "creative process" that enabled him to bring these qualities together in "a superior balance."[54]

Some preliminary sense of themes and concerns in *Gandhi's Truth* was therefore discernible within weeks of Erikson's arrival in India. Although issues of Indian childhood mattered, the nature of adult leadership was the primary focus. By 1964, when Erikson returned to India, he had lined up abundant financial support from the American Institute of Indian Studies, from the Shelter Rock Foundation, and from the Karmakshetra Educational Foundation of Ahmadabad. As the book progressed, free time away from Harvard was sponsored by the Center for Advanced Study in Palo Alto and the Field Foundation. Erikson had developed a facility for attracting research grants.[55]

At this point, he publicly identified himself in four different ways: positively as a clinician and a psychoanalyst, and negatively as a nonhistorian and a non-Indian specialist. "What 'discipline' there is to my enterprise is best revealed in the telling of its story"—the saga of the Ahmadabad strike. But Erikson was more than a storyteller; he also became a participant observer. In India, he and Joan resided in the affluent and protected Sarabhai family compound, where they mixed frequently and cordially with all of the Sarabhais and their friends, and where they enjoyed Western alternatives to the Indian foods they found difficult to digest. Erikson justified these quarters on the ground that "in India there is no reasonably safe travel for old people and young ones except as somebody's house guest or in expensive hotels." The Sarabhais became his protectors from the violence, unsanitary conditions, and disease of modern India; his excursions from the compound were usually quite limited. He assumed that he was too old to risk the potential health problems inherent in almost any sort of travel. Erikson felt especially indebted to Ambalal for protection "against the stark facts of Indian life" and for "a haven of friendship and sanitary safety." He also made the striking admission that he experienced "an unconscious transference" onto his host of "a father or older-brother role." The influence, safety, and security that Ambalal afforded were transformed into strong paternal qualities by this "fatherless child who found a loving stepfather in a foreign country." In 1918, Ambalal had supported and contested fifty-year-old Gandhi during "the Event." Erikson felt that he was entering a remarkably similar relationship as he studied how Gandhi forged a special truth in negotiations with Ambalal. Stepping into circumstances such as Gandhi had experienced within the family dynamics of the Sarabhais, Erikson ignored friendly warnings that he was overidentifying.[56]

After Erikson returned to Cambridge following his 1964 trip to India, he lectured and talked incessantly about Gandhi. His undergraduates suggested that he title his emerging volume "Middle-Aged Mahatma"—to match the seventh or generative stage in his life cycle model. Identifying strongly with the Gandhi of 1918 in his relationship with Ambalal, Erikson acknowledged that he, too, was "in my middle years" and "it was time for me to write about the responsibilities of middle age." He was sixty-two when he formally started the project and would cross the divide into old age as his research progressed. Indeed, the educated Indian professionals whom he met during the early 1960s already referred to him as a wise old man. Referring to subsequent research trips to "strenuous India," he sensed that he lacked abundant energy for traveling. "To the younger people 'one more trip' [to India] makes no difference," he wrote to Anna Freud, "but I am getting to the age where it does." Monitoring her husband carefully, Joan was to conclude, after a few additional trips, that they simply "can't afford the time and energy" for many more visits to India. The Gandhi project was both strenuous and energizing, exerting a subtle but significant effect upon Erikson's career as an intellectual.[57]

COTUIT

The beautiful Cape Cod beach town of Cotuit, near Hyannis and a few hours' driving time from Cambridge, offered a refuge from both Harvard and India during the early and middle 1960s. A relatively isolated location with a few local businesses, some modest art studios, and affluent home owners, Cotuit was a welcome retreat from Cambridge for long weekends and soon for summers as well. Eventually, the Eriksons purchased an attractive split-level home overlooking Poponesset Bay in Nantucket Sound. The house was hexagonal in shape; had a large, modern kitchen; and was surrounded by dense woods. Erik and Joan delighted in the view from their upstairs balcony, especially in the fall when, as Erik noted, the "black blue ocean" appeared "behind golden, red, orange, yellow, green leaves." They swam daily in the ocean and took walks along the beach. The couple prized their privacy, although they soon found that close friends from Cambridge like Gerald and Nina Holton might drive by, Benjamin Spock might dock his boat for a visit, and his new friend, the New York liberal Republican Jacob Javits, might greet the Eriksons on the beach. "Mom and I have to be outright antisocial in order not to run a visiting place for passing tourist friends," Erik wrote to Jon. He wanted his artistically talented second son to come and enjoy the colors and sounds of the southern Cape and to take in the area with his skillful photographer's eye.[58]

When the couple was not enjoying the beach, Erik wrote articles and grant applications for research in India and prepared for his Harvard classes. Joan's longtime interest in making jewelry had drawn her, by now, to a systematic study of the history and significance of beads. At Cotuit, Erik was delighted to see her gather information from art catalogs and the reports of archaeologists and historians and shape "a crazy and important story around those bitty things." Begun in 1961, Joan's *The Universal Bead* described how those small disks had signified rank and status, had conferred magical powers, and had served as currency. They not only symbolized the human need to turn the concrete into the symbolic; for Joan, beads represented the human eyes—the basic communication vehicle between mother and newborn that later became central to the nature of relationships between adults.[59]

The Eriksons allowed as few interruptions as possible during their joyful weekends and summers on the Cotuit beach, though they found themselves increasingly aware of the Kennedy compound in Hyannis, a few miles away. Every now and again a helicopter would hover overhead, transporting the Kennedys to their activities on the mainland. Erik watched with curiosity, especially after the president's assassination in 1963. Jacqueline Kennedy had learned of Erikson's reputation as an effective clinician from White House aide Richard Goodwin. She sensed that both of her traumatized children, especially John, Jr., were becoming distant and seemed to be blaming her for the loss of their father. There is some evidence (although it is not entirely conclusive) that several weeks after the murder she asked Erikson to help her son and possibly her daughter, as well. Whether Erikson first met the Kennedy children toward the end of 1963 or somewhat later, he acknowledged that he was "deeply touched by those two kids. What a fate, and they do think of their father." Erik found Jacqueline Kennedy to be "simple and friendly" despite her difficult circumstances. However, he compared the family compound to "a swank concentration camp" with guards. Erik also noticed Joan's irritation when Jacqueline and her children, with Goodwin, dropped by their Cotuit house unannounced. He was not captivated by the larger-than-life Kennedy "mystique" that emerged in the period after the president was murdered. But he seemed envious, at times, of the bold, the daring, the sometimes courageous, and always exciting lives of the Kennedy brothers. When Edward (Teddy), the youngest, came to his Cotuit house to consult about the psychological implications of a possible future run for the presidency, Erik urged him to consider another question instead. How, Erik asked, did he want to spend his old age?[60]

Their own children were far more central to the Eriksons' lives at Cotuit than were their neighbors from Hyannis. As early as the summer of 1962, Erik observed that "Cotuit proves to be a good spot for the family." By then both Kai and Sue had married and came regularly with their spouses. He was pleased that all four were "getting along fine" with him and Joan under the same roof.[61]

But it was the business of grandparenting that excited Erikson most. Kai and Joanna had given him his first grandchildren—Keith, early in 1963, and Christopher, the following year. He wrote to Gardner and Lois Murphy that he was "enjoying grand-parenting immensely." When he met the very pregnant Pamela Daniels soon after Keith was born, he could discuss almost nothing but the joys of parenting and grandparenting. But as excited as he was over the birth of his grandchildren, Erik (like many men of his generation) did not regard his role as a hands-on obligation. As with parenting, he contemplated the imperatives of grandparenting more than he applied them. On visits to the senior Eriksons, Joanna, Kai, and Joan attended to Keith and Christopher while Erik looked and touched and laughed—and then went off to write. As Keith and Christopher grew older, to be sure, Erik became interested in their drawings and sketches, and accompanied them on walks around Cotuit.[62]

While acknowledging the joys and shortcomings of his new grandfather role, Erik characterized Kai as "a *good* father (if and when he pays attention—you know)." Kai paid attention; he spent considerably more time with his children than Erik had with his. Although David Riesman found Kai "much less neurotic than his father," the son also became preoccupied with professional issues and a need to publish. Kai taught in the psychiatry department at the University of Pittsburgh School of Medicine with a joint appointment in the sociology department from 1959 to 1963 while completing his sociology doctorate at the University of Chicago. He then moved to Atlanta, spent the next three years with a similar joint faculty appointment at Emory University, and prepared *Wayward Puritans* for publication. The title was a takeoff on *Wayward Youth,* August Aichhorn's classic study of juvenile delinquency. In his book, Kai described how seventeenth-century New England Puritans had identified themselves socially and psychologically against "wayward" sinners (which they hoped they were not). He thanked Erik for "the counsel he gave and the discussions we shared." Kai's book won the Robert M. MacIver Prize of the American Sociological Association—one of the highest research honors in the field. Shortly before, he had accepted an offer to join the prestigious sociology department at Yale. Much as Joan left Stockbridge with misgivings and accompanied Erik to Cambridge so he could accept a professorship at Harvard, Joanna left Atlanta so Kai could become a Yale professor. Father and son were living similar lives. Both spent summers with their families in Cotuit, Kai renting for a few years before he built a house near his parents. During summers and many weekends, the two "establishments," as Erik called them, were more like one. They enjoyed joint sings, dancing, barbecues, and readings from books in progress.[63]

In 1961, Sue married Harland Bloland in a village near Nice where Erik was on leave writing and Joan pursued diverse craft and writing projects. After graduating from Oberlin College in 1959 with a philosophy major, Sue had moved to Berkeley and worked as a secretary in the Institute for International Studies. There she met Bloland, a handsome and athletic-looking doctoral student of Norwegian descent from Wisconsin. Highly regarded for his work in Berkeley's higher-education program, he had begun a dissertation on the roles of private philanthropic organizations in the shaping of American colleges and universities. Erik felt that Harland was a good match for Sue; he was "quietly strong with a good sense of humor." As the wedding approached, Erik noted that his quiet but wise and sensitive daughter seemed to radiate a "pervasive feminine happiness."[64]

The Blolands returned to Berkeley, where Harland continued work on his dissertation and began to establish an academic career specializing in the politics of higher education. Erik considered him, like Kai, an emerging intellectual. Sue took graduate courses in social anthropology, but because she needed to be a major breadwinner, she worked full-time, and made minimal progress toward a degree. Erik recognized that she was very bright and praised her graduate papers but did not encourage her to pursue a doctorate and assume a professional career. For him, Sue's role was akin to that of his mother and his wife. She was a possessor of the life force, and had tremendous strength, which her husband needed to help stabilize his life and career. Erik enjoyed visiting the Blolands' small house and was pleased when they came to his Cotuit home (which happened with increasing frequency). Nonetheless, a certain tension arose between Harland, the emerging scholar, policy critic, and academic who had writing blocks that delayed the completion of his dissertation, and a father-in-law who was a Harvard professor and distinguished author, and who published abundantly with apparent ease. Increasingly, Erik acknowledged that "the intellectual going is rough" between them on several occasions when he and Harland were together.[65]

With Kai and Sue, their spouses, and Kai's children visiting in Cotuit, Joan and Erik maintained a multigenerational household not wholly unlike Erik's Harvard classroom. However, they continued to be concerned that Jon remained unmarried and never visited. Jon continued as a San Francisco stage laborer and a proud member of Local 161 of the International Alliance of Theatrical Stage Employees. He enjoyed the physical work and, even more, the union-protected right to unpaid leaves for travel. Global travel, photographing much that he saw, was his passion. "To think you have never seen this place here," Erik wrote to Jon in 1964, "and yet are at home on all those Pacific Islands. . . . Cotuit may not seem very sensational after what you have seen, but it's not a bad place to touch home base in."[66]

Jon's troubled relationship with Erik partially accounted for his failure to visit. During a trip to Florence in 1953, the two felt that for the first time they were building a strong rapport. But the rapport did not last, and subsequent father and second son outings were rare. On those occasions when Jon let drop one of his humorously sarcastic one-liners and Erik laughed appreciatively, both thought of a return trip to Florence. Yet neither volunteered to plan it. Jon often blamed Erik's increasing preoccupation with writing for the distance between them. Once, for example, Jon wrote a letter to his father chiding him about time-consuming participation in "seminars" and asking sarcastically, "Why don't you write a book sometime?" Erik acknowledged that such barbs "sting particularly now when I am back at being a professor 200%—well, so I am writing. Mostly, to say we missed you all summer, and we think of you when all the [ocean] colors out there say that you should be here, with your eyes."[67]

In accounting for his reluctance to visit Cotuit, Jon took note of his heavy summer work schedule and the expense of cross-country airfares. But he recognized that Erik's shift away from his early artistic and bohemian past was more relevant. Erik believed that he could not combine psychoanalytically informed writing with work in the visual arts. He was Professor Erikson now, a prominent author and intellectual who taught at Harvard. Kai, the other Professor Erikson in Cotuit, was following his father's track far more than Jon. Because Jon realized that he represented a *Wanderschaft* past from which Erik was distancing himself, he knew that he would be uncomfortable in Cotuit. The problem was compounded by Jon's perspective on Neil, who was institutionalized not far from Jon's Bay Area residence. From the time in late adolescence when he had been told that Neil was alive, Jon had partially identified with that "outcast" sibling and wanted Neil to be included in the family. Jon considered the failure of his parents to rear Neil at home as a signal concerning his own wayward identity—that he, too, was not quite an Erikson. When Erik and Joan called Jon and Sue from Italy in 1965, instructing them to arrange for Neil's funeral, Jon felt all the more distanced from the family and was even less inclined to respond to his father's prompting to visit Cotuit. Erik, the father who never met or knew his own father, had a third son who did not know his father and a second son who was apprehensive of becoming a father. The past intruded upon the present, limiting and complicating connections between generations of the Erikson family.[68]

WRITING, REWRITING, AND PUBLISHING

Erikson concentrated on his writing more than on family concerns during his time in Cotuit. Once he had committed himself to a book on Gandhi and the strenuous foreign travel required, writing may even have come to outpace teaching among his priorities. Indeed, by the 1963–64 academic year, he had become so involved in various publishing projects that he was starting to identify himself primarily as an author. Increasingly, he found himself in front of a desk, pen in hand (still refusing to learn to type).

As Erikson worked on his new publications, the reputation of his first book began to spread. He had assigned selections from *Childhood and Society* during his first semester at Harvard, and David Riesman had also assigned parts of the book in his own large social science undergraduate course. General sales were respectable but not impressive. Attentive to publishing currents, Riesman explained to Erikson that the paperback revolution under way was based on a college market. The undergraduates were a captive audience, and the professor's order for required course reading guaranteed the sales of a book. The college bookstore gladly accepted all orders, and students appreciated the considerable savings of paperback over hardback editions. With these factors in mind, Riesman suggested to Erikson the possibility of a college paperback edition of *Childhood and Society.* Erikson broached it with his publisher. As it happened, the W. W. Norton staff had already been considering the possibility.[69]

George Brockway and Erikson had been friends since Brockway edited *Young Man Luther*. Although Storer Lunt technically remained head man at Norton until 1977, Erikson recognized that Brockway had been assuming Lunt's duties and influencing most publishing policies. Thus, Erik looked to Brockway to advance his interests in pertinent staff decision making. Brockway obliged, working to enhance Erikson's royalties. When Erikson suggested a special college paperback edition of *Childhood and Society,* Brockway was not long in agreeing to take it on. The hardback edition had sold roughly forty thousand copies since 1950, yielding a decent balance for a book targeted to a professional and scholarly audience. Erikson's Harvard professorship gave *Childhood and Society* even greater credibility with faculty. Brockway knew that several college instructors felt that its accessible style would appeal to their students and that they were willing to order the paperback for course assignments. Sociologists and psychologists in academia had been especially attentive to the book, and several had promised to assign a paperback version. Brockway hoped that the marked attention among historians to *Young Man Luther* would eventually induce some of them to assign a paperback of Erikson's first book. Finally, Brockway recognized that *Childhood and Society* was an interdisciplinary volume, like Riesman's *The Lonely Crowd,* and he suspected that important cross-disciplinary books of the 1950s such as these might command a substantial readership during the 1960s. Advertised as a "revised and enlarged edition," the college paperback of *Childhood and Society* was less than that, though some of the changes were significant.[70]

The decision to publish a paperback edition was prescient. The publication in 1963 was an instant success. The 1964–65 academic year provided the first real test of the college market, and it sold almost 28,000 copies. In March of 1965, Brockway wrote to Erikson that *Childhood and Society* was "rapidly becoming one of the best selling [college] textbooks in America" and predicted 50,000 purchases during the 1965 calendar year. In the 1970–71 academic year, sales for this twenty-year-old volume remained very high, exceeding 37,000 copies. By then Norton had developed a sophisticated long-term marketing strategy with considerable money behind it, and the payoff was obvious. Almost every college and university bookstore in the nation included paperback stacks of *Childhood and Society.* Professors in a variety of fields wrote to Erikson of their decision to assign his paperback edition. Berkeley sociologist Robert Bellah confirmed that the book had enormous appeal to undergraduates: "If there is one book you can be sure undergraduates have read, it is Erikson's first one. You can't always be sure that they've read Shakespeare, but you know they've read Erikson."[71]

The very substantial success of the college paperback of *Childhood and*

Society motivated Brockway and his Norton colleagues to consider publishing other Erikson writings. Indeed, Brockway worried about other publishing houses that had contacted Erikson. The editor of *World Perspectives,* Ruth Anshen, had explained to Erikson that he would be wise to simultaneously offer future manuscripts to a variety of publishers, and start a bidding war. Erikson conceded to Anshen that "you are doing me a great favor by pointing out my lethargy in letting one publisher continue just because I started with him." Aware that they needed expert advice and representation, Joan and Erik retained David Cogan, an energetic New York City financial counselor from the accounting and investment firm of Cogan, Bell, and Company, to manage their finances. Cogan promptly engaged in prolonged negotiations with Norton concerning Erik's future with the house. In the end, Brockway and his colleagues assented to Cogan's demand for an advance of approximately $500,000 against the future earnings of *Childhood and Society* and all other Erikson books. For the time, this was a very substantial advance. Brockway considered it highly irregular and unprofessional and worried that it could jeopardize his relationship with his friend and star author. Nonetheless, he signed a contract in which Erik promised to place all his books with Norton until Norton recouped the advance through book sales. Erikson's public lectures were not covered by the contract. To head off offers by university presses to publish several of these lectures, Brockway offered various additional advances if Erikson allowed Norton to publish them in book form. One such advance totaled $25,000. A prominent author, Erik had become well-off financially. With Joan's periodic suggestions, Cogan invested the initial $500,000 plus subsequent publishing income as it arrived. His goal was to provide security for the Eriksons in their old age.[72]

The enormously successful 1963 paperback edition of *Childhood and Society* differed in several respects from the original 1950 edition. Erikson's artistic disposition made this inevitable, for he could never rest content with any of his writings. When Erikson began talking with Brockway in earnest about a paperback edition, he reported that "I have a copy marked up at home" with revisions that he had made over the years and that he had several more to make. One might regard the revisions as minor editorial changes. Erikson, however, considered them essential aesthetic and conceptual emendations. He had described the "original reciprocity" between parent and infant, for example, but revised it as "original mutuality." Seeking to broaden the appeal of the revised *Childhood and Society,* he ceased to describe it as "a clinician's book" and replaced the term *ego restriction* with *self restriction.* There were more formidable alterations as well. By 1963, for example, he had begun to enlarge his skeletal discussion of the seventh or generative stage of the life cycle. Pervasive emphasis on "the dependence of children on adults often blinds us to the dependence of the older generation on the younger one. Mature man needs to be needed." Central to generative adult psychological development, he now noted, was an emotional connectedness between the adult and younger generations. He also included a sentence in the revised edition indicating that intergenerational feelings of mutuality were easier for children than for adults because adults were more prone to "fixed character." In addition, the second edition illustrated Erikson's growing apprehensions about global survival if Cold War tensions prompted the use of nuclear weapons. Whereas in 1950, American sons were to preserve their freedom "on the basis of a new knowledge and a new identity," thirteen years later freedom was to be preserved with greater checks on "new technology" and deeper appreciation of "a more universal identity."[73]

Working over *Childhood and Society* line by line as he prepared it for a college paperback edition, Erikson regarded the revised manuscript as significantly different from the book of essays written between 1933 and 1950. Those essays had been pre-McCarthy and even pre-Hiroshima in their spirit, he explained to his SS 139 undergraduates. In contrast, the new themes and emphases of the revised edition were rooted in the concerns of a subsequent era. Indeed, Erikson hoped the paperback volume would be considered alongside his other books of the 1960s, *Insight and Responsibility* (1964), *Identity: Youth and Crisis* (1968), and *Gandhi's Truth* (1969).[74]

Insight and Responsibility resembled *Childhood and Society* in the sense that it was a collection of previously delivered addresses that had been published as articles. Unlike *Childhood and Society*, however, Erikson rewrote and amplified all of these articles and worked them into a single manuscript. He began the process at Cotuit and very nearly completed it on a fellowship at the Center for Advanced Studies in the Behavioral Sciences in Palo Alto during the spring semester of 1963. At the center, he met a wonderfully creative critic of his writing—Robert Wallerstein, a Jew born in Germany and a very talented Menninger Clinic psychiatrist and psychoanalyst who worked closely there with Gardner Murphy. Wallerstein and his wife, Judith, became lifelong friends of the Eriksons. Leaving Palo Alto, Erikson prepared a preface and made last-minute revisions at Cotuit. The entire process took less than a year. In December of 1963, Erikson wrote to Anna Freud that he intended to dedicate *Insight and Responsibility* to her. He characterized it as a volume on "the ethical implications of psychoanalytic insight." She never responded—not even after he sent her a copy of the published book. The breach between Anna Freud, representative of the Freud legend, and her analysand who identified deeply with that legend, had stretched beyond its third decade.[75]

Erikson stated the subject of *Insight and Responsibility* in the preface: "the light thrown by clinical insight on the responsibilities which each generation of men has for all succeeding ones." "Insight" was a "form of discernment" that included "preconscious assumptions which both precede and follow proven knowledge and formulated theory, and it included enlightened common sense and informed partisanship." The clinician often arrived at "insight" in the process of "interpreting, advising, or indeed lecturing." If his insights resonated soundly, the clinician would be exercising the "responsibility" of his generation for younger generations. Robert Coles astutely detected a tension between Erikson's twin aims. He was admonishing psychoanalytically informed clinicians like himself not only "to remain loyal to our clinical training" but also to "learn how life goes for men and women and children who are by no stretch of the imagination patients." Somehow the clinician had to be able to extend the "insight" that he derived from his work with patients; he had to understand and to benefit younger generations within the wider society. Erikson was never explicit on how the bridge between clinic and society was to be forged, and this constituted a certain amorphous quality in the book.[76]

Insight and Responsibility consisted of six chronologically arranged essays that Erikson wanted to be read and interpreted as a totality. The first essay was a slightly revised version of Erikson's 1956 address in Frankfurt at the centenary of Freud's birth. The second, "The Nature of Clinical Evidence," was the case write-up concerning the seminarian patient who had whetted Erikson's interest in young Luther, and it offered a powerful illustration of the psychoanalytically informed therapist's clinical "insight." "Identity and Uprootedness in Our Time," written for the World Federation of Mental Health in the late 1950s, responded to concerns about the plight of refugees and immigrants around the world. In the essay, Erikson underscored how a firm sense of identity afforded resilience in the face of dislocating changes.

The "Human Strength and the Cycle of Generations" essay represented one of the more substantial contributions to *Insight and Responsibility,* illustrating how the book picked up strength and momentum as it progressed. To prepare it for the book, Erikson took rough notes from a talk he had given before the San Francisco Psychoanalytic Institute and the Mt. Zion Medical Center and transformed these notes into a significant chapter. Because he had not allowed Norton to permit reprints of his enormously popular eight-stage life cycle chart without accompanying text, Brockway was pleased to be publishing this chapter; it enlarged Erikson's perspective on the cycle and would enhance sales. Erikson proposed a "schedule of virtues" for each of his eight stages:

Stage	Virtue
1. Trust vs. Mistrust	Hope
2. Autonomy vs. Shame	Will
3. Initiative vs. Guilt	Purpose
4. Industry vs. Inferiority	Competence
5. Identity vs. Role Confusion	Fidelity
6. Intimacy vs. Isolation	Love
7. Generativity vs. Stagnation	Care
8. Integrity vs. Despair	Wisdom

Each "virtue" represented an ego strength that was detectable in a certain inherent "animation" or "spirited" quality. As well, each virtue revealed a combination of strength, restraint, and courage. Without "virtues," man's "moralities became mere moralism and his ethics feeble goodness."[77]

A quasi-utopian vision of the human condition in the bewildered mid–twentieth century was sketched out in this chapter. Erikson augmented this vision by stressing rapport between generations. He maintained that "virtues" emerged through "the interplay of successive and overlapping generations, living together in organized settings." In each of these settings, every person's "life-stages are 'interliving' cogwheeling with the stages of others" of different ages and circumstances. Progression along the life cycle was therefore not so much an individual as an intergenerational process in which people at one stage assisted those at other stages. The *responsibility* each generation owed to the next was to provide solicitude and strength and support so that the next generation "can come to face ultimate concerns in its own way." Erikson was especially attentive to the primary responsibility of people in the adult generative stage for the "virtue" of *care*. Generative care was more than sexual procreation, involving as it did a "universal sense of generative responsibility toward all human beings brought playfully into this world."[78]

Clinical *insight* was not central to the "Human Strength" essay. Erikson argued that the clinician should mark "improvement" not by the disappearance of a patient's symptoms but by "an increase in the strength and staying power of the patient's concentration on pursuits which are somehow right." This "strength" and tenacity was essentially a virtue. Erikson's focus on people of different generations in settings where they conducted themselves "virtuously" toward one another (gaining by giving) prompted him to delineate universal social rituals through which such "virtue" was exhibited. Accompanying each of his eight developmental stages and each matching "virtue," Erikson noted a ritualized interplay between people with "adaptive value for the respective egos of both participants." The first or *numinous* ritual, for example, could be "fully met by the way in which a mother and her baby greet each other in the morning." There followed the *judicial* ritual at the second stage, the *dramatic* at the third, the *formal* at the fourth, a *convictional* ritual at the fifth, an *affiliative* ritual at the sixth, the seventh involving a *generational* ritual, and, the final stage, an *integral* ritual. Erikson did not elaborate on the eight rituals in this chapter, doing so in a London presentation the year after *Insight and Responsibility* was published. If, instead, he had coupled his list of "virtues" with his perspective on "rituals" and then connected his discussion to the literature on ceremonial rituals as integrators of the self into family, community, tradition, and worship, *Insight and Responsibility* would have contained Erikson's most important elaboration of the life cycle model since *Childhood and Society*.[79]

The final essays in *Insight and Responsibility* illustrated Erikson's embrace of the ritualization concept in 1963 and 1964. In the chapter "Psychological Reality and Historical Actuality," he took notes and some text from an address he had delivered before a plenary session of the American Psychoanalytic Association and turned them all into a polished product. Erikson wrote how psychoanalytically oriented clinicians had to become more *insightful* about the world of their patients. They were so concerned about removing distortions to the patient's view of reality that they were insufficiently attentive to his or her engagement with "actuality"—"the world of participation, shared with other participants with a minimum of defensive maneuvering and a maximum of mutual activation." The key clinical test for the "truly recovering patient" was the capacity to "direct his needs for activation toward those who in turn will be activated by him." Joan's remarkably effective patient activities program at Austen Riggs was decidedly influencing her husband's formulations as he prepared this 1964 book of essays.[80]

Erikson concluded *Insight and Responsibility* with the most powerful and significant essay of all: "The Golden Rule in the Light of New Insight." Originating in very undeveloped form as the George W. Gay Lecture on Medical Ethics at Harvard Medical School in 1962, the essay was perhaps his best writing during this interval. He elaborated it more fully in January 1963, at the end of his first trip to India, as an address to the India International Centre in New Delhi. As he revised it further for *Insight,* he was thinking in earnest about a full-length study of Gandhi and provided hints of the issues that *Gandhi's Truth* might address. Why, Erikson asked, had humankind been captivated by the Golden Rule? It seemed to provide "a mysterious meeting ground between ancient peoples separated by oceans and eras" and appeared to represent "a hidden theme" in many of civilization's most memorable sayings. Rabbi Hillel had alluded to it in explicating the meaning of the Torah: "What is hateful to yourself, do not to your fellow man." There was also, of course, the Christian injunction to "love thy neighbor as thyself." Erikson was beginning to pursue the equivalent formulation in Hindu philosophy and culture.[81]

Erikson's more basic agenda was to offer his own psychological reformulation of the Golden Rule along lines congruent with his prior "Psychological Reality" essay: "It is best to do to another what will strengthen you even as it will strengthen him, that is, that will develop his best potentialities even as it develops your own." A process of mutual interaction allowed each partner to become, in William James's words, "most deeply and intensely active and alive." For Erikson, this mutuality "strengthens the doer even as it strengthens the other." Significantly, he linked this formulation to his life cycle model. He characterized the Golden Rule as an intergenerational process involving people at different stages of the life cycle—a process not wholly unlike that between professor and students or between Gandhi and the residents of Ahmadabad during the textile strike of 1918.[82]

For Erikson, then, the Golden Rule offered penetrating psychological insights. But it also carried a personal appeal to a man who felt he had lived marginally through much of his life. After all, the rule attempted to make "all inclusive" what various tribes, castes, classes, nations, moralities, and ideologies had regularly made exclusive. These agencies of exclusivity had "proudly, superstitiously, and vicariously [been] denying ethics to those 'outside' " the fold, whereas the mutuality of the Golden Rule regarded the "outsider" as the "insider." Succinctly, the Golden Rule mandated what Erikson called a "species-wide identity" coupled with "truly universal ethics." He waxed utopian by assuming that this state could be reached. Indeed, he suspected that Gandhi had progressed a long way toward that goal. The world's adults would feel "universal responsibility" to care for "every child conceived," and international hostilities would recede. Instead of running the risk of nuclear war, nations would maintain a "mutuality in international relations" by imitating the conduct of their citizens.[83]

An inspiring essay in its own right, "The Golden Rule in the Light of New Insight" restated in a strong and evocative way essential elements prevalent in most of the early chapters of *Insight and Responsibility,* highlighting an underrated book of essays. But book buyers were not abundant. Marketed as a college edition paperback, it sold less than 7,200 copies during the 1964–65 academic year, peaked at slightly over 8,500 copies by 1970–71, and dropped to 2,500 copies by 1975–76. Erikson's undergraduates read only select chapters. This pattern of examining a chapter here and there at different times and in different contexts was not a wholly inappropriate way to deal with the volume, for most of the essays circled around the same essential themes. What was lost through such particularized reading was the slow but progressive sense of depth, profundity, and coherence. *Childhood and Society* was also a book of separate essays prepared over several years for different occasions. But though sales for the 1963 edition of *Childhood and Society* far outdistanced sales for *Insight and Responsibility,* it did not have the same cumulative effect; the essays in *Childhood* did not cohere.[84]

Insight and Responsibility differed from *Childhood and Society* in still other respects. Whereas the essays in *Childhood* had been based on considerable clinical, anthropological, cultural, or historical evidence, those in *Insight and Responsibility* were oriented toward very broad themes and contained only sparse, undeveloped illustrations. The quality of Erikson's writing was becoming more vague and abstract. He had three major goals: to offer fresh visions about clinical "insight," to accent the ethical "responsibility" of the different generations of humanity for one another, and, most important, to appreciate how each individual self existed by connecting to other selves. (Indeed, to other people, one's self was the other.) In no small measure, this book stood as a forerunner of the ethical and prophetic mode of presentation that would characterize *Gandhi's Truth,* which Erikson had decided to start the year *Insight* was published.

Because *Childhood and Society* was written in the 1930s and 1940s and not fundamentally rewritten for its second edition in 1963, it did not reflect Erikson's experience as a full-time college professor. *Insight and Responsibility* did, and decidedly so. A book about "mutual actualization" along an intergenerational life cycle, it reflected the rapport between Professor Erikson and his Harvard students as he transformed lectures and essays into polished chapters. Quite consciously, Erikson gave the students a course that focused on what they wanted most—insight into the frightening social and psychological processes they were experiencing as young adults. While he had not always had someone to help shepherd him through his own exceedingly painful identity crisis, he had been available to his students. During at least his first four or five years at Harvard, he thrived on "mutual actualization" with his students within the boundaries of the traditional academic setting. Consonant with his psychology of the Golden Rule as described in *Insight,* he gave to them and thereby got from them a sense of the otherness within himself and within the web of the intergenerational life cycle. David Riesman, Robert White, and other trusted friends on the faculty who attended some of his undergraduate lectures assured him that he was connecting in this way with the students.

Insight and Responsibility less perfectly mirrored the rapport between age groups within Erik and Joan's house in Cotuit. To be sure, Kai and Joanna as well as Sue and Harland often visited. Erik was able to support and encourage Kai and Harland—two new professors—with some degree of success.

He loved Kai's two young sons but did not dote on them. He may have been a somewhat more attentive father to his daughter-in-law, Joanna, who was nearby, than his daughter, Sue, in California, although he was less than fully available to either. Jon did not visit. When Erik instructed Sue and Jon from abroad in 1965 to attend to the burial of the brother they had never met, this hardly testified to a "mutual actualization" process of intergenerational enrichment. Rather, this behavior was consistent with a man who, despite his theories and his teachings, often tended to distance himself from personally difficult situations, much as his biological father had distanced himself from Erik.

AN ODD SEASON: FALL 1965

Insight and Responsibility was completed during the 1963–64 academic year, during which time Erikson occasionally attended a special Harvard faculty seminar. Paul Tillich of the Divinity School spoke at a session of the seminar, describing how his life and thought had involved navigating between diverse types of boundaries—geographic, conceptual, religious, and cognitive, to name a few. Erikson was deeply engaged by the presentation and attended other talks Tillich gave on campus. Soon, the two became friends and were struck by the coincidence that they both admired Kierkegaard. James Luther Adams, the eminent Harvard theology professor who had helped Erikson with *Young Man Luther*, had translated some of Tillich's writings from German for publication in English, and this interested Erikson. He began to read everything by Tillich that he could find. Adams encouraged and assisted him.[85]

Erikson was especially impressed by *On the Boundary*, Part I of Tillich's *The Interpretation of History* (1936). He read and reread this autobiographical essay, almost committing it to memory. Tillich maintained that "the concept of the boundary might be the fitting symbol for the whole of my personal and intellectual development. At almost every point, I have had to stand between alternate possibilities of existence, to be completely at home in neither." To stand on the boundary was to experience "the unrest, insecurity, and inner limitation of existence in many forms." It made for neither serenity, security, nor perfection "in life as well as in thought." But it was the ideal place to acquire knowledge. Erikson found himself especially attentive to two of Tillich's more specific boundary lines—between Lutheranism and socialism, and between his native land (Germany) and the alien land he came to love (America). Having lived much of the American part of his life near water (usually the Atlantic or the Pacific Ocean), Erikson appreciated

Tillich's designation of the coastline as still another boundary. All in all, Erikson recognized great profundity in the theme of *On the Boundary*. It helped him to understand aspects of his own life in a special way. He saw more clearly how "I had to succeed in making a professional life out of my early existence on what Paul Tillich has described as a life on boundaries."[86]

Tillich referred to Kierkegaard in his autobiographical essay as "the real founder of existential philosophy." Unlike Erikson, Tillich had mastered the intricacies of a tradition of theological existentialism that extended from Kierkegaard to Reinhold Niebuhr, as well as philosophic existentialists like Paul Ricoeur. Like those thinkers, Tillich thought the most formidable boundary line was inherent in one particular ambiguity: Man needed transcendence—that is, to be able to imagine infinitude and the absolute. Yet man also needed rootedness—finitude and particularism. For Tillich, it was at the boundary between transcendence and finitude that man explored issues of "Ultimate Concern." The exploration promised no final security. Ultimate Concern united superpersonal and personal elements. It was both a cognate of God and a human state of mind or consciousness. What mattered most was that at a given moment or historical circumstance, man could transcend himself and move toward freedom and self-determination. This connectedness of the personal to the superpersonal at a particular point in time represented the closest proximity to ultimate meaning that one could expect.[87]

Borrowing loosely from the language and thought of existentialism in its theological and philosophic contexts, Erikson was far less rigorous than his friend. He felt that Tillich's Ultimate Concern involved a lifelong tension between faith and doubt and suggested as well a complementarity between "the great Nothingness and the actuality of the cycle of generations." Tillich had long worried about any disintegration of the consciousness-centered personality. He had told Erikson his apprehension that psychoanalysis "streamlined" human existence, making man feel so "adapted" and comfortable with his situation that consciousness receded and man could not face Ultimate Concerns. Erikson had retorted that "concerns can begin to be ultimate only in those rare moments and places where neurotic resentments end and where mere readjustment is transcended." Tillich listened closely. Erikson felt that he understood that psychoanalysis need not stand in the way: "I think he agreed." In other conversations, the two friends found themselves distressed by the ways in which Protestantism had eliminated much of the female element from the symbolic expression of Ultimate Concern, such as that which the Virgin Mary represented. Erikson was pleased that Tillich had substituted the "Motherhood of God" for "the demanding father image." In yet another conversation, Erikson had explained how his course on the life cycle was really Tillich's course, focused as it was on the movement from youthful issues of identity and ideology to ethics and relativity and the caring for other people and generations. This focus, he felt, was at the boundary of Ultimate Concern. Tillich was not entirely convinced. He was interested in Erikson's identity concept to be sure, but was uneasy over the way it was being popularized and emptied of serious content.[88]

When Tillich died in the fall of 1965, Erikson volunteered to deliver a memorial address at a special Harvard service. This willingness seemed to signal his disposition toward a somewhat more public presence. He was allowing himself to become a more visible intellectual. In his address, Erikson summarized the salient points of *On the Boundary* plus crucial moments from their conversations together. An immediate backdrop was the death of his third son, Neil, a few months earlier. When Erik noted, toward the end of his address, that Tillich "has now gone beyond the borderline—unspeakable and inexorable—of all borderlines," Neil may not have been wholly absent from his thoughts.[89]

As Erikson characterized Tillich before the Harvard academic community, he was also describing himself. *Auf der Grenze sein* (being on the boundary) was an underlying theme in both their lives. Erikson explained how Tillich had lived on the boundary between homeland and foreign country (*Auf der Grenze von Heimat und Fremde*)—between his native Germany and the United States, land of his citizenship. Erikson had crossed those same national boundaries and a third, Denmark. He explained how Tillich regarded "the boundary as an existential design" and made it central to his Protestantism. Tillich's boundary was Luther's "Here I stand." By the 1960s, if not earlier, this reckoning with an existential boundary had become Erikson's way of accounting for his Protestantism—and his Judaism. Asked once by his friend Robert Lifton whether he was a Protestant or Jew, he answered, "Why both of course." Like Tillich, he rarely attended church—or synagogue—as he engaged this boundary.[90]

Much of Erikson's address concerned Tillich the personality theorist. He recounted conversations with Tillich about psychoanalysis, bridging in his own way the boundary between Freud, the confirmed atheist, and his theologian friend. Erikson insisted that both felt man had to be aware of his finitude and of responsibility for his own acts "in spite of the element of destiny in them" (quoting Tillich). Indeed, Tillich had acknowledged the superiority of Freud's discoveries on the ambiguity of goodness and evil over the "flabbiness" of much of doctrinal Protestantism, including his own. By underscoring these links between Freud and Tillich, Erikson was describing his own profound indebtedness to both. At this moment, he even seemed to discover a connection between Tillich's treatment of existential contradictions "as opposites to be bridged and thus transformed into creative polarities" and the polarities at each stage of his own life cycle model. For the first time, Erikson seemed to acknowledge publicly that polarities between trust and mistrust, for example, or between integrity and despair—polarities that he had worked to articulate for two decades—had a special autobiographical significance. They represented his own commitment to living and thinking on the boundary.[91]

Toward the end of his presentation, Erikson spoke of Tillich's "blend of realism and faith, his utter sensual and spiritual Hereness." When the memorial service concluded, he took a long walk with one of his teaching assistants, Richard Hunt, who had also attended and was completing a doctorate in German history. Erikson told Hunt about the appeal of Tillich's Protestant Lutheranism and of *On the Boundary* and other of Tillich's writings. He also noted how Tillich had been a model for him as a teacher, a writer, and a thinker. During this period, Hunt felt himself linked intergenerationally to the "Hereness" of both Erikson and Tillich as if they were one. Both were men of faith and spirituality, and both broadcast an unmistakable sensuality and realism. Both had crossed multiple boundaries again and again with the same facility, energy, and inspiration as he and Professor Erikson now crossed and recrossed the streets and parks near Harvard Square.[92]

Erikson felt comfortable and even energized by speaking publicly about Tillich, his thought, and his spirituality. This good feeling contrasted with another important, if more frustrating, experience he had had that same fall with the president of the United States. Although he never proclaimed his politics, Erikson was a liberal Democrat. He venerated Franklin Roosevelt and the New Deal, and he firmly supported John Kennedy's New Frontier domestic reform initiatives as well as those of Lyndon Johnson's Great Society. Indeed, Erikson was comfortable with the extension of federal jurisdiction and funding in matters of welfare, social services, and civil rights. He assumed, without much reflection, that there was "a natural alliance of psychoanalytic with liberal thought." Both had been grounded in the Enlightenment spirit of reasoned inquiry. Erikson was "not acquainted with such unlikely enlightenment as may have penetrated conservative circles." Because of his political allegiances and the recognition that he was an important public figure, he was invited to a small White House reception in November of 1965 with President Johnson, Vice President Hubert Humphrey, Secretary of Labor Willard Wirtz, and prominent African-American leaders such as Martin Luther King, Bayard Rustin, and Andrew Young.[93]

At that gathering, President Johnson announced that he would press for federal legislation to ensure that local southern juries would be less flagrantly racist, all-white institutions. Erikson was happy and relieved. Indeed, as the discussion progressed, he was deeply impressed by "the spirit of dedication" to civil rights within the Johnson administration. He wished that Robert Coles, his friend and teaching assistant who had participated in Mississippi Freedom Summer and similar efforts, could have been present. But Erikson was also profoundly apprehensive of the president's escalating military actions in Vietnam following the Tonkin Gulf Resolution of 1964, especially the bombings of North Vietnam and the authorization of increasing numbers of U.S. combat troops. It was Johnson's firm domestic initiatives for justice and equality "which made the Vietnam issue that much more incomprehensible and nightmarish." Erikson felt somewhat disposed to speak out, to warn this good president that America's presence in Vietnam threatened to undermine the Great Society's commitment to civil rights and related domestic programs. On deeper reflection, Erikson sensed that Johnson was already painfully aware of this danger, "but thinks that nobody has pointed to a workable alternation [sic]" to address the instabilities in Southeast Asia. He could not quite summon the words to respond to Johnson's apprehension—to tell the president that he must disengage from Vietnam, whatever the costs. Had Erikson spoken up, he knew that Johnson would have listened and taken his advice seriously. But he did not feel sufficiently comfortable in a White House setting. It was one thing to speak honestly and forcefully at a Cambridge memorial service for his friend Paul Tillich, quite another to speak out on a difficult matter to the president of the United States. Erikson said little at the gathering. In a private "White House Diary—Postscript" account, he remarked that "I think I learned something about political and economic realities and about people 'in the know'— enough to stick to my writing." By this point in his career, however, authorship was hardly a retreat from the public realm; his writings were engaging public issues more fully and more directly than ever before. Erikson was becoming a significant public intellectual. The next time he was invited to the White House, he would confront the president and his advisers.[94]

RESEARCH AND WRITING PRESSURES

Less than a year after the meeting in the Johnson White House, Erikson consented to publish some preliminary writing in his slowly evolving book on Gandhi for the *American Scholar*. He had been named to the editorial board of this Phi Beta Kappa journal and felt that he could not refuse a solicitation for an essay. His essay revealed that he was already well along in the research phase of the project. He had talked extensively with Susanne Rudolph, a young Harvard faculty specialist on India. He had also studied two Gandhi biographies—one by B. R. Nanda and the other by Gandhi's longtime secretary, Pyarelal Nayar. The essay, however, also revealed that he was experiencing considerable difficulty with Gandhi's published autobiography. Pondering crucial passages, Erikson found that he still could not visualize or hear the Mahatma in his middle years, especially at the point when Gandhi left South Africa and took command of the textile strike at Ahmadabad in 1918. This was unfortunate, for Erikson was determined to focus his study on that event. Nevertheless, he had already made considerable progress in understanding Gandhi's childhood. He discovered the development of a teasing quality in young Gandhi—a "seasoned playfulness"—that would become an important asset in Gandhi's leadership style. Erikson needed more time to explore how this "teasing and testing" played itself out with Gandhi in middle age as politician and national liberator. He realized that this focus would necessitate additional visits to India, especially to speak with those who knew Gandhi best.[95]

Feeling his years and wanting to conserve his energies in the mid-1960s, Erikson took several well-planned trips to India with Joan. Although they visited New Delhi and a few other locations, they spent most of their time in Ahmadabad. And like their earlier visits, they resided much of the time in the Sarabhai family compound. Even more than during his earlier trips, Erikson felt deeply attracted to Sarabhai family life, and he knew that Gandhi felt this same sense of attachment. For better or worse, Erikson therefore found himself connected emotionally to Gandhi. He spent a great deal of time talking with the old family patriarch, Ambalal, who had represented the mill owners during the strike, and with his sister, Anasuya, who had assisted Gandhi. He also sought out Shankerlal Banker, one of the key organizers of the striking workers, and others who had known Gandhi well. Erikson's interview technique defied the conventions of social scientists and oral historians, approximating instead the techniques of a clinician in a therapeutic context. He had no questionnaires or interview protocols or even a list of issues to discuss. Rather, he simply talked with elders who had participated in "the Event" of 1918, usually in English but periodically with an interpreter, for he had made no effort to learn Indian languages. Erikson would "jot down only an occasional word." There were quotations in his text, but these were "approximations of what I remembered from my informants to have said, in word and in tone." What mattered was Erikson's direct personal rapport with the interviewee. He was "the kind of worker who must find his way from personal observation to what seems relevant enough to be recorded." He had to "find my [his] way from strong esthetic impressions to what survives as ethically urgent." Erikson's friend Robert Coles conducted himself similarly when he met with children who had been involved in school desegregation in New Orleans and Atlanta. Like Coles, Erikson was intent on "letting sub-jectivity and even circumstantiality reign." The task was to relax or "loosen" his interviewees (as he had his patients) to the point where they moved with him beyond fixed "formulas" that defined Gandhi either as a saint or a sinner. The source of these fixed "formulas" was the fact that Gandhi had "simply made too great demands on all of us as well as himself and must, therefore, be disposed of somehow."[96]

As he progressed with his research and preliminary writing, Erik relied on helpers. As usual, Joan was around to discuss problems and to evaluate out-lines and drafts. In addition to her considerable duties managing his under-graduate course, Pamela Daniels put aside her own dissertation research on Gandhi and devoted herself to Erikson's project. She went over every sentence and paragraph that Erikson wrote, again and again, to help him capture qual-ities that words seemed unable to represent very adequately. The two talked constantly about Gandhi, India, and "the Event." Daniels felt that she encouraged Erikson as much as she critiqued his work. Kamla Chowdhry's nephew, Sudhir Kakar, also helped. He had recently completed a master's degree in economics in Germany, enrolled at Harvard, and served as one of Erikson's teaching assistants. Kakar thought increasingly of leaving eco-nomics for psychoanalysis, especially after conversing with Erikson, but worried that he had never studied psychology. "Neither have I," Erikson reas-sured him. As their vocations began to blend, Kakar proved indispensable in helping Erikson understand Hindu belief and social psychology, whether in Cambridge or during regular evening conversations when they were both in Ahmadabad. Kakar also reviewed pertinent portions of Erikson's writing with an eye to faulty translations and imprecise assertions concerning Indian cul-ture. Whenever Erikson was in Stockbridge, he depended on Austen Riggs secretary Julie Negrini to transform handwritten paragraphs connected by green triangles, blue circles, arrows, and other directives into conventional typescript. Unlike work on prior books, he even asked Kai to look over pre-liminary chapters and shorten them through "gentle severity." If not for his helpers, Erikson knew that his research and writing would have been weighed down by mistakes and would have spurted off in too many directions.[97]

By late 1966 and early 1967, Erikson found that he could not devote suf-ficient time and energy to his work on Gandhi. More than teaching and administrative commitments were distracting him. Identity had long been one of his most powerful concepts, and by using it as a primary referent, he had finished *Young Man Luther* rather quickly. *Insight and Responsibility* seemed to cohere, at least modestly, because identity was treated as the basis for the intergenerational life cycle. With these and other successes, Erikson had gained such widespread popular recognition for his identity crisis formulations that W. W. Norton was pressuring him for another book-length manuscript. Norton wanted it pegged to the paperback college textbook market and calculated that such a volume would help to recover his $500,000 advance. Erikson agreed to put out a volume on identity, but to finish it quickly so that he could return to his Gandhi project.

Identity: Youth and Crisis came of these circumstances. The book represented an amalgam of previously published essays reaching back to "Ego Development and Historical Change" (1946). "The Problem of Ego Identity" (1956) on the identity crisis of young George Bernard Shaw was by far the most significant and arresting essay, for Erikson had brilliantly characterized identity as a persistent sameness within oneself and a persistent sharing of a sort of "essential character" with others. The essay had also powerfully addressed the nature of youthful intimacy, the psychological components of youthful ideology, and the place of the identity construct in the evolution of psychoanalytic theory. To fill out the *Identity* book, Erikson selected previously published essays on racial identity, gender identity, and even portions of his "The Dream Specimen of Psychoanalysis" article. Some of these publications were broken up, abbreviated, and knit together to forge chapters. Others were simply reprinted as self-contained chapters. Assisted by Joan and Pamela Daniels, Erik devoted six weeks to transforming all of these essays into a book. Much of his work during this period involved the preparation of a preface, a prologue, and a long final paragraph.[98]

While he worked on *Identity: Youth and Crisis,* Erikson experienced misgivings, for he realized that it was less a book on the essential architecture of identity than a group of earlier essays. He could offer only a lame justification: "I am apt to present the same observations in various contexts, hoping each time that understanding may be deepened." Wisely, he deleted this sentence prior to publication, though he did acknowledge that "it is disquieting to hear oneself talk in different tongues to different audiences, especially if one has forgotten to whom in a given audience—and against whom—one was talking at the time." For a clinician and writer who believed that "context is everything," it was distressing to be republishing articles with no clear memory of the circumstances that had motivated him to write them in the first place. Part of the problem was that between 1946 and the mid-1960s, Erikson frequently modified his perspectives on terms like *identity crisis, self-identity, sexual identity,* and even *moratorium.* Consequently, their meaning in one chapter of *Identity: Youth and Crisis* sometimes differed from their meaning in another chapter. He assigned Pamela Daniels to edit the chapters for redundancy and to amplify those passages in the reprinted articles that had confused his undergraduate students. But six weeks was insufficient time to begin to clear up these matters.[99]

Defensive about doing a book so hastily, Erikson was less than certain about what he had created. Just before publication, he changed the subtitle from "Youth and History" to "Youth and Crisis." He told the reader that the main title indicated that the book was "a successor to *Childhood and Society*," but in the prior sentence, he had described it as "a companion book" to *Young Man Luther*, which elaborated, through a single life, "what this book roamingly explores in many lives and times."[100]

Identity: Youth and Crisis roamed loosely and often sloppily. There was little careful reflection or systematic writing and rewriting. Robert Coles devoted considerable space and attention to *Insight and Responsibility* as a book of essays in his thoughtful 1970 volume concerning Erikson's publications. In contrast, Coles referred to *Identity: Youth and Crisis* only twice and without the briefest summary statement. Taken as a whole, the volume probably merits more attention, but not a great deal more. As Erikson was coming to understand in his expanding public role, however, quality in commercial publication rarely correlated with successful sales figures. W. W. Norton heavily promoted the *Identity* book. Promotional literature resonated to the catch themes and visions of contemporary American college students. The hardcover sold over 10,000 the first year it came out. The book was then quickly discounted as a paperback text for college bookstores. By the 1970–71 academic year, nearly 31,000 paperbacks were purchased; that was impressively close to sales figures for *Childhood and Society*. Five years later, paperback sales had dropped to slightly below 15,000. But this exceeded all other Erikson publications except *Childhood and Society*.[101]

Publication success aside, *Identity: Youth and Crisis* represented conceptual progress in a few areas. For one, Erikson made it transparently clear why he preferred the concept of a "sense of identity" over psychoanalytically informed constructs like "character structure" or "basic character." The latter were static and failed to address the changing experiences and conditions that enhanced or threatened a person's sense of what he or she was and was becoming. Perhaps taking a page from his own life, he insisted that activity and process were the keys to a person's feeling of identity. William James was on the mark, Erikson charged, by describing the "sense of identity" as a feeling of being and becoming "most deeply and intensely active and alive."[102]

Erikson also used *Identity: Youth and Crisis* to accent a special spiritual and cognitive aspect of identity. It was clear from his 1923–24 journal that he had been impressed by Meister Eckhart and other German mystics who designated the eye as a primary center of awareness and the self as considerably more than the adaptive ego. Erikson had given some sign of this orientation in *Young Man Luther* when he described Luther's sense of identity. He used *Identity: Youth and Crisis* to elaborate modestly, referring to the "sense of I" as the most essential element in selfhood. The "I" involved a conscious dimension that the ego lacked and was rooted in mutual recognition—connection with another person and assuredly with the "*ultimate other*." The "I" was at once a cognitive, social, and spiritual facility.[103]

As *Identity: Youth and Crisis* was about to go to the printer in 1968, Erikson penciled in a few final sentences in which he noted that youth's quest for ideology (a prerequisite for identity) was coming "to dominate the collective mind." This was altogether natural in a period of "radical change." In a year when the Nixon-Agnew presidential ticket was capitalizing on the growing backlash against the "radical" assertions of activist youth, Erikson wanted to come to their defense and conceived of his book as a primary vehicle for doing so. In the prologue, he voiced relief that American youth exhibited none of the "ideological undernourishment" evident during the McCarthy era. In the period when he had left his Berkeley professorship, he recalled how many students had been indifferent to the repressive dangers of the loyalty oath. Fortunately, times had changed. By embracing the Peace Corps, civil rights, and arms control, and by opposing the accelerating war in Vietnam, "youth have proven more foresighted than many, many adults. To the horror of a parent generation brainwashed by McCarthyism, they have reinstated some of their own parents' abandoned ideals." Writing with a more strident tone than he usually exhibited, Erikson also replied to conservative social critics who had accused activist youth of a "de-sacrilized" social and political existence. He included in *Identity* portions of a public letter he had prepared for the "Commission on the Year 2000" that spoke to a greater "re-sacrilization of life in our youth than in us." By pressing for "new logical and ethical boundaries," youth was bringing a new spirituality to society that their parents could not see owing to the parents' "dogmatic rationalism," their appetite for consumer "gadgets," and their "denial of the infinite."[104]

Other republished essays in *Identity* would embroil Erikson in public controversies in the years ahead. He felt the book would reflect "the overriding issue" of the day for humankind: global survival in the face of the destructive potential of modern weapons. Artificial ethnic, national, religious, and other divisions that justified one group or "pseudospecies" clashing with another "can now spell the end of the species." The great hope was that such "pseudospeciation" might ultimately be overshadowed by "a more *universal identity*," one that embraced "all the diversities and dissonances" of the modern world. Such universality, he discovered, had been central to Gandhi's efforts. The new ethics that facilitated the "universal identity" had to be rooted in generative caring for others—"the test of what you produce is the *care* it inspires." In essence, Erikson was advocating a "belief in the species" that would make the care for every child on the globe "a welcome trust."[105]

Although *Identity: Youth and Crisis* was a flawed volume (by no means comparable to Erikson's three earlier books), it was not devoid of merit. One could scarcely turn from a serious reading without thinking more deeply about the strengths and fragilities of identity in the contemporary world. While Erikson literally reprinted essays he had written during the two decades after World War II, portions of his text forecast concerns that he would emphasize for the rest of his life. Many would appear more compellingly, as spiritual and prophetic calls to humankind, within the pages of *Gandhi's Truth*—a volume that he now yearned to complete.

THREE GENERATIONS

Periodically throughout his *Identity* book, Erikson took short jabs at psychoanalytic orthodoxy. He criticized his Freudian analytic colleagues for their unwillingness to take the ideas of Jung, the rival, seriously. He himself had profited substantially from dialogues with his Jungian friend Joseph Wheelwright. Erikson also criticized Freudian analysts for invoking the vague term *outer world,* as Anna Freud did when he worked with her in Vienna. Preoccupied as they were with vertical excavation into an individual's "inner world," orthodox analysts had failed to address the social milieu surrounding the individual—the horizontal plane—as a basic force shaping psychological development. Erikson could not tolerate "patronizing tributes to the role 'also' played by 'social factors.' " But critical as he was of the psychoanalytic establishment, he would not break from Freud and his traditions. The Vienna Freudians had given him his "foundation"—his first job, his profession, and his first coherent intellectual system. Erikson attacked "psychoanalytic 'revisionists' " for having "taken unnecessary chances" with basic psychoanalytic ideas. He distinguished himself from neo-Freudians, in particular, despite emphasis by many of them on social factors, because their perspective "overadjusts some basic Freudian notions to a new climate of discourse." His *Identity* volume thus illustrated both his continuing attraction to and his discomfort with Freudian orthodoxy.[106]

While Erikson worked to complete *Identity: Youth and Crisis* and to return to his more important Gandhi project, he found himself involved in a psychoanalytic controversy that became another detour. Sigmund Freud had purportedly co-authored, with William C. Bullitt, an American ambassador, politician, and journalist, a book concerning the psychology of Woodrow Wilson. Despite Erikson's reputation within the college community, and despite profound respect for his writing by important European as well as American intellectuals, he was not held in the highest regard by many psychoanalysts, owing in part to Anna Freud's strong misgivings, which she did not keep to herself. Some analysts also criticized Erikson for failing to elaborate his identity concept with sufficient rigor. Even neo-Freudian Abram Kardiner characterized Erikson as "an adventurer—reckless, inconsistent, the right hand not knowing what the left is doing." Such perceptions of his work within the analytic community made Erikson uncomfortable, of course. He was a successful professor, author, and intellectual, but he also identified professionally as a Freudian and a Vienna-trained psychoanalyst. The role that he played in the erupting controversy over a book that endangered Freud's reputation could make or break his fragile reputation among psychoanalysts.[107]

Bullitt had approached Freud in 1930 about working with him on a manuscript concerning Wilson's psychology, and Freud had agreed. Freud's esteemed biographer, Peter Gay, concluded that while Bullitt did most of the work, Freud had made definite contributions. The volume was essentially completed by 1932. Freud approved the general intellectual framework, wrote the introduction, and referred to Bullitt as his "collaborator." He acknowledged that he was more than a mere consultant and that he shared Bullitt's less than flattering assessment of Wilson. Nonetheless, Freud had apparently balked at publishing the manuscript until his move from Vienna to London following the *Anschluss*. Bullitt had facilitated this move, and Freud was grateful. In ill health and with more important matters on his mind, Freud gave Bullitt his consent to publish. After Freud died in 1939, Bullitt apparently revised all but Freud's introduction. He crowded the manuscript with stylistic infelicities and mechanistic applications of psychoanalytic constructs, but prudently delayed publication until after the death of Wilson's widow in 1961.[108]

Early in the fall of 1966, Erikson learned of the existence of the Bullitt-Freud manuscript through his connection to the Kennedy family. A former John Kennedy aide who liked and respected him (almost certainly Richard Goodwin) had wanted to be helpful. He informed Erikson that Houghton Mifflin would soon publish the volume. Indeed, excerpts appeared in a December issue of *Look;* additional publicity would certainly follow. Even before the *Look* publication, however, an editor at the *New York Review of Books* had asked Erikson to write a lengthy review essay. To facilitate that task, Houghton Mifflin sent him galley proofs of the entire text.[109]

Erikson's immediate reaction was negative; the book was a crude and insensitive polemic that would damage Freud's reputation, and he urged Houghton Mifflin not to publish it. At a minimum, the publisher had to designate Bullitt as the principal author. Erikson also requested that Houghton Mifflin delete Bullitt's claim that Freud had signed each chapter of the book (attesting to his approval). Houghton Mifflin refused all of his requests. Freud promoters and former associates, such as Max Schur, Marianne Kris, and Kurt Eissler, were grateful for Erikson's efforts. Indeed, they were counting on him to vindicate Freud in the *New York Review of Books* and sent him information to tarnish Bullitt's character. They also urged Anna Freud to cooperate with her former analysand.[110]

At this point, Erikson wrote the longest letter he had in years to Anna Freud and focused it on his role in the controversy. He informed her that her father's introductory essay to *Wilson* differed dramatically from the dismal chapters composed by Bullitt. Moreover, "the interpretations supplied by him [Freud] vastly outdistanced Bullitt's capacity to understand, to translate, and to formulate." Erikson attached to the letter a questionnaire on publication specifics, asking Anna Freud to detail precise portions of the manuscript her father had assisted with and how he had done so. Erikson also asked about issues of translation from German to English and about the legal relationship between Freud and Bullitt in this publication venture. Anna Freud replied immediately, thanking Erikson for attending to "a great worry to me." She confirmed Erikson's view that Freud had written only the introduction. She also commended him for questioning whether her father had signed off on the chapters. But her letter was not warm; it carried little emotion of any kind.[111]

Erikson sent the same questionnaire to Freud's personal physician, Max Schur, knowing of his reputation and influence among psychoanalysts. Schur provided very detailed responses. He also instructed Erikson on just what "*can* and *should* be done" in the *New York Review* essay. Erikson was to stress that "Bullitt did not understand the subtleties and intricacies of analytic interpretations." Erikson was also to "trace some of the grand design of Freud's Introduction" to the book. Schur intimated that Anna Freud shared these expectations for the *New York Review* essay. Over the next several weeks, Erikson drafted the essay and sent it to both Anna Freud and Schur so that they could correct any "misrepresentation."[112]

Erikson's draft and his published essay pleased Anna Freud, Schur, and other Freud loyalists, bolstering his fragile reputation among them. Indeed, the *International Journal of Psycho-Analysis* reprinted the essay. However, it hardly counted as one of his more thoughtful publications, for he had complied too meticulously with Schur's instructions. He took care to distinguish Freud's introduction from the main text of the book, and he assured readers that Freud's tone of animus toward Wilson and America was "more than a personal gripe or prejudice." Wilson had failed to make the world safe for democracy after World War I; he had only raised false hope. Erikson complied with another Schur directive by insisting that Bullitt did not understand Freud's analytic subtleties. Bullitt was "an avid student with no special gift" for nuances who described crudely what Freud had "tried to convey to him." To bolster his case, Erikson cited example after example of Bullitt's crude misuse of Freud's ideas. Whereas Freud had an "abiding respect for his patients," he noted, Bullitt's "totally un-Freudian bias" produced "a petty denigration" of Wilson.[113]

Almost entirely missing from the *New York Review of Books* essay was the suggestion of an alternative approach to Wilson. Erikson had hoped Bullitt might have elaborated on aspects of the president's early life, religion, and culture—factors that helped make Wilson a charismatic statesman. Yet he refrained from providing this elaboration himself when Bullitt fell short. That task was left to historian Richard Hofstadter in a rich sequel to Erikson's essay in the same issue of the *New York Review*. Erikson also failed to characterize Freud as the founder of psychoanalysis with much insight even though he lavishly praised him. One finds none of Erikson's customary, thoughtful reflections on Freud's historic setting and innovations.

Clearly, Erikson had elected to write a very pedestrian essay that refurbished his reputation among Freudians generally and Anna Freud in particular. The results of this strategy were modest and temporary. While Anna Freud was grateful for the essay, she expressed private reservations over Erikson's citation of numerous examples of Bullitt's awkward use of psychoanalytic constructs. Indeed, she urged the editors of the *International Journal of Psycho-Analysis* to limit the examples when they reprinted the article. At the 1971 International Congress on Psychoanalysis in Vienna, Anna Freud and Erikson appeared uncharacteristically friendly, to be sure, and she acknowledged his professional writing. But comments by both at a psychoanalytic forum in Philadelphia two years later indicated that the period of apparent goodwill did not last long.[114]

Intent as Erikson was during the Freud-Bullitt controversy to demonstrate his bond with the founder of psychoanalysis—the man he regarded as the seminal intellectual in the generation that preceded his—he also wanted to connect with Robert Jay Lifton, a very important intellectual in the generation that followed his. Succinctly, Erikson found himself pulled in two directions, with the increasingly complex Gandhi project still needing to be completed. Lifton had broken away from organized psychoanalysis and its institutions, departing very fundamentally from Freud. Yet the young man appealed to Erikson, enormously so.

Their friendship can be traced back to 1956, when Lifton had completed a psychiatric residency in New York City and was researching his first book concerning Maoist "brainwashing" in China. He was not entirely clear why "brainwashing" techniques affected some victims but not others. After he read Erikson's article, "The Problem of Ego Identity," in the *Journal of the American Psychoanalytic Association,* he announced, "That's my answer." Lifton concluded that Maoist "brainwashing" was really an attempt "to bring about a change in identity in the participant." It was "a coercive form of psychotherapy" designed to obliterate one's old identity and to establish a new one. Hastily, Lifton wrote to Erikson explaining his project and requesting an appointment.[115]

They met at Erikson's home in Stockbridge. Within minutes, the tall, slim Lifton with dark, broad-rimmed glasses and the more stylishly attired immigrant several decades his senior began walking in European fashion, as Erikson and David Rapaport had done quite regularly, past the Austen Riggs Center and all over town, so immersed in conversation that they scarcely recognized where they were headed. Erikson was impressed with Lifton's use of his concept of identity to clarify Maoist "thought reform." He confided that when he had trained under Anna Freud in Vienna, there had been an element of "thought reform" not unlike Maoist "totalism" within the psychoanalytic community. Lifton had just begun a training program at the Boston Psychoanalytic Institute, and as he listened to Erikson, he began to connect that training to his Maoist project. In fact, he reflected on it for the next several years and concluded *Thought Reform and the Psychology of Totalism* with several pages linking the process of Chinese thought control with psychoanalytic training. Both processes sought to break down a person's identity and to manufacture a new one. Lifton had completed his analysis by the time his book was published, but had yet to tackle analytic control cases. And he never did, which amounted to deciding not to become a psychoanalyst. That decision, plus Lifton's charge in *Thought Reform* that analytic training resembled Maoist "brainwashing," marked his secession from the psychoanalytic movement. Erikson may have been uneasy over Lifton's course of conduct, and would never have taken it himself, but he did not try to dissuade the young man. If Lifton was no obedient student, Erikson was not the traditional mentor who demanded that the student's training replicate his own.[116]

A personal dimension to the relationship developed when Erikson became especially close to Betty Jean Lifton, Robert's wife and a pioneer in the movement for the rights of adopted children. She had struggled for years to find her biological mother, and Erikson, of course, had always wanted to learn the identity of the man who had fathered him. She succeeded where he had not, but they talked frequently about adoption and biological parents. Robert Lifton also grew quite close to Kai; the two belonged to an emerging generation of young, university-based public intellectuals who were too young to have profoundly experienced either the Holocaust or World War

II. Lifton appreciated Kai's technique of developing the identity theme in *Wayward Puritans* through collective social psychology. Kai's second book, concerning a disastrous flood in Buffalo Creek, West Virginia, drew as heavily on Lifton's work on collective death anxiety as it relied on Erik's view of the resiliency and decline of viable selfhood. Kai and Joanna became fast friends with the Liftons.[117]

The ties between the Eriksons and the Liftons were augmented by the Wellfleet psychohistorical meetings in the summer at the Liftons' beach home. Robert Lifton and his Yale colleague Kenneth Keniston (Erik's first "chief section man") established the "Group for the Study of Psychohistorical Process" in 1966 as a forum for Erik's ideas and writings. Next, Lifton built a long and rather rustic room adjacent to his house and occupied it with a large seminar table to accommodate the group. Associates with whom Erik felt comfortable were invited to attend and to bring their families for several days on the Cape each summer. None were orthodox psychoanalysts and most were of Lifton's and Kai's generation. Erik brought work-in-progress and was expected to report informally about it. Unlike his dealings with Freudian loyalists in the Bullitt controversy, Lifton encouraged Erik to pursue his own interests and projects at Wellfleet in his unique, idiosyncratic way. According to the predesignated format, Erik's report about his ongoing work was to signal a point of departure for all other presentations.[118]

The Wellfleet meeting was supposed to generate the institutional structure of an Eriksonian movement, but this did not happen. Not even the kernel of such an agency was discernible at the initial August 1966 gathering or at those that followed. With tough-minded, critical intellectuals like Philip Rieff, author of important studies of Freud and his legacy; prominent historians Bruce Mazlish and H. Stuart Hughes; plus Lifton and Keniston, Erikson was regarded as a very distinguished and creative senior scholar but not as the leader of a movement or school. While his informal work-in-progress presentations were appreciated, they rarely dominated more than half a day of discussion. Erikson did not treat other participants as followers or successors. Lifton presided over the meetings, and without his prodding, Erikson would have said little. Those whose thinking most closely approximated Erikson's—Keniston, Lifton, and Robert Coles—rarely dwelled upon or elaborated his ideas. Wellfleet was not the sort of hierarchic psychoanalytic forum that Erikson had attended in Vienna and had seen replicated in the United States. His propensity toward a more egalitarian horizontality was more conspicuous at Wellfleet than Freud's disposition toward a graded verticality.[119]

At the first Wellfleet psychohistorical meeting, Erikson presented material from his Gandhi project. In turn, Lifton talked of the *hibakusha* victims of America's atomic bombing of Hiroshima in 1945—the basis for his book in progress, *Death in Life: Survivors of Hiroshima.* The two friends continued to use Wellfleet gatherings to engage in dialogue about their respective projects until both books were completed. As each became more familiar with the other's project, Erikson and Lifton recognized that both volumes were being written in the context of an escalating American military presence in Vietnam and the danger of Soviet-American nuclear missile attacks. Lifton sensed a new historic level of danger for humankind that could exceed the tragedy of Hiroshima. Global destruction was no longer a remote possibility. But Erikson's project left Lifton hopeful for a viable alternative to war and nuclear destruction—emphasizing Gandhi's legacy of tough and realistic but nonviolent resolutions of conflicts. As Erikson familiarized Lifton with Gandhi's complex pacifistic principles and practices, he sensed that he was helping his friend get beyond the trauma produced by American bombs in Hiroshima and now in Vietnam. In turn, Erikson's encouraging assistance to Lifton provided crucial context for his approach to *Gandhi's Truth.* Erik came increasingly to feel that Gandhi's nonviolent strategy or *Satyagraha* (active perseverance in truth) was a gift to humankind to avert mass violence and military catastrophes. Essentially, Gandhi's *Satyagraha* represented an intergenerational act of generativity—a wise adult giving to and supporting younger generations. As he began to construe *Satyagraha* as a supremely generative act, and related to the more optimistic global perspective that he was providing Lifton, Erikson found that he could flesh out as never before the very concept of generativity (the seventh stage of his life cycle model and the central psychological task of adult life).[120]

As Lifton and Erikson discussed their major research projects, they related their theoretical perspectives to classical psychoanalytic formulations. The springboard for both was Freud's image of instinct (mostly sexual) and defense (mostly repression of instinct). For Freud, demonic instincts or drives battled against a fragile superstructure of civilized human reason. Erikson had drawn on Freudian instinct and defense for his theory of identity; Freud's perspective helped to shape his delineation of the search for a sense of coherence and continuity in the course of the life cycle. Erikson had been oriented along these lines in his characterization of young Luther and was proceeding with that orientation again in his book on Gandhi. For Erikson, the search for identity had its own particular *configuration*—the pattern or shape of the convergence between a person's emotional concerns and pertinent issues within the society and culture about him. In a sense, Erikson's configuration liberated Freud's imagery from its mechanistic clash between drives and defenses as well as from its preoccupation with the inner psyche. In contrast to Erikson, Lifton advanced what he called formative theory, which effectively abandoned Freud's drive theory. Lifton used Freud's concept of a life instinct at war with a death instinct only as his preliminary launching point. From there, he argued for a controlling image (not instinct) of death and the continuity of life. In individual but especially in group experience, Lifton focused on the shapes or forms that symbol making took as people like the *hibakusha* struggled to maintain life in the face of death. Their struggle was between the continuity and discontinuity of life, and it rested less on the premise of a fixed and continuous self than did Erikson's configurational approach to the quest for identity. As a Jew, Lifton's abiding interest in Holocaust survivors may have sparked his interest in the *hibakusha,* motivating him to interpret their particular struggle in the broader realm of human survival. Yet he noted that all generations were preoccupied with symbolic mortality; parents needed to create symbols of continuity over time and space for their children, a spirituality that transcended death, and a sense of psychic transcendence that overcame the passing of time and the inevitability of death. Most concisely, Lifton studied people struggling to evoke and preserve images of selfhood that were alive, individually and collectively, and avoiding images of the self as dead.[121]

Eventually, Lifton began to characterize his imagery (what he called psychoformations) as an extension on Erikson's work, in the sense that it moved beyond Freudian drive theory and embraced common collective experience more comprehensively. Most important, it "carries Erikson's principle of configuration still further. I interpret individual feelings and actions on the basis of immediate struggles to harmonize and recast the forms and images that have been evolving over the course of the life cycle." Erikson did not describe Lifton's imagery as an extension of his own work or inferior to it; Lifton's work was simply different from his. Yet he felt free to borrow from Lifton's work owing to its simultaneous emphasis on psychobiology and culture, its concern with the life cycle, and its emphasis on the form or shape of psychic experience. The difference in the ways the two friends regarded each other's framework suggests that Lifton viewed their relationship more from a mentor-student perspective than Erikson did. Lifton, the student, felt that he had affirmed, enlarged, and extended the perspective of the mentor. For Erikson, both he and Lifton were engaged in interesting work from which they both shared and borrowed intergenerationally. Neither advanced beyond Freud or beyond one another.[122]

Even given the differences between Erikson and Lifton on theory and legacy, neither could tolerate the closed, self-protective, and semi-authoritarian perspectives that sometimes emerged within the psychoanalytic movement. By the 1960s, Erikson felt less fully a part of that movement than in earlier years. The premium that he now placed on intergenerational rapport, most evident in his undergraduate course and in *Insight and Responsibility,* helps to explain why. Hierarchy and dictates from a senior to a junior were not the stuff of free-flowing reciprocity or mutuality along the intergenerational life cycle.

By the time the Wellfleet meetings had been organized, then, Erikson could respect and profit from Freud and Freud's followers, but also from Lifton and others who felt disconnected from the psychoanalytic movement. He could protect Freud's reputation in the controversy over the Bullitt-Freud volume on Wilson but also speak out on Lifton's behalf when orthodox analysts cavalierly dismissed Lifton's work. Erikson's ability to genuinely esteem both Freud and Lifton paralleled the nature of his intergenerational focus as a writer and a teacher. More than either Freud or Lifton, Erikson found vitality and engagement by shifting not only between different generations, but between different forums, theoretical formulations, and even occupations. A psychoanalyst and a clinician, he was also a writer and a professor. By now, he had also become more visible as a public intellectual.

CONCLUSION: A PUBLIC PRESENCE

In the Erikson-Lifton relationship, Lifton was much more the political activist, regularly protesting various controversial issues like racial discrimination and the Vietnam War. Although Erikson shared Lifton's views and was regarded as a more eminent national figure, he did not always speak out publicly. Indeed, he refused to sign antiwar petitions when they were circulated at Wellfleet gatherings. Stanley Hoffmann, his good friend on the Harvard faculty and a favorite of left-leaning students, was unable to mobilize him in protests against Dow Chemical Corporation's recruiting visits to Harvard or campus ROTC operations. Nor would Erikson consent to speak at antiwar rallies. This did not mean that he was unsympathetic to the young protesters, who included many of his students. Rather, he never felt entirely comfortable in the role of dissident activist. Indeed, he picked and chose his moments of public protest very judiciously. At those times, however, he seemed to speak with new strength and presence.

Apparently at the urging of Richard Nixon's domestic policy adviser, Daniel Patrick Moynihan, Erikson was asked to address a White House staff dinner early in June of 1969. It was his first trip to 1600 Pennsylvania Avenue in four years. The Vietnam War had escalated considerably, campus protests had accelerated, and President Nixon sought advice on whether federal funds should be withdrawn from colleges and universities characterized by vociferous opposition to the war. Whereas Erikson said little when he visited Lyndon Johnson's White House, this time he arrived with a prepared text and read it with considerable feeling. He characterized protest by young people as understandable in a world where "the technicians of government, commerce, and technology" were "poised, every minute of day and night, for overkill" that could produce the "self-destruction of mankind, planned and perfected." Young protesters expressed "a deep ethical concern" for a better world that was not driven by the military imperatives of destructive technology. Speaking explicitly to President Nixon, who had "dropped in for drinks" and asked why protesters were not more interested in football, Erikson called for "a new covenant of cooperation" between ethical adults and rebellious or potentially rebellious youth. Participants in this "covenant" would seek a "new world wide ethics" and "such international and national teamwork as may secure . . . nuclear peace and the reconstruction of cities." Bringing his uncharacteristically strong and evocative presentation to a conclusion, Erikson complained that "there is not a single woman at this dinner" of presidential advisers. He handed his typed text to Moynihan, who kept it for Nixon.[123]

Roughly five weeks after his presentation at the Nixon White House, Erik and Joan raced from Cotuit to New York City. Sue had just given birth to Per, their third grandchild. Erik watched Per with fascination and occasionally held him. He made a sketch of Sue nursing the baby and talked excitedly to Harland, the proud father. Erik was still unsure about the particulars of parenting, however, and let others care for Per. As Sue rested in bed with her son, Erik and Harland sat nearby watching the televised Apollo moon landing. Erik was captivated by the event and discussed it enthusiastically with Harland. Neither voiced dissent when a NASA official analogized the landing to the Creation. This was a happy and memorable week for Erik. If his own father had rejected him, he had embraced his children, and they continued to give him grandchildren. The generations had connected in the Bloland apartment as they had a few years earlier when Erik and Joan had traveled to visit Kai and Joanna's newborns. Amid this good cheer, Erik was awed by the success of his adopted country in outer space. A proud American citizen, he had a son-in-law, a daughter-in-law, and three grandchildren—all American born—and their country had accomplished the unthinkable by landing on the moon.[124]

Amid the joys of another grandchild, Erik had apparently lost some of his cynicism about technology and its misuses by American power brokers, from Hiroshima to Vietnam, such as he had voiced at the Nixon White House. But his euphoric appraisal of the moon landing quickly dissipated. By late September, he returned to his characteristic perspective in an address at Appleton Chapel on the Harvard campus. He began by alluding to "something I must get off my chest"—the real significance of the Apollo landing. The NASA spokesman had been wrong when he described the landing as

"the greatest week since Creation." Erikson profoundly distrusted the astronauts, who "invade the boundaries of the heavens" behind an American military program with "a comfortable margin of overkill." The Apollo astronauts
had "become the superbrains of machines invented by brains" and were
programmed to follow a potentially "lethal design which all human conquest
has helped to spread." In contrast to the ominous moon landing, Erikson
described Per Bloland's birth. The very sight of his grandson had made it
apparent that "every time a child is born, *there* is potentially the greatest week
since creation." The true challenge was not in space but on earth so as to
assure that each newborn would feel "at home in his body, mind, and senses"
and would gain a sense of trust in other humanity. "Without that priority on
earth," Erikson insisted, "all landings elsewhere remain footless."[125]

Erikson was espousing themes that he had developed in the classroom, in
his writings, and in public forums through the 1960s—the dangers of technologies with destructive capabilities and the centrality of intergenerational
rapport. Capable parenting, teaching, and general caregiving in rearing
trusting youngsters benefited adults as well as children. This focus offered the
most promise for a stable and peaceful planet. Erikson may have become
more appreciative of these themes as he felt the tensions, and saw the signs of
discord in the Bloland family as summer shifted into fall. Parents and grandparents as well as newborn were suffering. But there was also something
almost prophetic in Erikson's manner and intensity during his Appleton
Chapel presentation as he contrasted the birth of his grandson with the
Apollo landing. It was not unlike the way he had stated his message at the
Nixon White House in June. In manner and content, these two powerful
public presentations resembled addresses by Mohandas Gandhi as Erikson
characterized them in *Gandhi's Truth*. He had completed and published the
book that year. The experience of finishing that volume had literally transformed Erikson to the point where he was making Gandhi's prophetic
"Truth" his own. Neither a guru nor a national leader, he had become a
strong and forceful public intellectual with a vibrant prophetic streak.

CHAPTER EIGHT

Global Prophet:
Erikson's Truth

S tarted in 1964 and published five years later, many regarded *Gandhi's Truth* as a counterpoint, in style as well as message, to an aggressive and bureaucratic, technologically specialized, and ethically vacuous American military presence in Vietnam. Erikson's book stood for spiritual communality, the interplay of the body and the imagination, psychological wholeness, generativity, and an ethnically diverse global family. Erikson elaborated these themes—extensions of what Gandhi meant by "Truth"—for years after the book was published. The themes were discernible in his Godkin Lectures at Harvard in 1972 and in his National Endowment for the Humanities lectures in the nation's capital amid the Watergate scandals. In these presentations, Erikson linked Gandhi with two other personalities he characterized as wise prophets: Jesus and Thomas Jefferson. In the end, Erikson propounded his own prophetic presence and Truth. As such, he came to be regarded as perhaps the most highly regarded healer among America's public intellectuals. But there was a cost. His characteristically probing and well-crafted prose grew increasingly vague—sometimes downright illogical—as spiritual evocation was substituted for shrewd analysis.

TWO BOOKS AND ONE MARRIAGE

From the start of his investigation of modern India, Erikson felt that his primary task was to "search for the historical presence of Mahatma Gandhi and for the meaning of what he called Truth" or *Satyagraha* by focusing on "the Event" (the Ahmadabad textile strike of 1918). This proved to be an enormously difficult task, yielding many frustrating experiences. To start with, the very meaning of *Satyagraha* was problematic. According to some translations, it was a "persistent demand for truth," though some characterized it as "insistence for truth." Erikson settled upon "Truthforce as the shortest and most sloganlike term" to equate with *Satyagraha* as "an active and forceful quality" in contrast to "passive resistance." But he felt uneasy with this formulation in a world of specialists and linguists. Other difficulties arose. On one particular day, for example, Erikson struggled to connect four items on his writing pad. Three related to the year 1918—the "textile strike" (at Ahmadabad), "myself [at] 16," and "Wilson! 14 points" (Woodrow Wilson's postwar peace program). The fourth item was "Freud [at] 60." On another occasion, Erikson found himself confused. He had concluded that the British colonial legacy had thwarted the Indian capacity to write and speak "authentically." But then he questioned whether his conclusion was "unfair," coming as it did from "a stranger in India and an immigrant in his own country." At one point, Erikson tried to observe Indian children at play using American clinical research methods, including one-way observation screens and consistent instructions presented to each child. He discovered that these techniques simply got in the way of any real understanding of the children. Consequently, he tried to persuade himself "to forget about the scientific imperatives of psychologists at home" and to watch and "enjoy the social habits" of the children. Yet, was this a valid approach? he fretted. Recognizing that the Hindu concept of *darstan* elevated seeing over hearing, he found himself struggling to think visually whenever possible and not always succeeding. These constituted only a small sample of the problems plaguing Erikson. Indeed, the tasks and difficulties seemed to proliferate. But so did the potential to produce a new and important book. By 1967, Erikson had persuaded two associates in his undergraduate course on the life cycle, George Goethals and Norman Zinberg, to essentially take over for him. He needed time, especially after the tense and exhausting controversy over the Freud and Bullitt volume on Wilson, if he was to finally finish *Gandhi's Truth*.[1]

Joan was available to help, as she tended to be during difficult intervals. In his application to the American Institute of Indian Studies for travel funds, Erik had sought support for Joan, whom he designated as his "research assistant."[2] This was a gross understatement. She still served as Erik's primary editorial critic, though supplemented now by Pamela Daniels, Kai, and others, but she also worked on her own projects. Therefore, the support Joan provided differed in kind from her past involvement as the dynamics of the marriage changed.

Joan found herself engrossed with local arts during their trips to India. She discovered a great many materials for her research on beads, part of an ongoing project that culminated in *The Universal Bead* (1969), an abundantly illustrated coffee table volume on the diverse uses of beads in various cultures. The Sabarmati River was near Ahmadabad, and Joan often took excursions along its banks to study indigenous patterns of printing and the dyeing of textiles. However, her main venture, while Erik interviewed and read and wrote about Gandhi, was preparing her manuscript on St. Francis, another prophet from a different time and place. Reminiscing later on how the two book projects seemed to cross-fertilize, Erik characterized *St. Francis and His Four Ladies* as "one of my favorite books." He may have been overly generous, for it lacked his stylistic elegance and other compelling techniques through which he presented his own work.[3]

Joan had decided on the book in the mid-1960s while sitting in on Erik's graduate seminar. She prepared a paper that focused on the relationship between St. Francis and St. Clare, founder of a women's order. Consistent with Erik's characterization of the psychology of gender roles, Joan portrayed the Franciscan friars moving about through the countryside (outer space) while the women of St. Clare's order remained within convents (inner space). The work paralleled a similar paper that Margaret Mead's daughter, Mary Catherine Bateson, was preparing on the relationship between St. John of the Cross and St. Teresa of Avila. Joan took her seminar paper to India and expanded it into a book-length publication.[4]

In her research, Joan was even more detached from current historiography and primary written documents than Erik was in his. She characterized St. Francis as an alternative to twelfth-century mercantile society and its increasing obsession with hard currency, transferable wealth, plus worldly pleasures. He embraced celibacy, wed poverty, and cared for others with a mild and passive "femininity." Succinctly, Joan's St. Francis found "creative fruition" or consolidation of "the masculine and feminine elements of his nature" by meekly assisting the needy. Joan also celebrated the elevation of Mary in medieval piety to a position of power and influence. Through Mary's "Heavenly Personage," ancient pre-Christian female deities converged in their mystery and symbolism. This inclusion restored "a unity of rational and emotional spirituality denied by the Judaic roots of Christianity." Perhaps reflecting her upbringing as a provincial Episcopal minister's daughter, Joan was suggesting that Judaism had been less than hospitable to women and was also overrationalized. She narrated the "evolution" from an early Christianity that was heavily influenced by Judaism to a later Christianity that stood freer of those beginnings. If Erik did not embrace this perspective, which may have shaded into unintended anti-Semitism, he did not contest it either.[5]

As husband and wife worked on their books, St. Francis and Gandhi were compared, again and again. Both leaders drew power from their feminine as well as their masculine qualities. For Joan, this fact signaled their acceptance of "our basic bisexuality." Both leaders also harmonized "self-denying asceticism and receptive sensuality." Both gave primacy and structure to the lives of the poor and needy. Erik credited Joan with helping him to understand, through St. Francis, the high-spirited "kind of sainthood also found in Gandhi." Compared with St. Francis, Erik detected a great "locomotor restlessness and energy" in the Mahatma alongside more contemplative qualities. In time, Erik broadened the parallels. Whereas St. Francis confronted the bishop, Gandhi faced down the viceroy. While St. Francis embraced the lepers, Gandhi befriended the untouchables. Each leader headed a communal "household" that extended not only to family but to co-workers, followers, and eventually all of humanity. As Joan traced St. Francis's life, she emphasized that his father was a textile merchant, and she relied on images of cloth, clothing, repairing, and craftsmanship throughout her study. Erik's Gandhi weaved regularly, true to premodern habit; he was "a religious craftsman" as he taught, cured, and reformed. Most important, both Joan's St. Francis and Erik's Gandhi represented God and holiness and wholeness through their very presence. Both communicated the "infinite in the immediate and in the finite." In doing so, both exemplified "the stuff parables are made of."[6]

The thematic confluence of *St. Francis* with *Gandhi's Truth* said more about the Erikson marriage than the qualitative comparability of the two books. Both had been writing in the small mountain town of Perugia just south of Florence and very near to Assisi when they learned of their son Neil's death. Avoidance and guilt contributed to their decision to remain abroad, leaving burial and funeral arrangements to Sue and Jon. But there was a positive aspect, too—a rebuilding of a fragile, often troubled marriage that had been circumscribed by this often repressed family tragedy. The cross-fertilization of the two book projects and the two prophetic historic personalities appeared to infuse new vigor into the marriage. Joan published an article in the middle 1960s that characterized a gradual rejuvenation of Franklin Roosevelt's marriage to Eleanor after he was stricken with polio. If this was an exaggerated portrayal of the Roosevelts, it bore closer proximity to the evolving state of the Erikson marriage.[7]

WRITING TO GANDHI

When he started *Gandhi's Truth,* Erikson planned to focus his account of Gandhi and his leadership at Ahmadabad on the concrete, the tangible, and the physical. The backdrop of the book was the Sarabhai compound where Erikson had resided and where crucial events during the 1918 strike had occurred. Still, Erikson the developmentalist recognized that he had to begin his narrative before 1918, to describe Gandhi's transitions through the first six stages of the life cycle and even to discuss those aspects of seventh-stage generativity that preceded "the Event." To navigate all of these stages quickly and to capture the essential shifts in Gandhi's early life, Erikson seemed to merge the stages into a few broad intervals—childhood and adolescence (lasting well into Gandhi's twenties), mature adulthood, and finally senescence.

Beginning to write in earnest in 1965, Erikson wanted to move quickly through Gandhi's early years. His exposition was rich, elegant, and organized more closely than the balance of the book. He deemphasized developmental theory and simply narrated Gandhi's early life. Before he knew it, Erikson found that he had written a great deal—over one-quarter of what became the final manuscript (Part Two: The Past). He had characterized Gandhi's relatively comfortable early life in a large and prominent Indian family. The last of several children, Gandhi had been born in 1869 to an aging patriarch who was chief minister of Gujarat state and a twenty-five-year-old devout mother. The boy was indulged by both parents. Yet he learned that tact and self-control were important in a large family living in close quarters. The boy became a jokester who loved to tease, especially in difficult situations. Unlike many clinicians, Erikson did not characterize this teasing as a mask for anger or aggression. He emphasized instead that Gandhi had shown an undefinable sort of inner integrity—flexible yet willful, sensual yet tough.

With a minimum of psychoanalytic jargon, Erikson moved Gandhi through a precocious childhood and too early a marriage, in which he struggled to remake his wife, Kasturba, into a more cultivated person. Gandhi traveled to London to train as a barrister. There he learned to dress formally, to consider Christianity as an alternative to Hinduism, and to speak a cultivated English. Erikson's description here was wholly compatible with Frantz Fanon's characterization of the third-world middle class in Europe imitating the manners, morals, and insensitivity of the white Western colonialists. In England, Gandhi became socially and psychologically isolated; he had no caring relationships with friends or community. In this context, Erikson praised Fanon's general critique of the social and emotional damage that colonialism inflicted among people from Europe's African and Asian "provinces."

After completing the destructive English phase of his education, Gandhi, now twenty-four, traveled to South Africa. There he began to practice law with a group of Indian barristers who tolerated the insults of the British ruling elite and paid little attention to the poverty and desolation of the non-white masses. Within weeks of Gandhi's arrival, Erikson had the young man riding in the first-class car of a train from Durban to Pretoria. A white passenger demanded that Gandhi leave the car. Gandhi insisted that he had paid for a first-class ticket and remained seated until police unceremoniously evicted him at the Maritzburg depot. He spent the night at the depot, cold and miserable in the waiting room, seeking his confiscated luggage. This incident left Gandhi painfully aware of the color of his skin and of the fact that he was not a dignified British citizen, and never would be.

Gandhi had finally recognized his marginal status in the British imperial realm. Now, he was determined to fight racial and ethnic discrimination. He would begin by organizing the Indian masses throughout South Africa. As an activist lawyer in Pretoria, Gandhi combined a spirituality and an ethical commitment with a dogged pragmatism. Erikson ably accounted for his evolution into a mature, astute leader and tactician. Gandhi also emerged as an adept writer and practitioner of *Satyagraha* as he sought to combat the poverty and racism of an ethically vacuous British colonial administration. *Satyagraha* represented an original approach in ritualizing the struggle between colonized and colonizers, and was far more creative and humane than traditional armed conflicts. Gandhi was readying himself to return to India, a devout Hindu once more in touch with his ethnic and community roots. There he would begin his campaign to liberate the masses in his own country based upon the technique he had developed in South Africa. At this point, Erikson felt he had provided sufficient detail about "the Past." He was ready to begin the part of the narrative that had compelled him to write the book in the first place. He brought Gandhi, mature and middle aged, back to India in 1914. Gandhi knew who he was and how he was to conduct himself.

Erikson provided a wonderfully rich and critical description of social and political conditions in South Africa at the turn of the century under British rule and a vivid account of Gandhi's transformation. But just when he was about to begin his "real" narrative, Erikson found that he could not continue. He had to suddenly stop his narrative and prepare a twenty-five-page "Personal Word" in the form of a letter to the Mahatma. Addressing the Indian leader two decades after his death, Erikson discussed his inability "to continue writing *this* book because I seemed to sense the presence of a kind of untruth in the very protestation [by Gandhi] of truth; of something unclean when all the words spelled out an unreal purity; and above all, of displaced violence when nonviolence was the professed issue." He criticized the Gandhi he had become acquainted with for professing *Satyagraha,* Truth Force, while being harsh and cruel to those close to him. For Gandhi, rigid adherence to principles had been more important than caring empathy. Specifically, Gandhi had required young girls who admired him to cut off their hair in order to be less alluring to the boys at Tolstoy Farm, a South African communal settlement. In addition, he tried to force literacy upon his wife and to ignore her obvious distress when he required her to discard the waste of a Christian untouchable. When Harilal, his oldest son, wanted to get married, Gandhi repudiated him, and Harilal suffered deeply over his father's rejection. In marked contrast to his mission and his public crusade for *Satyagraha*, Erikson insisted that Gandhi's actions were coarse and arbitrary, wholly insensitive to those closest to him: "You were right wherever you could give to your arbitrary decisions a pervasive meaning enhancing *Satyagraha* and involving others in a clear and self-chosen mutuality, and you were dangerously wrong [as here] where you indulged in perverse arbitrariness." Although Erikson's letter interrupted the flow of his narrative, it was compelling and evocative. When he read it in his undergraduate course, Carol Gilligan (soon to become a leading feminist intellectual) and other students regarded it as the most powerful and thrilling moment of the semester, an unforgettable occurrence in their lives. What motivated Erikson to compose the letter? What made the letter the most arresting and biographically revealing part of *Gandhi's Truth*—the pages that shifted his emphasis from a rich biographical narrative to a personal dialogue with the Mahatma over fundamental issues concerning the human condition?[8]

Unlike *Young Man Luther*, Erikson had not been able to bring *Gandhi's Truth* to a speedy conclusion after a period of intensive writing. Rather, through the winter of 1966–67 and extending into the spring, a man who wrote compulsively, skillfully, fluently, and productively (though never easily) suffered from the most serious writing block of his life. He realized that his subject (perhaps the most generative and caring leader since St. Francis) had a terrible blind spot in his close relationships. Having idealized Gandhi, Erikson was distressed over the recognition that the Mahatma could be cruel, even violent. Erikson felt an "impulsive need to answer him 'in person' before I could go on with my book." As a psychoanalyst, he knew that he could harbor shocking thoughts about his analysand but was not to voice them in the consulting room. And yet he felt "all manner of countertransference" with the Mahatma and desperately needed to address certain issues that might help to relieve his distress.[9]

Kamla Chowdhry, who had done much to facilitate his travels to India, warned Erikson that he had no hard evidence to confirm that Gandhi had verbally abused family members and others close to him. Rather, Erikson had not fully appreciated the circumstances. If Gandhi had, in fact, mistreated others, particularly young girls and women, Chowdhry insisted, this behavior was not unusual for a Hindu man of his caste and class. Her nephew, Sudhir Kakar, got to know Erikson well in the course of his graduate studies at Harvard, and he had been a teaching assistant in the undergraduate course. Indeed, he had become Erikson's trusted adviser on matters of Indian languages and cultures. Kakar realized how troubled Erikson was over Gandhi's aggressive behavior, and Erikson confided in Kakar questions that pressed on him. Was his evidence correct? Was Gandhi's conduct toward others a universal form of aggression or was it specific to Hindu culture? Should he even be writing a book about India? Hoping to provide Erikson some peace of mind, Kakar urged him to write a letter to Gandhi, stating quite bluntly the nature of his turmoil.[10]

There were nineteenth-century precedents for writing public letters to the deceased. Even as they ceased to be literary conventions in the twentieth century, they reappeared from time to time, as in Saul Bellow's *Herzog*. But philosopher Martin Buber's 1939 "Letter to Gandhi" may have offered the most pertinent precedent. Erikson had often placed Buber alongside Kierkegaard and Tillich when considering a spiritualized psychodynamic of the self and the other, "I" and "Thou." In his letter, Buber responded to a two-point statement issued by Gandhi late in 1938: (1) Jews in Germany should deploy *Satyagraha* against Nazi atrocities; (2) Zionists and other Jewish settlers in Palestine had to redress the injustices they had inflicted upon the Arabs, whose land they occupied. Writing a rebuttal from Jerusalem, Buber insisted that *Satyagraha* was ineffectual against the Nazi killing machine, and that Palestine had become an indispensable "home centre" to the dispersed Jewish population. Buber's letter concluded with respect for the goals of *Satyagraha* and Truth that Gandhi (who could find a basis for combat) must have respected and even partly embraced:

> I do not want force. But if there is no other way of preventing the evil destroying the good, I trust I shall use force and give myself up into God's hands. . . . If I am to confess what is truth in me, I must say: There is nothing better for a man than to deal justly—unless it be to love; we should be able even to fight for justice—but to fight lovingly.

Buber admitted that painful weeks had passed as he reflected on the Mahatma's initial statement and feared that it would be a "grievous error" for him to reply. Only after powerful promptings from "friends and my own conscience" did he do so.[11]

Erikson was neither a passionate nor a systematic reader, and he never mastered the large body of Buber's writing. But it is almost inconceivable that he was unfamiliar with Buber's "Letter to Gandhi." He might have learned about it initially during his work with the OSS on Hitler's appeal to German youth. Several of the philosophers, theologians, and intellectuals he had met since (Tillich and Lifton, for example) had read Buber's "Letter." Some must have mentioned it to him when they learned about his research on Gandhi. Buber's writings were exceedingly popular on college campuses during the 1960s, and any of Erikson's many students may have reminded him about the "Letter." When he visited Israel to see his mother and younger sister, to give presentations, and to discuss Gandhi, many people that he met had read Buber, and the "Letter" could have been mentioned.[12]

As he drafted his own letter to Gandhi, Erikson was preoccupied with Gandhi's aggressive behavior toward others, especially women. Gandhi's violence shocked him. Moreover, the contradiction between the Mahatma's benevolent demeanor and his conduct had touched on difficult aspects of Erikson's own past. There was the talented biological father whom he continued to honor and to pursue but who had abandoned him, the "wonderful" mother and stepfather who had lied to him about his paternity, and his own flawed efforts to do "right" during the painful family crisis over Neil's birth.

At a *Daedalus* symposium in 1967, Erikson described how Gandhi at sixteen satisfied a desire for intercourse with his pregnant wife while his father was dying elsewhere in the house. His callousness had been unconscionable. Gandhi was never able "to efface or to forget" that tainted Oedipal occurrence in which he had shown contempt for his father. Nor could Gandhi ever forget that his wife subsequently aborted the baby she was carrying. Erikson borrowed from Kierkegaard here in claiming that sexual intercourse while his father died had produced "the Curse" on Gandhi's life. It compared to the "Curses" that dogged the lives of "comparable innovators with similar relentless consciences." Erikson had also experienced his share of "Curses," which often also involved relationships between fathers and sons.[13]

The completion of the letter to Gandhi had a salutary effect. Erikson's writing block soon disappeared, and he finished *Gandhi's Truth*. At Robert Lifton's annual Wellfleet gathering in the summer of 1967, Erikson read a draft of his letter to Gandhi. Lifton found it a remarkable document, but also felt that it was incongruous with the rest of Erikson's manuscript. Most of the others at Wellfleet agreed with Lifton. So did most friends with whom Erikson shared the letter, including Henry Murray. Erikson persisted doggedly with the letter, however, and would not place it as an epilogue or as an appendix essay. He realized, as others did not, that it was transforming his book from a conventional narrative into a personal and intellectual exploration of pressing issues. Joan understood; the letter marked the point at which the book came to emphasize Erik's Truth.[14]

Erikson's "A Personal Word" appeared under the title "Letter to Gandhi" in the *New York Review of Books* in 1969 almost simultaneously with the publication of *Gandhi's Truth*. The letter attracted much attention and probably motivated some readers to take up the entire book. But the essay could stand on its own. With sharpness and vigor, it registered some of the ethical and psychological concerns that Erikson discussed elsewhere in his volume. Above all, Erikson maintained throughout the letter that the emotional violence Gandhi had inflicted on people close to him was as serious as physical violence. The "mere avoidance of physical cruelty" was not enough to meet the requirements of *Satyagraha*. Gandhi had treated "those closest to you [him] as possessions and whipping posts." He had especially done violence by his "unilateral coercion or threat" against children when he forced "on them decisions for which they are not ready." The human psyche contained conflicting or divided elements; coercive child rearing exacerbated those divided functions by setting "one part of him [the child] against another." When adults agitated the divided functions within children and refused to accept their own grown-up feelings of ambivalence, they promoted the spirit of violence. Gandhi had done just that.[15]

Erikson advocated "mutuality" as an alternative to violence in all its forms. "Mutuality" spoke to empathy, understanding, and connectedness between people. It permitted action with the willing consent of the affected other and did not tolerate "unilateral coercion or threat." Gandhi was wrong to equate sexual relations with violence and to embrace abstinence, Erikson charged. Although "taking sexual possession" of another was violence, "mutual consent and artful interplay" in sex and all else in human relations were not. By seeking to maximize "mutuality" and to minimize coercion, one gradually succeeded in *Satyagraha* or the "experiment in truth." It was an evolving process in which one participated in relative degrees, never absolutely or irrevocably. It was what "I, as a post-Einsteinian and post-Freudian[,] call the *relativity of truth,*" and it was most consequential in "the meeting of adult and child."[16]

Clearly, Erikson's preoccupation with intergenerational relationships had become vital in his letter to Gandhi, and mutuality became indispensable to the spirit of *Satyagraha* and Truth. Erikson ended his letter "more truthfully." Having "told you all this" (about Gandhi's violence), he could "conclude with abiding and affectionate respect" and "now simply narrate . . . the years of ascendance to the job of prophet of his own country." Erikson, the Dane-German-American, had arrived at a profound level of empathy and understanding for a leader whose people were oppressed by Western imperialists. Toward the end of *Gandhi's Truth,* he emphasized that Gandhi's successes in India, starting at Ahmadabad, all came because he had "listened to [an] inner voice, heard the clamor of the people." Unlike Freud's vision of the leader who stood above and apart from society, Erikson's Gandhi belonged to society. Erikson speculated here, boldly, personally, and empathically: "It may be just this alliance of inner voice and voice of mankind which must make such a man at times insensitive to those closest to him by familial bond."[17]

GLOBAL PROPHECIES

Erikson's letter to Gandhi addressed universal issues, but it was also a remarkable cross-cultural discussion between West and East. The balance of *Gandhi's Truth* narrated "the Event" and its aftermath. While set in India, the core issues in Erikson's narrative perpetuated the tension between cultural particulars and human universals. In this sense, Erikson's letter did not interrupt or separate the two parts of his book ("the Past" and "the Event") so much as it illuminated his essential concerns. Indeed, Erikson's narrative of the Ahmadabad strike and the subsequent developments was not a continuous story but a series of expositions on four fundamental if overlapping issues that he needed to take up with Gandhi. In this sense, Erikson's letter to Gandhi became the organizational center of his book. The process of composing the letter made it clear to him, so that he could make clear to his readers, that the issues discussed were far more important than the story line.

The story line was straightforward. Erikson portrayed Ahmadabad as a plague-infested city of textile mills where the elite prospered while workers and their families suffered. Early in the strike, Gandhi allied with Anasuya Sarabhai and the mill workers in their demands for a 50 percent wage increase, better living conditions, and improved education for their children. Gandhi persuaded them to reduce their salary demands to a 35 percent increase, which he felt the mill owners could afford and which represented a gesture of conciliation. All the while, Gandhi maintained open communication with Ambalal Sarabhai and the other mill owners, who made a counteroffer of a 20 percent wage increase. Erikson analyzed the leaflets that Gandhi distributed to the workers to acquaint them with national and global labor inequities. In the end, Gandhi's prolonged period of fasting proved decisive. Not wanting his death on their hands, the mill owners acceded to the conditions Gandhi set forth when the strike began. But he was not overjoyed by the victory; he had much more work. The Mahatma left Ahmadabad for nearby Kheda to help suffering peasants and then to other locations as he built mass support for the liberation of India. Erikson's primary concern, as his narrative advanced, was not the historical detail but the importance of elaborating his four fundamental issues.

Throughout *Gandhi's Truth,* but especially in the chapters covering Gandhi's India campaigns, Erikson was preoccupied with one of the four issues: the connection between his purportedly universal eight-stage life cycle and the Hindu view of the life cycle. This was a troublesome task. The variables to be reckoned with seemed to multiply as the years passed and hardly ceased after *Gandhi's Truth* went to press. The Hindu theory of *asrama* (stages of life) had developed between the sixth and third centuries before Christ. Initially, Erikson felt that it approximated his own framework, for it viewed human development in terms of distinct stages of life; each individual life cycle registered wholeness and each was cast within a sequence of generations. However, whereas Erikson's life cycle model centered on early childhood and was rooted in Freud's oral, anal, and phallic phases, the Hindu cycle did not. Instead, the Hindu cycle was anchored in a succession of previous lives. Erikson's model was clinical. While it was decidedly value laden, it purported to be *real* and to describe *what is.* In contrast, the Hindu perspective was *ideal* and was directed toward *what should be.* Whereas Erikson's model included eight stages, he felt that the Hindu life cycle essentially addressed three: *Antevasin* (youthful apprenticeship), *Grhastha* (householder, generativity), and *Vanaprastha* (inner separation from all ties of selfhood, communality, and body-boundedness).[18]

The year before *Gandhi's Truth* went to press, Sudhir Kakar, working assiduously to reconcile Erikson's model with the "Hindu Scheme," managed to chart the Hindu equivalent of Erikson's eight stages. By his own acknowledgment, the effort proved highly problematic because stages seemed to differ in their timing, their intensity, and even their content. The first three Erikson stages (infancy and trust, early childhood and autonomy, play age and initiative) had no Hindu equivalent save for the individual's "prehistory." The concept of industry in stage four, school age, had to be collapsed into Erikson's crucial stage five of adolescent identity crisis to find a very rough equivalent in *brahmacharya,* or apprenticeship. Intimacy-isolation of young adulthood (stage six) bore some proximity to *Gårhasthya,* or the Householder. Kakar's effort to equate adult generativity (stage seven) with *Vånaprastha* (withdrawal) and old-age integrity-despair (stage eight) with *Såmyasa* was inconclusive.[19]

As Kakar talked with Erikson about problems in reconciling the two characterizations of the life cycle, he sensed that Erikson's priorities were changing; he was less interested in adolescent identity and more concerned with midlife and beyond. Indeed, Erikson appeared more than willing to accommodate the Hindu disinterest in matters of youthful identity in order to explore the Hindu emphasis on the last half of life. After all, he had rushed through Gandhi's early years in order to focus upon the older, more seasoned leader. For a psychoanalyst schooled in Freud's Vienna on the primacy of early development, this was a very consequential decision.

Kakar recalled that Erikson shifted his focus as he discovered that the striving for initiative, autonomy, and identity (all central to Western childhood) was not nearly as important in Indian childhood. Indian children were taught to remain dependent on parents and family; interdependence and hierarchy were central to their early years. Kakar also recognized that Erikson's concentration on adulthood corresponded with his growing awareness of his own old age. In the course of the 1960s, Erikson had been especially attentive to fleshing out the seventh or generativity stage. Unlike Kakar, he did not connect generativity with withdrawal but with the Householder. Erikson felt the Hindu image of the Householder began with "love in mutuality" (stage-six intimacy) but found fruition and meaning in *caretaking*—parenting children, making goods and ideas, helping the needy—the "ability to *take care*" wherever life required. A Householder engaged in "maintenance of the world" by caring for the generations before and after him. Postulating that the Householder was a caregiver, Erikson asked Kakar for Hindu terms corresponding with "care" in the generational life cycle. Kakar offered *Dama* (restraint), *Dana* (charity), and *Daya* (compassion), which Erikson took to mean "to be careful," "to take care of," and "to care for." He was struggling here to give meaning to *Satyagraha* as Gandhi, now middle aged, invoked it during "the Event" and after. *Satyagraha*—"perseverance in truth"—was Gandhi's supreme "gift of giving and accepting actuality." *Satyagraha* corresponded with the emergence of a flesh-and-blood caregiver for others. The Mahatma's very existence and Truth Force rested within the other for whom he cared.[20]

Erikson was settling for his own idiosyncratic connection between generativity and the Householder because that was crucial to his discussion of Gandhi. He went beyond Kakar's admittedly flawed chart here comparing his life cycle with the Hindu cycle, but he left the remainder of the chart in place. In the end, Erikson simply concluded that it was "impossible to [adequately] compare these schemes point by point." What mattered was the epigenetic principle "which makes them comparable at all." This principle postulated that "in each stage of life a given strength is added to a widening ensemble and reintegrated at each later stage in order to play its part in a full cycle—if and where fate and society permit." Erikson had not, of course, actually made a case for such a principle within the Hindu life cycle, and he had already conceded that the dynamics of Hindu childhood and youth were quite unlike those of Western youngsters. Essentially, he was postulating a universality to his eight-stage cycle and hoping for the best.[21]

The basis for Erikson's hope that the two life cycles could be reconciled was his assumption that they connected to powerful, pervasive, and *equivalent* idea systems—psychoanalysis and *Satyagraha*. Equivalency represented the second fundamental issue that Erikson addressed, especially within his narration of "the Event." Erikson's accumulating reservations about psychoanalytic orthodoxies, with their constrictive effect on his explorations, were relevant here. The task of connecting psychoanalysis with *Satyagraha*, Freud with Gandhi, precluded narrow construction and use of the doctrines of the

Vienna founder. Erikson refused, for example, to demand that "the nonsexual always symbolized the sexual." When Gandhi protested the British tax on salt by refusing to use the substance, the context of protest made it abundantly clear that "salt means salt" and not semen. Similarly, Erikson felt free to substitute "mutuality" for Freudian "genitality" whenever it seemed appropriate. "Instinct" in its narrow biological sense "has become an embarrassing term," Erikson charged. The concept was useful only to capture "the energetic and the driven aspect of man's behavior." He regretted that he had "never learned in Vienna" what Joan's approach to St. Francis made abundantly clear, that "there's a deep mythical person in us," a very special "sense of being related to a fate, which makes you a very special person."[22]

The tendency of psychoanalytic orthodoxy to focus on a person's deficiencies rather than his strengths became the primary obstacle to linking Freud's perspectives to *Satyagraha*. It was necessary "to proceed from the case history to the life history, from the symptoms of human conflict to the signs of human strength, from man's adaptive and defensive maneuvers to his generative potentialities." This was why "I consider any attempt to reduce a leader of Gandhi's stature to earlier as well as bigger and better childhood traumata both wrong in method and evil in influence." Erikson did not, for example, dwell on Gandhi's "obsessive symptomatology" where his "dispositions and preoccupations help to release a new energy capable of awakening corresponding energy in others." Instead, he described a more general process of connectedness between leader and followers through "creative ritualization."[23]

Because of his insistence on a broad definition of Freud's legacy and his attention to the creative strengths of a man like Gandhi, Erikson felt confident in equating the Mahatma's *Satyagraha* or "perseverance in truth" with psychoanalysis. The two were "joined in a universal 'therapeutics,' committed to the Hippocratic principle that one can test truth . . . only by action which avoids harm—or better, by action which maximizes mutuality and minimizes the violence caused by unilateral coercion or threat." More specifically, *Satyagraha,* like psychoanalysis, "confronts the *inner* enemy nonviolently." Both revealed "the poisonous pollution of man's inner motivations and the abysmal self-deceit and destructiveness" within. Thus, each was an "instrument of enlightenment." As Freud and Gandhi engaged in self-analysis and became enlightened about their own motives and hidden demons, they created a perspective that enlightened humankind. Thus, psychoanalysis produced a "*truth method,* with all the implications which the word has in *Satyagraha.*" Both were at once "encounters" within the self and between the self and the other, and both involved "militant probing of a vital issue by a nonviolent confrontation" rather than repressive "moral suppression." To be sure, the method both used was "disciplined self-suffering" while exploring the inner self. The result was a therapeutic transformation "where man learns to be nonviolent toward himself as well as toward others." Whether one called it psychoanalytic insight or "truth in action," the outcome was successful when a person acquired the capacity "not only to think clearly" about himself but also to enter into "an optimum of mutual activation with others."[24]

By arguing forcefully and repeatedly in *Gandhi's Truth* for the essential convergence of *Satyagraha* and psychoanalysis in a "universal 'therapeutics,'" Erikson broadened his portrayal of both. *Satyagraha* stood not only for "perseverance in truth" but for other vintage Erikson notions—mutuality, actuality, and relativity. The Truth-seeker connected to others by giving and in actuality, yet one person's perspective or gift was not to be imposed on another. Similarly, Erikson discarded the constrictive psychoanalytic practices to which he objected. His portrayal of young Gandhi addressed serious inner conflicts, to be sure, but not as extensively as he had addressed them in young Luther. In his focus on Gandhi's middle years, Erikson did not elaborate neurotic conflicts or note Gandhi's debilitating psychic tensions. Indeed, he did not really discuss Gandhi's ego crises (as he had Luther's). Instead, he characterized an ego that could accommodate experiences of the self in the realm of value and spirit. By giving broad new shape to Gandhi's Truth, he was articulating his own. As Erikson worked on the convergence of *Satyagraha* and psychoanalysis in a Truth uniting East and West, his tone was prophetic.[25]

Critics have belittled this convergence. Some have emphasized that the Western psychoanalytic perspective was rooted in the experience of children being reared by their primary caretakers (mother, parents), while in India the Hindu mother encouraged her child to accept supplemental mothers and involvement in an extended family. Certainly, Erikson discounted important cultural distinctions such as this as he equated psychoanalysis with *Satyagraha*. Embracing a prophetic role, he was indisposed to close comparative analysis. The closer *Gandhi's Truth* came to completion, the more Erikson strained to see himself on a mission to save humankind from itself.

His concept of "pseudospeciation" testified to this perspective and became the third fundamental issue he addressed. At a Royal Society of London meeting in 1966, Erikson had spoken of man's "pseudospecies" mentality. Intrigued by Erikson's concept, the renowned biological thinker Konrad Lorenz suggested "pseudospeciation" as a modest descriptive modification. Unaware that Lorenz had once found a certain appeal in Nazism, Erikson appeared delighted and chose to develop the concept of pseudospeciation in *Gandhi's Truth*. He characterized the concept as a deeply rooted propensity in relatively homogeneous groups to deny the fact that humankind is "obviously one species." People seemed disposed to irrationality by ignoring this fact. They preferred to "split up into groups (from tribes to nations, from castes to classes, from religions to ideologies) which provide their members with a firm sense of distinct and superior identity— and immorality." A pseudospecies invented for itself a special "place and a moment in the very centre of the universe" and looked upon itself as "superior to all others, the mere mortals." "Pseudospeciation" tended to harden "mutual differentiations" among groups "into dogmas and isms which combine larger and larger human communities into power spheres" of exclusiveness that simply became new "examples of a *pseudospecies.*"[26]

Much as Erikson, the clinician, accented psychic strengths over disabilities, he heralded "universal specieshood" over "pseudospeciation." Congruent with Wendell Willkie's *One World* (1943) and Edward Steichen's *The Family of Man* photography exhibit during the mid-1950s at the Museum of Modern Art in New York, Erikson embraced a universal cosmopolitan perspective, traced to the Enlightenment, which held that particularistic loyalties were irrational and had to be countered by reformist pedagogy. Through *Satyagraha,* Erikson asserted, Gandhi had succeeded in reconciling brother and sister Sarabhai, mill owner and workers. Gandhi's settlement of the strike enriched and dignified all contesting parties by appealing to their common humanity. The Mahatma proceeded to build on this achievement and free his country by reconciling the British authorities to the idea of Indian independence. In this way, Erikson insisted, Gandhi "*may have* created a ritualization through which men . . . can face each other with a mutual confidence analogous to the instinctive safety built into animals' pacific rituals." Gandhi equated this mutuality with the Hindu *dharma,* which connected self with society for the "maintenance of the world." Erikson portrayed Gandhi's method as a ritualized process by which a man "actualizes both in himself and in the other such forces as are ready for a heightened mutuality." Two antagonistic "pseudospecies" thereby "join their identities in such a way that new potentialities are activated in both." Erikson hoped that a world recovering from the Holocaust and immersed in Cold War confrontations in which nuclear weapons were brandished would heed Gandhi's example of a new universal ethics: "For all parts of the world, the struggle now is for the *anticipatory development of more inclusive identities*" and ultimately the recognition of "universal specieshood." Modern technology had built weapons for "pseudospecies" warfare, but technology could also be used to enhance communication and understanding "in a sense of widening identity which helps to overcome economic fear, the anxiety of cultural change, and the dread of a spiritual vacuum."[27]

While Erikson, aided by Lorenz's suggestion, used the terms *pseudospeci-ation* and *universal specieshood,* the concepts behind the terms had been around for a long time. For example, "pseudospeciation" connected to the German romantic movement of the late eighteenth and early nineteenth centuries, with its emphasis on the special genius of the German *Volk*. In contrast, the civic nationalism of the American and French revolutions was congruent with "universal specieshood" in the sense that the national com-munity welcomed all residents as equal citizens united in mutual respect. In some sense, Goethe's view of *Weltliteratur* and the need for mutual tolera-tion and borrowing among diverse nations also suggested "universal species-hood." When W. E. B. Du Bois, the great African-American leader and intellectual, postulated in his 1903 classic *The Souls of Black Folk* that the "problem of the twentieth century is the problem of the color line," he was predicting that the major conflicts ahead would be rooted in allegedly per-manent group characteristics like race, ethnicity, and nationality. With the courageous anthropologist Franz Boas, DuBois had led a frontal assault dur-ing the interwar period against the racist theorizing that had postulated this permanent distinctiveness. By mid-century, intellectuals and researchers like Gunnar Myrdal, the well-known Swedish economist and principal author of *An American Dilemma,* and Columbia University social psychologist Otto Klineberg, who published the classic study *Race Differences,* were working assiduously to connect the concept of specieswide commonality to Enlight-enment notions of knowledge and rights. They felt threatened by the resur-gent popularity of nationalist chauvinism and religious and racial bigotry.[28]

Like Myrdal's and Klineberg's works, *Childhood and Society* had railed against contrived particularisms. As Erikson developed his perspectives on the "identity crisis," which he postulated as universal, he also came to acknowledge the importance of "contending and even conflicting identity elements." "Wholeness and Totality," his paper for a 1953 conference of the American Academy of Arts and Sciences, advocated the acceptance of humankind without totalistic, exclusionary borders such as those espoused by the Nazis. But it was only after Erikson had begun his book on Gandhi and *Satyagraha* that he became deeply committed to the idea of transcend-ing "pseudospeciation" and pursuing a pervasive sense of "universal species-hood." Working closely with Erikson on all phases of the book, Pamela Daniels sensed that he felt a special calling to propound "universal species-hood." While not disputing Daniels's observation, John Ross, Erikson's Harvard student and friend at the time, cautioned her not to overlook Erik-son's special sensitivity during the early 1960s, after the death of his mother, to the conflicting elements in his own religious and national identity. Was he Jew or Gentile, and was he Danish or German or American? Erikson's sympathy with the American civil rights movement was also relevant. So was his early abhorrence of an American military presence in Vietnam, which he feared could lead to a global nuclear war. Clearly, there were multiple sources for Erikson's preoccupation with the dangers of "pseudospeciation." Still, it is noteworthy that as early as the spring of 1964, before these sources had all come fully into play, he had lectured at Harvard's Appleton Chapel on how Gandhi's "perseverance in truth" had brought lasting "industrial peace" between workers and mill owners in Ahmadabad. It had also "led to unheard-of efforts of actual tolerance and social welfare." Emphasizing the accomplishment of Gandhi's prophetic Truth at this early date, Erikson had launched himself on a crucial mission to reveal that Truth to the dangerous world of the late twentieth century.[29]

Erikson's appeal to revive *Satyagraha* and to recognize "universal species-hood" had grounding in evolutionary biology. If Lorenz had modestly helped him to coin the antithetical term *pseudospeciation*, another prominent biologist who spoke out on matters of race, ecology, and evolution, Stephen Jay Gould, agreed with Erikson that "pseudospeciation" was not an inborn disposition of humankind. The genetic distinctions among racial groups were demonstrably trivial, Gould asserted. Acceptance of Erikson's view that "we are truly one biological species" was proper, Gould held, because the human was a large-brained neotenic primate and had the ability to overcome long-standing cultural habits of "pseudospeciation."[30]

Over the years, Erikson came to increasingly rely on these and other scientists investigating biological evolution. His emphasis in *Gandhi's Truth* (especially in the narrative that followed his "Personal Word"), however, was for a new international politics that would encourage "universal species-hood." In this regard, and through his coverage of "the Event" of 1918, Erikson spoke quite directly to the fourth of his fundamental issues: the efficacy of a spiritual kind of political leadership. He sought to demonstrate that Gandhi exemplified a special type of political leader—a "religious actualist"—who could unite opposing groups, teaching them in the process the advantages of *Satyagraha*. Gandhi had demonstrated a new integration of ethical and political identity—for India and for the planet.

For Erikson, Gandhi was a new type of world leader who, through his success at Ahmadabad, contrasted with more traditional political leaders who promoted a "war to end war," who failed to achieve peace at Versailles, and who (in the Russian context) conducted a reign of terror that was to "initiate an eventual 'withering away of the State.' " Rejecting formulas that justified bloodshed and violence, Gandhi had "confronted the world with the strong suggestion that a new political instrument, endowed with a new kind of religious fervor, may yet provide man with a choice." Unlike Wilson,

Clemenceau, or Lenin, Gandhi had decided in Ahmadabad against "recip-rocal coercion," opting instead for a settlement providing "an opportunity for all—the workers, the owners, and himself—'to rise from the present condi-tion.' " Gandhi's terms were for a new type of *"justice which does not harm either party to a dispute."* Unlike Versailles or revolutionary Russia, none had suffered "economic disadvantage, social indignity, loss of self-esteem, and latent vengeance." Gandhi had practiced an ethical leadership that translated "age old spiritual insights into political action." He had adhered zealously to "rock-bottom principles" of ethics and spirituality, especially the Golden Rule. Having this firm grounding in the ethical and the "saintly," Gandhi embraced the politician's "crafty and cunning" qualities of bargaining and compromise without "seeing any contradiction between these qualities"; he merged the traditional division between the spiritual and the political. Then he immersed himself in Truth-pursuing action in the here and now—an "actualism" fitting a context of specific historical circumstances. He operated in the political arena while remaining attuned to an "inner voice."[31]

Erikson not only admired Gandhi's new style of political leadership, but identified with it, almost as if he were a Gandhi apostle. "Gandhi would study the evil to be attacked most searchingly; he would shrewdly choose the time and place for the attack," and announce his intentions to his oppo-nents. Then he would "persist relentlessly" through *"engagement at close range"* in a way that involved "the meeting of bodies; the facing of the oppo-nent 'eye to eye,' the linking of arms in defensive and advancing phalanxes, the body 'on the line.' " Erikson characterized this "solidarity of unarmed bodies" pursuing a solution beneficial to all as a powerful "leverage" even against "the cold and mechanized gadgetry of the modern state." This soli-darity gave *"the opponent the courage to change* even as the challenger remained ready to change with the events."[32]

Embracing Gandhi's politics, Erikson emphasized that his active "perse-verance in truth" was not tantamount to passive resistance. Rather, Gandhi's method required great effort in learning to "discipline rage" in the interests of "true self-control"—that is, only "a very self-disciplined use of force can lead to disciplined nonviolence." To acquire this self-discipline, Gandhi canceled *Satyagraha* campaigns where they yielded to rioting. His followers had to become masters in their use of force. Next, they had to show their country-men how to participate in the organized military defense of the British Empire so as to master "the virtues of disciplined violence." Only with this new sense of discipline could *Satyagraha* be reestablished. Interpreting the Mahatma's strategy in this way, Erikson probably agreed with Buber's asser-tion in his "Letter to Gandhi" that German Jews were not ready for *Satya-graha* against the Nazi war machine; they had first to "fight for justice—but to fight lovingly." Indeed, Erikson was so intent on the point that he blundered toward the conclusion of his narrative of "the Event." Without qualification or substantiation, he asserted that anti-Semitism had been augmented by the historic incapacity of Jews to fight in their own self-defense. The belated demonstration by "Israeli soldiery" that "Jews *could* fight a national war" partially addressed the disability of "the Jews of the diaspora." Through their "superb" mastery of "military methods" against Arabs, the Israelis helped to "make peace-loving Jews everywhere better potential *Satyagrahis.*" This was a problematic appraisal of Israeli military ventures in the Middle East and a stereotypically upbeat view of world Jewry. Certainly this appraisal clashed with Erikson's broad sympathy, evident throughout *Gandhi's Truth,* with the struggle of third-world peoples against Western imperialism.[33]

The very process of characterizing Gandhi's politics of spirituality and actualism emboldened Erikson, and he seemed to want to test this new persona and method in the rough-and-tumble of backroom political decision making. The June 1969 dinner at the Nixon White House was only a start. A more fruitful opportunity presented itself a month later, just as W. W. Norton was moving *Gandhi's Truth* into production. New York City mayor John Lindsay's human resources director Mitchell Ginsberg had convened a group of specialists and theorists in urban policy and administration during a difficult point in the city's history, for the Vietnam War had drained significant federal dollars away from urban projects. The group met over several months and was to report back to the mayor on ways to enhance New York's massive, often poorly coordinated and underfunded array of social services. Participants included community action commissioner Major Owens, New York University social work professor Alvin Shorr, Harold Pinckney of the Bronx Model Cities Policy Committee, Michael Sovern of Columbia Law School, and Lindsay's hands-on special counsel Norman Redlich. Ginsberg invited Erikson to join the group as a consultant. He accepted and invited Harland Bloland, his son-in-law, to accompany him. With Gandhi's mix of ethics and political craftsmanship as his obvious point of departure, Erikson carried on enthusiastically even though he had no technical knowledge or experience in urban planning. In a decidedly spiritual manner, replete with his well-worn formulations, he admonished the specialists that a New York City services administrator had to commit himself to enhancing the lives of "those left out"—the economically and socially disadvantaged. In doing so, both the administrator and the disadvantaged would be inclined "to make a personal issue out of something that is not personal"; the administrator and not his policies would be judged trustworthy or lacking. Serving in "a conscientious, self-aware, directed kind of way," the administrator had to connect his own evolving life cycle to the life cycles of those he assisted much as Gandhi had during "the Event." Erikson insisted that by helping needy clients, the local administrator enhanced his own sense of being. Above all, Erikson admonished, a city services administrator had to persevere in a spirit and Truth that enriched the physical and spiritual welfare and trust of the needy and the dispossessed.[34]

Erikson's tone and themes during these New York meetings, beginning in mid-summer 1969, suggest that he had internalized the Mahatma's politics of *Satyagraha*. Indeed, Erikson had confessed to his students and various audiences that he had essentially become Gandhi's messenger to the late twentieth century. "When I came to Ahmadabad," he told a *Daedalus* symposium on leadership, "it had become clear to me that man as a species cannot afford any more to cultivate illusions" of the superiority of a "pseudospecies" over its enemies in a world with "arsenals capable of global destruction." He recognized that only Gandhi "had visualized *and* demonstrated an over-all alternative" to weaponry through *Satyagraha,* and he was publicizing that alternative. Erikson corrected Tagore for characterizing an invitation to Gandhi from the viceroy to meet in May of 1930 on the future of British rule in India as a sign that Asia had started to look down on, rather than up to, Europe. "Gandhi, as I read him, might have said it differently," Erikson insisted, offering his own take on the transition away from Western colonialism: "Asia could now look Europe in the eye—not more, not less, not up to, not down on. Where man can and will do that, there sooner or later will be mutual recognition." Erikson was regarding himself as the guardian of Gandhi's words—and his message. In a 1964 essay for *Daedalus,* titled "The Inner and the Outer Space," he had characterized women (quite problematically) as agents of human connectedness and caregiving. He had argued that with an infusion of these qualities and a decided female presence, governments would function better. This perspective deepened as Erikson recognized that Gandhi seemed to draw on the "inner space" qualities within himself that were rooted in "his relation to his mother." The qualities also derived from what Erikson judged to be a feminine Indian culture. (He did not dwell on the harsh ways women were treated within that culture.) Like none before him, Erikson insisted, Gandhi was able "to unite the feminine and the masculine aspects of religiosity." The confluence of Gandhi's Truth Force and Erikson's was no more apparent than during a lecture to his Harvard undergraduates explaining why he had to complete his work. The fate of humankind would be determined, he told them, by two fundamental but contrasting third-world perspectives. Against Frantz Fanon's prescription of violence to resurrect the degraded self, he served as messenger for Gandhi's *Satyagraha.*[35]

It would have been exceedingly helpful and appropriate if Erikson had discussed the evolution of the American civil rights movement at this juncture. Given the strong civil rights advocates among his friends, including Robert Coles, Benjamin Spock, and Robert Lifton, he was almost certainly urged to connect this movement to Gandhi and *Satyagraha*. As he lectured and wrote on Gandhi, the movement was shifting tactically and ideologically from the nonviolent resistance of Martin Luther King, Jr., toward varieties of black nationalism, some of which exalted Fanon and sanctioned violence. This shift in focus worried Erikson. Following King's death, he decided to dedicate *Gandhi's Truth* to King's memory. But he neglected to develop the obvious parallels between Gandhi and King. Both came from privileged backgrounds, for example, and it took the brutalities of racism to force them to recognize their outcast status. Gandhi's *Satyagraha* approximated but was by no means identical to King's "militant nonviolence." After both leaders were assassinated, they became symbols of justice and hope in their respective nations. Such comparisons could hardly be discussed in the two sentences Erikson allocated to King. Erikson seemed so preoccupied with broad global principles that he failed to address the obvious focus of many of his American readers on Freedom Riders, "Mississippi Summer," the Student Nonviolent Coordinating Committee, Malcolm X, and black power. With only modest effort on Erikson's part, *Gandhi's Truth* could have been a primary document for the second Reconstruction era in American history as well as a commentary on universal human rights.

Through his elaboration of Gandhi's spiritualized politics during the strike, Erikson appeared to be drawing into himself some of the very doctrinal and leadership qualities that he described. This propensity to invoke and absorb vital aspects of the Indian leader was most apparent when he emphasized Gandhi's most striking quality—his personage. Erikson came increasingly to internalize Gandhi's presence. He "wanted to get closer to what religious genius is" through a very personal "search for Gandhi's presence." "I have been trying to visualize him and to 'hear' him," Erikson acknowledged. Once this was accomplished, once Gandhi's presence was fully absorbed, Erikson felt obligated to somehow radiate it and offer it to his students, his colleagues, and his readers.[36]

This presence that Erikson fixed upon was of "a man who, while small and ascetic, was of infectious agility and energy, totally serious and yet of a pervasive gaiety, always himself and yet attuned to each counterplayer, and most of all utterly and always *there*." One of the parts of being "*there*" that most impressed Erikson was Gandhi's "feminine imagery." He "prided himself on being half man and half woman" and appeared "more motherly than women born to the job." Erikson was far more intrigued with Gandhi's physical presence than he had been with young Luther's. He was impressed by the Mahatma's toothless smile, his spinning wheel and homespun robes, a kind of asexuality alongside a motherliness, and the simple homilies that he invoked in order to revive the spirits of his followers.[37]

These qualities called to mind another powerful presence that Erikson insisted he felt before *Gandhi's Truth* was formally begun. On the way to India, he and Joan had stopped in Israel and had wandered along the shores of the Sea of Galilee "thinking of Him who had spoken on these shores to the fishermen." During "the silent nights" by the sea, and doubtlessly prompted by what William James called the will to believe, Erik claimed that he and Joan were able "to visualize that presence, which had evoked such elemental forces both for the best and the worst in man." With Jesus and his Galilean ministry deep in their thoughts, the Eriksons continued on to Ahmadabad, where they seemed almost determined to connect Jesus' presence with Gandhi's. There "we encountered the persistent presence of another one of those rarest men who did speak the language of the people and of the spirit in words which moved mountains." With both leaders, there was "as pervasive a presence as only silence has when you listen." Intense desire to join with that presence seemed to be interfering with Erikson's substantial capacity to analyze critically.[38]

Part of Gandhi's Jesus-like presence, Erikson felt, was as a caregiver—a generative man. Gandhi was already middle aged during "the Event." As Erikson shifted between mid- and late life, he empathized with the nurturing requirements of those years. People in midlife—the Mahatma and he himself—had to be clear on "what and whom they have come to care for, what they came to do well, and how they plan to take care of what they have started and created." For Gandhi, the generative obligation was motivated by the Hindu view of "maintenance of the world"—a time when one "*must* forget death for the sake of the newborn individual and the coming generations." This was essentially a midlife version of the Golden Rule, which required one "to enhance the potentials" of others. Special men like Gandhi enjoyed this generative presence even as children, Erikson added, for they "have to become their own fathers and in a way their fathers' fathers while not yet adult." Certainly Erik, the son without the father, who became Erik-*son*, was speaking of men like himself as he described Gandhi's presence.[39]

The element in Gandhi's personality that most captivated Erikson was his craftsmanship. Throughout *Gandhi's Truth*, but especially after Erikson's "Personal Word" to the Mahatma, one finds the image of a "religious craftsman" who "repaired" by caring, teaching, reforming, governing, and otherwise giving to others. Gandhi's success in the Ahmadabad strike was characterized as "a craftsmanlike rehearsal" for the broader campaigns for Indian independence. Joan's decades of involvement in weaving, jewelry making, and other crafts must have also contributed to Erikson's emphasis on craftsmanship. Above all, Erikson was struck by the Mahatma encouraging others to work at the traditional spinning wheel—"an economic necessity, a religious ritual, and a national symbol." In some sense, the crossing and recrossing of threads also appealed to Erikson's pleasure with multiple crossings of all sorts. British rule had undermined artisan crafts generally, the skillful spinning of yarn and handloom weaving of textiles in particular. Yet "the skills necessary to produce excellent things are a prime source of identity." The image of Gandhi sitting by a spinning wheel and championing the handloom represented, therefore, "the symbol of a lost and regained identity." But although the concrete, physical Gandhi was very important to Erikson, there was more to the presence of the Mahatma rallying behind the traditional trades. There was a broader "spinning, praying, and ascetic living according to faith which never left him." Gandhi had struggled "to build a community around the cultivation of spinning and weaving." By doing so in the midst of British imperial rule, the Mahatma became a "crafty politician." To Erikson, this meant that he was more than a calculating, public relations–minded Indian nationalist. Embedding politics in presence, Erikson characterized Gandhi, the textile weaver, as a metaphor for linkage or connectedness, Gandhi "weaving" his actual being to his countrymen, to other generations, to other times and places and cultures, and to *Satyagraha*. The diminutive man who spun thread on a hand-powered wheel was essentially weaving identities, interpersonal connections, and Truth Force.[40]

In a broader sense, then, Erikson heralded Gandhi as a weaver of ideology and as a personality that bound spirituality with secular action. The Mahatma spun and wove together the whole Indian nation with a new image of connectedness and universal humanity. As Erikson described the Indian leader, inseparable from spinning and weaving imagery, and against the backdrop of a textile strike, he was also engaged in a similar task. Erikson was spinning out and weaving together an enormously complex and layered narrative about history, ethics, race, gender, and international relations, among other topics. The final product contained many "loose ends" and stray "threads." But by writing a volume that examined Gandhi's presence and Truth for a wider public, Erikson had added another element to the intergenerational weaving begun when he arrived at Harvard in 1960 to teach young students and to write and think about the intergenerational life cycle. Through his teaching and his writing, and especially through Gandhi, he ended the decade feeling that he had become more than a teacher and an author, that he was something of a prophet as well.

This prophetic quality was certainly detectable toward the end of *Gandhi's Truth* as Erikson shifted from amplifying his four fundamental issues to describing what he referred to vaguely and imprecisely as the sense of "I." The "I" occupied an existential sphere that transcended both the ego and psychosocial development generally. The sense of "I" seemed to occur when Gandhi felt his existential and ethical nothingness before God; it marked his sense of identity with all of humanity—a real yet immortal identity. Gandhi realized "that each of us exists with a unique consciousness and a responsibility of his own which makes him at the same time Zero and everything, a center of absolute silence, and the vortex of apocalyptic participation." Such a sense of "I" represented "a glorious and yet miserably fragile sense of immortal identity, defined status, and collective grandeur." It occurred when Gandhi and humankind "faces the central truth of our own nothingness—and, *mirable dictu,* gain power from it."[41]

When he described this "glorious and yet miserably fragile sense," Erikson was writing of himself: "a man who looks through the historical parade of cultures and civilizations, styles, and isms." He had begun to write about this "parade" in fashioning the experiences, observations, and texts that became *Childhood and Society.* In *Young Man Luther,* he described the young seminarian fashioning an identity that included the "I." In *Gandhi's Truth,* the sense of "I" emerged fuller still, rooted in Erikson's personal presence within the family and location of "the Event." He wrote of the way Gandhi (like "such men as St. Augustine, St. Francis, and Kierkegaard") would "involve the very persons he must depend on in an intimate struggle." In this struggle, a man like Gandhi sought "to wrestle from them [those persons] all possible strengths without losing any of his precious inviolancy." In time, however, a leader like the Mahatma was to "reverse positions and become the giving and judging and, in fact, the *parental agens.*" Once more, Erikson was placing himself alongside Gandhi. Recognizing that much of the third-world anticolonial movement had shifted away from Gandhi's focus on universal rights and toward Gamal Nasser's semi-authoritarian embrace of particular loyalties, Erikson took up Gandhi's torch. "Involved" as he had become with the Mahatma, he identified deeply with Gandhi's "strengths." In conveying Gandhi's presence and *Satyagraha* to the late twentieth century, especially through his "Personal Word," Erikson had partially reversed "positions and become the giving and judging" plus the societal parent. Erik the fatherless son was parenting Gandhi and the Truth Force for an imperiled planet.[42]

THE RECEPTION OF *GANDHI'S TRUTH*

W. W. Norton launched a vigorous advertising campaign to promote *Gandhi's Truth.* George Brockway worked assiduously and successfully to have the volume reviewed in the *New York Times,* the *New York Review of Books,* the *American Scholar,* and *Harper's Magazine,* among other forums for an intelligent general readership. The book won more prestigious awards and acknowledgments than Erikson's previous volumes, including the Pulitzer Prize in general nonfiction and the National Book Award in philosophy and religion. *Gandhi's Truth* also garnered the Frederick G. Melcher Award of the Unitarian Universalist Association for "the most significant contribution to religious liberalism." The *New York Times Book Review* listed it among "Twelve Books of Uncommon Excellence" for 1969. By early 1971, a German edition was in print while Japanese, French, Swedish, and Spanish editions were being prepared.[43]

However, sales for *Gandhi's Truth* disappointed the publisher. Hardcover sales approximated 18,000 the first year, but then fell steeply because Erikson insisted that Norton bring out a college paperback edition for classroom adoptions. Paperback sales peaked at roughly 37,400 for the 1970–71 academic year, equaling *Childhood and Society,* but dropped by more than 60 percent the second year and declined to less than 3,100 by 1975–76. In London, Faber and Faber published a special British edition that stayed in print for a few years but sold less than 4,000 copies in all. The Richard Attenborough film on Gandhi later provoked modest resurgence in paperback sales. Norton reported about 10,700 paperbacks sold in 1983–84, only to dive to the 3,000 to 5,000 range in subsequent years. Erikson's editors at Norton attributed the disappointing sales history to paltry American interest in India, a nation that received minimal attention in the undergraduate curriculum. They also worried because the book was vague, multilayered, and unfocused; faculties seemed reluctant to compel their students to master 448 pages of text that lacked a sharp unifying thesis.[44]

Erikson was not as disappointed by the sales figures. Purchase of his books had depended heavily on college course adoptions; he had never appealed to a large general readership like Norton author and psychologist Rollo May. Important intellectuals tended to read and discuss his books, and that was satisfying. Moreover, he sometimes regarded the sales record as secondary to the attention he enjoyed at award ceremonies honoring other renowned writers. While he had mixed feelings over a congratulatory note from President Nixon, he was anxious about the reviews that would soon appear in print. Indeed, he awaited those reviews "with considerable trepidation." "I do not really know India well enough to write this book," he acknowledged, for that would have taken "more years than are at my disposal." He feared that others more knowledgeable about India would take him to task.[45]

They did. Some pointed out that *Satyagraha* was not a universally valid method for ritualizing a confrontation in order to prevent violence. The approach worked in the specific context of British India owing to British ideas of fairness. Gandhi would have been less than successful against rulers like Hitler and Stalin who did not share those ideas (Buber's point). Erikson conceded that perspective and regretted that he had not developed it. Bowdoin College scholar L. N. Gupta went farther, suggesting that like the British imperialists in India, Erikson held a circumscribed view of the colonized. He did not understand, for example, that *Satyagraha* was a "weaker" term than Truth Force. In context, Gupta pointed out, Gandhi was insisting that both the Indian masses and the British in India "demand and pursue the truth rather than prevalent law." Reviewing *Gandhi's Truth* in the preeminent *Journal of Asian Studies,* Floyd Wylie of the University of Michigan charged Erikson with reluctance to ease up on his "*very* Western" psychoanalytic perspective, to open himself to very different Indian viewpoints. Others chided Erikson for characterizing the 1918 strike as such a decisive "Event." It was not the seminal occurrence in Gandhi's career as a leader. After all, Ambalal Sarabhai believed in Gandhi's goals and had patronized him before the strike; he was hardly an opponent who thoroughly tested the Mahatma's reliance on *Satyagraha.*[46]

Erikson took special note of India scholars who faulted his connections between East and West concerning identity and the life cycle, and who dismissed his equation of psychoanalysis with *Satyagraha.* He found a review in *Contemporary Psychology* by Pamela Daniels's mentor, political scientist Susanne Rudolph, especially disturbing. He liked and respected her, and she had taught him much about modern India. Rudolph criticized Erikson for a general approach to Indian culture that was vague in time and circumstance and that ignored the average nuclear family. His account of "the Event" had "more the wondrous air of a folk myth than the concrete air of social history." Rudolph even disputed Erikson's "Personal Word" attacking Gandhi for cruelties against those close to him. If Gandhi's acts against them represented "moral sadism," she charged, they were wholly consistent with the conduct of men of Gandhi's caste, class, and religious disposition. Erikson was inappropriately wielding a Western measuring stick to evaluate Indian behavior.[47]

Reviewers in psychoanalytic publications were also critical. Several accused Erikson of turning his back on his Freudian intellectual legacy. Writing in the *International Journal of Psycho-Analysis* well before his widely acclaimed break with psychoanalytic orthodoxy, Jeffrey Masson charged Erikson with being "not unimpressed" by Jung and with failing to analyze Gandhi's "innermost being." Alan Grey accused him of being a "culturalist" and ignoring inner psychic drives: "Erikson's orthodoxy is a colorful Joseph's coat taking generous swatches from a cultural orientation and patching them over the libido theory." Erikson's friend, the psychoanalytically trained psychologist Lester Luborsky, who had worked with David Rapaport, voiced this reservation about his orthodoxy more generously. Although the book "refreshed the fragment of me that has a kinship with Gandhi," there was a "larger" loyalty to Freud that Luborsky wanted upheld.[48]

Assailed by some for being insufficiently attentive to Indian culture and custom, Erikson was also criticized by others for straying from Freudian orthodoxy by being too culture-bound. Few reviewers accepted Erikson's book on its own terms with its own agenda. Perhaps one had to know Erikson to discern that agenda. The India scholar G. Morris Carstairs congratulated Erikson for a "brave attempt to resist your revulsion against the less attractive features of Gandhi's personality." When Randall Kehler, a former student in Erikson's undergraduate course, was imprisoned in a federal facility in El Paso for refusing to fight in Vietnam, he read *Gandhi's Truth* in a violent, noisy, and overcrowded cell. Instantly, he felt himself connected both to Gandhi's and Erikson's presence in their experimental pursuit of wholeness and integrity and Truth. Robert Lifton characterized Erikson's sense of attachment both to Freud and Gandhi. All three sought to "test the truth" through action that maximized mutuality and minimized the violence of unilateral coercion. For Lifton, Erikson and Gandhi had essentially participated in a mutuality "in which the insight of each illuminates that of the other." Robert Coles acknowledged a similar kinship; he felt drawn both to Erikson and to the Mahatma. In the course of *Gandhi's Truth,* Coles noted that "Gandhi's 'truth force' becomes—modestly and affectingly— Erikson's 'truth force.' " Through a dialogue across time and place, the two men "came together with no loss of dignity to either."[49]

Despite these appreciative readers, *Gandhi's Truth* did not revolutionize the study of culture and identity as *Childhood and Society* had. Important as it was, it did not represent a groundbreaking contribution to contemporary concerns. It could have been Erikson's most important book if he had been as attentive to the complex currents in society as he had been when he prepared his first book. With Frantz Fanon's *The Wretched of the Earth* (1961)—a revolutionary manifesto against colonialism for the extreme psychological damage that it inflicted on the colonized—*Gandhi's Truth* might have come to be regarded as one of the primary intellectual manifestos of decolonization. It might have emerged as a profound challenge to a Western historicism that viewed Europe as the dominant center of the world and drew binaries between the center and the periphery, the metropolis and the colony, the technological base and the "primitive source." With public intellectuals like the aging phenomenologist Emmanuel Levinas, Erikson had struck at a foundational assumption of colonialism: that the self could ethically assimilate the other. Levinas prescribed a relationship between the self and the other, conversing face-to-face, that breached and defied totality. Erikson propounded direct personal reciprocity, eye to eye, getting by giving to the other in a spirituality of respect and connectedness. There was no self without the other, both free and independent but acting with mutuality.

Erikson belonged to a generation of cosmopolitan Western intellectuals who reached out, to some degree, for what was to become the rich postcolonial perspective of Fanon, Edward Said (the prominent critic of Western "Orientalist" stereotypes), and leading Indian intellectuals like Homi Bhabha and Gayatri Spivak. The Western cosmopolitans had advocated a "Family of Man" and universal brotherhood in the wake of the Holocaust and World War II, but they did not seek aggressively to dismember the foundations of Western imperial hegemony. Instead, they backed programs offered by the American government, the Rockefeller Brothers Fund, and the Ford Foundation for technical assistance to aid economic development in newly independent third-world nations. They did not actively promote full agency for the former colonists, and they rarely critiqued the cultural hierarchy forged by persisting Western prejudice and NATO troops. Consequently, third-world thinkers like Fanon, Said, Bhabha, and Spivak became critical of the cosmopolitans.

Erikson was a cosmopolitan Western intellectual with a difference. Owing to his extensive contact with Clyde Kluckhohn, Margaret Mead, and other leading anthropologists who studied and appreciated "native" societies, he deeply valued the cultures of the colonized. Indeed, as he composed *Gandhi's Truth,* he sometimes forged ahead of his cosmopolitan colleagues to promote a mapping of the world in which the Western powers ceased to occupy the center. Erikson's effort at postcolonial mapping was obvious in his "Personal Word" to Gandhi—the point where he found failure and weakness and therefore humanness in the Mahatma. This effort allowed him to connect his own flaws with Gandhi's as he completed his book, to identify profoundly with a non-Western man. The problem was that despite his urging for strong reciprocity in human relationships, by making the Mahatma's Truth his own Truth, Erikson had essentially (if unintentionally) absorbed Gandhi.

By becoming a spiritual Gandhi, Erikson could reshape the Mahatma's message. Thus, although he tried to portray Gandhi fairly as a crafty South Asian politician working to free India from British hegemony, his Western perspectives periodically redirected the Mahatma in problematic ways. Erikson endorsed the fighting capacity of Israeli soldiers against the Arabs, for example, and claimed that this capacity had promoted Gandhi-like *Satyagraha.* He provided a constrictive view of Fanon's emphasis on violence to resurrect the colonial's degraded sense of selfhood by overly accenting the difference between Fanon's analysis and Gandhi's. And he waited for a decade after the publication of *Gandhi's Truth* before he was ready to modify his equation of *Satyagraha* with psychoanalysis. Only then did he ask an international congress of psychoanalysts to cease universalizing so uncritically the Western premises of psychoanalytic thought.[50]

FROM CAMBRIDGE TO OAKLAND, 1970–71

Erikson wrote to a friend that the acclaim of having won both the Pulitzer Prize and the National Book Award for *Gandhi's Truth* helped to encourage him "to retire earlier from professional work and to write some more." He taught SS 139 for the last time in the spring semester of 1970 and retired in July; more than book prizes were involved in this decision. President Nathan Pusey had been trying to lower the mandatory faculty retirement age at Harvard to sixty-seven. Most faculty retired at sixty-five but were not required to retire until seventy. Still quite proud of his professorship status and continuing to enjoy his undergraduate course, Erik preferred a reduction of his university duties rather than emeritus status as he neared sixty-eight. When Pusey insisted that his mandatory policy was firm, Erikson accepted Harvard retirement benefits and abandoned efforts at negotiation.[51]

In any case, the Eriksons did not depend upon Erik's faculty salary. Retirement income from Austen Riggs and Harvard, more offers of clinical consultantships than Erik could possibly handle, plus investment income from Norton's substantial book advance combined to produce a very comfortable income. In addition, George Brockway, the new chairman of Norton, recognized that during the 1970–71 academic year, paperback sales for all of Erikson's books approximated 140,000. As well, university presses eagerly offered to publish Erikson's public lectures in book form. Since these lectures were not covered under Norton's advance, Brockway pledged considerably more than university presses could afford to put them out as books. He offered a $25,000 advance, for example, for the right to publish Erikson's 1972 Godkin Lectures.[52]

Gradually, during the course of the 1960s, the Eriksons found themselves spending not only summers in their Cotuit house, but more and more time during spring and fall in Stockbridge. The quiet town in the Berkshires appealed to them over the faster pace of Cambridge, especially after Erik stopped teaching at Harvard. As "an immigrant . . . there are very few places where I feel at home," he acknowledged, and Stockbridge was one. Leaving Cambridge permanently in mid-1970, Erik and Joan bought a very large house on Main Street, across the street from the Austen Riggs Center, with ample writing studies for both and a ballroom where they could revive their considerable talents for the waltz. They also renewed old friendships with playwright William Gibson, screenwriter Arthur Penn, who had bought their first Stockbridge house, and others. As well, they assumed informal mentor roles for area writers, craftspeople, and clinicians. If work on the global issues that converged in *Gandhi's Truth* had made Erik more somber and prophetic in his manner, the return to Stockbridge seemed to enhance his sense of humor. He was always ready with a joke or a funny remark. A steady flow of friends vacationing in the Berkshires came to visit, including pediatrician–peace activist Benjamin Spock and Senator Jacob Javits. Regular correspondence from intellectuals such as psychologist Lester Luborsky and Stephen Graubard of the American Academy of Arts and Sciences also kept him busy. But what Erik most enjoyed when he was not writing was to attend Austen Riggs case conferences without the press of day-to-day clinical duties. Younger clinicians like M. Gerard Fromm and Stephen Schlein seemed to hang on his every word at these sessions, especially when he bemoaned the fact that current diagnostic nomenclature seemed remote. Erikson supervised a few clinicians in his home. He also offered informal clinical seminars in his study—often occasions for testing his papers or chapters or possible book projects. Riggs remunerated him well for what he was willing to do.[53]

Erikson's routine reflected his acceptance of old age. In the fall of 1970, he was hospitalized for treatment of a serious but nonmalignant internal disorder. Joan required him to nap after lunch and sometimes at other times of the day in order to conserve his strength. He referred to himself publicly as "a psychoanalyst at the end of his career." While Erikson did not yet feel fully the eighth-stage pull between "integrity" and "despair," he projected himself as a graying sage rather than as a driven professional. This was evident at a ceremony late in 1971 marking Peter Blos's retirement from work at New York City's Jewish Board of Guardians. Since Erikson left Vienna, he had not seen or corresponded with Blos very often. In underscoring his old friend's "workmanship and *Geistigkeit* . . . which old age tends to conserve and to deepen," Erikson seemed to be characterizing himself as well. If the grave was now much closer than the cradle, it was not starkly in view.[54]

Awards and honors abounded, especially from within academic and clinical circles, where his book sales were strongest. Honorary doctorates were awarded by Brown, Yale, and Berkeley. Erikson was especially gratified to be the first to hold the Freud Memorial Chair in Psychoanalysis at University College, London. This had "special meaning in my lifetime." The National Association for Mental Health selected him for its third annual Research

Achievement Award and provided a $10,000 stipend. Memories of his Montessori training in Vienna were rekindled when the Montessori Institute of America gave him its Gold Medallion Award for his contributions to childhood education. He was elected to the National Academy of Education. With this "notoriety I have acquired in recent years," he told a friend, he had to spend much time attending to his correspondence so as to ward off additional intrusions into his life.[55]

Erikson was becoming a cultural hero of sorts and something of a cult figure. Walking from their Manhattan hotel one Sunday morning in the spring of 1970 to buy the *New York Times* at a newsstand, he and Joan were uncomfortably aware that people were pointing at them. The cover of the *Times Magazine* provided the explanation: a full-page color photograph of a sixty-eight-year-old man in a dapper dark brown jacket, white shirt, and dark tie. He was in a reflective position, hand to chin, with his massive white mane, ruddy complexion, and penetrating eyes conveying profundity and balance; the caption read "Psychoanalyst Erik Erikson: Beyond Freud." There and in the *Saturday Review,* psychologist David Elkind maintained that Erikson's concepts had become an integral part of the basic education of psychiatrists, psychologists, educators, and social workers. *Newsweek* ran a similar feature article, "Erik Erikson: The Quest for Identity," quoting Berkeley sociologist Robert Bellah on American undergraduates: "You can't always be sure they've read Shakespeare, but you know they've read Erikson." In the *New York Times Book Review,* London psychoanalyst Peter Lomas described him as "the most influential of living psychoanalysts." An official from Random House Dictionaries asked Erikson to review its entry for "identity crisis." The Institute of Religious Studies at the University of California, Santa Barbara, brought in Bellah, historian Natalie Davis, and other renowned scholars and intellectuals to join with Erikson in a special symposium in his honor. More and more, there were references to "Eriksonian psychohistory," which made him uncomfortable: "I didn't intend to set up an interdisciplinary *field*" through his books on Luther and Gandhi.[56]

There was more. Belated recognition came from segments of American popular culture that Erikson's configurational approach could be adapted visually. An article in *School Library Journal* showed how E. B. White's well-illustrated tale *Charlotte's Web* rested upon Erikson's view of the life cycle. Nine million Americans watched a CBS television special featuring John and Faith Hubley's animated film "Everybody Rides the Carousel," illustrating his eight-stage cycle. The Chicago Institute for Advanced Study in Child Development renamed itself the Erik Erikson Institute. Robert Coles wrote a series of articles for the *New Yorker* discussing with considerable feeling many of the publications of "a clinician and professor I know and admire."

Little, Brown and Company convinced Coles to publish them in expanded form as *Erik H. Erikson: The Growth of His Work.*[57]

Erikson felt awkward and sometimes downright distressed about all the media attention. Much as he considered himself to have a prophetlike mission as he completed *Gandhi's Truth,* he had not cultivated the relatively easy public presence of the Mahatma, preferring to live in secluded "Magic Mountain"–like locations. Pleased that he was being quoted and summarized so abundantly, Erikson nevertheless disliked the fact that the preponderance of the citations were grossly simplified, distorted, and misapplied. He recognized, too, that much of his writing intersected with Erich Fromm's; the attention he enjoyed could pass as quickly as it had from that creative psychoanalyst and intellectual. He attributed some of the attention among college students to his elderly presence: "Young people today distrust their parents. They want to trust a grandparent." He did not quite know how to respond when the Robert Wood Johnson Foundation presented him with an award, money, and a plaque. Despite this uncertainty, he drove from Cotuit to Harvard to discuss with a former colleague just where in William James Hall the plaque was to be hung. Erikson felt somewhat ill at ease when Robert Coles's *New Yorker* articles about him were published. However, the articles provided him a rationale for refusing to cooperate with six national newsmagazines clamoring to publish features on him; it had already been done. Similarly, he almost always rejected invitations for lectures; he cited his schedule, his health, or almost any other excuse that came to mind. As time passed, Erikson acquired trusted techniques for curbing media intrusiveness while not entirely squelching favorable publicity. Communication, he insisted, was to take place through the mails. He would send the appropriate newspaper or magazine or commentator a photograph along with carefully crafted written responses to specific questions. Early photographs (potentially revealing) would not be supplied and questions about personal issues were usually ignored. "I already say more about myself than is usual for somebody in my field," he told a *New York Times Magazine* reporter. To the consternation of his editors at W. W. Norton, he refused to permit advance excerpts from books about to be republished. He also lost potential publicity and revenues by denying applicants the permission to reprint his chart of the eight-stage life cycle unless they accompanied it with explanatory text.[58]

It was one thing to fend off media agents. It was another matter when Kai urged his father to participate in a public dialogue with Huey P. Newton, cofounder, field marshal, and prime minister of the Black Panther Party. The party patrolled the streets of Oakland armed, purportedly, to defend local blacks against the racist and violent city police. Newton had called for a

United Nations supervised plebiscite for blacks to determine their national destiny and heralded guns as tools of national liberation. While embracing black solidarity, Newton had also suggested a coalition with Marxist-Leninist white revolutionaries in a class war against capitalist imperialists.

The Huey Newton–Erik Erikson dialogue came about quite by chance. Donald Freed of the Defense Committee of the Black Panther Party was in New Haven early in January 1971 for the murder conspiracy trials of Bobby Seale and Ericka Huggins. He called Kai, then teaching at Yale, to inform him that Newton and others in the Panther high command would be in town for the trials. Freed asked Kai to arrange for Newton to talk with Yale students, and Kai jumped at the opportunity.

In the aftermath of the American invasion of Cambodia and the shooting of students at Jackson State and Kent State universities, tensions were very high at Yale. Earlier Panther murder trials had taken place in New Haven, where the Yale student body together with New Left leaders like Abbie Hoffman, Jerry Rubin, and Tom Hayden had publicly supported the Panthers as a show of solidarity with black America. Liberal celebrities like Harry Belafonte, Otto Preminger, and Jane Fonda also rallied behind the Panthers, and Yale president Kingman Brewster was sympathetic. Close to Brewster and master at Trumbull, one of Yale's colleges, Kai arranged an informal seminar there so that Newton and Trumbull students could discuss their concerns about various troubling issues. With Newton's permission, Kai invited his father to participate in the seminar.[59]

Erikson eagerly accepted the invitation. He had become increasingly interested in American race relations and white-nonwhite rapport in general. As a white immigrant enamored with FDR's America, Erikson had been slow to appreciate the insidious effects of racism at home. Working in the San Francisco Bay Area in the 1940s, he began to notice the fallout from white-black tension, especially on black children. Consultations with children of working-class parents in Pittsburgh during the 1950s deepened Erikson's concern. He had also begun to read African-American novelists like Richard Wright, James Baldwin, and Ralph Ellison. Visiting Fisk University in 1956, he listened closely to civil rights discussions. Indeed, he had become more strongly committed to civil rights than several other leading intellectuals of his generation. Unlike Hannah Arendt and Reinhold Niebuhr, Erikson had no reservations about the Supreme Court decision in *Brown* vs. *Board of Education*. Unlike Walter Lippmann, he wanted more than gradual integration of southern schools. Rosa Parks's courage in refusing to move to the back of a Montgomery bus had impressed him, and he considered writing a book on her Luther-like "Here I Stand" position.[60]

At Harvard, Erikson was well aware of his students' and colleagues' involvement in the civil rights movement. He prepared several papers on problems of African-Americans in sustaining positive identities, including one as a full chapter in *Identity: Youth and Crisis.* Encouraged by civil rights activist and friend Robert Coles, he met with volunteers to the Mississippi Freedom Summer project in 1964, let himself be listed on the Board of Consultants of SNCC Educational Institutes, and observed troubled black children in the Boston schools. Ralph Ellison's exploration in *Invisible Man* of "faceless faces, of soundless voices" among African-Americans had more immediacy for him now. After *Gandhi's Truth* was published, he regretted that he had not done more to connect Gandhi's *Satyagraha* campaigns in India to King's nonviolent resistance in America. Erikson also found some salutary effect in the Black Muslims' effort to restore African-American identity; he would not dismiss black nationalism out of hand. Nor did he agree with the prevalent claims that "father absence" was responsible for pathologies in African-American families. Fatherless himself, Erikson insisted that a nurturing mother offered an important counterweight. Not long before Kai called him to meet with Newton, Erik had returned with Coles from a visit to Head Start schools in impoverished rural Mississippi where he had played with, observed, and drawn sketches for young black children.[61]

Kai's small Trumbull College seminar quickly escalated into the sort of national media event that Erik found distasteful. National newspapers sent correspondents to New Haven. The FBI assigned undercover agents, who investigated Erik's presumed ties to what it characterized as a "black extremist organization" that advocated "guns and guerrilla tactics to bring about the overthrow of the United States Government." A small audience, largely of students and faculty, sat around a seminar table. Almost from the start, Newton transformed what was to be an informal exchange into a formal debate. He recycled pronouncements concerning dialectical materialism and the philosophies of Marx, Hegel, and Kant. He avoided what people really came to hear—the specifics of Black Panther activism. No standout at the lecture podium, Erikson recounted a bit about his own background and sought to "translate" and comment on Newton's abstractions. Agreeing with Kai and Erik that this Yale gathering was a failure, Newton proposed that they meet at a friend's apartment in Oakland, his hometown, where he would feel more comfortable. The change of venue allowed for a much more relaxed second interchange despite the presence of armed Black Panther guards monitoring the streets and hallways. Jon came to shoot photographs and took sandwich orders for lunch. With everybody sitting around a table drinking scotch, Newton's posturing disappeared. Erik asked him about his childhood and the course of his life. The Black Panther leader appeared to enjoy the discussion. A friendship of sorts had begun.[62]

It was obvious, of course, that Erikson and Newton came from different generations with widely contrasting experiences. Erikson was from a generation of Western intellectuals that had "kept a close and personal eye on the emergence of Nazism in Germany" and was deeply suspicious of claims of unique ethnic and national virtue. Erikson acknowledged that he had been oblivious to the pervasiveness of American racism when he arrived from Europe; he had not been attentive to "the management of things and people" in a culture of "technological imperialism." Indeed, he now understood that since the FDR presidency, "the idea of the country liberating others from bondage has been reversed." Still, Erikson admitted to Newton that he continued to view the United States as a nation of immigrants and a center of cosmopolitanism—even an embodiment of "universal specieshood"— more than as a breeding ground for racist "pseudospeciations."[63]

Newton rejected Erikson's perspective, continuing to insist that the "official" ideology of the Black Panther Party be based upon dialectic materialism, and he was much less tolerant than Erikson of American bigotry. However, Newton became candid about his private life, confessing his own problems in growing up and relating to his parents, and his personal troubles as a Black Panther Party leader. A "debate" had become a conversation between two men who enjoyed being together.[64]

Each came to find strengths in the other, reassurance, even trust. Erikson formed a "personal" as well as an intellectual "impression" of the Black Panther leader—a perspective "without which I do not understand." He began to draw a specious connection between Gandhi's pacifism and Newton's resistance tactics. Like the Mahatma's militant pursuit of the Truth Force, Erikson asserted that the armed love of the Panther Party proclaimed by Newton was not aimed "to kill that human dignity" of the adversary. Instead, it was to make clear to the Oakland police that "the law of the land applied to the black ghetto" and that law enforcement officers could not behave like "outlaws." Erikson insisted that he could accept Black Panther armed neighborhood patrols and *Satyagraha,* too, for Newton, like Gandhi, had "sensed the representativeness of a dramatic theme in a circumscribed locality at the right moment in history." In the end, Erikson concluded that he would "respond to human love" in a black militant formula for ghetto dignity as he had responded to Gandhi's formulation of *Satyagraha.* He voiced relief that Newton could no longer "treat me as an adversary" while "I found it difficult not to admire him."[65]

Erikson felt that they both were on a quest for "universal specieshood." Although "our pasts were as different as any pasts could be," Erikson recalled, "our futures very much depended on each other." He had no idea that during their exchanges, Newton had secretly ordered Panther squads to beat up various disaffected party members. Nor did Erikson see that although Newton sometimes used the language of cosmopolitan universalism, the Panther leader was also dedicated to a retribalist perspective under newer forms of ethnic consciousness. Kai edited down a transcript of the tape recordings of the exchange and, as an act of friendship, George Brockway had W. W. Norton publish it under the title *In Search of Common Ground.* Newton arranged a book-signing party at Oakland's Community Learning Center for ghetto children, and Erikson attended.[66]

As Brockway suspected, *In Search of Common Ground* was not the sort of book that would sell widely. Nor did it contain much depth or subtle reflection. Instead, it served as a historic marker that a short-lived dialogue was possible between a young rifle-toting black militant espousing Marxist clichés and an aging European intellectual who relied on his own idiosyncratic blend of Goethe and Freud and never carried a weapon. The two of them tried to bridge the increasing polarization in American society over the war in Vietnam and unprecedented violence on college campuses as Martin Luther King, Jr.'s, hopes for racial conciliation were replaced by the rhetoric of black nationalism and white backlash.

The bridge between Erikson and Newton did not endure. When Erikson learned of Newton's involvement in shoot-outs and violent clashes with civil authorities, he promptly ended the relationship and refused to aid Newton's legal defense efforts.[67]

GODKIN LECTURER

In the early spring of 1972, a year after Erikson met with Newton in Oakland, he lectured on the Harvard campus in Cambridge before a very different audience. Although his range of listeners never approximated Gandhi's, it was significant for a man two months shy of seventy to be "invited from retirement" for a major presentation. Harvard's John F. Kennedy School of Government sponsored the annual E. L. Godkin Lectures on "the essentials of free government." Named after the prominent nineteenth-century reformist magazine editor and intellectual, the format involved two formal presentations accompanied by a few special interdisciplinary seminars for faculty and students. Seminar participants were nominated by Harvard department chairpersons. Erikson asked his former "chief section man" Pamela Daniels to take charge of all arrangements. He seemed more concerned with seminar arrangements than lectures. With Daniels, he would interview everyone nominated for the seminars so that he could make the final selections.[68]

His lectures, titled "Play, Vision, and Deception," sought to cover the relationship between childhood play, which he had observed and analyzed since his Vienna training, and "the political imagination." Gandhi's creative politics of *Satyagraha* was on his mind as a stark contrast to America of April 1972, where, Erikson later wrote, "a curtain has come down over Vietnam and another has opened . . . on the home-town spectacle of Watergate." In preparation for the lectures and seminars, Erikson focused on two sources: his "Ontogeny of Ritualization in Man" talk in 1965 at the Royal Society of London, where he had designated eight social rituals (numinous, judicial, etc.) to accompany each of his eight developmental stages; and William Blake's observation, "The child's play and the old man's reasons are the fruits of two seasons." Attentive to ritual in the course of human development, Erikson proposed to capture "the child's innocent eye" as he or she registered the sensory universe during play. From the other end of the life cycle, he would examine the mature "reasons" of old men like himself. He would include, too, the artist in himself capable of weaving perceptions into a whole.[69]

By April 11, when he was to give the first lecture, Erikson had twenty-four double-spaced pages of text ready to read, and twenty-three pages for the April 12 lecture were also finished. Traditionally, the Godkin Lectures were held at the Ames Court Room in the Law School. Long before lecture time, however, Ames was filled and hundreds more waited outside. Sanders Theater was available across campus, and thirteen hundred students, faculty, friends, and family traipsed over to the theater. The facility was striking, with varnished wood and rows of seats curved to embrace the stage. But Erikson disappointed, reading his text in a low and boring monotone, with a decided German accent and minimal eye contact. If listening was a trial in the auditorium, the seminars were captivating. Roughly twenty different applicants had been assigned to each session. Erikson was much more relaxed and animated in that setting than as a lecturer; he was full of wit, wise observation, and humor. Brockway had committed W. W. Norton to publish a volume consisting of revised versions of the lectures supplemented by materials from the seminars; he had given Erikson a respectable advance on the final manuscript. Based on written comments from those attending the seminars, notes after he gave the lectures, and advice from Daniels, Kai, Joan, and others close to him, he transformed the forty-seven pages of text into a short book, *Toys and Reasons,* and dedicated it to Joan "because of her lifelong devotion to the grace that is play."[70]

Neither the lectures nor the book stayed focused on the Blake quote or the "Ontogeny of Ritualization" essay. Neither developed systematically the relationship between children's play and the political imagination. A few weeks after delivering the lectures, Erikson confided to the dean of the Kennedy School: "It was obvious that I was not yet master of my themes."

Reviewers spotted the same shortage of direction and mastery in the published volume. Robert Coles charitably attributed this "ever moving back and forth" aspect of the book to Erikson's attentiveness to the dangers of "entrapment by categories of determinism." Culture commentator Rosemary Dinnage felt Erikson needed to work through specific materials to connect "inner dramas" in the self with "public ones." *Gandhi's Truth* had depended, according to Dinnage, upon a concrete event (the Ahmadabad strike) to anchor a narrative that wheeled in various directions. Otherwise, readers would have been left with page after page of Erikson's pontifications but little sense of connectedness. Dinnage felt that it was this dearth of concrete materials that made for the anchorless quality in his Godkin presentations.[71]

When Erikson arrived in Cambridge to deliver the lectures, he had no ongoing book project for the first time in decades. Years of work involving travel to complete *Gandhi's Truth* made him leery of new long-term projects like a biography of Golda Meir or Rosa Parks or two interesting Danes—Søren Kierkegaard and Hans Christian Andersen. But as the date for the Godkin Lectures approached, there was one possibility. With Joan and with his Stockbridge psychologist friend Peggy Penn, he had spent parts of the past few years observing play constructions of four- and five-year-olds in rural Mississippi, at a child study center in Chicago, in Boston public schools, and even abroad. His work was similar to the work Robert Coles was engaged in for his *Children of Crisis* series. Erikson sketched, made notes, and occasionally photographed as the child would construct shapes from blocks and toys and then "tell a story" about the scene he or she had created. In lieu of a book in progress, Erikson hoped that he could find a book in this new work without too much difficulty. The most substantive, compelling part of the Godkin Lectures and *Toys and Reasons* drew on this observational material concerning the nature of play. The book would have been much more persuasive if it had been organized around those observations.[72]

Erikson had always valued play; he exalted its utility. Children's play was a precursor to conceptual thought and eventually to "old man's reasons." To support this view, and relying on materials from physician and science historian Gerald Holton, Erikson cited the case of Albert Einstein. As a child, Einstein loved to play with puzzles. This play grounded his exceptional visual and conceptual capacity as he later began to investigate energy and mass, inertia and gravitation, space and time, and eventually conceived the theory of relativity. This was why Einstein "characterizes his thinking . . . [as] play." More broadly, children's play "provides the infantile form of the human propensity to create model situations in which aspects of the past are re-lived, the present re-presented and renewed, and the future anticipated." Play therefore rested on participation in the ritualizations of the life cycle that helped people to "reach out and know your [their] innermost resources" and to feel "grounded." From infancy to old age, playfulness was "a symptom of aliveness" that conferred a special "leeway" for experimentation within the context of society. The Germans were attentive to it in what they called "*Spielraum:* space to *play* in" with leeway. Neither Freud's nor any other developmental perspective, Erikson insisted, could avoid *Spielraum* and the playful concern with "what is given, what is developing." For further support, he cited the observations of his prominent Harvard faculty friend Jerome Bruner concerning infants at play and what Bruner had taught him about Piaget's reflections.[73]

Play offered both the child and the adult a way to transcend limitations on self-expression that was both nonverbal and verbally poetic. Erikson agreed with Blake that an old man's "reasons" at their best were "blessed by playful childlikeness." Playfulness afforded "a simple integrity" through which "old people and children feel an affinity for each other." The earliest and latest rituals on the life cycle circled into each other through play. At a 1970 presentation in Chicago, Erikson defined "actuality" as "the leeway created by new forms of interplay." Actuality had constantly to "retest reality to remain truly playful." Reiterating this perspective in Cambridge, Erikson asserted that modern life, with its political and technological imperatives, was interfering excessively with "playful experimentation within limits." Society was imposing more limits on people than social order required. This trend toward excessive limitations underlined the importance of the playful ritualizations that Gandhi had offered humankind—a gamesmanship of skill and chance in which the adversary was accepted as "equally human," meriting benefits, and deserving dignity. That was the lesson of Ahmadabad and *Satyagraha.*[74]

Erikson did not feel that it was sufficient to focus on the way Gandhi's playful gamesmanship integrated children's play and the political imagination. He had already told the Mahatma's story. In the course of preparing his lectures, he also feared that he had not amassed enough fresh data on the play of four- and five-year-olds to sustain an entirely new study, fused perhaps with his "Ontogeny of Ritualization" essay. In the end, Erikson elected to fill out the Godkin Lectures and seminars and to publish them in a book-length work by including quick, unfocused comments on a myriad of prophetic "truths"—usually only very tangentially related to play, playfulness, and the political imagination.

Erikson noted, for example, that he "had some conversations recently" with Huey Newton, who, with Bobby Seale, had created an institution for "armed young black men to patrol the streets of Oakland" protecting residents from police brutalities. This venture by the Black Panther Party represented a "desperate kind of playfulness" against public injustice. Without referring to the Panthers and the Oakland ghetto or even to his seminars with Lindsay administration officials and others in New York, Erikson discussed at one of the Godkin seminars the sort of urban neighborhood where people of all races and ages and life stages "have greater leeway" for play in their lives and a sense of responsibility for local children not their own.[75]

In both his second Godkin lecture and a separate seminar focused on the "New Woman," Erikson recognized that he had to respond to feminist attacks on his 1964 essay "The Inner and the Outer Space," which had been republished in *Identity: Youth and Crisis.* He insisted that his long-standing observations concerning significant differences in the play constructions of boys and girls had to be taken more seriously. It saddened him how "some women now declare, I should not have observed, or, at any rate, not pointed out" these differences. Feeling that several female participants at the "New Woman" seminar were too serious and lacked playfulness, he inappropriately urged them to prepare memoranda that he could consult when he revised his lectures for *Toys and Reasons.* But he did not elaborate on the issue of gender difference and playfulness, which might have eased the tension. Instead, he exacerbated matters by moving away from the issue of play and insisting (congruent with his image of Gandhi) that "we are all bisexual, let's face it." Erikson also spoke to a need for certain nurturing qualities—which he attributed to women—as a defining feature of the American presidency. Yet he cautioned feminists that "roles to experiment" were "different for boys than for girls" and that these should not be patched over in an effort to gain "new leeway" for the female. The mood of the seminar grew more somber. When Erikson left, he confided his disappointment to a friend.[76]

Since his investigation decades earlier of the Nazi appeal to German youth, Erikson had fretted about advancing technologies outdistancing the human capacity to master them. The Godkin Lectures and seminars and the resulting book afforded the opportunity to delineate how these technologies threatened to undermine playfulness and to check the political imagination. However, he did not elaborate on these concerns. He spoke, for example, of "the incomparably greater awareness and the greater power" provided by new science and technologies, which "makes man lonelier in the universe" and prone to "totalistic . . . ideologies." The unstated implication was that scientific technologies could dispose man to constrict his "leeway" and playfulness, and the richness of his unique imagination. Just before the Godkin Lectures, Erikson wrote of the increase of "mass produced roles, of standardized consummerism, and of rampant bureaucratization" and how this technological mind-set served to "take the play out of work." But he left the observation and its connection to politics out of his text.[77]

In the Godkin Lectures, Erikson articulated his distress over an American propensity to use sophisticated technology to promote pseudospeciation and violence. Certainly influenced by friends in the peace movement like Benjamin Spock, William Sloan Coffin, and especially Robert Lifton, he spoke of the "American Way of Death, which means the passionless use of overkill against other species" that had "reached its climax in Hiroshima." He suggested that American qualities of playful experimentation and even "showmanship" had been bypassed by the "aimless and voiceless detail in a blueprint" that culminated in the deployment of the atomic bomb in August 1945. Concerning the American military presence in Vietnam, Erikson made the connection between play and technology in a careless, almost trivial way that skipped over the points he wanted to establish. He postulated that the U.S. massacre at My Lai using modern technology exemplified "the deadliness which takes over when all gamesmanship has gone out of an adult scenario." Indeed, the whole "colonial war" in Vietnam required "technological means of overkill" because of the lack of playfulness and the utter "loss of imagination" as unsure leaders felt impotent to end the technology-driven slaughter. If Erikson had used the Godkin Lectures to carefully amplify these thoughts, placing them more squarely in the context of racial and colonial aspects of American military expansion, as Lifton, Kenneth Keniston, and other antiwar activists at the annual Wellfleet meetings had urged, they would have cohered around a compelling historical narrative.[78]

Erikson had required participants in one of his Godkin seminars to read his "Ontogeny of Ritualization" essay. Seeking to transform forty-seven typed pages of Godkin Lectures into a book-length entity, he decided to expand the essay so that it occupied roughly one-third of *Toys and Reasons*. He hoped that the expanded essay would show that the "concept of ritualization has proved so essential a link between the ontogeny and the phylogeny of human playfulness." Had Erikson explored this theme systematically, including extended commentary on how ritualization at each of the eight stages of his life cycle model connected to a person's evolving political imagination, the middle section of *Toys and Reasons* would have been integrated and reinforced his more general theme of play and political ingenuity. But this was not the case; the "Ontogeny of Ritualization" essay was not revised significantly—certainly not along his proposed lines. Much like *Identity: Youth and Crisis* and even several of the essays in *Insight and Responsibility*, Erikson elected to recycle previous publications rather than to rewrite extensively. Reflective friends like psychoanalyst Robert Wallerstein, sociologist Neil Smelser, and historian Nathan Hale had offered critical suggestions for revision, but he bypassed revisions that entailed time and effort. If the financial incentives Norton offered for "new" books contributed to

Erikson's disposition toward hasty recycling, so did advancing age. In his early seventies, exhausted over the final push to complete *Gandhi's Truth,* he was not disposed toward extensive rewriting.[79]

More than in *Gandhi's Truth,* periodic comments in *Toys and Reasons* signaled a growing interest in matters of Ultimate Concern. Discussions with Helmut Wohl, a Stockbridge neighbor and fellow scholar, had intensified Erikson's interest much as contact with Paul Tillich had some years earlier. Beginning at infancy with the numinous ritual of mutuality of recognition between mother and child, and extending through old age, Erikson spoke of the "sense of 'I' renewed by the mutual recognition of all 'I's' joined in a shared faith in one all embracing 'I Am.' " This sense of "I" assured "a *separateness transcended* and yet also a *distinctiveness confirmed.*" The newborn and the mother smiling at each other prompted mutual recognition and lifted both up to "feel central and new." The process continued through late life when the elderly person went to his grave assured of "the desired presence of the providing person"—God and simultaneously all of humankind. This process involved the sense of "an all-human consciousness." In a way, Erikson suggested, this sense of "I" was not terribly different from what he had learned as a German youth as a worldview or weltanschauung of shared visions that held life together in an "all-human consciousness." On the other hand, it was more than "a remnant of my humanist schooling" in a Karlsruhe gymnasium. The sense of "I" was commanding the attention of an aging man who was disposed to go beyond psychological constructs like "ego" and "identity." More than ever before, he wanted to explore spirituality and the supernatural.[80]

THE JEFFERSON LECTURES

Whereas *Toys and Reasons* began as Godkin Lectures in 1972, the revision and completion were delayed until 1977. During much of that time, Erikson was preoccupied with preparing for the most important lectures of his life and with meeting a tight deadline to ready them for publication. The National Endowment for the Humanities (NEH) selected him from roughly two hundred nominees to follow Lionel Trilling and deliver its second annual Jefferson Lectures in 1973. The NEH provided a $10,000 honorarium but required him to transform the lectures into a book soon after they were delivered. Erikson presented in early May of 1973 amid the growing Watergate crisis, and in the middle of a move from Stockbridge to the Tiburon-Belvedere area overlooking San Francisco Bay.[81]

If the precise timing for the move to the West Coast was unanticipated, conditions that dictated the move were not surprising. To escape another cold and snowy winter in western Massachusetts, Joan and Erik had rented a house in Tiburon in the early months of 1973. Joan suffered from an arthritic hip that required surgery, and the condition had been compounded by a bad fall on the ice. She needed a warmer climate. So did Erik, who felt "footloose" after two decades in the East. Jon still lived in the Bay Area, and Joan and Erik hoped that geographic proximity might improve their relationship with him. Old Bay Area friends like Thomas and Martha Proctor urged them to return. Robert Wallerstein, chief of psychiatry at Mt. Zion Hospital in San Francisco, who had been close to the Eriksons for nearly a decade, promised flexible part-time jobs for both of them. Joan could assume whatever duties she wanted in the Mt. Zion activities therapy program. Through funds Wallerstein procured from an external grant, Erik could teach and consult and write at his leisure.[82]

In late winter of 1973, the Eriksons sold their Stockbridge house and bought another with a heated outdoor pool in Tiburon. Reflecting his affection for the Austen Riggs Center, Erik kept his seat on the Board of Trustees. The move proved "most difficult"—sometimes chaotic. The Eriksons took a full month to move and get settled in the new house. Erik promised Joan "what help a husband can give in such matters." For him, this was not much. In the packing, shipping, and unpacking of a great many boxes, a number of very important files of Erik's clinical case notes covering his crucial years at Riggs were mailed to and apparently arrived in Tiburon. If they were delivered to the Eriksons' new home, they have never been seen since. This loss left a critical gap in the documentation of his work as a therapist and a clinical consultant.[83]

The Jefferson Lectures occurred at a time when the Eriksons were flying back and forth between western Massachusetts and northern California attending to the details of their move. The task of preparing, then revising, such important presentations proved difficult for the same reason the Godkin Lectures had been difficult. Despite his persistent desire to write, Erikson still had no ongoing research project upon which to draw. The kindly Wallace Edgerton, former head of the Institute of International Education and acting director of NEH, offered him the choice of a topic; Erik settled on the versatile and artistic third American president. He acknowledged special curiosity concerning Jefferson's views about human nature, for they represented a holistic eighteenth-century perspective, potentially a healthy counterpoint to twentieth-century fragmentation. Edgerton advised him to consult historian Dumas Malone, generally acknowledged to be the foremost Jefferson scholar and the author of a definitive multivolume biography.[84]

Erikson wrote to Malone, describing himself as "a man from another field [who] wants to browse around in yours" and to arrive at "some deep insights." When Malone indicated a disinterest in any parallels between Jefferson's emotions and his public pronouncements, friends urged Erikson to consult the more controversial UCLA historian Fawn Brodie, who had been excommunicated from the Mormon Church for an unflattering biography of Joseph Smith. At the time Erikson contacted her, she was writing a biography of Jefferson focusing on his emotional life and broader social circumstances. Erikson was excited because Brodie was willing to explore data that more traditional male Jefferson biographers ignored. She responded intuitively "both to the woman (and I don't mean the 'passive man'!) in Jefferson and to what he looked for in a woman." As a psychologically oriented historian, Brodie shared Erikson's reservations about the emerging field of psychohistory. Both disapproved of the disposition by some psychohistorians to treat the public statements of a prominent figure as if they originated in a therapeutic clinical setting. Brodie urged Erikson to consult the standard published primary sources on the Sage of Monticello, including his *Notes on the State of Virginia,* his autobiography, his correspondence with John Adams, and similar easily accessible documents. Erikson did not go far beyond this very preliminary list. Brodie soon realized that he was no prodigious or systematic researcher and pursued whatever interested him. But she liked and respected Erikson. Consequently, she volunteered her own wealth of historical and biographical knowledge to provide context for his preliminary characterization of Jefferson.[85]

Even with Brodie's help, Erikson recognized that his knowledge of Jefferson was fragmentary. As the date for his address approached, he told distraught NEH officials that he would not be satisfying their requirement of a full text from which he was to read; he had not yet achieved sufficient mastery of the subject and would be speaking from notes. He also requested that lecture invitations be sent to students in the Washington area as well as to staid, over-forty local cultural patrons—that is, he wanted the occasion to be multigenerational. Even with these changes in format, Erikson was uneasy. He presented a trial run of the lectures on the Virginian in a distinctly Yankee forum—the Stockbridge Town Hall—where friends and former Austen Riggs colleagues voiced approval, including John Demos, a young Brandeis historian whose well-received book on family life in the Plymouth colony owed a debt to Erikson's developmental schema.[86]

Five weeks before Erikson was to deliver the Jefferson Lectures in Washington, Robert Lifton stayed overnight with him in his Tiburon home. Lifton had lectured in Berkeley and wanted to visit before returning to New York. When Erikson greeted him at the door, Lifton sensed instantly "how much he has taught me, how much he has meant to me." The feeling was reciprocal. Soon after Lifton arrived, Erikson confessed the secret of his third son, Neil, indicating how much this Down Syndrome child continued to weigh on him almost a decade after his death. Not knowing how to respond, Lifton switched the subject and asked Erikson about the state of his NEH lectures. Erikson answered "with great flow" through the afternoon, the evening, and the following morning.[87]

Erikson admitted his scant knowledge of Jefferson and that he planned to use the third president as a springboard for larger topics. For instance, he planned to speak about Jefferson's "protean" or ever-changing personality—characterized by effusiveness and reserve, facade and feeling, informality and elegance. In *Childhood and Society,* Erikson had dismissed the "misconception" that a person achieved a sense of identity "through the indefinite adaptation to the demands of social change." But in the course of the 1960s, both he and Lifton were taken by the proliferation of protean qualities in contemporary society. At a Rockefeller Foundation–sponsored Bellagio Center conference in 1968, just before the first of Lifton's two articles on "Protean Man" was published, Erikson had noted the difficulty for modern youth to say "Here I stand" as young Luther had done, for "change is now self-sustaining." Between Luther's day and present times, Erikson insisted, a person had come to need "an ethical flexibility, a capacity for being with it." Change had become a constant, and a protean personality responsive to change in contemporary life was required. At this point in his work, Erikson, like Lifton, seemed to be anticipating qualities associated with a decentered, postmodern state of affairs.[88]

Discussion of proteanism consumed most of the time Lifton spent with Erikson since it represented a major shift in Erikson's perspective on identity. He wanted to be sure that he was on firm ground before giving his NEH lectures, and Lifton had thought long and hard about the concept. To be sure, the two ate, drank, and talked avidly about other matters, but the old man always returned to the protean Virginian.[89]

Buoyed by his visit with Lifton, Erikson flew to Washington for two days of lecturing. Edward Kennedy, the senator from Massachusetts and a neighbor on the Cape, hosted a luncheon for the Erikson family prior to the first lecture. Several Senate liberals also attended; Erikson was gratified to see his friend Jacob Javits among them. After the first lecture, there was a black-tie dinner in the Benjamin Franklin Room of the State Department. Senators Claiborne Pell and Javits attended. So did Supreme Court Justice Byron White, a Kennedy appointment, and Kennedy Center chairman Roger Stevens. Edgar Shannon, Jr., president of the University of Virginia, founded by Jefferson, was on hand. Erikson had to be pleased when Leonard Garment, Nixon's adviser on Watergate matters and an NEH supporter in the administration, called to voice regrets, for the moral gap between Jefferson and Nixon had been on everybody's mind. During the balance of his stay in Washington, Erikson tried to fend off reporters, especially one from the *Washington Post* who requested a short and simple definition of pseudospeciation. A *New York Times* reporter asked how seriously Erikson regarded the women's liberation movement. "I take the subject very seriously indeed," he responded in a dismissive tone.[90]

Uneasy about his public-speaking skills, Erikson regretted that the lectures were being broadcast live on radio. The congressional hearings on Watergate were about to begin, and the capital was unusually tense. Erikson thought it best to punctuate his lectures with humor. Wearing a conventional dark suit, a white shirt, and a dark tie—unusually conservative attire for him if appropriate for the occasion—he began by trying to relax the audience. It was difficult to find a suitable title for the lectures, he announced. "Dimensions of a New Man" was sexist while "Dimensions of a New Man and New Woman" was awkward. "Dimensions of a New Person" looked too much "like a compromise to me." Finally, he came across "Dimensions of a New Identity," which was "what you would expect me to talk about anyway." And "it is bisexual." The audience laughed and tension dissipated. At another point, as Erikson felt the tension returning, he referred to pseudospeciation as "a new concept of mine which I cannot pronounce." This drew light laughter. Humor now came easily to him.[91]

During Lifton's visit with him, Erikson had indicated that the NEH audience would expect some reference to the controversial Nixon presidency. As early as June 1969, while attending a White House staff dinner, he had sensed that this would be a troubled administration. Erikson told Lifton that he wanted to mention Nixon's punitiveness and vindictiveness, "but I don't want to use names." There were no explicit references to Nixon in the NEH lectures, but allusion to "events in this city of Washington and in high places" that evidenced "the pervasive power of atavistic strivings, and of how the man out front, the erstwhile warrior and hunter, has perpetuated himself." Erikson noted "the sudden shift of attention from military atrocity in foreign lands [Southeast Asia] to political scandal at home." Discussion of Jefferson against the backdrop of a besieged chief executive who had "overadjust[ed] to power, the *suppression* of adversary opinions, and the ready *oppression* of foreign people" was what he intended to address. Clearly, the Sage of Monticello was to be a prop, a point of departure for a prophetic message.[92]

The task at hand, Erikson instructed his audience, was to explain why "the geopolitical foundations of the American identity have changed beyond recognition" since Jefferson's day, and why it had become so difficult for Americans to demand "disengagement from such adventures as the war

in Southeast Asia." "How can we really grasp, in one lifetime . . . the Holocaust, Hiroshima, [and] the moon landings," Erikson asked, to say nothing
of Vietnam and "our moral malaise at the height of our mechanized power
of destruction?" The focus in America had shifted in "emphasis from what
you were (that is, made of yourself by hard work) to what you had (that is,
acquired and conspicuously possessed) to what you could consume." And
yet there was hope, Erikson explained, by rediscovering what Lincoln meant
by America as "an almost chosen people." If the rest of the world "abhors
our excesses in the use of mechanical power" and other "crudities," it "still
looks to America as one model, however tainted, of a historical miracle."
Contemporary Americans should look beyond their "industrial complexes,
and telecommunications," and acknowledge their guilt "over having transgressed against humanity and nature." Understanding Jefferson and his
vision for America just might promote "the *inner liberation* necessary to
plan the global politics of technology shared by one species." The American
assignment was to move beyond the pseudospeciation represented by U.S.
destruction in Hiroshima and Vietnam, and to embrace "universal specieshood"—"to be activated by and to activate" humanity everywhere. In this
way, Jefferson's lost vision would be recovered.[93]

Prophetic in tone, identifying with an eighteenth-century public intellectual with strong aesthetic proclivities, Erikson translated Jefferson to America and the world as he had translated Gandhi and *Satyagraha.* Indeed, he
explicitly connected the two in a common "faith in a self-aware, all-human
identity." Erikson reminded his audience of Gandhi's proclamation that
"God . . . appears to you in actions" and that Jefferson "could have said
that." He added that "if Gandhi meant nonviolent action, I think one can
find a strong temperamental trend—'peace is my passion'—toward solutions without violence in Jefferson's policies." Both leaders had sought "a
new actuality with infinite possibilities" for all of humankind. While Jefferson's view of the "earth" meant the literal soil under one's feet "bounded by
property lines in a new land still defining its over-all boundaries," it also
must "mean to us the globe inhabited by one mankind." Gandhi had shared
that vision even as he redeemed Indian soil from British occupation.[94]

The problem was that Erikson had spent far more time and effort investigating Gandhi's "ecology of greatness" than he had Jefferson's. His attempt
to sketch Jefferson's "ecology" was fragmentary at best. He prepared no "Personal Word" to Jefferson concerning his faults as he had to Gandhi. Rather,
he worked to reinterpret a few of Jefferson's potential blemishes as paths to a
more inclusive American identity. Race was a major case in point. Erikson
skirted Jefferson's racism and his commitment to slavery. While he acknowledged that Jefferson had opposed miscegenation and had "tentatively advo-

cated colonization" of American blacks in Africa [an understatement], Erikson insisted that the Virginian had still intended to guarantee to blacks "the status of a 'free and independent people.' " If Americans of Jefferson's day sometimes incarcerated orphans, the destitute, and the deranged, Erikson cited Jefferson's letter to his daughter, Martha, which insisted that America mark "itself off against those negative potentials that each man must confine and repress, deny and expel." Ultimately, Erikson's Jefferson was wrestling doggedly to transcend America's bigotries and discriminations.[95]

Straining to present Jefferson as a champion of "universal specieshood" and a proponent of "a wider human consciousness," Erikson urged his NEH audience to see beyond the "practical as well as intellectual racism in his own writings." Jefferson had written that "the earth belongs to the living," which rvealed the truth "that all men are created equal" and that "each child born has a right to expect a chance to develop such [his] potential." It also meant "the right to live in a community which chooses to guarantee . . . the fullest development of each of its members." Erikson was obviously pushing well beyond his evidence. He insisted that Jefferson favored existence in relatively small "optimal communal units to be built into a future megalopolis" because he realized that this was essential for optimal human development. Jefferson realized that American democracy required "direct personal and communal communication." Proximity and personal interchange represented two of Jefferson's methods for warding off "odious peculiarities" or what Erikson called pseudospeciation.[96]

Erikson's case for Jefferson and his America derived from personal identification with the Sage of Monticello, who lacked the personal presence and prophetic aura of Gandhi. Jefferson "never was an eloquent orator; he *wrote* with supreme oratory." Erikson could identify with a less than charismatic prophet who led through the power of his ideas and his writings. More fundamentally, he insisted that Jefferson had the qualities of a developmental theorist, as Erikson had. After all, Jefferson found an ethical core in man that, "if given leeway to manifest itself in mutual activation with others[,] will tend to make ethical and rational choice[s]." This was "a basic developmental truth." Both Erikson and Jefferson prized personal introspection "to face the worst and best in us." Finally, following introspection, both advanced the same therapeutic regime for man—"the informed love of humanity—in others, in himself, and in his children." As he concluded his remarks on Jefferson's philosophical and psychological insights, Erikson began to whistle the "Star Spangled Banner"—if only for a split second. The European immigrant was straining to locate America's humanistic beginnings in a chief executive who, unlike several other Virginia planters, had refused to manumit his slaves and had concluded that blacks were innately inferior to whites. His enthusiasm for Jefferson outdistanced his evidence.[97]

Erikson was especially captivated by Jefferson's devotion, during his presidency, to Jesus' precepts. This devotion illustrated the connection that Erikson made between Gandhi's and Jefferson's spiritualized politics. In the NEH lectures, Erikson traced the history of a scrapbook or booklet completed by Jefferson in 1805 that consisted of selections clipped and pasted together from the New Testament in various languages under the title "The Philosophy of Jesus of Nazareth." In the 1820s, Jefferson enlarged the booklet into a compendium that came to be called *Life and Morals of Jesus of Nazareth.* Jefferson had selected accounts of Jesus' life and teaching presented by Mark, Luke, and John that "spoke to him as the voice of Jesus." For Erikson, these "authentic" selections demonstrated that Jefferson "believed strongly in the singular presence of Jesus among men" and not in his divine status. Although Jefferson was not a devout churchgoer and was uninterested in religious power struggles, he had been deeply attentive to "the genuine precepts of Jesus himself." Erikson not only studied Jefferson's selections in the published compendium, but made much of Jefferson's failure to include "the decisive therapeutic event in the Gospels" cited in Luke 8:48 and Mark 5:25–35—the story of a woman who had lost her blood and her money but who touched Jesus' clothes and felt whole. For Erikson, it was "her faith in his mission that had made her whole." Because Jefferson "believed in the preventive powers of an active life" more than the healing arts, Erikson understood why he had neglected this episode. The president had intended his initial booklet as an abridged scripture for American Indians. Erikson, long interested in Native Americans, characterized the booklet as "something of a native, an American Gospel."[98]

More than any other source, Erikson depended on Jefferson's *Life and Morals of Jesus of Nazareth.* However, he never became well informed concerning Jefferson's interest in Jesus. Fawn Brodie criticized him privately for failing to explore the specific biographical context of the compendium. She explained to Erikson that had he researched his subject, he would have learned that Jefferson felt crucified because the Federalist press exposed his probable liaison with a slave woman (Sally Hemings); that situation helped to account for material in Jefferson's compendium on Jesus' crucifixion. But if Erikson was no Jefferson scholar and hardly a Jesus scholar, he identified with Jefferson's decision to put aside his distaste for institutional religion in order to study Jesus' precepts. Erikson seemed to be emulating the Virginian. He found himself examining New Testament passages for the "presence of Jesus among men." Like Jefferson, Erikson studied that presence to fathom an ultimate reality in which human trust for another and The Other might rest. More abstractly, he wanted to explain how the lonely "I" might connect itself with all of humanity and simultaneously with God. More than in *Gandhi's Truth,* where he felt Jesus' presence as he stood at the Sea of Galilee, Erikson was moving toward the concerns of his last major publication, "The Galilean Sayings and the Sense of 'I.' "[99]

At various times during his two days of NEH lectures, Erikson alluded to the dangerous "age of nuclear destruction" with "the ritualization of warfare." The fateful questions, he said, were whether society was willing to repress the need of people to connect to others in caring, loving ways and whether humankind was willing to annihilate the world at large. A globally suicidal course could be initiated by American actions, as well as by those of any other superpower, for "no nation with superweaponry . . . is above the temptation to exterminate (in occasional massacres or planned bombardments) what it considers to be an expendable species." Against this disastrous course, Erikson juxtaposed the trust established in the parent-child relationship. He concluded his final NEH lecture by emphasizing the importance of capable parenting—adults nurturing younger generations. The adult needed, above all else, to feel empowered "to take care of what he most cares for, what he cares to be, and what he cares to cause to be." This caregiving was not relegated to one's own progeny; rather, it involved "personal and communal responsibility for all those born, and the application of parental concerns to the preservation of what enhances the whole cycle of life." To "take care of" corresponded to the Hindu concept of "maintenance of the world" and represented "the only adult meaning of that strange word *happiness* as a political principle." Erikson ended the final lecture by alluding to Jefferson's "pursuit of *happiness*" along lines that called to mind Hannah Arendt's reference to Jefferson as the advocate of public happiness. His last words represented at once an admonition and a greeting: "TAKE CARE." The audience responded with respectful but less than overwhelming applause.[100]

After Erikson delivered the Jefferson Lectures, he spent "a most difficult summer" revising them to meet NEH requirements for prompt publication. Revisions were primarily literary, not substantive, and "I [he] have endeavored . . . to maintain a spoken rather than a written style." His eyes tired easily, and his vision was flawed. Much of his spontaneous humor and certain specific references to Watergate and Vietnam were not included in *Dimensions of a New Identity.* Erikson inserted "subtitles" for *Dimensions* so that the two lectures were presented as eleven short chapters. Yet he did not choose to deepen his evidential or analytic perspective on Jefferson or to flesh out other important aspects of the lectures. Erikson acknowledged that his only truly substantive addition was an elaboration on "the long-range convergence of contemporary concerns with my main themes." This resembled his follow-up work on the Godkin Lectures. He was disturbed that Norton provided a white, red, black, and yellow dust jacket; it was "so loud as to suggest almost anything—except Jefferson lectures."[101]

After *Dimensions of a New Identity* was published, Erikson wrote to Wallace Edgerton of the NEH that "I have received very few letters about the Jefferson lectures" and that early reviews ranged from very good to bad and "even vicious ones." He sensed "that many people did not quite know what to do with them" and that he had been perhaps too conscientious about the assignment. He was particularly upset over a review in *Commentary* by the well-known University of Michigan psychologist David Gutmann, which asserted that Erikson had shifted from a richly complex and positive view of America in *Childhood and Society* to a flat, negative evaluation of his adopted country in *Dimensions*. Erikson drafted a reply defending the Jefferson Lectures for presenting both the "very special humanity" and "very special forms of inhumanity" that "come to the fore in the history of all empires." He felt duty bound to delineate these "inner contradictions" in the American psyche. The preparation of this response seemed to afford sufficient relief; Erikson decided against sending it to *Commentary*. Conservative social commentator Edwin Yoder's review in the *National Review* was even more critical. Like Gutmann, Yoder faulted Erikson's critique of America. More disturbing, Yoder prescribed "a few hours of Strunk and White" to improve an obtuse style; Erikson "does not write English very clearly."[102]

Despite some negative reviews, *Dimensions of a New Identity* sold respectably when it was released in 1974. The combined cloth and paperback sales approximated twenty thousand the first year out and then scaled down, but exceeded *Toys and Reasons*. Erikson's former students and close colleagues were effusive in their praise of *Dimensions*. His friend John Demos, a specialist in early American history, wrote to him that "you have done extremely well at *seeing Jefferson in his context*." Robert Coles agreed, noting in a book review that Erikson showed sensitively and subtly "how a given era's social and cultural tensions work their way into the most gifted, private, and introspective individuals."[103]

Two commentators, University of Virginia historian Robert Brugger and Yale chaplain friend and peace activist William Sloane Coffin understood that, like *Gandhi's Truth* and *Toys and Reasons,* the Jefferson Lectures underscored Erikson's sense of himself as a global prophet with an urgent message. Gandhi's Truth and Jefferson's Truth were ultimately Erikson's Truth. Brugger characterized Erikson as "a kind of statesman" who "contends for the 'inner emancipation' necessary for the politics of a globe humankind needs to share." Coffin felt that Erikson realized, even more than Jefferson, "that in the sullied stream of human life it is not innocence but holiness that is our only option." If "holiness" was Coffin's term and "wholeness" was Erikson's, Coffin acknowledged that "the concept is yours [since] whole and holy come from the same root." Erikson's Truth was that "pseudoinnocence" about man's inner demons provoked the pseudospeciation that threatened global survival.[104]

Coffin and Brugger were relatively tolerant of Erikson's prophetic approach, but several older friends, like Henry Murray and Margaret Mead, found that this manner placed a strain on their relationships with him. In contrast, young students and political activists like Janice Abarbanel, Mark Gerzon, and Randall Kehler considered his manner charismatic and alluring. Of Erikson's two closest Indian colleagues, Kamla Chowdhry was a bit put off while her nephew, Sudhir Kakar, found a certain magic in his manner. Friends from a generation of emerging public intellectuals like Robert Lifton, Robert Coles, and Robert Wallerstein, who considered Erikson a mentor, regarded the prophetic mode as interesting and exciting although not quite the "right fit" for a man they thought they knew. Senior scholars like Jerome Bruner, David Riesman, Gerald Holton, and Gardner Murphy continued to focus on the content of Erikson's work, deemphasizing this new aspect. But those closest to Erikson, especially Joan, Kai, and Pamela Daniels, felt that the prophetic quality was but another variation of a fascinating and constantly changing individual.

By 1973, Erik Erikson, second Jefferson Lecturer, appeared to have transcended the diffident, insecure European immigrant who happily and gratefully made his way in FDR's America. He had received a very significant honor for an American intellectual—delivering the annual NEH lectures. People in very high places watched as he urged Americans to rediscover aspects of their Jeffersonian legacy—his Truth and the third president's. The enormous praise and honors Erikson received during the early 1970s, however, would soon be accompanied by blistering criticisms that made David Gutmann's and Edwin Yoder's reviews pale by comparison. As these criticisms mounted, Erikson's old self-doubts and insecurities resurfaced.

CHAPTER NINE

Public and Private Matters
of Old Age

In 1975, Erik Erikson published another collection of essays, *Life History and the Historical Moment.* Most had been previously published and were simply lightly revised. Only a paper that Erikson had given in 1974—"Psychoanalysis: Adjustment or Freedom?"—had not previously appeared in print. However, the argument of that paper—that the effective analyst and analysand experienced "mutual activation"—was a familiar theme. Other essays included an "autobiographic perspective" that he had published twice before, his 1955 review of Freud's *The Origins of Psychoanalysis,* a twice-published review of Sigmund Freud's collaborative volume with William Bullitt on Woodrow Wilson, a research report published in 1968 on his Gandhi project, and a lecture delivered in 1968 at the University of Cape Town on the South African origins of *Satyagraha.* Finally, the book included a twice-published essay on youth protest and another that he had revised and republished several times on womanhood and "inner space."

One factor behind publication of this volume was the pressure W. W. Norton was putting on Erikson to earn back a very large advance. But he was also anxious to justify the book. In a prefatory note, he claimed that the "main" essays were presented at interdisciplinary symposia convened by the American Academy of Arts and Sciences, publisher of the journal *Daedalus.* At these symposia, he represented psychoanalysis in its relationship to other fields and to themes that crossed many fields. He insisted that "one over-all theme 'orchestrates' all of these occasions"—the relationship of the life histories of leaders and their followers to particular "historical moments." Part of this phenomenon was represented by "the awakening of whole groups of contemporaries (young people, modern women) to a need for inner as well as political liberation." The volume was also united by the "life histories of us, the observers, defined as we are by our own past, by the history of our field, and by the tasks of the times." Clearly, Erikson was inflating his "theme" to justify inclusion of very disparate essays that had been prepared over a twenty-year period and in very different settings. He wrote lengthy introductions elaborating the context for each essay, but his Norton editors persuaded him to delete them. He thanked Pamela Daniels, who continued to assist with his writings and public appearances, for helping him to select and edit each essay in the book, and dedicated it to her and other teaching staff and students of the Social Science 139 life cycle course at Harvard.[1]

More than a year after publication, Erikson characterized *Life History and the Historical Moment* as "my least successful book," and paltry sales were not the most important reason. The volume was simply not well received. Because of his popularity, Erikson felt, an increasing number of critics had been using him "as a straw man" and liked to "take pot shots at me." This publication was but the most recent example. David Lipset, a social critic and one of the more charitable reviewers of *Life History,* offered a somewhat more cogent appraisal. Erikson's renown and his "indisputable creativity" had generated very high expectations within the intellectual, scholarly, and professional communities, Lipset pointed out. Readers in these communities "may be asking too much from this thinker precisely because he has already given us so much." Lipset warned that they would carp at this "collection of minor writings connected in only the loosest way."[2]

Both Erikson and Lipset had been right. Readers had been carping since the late 1960s as Erikson rose to intellectual stardom. Some of the more perceptive critics observed that his facility to analyze and to organize his materials was declining, and that his vague ethical assertions represented inadequate substitutes. Indeed, the publication of *Life History* opened a floodgate of Erikson bashing that he found devastating.

CRITICISM: BEFORE *LIFE HISTORY*

By the early 1970s, criticisms of Erikson's writing were rather frequent. University of Illinois psychologist J. McVicker Hunt spoke out, for example, about the level of simplification within Erikson's constructs; they "don't lead me to empirical kinds of things that I can go and test." They never could, of course. More pointedly, University of Rochester child psychologist David Elkind, who had praised Erikson highly, was keenly disappointed with the high level of generality in Erikson's writings and the vagueness of his assertions. These elements often precluded application "to here and now real problems." Not long after *Gandhi's Truth* won major book prizes, a methodologist in social research James Phelps, prepared a fifty-page critique of select Erikson publications, attacking him for failing "to define his terms operationally" and for confusing correlation with causation, cause with effect. These charges reflected a complex and shifting intellectual and scholarly climate, especially in psychology and other areas of the social sciences. While variations of Freudianism and neo-Freudianism retained support in some quarters, and broadly humanistic interdisciplinarity still enjoyed wide currency, there was increasing stridency among heirs of diverse positivist and behaviorist traditions. They valued empiricism, quantification, and cautious assertion, and were often unsympathetic with Erikson's wheeling exploratory style (typical of the World War II generation of cosmopolitan intellectuals).[3]

During the early and middle 1970s, some of the historians who had initially heralded *Young Man Luther* and *Gandhi's Truth* as groundbreaking psychohistorical studies now expressed serious second thoughts. Frank Manuel questioned whether Erikson's life cycle model was universally applicable. More probably, it captured only select aspects of "twentieth-century psychoanalytic experience" and lacked relevance "to other cultures and periods." Howard Kushner came to this same conclusion after attending a seminar (in 1974) in which Erikson doggedly defended the universality of his life cycle model. Kushner was especially upset because Erikson dismissed Philippe Aries's evidence that concepts of childhood were historically grounded in time and place. During this same interval, Fred Weinstein and Gerald Platt warned of a "Coming Crisis in Psychohistory" rooted in overreliance upon Erikson's works. Erikson blinded scholars to underlying social structures, they charged, and simplified their portrayal of mass uprisings. Patrick Dunn, who had read Erikson zealously, reprimanded him for reprinting familiar essays in *Life History* and for writing little that was not recycled. Although John Demos remained a friend and admirer, by the 1970s his research on witchcraft hysterias diverted his attention from Erikson's work and toward what came to be called self psychology.[4]

As important historians ceased to value Erikson's work as a model for psychohistorical endeavor, leading psychoanalysts also voiced disenchantment. Like the historians, psychoanalysts were emphasizing different theoretical orientations. Although so-called late ego psychologists like Otto Kernberg and Margaret Mahler continued to appreciate Erikson's contributions, they began to alter their focus. British object relations theory represented by W. R. D. Fairbairn, D. W. Winnicott, and others was coming to capture a significant following. Heinz Kohut's "self psychology" attracted increasing support as the 1970s progressed. Most adherents of these three overlapping psychoanalytic "schools" departed from Erikson by concentrating on early development, by viewing infancy as a period where clear differentiation or self-distinctiveness in the youngster's self-image was lacking, and by being more attentive to severe pathology than to normal development. While

Kernberg and Winnicott acknowledged a large debt to Erikson's formulations, Kohut distinguished his "depth" concept of the self from the "psychological surface" covered by Erikson's identity construct. Erikson was distressed by this shift in the psychoanalytic landscape. He was most upset with Kohut because "he simply tries to do away with me." Kurt Eissler's charge that Erikson's theoretical system was not psychoanalytic and that Erikson was a psychotherapist instead of an analyst also hurt. Nor could Erikson take comfort in a poll of ninety psychoanalysts released in 1972. The majority of those canvassed considered him a psychoanalytic innovator but acknowledged that their clinical applications of his ideas were minimal.[5]

Before *Life History* was published, barbs were also aired from the academic left. Attentiveness to the works of Walter Benjamin, Jürgen Habermas, Louis Althusser, and Antonio Gramsci signaled the rebirth of academic Marxism along varied lines. In this climate, veteran neo-Freudian and Marxist Erich Fromm spoke out. Fromm had long been upset with Erikson for borrowing from his writing (especially from *Escape from Freedom*) without adequate acknowledgment. For decades, Fromm had also felt that Erikson had been deficient in his critique of dominant economic and social institutions. In *The Crisis of Psychoanalysis* (1970), Fromm went public, attacking Erikson for failure to pursue "in a more radical way" the theme that social organization and values could cripple the individual self, and leave a person with a fake sense of identity. This set the tone for criticism from younger voices on the left. By 1973, Tufts political scientist Tony Smith was circulating a paper characterizing Erikson as an apologist for an oppressive status quo. Erikson's notion of reciprocity between the individual and society obscured the fact that society's conformist pressures on the individual far exceeded the individual's effect on society. In short, Erikson was advocating individual adaptation to socially prescribed norms. The following year, social critic Joel Kovel of the Albert Einstein College of Medicine advanced a less temperate critique, characterizing Erikson as a second-rate thinker and an apologist for the established order. In *Gandhi's Truth,* for example, Erikson had turned "mistily to God . . . without criticizing what society has established in the way of morality and law." Kovel claimed that Erikson avoided analysis of "real power, the economic and political kind," and failed to confront the fact that "there is real destructiveness in the world."[6]

These and similar charges hurt Erikson deeply. Had critics like Smith and Kovel, who were characterizing him as a social conservative and a status quo theorist, failed to read his texts carefully? Had they overlooked his warning that "we must refuse to be technicians of adjustment" and that "true *adaptation,* in fact, is maintained with the help of loyal rebels who refuse to adjust to 'conditions' "? To make matters worse, Erikson's good friend

David Riesman sometimes accused him of political "centrism." Had Riesman failed to understand that Luther, Gandhi, and Jefferson, whom he portrayed so positively, were revolutionaries? Why had critics on the left failed to see that, book after book, he had endorsed revolution?[7]

In short, Erikson had more than his share of adversaries. The decision to reprint a lightly revised version of his 1964 *Daedalus* article "The Inner and the Outer Space: Reflections on Womanhood" in *Life History and the Historical Moment* augmented what was already a groundswell of hostile feminist criticism. The article had grown out of his observations, since the late 1930s and early 1940s, concerning gender differentiations that were detectable in children's play constructions. Many of his points in the essay were decidedly pro-feminist. But when the essay reappeared in *Identity: Youth and Crisis* (1968), intense criticism arose over Erikson's equation of girls' inward turning (enclosing) genitalia with play constructions that suggested nurturing others, and boys' outward protruding (penetrating) phalluses with play constructions indicating dominance and bellicosity.

At the time, many American feminists had embraced egalitarian values to the point of deemphasizing physiological differences. They were influenced by a strain of Anglo-American political theory that had been vibrant since John Stuart Mill's *The Subjection of Women* (1869), which considered the individual (irrespective of gender) as the basic unit and entitled to the same rights and privileges as any other individual. Confusing Erikson's observations on differences between the sexes with an endorsement of inequality, they retorted that women were the equal of men, entitled to the same choices, spheres, autonomies, and opportunities for self-realization. Several feminists accused Erikson of clinging to the traditional Freudian view that women were guilty of penis envy and feared inner emptiness. Admittedly, Erikson's long-standing preoccupation with the shape and importance of the genitals, while he elaborated on Freud, had helped to feed this charge. Most critics, however, failed to recognize that his perspective was also compatible with a continental European (primarily German and French) feminism that elaborated and celebrated womanliness—essentiality—and lauded male-female complementarity in differences. Continental feminists drew on essentialist nineteenth-century writers such as Hubertine Auclert and Bertha von Suttner. Like Erikson, they emphasized woman's unique capacities for relationships, healing, and general caregiving, and they found special benefits in modifying the militaristic nation-state with maternal qualities. They linked woman's capacities to her distinctive biology as a child-bearing creator of life.[8]

American feminist attacks on Erikson began with psychologist Naomi Weisstein's widely publicized 1968 pamphlet *Kinder, Kuche, Kirche as Scien-*

tific Law. Lumping Erikson with psychoanalysts Bruno Bettelheim and Joseph Rheingold, Weisstein insisted that all three replaced empirical evidence and close observation of social forces with a subjective quest for imagined inner female traits. The problem with their flawed quest for the intrapsychic, Weisstein maintained, was that it served to maintain cultural myths that sustained male domination. Two years after the Weisstein pamphlet, the criticism extended into the wider culture with the publication of Kate Millett's much heralded *Sexual Politics.* In Millett's view, Erikson and Freud were part of a "counterrevolution" against opportunity for women. His "inner and outer space" dualism was "built on psychoanalysis' persistent error of mistaking learned behavior for biology." In her book, Millett failed to distinguish Freud's focus on what females lacked (the penis) from Erikson's emphasis on what they possessed (unique strengths of connectedness that were rooted in their "inner space"). For Millett, Erikson's "beliefs in the existence of innate sexual temperament" were distressing; his "inner space" concept confined female creativity to maternity and "remote moral assistance to the male." Indeed, "Erikson is pained when ova go unfertilized." A "Radical Caucus" of feminists distributed a printed "Credo" at the 1970 annual meeting of the American Psychiatric Association; linking Erikson with Freud, much as Millett had, the credo asserted that both penis envy and "inner space" compounded women's problems and that a sexist social structure had to be confronted.[9]

By 1971, the feminist criticisms of Erikson—and Freud—were abundant. Germaine Greer's national bestseller *The Female Eunuch,* for example, perpetuated the Millett equation of Freud and Erikson. In addition, Erikson was singled out for inventing "the lunatic concept of *inner space* in a woman's *somatic design,* a hole in the head as it were, which harbors the commitment to take care of children." In *Man's World, Woman's Place* (1971), Elizabeth Janeway was slightly more circumspect; she rejected Erikson's "idea of innate sexual separatism" for its essential Freudianism. According to Janeway, the "inner space" concept postulates that "any attempt on their [women's] part to come out of their inner space and mix in men's world is unnatural." Judith Hole and Ellen Levine's *Rebirth of Feminism* (1971), influenced by Millett, insisted that Erikson had replaced Freud's penis envy construct with "the joy of 'inner space.' " Phyllis Chesler joined the fray in *Women and Madness* (1972), claiming that Erikson, Freud, and other psychoanalysts all viewed women as imperfect beings who required men. By this time, less polemical feminist scholars were beginning to complete replication studies of Erikson's play constructions of young boys and girls, and their tests indicated that the children did, indeed, make constructions that reflected "inner" and "outer" space. However, the types of constructions bore no correlation to their genders; Erikson's observations simply did not hold up. At this point, George Brockway was apprehensive both as a W. W. Norton executive and, by now, Erikson's close friend, for the persistence of feminist attacks had begun to make inroads on the sales of Erikson's books.[10]

While criticisms from historians, psychoanalysts, and leftist academics were disturbing, Erikson found the feminist attacks most painful of all. He had always been appreciative of strong, unconventional, free-thinking women like Margaret Mead, Ruth Benedict, and Pamela Daniels—not to mention his wife, Joan, and his mother, Karla. Although he probably valued their assistance and protection more than their intellectual prowess, he conceived of himself as a genuine feminist and was sure that he was being misunderstood and erroneously stereotyped. Some "women writers" had been "so angered by what they think I said that they never read my conclusions," he pointed out. Despite the obvious anatomical differences, he had concluded that males and females "have joint histories and separate [individual] personalities." He wanted to get around the canned summaries of his thought, which categorized him as a Freudian who had denigrated women, for "there is much in the radical endeavors of today's women students which is at least consonant with the general trend of my writings." He found public forums on his "Inner and Outer Space" essay exceedingly painful. At a Berkeley symposium in which a feminist construed one of his comments as "penis envy," Erikson exhibited rare anger: "You '*understood*' my remark as 'assuming' something I did not say" so that it could fit "your ideological stance." Deeply saddened by the barrage of criticism, Erikson asked former SS 139 undergraduate Jean Strouse "how best to answer my women critics." He also urged W. W. Norton to limit republications of the controversial essay. On the other hand, he agreed to let Strouse print a somewhat revised version of the essay that politely refuted some of his critics. She inserted the essay in her own collection of articles, *Women and Analysis* (1974). Erikson then republished his revised essay in *Life History*.[11]

To some extent, Erikson was victimized by shifting feminist perspectives. By the time *Life History* appeared in 1975, important segments of American feminist thought were shifting from the egalitarian-environmental paradigm dismissive of intrapsychic life toward an "essentialist" and "culturalist" posture popular in continental Europe. But suspicions of arguments based on sex differences persisted, especially those connected with woman's physiology and nurturing capacities. This was especially true when the arguments were advanced by Erikson and Ashley Montagu's postwar generation of male writers who had professed knowledge of the special nature of women. Consequently, even though Erikson's "inner and outer space" perspective was not antagonistic to the new "cultural" feminist emphasis on woman's capacity for caretaking and human connectedness, he continued to be castigated. The charges of feminist egalitarians were perpetuated by the feminist culturalists. Nancy Chodorow, for example, characterized the mother-daughter relationship as one encouraging women to develop less competitive, more relational views of the world than men. However, she still chastised Erikson, insisting that he was too close to Freud in his gender distinctions.[12]

The criticisms of Erikson's former teaching assistant Carol Gilligan upset him even more. Although she had heard him lecture on "Inner and Outer Space" and had read the paper in published form, she did not acknowledge it as a building block in her own evolving theory. During the winter of 1975, Gilligan drafted the essay "In a Different Voice" that was subsequently published in the *Harvard Educational Review* and expanded into a major book. One of her central arguments was that women's life cycles at every stage were deeply relational. Mutuality, respect, and caring were central to a woman's development. Erikson's "The Inner and the Outer Space" perspective pointed her in this direction. But as Gilligan prepared the first draft of her essay, she felt that he did not go far enough in his work. A male from an earlier generation, Erikson seemed too Freudian and too old to rework his life cycle chart to reflect woman's distinctive voice and developmental pattern from infancy to adulthood. If the chart registered male development accurately, it did not serve women well. According to Gilligan, women were much more preoccupied with relational concerns of intimacy than with separation-independence. While Erikson acknowledged that female identity had as much to do with intimacy as with separation, Gilligan insisted that identity's architect needed to prepare a separate developmental chart for women. She attacked him with these points in her paper, her article, and her book. Erikson did not respond publicly. Privately, he was annoyed and hurt that Gilligan had not acknowledged his contribution to her work or the proximity of their views. Erikson was also concerned because his daughter, Sue, a mother well into her thirties, could not plot her own life along his developmental chart. She felt that she had yet to reach his fifth or identity stage. Sue agreed with Gilligan that a separate developmental chart would be helpful.[13]

THE BERMAN CONTROVERSY

One of Erikson's worst tactical errors, then, was to have included a slightly revised version of "Inner and Outer Space" in his *Life History* volume. It appeared as a sign of defiance to his feminist critics, exacerbating attacks that persisted well into the 1980s. The decision to open *Life History* with the twice-published essay " 'Identity Crisis' in Autobiographic Perspective" proved to be an even greater blunder for a man who found no comfort in controversy or notoriety.

In 1969, Erikson presented a draft of that essay to an American Academy of Arts and Sciences conference at Lake Como, Italy, then published it in *Daedalus,* the academy's journal. The conference concerned the "biography" of innovative twentieth-century ideas and Erikson had taken the assignment very seriously. He had elected to treat his most widely discussed concept— the identity crisis—as it evolved in the context of his own life and career. When Freud was his age, he had written "An Autobiographic Study" along similar lines. Erikson felt that it was appropriate to do the same, later acknowledging "that autobiography is almost impossibly complex for a psychoanalyst" and that he became "uncomfortable about its publication." He began his essay with a hasty discussion of identity as a concept, then launched into a review of his own life by beginning with his work in Vienna. Next, he dropped back chronologically to his pre-Vienna years and went forward to the post-Vienna decades. The Vienna training period was therefore pivotal—when his sense of professional and personal identity, and perhaps even the identity construct itself, had begun to cohere.[14]

Erikson's autobiographic essay was no small or insignificant document. Since the mid-1930s, psychologists had been perhaps more disposed than any other profession toward autobiographical publication; the microcosm of an individual life was to reflect the macrocosm of the discipline. Erikson saw this as the point of his essay. He would review his life as it shed light on his discipline of psychoanalytic psychology and his major contribution to that discipline, the identity crisis concept. But he was guarded, distant, and inclined toward the third person. A few years earlier, when he had written about Gandhi's autobiography, Erikson had acknowledged that "autobiographies are written at certain late stages of life for the purpose of re-creating oneself in the image of one's own method; and they are written so as to make that image convincing." He seemed to be doing just that. He was recasting his life in the context of his major methodological contribution—a developmental model that involved the working toward and consolidating of an identity over the eight life stages. Erikson revised part of the essay for his friend Gerald Holton's 1972 collection, *The Twentieth-Century Sciences: Studies in the Biography of Ideas,* and revised it again as the first essay in *Life History.* Detailed textual comparison of these three versions reveals much, showing Erikson the artist at work, forever polishing his prose, rearranging words, sentences, and paragraphs to make them aesthetically pleasing. It also suggests some effort to manage an "official identity, the moment when life suddenly becomes biography." In the version published in 1970, for example, he had written of "an *ambivalent* identification with my stepfather" (Theodor Homburger); whereas in 1975 he revised it to read "*some strong* identification with my stepfather." But the pattern was inconsistent; sometimes he revealed more in the 1975 version than in 1970 or 1972.[15]

In a revised essay, "On the Nature of 'Psycho-Historical' Evidence," which appeared elsewhere in *Life History*, Erikson had warned that "nobody likes to be found out" and that the autobiographer "spars with his reader and potential judge." He told Betty Jean Lifton that he had revealed only "what I have wished to tell about myself" in the versions of his autobiographic essay; he would not permit her to include additional information concerning his early life in her publications on adopted children. But in sparring with his reader, Erikson allowed one fundamental fact to be "found out." His narration of the stages of his own life did not quite fit with his eight-stage life cycle model. He had charted his own life along six rather than eight stages:

Eight-Stage Life Cycle
1. Basic Trust vs. Mistrust (infancy)
2. Autonomy vs. Shame, Doubt (infancy, early childhood)
3. Initiative vs. Guilt (play age)
4. Industry vs. Inferiority (school age)
5. Identity vs. Role Confusion (adolescence)
6. Intimacy vs. Isolation (young adulthood)
7. Generativity vs. Stagnation (adulthood)
8. Ego Integrity vs. Despair (old age)

Autobiographical Life Stages
1. Childhood, Youth, Early Adulthood (1902–27)
2. Training in Freud's Vienna (1927–33)
3. Making of *Childhood and Society* (1933–50)
4. Clinician of Voice and Identity (1950–60)
5. Professor–Ethical Philosopher (1960–75)
6. Old Age[16]

Because Erikson's eight-stage model represented an elaboration of Freud's developmental theory, it had concentrated on infancy and childhood and on issues concerning sexuality and impulsivity. In his autobiographical essay, which was intended more to summarize his life course than to single out specific stages, he essentially consolidated the first five of the eight stages into a single stage. This stage covered his first twenty-five years—his inauspicious origins, his childhood and schooling in Karlsruhe, and the artistic and intellectual aspects of his *Wanderschaft.* The theme uniting these decid-edly non-Freudian issues was "my *personal* identity." Next, the autobio-graphical essay took up the central vocational, ethical, and philosophic concerns of Erikson's adulthood. There was the 1927–33 training period in Vienna. Then came the professional concerns in America that led to *Child-hood and Society.* Although Erikson distinguished "the thirties" on the East Coast from "the forties" in California, his discussion of trends in these two decades made for one distinctive autobiographical interval. It was followed by his clinical work at the Austen Riggs Center, then his Harvard years as a professor pursuing ethical and historical issues. The sixth and final stage in his autobiography—spiritual and prophetic old age—was implied. The dis-parity between the universal eight-stage life cycle and Erikson's six-stage autobiography was in character. He had always regarded his developmental model as a tool to be applied flexibly, especially when specifically reviewing someone's life. Moreover, he tended to regard formal psychological and social models as prescriptions for normality that rarely could be fully met.

The first two versions of Erikson's essay appeared in comparatively obscure publications and did not attract much notice. The third version, as the opening essay in *Life History and the Historical Moment,* attracted the most personal and damaging critique Erikson had ever received. Feminist criticisms paled by comparison. It was the most widely discussed essay in the book; some readers never got beyond it to the other seven essays.

The focus on the autobiographic essay in *Life History* occurred largely because of an arresting essay on the cover page of the *New York Times Book Review* in late March 1975, featuring a recent photograph of Erikson with his impressive white hair, well-groomed mustache, penetrating eyes, and characteristically reflective countenance. Above the photograph was the caption: "Erik Erikson, the man who invented himself." The essay on *Life History* was written by a former Harvard graduate student Marshall Berman, who had periodically attended Erikson's graduate seminar during the late 1960s. Berman had read and reflected deeply upon most of Erik-son's publications.[17]

Finishing his doctorate, Berman taught political science at City College of New York, where he completed *The Politics of Authenticity* (1970). The book sought to chart a transition in Western culture from values of "sincer-ity" to those of "authenticity." Berman argued that Rousseau and Mon-tesquieu had elaborated the nature of the "authentic"—a full sense of one's power to experience, to pursue happiness, to achieve, and to enjoy genuine relationships with others. An atmosphere of personal trust, candor, and inti-macy was crucial to establishing this authentic. Berman felt that Erikson had wonderfully exemplified this authentic quality in his "Personal Word" to Gandhi. Indeed, authenticity was evolving into his litmus test for appraising Erikson's writing.[18]

Early in 1975, *New York Times Book Review* editor John Leonard asked Berman to review *Life History and the Historical Momement*. Manager of a publication that reached roughly 1.6 million readers and commanded vast advertising sums from book publishers, Leonard was one of the most influential figures in the book world. Highly regarded and ambitious, he encouraged lively, thoughtful essays. He was also Berman's friend, thought well of *The Politics of Authenticity*, and was pleased with the provocative reviews that Berman had prepared for him on R. D. Laing, Edmund Wilson, and Erving Goffman. Berman had told Leonard of his interest in reviewing Erikson, and the publication of *Life History* provided that opportunity. Leonard selected it for a page-one review, which would influence book sales and Erikson's reputation quite decidedly.[19]

Leonard had no interest in encouraging a hostile review, especially after George Brockway, Erikson's influential editor, wrote a letter to leading literary agents accusing the *Times Book Review* of "smart ass" and "stand-up comic" reviewing. However, he understood the internal politics of the *New York Times* and recognized that the newspaper had assumed some of the pervasive Watergate era cynicism toward heroes and ideals. Leonard also saw that influential *Times* editors were becoming more conservative. By the early 1970s, several sympathized with public intellectuals like Irving Howe, Seymour Martin Lipset, and Nathan Glazer, who attacked the New Left for questioning "democratic Israel," for opposing American actions in Vietnam, and for embracing affirmative action for blacks (but not for Jews). *Times* editors regularly printed or summarized parts of this critique, usually unaccompanied by alternative perspectives. Leonard did not sympathize with the critique. However, he could hardly ignore the orientation emerging in the op-ed page, the *Sunday Magazine,* and other parts of the *Times*.[20]

What Leonard found in Marshall Berman was an exceedingly bright Jewish New Left intellectual, decidedly against the American presence in Vietnam, no apologist for Israeli militarism, empathetic to the civil rights movement, and rendered somewhat cynical by the events of Watergate. Berman was also troubled by Jews like I. F. Stone and Noam Chomsky, who seemed to deny their Jewishness, often by failing to align with Jewish traditions and perspectives. He felt that this failure was a telltale sign of the *inauthentic*. With adequate cause, Berman was willing to expose it in a man like Erikson, whom he had admired. The exposé would hardly displease powerful *Times* editors like A. M. Rosenthal, but it would not make the *Times Book Review* appear to be a front for intellectual conservatism, which it most certainly was not.[21]

Berman's notes and some preliminary jottings for his review indicate that he was impressed by the importance of his assignment. He acknowledged that "Erikson has reached a steadily wider public, penetrated deeper and deeper into our collective consciousness, and become the closest thing to an intellectual hero in our culture today." Yet Berman also registered a troubled initial response to the autobiographical essay in *Life History:* "E[rikson] asserts his universality by derogating his particularity—i.e., Jewishness!" This evasiveness made all of Erikson's "affirmations ring esp[ecially] hollow." Berman's initial concern about evasiveness was augmented when he telephoned Ernest Schachtel, a German-Jewish émigré who had lost track of his Palestine-based parents during the war. He had been an early member of the Frankfurt School for Social Research and a collaborator with Erich Fromm. Schachtel warned Berman that many German-Jewish émigrés were elusive about their pasts; he himself had long been suspicious of Erikson's candor. Schachtel also discussed his apprehensions about Erikson after reading *Young Man Luther* and realizing that Erikson had not come to grips with Luther's virulent anti-Semitism. This point was not lost on Berman. The telephone conversation completed, Berman remembered stories in his own family of Jews who, like Erikson, had changed their names and denied their Jewishness. Clear now about the focus of his review, Berman wrote it through to completion.[22]

His essay in the *Times Book Review* was long and engaging. Early on, Berman praised Erikson's concrete, earthy writings during his initial decades in America. But he found the man's more recent publications distressingly vague: "There is no animating vision, no vital energy to light it up. Where is Erikson himself in the picture?" Erikson's strong presence, vision, and Truth had, of course, been transparent in his works on Gandhi and Jefferson. By insisting that he could not locate Erikson in these latest books, Berman had begun to launch his attack.[23]

The review was scathing. Berman characterized the autobiographical essay in *Life History* and the issue of Jewishness as the primary test of authenticity. By changing his surname from Homburger to Erikson, Berman argued, he had repudiated his stepfather's Jewish name. Joan's considerable role in this context (and as a non-Jew) went unnoticed. Berman emphasized that Erikson could not even bear to reveal that his mother was Jewish. He characterized the name "Erikson" to mean that Erik was "his own father, in the most literal sense a self-made man." This was "cosmic *chutzpah.*" For Berman, Erikson's fundamental problem was that "he cannot bear to say: that he is a Jew." Like the recent Watergate scandal, however, Erikson had covered up this issue. By evading his Judaism, Erikson had weakened his identity concept, which had stood for wholeness and integration. His "evasion of Jewish identity" also undermined his claim for a universal identity. If a universal identity "can be attained only by suppressing one's own particularity," then it "is a phony universality, built on a lie, rotten to the core."[24]

Berman concluded by noting how striking it was that a Jewish psychoanalyst—a student of Freud—had cultivated a self-image and an identity concept "built on systematic repression and 'noble' lies." Erikson had even repressed the fact that because he was a Jew, "he had to go" from Europe to America as Nazism swept through Europe. (This was not the case.) Only at the very end of his essay was Berman willing to moderate his attack and to turn modestly charitable: "Maybe we can love him [Erikson] more authentically now that we can see him as a [flawed] man like ourselves."[25]

Although Berman had missed relevant biographical information and skewed some important particulars, several of Erikson's closest friends and family realized that he was not wholly off the mark. They knew that Erikson had sometimes been confused, sometimes ambivalent about his parentage, his Jewish/Christian identity, his nationality, and much else. While Berman did not understand the Erikson who lived on multiple and shifting borders, he had brought some of Erikson's uncertainties to light.[26]

Erikson was especially upset by the caption for Berman's review: "Erik Erikson, the Man who Invented Himself." The blunt crudity of the characterization was appalling. "Really: I don't want to be great or even right," he confided to Munich friend Kurt von Fritz. As one child that Erikson had observed told another who had been critical of the details of a drawing: "I just wanted you to say it is nice." "The review was nasty," he told another friend, and he hoped it was "generally rejected by the readers." The problem was that Berman "did raise questions" that required responses.[27]

Erikson decided to go public by writing a letter to the editor of the *Times Book Review*. In a draft of the letter, he insisted that the autobiographic chapter in *Life History* was hardly "my last word" on parentage and religion. This was an exceedingly complex matter: "Certainly, to 'simply say' one is a Jew and 'move on' (as your reviewer suggests) does not always settle the identity issue authentically." Brockway advised Erikson not to send the letter. Trusting his Norton editor, he obliged. Kai contemplated writing a letter to point out Berman's imprecisions but reconsidered. Some friends and former students mailed letters to the *Book Review* defending Erikson, and a few were published. Berman responded to them by insisting that *Life History* was "turbid and turgid" and "light years away from 'spiritual freedom.' "[28]

Berman had gotten the best of a man in his seventies who often felt uncomfortable in public controversy. In the end, Erikson instructed Brockway to add a brief explanation of his name change for future editions of *Life History:* Theodor Homburger had given him his last name "which I kept as my middle name, when, later, on my becoming an American citizen, my family assumed its present name." Readers were to know that he had not repudiated his stepfather even though he had replaced "Homburger" with the middle initial "H" long ago and was usually referred to simply as "Erik Erikson."[29]

Erikson wrote to his half sisters, Ruth and Ellen, "how sorry I was about the so-called 'book review' in the *New York Times,* which must have been a shock to you." Since "I am an artist" and "wrote to be read with some pleasure," he had not seen the need to explain all the particulars that Berman had raised. Because of "the information which I had pieced together over the years" on his real father, it was "impossible for me (as suggested in the *N. Y. Times*) to simply call myself a Jew and 'to move on.' " Any fair reader of *Life History* would realize that "without a deep identity conflict I would not have done the work I did."[30]

By June of 1975, Erikson had formulated a short private "Memorandum" summarizing his position for Anna Freud and other "friends and family." He had changed his name from Homburger to Erikson during the naturalization process, after he had lived in America for six years. The change was a family decision. "My mother was a Danish Jewess, my original father was a non-Jewish Dane," and his stepfather had approved of the change to a name that "is rather common in Scandinavia." Erikson was preparing a narrative for the public record that appeared to resolve a matter that had not been resolved in fact. He did not know for sure whether his real father was "a non-Jewish Dane" and whether he was the son of Erik or of any other Scandinavian Gentile.[31]

In July, Erikson drafted a two-and-a-half-page typed "Dear Friend" form letter that he sent to inquirers. It noted that his mother, a Danish Jew, had married Valdemar Salomonsen, who left her "years before my birth." Erikson was "the offspring of a love affair between my mother and a Danish man who, so my family have told me, was not a Jew and whose name was kept secret from all but a few who have long since died." He was acknowledging, but not quite admitting, that he had no solid information about his father.[32]

Erikson prepared other general letters to inquirers over the next several years. But there was no consistent pattern. An August 1977 letter told less, for example, than his July 1975 account. An undated 1978 version, "Notes on My Parentage," added new details on Valdemar Salomonsen. It also recounted how "I was the offspring of a love-relationship with another Dane" and how his pregnant mother "was forced to leave Denmark" and to give birth in Frankfurt. She never told him who his real father was, though he "had concluded from accidental impressions" over the years that he was "a Gentile Dane 'from a good family' and 'artistically gifted.' "[33]

Much as Erikson had written and rewritten his autobiographical essay, he had composed and recomposed responses to the Berman review. Some responses revealed more than others. Some ticked off points flatly while others were composed with style and elegance. The old man was not at peace with himself. As his friend Fawn Brodie observed, he retained "an unquenchable hunger that all his private healing and public teaching never totally assuaged."[34]

In part, Erikson was so "hungry" and distressed because Berman's essay in the *Times Book Review* was exceedingly damaging. Book sales plummeted. During the 1970–71 academic year, Norton registered nearly 139,000 total paperback sales for all of his books from *Childhood and Society* through *Gandhi's Truth*. In the course of the 1975–76 academic year, which began five months after the Berman review appeared in the *Times,* the total for those books had declined to roughly 66,400. Sales had been declining in recent years, to be sure. Brockway felt feminist criticism was primarily responsible for the earliest manifestations of the decline, but criticism from the academic New Left, from political conservatives, and from others had also contributed. Exciting, innovative new books during the early and mid-1970s might have given Erikson's sales a boost, but *Dimensions of a New Identity* and *Life History and the Historical Momement* did not meet this need. The shift in American undergraduate education since the 1960s, from course requirements that included provocative topical paperbacks to the traditional pattern of a single course textbook with supplementary reader, certainly diminished Erikson's college market. But even counting a large array of factors involved in cutting Erikson's book sales in half, it is folly to dismiss the influence of Marshall Berman's essay.[35]

The essay provoked an outpouring of letters. Kimberly Wiar of the University of Chicago Press wrote Berman to inquire whether he had a book in preparation that was not already committed to a publisher. Editors of *Mainstream* and *Moment,* two intellectually oriented Jewish journals, invited him to publish essays with them. Lionel Trilling, whose *Sincerity and Authenticity* (1971) paralleled Berman's *The Politics of Authenticity* on the rise of the moral imperative of revealing one's feelings and convictions, congratulated him for "a good and useful job you have done on Erikson! . . . I've suspected everything since *Childhood and Society.*" Berman's essay gave Trilling reasons to question Erikson's authenticity. MIT historian Bruce Mazlish, who had seen Erikson in lectures and seminars, had read all of Erikson's books, and had done important work himself in psychohistory, thanked Berman for saying publicly what a number of people had considered privately. Todd Gitlin, a leading student activist of the 1960s and well-known sociologist, congratulated Berman for refusing to allow Erikson to escape, through public charm, the difficulties inherent in his overly schematized worldview.

Psychoanalytic Quarterly editor Jacob Arlow confided to Berman that because Erikson and other analysts of his generation had often failed to come to terms with their inner identities, they had impaired the profession scientifically and therapeutically.[36]

To be sure, friends and neighbors rallied to Erikson's defense. Joan's Episcopal rector in the Tiburon-Belvedere area, John Thornton, and local architect John Payne were among them. Former Harvard students of his like Mark Gerzon and John Ross dashed off letters to the *Times* to deflate Berman's charges. Ortiz Walton, professor of Afro-American Studies at Berkeley, was disturbed by the transparent enmity behind Berman's essay. His letter warned that Berman could not expect to invalidate Erikson's theories simply by dwelling on the man's autobiographical recollections. The prominent Harvard political scientist Martin Kilson underscored how "great minds like Erikson" unlocked their creativity by recasting but never resolving the crises of their lives. Erikson was creative because his life and theory involved the never-ending process of becoming. A full-scale debate erupted consisting of many exceedingly passionate letters—the few that the *Times* published and the preponderance that it did not.[37]

To an important extent, Paul Roazen's *Erik H. Erikson: The Power and Limits of a Vision* (1976) represented an extension of the Berman controversy. Roazen had met Berman at Harvard, where both had been graduate students interested in political theory. Erikson's graduate seminar had helped Roazen to begin what became a profoundly informative and inciteful classic, *Freud and His Followers.* He grew quite fond of Erikson, admiring him for questioning some basic Freudian premises in fresh and creative ways. However, Roazen was exceedingly disappointed when Erikson did not select him as a graduate assistant for his undergraduate course, feeling "I was never important enough for Erikson to have invited me to be one of his teaching assistants."[38]

When he read Berman's essay in the *Times Book Review,* Roazen was deeply upset. He had written a preliminary draft of a book intended to give "critical scrutiny" to the concepts developed in Erikson's published writings. It was critical but favorable; he had characterized Erikson's work as providing "what is of enduring value in psychoanalysis." But Berman's observations on Erikson's apparent evasions changed Roazen's direction. He waited for Erikson's public rebuttal. Instead, Roazen received one of the several private memoranda Erikson prepared which "did little, I thought, to put to rest the original piece." A month after the *Times Book Review* essay, Roazen wrote to Berman to describe his astonishment at what Berman had discovered about Erikson, especially about his parentage, his illegitimacy, and his Judaism. Roazen then completely rewrote his manuscript on Erikson.[39]

Roazen's book was learned, intelligent, and scholarly. (It remains a very useful volume.) But the tone was critical. Roazen accepted Berman's central points of criticism and agreed that Erikson was "disguising the simple facts of his family religion." He also accused Erikson of a general vagueness in his writing "calculated to protect a mythic continuity with Freud." Roazen sided, too, with the egalitarian feminist critique of Erikson. Finally, he emphasized a perspective of several New Left academics that Erikson had endorsed individual adjustment to the dominant culture about him: "Erikson's fundamental outlook is conservative." This helped to explain why he had "remained publicly silent and aloof from the antiwar movement"—the opposition to an American presence in Vietnam.[40]

"I imagine you must have mixed feelings, or worse than that, about Roazen's rather uneven work," Williams College psychologist James Anderson wrote sympathetically to Erikson. In fact, Erikson was distressed beyond measure, and did not see that Roazen had treated his publications as profoundly important documents. Erikson explained to one sympathizer that Roazen had violated a personal trust: "Believe it or not, the man never sent me his book on me!" He told Brockway that Roazen "never consulted me on anything" and had accepted Berman's review uncritically. Worse yet, Roazen "quotes so many sentences (and half-sentences!) out of *my* context and diagnoses them, that I feel I am being autopsied alive." Roazen's short quotations were "destroying all aesthetic context" in his writing. Erikson remarked that he composed like an artist, with a broad brush and attention to the flow of words and images; the close and constrictive textual analysis throughout Roazen's book did violence to the nature of his authorship. When Erikson learned that his Vienna friend Maria Piers was preparing a review of Roazen's volume, he informed her that he was especially hurt because Roazen had believed Berman on the issue of his parentage and religion. On the other hand, he was relieved by "the evident lack of public interest in this book." Especially when his publications were involved, Erikson had little taste for direct, open debate among scholars, and assumed that his name and publications would survive Roazen's, though he could not be certain. With minimal fanfare, Erikson prepared a private memorandum for the Freud Archives at the Library of Congress to correct three errors made by Roazen concerning aspects of his relationship with Sigmund Freud. For an audience of serious researchers, he would try to discredit Roazen, if only on a few points. The Berman controversy had become the Berman-Roazen controversy. By 1977, a battered Erik Erikson hoped that it had passed.[41]

RETIREMENT: A PARTIAL "RETREAT"

As the controversies surrounding Erik's work mounted, rural Marin County overlooking San Francisco Bay seemed to offer a sense of protection for him and for Joan. "Old Tiburon" had been a terminus for trains that carried lumber from the redwood forests of northern California to build San Francisco homes and businesses. Those boom days had long passed, and Tiburon had become a quiet beach community of professionals and artists, with a socially conscious business community. Erik wrote Peter Blos (reflecting the recent revival of their friendship) that the town was a "retreat" that helped him "to recover from my all too extroverted years." Indeed, he considered it another "magic mountain." The Eriksons lived in a lovely three-level turn-of-the-century house. Joan's work area was on the top level, and Erik had a large, secluded study on the bottom. Trees and shrubs surrounded the living area. A small exercise pool was constructed (partially heated by solar panels) so the two could swim daily. The view of the Bay Area was spectacular, including both the Golden Gate and the Bay Bridges and the city of San Francisco. "The scene is awesome, a bit less than real," Robert Lifton noted during his first visit. The Eriksons felt safe, secluded, and comfortable there. They moved to a more conventional single-level house within easier walking distance of the grocery store and post office only after it became too difficult to climb the hilly terrain and the surrounding streets, which lacked sidewalks.[42]

Joan had made an offer on the spectacular split-level house before Erik had seen it. David Cogan, who managed their financial resources, had advised Joan not to take the down payment for the house from the principal of their portfolio, since that was investment money for retirement income, but Joan withdrew from it anyway. Cogan realized that, by the late 1970s, the Eriksons' finances had become problematic. While they lived comfortably, their income depended on checks from awards, prizes, and honoraria; there were no significant salary checks in the mail. Because income from book sales continued to pay off the $500,000 Norton advance, that, too, was unavailable. Arguments between Joan and Cogan intensified as the Eriksons' financial situation became more precarious and Cogan advised greater financial caution. Joan refused to accept many of Cogan's directives and dismissed him in the early 1980s. At that point, Brockway (who had encouraged the break) allowed Erik to keep the remainder of his Norton advance and to receive additional income from any new books he might publish. By then, however, his books hardly commanded the attention and sales they once had. Financial problems therefore remained a concern during the couple's final years.[43]

Retirement in Tiburon did not keep Erikson entirely out of the public eye. Invitations to special events and a vast stream of correspondence persisted. He retained a private secretary for form-letter responses "to get people who want something from me, off my Buckle." Many of the letters concerned requests to endorse new books, to give lectures, or to provide clinical treatment. The response to almost all of these inquiries was negative, citing his "retirement" (clinical, academic, and literary). Still, he could not entirely avoid publicity. When a prominent liberal Democrat presidential and policy adviser like Joseph Califano visited the Eriksons, reporters were not far behind. When Margaret Mead proclaimed that Erik "is one of the greatest men in the *world!*" news stories appeared in print.[44]

Health problems made it increasingly difficult for the Eriksons to write or travel. Joan's ailments were less formidable than Erik's. During the winter of 1973–74, severe arthritic pain led her to surgery for a unilateral hip replacement. Subsequently, there was abnormal bone growth near the prosthesis, which required constant monitoring. After recovery, Joan labored even more systematically than earlier to enhance her health as well as Erik's. She insisted that they swim regularly, eat sensibly, and avoid demanding public events. Other than *Masterpiece Theater* and the evening news, they watched little television. Every day they took long walks hand in hand, and were in bed by ten. Joan was delighted when Erik occasionally felt energetic enough to stay up late to dance a jig, for that was now quite rare. She overlooked his secret late-evening raids on the freezer for a few spoonsful of ice cream.[45]

Erik's physical decline was unmistakable. Hearing aids helped in small settings but not in large auditoriums. His eyes watered frequently owing to chronic blepharitism, while an eye muscle abnormality made prolonged reading difficult. Such visual problems "influences my mood greatly," he confided to Peter Blos, though he was pleased that medical interventions had helped. Erikson was diagnosed with prostate cancer and had operations in 1974 and again in 1975. Catheterization to facilitate urination was a problem after both operations, producing serious infections and significant urinary tract difficulties that persisted for the remainder of his life. Moreover, long-term medications prescribed to fight recurrence of cancer made him feel drugged and lethargic, and his resistance was poor. A year after the second surgery, Erik complained how "with me, a cold easily means pneumonia." Despite these troubles, he tried to retain equanimity. When a friend visited him in Marin County Hospital after one of his surgeries and realized that he was catheterized, Erik downplayed the tubal insertion: "I didn't know this is what the penis is for." Chided for having to put up with reduced sexual activity, he retorted: "My whole body is sexual."[46]

Joan remained energetic as Erik's medical problems increased. When automobile transportation was necessary, Joan usually drove, for Erik's control of the steering wheel had become suspect. When there was marketing or banking to be done or a social occasion to be planned, Joan assumed the tasks. She was less willing, now, to subordinate her interests and career to Erik's and began to set the agenda for joint research ventures on the last stages of the life cycle. Erik noted that he could "rarely travel to meetings without Joan, and we are, in fact, working together on problems of aging (as well as sharing them)." By 1981, they spent part of each week together in Berkeley on a research project that produced *Vital Involvement in Old Age* (1986).[47]

A minister's daughter, Joan also became very active in St. Stephen's Parish (Episcopalian) in Belvedere, not far from home, and in an inner support community within the congregation. She seemed to inspire the young intellectual rector, John Thornton, and to rally kindred spirits (Maia Aprahamiam, Richard and Zoila Schoenbrun) who shared her artistic and devotional interests. Erik especially liked Thornton, considering him "singularly able to convey the basic terms of original Christianity" and "hospitable toward my kind." Indeed, Erik occasionally honored Joan's request to join her in a Sunday church service "to affirm and to receive affirmation from the ritual formulations of a devotional community." Form and ritual concerned him far more than theology. He lectured to St. Stephen's special Torah and Gospel group on Kierkegaard, played one of the three Wise Men in the parish's Christmas pageant, and participated in the liturgical dance program. At Thornton's urging, Erik took communion with Joan at a special ceremony at Grace Episcopal Church in San Francisco to honor a monk whom she admired. Communion required baptism or, in this case, presumably the pretense of baptism. In time, Erik and Thornton became good friends and intellectual colleagues. Erik advised him not to be neglectful of his boyhood dream of becoming a farmer. He also confided to the young minister that his personal religious concerns were connected heavily to the mystery of his paternity.[48]

On Thursday evenings, Erik met with a few local clinicians to review current and sometimes even decades-old case files on schizophrenic patients. The group met at the home of Robert Rubenstein, director of inpatient psychiatric services at Mt. Zion Hospital in San Francisco. Former Austen Riggs director Otto Will and his wife (Beulah Parker), Beatriz Foster, and one or two others attended. Erik rarely missed a meeting. Routinely, he kicked over the Rubenstein cat's water dish as he entered the kitchen. Once when he avoided the dish, he chided others in the group: "You thought I was going to kick the bucket, didn't you?" Although Erik had not worked with many psychotic patients, he was fascinated with unusually open discussions of their subjective worlds and the vulgarity sometimes discernible in their language and behaviors. Joan was pleased that the group seemed to revive Erik's clinical interests.[49]

Joan and Erik both looked forward to meeting socially with old friends, particularly Robert and Judith Wallerstein. The Wallersteins were sometimes accompanied by Martha and Thomas Proctor (close friends since the 1940s), and by former Riggs clinician Allen Wheelis and his wife, Ilse Jawetz. A psychoanalyst and psychiatrist at Mt. Zion Hospital and at the San Francisco medical campus of the University of California, where he was head of psychiatry, Robert Wallerstein developed a relationship with Erik that resembled Erik's earlier friendship with David Rapaport. Like Rapaport, Wallerstein looked out for Erik's professional and intellectual interests. He persuaded the Maurice Falk Medical Fund to support Erik on a part-time basis in a new doctorate of mental health program at Mt. Zion that was affiliated with the medical campus. The job involved periodic supervision of doctoral candidates, psychiatric staff conferences, and a seminar on adolescents. As well, Wallerstein tried to assure Erik that the psychoanalytic profession could accommodate his ever-expanding range of interests. He kept Erik modestly involved with the San Francisco Psychoanalytic Institute and organized a special seminar for him on the adult years of the life cycle. Wallerstein also encouraged Joan to establish a patient activities program at Mt. Zion along the lines of her pioneering Austen Riggs program. As Jews, Robert and Judy Wallerstein felt uneasy about Erik's interest in St. Stephen's Church and its young rector, but this did not deter them from visiting regularly around the Eriksons' outdoor pool with the Proctors, Wheelis, and Jawetz.[50]

Their children continued to concern Erik and Joan as they moved into semiretirement. One motive for the move to Tiburon had been to be closer to Jon, who lived in Sausalito and worked as a stagehand near San Francisco. Jon had also become a free-lance photographer and proved to be very talented. He had an artist's eye for form and shape, and this delighted his parents. Jon's photographs often emphasized a particular quality like a human eye or the contours of a head or the pattern of a shadow. Erik remarked that he and Joan were "glad when our son is interested in our interests." He sought information from the president of the Guggenheim Foundation concerning Jon's eligibility for a fellowship in photography. When Jon came to his parents' home for dinner, he took off a tool belt he needed as a stage crew member, and Erik always examined it. He admired people who (unlike himself) could fix things. Jon liked to watch Erik swim with a slow breaststroke and to register satisfaction ("Ah, that's wonderful") as he left the pool. He heated up frozen dinners when Joan was out of town, and was pleased that his father was no gourmet. Erik and Joan sometimes worried because Jon often seemed a bit depressed and was not married. Nonetheless, they were pleased that they were on better terms with him than they had been in the past.[51]

Their only daughter, Sue, also experienced difficult times. In 1976, she and Harland divorced. Erik and Joan worried about her supporting herself and her son, Per. "I never thought the man was the right one, from the first moment I saw him," Erik confided to his half sister Ellen, contradicting his initial impression of Harland. "We are worried but Sue handles it [the divorce] all admirably," he told Ruth, his other half sister. He remarked to his friend Kurt von Fritz, half-jokingly, that Sue was "liberating herself from the Columbia professor." Indeed, she was struggling with her new independence. Sue worked at the Hubley Studio in New York and took graduate courses in anthropology and sociology at the New School for Social Research. Erik tried to help her out. He asked acting NEH director Wallace Edgerton, for example, to advise Sue on her education and her career. He also inquired of a high Danforth Foundation official about fellowships for women interested in completing graduate work. Essentially, he was telling her to pursue a career on her own, but also that he would help her to establish it. During this difficult time, when she was deeply involved in psychotherapy, Sue sometimes brought Per to visit with her parents. Although Joan spent more time with Per than Erik, and Per adored her, he also liked to set up his train sets and other toys on the floor of Erik's study. Erik usually wrote at his desk as Per played. Periodically, he got down on the floor to participate. Occasionally, he took Per for a walk to the beach or to a restaurant. Sue was not as anxious as her parents were about supporting Per and herself. However, she also felt that she was not like Erik's much admired friend Margaret Mead, who could clear her own path and subordinate spouses to her professional interests. Sue's very talented mother had a man—and for nearly fifty years.[52]

The Eriksons were proudest of Kai. Indeed, Erik was starting to regard Kai as the closest of all of his friends and colleagues. Very successful as a scholar, Kai was also achieving a reputation as an academic administrator. In 1969, Yale president Kingman Brewster had appointed him as one of the youngest masters of Trumbull College. On extremely good terms with Brewster, Kai subsequently became chair of two academic departments (American studies, then sociology). He assumed the editorship of the *Yale Review* in 1979 and extended the *Review*'s scope of issues beyond literary concerns. Along with managerial abilities that Erik lacked, Kai was, according to David Riesman, "much less neurotic than his father." Nonetheless, Kai labored under the very considerable burden in academic, intellectual, and cultural circles of being "the son of psychoanalyst, Erik Erikson," for that was how he was often identified. That onus had the effect of making him push himself all the harder toward scholarly perfection and to be more guarded than Jon or Sue. "I obviously do not have Pop's knack for keeping out of trouble," he remarked in the midst of a dispute with other sociologists. Added to the complex dimensions of Kai's relationship with Erik was the son's propensity to take the father's perspectives on identity, selfhood, and the psychosocial and apply them to general social situations. Skillfully and creatively, Kai elaborated on these perspectives in a book tracing the decline of New England Puritanism and in another book about the trauma visited on a West Virginia mining community after a massive flood. In turn, Erik tended to borrow from Kai's case studies to help ground his more amorphous, abstract, and increasingly spiritual probings. Father and son often acknowledged this mutual borrowing. Indeed, more than anyone else, Kai probably provided intellectual stimulation for Erik during his retirement. "Don't you think your conclusions regarding my conclusions and mine concerning yours are related?" Erik asked in 1976 as each worked over drafts of the other's book manuscript.[53]

In the summer months, Erik and Joan returned to Cotuit, and Kai and Joanna and their children drove up from New Haven. Kai had a modern, rather idiosyncratic house constructed adjacent to his parents' beach home, so the two families were often together. Entertainment revolved around Erik and Kai reading aloud from their works in progress, around card games and group sings, and around grandchildren Keith and Christopher. The boys were teenagers and increasingly "sensitive and active," Erik boasted to Ruth Hirsch. He admired Keith's drawing ability and his attentiveness to the natural world, and especially Keith's hard work in dealing with dyslexia to achieve a solid academic record. Christopher was more playful, a freer spirit. Erik was impressed with his musical ability and even by the rock band that he had formed. Thinking about Keith and Christopher when he traveled, Erik often sent them postcards reflecting their special interests and jotted down remarks to humor each boy.[54]

Kai's relationship with Erik probably would have thrived even without summers in Cotuit. They conversed about their work at every conceivable opportunity, especially as overnight roommates at Lifton's Wellfleet meetings. Two topics especially engaged them. The first was Erik's concept of pseudospeciation, which he had been elaborating since his presentation at the Royal Society in 1966. Indeed, Erik joked that neither Julian Huxley nor Konrad Lorenz had critiqued his concept in 1966 as thoroughly as Kai had been doing for a decade and more. "Do you want to let me have it about pseudospecies," Erik inquired playfully during one Wellfleet session. "Yes," Kai replied invitingly. While Kai felt the concept engaged psychoanalysis and the social sciences in powerful ways, he disputed the term *pseudo,* preferring "psychosocial speciation." "Pseudo" made the human propensity to form artificial groupings, which distinguished one collectivity from another, seem to be a counterfeit or fake phenomenon, Kai insisted. Psychological and espe-

cially social factors that were neither artificial nor biologically inn
explained group clinging or speciation, Kai argued. Erik fired back that
there was "a pseudospeciation *within* the psychosocial one"—the "pseudo"
involving an "often unconscious combination of prejudices, illusions, and
suspicions in regard to one's own human kind *and* to other kinds." The father
trained in psychoanalysis in Freud's Vienna was contesting the sociologist son,
who was more suspicious of universals in the human condition.[55]

The second topic that engaged them was Erik's increasing disposition to
move beyond the concept of ego and even identity to the subjective sense of
"I." This sense activated the individual, he felt, as it simultaneously activated
others important to the individual. It was the numinous ritual of infant and
mother writ large. Indeed, the subjective "I" extended to all humankind and
promoted a sense of universal specieshood and devotedness to an Ultimate
Other—an indispensable check on pseudospeciation. Kai was responsive to
the pseudospeciation connection here, but less concerned than his father with
the subjective "I" and the Ultimate Other. He had not been engaged keenly
by Erik's abiding interest, since *Young Man Luther,* in issues of Ultimate Concern. Nonetheless, Kai felt obligated to listen to Erik on this matter.[56]

As his hearing deteriorated, and he began to ramble when he spoke, Erik
avoided speaking engagements and concentrated even more on discussions
with Kai over his writing projects. But writing, too, became laborious. He
was increasingly aware that "one could be more precise than I am" in draft-
ing text and sensed that "training in logic would have helped a lot." A man
who had grown accustomed to constant work seemed to push himself all the
harder. He continued to wake up early, eat his customary breakfast of soft-
boiled eggs mixed with catsup and bits of toast, and go to his study. When
family and friends urged him to take a break, he insisted that "I have much
overdue writing to do." His connection with the public through formal
papers, articles, and books had long been crucial to his sense of purpose.
Erikson listened as others warned him not to place such a burden on himself, but acknowledged that "I can't stop, no matter what 'they' say."[57]

WILD STRAWBERRIES:
AN EIGHTH-STAGE PERSPECTIVE

Through the late 1970s and into the 1980s, Erikson worked as much as his
circumstances would allow to flesh out the Integrity vs. Despair conflict of
old age, a conflict he was on intimate terms with, for there was no getting
around the fact that he was negotiating the last stage in his life cycle model.
"Without a bit of despair (quite a bit) there can't be any integrity," he told

Ellen Katz. "That's what I said long ago, and (dammit) it is even true." The despair came from "a sense of being lost on the periphery" with "the stigma of chronic impairment and the sentence of inactivation." The integrity came with the discovery of Wisdom. Like the astute Jungian M. Esther Harding decades earlier, Erikson described this Wisdom of old age as a reprieve from the overcommitment of adulthood pressures to adapt to inner psychic and outer social necessity. In old age, there was no longer the prompting "to emphasize as mutually exclusive" qualities like rationality and intuition, sociability and privacy, action and reflection, "hereness" and spirituality. The eighth stage emphasized the ritual of integration.[58]

As he neared eighty, Erikson became deeply concerned about the integration of early and late life. There was "a certain childlikeness in old age" linked to the "slowing up of responses, caution in judgment," and other so-called cognitive defects. The eighth stage seemed to circle into the early stages; "in advancing years one thinks back to one's beginnings." Erikson found himself thinking increasingly about connections between "my adult life here in America and the memory of my childhood in Karlsruhe." He reflected on his stepfather's house "besides the Schlossplatz and the Theater, many places to which I owe so much of my basic *Bildung*." He also recalled how he had wandered as a youth all over the Schwarzwald. "Say hello to the Schwarzwald," he told a German friend. He thanked Kurt von Fritz for storing many of the woodcuts he had made as a youth and noted that "I am even beginning to have ideas for new woodcuts!"[59]

As he reexamined and elaborated on the life cycle from the perspective of old age, Erikson completed an exceedingly important article on Ingmar Bergman's film *Wild Strawberries*. It was the first of his major later writings in which he began a review of his life cycle model at the eighth stage, rather than the first, moving from the elderly state toward infancy.

The article had been a long time in the making. Throughout the 1960s, Erikson had anchored his undergraduate course at Harvard with *Wild Strawberries*. As Swedish physician Isak Borg traveled in the course of the film from his retirement city toward Lund to receive an honorary doctorate, the automobile trip became a symbolic pilgrimage through Borg's own life. Erikson felt there was no better overview of the life cycle. After his students saw the film, they read a short paper he had prepared on it. Then he offered a full lecture elaborating the paper. As the 1960s progressed, the paper grew longer and became increasingly important. Erikson felt his essay registered the riches provided by Bergman—the "most perfect combination of *artistic form and psychological comprehension + existential religiosity.*" When he retired from Harvard in 1970, he decided to transform the paper into a more formal presentation for professional conferences and ultimate publication. He had students and colleagues in psychiatry, psychology, and social work at the Mt. Zion Hospital in San Francisco review the essay. Erikson also presented it at various gatherings of the American Academy of the Arts and Sciences, promising the paper to *Daedalus*. A few months before it was published, he offered it as the keynote address for the important and prestigious Symposium on Human Values and Aging at Case Western Reserve University. This represented his most polished and significant public presentation of the paper. When he arrived in Cleveland, Erikson cut a striking figure with his snow white hair and mustache, visible hearing aids, a brown herringbone jacket, thick suspenders as well as a belt, a large colorful ring on his finger, and an old letter envelope–style briefcase tucked under his arm. He was a more scholarly, elegant, and zestful Isak Borg—at least until the moment when he had to be extricated from the backseat of a host's small Volkswagen![60]

The connection between Erikson's life and his narration of Dr. Borg's trip in *Wild Strawberries* had interested his undergraduate students throughout the 1960s. Indeed, when the article was finally published in 1976, Erik was only four years younger than Borg. A house servant attended closely to Borg much as Joan attended to Erik. Joan's given name was Sarah. Sara was Borg's earliest love. She provided Borg's life with a healthy mix of passion and balance much as Sarah Serson had provided to Erik in Vienna. Borg's son, Evald, did not want his wife's unborn baby, while Erik was tormented by Neil's birth. Indeed, Erik acknowledged two other connections to the old doctor. Borg was heading to Lund—just across the Øresund from his Abrahamsen uncles' country houses where Erikson had spent the "sunniest summers" of his early years (they had been drearier in Karlsruhe). Three young-adult characters in the film, including a fascinating and lively second Sara, were hitchhiking to Italy. They were out "to Find Themselves and Their Ideologies," Erikson remarked, much as "all Northerners, including myself" had to do. Through these parallels, one is struck by the personally situated aspect of Erikson's narration. Isak Borg was anticipating the end of his life. A decided gap existed between Borg's hopes and his accomplishments, and this gap signified that Borg had not yet found the Wisdom of old age—a "detached yet active concern with life itself in the face of death itself" that "conveys the integrity of experience, in spite of the decline of bodily and mental functions." Erikson had not entirely found Wisdom either.[61]

Had Ingmar Bergman reviewed Erikson's Cleveland presentation and final article, he might have criticized Erikson for deemphasizing the particularities of Swedish culture and for making too little of Bergman's disposition to illustrate how remote, withdrawn women like Borg's mother gave birth to withdrawn children. Carol Gilligan took issue with Erikson for deemphasizing female development generally, especially the caring qualities of Borg's daughter-in-law, Marianne. But Erikson's unwillingness to elaborate on the women in *Wild Strawberries* was caused primarily by his abiding interest in Isak Borg. As early as 1950, Erikson had acknowledged "dreams of getting an honorary degree sometime in my old age." And by the mid-1970s, invitations to accept honorary degrees abounded. Owing to his desire to be considered Scandinavian, Erikson felt deeply honored by an invitation from the university at Lund: The degree would be presented at the very cathedral where Borg received his. Borg's ceremony recognized his years of service to his patients. He had delivered their babies and cared for them when they were ill. "His patients had provided the renewal in his adult life of the strengths he had developed"—namely purposefulness and competence and fidelity. Borg had practiced "the ethical rule of adulthood . . . to do to others what will help them, even as it helps you to grow." Erikson felt that the elder Borg, who had ceased to practice medicine, mourned for that more productive period in his life. Erikson was at least modestly mournful, too; he had ceased to be a clinician, a teacher, or even a prolific writer.[62]

If Erikson looked back nostalgically with Borg to the more creative, generative period of his life, he also shared some of Borg's anxiety concerning the death that lay ahead. Erikson noted that Borg was anticipating his own death quite graphically through a dream sequence of himself in a coffin. The problem was that he had not yet learned to die. As one who was close to death, Borg "must yet learn to affirm life." He had learned "to work, but *not* to love," and Erikson sometimes felt that he had not loved sufficiently either. As the film progressed, the older Borg arrived at a fuller self-awareness. He became conscious of being an actor in his own life and experiences; he could promote or change previously feared inevitabilities. This consciousness deepened as Borg approached Lund and more fully reexamined his life. The entire trip represented "a pantheistic reunification with nature, a Christian pilgrimage to salvation—and, indeed, a modern self-analysis." The trip and the ceremony that followed did not leave Borg depleted; rather, he had ceased to be a compulsive old man, somewhat depressed and paranoid. For Erikson, Borg ended up with a dream in which the smile of Sara, his early love, "seems to restart the trust of the first stage, without which Isak could not have become what he is and could not have dreamed as he did." In the end, a narrow, compulsive, obsessive old man who appeared to "go wrong in each stage" of his life had reached out and affirmed what had also gone right at each developmental stage. By the end of the film, Borg's fear of impending death had receded. Erikson's must have, too, for he considered himself healthier than Borg and with more emotional resources.[63]

Erikson's article on *Wild Strawberries* was hardly a traditional Freudian narrative, and he had not been intent on excavating through Borg's repressions and compulsions to find the roots of his distress—the original primal scene of imagined parental lovemaking. Instead of vertical Freudian probing of psychic depth, Erikson's narrative mapped the horizontal cultural surface, an old man's journey from the compulsive rituals of his lonely life "through some everyday ritualizations of his culture, to a grand ritual which both seals and permits a transcendence of his over-defined professional existence." This journey culminated in the security of an honorary degree. Borg had become conscious of the strengths, the weaknesses, and, above all, the continuities and the wholeness of the life cycle. The "first revelation of the life cycle" came as the child's eye connected to the maternal other. This was also "the hope of old age," which Borg had finally realized.[64]

In the end, Borg understood that there was no sense of "I"—of wholeness or completeness—without a shared Other. Borg's journey was successful precisely because it brought back memories of important Others in his life and reaffirmation of the Ultimate Other. Erikson used Other as a positive construct here, a complementarity. He had not yet completed his journey over space and time. But by reading his paper in Cleveland, and then publishing it in *Daedalus*—after so many years of wrestling with Bergman's film—Erikson almost certainly sensed that he was not far off course. If Borg could complete the journey, he could, too.

"THE GALILEAN SAYINGS
AND THE SENSE OF 'I' "

Erikson's article on *Wild Strawberries* represented an important effort to elucidate his model of the life cycle from the perspective of old age. Over the next several years, he worked on his last truly innovative essay—"The Galilean Sayings and the Sense of 'I' "—for the *Yale Review*. The essay marked a departure from his training in ego psychology and even from his concept of identity, as it primarily concerned the "I" in relationship to Others and to the Ultimate Other. A broad-ranging and deeply spiritual essay, it also represented Erikson's last significant attempt to engage his psychoanalytic colleagues. By focusing on the sense of "I," he held out for an innovative alternative to Heinz Kohut's emphasis on the self, which was commanding increasing attention from analysts. Whereas Kohut saw the self appropriating the strength of another, Erikson described the "I" as a spiritualized appropriation from (and with) Others and a relationship with the Ultimate Other.

For many years, Erikson had pondered William James's notion that the self was what "I" can perceive. By the time of his NEH lectures on Jefferson in 1973, the sense of "I" had assumed such an urgency in his investigations that it became the most striking and innovative part of his inquiry into the third president. Jefferson had sought to register the sense of "I," among other goals, by compiling Jesus' more "authentic" remarks. Erikson found the Virginian's inquiry captivating and fruitful. Prompted by Jefferson, Erikson began his own inquiry into the sayings of Jesus during the Galilean part of his ministry. But this inquiry was not, at first, part of a major writing project.

Rather, by the mid-1970s, Erikson had intended to address the nature of the "I" and other issues by writing about Søren Kierkegaard. As Berman had failed to appreciate, Erikson regarded himself far more a Dane in origin than a German or a Jew. By studying Kierkegaard, he hoped to deepen his under-standing of his Danish roots and identity and to better comprehend the sense of "I." Erikson knew, of course, that the nineteenth-century Danish theolo-gian, whom his mother often read when he was young, had been regarded as the first modern existentialist. Kierkegaard had insisted that man's duty to God required rigorous self-analysis of feelings and dispositions. Ultimately, man had to reckon with the complex, devious, hard-to-fathom workings of his mind, which was split between self-interest/self-expression on the one hand and ethical responsibility on the other.[65]

Erikson tried to pursue this philosophic, ethical, and psychological inquiry within a religious context, as Kierkegaard had done. He quickly felt that the inquiry would suggest new meanings and hopes for humanity. He would explore Kierkegaard's life and thought as it was bound together through rela-tionships and dialogues. At a seminar in Marin County in 1977, Erikson described the basic concern of his project: Like Freud, Kierkegaard postulated "a deeply committed and deeply gifted 'I' turning analytically upon itself—and not only surviving his own method, but describing the results with lit-erary creativity." Erikson got as far as a twenty-two-page typed manuscript, "Themes from Kierkegaard's Early Life." But after a few years of work, he concluded that he could not make much of a scholarly contribution. He could not read Danish and had little background in Danish history and cul-ture. Deficiencies in language and background had contributed to the length of time required to write *Gandhi's Truth*. Erikson knew that he did not have the better part of a decade to work on Kierkegaard. Perhaps even more important, he seemed to have difficulty relating to Kierkegaard's sense of reli-gious commitment as absolutely binding and specific. Erikson liked the idea of religion without being religious in any profound creedal sense. His disposition was too playful, and his interests were too broad and changing for that sort of commitment. Even with his cousin Edith Abrahamsen helping with translations, he put the project aside.[66]

As he cut short the project, Erikson returned, more intently, to the topic of Jesus in Galilee, even as he toyed with investigating David Ben Gurion as an old man. He had written enough on Jesus' sayings for *Dimensions of a New Identity,* his Jefferson volume, to have confidence in his power to describe how Jesus, like Kierkegaard, had probed the " 'I' turning analytically upon itself." For Erikson, the sense of "I" involved the person conceiving of his or her self in an individualized Jamesian sense, but it also involved "the presence of another" and Others. If he had succeeded in explaining the existence of the "I" in Gandhi, one of "Jesus' modern followers," he could surely write a significant book about Jesus himself and his Galilean ministry.[67]

Soon after Kai had become editor of the *Yale Review* (1979), he encouraged Erik to prepare an essay for the journal, an installment of the book on Jesus. Recognizing that writing was increasingly laborious for Erik, Kai would assist him. A finished article was preferable, Kai felt, to an incomplete book. Erik was receptive, for he regarded Kai as his closest intellectual colleague—the first male with whom he had been able to work closely on his writing without an unpleasant competitive undercurrent.[68]

As he reviewed old notes on Jesus and related subjects for the article, Erik felt that he was working over a concern that had interested him since his *Wanderschaft* years, when he made a woodcut of Mary holding the Christ child in her arms. His discovery of the work of Norman Perrin of the Divinity School of the University of Chicago proved exceedingly helpful to his investigation. Erik was aware that for centuries biblical scholars had tried to distinguish the actual words of Jesus from those composed by early Christians after the crucifixion. But he had not wanted to get involved in the vast literature on detecting the "authentic" Jesus. Perrin's *Rediscovering the Teaching of Jesus* (1967) would do instead. With considerable care and erudition, Perrin reviewed the oral tradition of Jesus' sayings in the Galilean part of his ministry and noted that the sayings were later collected in various written forms. Indeed, Perrin had mastered form criticism, which supposedly allowed him to discern which of Jesus' early sayings were probably "authentic." Erikson accepted Perrin's proficiency and did not probe for alternative perspectives. With Perrin's book guiding him through the sayings, he felt prepared to describe Jesus' essential character at the origin of his Galilean ministry—the "genuine presence of a singular man."[69]

As Erikson began to draft portions of his article for the *Yale Review,* he found himself presenting a broad-ranging drama that included a large number of historical figures from Hitler to Luther to Gandhi to Jefferson, plus an enormous number of ideas and comments on personal relationships. It was as if he was preparing an autobiographical work—a fully staged drama of characters and issues that had impressed him. In conjunction with his interest in Einstein, for example, he discussed the nature and limits of linear time. He portrayed the essence of Jefferson's humanity in the process of studying, clipping, and pasting Jesus' sayings for a special Bible. He also discussed the personification or presence of the leader, the power of transforming language, the crisis of young-adult identity, and the importance of basic trust in parenting—concerns that had been evident since *Childhood and Society.* Briefly, Erikson was inquiring how time and place, personification and leadership, sickness and healing, play and development, parenting and caregiving, and even the roles of fathers and sons provided a framework for understanding Jesus, his Galilean ministry, and his sayings. He appeared to be charting a magnum opus, only to realize that he lacked the energy, discipline, and concentration to draft a full outline much less a polished essay.[70]

In August 1980, Erikson brought extensive notes and several sections of the essay to the annual Wellfleet meeting at Robert Lifton's Cape home. Longtime friends like psychologist Margaret Brenman-Gibson and science historian Gerald Holton, plus Kai and Joan, sat around Lifton's familiar seminar table in his rustic book-lined study. Erikson sat at the head of the long dark table in front of an imposing brick fireplace. Discussion, often animated at Wellfleet gatherings, was especially intense. Casually dressed with open shirt, his flowing white hair a bit untidy, Erikson began by warning the group that "I really have just started to put this material together, [and am] quite unsure about my conclusions." He noted that he had "always wanted to come to grips" with Jesus and that Perrin's book had finally made it possible. From Perrin's work, Erikson was able to put into context Jesus' sayings as a rabbi from Galilee who "is always on the move." Erikson insisted that Jesus' essential message during his Galilean ministry was probably "the main phenomenon of human existence"—the sense of "I." Jesus' ministry was less about the ego and the sense of self, and more fundamentally about "a sense of lightness, of having a light, or being in a center of something." It represented a special, existential sort of magic moment.[71]

At this point, Wellfleet regulars began to pepper Erikson with questions about how the sense of "I" related to their particular research interests and concepts. (This disposition to fit Erikson's contributions into perspectives other than his own would increase as he aged and his vigor receded.) Erikson struggled to advance one last point. Quite uncharacteristically, he explicitly rejected Freud's premise that the image of God was a mere father transference. Instead, "His (God's) *I am* is connected with my *I am,* which gives me a certain substantive existence in the world." Man knows about God only as God knows about himself in man. The sense of "I" linked man and God to each other.[72]

The balance of the Wellfleet session explored many directions. For example, theologians like John Dunne and Colin Williams prompted Erikson on specifics of Jesus' ministry and on the apostles. Psychoanalysts and psychologists queried him on how the "I" superseded the ego and bypassed Heinz Kohut's concept of the self. Holton asked Erikson to connect his discussion to Einstein's space-time concepts, while Lifton raised the issue of a broken connection in people's sense of the continuity within their lives. Rather than argue that these queries were tangential to his presentation, Erikson was relieved that others were now monopolizing the discussion. He sensed that he knew too little about his subject and appeared unnerved.[73]

Seven months later, the essay appeared in the *Yale Review.* Having listened to Erik's presentation at Wellfleet, Kai had a good idea of his father's themes and felt compelled to bring the essay to some form of completion. After the conference, he worked assiduously to tighten and clarify the various segments of the essay so that readers would better understand the main themes. Erik was grateful. Indeed, he referred to the final edited draft as "Kai's version." But it remained very much Erik's paper and there was no getting around the fact that his writing capacity had substantially diminished. Even with Kai's editing, the final product remained exceedingly difficult to follow. It tended to lack clear focus and the phrasing was often quite imprecise.[74]

Although the *Yale Review* essay rambled among many topics, the most arresting part was Erikson's amplification of Jesus' articulation of the sense of "I." Jesus' message at Galilee represented a crossroads in human conscious-ness, for in Galilee, Jesus made it clear that all humans were of one species. In addition, everyone who heard Jesus felt "a transcendent sense of awareness lodged in an earthly human shape." Jesus personified the trusting father who supported man's identity and moral purpose; he was restored to all people who believed in him. By truly hearing the words of Jesus, a listener discovered a vital inner core—an "I"—that connected him or her to all humanity and to God.[75]

More than in his Wellfleet presentation, Erikson elaborated the sense of "I" in the article along lines congruent with the Quaker inner light. When he noted how the sense of "I" comported with discovery of "the shining light," he was very close to the Quaker "light within." The "I" was "an inner eye full of light." One saw God through this "inner eye" as God simultane-ously saw man through it. When man connected to God and God to man in this way, the reward was profound: Man found "a sense of being alive and more, of being the vital condition of existence."[76]

Erikson argued that this sense of "I" originated within the ritual of mutual recognition between infant and parent. This called to mind Jacques Lacan's portrayal of the "mirror stage" where the young infant "projects himself, with the phantoms that dominate him" upon his parents and the world, only to see the projection reflected back upon himself. Erikson did not directly respond to the French psychoanalyst's well-known formulation

(1936, 1949). Instead, he underscored how the "innocent eye" of the child met that of the mother; there was a stronger and more direct personal reciprocity between the two than Lacan had addressed. "The beginnings of the sense of *I* itself," Erikson explained, "can emerge in a newborn out of a counterplay with a sense of *You* in the maternal caretaker." This "original interplay of *You* and *I* remains the model for mutual recognition throughout life." Jesus' sayings at Galilee were principally important because they helped to sustain the spirit of the original infant-parent interplay. They rekindled memories of that interplay and thereby connected people to each other and to God.[77]

Although the *Yale Review* article emphasized the developing sense of "I" during early life, Erikson expressed interest in how the "I" played out much later in the life cycle, especially as death neared. Life and the "I" began with *hope*. As hope matured, it culminated with old-age *faith*. When an elderly person had to "face the border of life," he or she embraced a sense of existential identity—an "I" bounded ultimately by death. In the process, the elderly person experienced "various dreads" that were unsettling but difficult to articulate. Erikson confessed to his friend Kurt Von Fritz that he experienced these dreads in his dreams.[78]

If Erikson had been able to maintain a clear, sustained focus on the sense of "I" and to avoid diverse other topics only remotely related to his theme, his "Galilean Sayings" article might have commanded more attention. But the response was minimal, even among theologians, and it was rarely cited. This did not trouble Erikson, for he regarded it simply as a very preliminary piece and intended to do more work. Five months after the article was published, he drafted a page of notes entitled "Some Dimensions of the Sense of 'I.' " In the left-hand column, he listed qualities that co-existed with the "I" and in the right-hand column the qualities that did not:

Luminous	Obscure
Active	Inactivated
Central	Peripheral
Whole	Fragmented
Coherent	Incoherent
Continuous	Scattered
Generative	Impotent
Inclusive	Isolated
Aware	Numb
Indivisible	Divided
Chosen	Bypassed
Safely Bounded	Invaded

The "I" represented special, revealing, and connective qualities while the alternative represented almost deathlike incapacity and disintegration. Erikson had his secretary type up the list. As he perused it—two sparse columns without illustrative examples—he realized that his article had failed to include the old-age struggle between Integrity and Despair. Consequently, he wrote "Integrity" atop his left-hand column and "Despair" atop the right-hand column. The implication was obvious. The eighth-stage struggle between Integrity and Despair in his model of the life cycle was part of a larger phenomenon—the effort to secure and maintain the sense of "I" from birth to the border between life and death.[79]

Erikson was also not entirely satisfied with another aspect of his *Yale Review* article: his portrayal of Jesus as a healer in his time and for the contemporary world. In *Dimensions of a New Identity*, he noted that Jefferson had neglected the New Testament story of the hemorrhaging woman who had touched Jesus' clothes and felt whole. In the *Yale Review* essay, Erikson cited Jesus telling this woman: "Your faith has healed you." Jesus had been a master therapist in this instance, revitalizing the numinous ritual between child and parent. He had prompted mutuality and trust, which facilitated identity, the sense of "I," and the healing process. Erikson recognized that though his article emphasized Jesus' words as healer, it did not properly characterize Jesus' healing presence. The living Jesus never quite emerged. Still, Erikson was pleased that the essay had connected Jesus as healer with Freud. Like Jesus centuries earlier, Erikson had noted how Freud had essentially depended on the biblical language of miraculous cure. As he proceeded with his book on Jesus, Erikson planned to compare the healing essence of Jesus and of Freud more comprehensively.[80]

In his later years, then, Erikson identified very closely with Jesus, the wandering rabbi at Galilee—the Jew who crossed new territory and launched Christianity. It was this perennial movement of Jesus on several important levels that he found especially compelling. After Christmas in 1976, Erikson had written a long, beautifully composed, and strikingly revealing letter to Hope Curfman, a correspondent from the Montview Presbyterian Church in Denver, explaining to Curfman that "historically and psychologically, Jesus most assuredly was a Jew, if one of a new kind." He also admitted to Curfman that Joan characterized him as "a Christian apprentice," and that seemed to offer sufficient flexibility in crossing and recrossing "the frontier on which one is struggling for insight and community." Erikson insisted to Curfman that he was "determined to live on the shadowy borderline of the denominational ambiguities . . . into which I seem to have been born." He found a healthy unity of soul and body in the tradition of both the Hebrew Torah and the Christian Gospels. To be sure, he was drawn to leading Christian historical figures. But he also insisted "that nobody who has grown up in a Jewish environment can ever be not-a-Jew" and that he himself "would have been eligible for the Holocaust."[81]

Because Erikson viewed Jesus as a "new kind" of Jew and shared with Paul Tillich a taste for the "shadowy borderline," he did not characterize the Galilean ministry and Christianity as an evolutionary step up from Judaism. Rather, he portrayed the Jewish acceptance of monotheism and the worship of Jehovah as a decisive turning point in history, producing "a lasting sense of ethnic and religious identity and, in fact, of some lasting moral mission." Nonetheless, despite Jehovah's rule, the Jewish homeland had been in continuous danger of invasion and occupation. A temple in Jerusalem had existed by dint of Jewish accommodation to Roman authorities, and this violated "every dimension of that sense of I which any collective must provide . . . such a nation had no identity with a chance of survival in centuries to come." Consequently, Erikson claimed that the plight of the Jews "helped to open some ears to Jesus' great existential message." This message represented a stage in the unfolding of the sense of "I" and the potential for diverse " 'I' 's to become "We." Jesus' sayings at Galilee influenced human evolution toward a more inclusive and self-conscious humanity. As Erikson told Curfman, there was "shining newness" in Jesus' parables even though his teachings would have been "unthinkable" without the elemental steps of Judaism. Moreover, Jesus' sayings were subsequently promoted by various Jews "dedicated to the messianic tenents of a more universal love" and "radical ways of realizing it." Erikson was, of course, one of those promoters. Too cosmopolitan and too content with Jewish-Christian indeterminacy to chart a clear evolution from Judaism to Christianity, he came dangerously close to doing so in his *Yale Review* essay and in parallel statements. But he ultimately drew back, even as Joan's "Christian apprentice," for he would not seek to bolster "one's identity by the categorical exclusion and rejection of otherness."[82]

Perhaps the most disorganized of his publications when it appeared in 1981, Erikson regarded the *Yale Review* article as a springboard for his first major writing project since *Gandhi's Truth*. Kai was skeptical, but Erik assured David Cogan that "I am now making a book of it. This will take a while." Erik confided to his former Stockbridge neighbor Helmut Wohl that it would have to be a short book, for his power of concentration was not what it once had been. Combined with periodic visual problems, the writing process had become very slow and difficult. Joan and friends like Margaret Brenman-Gibson brought Erik stacks of books and articles on Jesus to encourage him in his work. Through the 1980s, he sat at his writing table, hoping the thoughts and words would come. He had wanted to elaborate, fully and systematically, the Judeo-Christian traditions of healing as a counterpoint to modern technologies. He had also wanted to invoke those traditions as a wedge into the spirituality and the apprehensions of the elderly. Finally, he had hoped that by writing about the Judeo-Christian healing traditions, he could become a better traveler in the borderlands between life and death. However, as the years passed, he wrote fewer and fewer sentences on the notepads in front of him. This long and important phase of his career was almost over.[83]

CHAPTER TEN

"The Shadow of Nonbeing"

When Erik Erikson first publicly presented his model for the full eight-stage life cycle in 1950, the seventh or generativity stage and the eighth on old age had been the least developed. *Gandhi's Truth* represented perhaps his fullest effort to amplify the psychological and ethical needs and obligations of seventh-stage adulthood. While lecturing and writing about *Wild Strawberries* and on Jesus' Galilean sayings, Erikson began to focus on the eighth stage, and eventually, the last part of the eighth stage with its boundary between life and death. He referred to this boundary as "the shadow of nonbeing."

By the early 1980s, Erikson's writing projects were erratic; they required more energy and perseverance than he could summon. Joan helped enormously, husband and wife frequently discussing the distinction between the early and later segments of old age. Indeed, Joan began to describe a distinctive ninth stage covering late old age as if it represented a logical extension of the life cycle model. This pointed to a more general occurrence during Erik's last years: Family and friends often tended to appropriate aspects of his thought within their own conceptual agendas. At the annual Wellfleet meetings, for example, Robert Lifton borrowed from Erik's identity formulation in *Young Man Luther,* Kai from Erik's ideas on pseudospeciation, Margaret Brenman-Gibson from his clinical insights and biographical perspectives, and John Dunne from his formulations of the sense of "I." Because of his diminished powers of observation and articulation, Erik seemed unable to take the initiative as others "crowded" in and incorporated their own versions of his work.

Nor could he do much new work of his own. Erikson's efforts to amplify the divide between late life and death fell short in an intellectual, literary, and aesthetic sense. So did his efforts to restate and modify his earlier formulations. Nonetheless, he kept trying to make a major conceptual contribution as his hearing, sight, and energy faltered.

THE LIFE CYCLE COMPLETED—ALMOST

While Erikson was writing about the Galilean sayings, he completed an essay of approximately fifty printed pages for a three-volume collection, *The Course of Life, Psychoanalytic Contributions toward Understanding Personality Development,* commissioned by the National Institute of Mental Health. In this essay, Erikson followed the pattern of his article on *Wild Strawberries,* beginning with adulthood and old age and working backward toward youth and infancy. Since this NIMH essay was reasonably clear, Erikson (helped substantially by others) turned it into a book. He wrote a brief preface and introduction, and he drew on a few other previously published materials, revising them very sparingly. Reflecting his emphasis on the perspective of old age, he titled the very slim volume *The Life Cycle Completed: A Review* (1982).

Erikson's justification for this collection of already accessible material was insubstantial. It "seemed to me pointless to rephrase what seems already to have been rather fittingly formulated." Because he had "said it all (or most) before, I must paraphrase and, here and there, even quote myself." He admitted that he had not taken up those "institutional structures and mechanisms" that helped to account for the place of aging individuals in "the politics of community." Because this vital context had not been included, he had not fashioned the richly textured psychosocial account that was needed on aging and the life cycle. Consequently, he inappropriately referred readers to some social science literature and to his work on Luther and Gandhi to help enhance his discussion. These apologetics masked the failure of *The Life Cycle Completed* to approximate Freud's *Outline of Psychoanalysis* as an effective late-life overview of salient ideas and perspectives. As Erikson's inability to make much progress on his biography of Jesus also indicated, he had become incapable of writing serious books. Even with rising national interest in issues concerning the aging process, sales figures for this last volume never remotely approximated sales for books like *Childhood and Society, Identity: Youth and Crisis,* and even *Dimensions of a New Identity.* Months after *The Life Cycle Completed* was published, Erikson complained that "I have received only one letter saying, hey, thank you, that's a good book, one letter and you can imagine how many readers I had, you know."[1]

This is not to say that one should wholly discount Erikson's last book. Through his selection of materials and his rewriting, he revealed important dimensions of how he was approaching and viewing his own late life. For one, there was a decidedly historical perspective at several points in the volume—a sense not only that the past was vital to the present but that Erikson and his ideas were becoming part of that past. In his preface, for example, he summarized his professional career since 1933, when he arrived in America, and how he and Joan had collaborated on life cycle work since the Midcentury White House Conference. The introductory essay that followed elaborated on some of these ventures but focused on Freud's Vienna, where he was trained. That, too, was written from a decidedly historical perspective. He observed that psychoanalysis at that time adhered to a scientific model derived from physics—quantities of energy were shifted about through mechanistic drives and restraints inherent in a person's "inner" psychic world. Yet his work at that time with children, child analysts, and teachers had moved "the reductionist language of scientistic theory" into the background and made him more attune to "this century's emphasis on complementarity and relativity."[2]

Perhaps because Erikson was sensing greater proximity to his own death, random portions of *The Life Cycle Completed* registered acute awareness of historicism. Indeed, he asserted that history and psychoanalysis were very much the same enterprise. He underscored R. G. Collingwood's classic and decidedly Hegelian observation in *The Idea of History* (1956): "History is the life of the mind itself which is not mind except so far as it both lives in the historical process and knows itself as so living." Erikson insisted that this was the essence of the psychoanalytic approach: "These words have always impressed me as applicable to the core of the psychoanalytic method." Indeed, he proposed a massive international research project comparing the transference between analyst and analysand that would factor in nation and region, age, gender, cultural differences, and other variables so as to better determine what was shaped by "*developmental* and *historical relativity* in human experience." The ultimate goal of this undertaking was "to register the fate of the basic human strengths and core disturbances under changing technological and historical conditions."[3]

If several of Erikson's observations in *The Life Cycle Completed* showed how profoundly historical his orientation had become, the more primary task was to reconsider the meaning of old age and the death that lay ahead. He acknowledged that he and Joan had formulated the eighth stage (the old-age clash between integrity and despair) in the 1940s when they were "in our 'middle years.' " That was "a time when we certainly had no intention of or capacity for imagining ourselves as really old." Now in their eighties, husband and wife had joined an increasing "group of mere 'elderlies' " and they could understand more about the last stage of life.[4]

Erikson expressed the firm conviction in this final book that late life involved more than a regressive fixation on the problems and tasks of earlier stages. Indeed, old age could be likened to "an epigenetic recapitulation on a higher developmental level." The despair of late life often represented a "mourning not only for time forfeited and space depleted but also . . . for autonomy weakened, initiative lost, intimacy missed, generativity neglected—not to speak of identity potentials bypassed or, indeed, an all too limiting identity lived." Against these qualities, Erikson emphasized the opposite pole of the eighth developmental stage—integrity. He insisted that integrity meant more than the ethical virtue of "wisdom." With the integrity of old age came a broad philosophical disposition rooted in "faith" and "hope," a disposition of both existential and sensuous qualities. An elderly person received some preview of the "existential preoccupations of the kind that can 'come of age' only in old age" during adolescence, when an "ideological worldview" first appeared. But that adolescent perspective was replaced by the business of adulthood and its responsibilities—a time when one was too preoccupied with everyday activities to consider "the shadow of nonbeing." As the older person contemplated that "shadow," Erikson observed, and before senility set in, he also found himself experiencing an important "final psychosexual state" that involved "a *generalization of sensual modes* that can foster an enriched bodily and mental experience even as part functions weaken and genital energy diminishes."[5]

Clearly, *The Life Cycle Completed* presented a very upbeat view of old age—a richly engaging period spiritually, philosophically, and sensually. The total experience went beyond Erikson's initial term ("integrity") and even beyond "wisdom." It involved a hopeful wholeness, a new kind of inner and outer vitality. Unfortunately, Erikson lacked the energy and the power of concentration to elaborate further. While he sensed the richly textured nature of late old age, he lacked the capacity to communicate it fully to his readers. What is most striking, however, is that Erikson seemed intent on emphasizing the connection between the eighth stage and the first. This was not the first time he had discussed the idea. But his intensity—almost a sense of urgency—was important. Indeed, the connection of early infancy to late life represented the single most salient point he wanted to convey to his readers about the completion of life and the approach of death. Owing to his determination to connect the two, he probably overemphasized the cognitive and sensory capacities of infants.

At eighty, Erikson wanted to stress what Shakespeare, in *As You Like It*, had stated less positively through Jaques's famous speech on the seven ages of man—that the infant and the very old person shared crucial essentials. Because "the last stage of life seems to have great potential significance for the first," one could understand why "children in viable cultures are made thoughtful in a special way by encounters with old people." Unlike generative adulthood, which was preoccupied with the here and now, the young and the old lived in "the times that dream of rebirth" and attentively contemplated "the shadow of nonbeing." The two were drawn together because both acutely sensed the border between existence and nonexistence.[6]

The initial pattern of mutual recognition between newborn infant and mother ("the *primal other*") first established this sense of a divide. The ritual that connected newborn and parent fostered in both the assurance of "*separateness transcended* and yet also of *distinctiveness confirmed*" and this represented "the very basis of the sense of 'I.' " With a successful ritual of initiation into the world, "the human being will thereafter feel confined by 'uplifting' encounters" between the I and the Other through his life. Throughout his existence, he felt "the *numinous,* the aura of a hallowed presence"; he had a sense of connection to others and also a sense of distinctiveness. By the time he reached old age, his connection with the mother and then with others had transferred "to the *ultimate other* who will 'lift up His countenance upon you and give you peace.' " For Erikson, then "infantile trust" established the "aura of hallowed presence," and it had evolved by old age into "mature faith" in the "*ultimate other.*"[7]

Erikson therefore considered the "completion" of the life cycle, like its initiation, within an "aura of hallowed presence." He wanted to do more, to corroborate and elaborate this and other of his observations on late life. Indeed, he felt that *The Life Cycle Completed* was only the beginning of the effort. After it was published, he used green and red ink to pen in numerous small corrections and to emphasize particular words and phrases, perhaps in the hope of facilitating a more comprehensive revised edition. With key words and bits of doodling in the margins, he marked up his copy of *The Life Cycle Completed* from cover to cover. But intellectual and physical vitality had ebbed, precluding significant rewriting, and no revised edition was possible.[8]

In these circumstances, Joan pursued what she considered the next best course. She turned to Helen Kivnick, a young clinical and research psychologist with whom she had worked in the activities program at San Francisco's Mt. Zion Hospital. Kivnick's dissertation had been on grandparenthood and, more generally, on the nature of late adulthood. As it became obvious that Erik was incapable of producing a new edition of *The Life Cycle Completed,* Kivnick and Joan started a special compensatory project, interviewing some of the children that Erik had observed during the early 1940s as part of Jean Walker Macfarlane's longitudinal developmental study at Berkeley. Most were now parents and grandparents themselves, suitably positioned to discuss the life cycle from the standpoint of the seventh and eighth stages. Kivnick directed day-to-day research and writing for the project, though Joan's advisory role was not inconsiderable. They listed Erik as the third author, and he seemed to understand that this was to assure a wider readership.[9]

Vital Involvement in Old Age (1986) came of this undertaking. It was not a book that Erik could possibly have written. There was almost no discussion of the border between late old age and death that had so deeply concerned him in *The Life Cycle Completed.* The volume had none of his penchant for layered, multivariable explanations, complex ambiguities, periodic ramblings, or his zest for crossing disciplinary and thematic boundaries. His aesthetic and literary artistry was missing. Instead, *Vital Involvement* represented a rather flat, concrete, and linear recapitulation of his life cycle model from the eighth to the first stage plus extensive illustrations from the "voices" of the subjects. Because Kivnick saw no viable connection between the last stage and the first, that was not emphasized. Intergenerational connectedness, the psychosocial perspective, the sense of "I," and other of Erik's ideas were presented with perhaps excessively tangible concreteness and little sense of dynamism. Decidedly a Kivnick production and heavily influenced by Joan, the book clarified and simplified for a general audience some of Erik's views on the life cycle. If not for Joan's connection to the work, he would not have paid a great deal of attention to it.

MOVING EAST AND WINDING DOWN

Although Erikson published his last book in 1982, clinical psychologist Stephen Schlein offered a valuable volume five years later that represented half a century of Erikson's unpublished and obscurely published writings (*A Way of Looking at Things: Selected Papers from 1930 to 1980*). Schlein first met Erikson in 1971, when he was a postdoctoral fellow at Austen Riggs. He was impressed by the older man's clinical skills and professional writings. Schlein gathered together forty-seven papers, twelve of which had never been published. He added thirteen sketches Erikson had made over the years of people important to him. Materials relevant to every period in Erikson's life from his Vienna years through the 1970s were included, and there was a comprehensive bibliography. Erikson was deeply touched that Schlein had been willing to spend several years to produce the collection. Schlein regarded the project as the thrill of his life.[10]

Erikson enjoyed meeting with Schlein to help with selections for the collection. The materials concerning his Vienna training and his relationship with Anna Freud and Dorothy Burlingham were especially important to him. Erikson also liked the section of brief portrait sketches of friends like Joseph Wheelwright, Larry Frank, and Paul Tillich. He was pleased, too, that Schlein was including his elegy for a former patient who had committed suicide. Finally, he strongly approved of Schlein's decision to conclude the book with his 1969 talk at Harvard's Appleton Chapel, in which he asserted that the birth of Per

Bloland, his grandson, was a more humane achievement than the first moon landing. W. W. Norton published *A Way of Looking at Things,* but neither sales nor royalties were substantial. Republication in 1995 as an eighteen-dollar paperback assured that Erikson enthusiasts and researchers would have the opportunity to read a large array of writings in a single volume.[11]

No longer capable of undertaking his own books, Erikson enjoyed helping Robert Lifton with his exceedingly difficult study of the motives of Nazi doctors who had participated in medical genocide. He critiqued portions of Lifton's text, convincing him that the doctors had an ideological rather than a religious perspective. Erikson also insisted that the doctors' rationalizations for their killings—to eliminate "genetic danger" and to preclude "miscegenation"—were variations of pseudospeciation. He shared personal memories of life in Germany and Austria that he had never before mentioned to Lifton. Erikson found himself captivated by Lifton's conclusion that the Nazi doctors were not demons but ordinary people, sometimes very decent, but also motivated to do great evil. This was congruent with Erik's take on German culture, with its normal and benevolent side and its propensity toward demonic and totalistic solutions. He wrote to Lifton that "you have done the nearly impossible, namely, finding a quiet and strong tone for a set of observations which in their emotional substance are really unfathomable." As these friends of thirty years discussed the particularistic and the universal aspects of Nazi conduct, their relationship became even closer. In appreciation, Lifton presented a cartoon of one bird saying to another "An [s]elf inside a wise man I can understand. But how can a wise man fit inside an [s]elf?" The other bird replied: "80 years of practice."[12]

Honors and recognition for Erikson abounded during the 1980s as the force of feminist attacks and Marshall Berman's article diminished. The San Francisco Psychoanalytic Institute renamed its reading room the Erik H. Erikson Library. He was one of the five most cited authors in American psychology textbooks. On Erikson's eightieth birthday in 1982, a special celebration in Cambridge attracted more than two hundred friends and colleagues. Robert Coles, John Mack, and William Gibson offered tributes, while the director of Austen Riggs, Daniel Schwartz, announced a new funded staff position: the Erik H. Erikson Scholar. In 1984, Erikson was invited to address a plenary session of the American Psychiatric Association. With fading voice and unsteady body, he advised understanding the otherness in ourselves as the best counter to the pseudospeciations that heightened international conflict in a nuclear age. Three years later, the Psychiatric Clinic of Karlsruhe (Germany) dedicated a special child and adolescent unit as the Erik Homburger Erikson House. The eminent developmentalist Jerome Bruner declared publicly that "Erikson must surely be the most distinguished living psychoanalyst." By 1991, the Cambridge-based Center for Psychological Studies in the Nuclear Age honored the Eriksons jointly at its annual recognition award ceremony. The founder, Harvard psychiatrist John Mack, lauded them as breakers of artificial boundaries between people. Robert Lifton underscored his appreciation, and Kai explained that he was standing in for his father, who was too infirm to attend the ceremony.[13]

Many of these recognitions took place in Cambridge because the Eriksons came increasingly to regard it as their home base. Their return to the area after spending most of the 1970s and the early 1980s in Tiburon was incremental. The founding of the Erik H. and Joan M. Erikson Center, an adjunct of the Cambridge Hospital psychiatry department and the Harvard Medical School, was a compelling motive for the move. The center had been established in 1982 to provide training, research, and teaching opportunities for mental health professionals and humanists interested in drawing on clinical insights. Because the center was also to serve as a link between the old and the young, it was appropriate to have the Eriksons around, and every fall they came and conducted a short course on the life cycle. Joan was the principal instructor. She prized the center as an opportunity for intergenerational and interdisciplinary activity on the Harvard campus, and provided a $100,000 loan to cover unanticipated center expenses.[14]

The impetus for a full move back to Cambridge occurred in the spring of 1987, not long after Joan and Erik had a wonderful time dancing—slowly, joyously, and with eloquent presence—at the wedding of Robert Wallerstein's daughter, Amy, in nearby Sausalito. Neither quite knew where the energy came from. During this interval, Margaret Brenman-Gibson and John Mack, who had taken the lead in establishing the Erikson Center, found themselves overcommitted, and they brought Dorothy Austin in to take charge. A young minister with a theology degree and a psychotherapist with a gregarious personality, Austin realized that the permanent presence of Joan and especially Erik would greatly enhance her efforts to promote the center. Consequently, she visited Tiburon with center board member David Wilcox to persuade the couple to move East. Austin's timing was auspicious, for the unit at Mt. Zion Hospital where Joan consulted had been closed. In addition to keeping herself busy, Joan worried about Erik's health care needs as he declined. She feared that she might have to move with Erik to a nursing home or other special care facility, a decision that she regarded as a death sentence. Austin understood Joan's concerns and presented an attractive proposal: an intergenerational home in Cambridge. She and Diana Eck, a young professor of comparative religion and Indian studies, would buy a house with the Eriksons and be available as caregivers, attending to their needs.[15]

Joan found herself deeply attracted by Austin's youth, her intelligence, her feminist independence, and her enthusiasm. Joan knew, too, that Eck would appeal to Erik, especially considering her interest in India and Gandhi. Indeed, Joan realized that Erik would delight in a household of bright and supportive women. Austin's proposal seemed, as well, to promise far more autonomy and dignity than institutional assistance; Joan felt she would be free to come and go as she wanted, assured that Erik would be well cared for while she was out. Joan consulted Kai, who may have been uneasy over Austin's proposal but saw the benefits; it resolved his parents' day care needs in their final years. Joan accepted the proposal. "Living communally is an adventure at our age," she proclaimed enthusiastically. With Austin and Eck, Joan found a rambling three-story Victorian house on Trowbridge Street a few blocks from Harvard and equally close to the Erikson Center. It sold for $415,000; another $150,000 had to be spent to make the place livable. The four would own the house as joint tenants; in the event of death, the surviving tenants would inherit that person's interest. Austin instructed the Eriksons to place $200,000 in an escrow account to buy the Trowbridge house. Next, she persuaded W. W. Norton to give the Eriksons a $100,000 bridge loan to help with the Trowbridge purchase while they sold their house in Tiburon (valued at roughly $400,000) and liquidated certain other assets. Thus, the Eriksons committed a significant portion of their retirement reserves for the house. For their part, Austin and Eck assumed responsibility for the mortgage. Record keeping and dollar figures on all phases of this venture were imprecise and haphazard, while the promise of caregiving was never recorded.[16]

Although the move to Cambridge began on a hopeful note, problems arose. Not long after the Eriksons unpacked, the *Harvard Crimson* ran a story about a scandal at the university's John F. Kennedy School of Government. Kennedy School officials had promised a wealthy Texas couple a special honorary type of affiliation with Harvard, including modest privileges, in exchange for a $500,000 contribution. To justify their actions, School of Government officials charged that the Erikson Center had already granted the same couple Harvard library privileges and an insurance plan in exchange for a $150,000 donation. This bizarre revelation caught the Erikson Center in the larger scandal of the Kennedy School, resulting in close scrutiny of all aspects of its financial operations. Some officials at Cambridge Hospital wanted to disaffiliate the Erikson Center from their Department of Psychiatry unless Austin resigned. Joan supported Austin. So did Carol Gilligan, who sat on the center's governing board. But several influential members of the board resigned, participation in center activities declined, and its ambitious educational program was undermined; teachers and lecturers left and replacements were difficult to attract. Services for the elderly became the center's primary focus.[17]

By the early 1990s, life in the Erikson-Austin-Eck household also became difficult. Because of Eck's scholarly and intellectual commitments, she was rarely home. Austin was away more, too, after she accepted a position at Drew University in Madison, New Jersey, and commuted from Cambridge. As the promised caregiving from housemates evaporated in the face of important career opportunities for both women, Joan was required to hire attendants and nurses to care for Erik. They often proved unreliable, and Joan sometimes had to take over on short notice. She compounded the difficulty by refusing to delegate authority over any aspect of Erik's care. When the grandchildren visited, they could not speak loud enough for Erik to hear them. Joan assumed that she had to be present to serve as the go-between. She also tried to provide good cheer to her children, and, in a sense, to herself, for the entire family found it difficult to see Erik deteriorating. Indeed, Joan felt a personal stake in maintaining the appearance that Erik was still reading and thinking. All the while, she realized that her life was becoming heavily constricted with mounting, sometimes self-imposed burdens. She was not even able to get outside very much to exercise. As time went on, it became increasingly clear to Joan that one day she would have to sell the Erikson interest in the house to Austin and Eck and to move with Erik into a nursing home.[18]

Erik's role had been minimal in the decision to return to Cambridge. Indeed, he watched and acquiesced as some of his personal notes, files, and correspondence were discarded in the course of the move from Tiburon to Cambridge. Joan had become the senior partner of the marriage. Through most of her married life, she had subordinated her creative projects and opportunities to Erik's professional and intellectual advancement, but was determined, now, to emerge from his shadow. With Erik's assent, Joan assumed a proprietary interest in his writings and many of his ideas. When Erik referred to his publications and concepts as the creations of "Joan and I [me]," she was deeply gratified. Whereas his Midcentury White House Conference paper on the life cycle listed Joan as his collaborator, *The Life Cycle Completed* referenced that same paper as the work of "J. M. Erikson (with Erik H. Erikson)." This probably reflected the fact that Joan had taken an intense interest in the eight-stage life cycle model. When the couple was asked to make presentations about the model, Joan did most of the talking. She offered a very clear, exacting sequential presentation of the stages illustrated by her weaving and her experiences. Whereas Erik rarely underscored distinctly separate stages and was interested in the ways that stages merged into each other, Joan thought increasingly about a distinctive ninth stage of old age beyond Integrity versus Despair. When Joan compiled a short volume of Rilke poems, the couple reversed long-standing literary roles. Erik helped with translations from German and prepared a few decorative woodcuts to help support Joan's efforts. Erik rarely objected to Joan's increasing control over their lives. At dinner, he sometimes cut his dessert chocolate in half again and again, handing each new half to Joan as a sign of his feeling for her. Once he traced his fingers on the table to frame a portrait of her, remarking: "She's beautiful, isn't she?"[19]

Joan's expanding role involved serving as an intermediary between Erik and others. She limited contact between him and his Homburger half sisters, especially Ruth, who turned to Sue Bloland for an explanation. Sue felt better about her relationship with her parents now, for she sensed that she was proving herself professionally. At fifty, she decided to become a psychotherapist and a psychoanalyst. She took a master of social work degree from New York University and a certificate in analysis from the Manhattan Institute for Psychoanalysis. A co-founder of the Center for Midlife Development, she dialogued with Erik's life cycle formulations. Joan felt closer to her more self-assured daughter, and the two discussed personal matters more candidly. Jon also felt better about his parents, especially during his many telephone conversations with Joan. But Kai, not far away in New Haven, remained the sibling upon whom Joan most depended for practical advice and support.[20]

In the course of the late 1980s and early 1990s, Erik steadily declined. In 1987, his Bay Area friend Daniel Benveniste characterized him as "a great oak swaying in the wind with roots losing their hold on the ground below." His eyes still sparkled and his smile imparted confidence and good cheer, but there was a faded quality to his countenance. Customarily a meticulous dresser, Erikson's clothing fit less well, for he had become quite gaunt. Indeed, he was very fragile, requiring a cane to walk even a few feet. He tired easily, and his hearing aids picked up less. G. Stanley Hall had referred to senescence as "the Great Fatigue" that increasingly narrowed one's existence. Whether we characterize Erikson's "fatigue" as Alzheimer's disease or simply senility, he moved in and out of it. When Benjamin Spock visited, he was shocked by Erik's appearance. He thought his old friend "looked like a corpse." Any serious cold could lead to pneumonia. Prolonged illness lengthened the periods of "fatigue." He began to mix German conversation with English, and distant childhood memories became more vivid than recent occurrences. If he became more inward and asocial in decline, his eyes were no less active or observant; they brought him meaning as the other senses receded and people engaged him less.[21]

Until his last months, Erikson continued to exhibit some level of intellectual activity. When he could summon the energy, he felt that he could become "entirely preoccupied with old age." He was trying to "learn to accept the law of life, and face the fact that we disintegrate slowly." He did not find that old age was overwhelmingly depressing. Instead, he detected that he was moving from the activity and responsibility of mature adulthood toward a new childlike zest—to "wonder, joy, playfulness—all those things that adults often have to sacrifice for a while." Indeed, he considered returning to an early preoccupation—woodcuts and prints. Now, too, there seemed to be a greater potential for humor: "I can't imagine a wise old person who can't laugh. The world is full of ridiculous dichotomies." Always ready with a joke, he tried to laugh about the final border crossing that separated life from death. When he was taking a short walk in Cambridge with a friend, for example, he asked where they were going. She replied that they were headed toward heaven. "And do you know the way?" he inquired, smiling broadly.[22]

The crucial issue of late life, Erikson noted, was the same "for every living creature, what's going to happen to me next? Who is going to be there, how do I get there?" Religions were especially helpful with these questions, for they provided "something that can be anticipated, something that can be prayed for, and so on." As one began to cross the divide between life and death, one needed "to experience something of an existential identity encompassing one's own singular existence." Reinhold Niebuhr, his Stockbridge friend, had written about being "on the sidelines of life." Erikson thought that perspective was too gloomy. He was impressed with a heightened sense of "I" at life's end that placed him instead "on the border of life." In that position, one could feel "a certain freedom from the despair associated with unlived or mis-lived" parts of one's past. And yet, Erikson cautioned, deterioration of the physical body made it difficult always to assure integration of mind, body, and spirit. That integration became a pressing goal as death approached. He insisted that one never ceased to require wholeness, coherence, the "I," and the "Other."[23]

Before death, Goethe had asked for "More light." Erikson seemed to be asking for the same, for he still had important tasks to complete. One of the most important was to manage his final clinical supervision.

Late in 1987, David Wilcox, a bright and enthusiastic young student who had participated on the governing board of the Erikson Center, required clinical supervision from a staff member at Cambridge Hospital so he could complete a Harvard doctorate in human development and psychology. He concluded that nobody in the Boston area was more appropriate than an eighty-five-year-old professor emeritus of human development and asked Erikson to assume the task. Erik had not supervised in decades and feared that Cambridge Hospital would not allow him to, especially from his home. But permission was granted. Wilcox spent many hours over the next two and a half years in Erikson's study discussing two of his patients—an adult and a four-year-old boy.[24]

Wilcox's clinical work with the boy proved to be deeply engaging. The boy frequently soiled and wet his pants. Erikson instructed Wilcox to bring to his house the same toys that the boy had played with during therapy sessions and to arrange them on the floor as the child had done. He also insisted on seeing the pages of the many tic-tac-toe games that the boy and Wilcox had played. Erikson explained how the toy arrangements and marked tic-tac-toe grids and other aspects of the child's play process had to be analyzed like an adult's dream recollection. Like the dream, play opened the door to the child's unconscious. But while Erikson was attentive to the child's psyche, he emphasized that social circumstance was no less important. Wilcox needed to understand how the toy arrangements and tic-tac-toe grids reflected the boy's specific social and familial circumstances. Erikson explained that during his own training, August Aichhorn had taken him to Vienna neighborhoods and playgrounds to establish that the child's "outer world" was no less fundamental than the "inner world."[25]

In this supervisory capacity, Erikson was essentially passing along lessons from his European training that had cohered during his first significant American case at the Judge Baker Clinic more than fifty years earlier. At that time, he had worked with a six-year-old boy who also had problems of incontinence. The youngster had taken toys (balls of clay) and shaped them into a revealing configuration. From that configuration, Erikson discovered how the child's emotions and social circumstances converged in his day-to-day life. The astute clinician was concerned with all the details involving the patient and nothing could be left out. "Remember," Erikson emphasized to Wilcox as he had on earlier occasions, "everything is our business." He was passing on a crucial aspect of clinical observation.[26]

Supervision of Wilcox helped Erikson to become focused and coherent for a few hours during supervisory days until the training period ended in mid-1990. Two old Stockbridge friends found that one topic in particular remained almost a surefire way to break through Erikson's "Great Fatigue." Helmut Wohl, his old Stockbridge neighbor, and Margaret Brenman-Gibson, his close friend and longtime Riggs clinical associate, discovered that he would still perk up and reflect, even as late as 1991, on the issue of his paternity. He still seemed distressed that he did not know who had fathered him. Erik kept a small Danish flag in his study and a framed honorary degree from a Danish university not only because his mother had come from Copenhagen. They were reminders that his father had probably also come from Denmark. Before he died, he hoped to learn his father's name.[27]

DEATH

The last two years in Cambridge with Dorothy Austin and Diana Eck were especially difficult. Between early bedtimes and long naps, Erik slept much of the time. He spoke more German than English, which made it hard to communicate with some of his friends. Failing hearing turned his life even more into itself. Yet there were still good periods, such as one morning in the late winter of 1991. A visitor showed him Hetty Zock's new book, *A Psychology of Ultimate Concern: Erik H. Erikson's Contribution to the Psychology of Religion,* and told him that it was impressive. He replied that he did not feel comfortable with the phrase "Ultimate Concern"; it seemed too vague and pretentious a way to characterize his thoughts. He grew increasingly uneasy, at this point, for Joan was away at a dental appointment. He walked a few steps here and a few there, hoping she would appear. When Joan returned, Erik relaxed and offered several humorous observations in German. He was back to some of his old habits; he had become a worrier again, joked, and split hairs over the way a thought was expressed.[28]

In the spring of 1992, Erikson fell and badly fractured his hip. Surgery was difficult. Rehabilitation therapy was unpleasant and disturbing, and he became despondent. He did not try to recover—to regain the capacity to walk. His face registered the downcast attitude. His eyes ceased to sparkle, his mouth tightened and puckered, and deep lines formed below his cheeks. His shoulders slumped badly now. He chilled easily, even in summer, and usually required a sweater or a blanket. He was confined to a wheelchair, where he slept much of the time. Incontinence became a problem. He was shifted to a soft-food diet and Joan or a hired attendant fed him.[29]

As the "Great Fatigue" progressed, there were still hopeful signs. His observant eyes, if dulled and narrowed, still remained active. He seemed content to glance out of the windows, to observe his surroundings, and to be quietly grateful for those who looked in on him. At times he scanned his Trowbridge Street study to see his Danish flag, photographs of Freud's Vienna, and other tokens from his past. "Wasn't it [life] beautiful," he remarked to Margaret Brenman-Gibson. In mid-1993, the Abrahamsen family in Copenhagen sent a photograph of his mother as a young woman. He looked at it, long and closely, remarking in a scarcely audible tone: "Fantastic!" Was this the bond of trust and the sense of "I" connecting mother and newborn, old man and "Ultimate Other"?[30]

As Erik declined, Joan suffered. She missed conversing, walking, and otherwise "doing" with her husband of more than sixty years. Her life seemed not only "very tough" but "very depriving," and she sometimes referred to Erik as if he had already died. To enhance their remaining time together, she began to consult with a German translator to prepare his 1923–24 journal, written during his *Wanderschaft,* for English publication. In reading his youthful ideas, she could see how several of them had anticipated his major conceptualizations. But that was not enough. Desperate to fill her lonely hours, Joan completed *Legacies: Prometheus, Orpheus, Socrates,* a short book arguing that the legends of the three Greek figures inspired hope, possibility, and human interrelationships, while helping to preserve the planet's fragile ecological integrity. Despite these projects, however, the large Trowbridge Street residence was coming to feel like a prison. Joan realized that it was time to leave. Austin and Eck became the sole owners of the house in exchange for a limited cash payment to the Eriksons.[31]

With Kai's assistance, Joan spent the spring of 1993 investigating facilities where she and Erik might move. They decided on one in Harwich, a small Cape Cod town that had no postal station, bank, or even much of a grocery. It had been settled by Indians more than ten thousand years earlier. In 1644, migrants from the Pilgrim settlement of Plymouth moved to Eastham. Some of their descendants embraced the "Congregational Way," supported themselves by farming and fishing, and eventually settled in Harwich. They organized the town about a "Church of Christ." Rebuilt several times, it became the First Congregational Church of Harwich, anchoring the community geographically and socially. By the end of the nineteenth century, Portuguese from the Cape Verde Islands also began to settle in Harwich and "summer people" from the mainland started buying lots to build cottages. But population growth was never substantial, and Joan had been especially impressed by the peacefulness of the town. She was also attracted by a small and convivial nursing home, the Rosewood Manor, which would give Erik attentive twenty-four-hour care. She would live nearby in the Winstead Elder-Care Facility and could visit Erik daily. Joan arranged to move in July. When she informed Erik, he summoned the capacity for perhaps his last coherent conversation, telling Joan that she had raised their children and had administered their house; she should not be required, at this point, to take care of him.[32]

In Harwich, Joan attended Congregational Church services regularly, sang in the church choir, cultivated friendships, and eagerly anticipated the annual cranberry festival. She soon felt compelled to leave the Winstead, however, as she disliked the always blaring television sets and an automobile transport system that discouraged the residents from walking. Drawing on dwindling retirement assets, she bought a modest two-family house adjacent to the Winstead and resided in the larger unit, renting the smaller apartment to two young women from the area. Kind and engaging, the two women cooked and cleaned for her, and they checked in on her regularly. Freed of daily responsibilities of caring for Erik and in a place that felt like home, Joan began to reflect, to gather together her notes, and to consider future writing projects and other ventures. She was trying to learn to live without her husband of sixty-three years but to keep alive his name, his books, and his ideas.[33]

The border between life and death became increasingly blurred as Erik lived out his last months in Rosewood Manor. Whenever she visited, Joan found him comfortable and serene. Attendants shifted him several times daily between bed and wheelchair. Because he was quiet, courteous, and appreciative of the care he received, Erik was a favorite of the Rosewood nursing staff. His eyes remained his most energized sense; he scanned all of the activity about him. However, he did not always recognize family or friends. When Sue visited on New Year's Day of 1994, for example, he said "I know you" but did not appear aware that she was his daughter.[34]

Joan, Kathy Benforado, her young friend and music instructor from Boston, and a Midwest guest visited the Rosewood Manor two weeks later when the snow was high and beautiful. Erik was sitting in a wheelchair in his room at the end of a long hall, looking out the window at a dull fence. He recognized Joan and was comforted by her presence. She handed him a piece of chocolate, which he ate instantly and enthusiastically. Then he kissed Benforado's hand, relishing its smell and texture. His small Danish flag and a photograph of his mother were quite apparent atop his dresser. There were very few books in the room, and the blare of television sets from guests in nearby rooms made it all too apparent that this was not a place for study or intellectual reflection. The milieu seemed to clash with the name-plate on the door—"Erik Erikson"—an author and intellectual. It was difficult to know what to say to a major thinker of the twentieth century who was crossing the line from life to death.[35]

By early May, Erik was rapidly failing. Catheterization to facilitate urination had produced another major infection plus great pain and discomfort. Joan recognized that Erik wanted to cross the last border. She convinced his local doctor and Rosewood Manor staff not to administer massive antibiotics or other medications to fight the infection. The staff did not understand why she insisted on being alone with Erik on May 11–12, his last day and night. As a young girl abroad with her mother, Joan had learned some of the old German songs and lullabies that Erik had been taught as a child. Now, she held his hand and sang these to him. Her singing appeared to soothe his pains and quiet his distress. He died at four in the morning. In "Love Song," a poem about his death, Joan wrote:

> If only the dying could smile
> At the instant of their parting
> Sharing with us the bliss,

> Of their complete surrender,
> Then perhaps, we could grasp
> The silliness of mourning
> And of dread.

Joan sat in Erik's room a few more hours. When she left for several minutes, Rosewood staff came into the room, wrapped Erik in sheets, and removed him through a special door reserved for that purpose. Joan had no time for a final good-bye. Jon subsequently prepared a summary statement of his father's last hours for the press and the public: "He died of old age, peacefully in his sleep."[36]

Joan planned for Erik to be buried in the cemetery of the First Congregational Church of Harwich. This plan seemed to cross the Jewish-Christian divide that Erik had usually navigated in life. Long before, both had told Kai of their preference for cremation (a procedure that has no sanction in traditional Jewish practice). Erik's ashes were returned to Joan in a small box for burial, and this distressed her. She hoped the ashes would pass quickly into the earth. The smallness of the grave plaque—"Erik H. Erikson 1902–1994"—was also cause for unease, as it sat rather inconspicuously in the shadows of several large gravestones.[37]

Joan scheduled a short private internment on June 15, a few hours before the memorial service at the First Congregational Church. It would have been Erik's ninety-second birthday, which was also the wedding day of his mother and stepfather. It was a Wednesday; a midweek service in a small town without motels and a two-hour drive from Boston mitigated against a substantial attendance. Joan planned the entire service with meticulous care, assigning friends to attend to flowers, invitations, choir music, the printed program, seating arrangements, the tape recording of all proceedings, and other particulars. She also called John Thornton, her former minister from St. Stephen's Parish in Tiburon, and asked him to preside over the service. She emphasized to Thornton, now bishop of the Episcopal diocese of Idaho, that she wanted a short and simple event—neither heavily academic nor theological—and that he should set the tone. Jon was the first of the children to arrive in Harwich for the service, several days in advance. He stayed with Joan and helped her with last-minute preparations. Jon brought photographs of a house he had just purchased in Port Angeles, Washington, along a body of water marking the American-Canadian border. Kai came from Vienna, where he had been teaching. Sue arrived from a trip to France with Robert Downey, her partner of seventeen years and a New York lawyer. While abroad, Sue had prepared remarks for the service. She had told Erik's half sister Ruth about plans for the service so that she could attend. Ruth then telephoned her sister, Ellen, in Haifa and reported that Erik would be buried in the graveyard of a Protestant church in a town that probably had no Jews. Ellen did not attend, though Ruth did. Quite old and in very frail health, Erik's oldest living friend, Peter Blos, could not attend the service. Blos wanted to, for his rapport with Erik had improved considerably after a long interval when they had rarely conversed.[38]

The day before the memorial service, Jon unburdened himself to an out-of-town guest. He talked intensely and cogently about his relationship with his parents, the problems of living with a celebrity father, the crisis over Neil, his connection with the artist-bohemian aspect of Erik, and the difficulty of being an Erikson. With rich and sensitive detail, Jon also described Erik's personal proclivities—the way he swam, the sweets he loved to eat, his appreciation of innovative photography, and his interest in the piano. As a photographer who had worked hard to capture his father through the lens of his camera, Jon had developed an eye for these qualities. He was proudest of a series of photographs he had taken for the *Harvard Magazine* in 1984 that captured Erik in the process of walking, sitting, and reading outside his Tiburon home. Large colorful pictures, they registered the old man's movements and changing expressions as few photographs have before or since. As the hours passed, Jon acknowledged that he had come to see much of his father in himself. He had cast off earlier resentments toward Erik, feeling that he had to love and embrace his father to accept himself.[39]

Henry James described memorialization after death as a process whereby those who held a person in high regard "compressed and intensified" his image so that it was "simplified and summarized" while the more subtle "shades have ceased to count." John Thornton's opening remarks at the memorial service complied with James's description. Before roughly 130 who attended, Thornton announced that talking with Erikson had made him feel "as if I were in the presence of God." Between exaltation of Erikson's sensitivity and curiosity and brilliance, Thornton underscored several of Erikson's humorous remarks. He concluded with the remark that Erikson drew on the themes of many religions and many personalities. Erikson had reconnected humankind with Luther, Gandhi, and other "spiritual giants" and had shown, in this way, that "he belonged to God."[40]

Next, Kai, Joanna, and Sue spoke. Especially close to Erik in recent years, Kai appeared stiff and distressed as he read a poem by W. H. Auden without much expression. He was coping with a difficult situation in his own way. Joanna, his wife, shared her vivid memories of Erik—joyously holding his first grandchild, mixing cocktails and dancing at family dinners, pretending ignorance at gin rummy games in order to win. Sue described her long struggle to establish a significant personal relationship with her father, often over lunches where both tried to put aside idealized images of what their relationship was supposed to be. As father and daughter acknowledged their vulnerabilities and frailties, Sue realized that Erik's clinical sensitivities were strongest when he connected his own profound confusions and apprehensions with those of his patients.[41]

Music permeated the memorial service. The mourners were invited to sing "Dona Nobis Pacem," and later, "We Will Remember." What drew everyone together most was the song "Music and Love." Joan and Kathy Benforado had worked it out with Maia Aprahamiam, a Marin County composer and friend:

> Music and love make the world go around.
> It never goes up, it never goes down.
> Love makes love and music makes song and
> the world goes around and around and around.[42]

In the year following this memorial, special commemorative services and forums were held, the overwhelming number being in the United States, where Erikson had lived for six decades and where he had his greatest impact. Although the services were often quite touching, only a few speakers, like his Bay Area friend Neil Smelser, had taken the time to reread Erikson's publications and to reflect deeply on his life and thought. This underscored a general failure to appreciate the fact that secondary source descriptions and distant memories were no substitutes for reading Erikson's writings themselves. Even Smelser's good efforts were not the equivalent of David Rapaport's profound reckoning, decades earlier, with Erikson's conceptual contributions. Erikson's prolonged period of decline seemed to leave many thoughtful friends and colleagues stale on matters relating to his intellectual accomplishments. In fact, for some years before his death, they had essentially been mourning. Consequently, salient thoughts identified with his name often went unmentioned.[43]

For instance, there was no discussion concerning Erikson's regard for the playfully reflective life. He valued "extravagant" and free-ranging cross-disciplinary speculation. This inclination was especially important in America, where the culture worshiped efficiency and the "bottom line." Learning and thinking were to be enjoyable and exciting and inspiring, often yielding the unexpected and even the erotic. Learning was not wholly unlike making love, which, he felt, flourished in a relationship freed of power and hierarchies and formulas. For this reason, Erikson abhorred the idea of heading an intellectual or psychoanalytic movement supported by docile, accepting followers. To be sure, he always needed others to acknowledge and affirm his insights and his actions, but through entirely voluntary, thoughtful reflection and caring affection. Related to this was the "everything is our business" aspect of Erikson's mind: his willingness to consider almost any topic or phenomenon, even when it got in the way of his evolving streams of thought and made him appear inconsistent. It was at once great fun and thoroughly exhausting to be contemplating and incorporating and changing thoughts and reflections every moment of one's day. Erikson not only left us with abundant ideas and reflections of his own, but he urged friends, colleagues, and students to continuously generate new thoughts of their own.

Robert Merton has pointed out that ideas often tend to be incorporated into general discourse without acknowledging the person who formulated them. This may happen with Erikson's thoughts unless readers resume the habit of pondering his texts. With or without acknowledgment, Erikson's major formulations will probably be with us for some time. Most importantly, he revived and did much to perpetuate the debate over the place of the individual self in society. Erikson rejected out of hand the notion of free, unfettered individuality that has been especially popular in American culture. He found little to admire in the self-made man or the isolated "American Adam." The self could hardly thrive without the Other, and the individual needed rapport with his or her society.

Like other ego psychologists of his generation, Erikson maintained that optimal selfhood required some adjustment to society's customs and expectations. New Left critics of the 1960s and 1970s pounced on this notion, characterizing him as an architect of adjustment whose focus on the individual search for identity obscured basic inequities of social class and imperialist global exploitation. On the other hand, Erikson provided fresh portraits of young Luther, middle-aged Gandhi, Jefferson the president, and Jesus at Galilee, revolutionaries who connected creatively and constructively with the Other in themselves and others in their societies. They all struggled to disrupt encrusted patterns of elite domination and social conformity, to promote radical new opportunities for humankind. As he aged, Erikson became increasingly interested in revolutionary change and less enamored with the benefits of social adjustment. (In this respect, he was not unlike Martin Luther King, Jr., whose later ideological transformations—some fairly revolutionary—have also tended to be slighted in the interests of a more centrist popular image.)

Erikson belonged to a generation of Western public intellectuals conditioned by the tragedies of Nazism, Stalinism, and McCarthyism. He joined the others in his embrace of a universal "Family of Man," a cosmopolitan perspective that might avert similar human tragedies over contrived differences (what he considered the fruits of pseudospeciation) among people. But in his insistence that people learn to recognize the Other in themselves through a multicultural perspective that embraced Native Americans, Germans, Russians, South Africans, and Indians, Erikson seemed to diverge from the cosmopolitan generation's broad (and hardly universalistic) Anglo-

American foreign policy perspective. To a modest degree, at least, he anticipated a younger generation of intellectuals, many from Africa, India, and
the Middle East, whom we have come to identify as postcolonial critics.

Erikson also endorsed a view of gender that is well worth remembering.
To be sure, it rested far too heavily on the assumption that women were captivated by their "inner space" and performed less comfortably in "outer
space" than men did. Yet it also promoted the idea that when we discover
the constantly altering feminine as well as the fluid masculine qualities in
ourselves and in our changing cultures, as Gandhi did at Ahmadabad, we
find a remarkably vibrant capacity for human connectedness and the ability
to mend dangerous breaches in the global family.

Whereas Freud provided Erikson with his first systematic set of ideas and
his profession, Erikson just might have preserved some of Freud's intellectual legacy. Almost all of Freud's assumptions—from the place of early
trauma in human memory to the role of drives and the organization of
intrapsychic life—have come under relentless attack in recent decades. No
letup appears in sight. Of course, in some sense, Erikson was also critical of
Freud, wanting his psychoanalytic colleagues to excavate less within the
inner self along the physicalistic lines that Freud had assumed. Through a
more decidedly hermeneutic framework, he urged them to map, as broadly
as possible (sometimes by drawing upon the patient's personal stories), how
the self connected to social circumstances. If concern with the mysteries of
human interiority is to survive the Freud bashers, it may be through Erikson's more open-ended interpretive perspective. Indeed, one detects a certain resonance with Erikson in efforts by psychoanalytic thinkers of the next
generation like Roy Schafer and Donald Spence to determine what makes a
personal narrative "feel true" and convey meaning.[44]

Erikson's thoughts on clinical endeavor derived, according to his colleagues, from his extraordinary skill as a practitioner. Most of his patients
improved. Erikson's capacity to understand the sense of crisis and confusion
of those he treated was remarkable. From his clinical encounters, he realized
that the therapist had to be attentive not only to patients' pathologies and deficiencies, but to ways to build upon the patients' strengths. As well, the clinician needed to take into account the patient's current social and emotional
world; that was as important as exploring the psychological origins of the
patient's malady. Indeed, Erikson characterized the premise that an early life
experience invariably determined subsequent psychological development as
the "originology" fallacy. Most important, he felt that the clinician must always
remember that the therapist-patient connection was essentially a relationship
through which both parties gained by giving. Successful therapy was largely
the practice of the Golden Rule—possibly no more and certainly no less.

As a social critic, Erikson was no friend of technology. Despite his Western, rather elitist education and training, he warned against the dangers of a specialized, efficiency-oriented technological society. Its values had undermined the serviceable folkways of the Sioux, the Yurok, and other traditional cultures. A corporate America that pursued technological efficiency had produced a generation of specialists trapped in circumscribed jobs and shortsighted ideologies who were insulated from life's rough edges and erratic turns. Erikson worried that these specialists were the parents of too many of his disturbed young patients at the Austen Riggs Center.

In the alternative, Erikson spoke to the possibilities of border crossing—the excitement and freedom of shifting ideas, moods, vocations, religious proclivities, geographic settings, and more. Indeed, he thrived, personally and conceptually, on border crossing. He never lived in one place for very long, and he constantly navigated the Jewish-Gentile divide. He was a Freudian in one paragraph, a cultural anthropologist in another, and an existentialist in still another. He was an artist, a clinician, a professor, and a public intellectual. Rarely was anything fixed or staid. Indeed, Erikson's life and his shifting identity, both reflected profoundly in his work, may have anticipated current discussions of the decentered sense of being that we have come to equate with postmodernism. Writing in the 1990s, his friend Robert Lifton has described the phenomenon optimistically as proteanism—a fluid and many-sided buoyancy responsive to the restless flux of the late twentieth century. Less positively, psychologist Kenneth Gergen has referred to "the vertigo of unlimited multiplicity" while psychologist Philip Cushman has characterized an unbounded and undifferentiated emotional hunger. However the postmodern condition is assessed, Erikson's life and writings would seem to present material for an instructive prologue.[45]

Erikson never elaborated fully how what he described as the sense of "I" was connected with his own border-crossing inclinations. The connection came at what he called the "invariable core" within the self. At seventy-nine, he jotted down a list of qualities that co-existed with the sense of "I." Essentially, he was delineating the benefits of perpetual border crossing—for himself and for humankind. One was "active" and "aware" and "continuous" and "luminous" as one crossed and recrossed borders and experienced the "I" of one's "existential identity." This deeply alive state of being engendered a sense of being "whole" and "chosen" and "indivisible" and "safely bounded." In the end, this elderly man was summarizing the lifelong excitement, tension, stimulation, and confusion of becoming Erik Erikson, identity's architect— a continuous process that seemed to end only with his death.

Postscript

Joan Erikson compiled a scrapbook concerning the events and ceremonies that followed Erik's death. She included letters of condolence from friends and admirers, among them one from President Clinton. The *New York Times* ran a front-page photograph of Erik, which she inserted in her scrapbook, along with a long, unsigned obituary essay reporting the familiar details of his life. More abbreviated newspaper stories about Erik and his death were included from the *Los Angeles Times,* the *Chicago Tribune,* the *Washington Post,* the *Boston Globe,* and other American newspapers. The foreign press was included, too, with stories from *Le Monde,* the *Guardian,* the *Jerusalem Post,* the *Times of India, Die Welt,* the *Independent* (London), *Weekendavisen* (Copenhagen), and other publications. Joan also inserted short essays from *Newsweek, Time,* and *Der Spiegel.* After more than six decades of marriage, she wanted to remain connected to her husband's name and reputation even as she had to find her way without him. Strong, assertive, and extraordinarily talented, Joan was also a woman of her generation. She found life awkward and difficult without Erik.

In addition to the scrapbook, Joan worked on a new edition of *The Life Cycle Completed.* Assisted by W. W. Norton, she republished the original edition and added material of her own. In the clear, concrete, and vigorous but sometimes less than felicitous style that distinguished her writing from Erik's, she discussed essential community support services for the elderly. She also wrote about the potential for peace of mind in old age through a rather cosmic and spiritual communion with the universe ("gerotranscendence"). But Joan was most preoccupied with the essentials of a ninth stage of the life cycle based upon her final years with Erik. She attempted to explain how he and many very old people felt as they declined and died. Whereas the eighth stage involved looking back on one's life with feelings of integrity and despair, the ninth brought up different issues. Retrospection was a luxury in very old age as mind and body disintegrated, and concerns about daily functioning became paramount. Success consisted of getting through the day intact with some measure of dignity.

Although Joan was more robust in her last years than Erik had been, she was also describing something of her own ninth stage. She remained an active citizen of Harwich, singing in the Congregational Church choir, and enjoying a steady stream of young visitors from the Boston area. Periodically, she visited friends in Cambridge and usually stayed overnight with her old friend Inge Hoffman. Nevertheless, age was taking its toll.

By the fall of 1995, Joan began to decline rapidly. One of her hips gave out and hospitalization was required. She had several major falls after that and was not successful at rebuilding the muscles around her injured hip. Walking even small distances became difficult. I visited in early July of 1996 and drove Joan the two blocks to the Stewed Tomato, her favorite local restaurant. When I visited again in October, her decline was more apparent. She occasionally felt dizzy, continued to have falling episodes, and required a night attendant in her home. Still, we spent hours together discussing her life with Erik. By December, Joan had moved into a nursing home in nearby Brewster. Periodically, and for very short periods, she appeared extremely ill, only to recover.

In late June of 1997, some friends and family traveled to Brewster to celebrate Joan's ninety-fourth birthday. She rose to the occasion. Although it was less than clear that Joan recognized her guests, she appeared to be her usual joyous self, laughing, joking, and smiling. But a short time later, she fell ill, with several comalike episodes. Jon flew in from Port Angeles and Sue came up from New York City. Kai, in nearby Cotuit, was very attentive. When Joan saw her three children together, she felt deeply content.

Joan Erikson died on August 3, 1997. She was cremated and buried next to Erik. A memorial service coordinated by Kai, Joanna, and Sue at Harwich's First Congregational Church was set for early September. At the service, Kai's son Christopher and Sue's son, Per, gave short but moving guitar performances. Kai described an old Native American perspective on death that Joan would have appreciated—that a loved one was not gone if he or she could still be heard and seen. Sue acknowledged difficulties in her relationship with Joan, but described appreciatively how Joan had elevated her spirits when she was a youngster by buying her a horse. Her European intellectual father had looked at the animal in wonderment. Other mourners remembered Joan's love for life and her playfulness. They noted her many talents: a skillful crafter of necklaces, rings, and shawls; a student of dance; a researcher; a poet; and an innovative activities therapist.

As I left the memorial service and walked through Harwich, I reflected on Joan and Erik's remarkable marriage. I wondered whether she had given

Erik more than he had given her, but was unsure. I also reflected on the invaluable contribution Joan had made to this book. When I began it in 1990, Erik was already in steady decline, and she became my most important source for information and insight. Without Joan, this would have been a very different biography. As I passed the Stewed Tomato, I wanted to ask her to join me there for a repast so that we could "talk Erik."

A Bibliographical Note

This study derived from a substantial and varied array of sources gathered from Copenhagen, Karlsruhe, Vienna, London, Washington, D.C., New York City, Berkeley, Akron, Chicago, and other locations. Endnotes provide running commentaries on specific primary and secondary sources. The voluminous Erikson Papers at Harvard's Houghton Library represent the single most important source for this volume. Without this collection, no scholarly biography would have been possible. To enhance the research benefits of the Houghton collection, I have donated important materials that I discovered elsewhere.

Several books, articles, and dissertations on Erik Erikson have been prepared over the years. Four especially influenced my reflections. Robert Coles's *Erik H. Erikson: The Growth of His Work* (1970) inspired me with its sensitive reading of Erikson's publications and its contagious enthusiasm for the man. Paul Roazen's hard-nosed and often deeply critical *Erik H. Erikson: The Power and Limits of a Vision* (1976) prompted me to be cautious about Erikson's assertions and of his use of evidence. These two volumes seemed to balance each other as I began this biography. David Andersen's important dissertation, "Erik H. Erikson's Challenge to Modernity" (Bowling Green State University, 1993), cautioned against quick reductionist summaries of Erikson's work. Quite persuasively, Andersen called for charting Erikson's thought along more flexible and layered trajectories of continuity and change. Hetty Zock's *A Psychology of Ultimate Concern: Erik H. Erikson's Contribution to the Psychology of Religion* (1990) characterized one of those trajectories quite skillfully—the interplay between Erikson's existentialism and his spirituality.

It was not easy to investigate Erikson's earliest years. Esther Ramon's *The Homburger Family from Karlsruhe: A Family Study, 1674–1990* (1992) afforded much helpful detail. A number of specific items in the Karlsruhe General Archive were invaluable. In Copenhagen, family historian Finn Abrahamsen provided me with abundant data extending over centuries on Karla Abrahamsen and her Danish family. The single most useful source on Erik as a young man, his mind and mood, was his 1923–24 journal, "Manuscript von Erik." In the possession of the Erikson family while I researched this volume, it needs to be translated professionally into English, to be annotated, and to be published. John Neubauer's *The Fin-de-Siècle Culture of Adolescence* (1992) helped to put the journal in context.

Thanks to important research and writing by Peter Heller, we have good data on the specific Vienna setting of Erikson's life between 1927 and 1933. *A Child Analysis with Anna Freud* (1990) detailed Heller's own life as a Hietzing School student who studied with Erikson. Heller's edited volume, *Anna Freud's Letters to Eva Rosenfeld* (1992), presented a crucial correspondence, some of which pertained to Erikson in important ways. Helpful, too, were Sheldon Gardner and Gwendolyn Stevens's *Red Vienna and the Golden Age of Psychology, 1918–1938* (1992) and Helmut Gruber's *Red Vienna: Experiment in Working-Class Culture, 1919–1934* (1991). The Anna Freud Papers in the Library of Congress were crucial to an understanding of the Erikson–Anna Freud relationship. I am also indebted to two Anna Freud biographers: Elizabeth Young-Bruehl (1988) and Robert Coles (1992). Unfortunately, the Library of Congress agreed to keep Peter Blos's account of the Hietzing School and other pertinent Blos documents for the period closed until well into the twenty-first century. Minutes after Thomas Aichhorn handed me the 1933 correspondence between August Aichhorn and Erikson (copies of which now exist in the archives of the Sigmund Freud House, Vienna), I realized that it revealed a substantial amount about Erikson's early life. Esther Menaker's *Appointment in Vienna* (1989) offered significant perspectives on the Vienna psychoanalytic community when Erikson lived there. Much useful data on the uprooting of Vienna intellectuals, artists, and professionals owing to the rise of Fascism came from *The Cultural Exodus from Austria* (1995), edited by Friedrich Stadler and Peter Weibel.

The Henry A. Murray Papers within the Harvard Archives, the Yale Institute of Human Relations Records, the Alan Gregg Diary in the Rockefeller Archive Center, and the Lawrence Frank Papers in the National Library of Medicine were important sources on Erikson's first decade in America. Forrest Robinson's *Love's Story Told: A Life of Henry A. Murray* (1992) and Steven Weiland's "Psychoanalysis without Words: Erik H. Erikson's American Apprenticeship," *Michigan Quarterly Review* (Winter 1992): 1–17, also afforded useful context. The Arnold Gesell Papers and the Margaret Mead Papers at the Library of Congress plus the Edward Boring Papers at the Harvard Archives contained several key documents for the period. Nathan Hale, Jr.'s *The Rise and Crisis of Psychoanalysis in the United States: Freud and the Americans, 1917–1985* (1995) provided a richly textured narrative of the psychoanalytic immigration to America and the U.S. institutional context for psychoanalysis within which Erikson worked.

Erikson's activities during the 1940s were covered in the Jean Walker Macfarlane Documents (Archives for the History of American Psychology, University of Akron) and the Margaret Mead Papers. The important anthropological context for his work was cogently discussed by Waud Kracke in "A Psychoanalyst in the Field: Erikson's Contributions to Anthropology," published in Peter Homans, ed., *Childhood and Selfhood: Essays on Tradition, Religion, and Morality in the Psychology of Erik H. Erikson* (1978). Portions of the Clyde Kluckhohn Papers, Harvard Archives, were also informative on Erikson's connections with anthropologists. The wartime context for Erikson's diverse policy-linked assignments was sketched out well in Carlton Mabee's "Margaret Mead and Behavioral Scientists in World War II: Problems in Responsibility, Truth, and Effectiveness," *Journal of the History of the Behavioral Sciences* 33 (January 1987): 3–13. The W. W. Norton Papers at Columbia University contained a preliminary and exceedingly important 1948 outline of *Childhood and Society* as well as correspondence on the production and publication of the book. Excellent general context for Erikson's work on *Childhood and Society* was provided in Ellen Herman's *The Romance of American Psychology: Political Culture in the Age of Experts* (1995); Steven Weiland's "Erik Erikson in America: *Childhood and Society* and National Identity," *American Studies* 23 (Fall 1982): 5–23; and William Graebner's "The Unstable World of Benjamin Spock: Social Engineering in a Democratic Culture, 1917–1950," *Journal of American History* 67 (December 1980): 612–29. I was much better able to place Erikson within a generation of liberal and cosmopolitan intellectuals through the works of David Hollinger and Wilfred McClay. Two Hollinger essays were especially helpful: "How Wide the Circle of the 'We'? American Intellectuals and the Problem of the Ethnos since World War II," *American Historical Review* 98 (April 1993): 317–37; and the fourth chapter of *Postethnic America: Beyond Multiculturalism* (1995). Chapters six through eight of McClay's *The Masterless: Self and Society in Modern America* (1994) were broad, rich, and insightful. Helpful, too, was Robert Fowler's *Believing Skeptics: American Political Intellectuals, 1945–1964* (1978).

Erikson's activities during the University of California loyalty oath crisis emerged from close scrutiny of his personnel file and diverse other documents within the archives of the Bancroft Library at UC Berkeley, the collections at the Institute for Personality Assessment and Research (UCB), and correspondence involving Donald MacKinnon and Alan Gregg deposited within the Rockefeller Archive Center. Some sense of Erikson's life at the Austen Riggs Center during the 1950s emerged from letters in the David Riesman Papers (Harvard

Archives), plus invaluable patient case files and other materials that Riggs allowed me to review. The way Erikson went about completing *Young Man Luther* emerged from letters within the W. W. Norton Papers and through a revised typescript of the manuscript at the Erikson Institute in Chicago. Finally, W. T. Lhamon, Jr.'s *Deliberate Speed: The Origins of a Cultural Style in the American 1950s* (1990) provided a very suggestive overview of the period.

Correspondence and other materials in the Erikson Papers at the Houghton Library proliferated greatly for the decade of the 1960s and especially for the 1970s. These were augmented by rich general studies of the period, especially Peter Clecak's *America's Quest for the Ideal Self: Dissent and Fulfillment in the 60s and 70s* (1983) and Theodor Roszak's classic *The Making of a Counter Culture* (1968). Abundant data that Pamela Daniels provided me for Erikson's Harvard undergraduate course during the 1960s combined well with Paul Roazen's suggestive essay "Erik Erikson as Teacher," *Michigan Quarterly Review* (Winter 1992): 19–33. Helpful context for some of the feminist perspectives on Erikson's "inner space" concept during this period is provided by Alice Echols's *Daring to Be Bad: Radical Feminism in America, 1967–1975* (1989) and Karen Offen's brilliant "Defining Feminism: A Comparative Historical Approach," *Signs* 14 (Autumn 1988): 119–57. Erikson's faculty personnel file at Harvard and syllabi for Erikson's 1960s courses (Harvard Archives) were quite informative. So was his correspondence with Robert Lifton (Lifton Papers, New York Public Library). It was exceedingly important to read and reread Erikson's "Autobiographic Notes on the Identity Crisis" essay as it appeared in *Daedalus* 99 (Fall 1970): 730–59, but was revised in *Twentieth-Century Sciences* (1975), edited by Gerald Holton, and revised again in Erikson's *Life History and the Historical Moment* (1975). These versions revealed much about the process of old-age reflections and reinterpretations of a life course. With coverage of Erikson's work during the early 1980s, Steven Weiland's "Aged Erikson: The Completion of the Life Cycle," *Journal of Aging Studies* 3, no. 2 (1989): 253–62, was also helpful.

Finally, let me emphasize how Stephen Schlein made a fundamental contribution to Erikson research with *A Way of Looking at Things: Selected Papers from 1930–1980. Erik H. Erikson* (1987). Schlein gathered together forty-seven unpublished and obscurely published Erikson writings, and accompanied them with excellent annotations. Short of the Erikson collection at the Houghton Library, students in a seminar on the Eriksonian legacy who are intent on discovering Erikson's unique voice should begin with this collection. In 1996, the journal *Psychoanalysis & Contemporary Thought* ran a special issue (vol. 19, no. 2) consisting of reflective review essays initially presented at an Erikson memorial conference in San Francisco. By the mid-1990s, *Contemporary Psychology* had also begun to publish thoughtful essays concerning Erikson's publications, particularly Irving Alexander's "Erikson's Gandhi and Erikson—Revisited" (41, no. 4 [1996]: 311–15) and Dan McAdams's "Three Voices of Erik Erikson (42, no. 7 [1997]: 575–78).

Notes

Collections

AP-SFH	Aichhorn Papers, Sigmund Freud House, Vienna
AHAP-Akron	Archives of the History of American Psychology, University of Akron
DRP	David Riesman Papers, Harvard College Archive
E-H	Erik H. & Joan Erikson Papers, Houghton Library
KAM	Karl A. Menninger Papers, Menninger Foundation Archives
LC	Library of Congress (Manuscript Division)
NLM	National Library of Medicine
RJL-NYPL	Robert J. Lifton Papers, New York Public Library
YIHR	Yale Institute for Human Relations

Interviews

PI	Personal interview
TI	Telephone interview
TRI	Tape-recorded interview

Abbreviated Names

EHE	Erik H. Erikson
JE	Joan Erikson
LJF	Lawrence J. Friedman

CHAPTER 1
TOWARD A NEW BEGINNING: INFANCY, CHILDHOOD, YOUTH

1 Robert Abzug, PI by LJF, Nashville, July 19, 1996.
2 *Boston Globe*, November 6, 1980, on "loving deceit." Betty J. Lifton, *Journey of the Adopted Self: A Quest for Wholeness* (New York, 1994), 66, quoting Blos. EHE, "Autobiographic Notes on the Identity Crisis," *Daedalus* 99 (Fall 1970): 744; EHE, "Erik Homburger Erikson," February 2, 1976 (revised June 22, 1977), E-H, "different background," "as a fact," "the pervasive love."
3 Finn and Martha Abrahamsen of Copenhagen, two extraordinary family historians, supplied a detailed family tree and much valuable information over the years. A visit with them in Copenhagen (May 8–9, 1993) plus much subsequent correspondence was crucial. See also Ruth Hirsch and Ellen Katz, TRI by LJF, NYC, August 16, 1991.
4 Finn and Martha Abrahamsen, TRI by LJF, Copenhagen, May 8, 1993; Ruth Hirsch, TRI by LJF, NYC, November 12, 1992; *Kracks Bla Bog* (Copenhagen, 1931), 30.

5 Finn and Martha Abrahamsen, TRI, May 8, 1993; letter from F. Abrahamsen to LJF, March 4, 1993; Ruth Hirsch, TRI by LJF, NYC, June 28, 1993.

6 Joseph Fischer, *Slaegten Salomonsen (Nyborg)* (Copenhagen, 1927), 63–64, on Salomonsen family history. EHE, "Notes on My Parentage," (n.d. [1978]), E-H; Finn and Martha Abrahamsen, TRI, May 8, 1993; Hirsch, TRI, June 28, 1993; Agnete Kalckar, PI by LJF, Cambridge, June 13, 1993; JE, TRI by LJF, Cambridge, June 12, 1993. Erik's birth certificate from the Frankfurt Standesamt is number 3235 and is dated June 21, 1902.

7 Letter from Ellen Katz to LJF, July 5, 1993; Hirsch, June 28 and TRI by LJF, NYC, November 8, 1993; Finn and Martha Abrahamsen, TRI, May 8, 1993; JE, TRI by LJF, Harwich, January 14 and October 20, 1994.

8 Letter from EHE to Robert J. Lifton, June 1976, RJL-NYPL, on Karla who "held all the confusing details." Hirsch, TRI, November 8, 1993, on Karla's friend at the Jewish hospital. Helene Abrahamsen, TRI by Martha Abrahamsen, Copenhagen (n.d. [1982 or 1983]), on Karla alone with her son and training as a nurse. EHE, "Autobiographic Notes," *Daedalus,* 742–43, on his "first male imprinting." JE, TRI, January 14, 1994, on people in Buehl noticing how Karla looked different from Erik.

9 Letter from Erik Homburger to August Aichhorn, September 7, 1993, AP-SFH, on "My earliest remembrance." EHE, *Life History and the Historical Moment* (New York, 1975), 31, on Karla as "pervasively sad" with "her ambitions for me." EHE, TRI by Robert Stewart, Cambridge, January 11, 1968, on how identity begins with the mother's smile. EHE, "Autobiographic Notes," *Daedalus,* 745, on Karla "deeply involved in reading." Letter from EHE to William Gibson (n.d. [June 27, 1963?]), E-H, on speaking Danish. See also Betty J. Lifton, *Journey,* 102, 206, and Erikson's remarks in a December 15, 1969, lecture on living with his mother, Janice Abarbanel lecture notes, Social Sciences 133, 1969–70, E-H.

10 EHE, "Autobiographic Notes," *Daedalus,* 742–43, "that intruder." Hirsch, TRI, November 12, 1992, and November 8, 1993; Helene Abrahamsen, TRI by Martha Abrahamsen (n.d. [1982 or 1983]). Finn and Martha Abrahamsen, TRI, May 8, 1993; JE, TRI, January 14, 1994; letter from Fred R. Homburger to editor, *New York Times Book Review,* May 7, 1975 (unpublished), Marshall Berman private papers. Donald Capps, *Men, Religion, and Melancholia: James, Otto, Jung, and Erikson* (New Haven, 1997), especially 186, 202–204, emphasizes Erikson's resentment with Karla over Theodor's "intrusion."

11 JE, TRI, June 12, 1993, and January 14, 1994; Abarbanel Notes, December 15, 1969, lecture, E-H; Betty J. Lifton, *Journey,* 205; Robert J. Lifton, "Talks (Dinner & Breakfast) with Erik Erikson on May 4–5–6, 1980, in Tiburon," RJL-NYPL.

12 Esther Ramon, *The Homburger Family from Karlsruhe: A Family Study, 1674–1990* (Jerusalem, 1992), especially 9, 18–20, 54–55, 75, 149. This is the best source on family history, including a chapter on Theodor and Karla written by their daughter Ellen Katz. See also Bernhard Schmitt, "Between Assimilation, Anti-Semitism, and Zionism, 1890–1918," in *Juden in Karlsruhe,* edited by Heinz Schmitt (Karlsruhe, 1988), 121–54; Joseph Werner, *Swastika and Yellow Star: The Fate of Karlsruhe Jews in the Third Reich* (Karlsruhe, 1988), 15, 28; Hirsch and Katz, TRI, August 16, 1991; Hirsch, TRI, November 8, 1993; Theodor Homburger, *Die Natürlich Beleuchtung in den Schulen* (Karlsruhe, 1895).

13 Ramon, *Homburger Family,* 75, plus the lengthy Abrahamsen family tree and data file in the possession of Finn Abrahamsen.

14 EHE, "Further Autobiographic Remarks: For Friends and Relations Only" (August 1977), 4, E-H, "promise to annul the past." EHE in *Boston Globe Magazine,* March 22, 1987, 34, "loving deceit." EHE, "Notes for Christian Gauss Seminar at Princeton," 1969, 8, E-H; EHE in Harvard Senior Seminar, "Perspectives on the Life Cycle," October 23, 1985, Harriet Harvey videotape, "felt all along." EHE, autobiographic remarks, June 22, 1977, E-H, "I was quietly convinced" and "cues." JE, TRI, October 20, 1994, on Erik reporting to her of often overhearing whispers.

15 Betty J. Lifton, *Journey,* 205, quotes Erik on his adopted father. JE, TRI, October 20, 1994, on Theodor being apprehensive of the real father.

16 The marriage certificate (*Heiratsurkunde*) of June 1905 for Karla and Theodor is found in the Standesamt of Karlsruhe. The July 1909 document of naturalization (Naturalizations-No. 4836) was sent to me by Ellen Katz. The 1902 birth certificate with the 1911 notation is in the Standesamt of Frankfurt. The Registry Books of the Karlsruhe District Court (*Abteilung* III, No. 3922, 1909; *Abteilung* V, No. 17351, 1911) are in the Karlsruhe General Archive. Erik notes 1908 as the date he assumed the name of Homburger in "Curriculum Vitae, Erik Homburger Erikson" (n.d. [1959]), Erikson Faculty Personnel File, Harvard University Archives.

17 *Begl. Abschrift. Übersetzung aus dem Hebraischen Testaments—Urkunde* (Haifa, 1942), in the Karlsruhe General Archive.

18 EHE, "Themes from Kierkegaard's Early Life" (n.d. [1977]), E-H, "I made many visits there." Finn and Martha Abrahamsen, TRI, May 8, 1993, on Erik staying with Axel Abrahamsen and being regarded as a Jew. Betty J. Lifton, TI by LJF, March 30, 1994, reports Erik describing the Danish king incident to her. Letter from Finn Abrahamsen to LJF, Copenhagen, February 24, 1994, describing the Roselund summer home. EHE, "Reflections on Dr. Borg's Life Cycle," *Daedalus* (Spring 1976), 4, recalling the Øresund and his "sunniest summers." Letter from EHE to Leunart Joelberg, March 29, 1979, E-H, on how he "looked across the Sund." JE, TRI, June 12, 1993, on Erik traveling to Copenhagen more often than his half sisters.

19 JE, TRI, June 12, 1993, on the close bonds between Abrahamsens and Homburgers, especially during World War I when Germans needed food. Letters from Ellen R. Katz to LJF, July 5 and August 12, 1993, elaborate the point. A copy of Erik's 1914 sketch for Henrietta was given to me by Finn Abrahamsen. Betty J. Lifton, TI by LJF, NYC, January 24, 1993, on how Blos, the previous day, had told her what Erik had said to him. Harvey videotape, with Erik remarking "Like I can imagine."

20 EHE, *Life History,* 27.

21 Ramon, *Homburger Family,* 75, on Elna. Theodor's ties to his daughters are discussed in a letter from Katz to LJF, August 12, 1993; Hirsch and Katz, TRI, August 16, 1991; Hirsch, TRI, November 12, 1992, and November 8, 1993. EHE, "Notes on My Parentage" (n.d. [1978]), E-H, on Karla encouraging his independence. Finn Abrahamsen of Copenhagen shared a few of Erik's early sketches with me.

22 Letter from Ellen Katz to LJF, August 12, 1993; Hirsch, TRI, November 12, 1992, and November 8, 1993; Ruth Hirsch, TI by LJF, September 4, 1994; Theodor Homburger, "Die Schulkinder während des Kriegsernährung, 1916–17," *Der Schularzt* 15, no. 8–9 (1917): 441–84.

23 Letter from Ellen Katz to LJF, July 5, 1993; Hirsch and Katz, TRI, August 16, 1991; Hirsch, TRI, November 12, 1992, and November 8, 1993; Ruth Hirsch, TI by LJF, NYC, June 9, 1991. Ramon, *Homburger Family,* 76; letter from EHE to William Gibson (n.d. [June 27, 1963?]), E-H, "forgot" Danish for "step-German."

24 Ramon, *Homburger Family,* 38, 75; Werner, *Swastika and Star,* 82, 98–99; Hirsch, TRI, June 28, 1993; JE, TRI, June 12, 1993; letter from Fred R. Homburger to editor, *New York Times Book Review,* May 7, 1975 (unpublished); letter from Hugo M. Schiff to Marshall Berman, March 30, 1974, Berman private papers.

25 EHE, "Autobiographic Notes," *Daedalus,* 743, on being the "goy" in the temple. For the sense of his real father as a non-Jew, see EHE in Harvey videotape. EHE, *Life History,* 27, on Theodor pressing Erik "to become a doctor" and on Theodor's "intensely Jewish small-town bourgeoisie family." EHE, "Gauss Seminar," 8, E-H, "intensely alienated". EHE, "Further Autobiographical Remarks: For Friends and Relations Only," 5, E-H, "my stepfather the pediatrician provided." See also Uwe Henrik Peters, *Anna Freud: A Life Dedicated to Children* (New York, 1985), 86; letter from EHE to Hirsch, December 20, 1975, and February 20, 1981, E-H.

26 Letter from Hugo B. Schiff to Marshall Berman, March 30, 1974, "he was aloof." EHE, *Life History,* 27–28, "*set out* to be different" and "our house." EHE, "Autobiographic Statement to Freshman Seminar" (n.d. [early 1960s]), E-H.

27 The likelihood that if Karla knew the identity of the missing father, it did not go beyond her generation is indicated in Finn and Martha Abrahamsen, TRI, May 8, 1993; Hirsch, TRI, November 8, 1993, and TI, June 28, 1993.

28 EHE, "Autobiographic Statement to Freshman Seminar," E-H, "MOTHER DECEIVED." Letter from EHE to Kurt von Fritz, December 20, 1976, E-H, "discordant signals."

29 Beulah Parker, TRI by LJF, Point Richmond, Calif., October 18, 1994, on Erik recalling to her what he had heard under the table. Betty J. Lifton, *Journey,* 205, reports Erik telling her in 1981 of the peasant woman incident, his mother's response, and later hearing as an adolescent that his real father was a Danish aristocrat. This is also reported in Betty J. Lifton, PI by LJF, Wellfleet, November 1, 1992. It is confirmed in a letter from Ruth Hirsch to LJF, December 17, 1993. Erik both espoused and suspected the Salomonsen as father story in Abarbanel Notes, December 15, 1969, lecture, E-H, and in J. M. Turner and B. Inhelder, eds., *Discussions in Child Development,* vol. 3 (Geneva, 1955), 16. Letter from EHE to Mrs. George (Hope) Curfman, Jr., December 30, 1976, E-H, "the gradual awareness." EHE, "Notes on My Parentage" (n.d. [1978]), 6, E-H, "They confirmed." See also EHE, "Further Autobiographic Remarks"; and EHE, "Autobiographic Note" (n.d. [c. 1977]), E-H. Betty J. Lifton, *Journey,* 206, quoting Erik on not pursuing his real father.

30 EHE, "Gauss Seminar," 8, E-H.

31 EHE, *Life History,* 27, on references to being Jewish and Gentile. Ilse Feiger, TI by LJF, Berkeley, January 4, 1993, on Erik's infatuation with Elizabeth Goldschmidt. Letter from EHE to Edward Tolman, April, 27, 1939, J. W. Macfarlane Docs., AHAP-Akron, "the scorn of German children" and "I developed my nationalistic German tendencies." Robert Coles, *Erik H. Erikson: The Growth of His Work* (Boston, 1970), 180, "to steal Schleswig-Holstein." EHE, "Autobiographic Statement to Freshman Seminar," E-H, "being a *German.*"

32 Ruth Hirsch, TI by LJF, July 6, 1993, and TRI, November 8, 1993, on the kosher dietary customs and spoken language within the Homburger home. Letter from EHE to Mrs. George (Hope) Curfman, Jr., December 30, 1976, and EHE to . . . (letter fragment) ("Is Erikson a Christian?") (December 1976), E-H, on his distress over synagogue rituals and writing to the rabbi. EHE, "Autobiographic Notes on the Identity Crisis," *The Twentieth-Century Sciences,* edited by Gerald Holton (New York, 1972), 16, on "transparent ceremonialism of a *Bürgertum.*" Letter from Hugo Schiff to Marshall Berman, March 30, 1974, on Erikson's less than complete bar mitzvah. Letter from EHE to Curfman, December 30, 1976, "part of a quiet alienation."

33 EHE, "Autobiographic Notes," *Twentieth-Century Sciences,* 16, "the Christianity of the Gospels." EHE to . . . (letter fragment) ("Is Erikson a Christian?") (December 1976), "I early received from my mother." Letter from EHE to Mrs. George (Hope) Curfman, Jr., December 30, 1976, "the core of values." EHE, TRI by Margaret Brenman-Gibson, Tiburon, April 1, 1983 (transcript), "there is a crucifix." Letter from EHE to Eugene B. Borowitz, April 8, 1976, E-H, "turn toward Christianity." EHE, *Young Man Luther: A Study in Psychoanalysis and History* (New York, 1958), 10, "Never having 'knowingly.' " See Bernhard Schmitt in *Juden in Karlsruhe,* 121–54, on Jewish assimilation to German Lutheranism. Robert J. Lifton, TRI, November 1, 1992, and Robert J. Lifton, "Talks with Erik Erikson on May 4–5–6, 1980, in Tiburon," 7, RJL-NYPL, on the power of Protestantism among German Jews and the meaning of hearing the Lord's Prayer.

34 EHE, "Themes from Kierkegaard's Early Life" (n.d. [1977], E-H, "introduction to Christianity" and "intensively Danish." EHE, "Autobiographic Notes," *Twentieth-Century Sciences,* 16, "that her family." EHE to . . . (letter fragment) (Is Erikson a Christian?")

(December 1976), "reverence for the existential." Coles, *Erikson,* 180, for Karla's account of Abrahamsen relatives.

35 EHE, "Generativity and the Future," Chautauqua [N.Y.] Institution Lecture (August 3, 1978), Chautauqua Library, 7.

36 Gordon A. Craig, *Germany, 1866–1945* (New York, 1978), 186–87, on compulsory primary school attendance and literacy. Hirsch, TI, June 9, 1991, and Coles, *Erikson,* 14, on Erik's *Vorschule* experience.

37 For general discussion of the German gymnasium, see Craig, *Germany,* 190, and Richard F. Sterba, *Reminiscences of a Vienna Psychoanalyst* (Detroit, 1982), 13–18. Peter Conzen, *Erik H. Erikson und die Psychoanalyse: Systematische Gesamtdarstellung seines theoretischen und klinischen Positionen* (Heidelberg, 1990), 16, and Coles, *Erikson,* 14, on Erik's years in the Karlsruhe gymnasium.

38 "Gymnasium Karlsruhe Studien Allgemeines . . . 1914–1927," 1919–20 school year, Karlsruhe General Archives, details Erik Homburger's studies and final examinations and that of his fellow students. See also "Gymnasium Karlsruhe Jahresbericht für das Schuljar 1918–1919" (1919) and "Abiturienten Zeugnis, Erik Homburger" (1920), both also in the Karlsruhe General Archives.

39 Ibid. Erik's dislike of all but Greek translation despite Karla's tutoring is reported by Hirsch, TRI, November 12, 1992, and JE, TRI, January 14, 1994. An "Arbiturfoto 1920" of Erik with his gymnasium class, sent to me by officials at the Erik Homburger Erikson House in Karlsruhe, provides the basis for the description of his appearance.

40 Letter from Peter Blos to LJF, June 13, 1991; JE, TRI, January 14, 1994; EHE, "Peter Blos: Reminiscences (Introducing the First Peter Blos Biennial Lecture)," *Psychosocial Process* 3 (Fall 1974): 5, "a very special." Also quoted in Stephen Schlein, ed., *A Way of Looking at Things: Selected Papers from 1930–1980. Erik H. Erikson* (New York, 1987), 710.

41 EHE, "Introductory Remarks: First Peter Blos Biennial Lecture," NYC, December 7, 1971, 1, E-H, "We both come." Peter Blos, TRI by Robert Stewart, NYC, May 22, 1966; Betty J. Lifton, TI, January 24, 1993 (based on Lifton's recent conversations with Blos).

42 EHE, "Autobiographic Notes," *Daedalus,* 744, "shared his father." Schlein, *Way,* 709–10, quoting Erik on Edwin Blos's beard, interests, *Geistigkeit,* and concern for Goethe and German "spirit." EHE, *Life History,* 9, and "Lecture by Erik Erikson," Santa Barbara, January 19, 1972, 3, E-H, on Gandhi. Letter from Peter Blos to EHE, January 5, 1978, E-H, on Edwin Blos and Erik *"über die Polarität."* Other data on the Erik–Edwin Blos relationship is noted in a letter from Peter Blos to LJF, September 18, 1992; Peter Blos, TI by LJF, NYC, May 8, 1991; letter from Victor Ross to LJF, August 25, 1992; JE, TRI, January 14, 1994; letter from Ellen Katz to LJF, July 5, 1993.

43 Betty Stonorov, TI by LJF, Phoenixville, Pa., December 12, 1992; Hirsch, TI, June 9, 1991; Hirsch and Katz, TRI, August 16, 1991 (noting Stonorov conveying to Erik an interest in piano).

44 JE, TRI, June 12, 1993, and January 14, 1994; Hirsch and Katz, TRI, August 16, 1991; Hirsch, TI, June 28, 1993.

45 Gustav Wolf, *Das Zeichen-Büchlein* (Karlsruhe, 1921), 8.

46 Ibid., 11–13.

47 Ibid., 15, 19, 22, 23.

48 Skeletal coverage of Erik in Munich is provided in Coles, *Erikson,* 15, and Conzen, *Erikson,* 17. EHE, "Autobiographic Notes," *Daedalus,* 743, on how sketching "can be a good exercise" and "enjoyed making very large woodprints." Erikson discussion with Mark Gerzon and Michael Lerner, TRI, Stockbridge, May 22, 1971, Reel 1, Tape B, Side B, E-H, "impressionistic," "alone w[ith] nature," "never learned to paint," "was where the inhibition was." Letter from EHE to Guillermo Delahanty, January 26, 1981, E-H, "black and white drawings."

49 EHE, *Life History,* 28, "always again." EHE, *Childhood and Society* (New York, 1985 edition), 8, "a German cultural ritualization" and "a more or less artistic." The German

Wanderschaft or wanderlust of the period is discussed intelligently in John Gillis, *Youth and History: Tradition and Change in European Age Relations, 1770-Present* (New York, 1974), 150–51; John Neubauer, *The* Fin-de-Siècle *Culture of Adolescence* (New Haven, 1992), 175, 193; Sterling Fishman, "Suicide, Sex, and the Discovery of the German Adolescent," *History of Education Quarterly* 10 (1970): 186.

50 Letter from Peter Blos to LJF (n.d. [June 13, 1991]), on the details of Erik's *Wanderschaft*. EHE to Kenneth Keniston, April, 24, 1961, E-H, "sat on the mountaintops." Conzen, *Erikson*, 17, on the route of the *Wanderschaft*. Erik's stay in Florence is discussed in Jon Erikson, PI by LJF, Harwich, June 14, 1994, and Stonorov, December 12, 1992. EHE, "Reminiscences," *Psychosocial Process* 3 (Fall 1974): 5, "we were waiting," "principles of artistic form," and "Fascism we took."

51 EHE, "Autobiographic Notes," *Daedalus*, 745, "the fortitude to." Letter from EHE to H. H. Thomas, October 28, 1977, E-H, "the strange boy." Karla's secret financial and other support for Erik in the face of Theodor's opposition is discussed in Hirsch, TRI, November 8, 1993, and TI, June 9, 1991; Hirsch and Katz, TRI, August 16, 1991. EHE, "Hitler's Imagery and German Youth," *Psychiatry* 5 (November 1942): 479, "the mother openly . . . the father was considered."

52 EHE, "Autobiographic Statement to Freshman Seminar," E-H, "almost Failure" and "mother believed." "Conversations with Erik H. Erikson and Huey P. Newton" in *In Search of Common Ground*, edited by Kai T. Erikson (New York, 1971), 98, "drop out." EHE, "Autobiographic Notes," *Twentieth-Century Sciences* (1975), 16, "*bürgerlich* confines." Coles, *Erikson*, 180, "This made me sturdy." Gerzon and Lerner, TRI, May 22, 1971, Reel 2, Tape A, Side A, "did not want to be" and "I had no image." For Erikson's diagnosis of his borderline psychotic condition, see EHE, "Autobiographic Notes," *Daedalus*, 742; EHE, *Life History* (1975), 26; Margaret Brenman-Gibson, "Erik Erikson and the 'Ethics of Survival,' " *Harvard Magazine* 87 (1984): 61; Gerzon and Lerner, TRI, May 22, 1971, Reel 2, Tape A, Side A. He provided more graphic lay terms in a December 15, 1969, lecture to his Harvard undergraduate class, Abarbanel Notes, E-H.

53 EHE, "Gregory Kepes" (n.d. [1970]), E-H, commenting on Courbet's painting and what it meant to him in his youth. EHE, *Insight and Responsibility: Lectures on the Ethical Foundation of Psychoanalytic Insight* (New York, 1964), 20, "nowhere to go."

54 When I conducted my research, Erik Homburger's 1923–24 journal was in the possession of his wife, Joan Erikson, and she did not permit photoduplication. Although the original manuscript was unpaginated, some pages were numbered and renumbered by people assisting her in preparing the journal for possible publication. There is no point in citing this random and temporary pagination. Consequently, meaningful endnote references to specific pages are not possible.

55 EHE, TRI, January 11, 1968, on how, as a youth, he found Freud absurd. For an excellent analysis of the conceptual similarities between Nietzsche and Freud, see Michael J. Scavio et al., "Freud's Devaluation of Nietzsche," *Psychohistory Review* 21 (Spring 1993): 295–300.

56 Ernest R. Hilgard, *Psychology in America: A Historical Survey* (New York, 1987), 561, recalling Erikson describe first seeing Michelangelo's work in Rome. Lerner and Gerzon, TRI, May 22, 1971, Reel 1, Tape B, Side B, "I was in many ways a nonfunctioning artist," "work disturbance," "there were simply months," and "doing anything at all." EHE, *Life History*, 26, also notes the "work disturbance."

57 Erik's return to Karlsruhe in 1925 is discussed in JE, TRI, May 6, 1991; Hirsch and Katz, TRI, August 16, 1991; Coles, *Erikson*, 16. EHE, "Psa & Ongoing," *American Journal of Psychiatry* (September 1965): 247, and Schlein, *Way*, 272, "Nietzsche once said." Betty J. Lifton, PI by LJF, Wellfleet, October 23, 1994, on Blos portraying to her Erik's fragile emotional condition.

58 D. Joyce Jackson, "Contributing to the History of Psychology: XXXV. Dorothy Burlingham," *Psychological Reports* 54 (1984): 857, and Blos, TRI, May 22, 1966, on Blos's ini-

tial activities in Vienna. His discussion with Ms. Freud is reported in Michael J. Burling-ham, *The Last Tiffany: A Biography of Dorothy Tiffany Burlingham* (New York, 1989), 183–84, and Blos, *Anna Freud Remembered: Recollections of Her Friends and Colleagues* (Chicago, 1983), 13–14.

59 Burlingham, *Tiffany,* 184, quoting Robert Burlingham, "a friend of." EHE, TRI, January 11, 1968, on his interview with Anna Freud: "hardly any idea" and "I didn't know." EHE, "Autobiographic Notes," *Daedalus,* 744, "regular hours." EHE and JE, PI by Michael J. Burlingham, Stockbridge, July 31, 1983, transcript 1–2; and Burlingham, *Tiffany,* 184, on the details of Erik being interviewed and hired. Blos, TRI, May 22, 1966, on Anna Freud letting him hire Erik if he took responsibility.

60 EHE, *Life History,* 22, "the very beginning of my career."

CHAPTER 2
VIENNA YEARS: PSYCHOANALYSIS AS A CALLING, 1927–33

1 EHE, *Life History and the Historical Movement* (New York, 1975), 37; letter from Raymond Dyer to EHE, July 3, 1977, E-H. "Erik Homburger," c.v. (April 1, 1936), Yale Archives (Institute for Human Relations); JE, TRI by LJF, Cambridge, October 28, 1992; Raymond Dyer, *Anna Freud Remembered: Recollections from Her Friends and Collegues* (Chicago, 1983), 10.

2 Robert Coles, *Erik H. Erikson: The Growth of His Work* (Boston, 1970), 21–22; Peter Gay, *Freud: A Life for Our Time* (New York, 1988), especially 571–73, 593–96; EHE, TRI by Robert Stewart, Cambridge, January 11, 1968; EHE, TRI by Nathan Hale, Tiburon, April 29, 1976.

3 Letter from EHE to Jerome Bruner, n.d. (1973), E-H (on Bruner letter to EHE, September 17, 1973), "Anna Freud and others." EHE, TRI, April 29, 1976, "could see Freud and Anna Freud," "close to the original atmosphere," and "Paulinian days." EHE, "Peter Blos: Reminiscences," *Psychosocial Process* 3 (Fall 1974): 6, "vocation in the area."

4 EHE, "Autobiographic Statement to Freshman Seminar" (n.d. [early 1960s]), E-H, Freud's "respect for form." EHE, *The Life Cycle Completed: A Review* (New York, 1982), 22, and EHE lecture of December 15, 1969, in Abarbanel Notes, E-H, on becoming a "clinical artist" with a "configurational" approach.

5 Dorothy Burlingham, TRI by Peter Heller, London, June 17, 1975; and Peter Heller, PI by LJF, Copenhagen, May 8, 1993, on Erikson being tense, joyless, and revealing little of his past. EHE, "Memorandum for the Freud Archives" (March 1977), E-H, on Freud's "stoic suffering." EHE, *Insight and Responsibility: Lectures on the Ethical Implications of Psychoanalytic Insight* (New York, 1964), 19, on his early months as a tutor. Howard B. Levine, "An Interview with Professor Erik Erikson," November 13, 1984 (transcript in Boston Psychoanalytic Society), 10, quoting EHE on "lack of training . . . I had a certain sense." See also EHE, TRI, April 29, 1976.

6 Analysis of the "Red Vienna" programs and reformers is provided in Helmut Gruber, *Red Vienna: Experiment in Working-Class Culture, 1919–1934* (New York, 1991), 43, 65–66, 75–76, 92–94; Mitchell G. Ash and William P. Woodward, *Psychology in Twentieth-Century Thought and Society* (Cambridge, 1987), 147, 150; Sheldon Gardner and Gwendolyn Stevens, *Red Vienna and the Golden Age of Psychology, 1918–1938* (New York, 1992), 98–99; Richard F. Sterba, *Reminiscences of a Vienna Psychoanalyst* (Detroit, 1982), 81. EHE, TRI, April 29, 1976, on Vienna social reformers like Bernfeld and Federn deeply impressing him. See also Ernst Federn, PI by LJF, Vienna, May 12, 1993, on Homburger's apolitical posture and contact with Federn's father.

7 For the turn to the right in Austria that followed in Vienna, see Myron Sharaf, *Fury on Earth: A Biography of Wilhelm Reich* (New York, 1983), 123–26; Gay, *Freud,* 591; Esther Menaker, *Appointment in Vienna* (New York, 1989), 10–11, 45–46, 68; Ivar Oxaal, Michael Pollar, and Gerhard Botz, eds., *Jews, Anti-Semitism and Culture in Vienna* (Lon-

don, 1987), 166–67, 183; "Noted Scientist Tells of Serious Austrian Problems," *San Francisco Chronicle,* February 10, 1929 (a lecture by Alfred Adler); Paul Hoffman, *The Viennese: Splendor, Twilight, and Exile* (New York, 1989), 209–10.

8 Peter Heller, ed., *Anna Freud's Letters to Eva Rosenfeld* (Madison, Conn., 1992), 16, quoting Rosenfeld, "I wanted to," plus Eva Rosenfeld, *Recollected in Tranquility* (n.p., n.d. [c. late 1970s]), 203–4, 209–10.

9 Anna Freud, *Introduction to Psychoanalysis: Lectures for Child Analysts and Teachers, 1922–1935* (New York, 1974), 47, "a school which is," and Elisabeth Young-Bruehl, *Anna Freud: A Biography* (New York, 1988), 178. For Burlingham's motives, see "Memorial Meeting for Dorothy Burlingham, 6th February 1980," 3, E-H; Burlingham, TRI, June 17, 1975. For Homburger and Blos's design of the building, see Heller, *Freud-Rosenfeld,* 32, and Rosenfeld, *Recollected,* 203–4.

10 Peter Heller, *A Child Analysis with Anna Freud* (Madison, 1990), is the best source on the school and its students, though it is also very helpful to consult Heller, "Recollections of the Burlingham-Rosenfeld School" (n.d.), E-H. See also Peter Heller, PI by LJF, Washington, D.C., May 2, 1992; Rosenfeld, *Recollected,* 20; Michael J. Burlingham, *The Last Tiffany: A Biography of Dorothy Tiffany Burlingham* (New York, 1989), 185; Heller, *Freud-Rosenfeld,* 87.

11 Heller, *Child Analysis,* xxxii; Heller, "Recollections," 3, "harsher social realities." See also Rosenfeld, *Recollected,* 206; Peter Heller, TRI by LJF, Buffalo, July 31, 1991; Peter Heller, PI by LJF, Copenhagen, May 10, 1993.

12 Blos as director is described in Heller, "Recollections," 1, and Heller, *Child Analysis,* xxviii–xxix; letter from Victor Ross to LJF, July 25, 1992; EHE, "Introductory Remarks: First Peter Blos Biennial Lecture," NYC, December 7, 1971, E-H, "to keep regular." Peter Blos, "The Dolphin Keeper: Recollections," March 1980, 1, E-H, on Robert Burlingham getting special favor. M. Burlingham, *Tiffany,* 186, on teaching areas of the staff. Use of the Deweyite project method for Winnetka is reported in Heller, *Freud-Rosenfeld,* 7; Rosenfeld, *Recollected,* 205; EHE, TRI, April 29, 1976; Heller, *Child Analysis,* xxxi–xxxii.

13 EHE (Wattmanngasse) (n.d. [ca. 1980]), E-H; JE, TRI by LJF, Cambridge, May 6, 1991. Copies of Hietzing School yearbooks for 1928 and 1929 were provided to me by Peter Heller.

14 Homburger's mannerisms, especially the proclivity to look into mirrors, is noted in a letter from Victor Ross to LJF, July 25, 1992, and Heller, *Child Analysis,* xxix. M. Burlingham, *Tiffany,* 195; Heller, "Recollections," 1; and the letter from Victor Ross to LJF, July 25, 1992, on his connection to the students.

15 For Erik's success with the students, see, e.g., letter from EHE to Dorothy Burlingham, October 14, 1974, E-H; M. Burlingham, *Tiffany,* 187; Heller, TRI, July 31, 1991; and Heller, PI, May 10, 1993. EHE, TRI, January 11, 1968, "immediately took to it." JE, TRI by LJF, Harwich, January 14, 1994, recalling how Anna Freud was taken by Homburger's effectiveness.

16 Anna Freud's posture ("All they know," etc.) is reported in Heller, *Freud-Rosenfeld,* 112, 125, and in Heller, TRI, July 31, 1991. Rosenfeld's position is indicated in Heller, *Freud-Rosenfeld,* 82, 112, and in Heller, "Drei Briefe von Anna Freud und Eva Rosenfeld," *Psyche* (May 1991): 444. Dorothy Burlingham's views are found in M. Burlingham, *Tiffany,* 230; Heller, PI, May 2, 1992; Paul Roazen, *Meeting Freud's Family* (Amherst, Mass., 1993), 81.

17 Blos, "Intimate History of the School in the Wattmanngasse, Vienna" was written around 1974. His refusal to lift restrictions against researchers or to explain why he imposed them is noted in a letter from Blos to LJF, December 14, 1991 ("I have no reason to explain my action nor do I intend to").

18 Homburger-Erikson's retrospective version of the school is found in EHE, TRI, April 29, 1976; Stephen Schlein, ed., *A Way of Looking at Things: Selected Papers from 1930 to*

1980. Erik H. Erikson (New York, 1987), 4–5; and EHE, TRI by Mark Gerzon and Michael Lerner, TRI, Stockbridge, May 22, 1971, Reel 2, Tape A, Side A. "Minutes of Closed School" (October 29, 1980), 7, Elisabeth Young-Bruehl private papers, for Homburger on "what Freud called."

19 Heller, *Freud-Rosenfeld,* 10–11.

20 Heller, *Freud-Rosenfeld,* has many letters illustrating the rapport between the three patrons, especially the Anna Freud–Rosenfeld relationship. Young-Bruehl, *Anna Freud,* 135–37, is also quite helpful (136, "You are me and I am you"). For good data and insight on the Burlingham–Anna Freud relationship, see Lisa Appignanesi and John Forrester, *Freud's Women* (New York, 1992), 282; *The Diary of Sigmund Freud, 1929–1939* (New York, 1992), 67; W. Ernest Freud, "Die Freuds und die Burlinghams in der Berggasse," *Sigmund Freud House Bulletin* 11, no. 1 (Summer 1987): 17–18.

21 Letter from Peter Heller to EHE, June 27, 1980, E-H, "spirit predominated." Peter Heller, "Reflections on a Child Analysis with Anna Freud and an Adult Analysis with Ernst Kris," *Journal of the American Academy of Psychoanalysis* 20 (1992): 64, "well-meaning dictatorship." Heller, *Freud-Rosenfeld,* 12, on the substitute family.

22 Heller, "Reflections on a Child Analysis," 66, "a tinge of hostility." EHE, TRI, January 11, 1968, "that atmosphere" and other useful insights on the gender aspects of patron and teacher roles. See also JE, PI by LJF, Harwich, October 22, 1994. The closing of the school is discussed in Rosenfeld, *Memoirs,* 213, and Peter Blos, TRI by Robert Stewart, NYC, May 22, 1966.

23 Harold and Brigette Eichelberger, "Montessori Pedagogy in Vienna," in *Kindersein in Wien: Zur Sozial eschichte der Kindes von der Aufklärung bis in 20 Jahrhundert* (Catalog of Exhibit of Vienna State Historical Museum, 1993), 84–86. Young-Bruehl, *Anna Freud,* 219–20; Raymond Dyer, *Her Father's Daughter: The Work of Anna Freud* (New York, 1983), 22; EHE comments at symposium, "Dynamic Psychology and Education," April 20, 1976, American Education Association, San Francisco, 2, E-H. Thomas Aichhorn, PI by LJF, Vienna, May 12, 1993; Dyer, *Anna Freud,* 10.

24 EHE, "Autobiographic Notes on the Identity Crisis," *Daedalus* 99, no. 4 (Fall 1970): 734, to "boast only of a Montessori diploma." EHE in *Children's House Magazine* 6, no. 4 (1973): 4, "deep and symbolic meanings . . . pay attention to and to repeat."

25 EHE in *Children's House Magazine,* 4, "meaningful activity." Coles, *Erikson,* 23, stressing Homburger's introduction to children's play. Hilde Federn, PI by LJF, Vienna, May 12, 1993, on Homburger's discomfort with how Montessori methodology ignored fantasies.

26 Esther Menaker, "On Anna Freud," *Journal of the American Academy of Psychoanalysis* 19, no. 4 (1991): 608, on Anna Freud's education. Menaker, *Appointment in Vienna* (New York, 1989), 45–46, provides a vivid account of anti-Semitism at the time at the University of Vienna.

27 See Erik Homburger's course transcript from the Archive of the University of Vienna, 1929–33, an analysis of it by the head university archivist (letter from Karl Muehlberger to LJF, Vienna, February 17, 1993), and an analysis of his Vienna coursework by the chairman of Harvard's psychology department (letter from Edwin Boring to Erik Homburger, June 16, 1935, Edwin G. Boring Papers, Harvard University Archives).

28 For comment on the Bühlers, their work at the University of Vienna, and their students, see Menaker, *Appointment in Vienna,* 151–52; Ash and Woodward, *Psychology in Twentieth-Century Thought and Society,* 150–51; Marie Jahoda, "The Migration of Psychoanalysis: Its Impact on American Psychology," in *Intellectual Migration: Europe and America, 1930–1960,* edited by Donald Fleming and Bernard Bailyn (Cambridge, 1969), 422–23.

29 Coles, *Anna Freud,* 13–14, quoting Homburger: "wasn't sure what that meant" and "could combine those interests." Erik Homburger to August Aichhorn, September 7, 1933, AP-SFH, on the resemblance to his early life with mother and aunts. EHE, *Life History,* 30, "to quote one's analyst" and "You might help to make them see" (reporting Anna Freud's direct advice to him). In film biographer Harriet Harvey's videotape of

Erikson's October 23, 1985, Harvard seminar, "Perspectives on the Life Cycle," he recounted Anna Freud reporting *as her father's advice* the "make them see" remark. He also reflected: "That kind of thing can decide your identity."

30 See, e.g., EHE, "Autobiographic Notes," *Daedalus,* 735; Harvey videotape; Daniel Schwartz, PI by LJF, Stockbridge, March 25, 1993.

31 Schlein, *Way,* 56, 68 (from the full "Fate of Drives in School Compositions" essay).

32 Richard I. Evans, ed., *Dialogue with Erik Erikson* (New York, 1967), 82, recalling Kris and other Vienna analysts with backgrounds in the arts. EHE, *Life History,* 30, "I soon detected in Freud's writings." EHE, Chautauqua talk (1978), 2, "to see, to restore his visual." Harvey videotape, on Freud's waiting room. Howard Levine, "An Interview with Professor Erik Erikson," November 13, 1984, (typescript, Boston Psychoanalytic Society), 5, and EHE, *Insight and Responsibility,* 20, on Freud's consulting room.

33 EHE, Chautauqua talk (1978), 2, "from art to psychoanalysis . . . could ever have made it." EHE, *Life History,* 30, "descriptions of his patients' memories and dreams." EHE, *Life Cycle Completed,* 21–22, on *Interpretation of Dreams* and "the rich interplay of form and meaning" and "the artfulness of manifest expression."

34 EHE, *Life Cycle Completed,* 21–22, on how dream analysis was the basis for his analysis of the forms of children's play and for some of his earliest psychoanalytic writings on children. He elaborated this point in the *Chautauqua Daily,* August 4, 1978; EHE, TRI, January 11, 1968; and EHE, "Epilogue [for Mt. Zion book]" (n.d. [early 1980s]), 4, E-H. Heller, "Reflections on a Child Analysis," 49, recalling that Anna Freud did not use play therapy in her child analyses of the late 1920s and early 1930s. M. Burlingham, *Tiffany,* 163, notes her analysis of daydreams and drawings.

35 "Remarks by Professor Erikson," Wright Institute, Berkeley, 1979, 2, E-H, "Freud's enormous visual talents." EHE, *Insight and Responsibility,* 20, "for a young man."

36 EHE, "The First Psychoanalyst," *Yale Review* 46 (1956): 40. Erikson's obituary in the *New York Times,* May 13, 1994, notes the family party and the mushroom hunting. Letter from EHE to (nameless) (n.d. [early 1970s]), E-H, on the automobile trip. Letter from EHE to David Riesman, November 19, 1957, DRP, on conversing with Minna Bernays. EHE, "Autobiographic Notes," *Daedalus,* 736, on his minimal discussion with Freud.

37 EHE, "Freud's 'The Origins of Psychoanalysis,' " *International Journal of Psycho-Analysis* 36 (1955): 10, "Freud had not left his parents'." EHE, *Insight and Responsibility,* 187, on Freud as "somewhat of a German nationalist." EHE, "Notes for Christian Gauss Seminar at Princeton," 1969, E-H, linking his own Judaism to Freud's. Letter from EHE to Riesman, November 19, 1957, DRP, on his memories of ties to the Freud household and "mannish intelligent women." Homburger read Freud's *The Question of Lay Analysis* soon after it was published. Freud's "to find their way" remark on children's work is reported in it. (See *Standard Edition of the Complete Psychological Works of Sigmund Freud,* translated by James Strachey [London, 1955], xx, 249.)

38 EHE, "Autobiographic Notes," *Daedalus,* 744, "What, in me" and "a kind of favored stepson identity that." EHE, "Gauss Seminar," 4, E-H, "had maybe too much of a mother" and "needed a father." In Harvey videotape, Erik directly linked his stepson existence in the Homburger household to his stepson existence in Freud's Vienna circle. EHE, "Autobiographic Notes," *Daedalus,* 744, as "close to the role of a children's doctor." EHE and JE, "On Generativity and Identity: From a Conversation with the Editors," *Harvard Education Review* 51, no. 2 (May 1981): 260, quoting Erik on Freud being "a doctor like my adoptive father" with "great interest in art" and Freud as "the most creative person."

39 EHE, "Gauss Seminar," 8, "great Jew . . . Their love made it . . ."

40 EHE, *Life History,* 37, and Dyer, *Anna Freud,* 82.

41 Anna Freud's emerging role is discussed well in Dyer, *Anna Freud,* especially 59–60, 93; Appignanesi and Forrester, *Freud's Women,* 281, 287; Young-Bruehl, *Anna Freud,* Chapters 4–5. EHE, "Studies in the Interpretation of Play," *Genetic Psychology Monographs* 22,

no. 4 (November 1940): 569, "the only safe technical statement." See also EHE, "Anna Freud—Reflections," *Bulletin of the Hampstead Clinic* 6 (1983): 53.

42 The pedagogy seminar is noted in Young-Bruehl, *Anna Freud,* 175; Daniel Benveniste, "Siegfried Bernfeld in San Francisco," *American Psychoanalyst* 26, no. 1 (1992): 12; JE, TRI, October 28, 1992. Homburger reflected on it in conjunction with developmental approaches and the general child analysis–education link in Schlein, *Way,* 72–73.

43 Sterba, *Reminiscences,* 42–43, and Young-Bruehl, *Anna Freud,* 157–59, properly distinguish *Kinder-seminar* from child analysis seminar. See also Anna Freud, *Introduction to Psychoanalysis,* vii; Menaker, *Appointment in Vienna,* 143, 147–48, 150. Homburger-Erikson often confused and blurred together the two seminars. EHE, TRI by Burlingham, July 31, 1983, transcript 4 on Anna Freud's gaiety and excited directing of the seminar. EHE, "Epilogue" (for Mt. Zion book) (n.d. [early 1980s]), 5, E-H, on the "*joy* which characterized." EHE, "Anna Freud—Reflections," 52, "I happened to be one of the very few men."

44 Coles, *Anna Freud,* 72. See also Anna Freud, "Normality and Pathology in Childhood," *Writings of Anna Freud* (London, 1965), vol. 6, 168.

45 Young-Bruehl, *Anna Freud,* 176–77; Menaker, *Appointment in Vienna,* 97, 148–49; Dyer, *Anna Freud,* 64; Anna Freud, *Introduction to Psychoanalysis,* 54.

46 For Anna Freud's desire to improve the social circumstances of children, see Young-Bruehl, *Anna Freud,* 177; Anna Freud, *Introduction to Psychoanalysis,* 175. EHE, "Reflections on Historical Change" (n.d. [c. 1978–82]), E-H, recording her advocacy of children's programs. Letter from EHE to Nathan Hale, November 12, 1975, E-H, recalling Anna Freud feeding child patients and calling it "an expensive business."

47 See, e.g, Anna Freud, *Introduction to Psychoanalysis,* vii; "Panel Report: The Ego and the Mechanisms of Defense," *Journal of the Philadelphia Association of Psychoanalysis,* 1 (1974): 37–39; Young-Bruehl, *Anna Freud,* 182, 187–88; Eugene Pumpian-Mindlin, "Anna Freud and Erik Erikson," *Psychoanalytic Pioneers,* edited by Franz Alexander (New York, 1966), 520; EHE, "Anna Freud—Reflections," 53, "form and presence."

48 Coles, *Anna Freud,* 13, quoting Homburger ("she suggested"). Letter from Erik Homburger to August Aichhorn, September 7, 1933, AP-SFH, "the moment I asked Anna Freud for an analysis" and "childhood which I spent." Peter Blos, PI by Betty J. Lifton, NYC, January 22 and 23, 1993 (notes supplied to LJF), on Homburger jumping at the opportunity for an analysis. Esther Menaker, TI by LJF, February 12, 1995, agreeing with Blos about Homburger's ambition.

49 Heller, *Freud-Rosenfeld,* 105, "Erik is making a drawing of me." EHE, "Gauss Seminar," E-H, "needed a father."

50 EHE, "Incomplete Vitae," July 2, 1938, J. W. Macfarlane Documents, Archives of History of American Psychology, University of Akron, lists a six-year period for his training analysis, though he was only on the roster of the Vienna Psychoanalytic Institute from 1929 to 1933. Usually, he claimed that the personal analysis portion lasted over three years (see, e.g., *New York Times,* May 13, 1994), and that seems reasonably accurate. In EHE, TRI, May 22, 1971, Reel 2, Tape A, Side A, however, he noted that the analysis ended when he met Joan Serson, his wife-to-be, in 1929, and this is inaccurate. Beatriz Foster, TI by LJF, January 23, 1996, recalls Homburger telling her the analysis was only temporarily suspended by Ms. Freud. In the May 22, 1971, Gerzon-Lerner interview, Homburger stressed how analysis with Anna Freud was frequently interrupted, especially when she went with her father to Berlin. This is supported by JE, TRI, October 28, 1992, and January 14, 1994. In both interviews, Joan Erikson emphasized his disinterest in being analyzed and his pleasure when his analytic sessions were canceled. One must regard this emphasis cautiously given Joan's dislike of Anna Freud.

51 Menaker, *Appointment in Vienna,* 147, describes the waiting room. Schlein, *Way,* 71, "would see the old 'Professor.'" EHE, "Autobiographic Notes," *Daedalus,* 735, "complex feelings." EHE, TRI, January 11, 1968, recalling feeling envy and sensing that he or Ms.

Freud was second-rate. EHE, "Gauss Seminar," 4, E-H, "complications of my position." Harvey videotape, "I often said . . . That was a training analysis." Gerald Holton, TRI by LJF, Cambridge, February 15, 1991, and David Wilcox, PI by LJF, Cambridge, March 31, 1991, recount Homburger telling of these diverse feelings in the waiting room.

52 Heller, *Child Analysis,* 72, on Anna Freud's daily schedule including Homburger and several of his students. Heller, *Freud-Rosenfeld,* 136, "Lizzie and Erik and little Peter"; 141–42, "I have sessions with . . . Erik in very good shape." Heller, TI, May 2, 1994, and Heller, TRI, July 31, 1991.

53 EHE to Alden Whitman, July 14, 1974, E-H, "the personal and the official." EHE to Anna Freud, March 1949, Anna Freud Papers, LC, "the high condensation." EHE, TRI by Howard B. Levine and Daniel Jacobs, November 13, 1984, transcript 4–5, "Anna Freud was my analyst . . . couldn't be, wouldn't be misused."

54 Coles, *Anna Freud,* 14, quoting EHE: "very methodical." EHE remarks for Erikson Institute, October 1983, E-H, "friendly listening." Letter from EHE to Alden Whitman, July 14, 1974, E-H, "a certain playfulness" and "a peacefulness and simplicity." EHE, "Play, Vision, and Deception," Second Godkin Lecture, April 12, 1972, transcript 2 (Margaret Brenman-Gibson private papers).

55 The knitting episode is reported in EHE, "Anna Freud—Reflections," 52, and Heller, *Freud-Rosenfeld,* 10; see also Arthur S. Couch, "Anna Freud's Adult Psychoanalytic Technique: A Defense of Classical Analysis," *International Journal of Psycho-Analysis* 76, Part I (February 1995): 169. Paul Roazen, "Erik Erikson as a Teacher," *Michigan Quarterly Review* (Winter 1992): 31, recounts discussing with Erikson in the 1960s the fact that Sigmund Freud analyzed Anna, with Erikson remarking to Roazen: "I always suspected incest!"

56 Letter from EHE to Anna Freud, March 1949, Anna Freud Papers, LC, on "tiredness" and "illness" and "you were quite right in letting me marry Joan." Foster, TI, January 23, 1996, on Homburger telling her of Ms. Freud's distress over his courting Joan.

57 Dyer, *Anna Freud,* 22–23, notes Anna Freud's attentiveness to the effect of absent fathers on children. Esther Menaker, TI by LJF, February 5, 1995, on the ship woodcut and Anna Freud's advice to sublimate the father issue. JE, TI by LJF, March 11, 1995, corroborating Menaker's interpretation of the woodcut. Robert J. Lifton, "Talks (Dinner & Breakfast) with Erik Erikson on May 4–5–6, 1980, in Tiburon," RJL-NYPL, on giving Anna Freud the woodcut. Betty J. Lifton, TI by LJF, May 5, 1993, on how her research on adopted children revealed that European analysts of the Anna Freud–Helene Deutsch generation discouraged youngsters from pursuing their parentage and their family scandals. Letter from Erik Homburger to August Aichhorn, September 7, 1933, AP-SFH, on his "betrayed father." With few variations, Homburger-Erikson told close friends again and again about how Ms. Freud dismissed what he felt he knew of his real father as fantasy. See, e.g., JE, TRI, January 14, 1994, and JE, TI by LFJ, December 13, 1993; Sue Bloland, TRI by LJF, NYC, November 8, 1993; Betty J. Lifton, PI by LJF, Wellfleet, October 30, 1992. Margaret Brenman-Gibson, TRI by LJF, Stockbridge, March 31, 1991, and Margaret Brenman-Gibson, PI by LJF, Stockbridge, May 29, 1991, March 20, 1992, and April 10, 1993, reiterated Homburger-Erikson telling her of the incident with the photograph (allegedly of his father).

58 EHE to Anna Freud, March 1949, Anna Freud Papers, LC, "only *after* my analysis" (emphasis added) and "I felt as if." Letters from EHE to Jon, Kai, and Sue (n.d. [1960s]), in possession of Jon Erikson, "the room where." Letter from EHE to Robert Wallerstein (titled "Homestead"), September 20, 1974, E-H, "a pretty good personal analysis." *New York Times,* May 13, 1994, quoting Erikson on "gave me self-awareness . . . in a liberating atmosphere." Letter from Lois Murphy to EHE, June 17, 1977 (unsent), E-H. Sue Bloland, TRI, November 8, 1993.

59 EHE, TRI, May 22, 1971, Reel 2, Tape A, Side B.

60 JE, TRI, May 6, 1991, and Harwich, October 24, 1994, and June 10, 1995. Sue Bloland,

TRI, November 8, 1993, and July 9, 1994. In my June 10, 1995, visit with Joan, I came across photographs of Serson family members and she stated: "So now you know."

61 JE, TRI, May 6, 1991; Coles, *Erikson*, 24–25. Mary Catherine Bateson, *Composing a Life* (New York, 1990), 50.

62 JE, TRI, January 14, 1994; JE and EHE, PI by M. Burlingham, Stockbridge, July 31, 1983, transcript 2–3; Christina Robb, "Partners for Life," *Boston Globe Magazine,* March 22, 1987, 19; M. Burlingham, *Tiffany,* 206; Heller, "Recollections of the Burlingham-Rosenfeld School,"2.

63 JE, TRI, January 14, 1994, and June 9, 1995; EHE, TRI by Benjamin White, Cotuit, July 22, 1978 (audiotape in Countway Library, Harvard Medical School); Sue Bloland, TRI, July 9, 1994. Menaker, TI, February 5 and 12, 1995, recalling how a Margo Goldschmidt and others persuaded Erik that he had to marry Joan, and on visiting Joan in the hospital after a difficult delivery.

64 Letters from EHE to Jon, Kai, and Sue Erikson (n.d. [1960s]), in possession of Jon Erikson, recalling the Anglican ceremony, for which we have no legal record. The civil ceremony, dated September 27, 1930, is registered as MA61-*Altmatrikenstelle* (#2492) in the *Rathaus.* JE, TRI June 9, 1995, and by LJF, Harwich, July 5, 1996, on the Anglican and the civil ceremonies. For the official record of the Jewish ceremony that contains data on the other two, see *Literal Excerpt from the Marriage Record Book of the Registrar of the Jewish Community of Vienna,* running document no. 427 (1930), Institut für Wissenschaft und Kunst, Vienna. For additional data on the Jewish ceremony, see Rosenfeld, *Recollections,* 211; EHE and JE, TRI by M. Burlingham, July 31, 1983, transcript 3; JE, TRI, January 14, 1994; letter from Finn Abrahamsen to LJF, Copenhagen, August 15, 1993.

65 Ruth Hirsch and Ellen Katz, TRI by LJF, NYC, August 16, 1991; Ruth Hirsch, TI by LJF, June 9, 1991; Hirsch, TRI, October 8, 1993.

66 JE, TRI, Cambridge, June 12, 1993, and Harwich, October 20, 1994; Hirsch and Katz, TRI, August 16, 1991; Hirsch, TI, June 9, 1991; Helene Abrahamsen, TRI by Martha Abrahamsen, Copenhagen (n.d. [1982 or 1983]); Sue Bloland, TRI, November 8, 1993; Menaker, TI, February 12, 1995.

67 JE, TRI January 14 and by LJF, Harwich, January 15, 1994, and June 9, 1995; EHE (Wattmanngasse) (n.d. [c. 1980]), E-H; Bateson, *Composing a Life,* 83, 215; Rosenfeld, *Recollections,* 210–11; Joanne and Kai Erikson, TRI by LJF, Hamden, November 7, 1993; Robb, "Partners for Life," 26; Menaker, TI, February 5, 1995.

68 Henry A. Murray, TRI by James W. Anderson, Cambridge, July 18, 1975, on the nonpassionate but trusting quality of the marriage. For the benefits Joan saw accruing to her from the marriage, see JE, TRI, January 14, 1994; Sue Bloland, TRI, October 8, 1993, and July 9, 1994. EHE, "Introductory Remarks: First Peter Blos Biennial Lecture," NYC, December 7, 1971, 4, E-H, on having "too much *Geistigkeit,*" which Joan alleviated. For Joan's marked effect on Erik's life, see Hirsch and Katz, TRI, August, 16, 1991; Hirsch, TI, June 9, 1991; Sue Bloland, TRI, October 8, 1993; Nina Holton, TRI by LJF, Lexington, Mass., April 30, 1991. Margaret Brenman-Gibson, TRI by LJF, Stockbridge, March 23, 1991, on how Erik expressed full agreement of Ellen Katz's appraisal.

69 Phyllis Rose, *Parallel Lives* (New York, 1984), 7.

70 For Jekels's background, see Elke Muhlteiter, *Biographisches Lexikon der Psychoanalyse* (Tübingen, 1992), 170–71. JE describes the course of her analysis with Jekels in JE, TRI, October 28, 1992, and January 14, 1994. She recounts the quilt incident in TRI, January 14, 1994. Menaker, TI, February 5, 1995, on Joan telling her of her anger when Jekels charged her for missing sessions. See also Coles, *Erikson,* 25, and John Thornton, PI by LJF, Bloomington, August 18, 1994, recounting a conversation with Joan about her analysis.

71 JE, TRI, June 9, 1995, on Freud with Kai in the garden. Roazen, "Erik Erikson as a Teacher," 31, reporting Joan Erikson's account of Hartmann's reprimand. Peter Heller, TI by LJF, February 5, 1994, contrasting Erik's with Joan's excitement over the psychoanalytic movement. In JE, TRI by LJF, Cambridge, December 17, 1990, and TRI, Janu-

ary 14, 1994, and June 9, 1995, she detailed her reservations concerning Anna Freud and the psychoanalytic movement, particularly Ms. Freud's impact on Erik. Letter from EHE to Anna Freud, March 1949, Anna Freud Papers, LC, reporting Ms. Freud's earlier warning that "dangers lie in such analytic alliances." See also Brenman-Gibson, TRI, March 23, 1991, and by LJF, Stockbridge, March 27, 1993; and Sue Bloland, TRI, November 8, 1993, and May 9, 1995.

72 EHE, TRI, November 13, 1984, transcript 3, "My God, all these things." EHE, Chautauqua (1978), 1, "the originators." EHE, TRI, January 11, 1968, "personal" and "more reliable."

73 EHE, "Autobiographic Notes," Daedalus, 740, "in terms of nineteenth-century physicalism," "drive enlivening inner structures," "verbal and visual configurations," "clearly suggested," "the very creativity of the unconscious." See also EHE, Life Cycle Completed, 16, on "Trieb." Schlein, Way, 39–69 ("The Fate of Drives in School Compositions"). Homburger recalls how he operated within mechanistic, physicalist Freudian terms but sensed their limits in EHE, TRI by Margaret Brenman-Gibson, Tiburon, April 1, 1983, Tape 2, 11. Levine, "Interview with Erikson," 12; letter from EHE to Robert R. Holt, December 31, 1979, E-H.

74 EHE, TRI, April 1, 1983, Tape 1, 30, on "inner" and "outer world" and "had completely neglected" their connection. EHE, Life Cycle Completed, 19–20, "the patient's mutual involvement." JE recalls discussion with EHE on "outside the analytic social world" in Harvey videotape. Erik notes how, despite Joan's prodding, he felt Sigmund Freud had room for serious consideration of the social world; see EHE, TRI, January 11, 1968; EHE, TRI, April 29, 1976, EHE, "Autobiographic Notes," Daedalus, 741; "seemed to me always implicit."

75 "Vereinigung," December 16, 1931, comment by Edith Jackson, Jackson Papers, Schlesinger Library, Radcliffe, "the discussion was sluggish." EHE, TRI, April 1, 1983, Tape 1, 26; Stephen Schlein, PI by LJF, Lexington, Mass., April 4, 1991; EHE, TRI, May 22, 1971, Reel 1, Tape B, Side A, "not be able to say."

76 Young-Bruehl, Anna Freud, 166–68, on the Klein–Anna Freud debate. EHE, TRI, January 11, 1968, recalling the Klein–Anna Freud debate during his Vienna years. Paul Roazen, "Transmission: Tausk, Erikson and Helene Deutsch," Le Cadre de L'Analyse (Paris, 1994), 19; Roazen, "Psychology and Politics: The Case of Erik H. Erikson," The Human Context 8 (1975): 580; and Roazen, Erik H. Erikson: The Power and Limits of a Vision (New York, 1976), 6–7, on Erikson being accused of being a Kleinian and reacting bitterly.

77 Schlein, Way, 27, "They spoke of aggression"; 54, on the girl's Oedipal wish to destroy her mother; 37, "which strains on the superego formation."

78 Letter from EHE to Dorothy Burlingham, October 14, 1974, E-H, on his presentations and work with Mabbie and Mickey. Schlein, Way, 68, on Dorothy Burlingham as teacher providing "the opportunity" and "confidence"; 56, "a boy with empty eyes"; 38, "Whatever behavior," "relationship is the crux"; xxii–xxiii, on how Homburger's Vienna papers underscored adult acknowledgment of the reality message within children's work. The point was made especially well in two 1931 papers: "Children's Picture Books" and "The Fate of Drives in School Compositions."

79 EHE review of Psychoanalysis for Teachers and Parents in Psychoanalytic Quarterly 5 (1936): 292–93, on Anna Freud telling "what may limit and endanger" and "illuminate the ego." EHE, TRI, January 11, 1968, on how his 1936 published criticism of Ms. Freud had been building while he attended her seminars. EHE, "Autobiographic Notes," Daedalus, 739, recalling being taken by Hartmann's discussion of ego adaptation.

80 Daedalus, 739, and EHE, Life History, 37, on Federn as an "obscure and yet fascinating teacher" who may well have used the term identity as he elaborated "ego boundaries." EHE, Identity: Youth and Crisis (New York, 1968), 9, recalling listening to Federn, an "inventive" man, elaborating on "ego boundaries." EHE, "Autobiographic Notes," See

also Dyer, *Anna Freud*, 107, and Sterba, *Reminiscences*, 127. The Tausk link to Federn is discussed in Paul Roazen, *Le Cadre de L'Analyse*, 14, and Roazen, *Freud and His Followers* (New York, 1976), 515.

81 Hetty Zock, *A Psychology of Ultimate Concern: Erik H. Erikson's Contribution to the Psychology of Religion* (Amsterdam, 1990), 56–57, provides an excellent discussion of Kris's influence on Homburger. EHE, TRI by Nathan Hale, April 26 and 29, 1976, on Reich's influence. See also EHE, TRI, January 11, 1968.

82 EHE, *Identity*, 20, quoting Freud's 1926 address using "inner identity." EHE, TRI, January 11, 1968, on his subsequent realization that the "ego" and "identity" issue was his personal and professional issue.

83 Letter from EHE to Alden Whitman, July 14, 1974, E-H, "a member of her 'inner circle.'" EHE, TRI, January 11, 1968, and EHE, TRI, April 1, 1983, transcript 23, on memories of being voted into full membership and its implications. Coles, *Erikson*, 30, describes the Vienna Psychoanalytic Society proceedings.

84 EHE, "Anna Freud—Reflections," 53–54, "an intellectual concentration on the inner dynamics." EHE, TRI, July 22, 1978, Countway Library; EHE, TRI, April 1, 1983, transcript 29; and EHE, TRI, January 11, 1968. In these interviews, he recounted the Austrian situation and the psychoanalytic community's response to Germany. See also a full discussion of Sigmund Freud's response in Gay, *Freud*, 593. JE, TRI, January 14, 1994, reviews all of the political factors in the decision to leave Vienna, especially her own political perspective and fears. Letter from EHE to Robert J. Lifton, June 1976, RJL-NYPL, suggests that his fears of Germany invading Austria were not as great as Joan's.

85 EHE, TRI, January 11, 1968, and EHE, TRI, April 1, 1983, transcript 29, on how he and Joan would have left Vienna even without the rise of Hitler. EHE, "Autobiographic Notes," *Daedalus*, 740, "growing conservatism." EHE, TRI by Forrest Robinson, Cambridge, August 12, 1970, transcript 2, "a community of believers." EHE, TRI, May 22, 1971, Reel 1, Tape B, Side A, echoes this point. In this same part in the Lerner and Gerzon interview, Erikson also noted the "ingrown group of hypermaternal" analysts and "Young men didn't exactly thrive."

86 EHE, Harvey videotape, on Joan's decision "to take us." For Joan's perspective, see JE, TRI, January 14, 1994, and June 9, 1995, and EHE and JE, PI, July 31, 1983, 5. Vienna city archives have no record of Erik and Joan applying for Austrian citizenship.

87 EHE, TRI, January 11, 1968, "I left with a great deal of ambivalence." EHE, TRI, May 22, 1971, Reel 2, Tape A, Side B, "The one thing I ever learned," and "not to do it differently" but "my own way." Gifford, "EHE-84," Side 2, 24–25, "the freedom from professionalization" and "to prove that you were a faithful follower." EHE, TRI, January 11, 1968, "my father was not a Jew." EHE, "Autobiographic Notes," *Daedalus*, 744, "my psychoanalytic identity therefore."

88 For Homburger's recollection of telling Anna Freud of his departure, see EHE, TRI, January 11, 1968, and letter from EHE to Anna Freud, March 1949, Anna Freud Papers, LC, "I needed to concentrate." Coles, *Anna Freud*, 15, quoting Homburger with Ms. Freud, "she shrugged her shoulders." Stephen Schlein, PI by LJF, Washington, D.C., May 1, 1992, recalling Anna Freud telling him about warning Homburger not to go to "the other side." Helmut Wohl, TRI by LJF, Boston, April 24, 1991, reporting Homburger's story to him of Freud at the railroad station. Wohl was a Stockbridge neighbor and close friend.

89 See Achim Perner, "Der Ort der Verwahrlosung in der Psychoanalytischen Theorie bei August Aichhorn" (n.d.), and Harold Leupold-Lowenthal, *Handbuch der Psychoanalyse* (Vienna, 1986), 49–50, for details concerning Aichhorn's background and activities. Gardner and Stevens, *Red Vienna*, 101, on Anna Freud's praise for Aichhorn. Blos, TRI, May 22, 1966, details Aichhorn's analytic perspective toward delinquent youth.

90 Transcript of conversation between Erik Homburger, August Aichhorn, et al., March 12, 1933, AP-SFH, on Homburger's seventeen-year-old patient and other connections between Aichhorn and Homburger. David W. Wilcox, "Reflections on a Supervision,"

Cambridge Hospital Symposium, October 29, 1994, 5, recalls Homburger emphasizing his Aichhorn supervision and what it taught him. Schlein, *Way,* 711, "eyes to the problem of youth." Aichhorn had also profoundly influenced Margaret Mahler and Heinz Kohut.

91 Letter from Erik Homburger to August Aichhorn, September 7, 1933, AP-SFH. The progress of Blos's career in Vienna and his contact with Aichhorn is discussed in Blos, TRI, May 22, 1966, and in Achim Perner, "Ein Interview mit Peter Blos über August Aichhorn," *Kinderpsychoanalyse* (June 1993). Ingrid Scholz-Strasser, PI by LJF, Vienna, May 11, 1993, comments on Anna Freud as the key to Blos-Homburger tension in Vienna.

92 Letter from Homburger to Aichhorn, AP-SFH, September 7, 1933.

93 Ibid.

94 Ibid. One wonders, here, whether Erik's story of fatherly betrayal was his personal translation of the theory of the son's Oedipal revolt against the father. Indeed, the story seemed to militate against his efforts to learn about the man who had fathered him.

95 Letter from Aichhorn to Homburger, September 17, 1933, AP-SFH.

96 Letter from Homburger to Aichhorn, September 29, 1933, AP-SFH.

97 Coles, *Erikson,* 180, "added a certain inner sturdiness."

98 Letter from Aichhorn to Homburger, September 17, 1933, AP-SFH, completed one chapter. Letter from Aichhorn to Blos, March 16, 1946, Thomas Aichhorn private papers, "not have pleasant memories" and "how his life."

CHAPTER 3
"THE MAKING OF AN AMERICAN": FROM HOMBURGER TO ERIKSON, 1933–39

1 EHE, *Insight and Responsibility: Lectures on the Ethical Implications of Psychoanalytic Insight* (New York, 1964), 84, "my status as an American immigrant." EHE, "Autobiographic Statement to Freshman Seminar" (n.d. [early 1960s]), E-H. EHE, *Life History and the Historical Moment* (New York, 1975), 43, on "identity" as "naturally grounded."

2 EHE, *Childhood and Society* (New York, 1963 ed.), 283, "always write about the way it feels to arrive or leave." Richard I. Evans, ed., *Dialogue with Erik Erikson* (New York, 1967), 41, "one of those very important redefinitions," "sensory and sensual impressions," and "conceptual images."

3 EHE, *Identity: Youth and Crisis* (New York, 1968), 227, "my own life history" and "prepared me for feeling at home."

4 EHE, TRI by Michael Lerner and Mark Gerzon, May 22, 1971, Reel 2, Tape A, Side B, E-H. JE, TRI by LJF, Cambridge, October 28, 1992. EHE, *"Lehrausschussitzung,"* Vienna, May 19, 1933, Freud Museum, London, on leaving Vienna without completing control cases.

5 EHE, TRI by Robert Stewart, Cambridge, January 11, 1968, "I was born a Dane." Ruth Hirsch, TI by LJF, June 28, 1993, recalled Erik telling her he hoped to learn more in Denmark about his father. EHE, "Memorandum to Freud Archives" (n.d. [March 1977]), 3, E-H, on helping Marie Bonaparte; see also Celia Bertin, *Marie Bonaparte: A Life* (New York, 1982), 189. JE, TRI, by LJF, Cambridge, December 17, 1990, October 28, 1992, and June 12, 1993, and Harwich, January 14, 1994.

6 JE, TRI, by LJF, Cambridge, May 6, 1991, and June 12, 1993, and January 14, 1994, and July 5, 1996.

7 JE, TRI, June 12, 1993, and January 14 and October 20, 1994; Agnete Kalckar, PI by LJF, Cambridge, June 13, 1993. The 300-kroner income from Joan's mother is noted in letter from C. B. Henriques to Ministry of Justice, June 10, 1933, Central Aliens Police File UDL, Case No. 35713, Danish National Archives.

8 Hirsch, TI, June 28, 1993; JE, TRI, June 12, 1993, and Harwich, June 9, 1996; Finn and Martha Abrahamsen, TRI, by LJF, Copenhagen, May 8, 1993.

9 Reimer Jensen and Henning Paikin, "On Psychoanalysis in Denmark," *Scandinavian Psychoanalytic Review* (1980): 109, on Naesgaard; 104, quoting Freud on Harnik as a

"manifest paranoic" and on Marie Bonaparte. Jensen and Paikin, 105, and Asger Frost, "The Reception of Psychoanalysis in Denmark" (n.p. [1992]), 5–6, concerning the Harnik episode. Myron Sharaf, *Fury on Earth: A Biography of Wilhelm Reich* (New York, 1983), 184–85, on Reich's difficulties in Denmark in 1933; see also Benjamin Harris and Adrian Brock, "Freudian Psychopolitics: The Rivalry of Wilhelm Reich and Otto Fenichel, 1930–35," *Bulletin of the History of Medicine* 60 (Winter 1992): 593–94. Evans, *Dialogue with Erik Erikson,* 85, Erikson on Reich, "the same bluish light." See also Bertin, *Marie Bonaparte,* 188.

10 Jensen and Paikin, "On Psychoanalysis in Denmark," 105, on Danish authorities failing to understand the Nazi threat. For the origins of Erik Homburger's legal appeal before the Ministry of Justice and the full documentation of that appeal, see Central Aliens Police File UDL, Case No. 35713, Danish National Archives.

11 Letter from C. B. Henriques to Ministry of Justice, May 15, 1993, Central Aliens Police File UDL, Case No. 35713, Danish National Archives, providing the Abrahamsen family narrative of appeal for the Homburgers.

12 Letters in Erik Homburger's behalf from Marc Kalckar, Lauritz Grun, Hugo Grun, and Viggo Sheitel are included in Central Aliens Police File UDL, Case No. 35713, Danish National Archives, as is Marie Bonaparte's letter of May 1, 1933. Einar Abrahamsen's sworn statement is reported in H. Wiene to Visa Section, State Police, Copenhagen, June 1, 1933, Case No. 35713, Danish National Archives.

13 National Board of Health to Ministry of Justice, June 8, 1933; letter from Ministry of Justice to C. B. Henriques, July 11, 1933, with a note by "E.B." on Homburger's German citizenship status and teaching at the University of Copenhagen. Both are in the Central Aliens Police File UDL, Case No. 35713, Danish National Archives.

14 Letter from EHE to Saul Rosenzweig, December 15, 1975, E-H, recalling "because I could not get my Danish citizenship back." For a contemporary report of Homburger's distress, see letter from H. Wiene to Visa Section, State Police, Copenhagen, July 19 and 21, 1933, Central Alien Police File UDL, Case No. 35713, Danish National Archives. Finn Abrahamsen, TRI, May 8, 1993, recalling his father, Svend, and his cousin Henny reporting how Erik was shocked by the ministry's decision.

15 EHE, TRI, January 11, 1968, and EHE, TRI by Benjamin White, Cotuit, July 22, 1978 (audiotape in Countway Library, Harvard Medical School), on why he and Joan rejected returning to Vienna. Letter from EHE to August Aichhorn, September 7, 1933, AP-SFH. JE, TRI, December 17, 1990, on Sachs recommending Boston.

16 EHE, TRI by Margaret Brenman-Gibson, Tiburon, April 1, 1983, Tape 1, transcript, 21; EHE, TRI, May 22, 1971, Reel 2, Tape A, Side B. Letter from EHE to Bernd Arenz, January 3, 1977, E-H; JE, TRI, May 6, 1991, October 28, 1992, and June 12, 1993, and January 14, 1994. EHE, Harvard Senior Seminar, "Perspectives on the Life Cycle," October 23, 1985, Harriet Harvey videotape, on how Joan "decided to take us to America."

17 JE, TRI, January 14 and October 20, 1994, on the role of Joan's mother in arranging visas and on the American official claiming Erik was ill. Ruth Hirsch and Ellen Katz, TRI by LJF, NYC, August 16, 1991, on Ellen's visit. Manifest of Alien Passengers for the United States . . . SS *Scanmail* from Copenhagen, September 30, 1933, U.S. National Archives (vol. 11638, p. 41, line 10).

18 EHE, "Written for Per Bloland," 1977, E-H. Jon Erikson, PI by LJF, Harwich, June 14, 1994, on the storms and seasickness problem.

19 EHE, "Written for Per Bloland."

20 EHE, TRI, April 1, 1983, Tape 1, transcript, 8, on Kennan as "the first American I met" and "That should be translated." Letter from George Kennan to EHE, November 7, 1950, E-H, "It is beautifully written" and "helped you in the problem." For other memories of conversations with Kennan on the *Scanmail,* see EHE and JE, PI by Michael J. Burlingham, Stockbridge, July 31, 1983, transcript, 5; JE, TRI, January 14 and October 20, 1994; Robert Coles, *Erik H. Erikson: The Growth of His Work* (Boston, 1970), 84.

21 Kai Erikson, ed., *In Search of Common Ground: Conversations with Erik H. Erikson and Huey P. Newton* (New York, 1973), 67, "I will never forget" and "at first narrows your perceptiveness." JE, TRI by LJF, Cambridge, March 12, 1991, and January 14 and October 20, 1994, on Stonorov picking the family up. Betty J. Lifton, TI by LJF, January 24, 1993, on Blos bringing the woodcuts. Betty J. Lifton, TI, January 24, 1993, on Blos telling her he brought the woodcuts. K. Erikson, ed., *Common Ground*, 124, "When you are welcome as immigrants."

22 Daniel Benveniste, "Siegfried Bernfeld in San Francisco," *The American Psychoanalyst* 26 (1992): 13, on the uncritical quality of Fenichel, Bernfeld, and Fromm. EHE, TRI by Nathan Hale, Tiburon, April 29, 1976. EHE, "Written for Per Bloland," on Roosevelt and "Happy Days Are Here Again." EHE, TRI, May 22, 1971, Reel 2, Tape B, Side A, recalling FDR as a "highly playful President" conveying *Spielraum*. EHE, *Dimensions of a New Identity* (New York, 1974), 97–98, on how FDR "appeared always erect" and lifted spirits. EHE, "Autobiographic Notes on the Identity Crisis," *Daedalus* 94, no. 4 (Fall 1970): 746, euphoric about New Deal America.

23 EHE, TRI by Forrest Robinson, August 12, 1970, transcript, 1, "the last moment" and "America still meant." EHE, TRI, April 1, 1983, Tape 1, transcript, 28–29, on the immigration office clerk's "welcome" and its meaning. See also Brenman-Gibson, "Erik Erikson and the Ethics of Survival," *Harvard Magazine* 87 (1984): 60.

24 EHE, "Autobiographic Statement to Freshman Seminar," E-H, on the "breaks," especially of language. EHE, in Abarbanel Notes, October 20, 1969, E-H, on old-world friends. Letter from EHE to August Aichhorn, October 7, 1933, AP-SFH, "I am expecting." EHE, TRI, April 29, 1976, on the visit to Brill who recommended St. Louis. Letter from A. A. Brill to Ernest Jones, November 17, 1933, Archives of the British Psycho-Analytical Society.

25 EHE, TRI, April 29, 1976, on the Brill visit, which he "never took seriously." Evans, *Dialogue with Erik Erikson*, 29, immigrants "gave up old national identities." K. Erikson, ed., *In Search of Common Ground*, 129, and EHE, "Insert p. 921," 1980, E-H, on how his own and America's "identity crisis" resonated with one another.

26 EHE, TRI, January 11, 1968; JE, TRI, January 14, 1994; and EHE, TRI, July 22, 1978 on Sachs's neglecting his promise but inviting the Homburgers to dinner. EHE, TRI, August 12, 1970, "I had to start from scratch." Letter from EHE to Sanford Gifford, February 12, 1982, E-H, "I was so involved." EHE, TRI, July 22, 1978, on the Cobb dinner invitation and Putnam's important role. See also Benjamin White, *Stanley Cobb: A Builder of the Modern Neurosciences* (Boston, 1984), 207, and Sanford Gifford, "Interview with Prof. Erikson and His Wife Joan," November 3, 1984, transcript in Boston Psychoanalytic Society, Side 2, 12. Letter from David Shakow to Erik Homburger, January 18, 1935, Shakow Papers, Archives for the History of American Psychology (Akron), inviting Homburger to visit Worcester State Hospital.

27 Jon Erikson, TI by LJF, August 31, 1996; JE, TRI by LJF, Cambridge, April 12 and May 6, 1991, and January 14, 1994; EHE, TRI, July 22, 1978; letter from EHE to Jon Erikson, October 31, 1966, E-H; Jon Erikson, TI, August 31, 1996. Kai Erikson, TRI by LJF, Hamden, November 7, 1993, on Erik being unwilling to learn about domestic practicalities. Jon and Kai were too young to have direct memories of family dietary and shopping habits; they were sources of family lore on these matters. Henry A. Murray, TRI by James W. Anderson, Cambridge, July 18, 1975, recalling Joan ordering at restaurants for Erik.

28 Homburger's early offices are noted in Gifford, "Interview," 1984, Side 1, 4; Brenman-Gibson, "Erikson and Ethics of Survival," 61–62. For Homburger's unorthodox analytic ways, meeting with children and their families, see, e.g., EHE, TRI, April 29, 1976; Richard Stevens, *Erik Erikson: An Introduction* (New York, 1983), 110; David Elkind in *New York Times Magazine* (April 5, 1970), 26; Florence Clothier at April 14, 1973, meeting of Boston Psychoanalytic Society, Archives of Boston Psychoanalytic Society. Letter from Hanns Sachs to Mark A. May, March 9, 1936, Yale Institute for Human Relations Records (YIHR), Box

9, Folder 67, on how Erik "succeeded." Paul Roazen, *Helene Deutsch: A Psychoanalyst's Life* (New York, 1985), 280, quoting Felix Deutsch on Homburger.

29 *Boston Globe,* March 31, 1992 (Taylor obituary); letter from Otto Rank to John Taylor, October 6 and December 5, 1930, Boston Psychoanalytic Society; Martha Taylor, TRI by LJF, Cambridge, March 6, 1991.

30 Martha Taylor, TRI, March 6, 1991. During this 1991 interview, Taylor stated that she wanted her therapeutic experience with Erik Homburger to be known.

31 George E. Gifford, ed., *Psychoanalysis, Psychotherapy, and the New England Medical Scene, 1894–1944* (New York, 1978), 334–35, on the Boston Psychoanalytic Society's 1930 reorganization and membership requirements; 390, on Homburger teaching the society's first child analysis seminar. Homburger recalled the relationship of his Vienna Psychoanalytic Society matriculation to his membership in the International Psycho-Analytical and the American Psychoanalytic associations in EHE, "Autobiographic Notes," *Daedalus,* 746, and EHE, TRI by Levine and Jacobs, November 13, 1984, transcript, 7. Ives Hendrick, ed., *The Birth of an Institute* (Freeport, 1961), 55, 49, on Homburger's "unusual creativity" on his case presentations, on his offering the Boston Society's first child analysis course, and on his becoming control analyst for children. Gifford, "Interview with Prof. Erikson," Side 2, 20, on Hendrick referring patients to Homburger. George Gifford, TI by LJF, Boston, March 3, 1991, on the general Hendrick-Homburger relationship. Letter from EHE to Saul Rosenzweig, December 15, 1975, E-H, clarifying his precise status in the Boston Society.

32 Letter from Anna Freud to Ernest Jones, November 29, 1934, Archives of the British Psycho-Analytic Society, on "good news about Boston." EHE, TRI, April 29, 1976, "In Vienna you had the feeling" and analysts "were all interested." "Erik H. Erikson: A Biography" (n.d. [1948]), in EHE Academic Personnel File, University of California, Berkeley, Archives, on appointment in 1934 to chair of the Committee on Psychoanalysis in Childhood and Adolescence. Coles, *Erikson,* 180, "had not completed any kind of college" and "I received only support." Letter from EHE to Henry A. Murray, May 23, 1957, E-H, "down-and-out."

33 Letter from William Healy to Mark May, February 29, 1936, YIHR, Box 9, Folder 67, "special gift" and "knows the psychoanalytic." Homburger on preventive checkups in "Symposium on the History of Early Psa. in Boston, April 1973," Florence Clothier Papers, Schlesinger Library, Radcliffe. B. White, *Cobb,* 291, on Homburger at Judge Baker case conferences.

34 EHE, "Studies in the Interpretation of Play," *Genetic Psychology Monographs* 22 (November 1940): 589–97 of this very long article (subtitled "A Six-Year-Old Boy's Secret—John"), is the Judge Baker case in point. Homburger sometimes lectured about this case; see Abarbanel Notes, November 3, 1969.

35 EHE, "Studies in the Interpretation of Play," 663–69, linking John's play configuration to those of other children to reveal the general meaning of play configurations.

36 For some sense of how Homburger was regarded in the Boston area for his success in the case of John, see JE, TRI, April 12 and by LJF, Cambridege, November 21, 1991, and January 14, 1994; Gordon Harper, TI by LJF, April 14, 1991.

37 The Murray-Cobb-Gregg connection and its significance was initially pointed out to me by Eugene Taylor, researcher extraordinary at Harvard's Countway Library. It is alluded to in Rodney Triplet, "Henry A. Murray and the Harvard Psychological Clinic, 1916–1938: A Struggle to Expand the Disciplinary Boundaries of Academic Psychology" (Ph.D. diss., University of New Hampshire, 1983), and in Caroline Nina Murray, PI by LJF, Cambridge, March 11, 1991. The topic cries for thorough research.

38 Triplet, "Henry A. Murray," 240–41, and EHE, TRI, July 22, 1978, both describe Cobb and his perspective. Letter from Stanley Cobb to Mark A. May, March 12, 1936, YIHR, Box 9, Folder 67, on Homburger as "rather speculative" but socially enjoyable and a natural therapist assigned "very difficult patients." Letter from Cobb to EHE, December 8,

1964, Cobb Papers, Countway Library, on Homburger characterizing psychoanalysis as a philosophy.

39 For Homburger's assignments and activities at MGH, see EHE, "Words in Memory of Frank Fremont-Smith" (n.d. [1974]), E-H, "the beginning of a certified career" and a "kind of homecoming," and B. White, *Cobb,* 207–208; EHE, TRI, July 22, 1978. EHE child analysis seminar announcement (n.d. [March 1935]), in David Shakow Papers, Archives of the History of American Psychology (Akron). EHE, TRI, April 29, 1976, "the beginning" and "kind of homecoming."

40 "Remarks by Professor Erikson," 1979, Wright Institute, Berkeley, transcript, 1, E-H, "an intercultural and interdisciplinary encounter." EHE, TRI, April 1, 1983, Tape 1, transcript, 26, "an interdisciplinary setting in America."

41 Murray's orientation and direction of the Harvard Psychological Clinic within the context of the psychology department is treated in M. Brewster Smith and James W. Anderson, "Henry A. Murray (1893–1988)," *American Psychologist* 44 (August 1989): 1153; Triplet, "Henry A. Murray," 11–12, 188–90, 276; Anne Bernays, "A Free-Wheeling Morning with Harry Murray," *Harvard Magazine* 83 (March-April, 1980): 70.

42 Letter from EHE to Henry A. Murray, May 23, 1957, E-H, on the clinic feeling "closest to home" with its "intellectual bunk" and its emphasis on James. EHE, TRI, August 12, 1970, transcript, 1, on Freud, Jung, and James; 9–10, on Christiana Morgan; 12, "the immigrant, the Jew"; 13, an American "sports event"; 12, "Anybody who hadn't come up socially or culturally."

43 Henry A. Murray, *Explorations in Personality: A Clinical and Experimental Study of Fifty Men of College Age* (New York, 1938), x–xi, 16–31; Triplet, "Henry A. Murray," 212; Stephen Schlein, ed., *A Way of Looking at Things: Selected Papers from 1930–1980. Erik H. Erikson* (New York, 1987), 137–38 *n.*15.

44 EHE, "Studies in the Interpretation of Play," 668 *n.*16, on how the Dramatic Production Test was really a clinical exploration. Steven Weiland, "Psychoanalysis Without Words: Erik H. Erikson's American Apprenticeship," *Michigan Quarterly Review* (Winter 1992): 4, quoting Homburger on "psychoanalysis without words." Murray, *Explorations,* 569, for Homburger on testing through play arrangements; 552, suggesting the play construction could be effective with psychotics. "Remarks by Professor Erikson," Wright Institute, 1979, E-H, transcript, 2, "Again I could see."

45 Lewin on Homburger's chapter in "Maturation and Disease as Reported in Configurations," Lewin Group, Smith College, December 29, 1940–January 2, 1941, Jean Walker Macfarlane Docs., AHAP-Akron. Nevitt Sanford, *Learning after College* (Orinda, Calif., 1980), 110. Murray, TRI by Anderson, August 18, 1975, on how Homburger's numerical ratings were off and his approach differed. Letter from Murray to Mark A. May, March 6, 1936, YIHR, Box 9, Folder 67, on Homburger being "not scientifically minded" and uninterested in experiments to test theories as a team player.

46 EHE, TRI, August 12, 1970; "Remarks by Professor Erikson," 1979, Wright Institute.

47 For Homburger's attentiveness to Murray's work on embryology in the development process, see Margaret Brenman-Gibson, TRI by LJF, Stockbridge, March 23, 1991; Bernays, "A Free-Wheeling Morning," 69. EHE, "Growth and Crisis of the Healthy Personality," *Psychological Issues,* Monograph I, vol. 1, no. 1 (1959):52, "anything that grows has a ground plan." Forrest G. Robinson, *Love's Story Told: A Life of Henry A. Murray* (Cambridge, 1992), stresses repeatedly how Murray emphasized normal development.

48 EHE, TRI, August 12, 1970.

49 EHE, TRI, August 12, 1970, "everybody told me that without a degree." For the Homburger-Boring negotiations over graduate credit and doctoral status, see letters from Erik Homburger to Edwin Boring, January 13, 1933 (1934 is the correct date), and n.d. (1934 or 1935); letters from Boring to Homburger, May 14, 1934, and June 19, 1935, both in Boring Papers, Harvard University Archives. Letter from Boring to Homburger, May 14, 1934, indicates that he dropped Psychology 22B. EHE, "Autobiographic

Notes," *Daedalus,* 734, "I flunked" the graduate course. Donald Brown, TRI by LJF, Ann Arbor, November 16, 1992, recalls Homburger telling him of tripping on the Emerson Hall steps when Boring was around.

50 JE, TRI, Harwich, October 22, 1994, on Erik's difficulty settling down in Boston-Cambridge and her discomfort at moving. JE, TRI, December 17, 1990, on Erik's need for more time to research and to write. Letter from EHE to Sanford Gifford, February 13, 1982, E-H, recalling being "so involved" and lacking "the overview." See also "Memo re: Alan Gregg's Interview at Institute of Human Relations, November 16–19, 1936," Record Group 1.1, 200 Series, Rockefeller Archives.

51 William Graebner, "The Unstable World of Benjamin Spock: Social Engineering in a Democratic Culture, 1917–1950," *Journal of American History* 67 (December 1980): 615, on Frank's general significance in the child development movement. Milton J. E. Senn, *Insights on the Child Development Movement in the United States,* monographs of the Society for Research in Child Development, Serial No. 161, vol. 40, nos. 3–4 (August 1975): 2, on Frank as "the catalyst." Letter from Margaret Mead to Frank Falkner, June 11, 1963, Mead Papers, LC, on Frank as father of child development. Margaret Mead, "Letter for Larry's Seventy-fifth Birthday," November 9, 1965, Mead Papers, LC, on Frank's "living networks."

52 EHE, TRI, April 29, 1976, on Frank as "the most maternal man," on his initial meeting with Frank in New York, and on the subsequent meeting in Frank's summer home. See also JE, TRI, May 6, 1991, and October 22, 1994.

53 Letter from Marian C. Putnam to Mark May, February 6, 1936, YIHR, Box 6, Folder 67, "He thinks freely." Letter from Mark May to Herbert W. Shenton, February 1, 1936, YIHR, Box 14, Folder 140, "the leading child analyst." May on Homburger having "no medical or scientific training" as quoted in Arnold Gesell, "Memorandum re: Mr. Homburger," April 8, 1936, Gesell Papers, LC. May, "Notes on Interview with Dr. Adolf Meyer, October 19, 1935," 1 YIHR, on fervor for psychoanalysis in Chicago and Boston.

54 Letter from Erik Homburger to Stanhope Bayne-Jones, October 16, 1937, Series I, Subseries III, General Education Board, Rockefeller Archives, explaining why he accepted Yale's offer with "cooperative research" opportunities. Letter from Herbert N. Shenton to Mark May, May 7, 1936, Lawrence Frank Papers, National Library of Medicine, outlining the Macy Foundation three-year salary package for Homburger. See also letter from Mark A. May to Lawrence Frank, April 10, 1935, Frank Papers, and May to Erik Homburger, April 8, 1936, plus May's "To Whom It May Concern" (n.d.), both in YIHR, Box 9, Folder 67. Don A. Oren, *Joining the Club: A History of Jews at Yale* (New Haven, 1985), especially 124–25, on the anti-Semitic, antiforeigner hiring policies. EHE, TRI, August 12, 1970, on Murray encouraging him to accept Yale's offer.

55 Esther Thelen and Karen Adolph, "Arnold L. Gesell: The Paradox of Nature and Nurture," *Developmental Psychology* 28 (1992): 368–69, 373, 379; Senn, *Insights on the Child Development,* 34; Ernest R. Hilgard, *Psychology in America: A Historical Survey* (New York, 1977), 554.

56 EHE, "Studies in the Interpretation of Play," 559 *n.*1; JE, TI by LJF, March 25, 1991; letter from Stanhope Bayne-Jones to Alan Gregg, October 6, 1938, Series I, Subseries III, General Education Board, Rockefeller Archives; "Erikson" (n.d.), YIHR, Box 9, Folder 67.

57 The study group research project is detailed in Mark May, "Yale University–Institute of Human Relations: Annual Report for 1936–37," 2–3, 19, Record Group 1.1, 200 Series, Rockefeller Archives; Milton J. E. Senn Oral History Collection in Child Development, 1967–75, National Library of Medicine (Edith Jackson interview, May 8, 1970). Louise Bates Ames, *Arnold Gesell: Themes of His Work* (New York, 1969), 235, comments on Homburger's finding that play constructions imitated the adult sex act. Schlein, *Way,* 103–4 (illustrations on gender differences in "Configurations in Play"). Homburger's detailed statistical tabulations on the shapes of boys' and girls' block constructions are reported in a 1938 array of papers titled "E.H. Erikson Research–Pre School Play–Yale," E-H.

58 Letter from Jean W. Macfarlane to Robert J. Havighurst, May 24, 1938, Macfarlane Docs., AHAP-Akron, on Washburn's departure and its effect on Homburger. Ames, *Gesell*, 235, on Gesell's distress with Homburger's seeming sexual emphasis. EHE, TRI, April 29, 1976, and Senn, *Insights on Child Development*, 30–31, reviewing the specific incident that triggered Gesell to deny clinical records. Letter from Arnold Gesell to Erik Homburger, October 20, 1937, General Education Board, Box 376, Folder 3925, Rockefeller Archives, and Arnold Gesell, "Memorandum re: Erik Homburger," October 15, 1937, Gesell Papers, LC, present his perspective on the controversy and the denial of records.

59 EHE, TRI, April 29, 1976, on Gesell becoming overtly hostile and not wanting him around. "Interview of Alan Gregg with Prof. Arnold Gesell at New Haven," October 20, 1938, General Education Board, Box 376, Folder 3925, Rockefeller Archives, on Gesell's inability to accept Homburger as a "free colleague." Alan Gregg diary, June 13, 1938, Rockefeller Archives, appealing to the medical school dean. Letter from Homburger to Stanhope Bayne-Jones, October 16, 1937, General Education Board, Box 376, Folder 3925, Rockefeller Archives, rejecting a "patch up" and seeking assurance of the right to publish. Letter from Stanhope Bayne-Jones to Alan Gregg, June 11, 1938, Record Group 1.1, Series 200, Rockefeller Archives, on "uncertainties" over Homburger's Yale future.

60 EHE, TRI, April 29, 1976, on the YIHR as the only part of Yale interested in psychoanalysis. Mark A. May, *Toward a Science of Human Behavior: A Survey of the Work of the Institute of Human Relations through Two Decades, 1929–1949* (New Haven, 1950), 65; letter from Erik Homburger to Mark May, April 25, 1936, YIHR; and J. R. Morawski, "Organizing Knowledge and Behavior at Yale's Institute of Human Relations," *ISIS* 77 (June 1986): 237, on Zinn, Dollard, Putnam, and the psychoanalytic role at the institute. EHE, "Autobiographic Notes," *Daedalus*, 747, Dollard's "remarkable interdisciplinary stimulation." John W. Whiting, TRI by LJF, Cambridge, March 28, 1991, recalling how Homburger treated Dollard's daughter and how it promoted their friendship.

61 John Dollard, *Criteria for the Life History* (New Haven, 1935), 3, "an account of how a new person," as well as 8, 24–25. May, *Toward a Science of Human Behavior*, 67–68.

62 EHE, "Notes on Freudian Theory" (n.d. [late 1930s]), 3, YIHR, Box 9, Folder 67, lists the four stages as he presented them to the institute.

63 Schlein, *Way*, 77–138, reprints the 1937 "Configurations in Play" article, and 105–14 presents and comments on the checkerboard chart. See 107, "the human organism in the successive stages"; 112, "general impulse to do something."

64 See Milton J. E. Senn, ed., *Symposium on the Healthy Personality: Transactions of Special Meetings of Conference on Infancy and Childhood, June 8–9 and July 3–4, 1950, New York, NY* (New York, 1950), 45, for Hendrick's recollection of listening as Homburger discussed his outline and diagram to institute colleagues plus Hendrick's insistence that this was an early version of the full life cycle model. Mead recalled seeing the same material in J. M. Tanner and Barbel Inhelder, eds., *Discussions in Child Development*, Proceedings of Meeting of World Health Organization Study Group, IV (Geneva, 1956), 141. Mead's reaction is also covered in a letter from Mead to Erik Homburger, January 10, 1936, Mead Papers, LC, B4, "laws of behavior"; Mary Catherine Bateson, *With a Daughter's Eye: A Memoir of Margaret Mead and Gregory Bateson* (New York, 1984), 207, and Jane Howard, *Margaret Mead: A Life* (New York, 1984), 176. See also letter from Erik Homburger to Mark May, February 24, 1936, YIHR, Box 9, Folder 67, seeking to work on correlating children's play constructions to developmental stages. This letter strongly supports the Hendrick and Mead view of what Homburger was up to.

65 The Hull project is covered in Morawski, "Organizing Knowledge," 234–37; May, *Toward a Science of Human Behavior*, 20, 65–66; Marie Jahoda in *The Intellectual Migration: Europe and America, 1930–1960*, edited by Donald Feming and Bernard Bailyn (Cambridge, Mass., 1969), 426–27; Robert Levine, PI by LJF, Cambridge, March 29, 1991; Regna Darnell, *Edward Sapir: Linguist, Anthropologist, Humanist* (Berkeley, 1990), 389–90.

66 Letter from Erik Homburger to Mark May, April 25, 1936, YIHR, Box 9, Folder 67, "to re-write the summary" and his distress with Hull disseminating his remark. EHE, TRI, April 29, 1976, and Darnell, *Sapir,* 389, on Homburger's disagreement with Hull's methodological effort.

67 "Memo re: Alan Gregg's Interviews at the Institute of Human Relations, November 16–19, 1936," Record Group 1.1, 200 Series, Rockefeller Archives, on Homburger's "great difficulty." Letter from EHE to Mark May (n.d. [1939]), YIHR, Box 9, Folder 67, "become a part of it." Letter from Erik Homburger to Mark May, April 25, 1936, YIHR, Box 9, Folder 67, "to work out quietly."

68 For Sapir and his interests and approach, see Darnell, *Sapir,* especially 146, 150, 384, 391–94, and Stephen Weiland, *Intellectual Craftsmen: Ways and Works in American Scholarship, 1935–1990* (New Brunswick, N.J., 1991), 24–25. Robert Levine, PI, March 29, 1991, on Sapir sensing anti-Semitism at the institute. George Goethals, Homburger-Erikson's teaching colleague at Harvard in the 1960s, has investigated his ties to Sapir at Yale. See Goethals, PI by LJF, Cambridge, March 27, 1991, and Goethals's presentation at Cambridge Hospital Symposium on Erik Erikson, October 29, 1994 (tape). John W. M. Whiting, TRI by LJF, Cambridge, March 8, 1991, recalled the Homburger-Sapir connection at Yale.

69 David Elkin, "Erik Erikson's Eight Ages of Man," *New York Times Magazine* (April 5, 1970): 27, "When I realized." Evans, *Dialogue with Erik Erikson,* 61, "before the white man came." Senn Oral History Collection, National Library of Medicine (Mead interview), on the Erikson-Mekeel contact.

70 EHE, "Observations on Sioux Education," *Journal of Psychology* 7 (1939): 101–56.

71 EHE, TRI, April 29, 1976, on Frank as his facilitator who introduced him to figures like Mead and Lewin; on "a continuation with what I had in Vienna"; "the basic ideas in *Childhood and Society.*" See also EHE, "Autobiographic Notes," *Daedalus,* 746.

72 Graebner, "Unstable World of Benjamin Spock," 625, on the Zachary seminar and its significance. Lois B. Murphy, *Gardner Murphy: Integrating, Expanding and Humanizing Psychology* (Jefferson, N.C., 1990), 168–69, recalling how the Zachary seminar was inspired by Homburger's presentations and how he "inspired my subsequent work." Lois Murphy, TI by LJF, June 10, 1991, recalling the presentation of the child distressed by the grandmother's death.

73 Kardiner's seminar and his ideas are treated well in Jerome Rabow, "Psychoanalysis and Social Science: A Review," *Psychoanalytic Review* 12 (Fall 1983): 34–35; Joan Te Paske Mark, "The Impact of Freud on American Cultural Anthropology, 1909–1945" (Ph.D. diss., Harvard University, 1968), 171, 176, 181; Darnell, *Sapir,* 356; Diana W. Warshay and Leon H. Warshay, "Situational Interpretation of Gender Relations," *International Social Science Review* 66 (Summer 1991): 113.

74 Robert Levine, PI, March 29, 1991; Abram Kardiner, TRI by Bluma Swerdloff, 1963, transcript, Columbia Oral History Research Office; W. H. Kracke, "A Psychoanalyst in the Field: Erikson's Contributions to Anthropology," in *Childhood and Selfhood: Essays on Tradition, Religion, and Modernity in the Psychology of Erik H. Erikson,* edited by Peter Homans (Lewisburg, Pa., 1978), 149–50; EHE, TRI, April 29, 1976.

75 For a very cogent analysis of young Mead, her attitudes, and her dispositions, see Helen Carr, "Coming of Age in America: Margaret Mead and Karen Horney," *American Cultural Critics,* edited by David Murray (Exeter, Pa., 1995), 141–56.

76 Howard, *Margaret Mead,* 329, on Mead and Homburger first meeting in Cincinnati. Senn, Oral History, NLM, on Mead recalling expanding Homburger's zonal formulations to the Balinese; see also Mead, *Male and Female* (New York, 1955), 289–90, and letter from Mead to Homburger, January 10, 1936, Mead Papers, LC, B4. Letter from Mead to EHE, June 23, 1939, Mead Papers, LC, B4, "I rely more and more on your" and "Please, please send everything."

77 EHE, "World Views" (n.d.), E-H, "psychoanalytic body image has only openings" and "a

special threat of disbalance." Letter from Homburger to Mead, January 7, 1936, Mead Papers, LC, B4, "every talk with you." Letter from EHE to Mead, June 6, 1939, Mead Papers, LC, B4, helping him with his writing. EHE, "Further Autobiographic Remarks: For Friends and Relations Only: August 1977," E-H, on Mead coaching him on public speaking. Letter from Mead to Homburger, January 10, 1936, Mead Papers, LC, B4, connecting Homburger with Benedict.

78 Ruth Benedict, "Configurations of Culture in North America," *American Anthropologist* 34 (1932): 2, "inner necessities"; 23, "configurations stand to the understanding"; as well as 4, 26. See also Mark, "Impact of Freud on American Cultural Anthropology," 112–14, 123, 126.

79 J. M. Tanner and Barbel Inhelder, eds., *Discussions in Child Development*, vol. 3, Proceedings of Meeting of the World Health Organization Study Group on the Psychobiological Development of the Child (Geneva, 1955), 17, "a similar language." See also EHE, TRI, April 1, 1983, Tape 1, 27–28.

80 Schlein, *Way* ("Configurations in Play"), 77–138; 78, scolding psychoanalysts for failing to see the "spatial configurations."

81 "EHE's Conceptual Structure" (n.d.), 2. YIHR, Box 9, Folder 67, "The greatest power."

82 EHE, TRI, May 22, 1971, Reel 2, Tape B, Side A, "The patients trusted you." EHE, *Identity*, 227, "a kind of moratorium" and "my abysmal ignorance." Letter from Tracy J. Putnam to Mark A. May, March 3, 1936, YIHR, Box 9, Folder 67. Henry A. Murray, TRI by J. W. Anderson, Cambridge, May 12, 1981, "taste for the language." JE, PI by LJF, Cambridge, April 23, 1991, and JE, TRI by LJF, Harwich, January 15, 1994, on her personal and editorial role. EHE, *Childhood and Society* (New York, 1985 ed.), 8, "guide my sentences."

83 Letter from EHE to Jean W. Macfarlane, October 21, 1938, J. W. Macfarlane Docs., AHAP-Akron, on the "Connecticut Yankee housekeeper" and the "old New England" furniture. JE, TI by LJF, September 14, 1996, and Jon Erikson, TI, August 31, 1996, on the piano. JE, TRI, May 6, 1991, noting private school arrangements for Kai and Jon.

84 In Mary Catherine Bateson, *Composing a Life* (New York, 1990), 215–16, Joan recounted the episodes of chicken pox and scarlet fever, as well as Jon's mastoid infection. The crisis over Jon's mastoid infection is also covered in Jon Erikson, PI, June 14, 1994. Letters from EHE to Wendell Johnson, March 30, 1956, E-H, "my wife was hindered," and EHE to Charles Van Riper, March 30, 1956, E-H.

85 The broad historic context for "rooming in," with Mead and Joan Homburger as pioneers, is provided in Raymond Dyer, *Anna Freud Remembered: Recollections from Her Friends and Colleagues* (Chicago, 1983), 162, and Bateson, *Composing a Life*, 216–17. See also Robert Rubenstein, "Erik Erikson" (n.d. [late 1980s]), 5, San Francisco Psychoanalytic Institute; Senn, Oral History, National Library of Medicine, for Edith Jackson's commentary.

86 The context for the departure of Ellen Katz and then her parents from Karlsruhe to Haifa is detailed in Hirsch and Katz, TRI, August 16, 1991; Hirsch, TRI, June 9, 1991; Esther Ramon, *The Homburger Family from Karlsruhe* (Jerusalem, 1992), 76–77. For the fate of the Homburgers in Karlsruhe, see Ramon, *Homburger Family*, 23, 39; Ramon, "Die Familie Homburger aus Karlsruhe," in *Juden in Karlsruhe*, edited by Heinz Schmitt (Karlsruhe, 1988), 467–68; Hirsch and Katz, TRI, August 16, 1991. EHE, *Young Man Luther: A Study in Psychoanalysis and History* (New York, 1958), 10, "the bleached bones."

87 The desperate financial condition of the Haifa Homburgers and Erik's $100 monthly payment is covered in Hirsch, November 12, 1992, and June 28 and November 8, 1993; Hirsch and Katz, TRI, August 16, 1991; Ramon, *Homburger Family*, 77–78. Letter from Erik Homburger to Mark May, May 16, 1936, "assumed the responsibility of supporting."

88 Hirsch, TRI, November 12, 1992, and November 8, 1993, and TI, June 9, 1991; Katz and Hirsch, TRI, August 16, 1991.

89 Last Will and Testament of Theodor Homburger, Haifa, 1942 (document in General-landesarchiv Karlsruhe).

90 United States of America Petition for Naturalization, November 30, 1938. See also United States of America Declaration of Intention, November 28, 1938. Both documents are in the Erik Homburger Erikson file, U.S. Immigration and Naturalization Service. Letter from EHE to Kai T. Erikson (n.d. [1960s]), on the details of his and Joan's naturalization process. A photograph taken of Homburger in 1938 and appearing in the *Daily Californian,* January 23, 1939, shows the dress he wore to file his petition and provides a good sense of his appearance.

91 EHE, "Further Autobiographic Remarks," E-H, "every new American" and "quite common among Scandinavians," as well as being connected to Theodor Homburger through his new middle name and Kai's middle name. Coles, *Erikson,* 181, "I have kept my stepfather's name." Letter from EHE to the editor, *New York Times Book Review* (n.d. [1975]; unsent), E-H, "the name Erikson was chosen." See also EHE, "Memorandum," June 1975, Anna Freud Papers, LC, 96; EHE, "Notes on My Parentage" (n.d. [1978]), E-H.

92 Robert K. Merton, *A Life of Learning* (New York, 1994), ACLS Occasional Paper No. 25, 9, listing several name changes by European Jewish immigrants. Moses Rischin, *The Promised City: New York Jews, 1870–1914* (Cambridge, 1977), 144, on name changes on the Lower East Side. Darnell, *Sapir,* 400, on Winternitz. For a good discussion of anti-Semitism and name changes within psychology, see Andrew S. Winston, " 'As His Name Indicates': R. S. Woodworth's Letters of Reference and Employment for Jewish Psychologists in the 1930s," *Journal of the History of the Behavioral Sciences* 32 (January 1996): 30–43. Letter from Jean Walker Macfarlane to EHE, October 10, 1938, and from EHE to Macfarlane, August 30, 1938, J. W. Macfarlane Docs., AHAP-Akron.

93 JE, TRI, June 12, 1993, and Harwich, October 20, 1994; EHE and JE in Harvey video-tape; letter from EHE to Avner Falk, November 12, 1963, and January 8, 1973, E-H; Sue Bloland, TRI, November 8, 1993; Jon Erikson, PI, June 14, 1994; letter from EHE to editor, *New York Times Book Review* (n.d. [1975]), E-H; Kai Erikson comment at "Erik Erikson's America" session, Wellfleet, October 31, 1992; Kai Erikson, TRI, November 7, 1993. In letter from Kai Erikson to LJF, January 17, 1998, he voiced skepticism over the family account of his role in the name change.

94 Harvey videotape, Erik on "we decided" and then "Joan decided." In this videotape, Joan then gave her full version of the family meeting and her role in it. Letter from Erik Homburger to Jean W. Macfarlane, September 20, 1938 (Joan wanting to be known as "Mrs. Erikson"), and October 21, 1938 (Jon and Kai being thrilled at the name change), both in J. W. Macfarlane Docs., AHAP-Akron. See also Kai Erikson, TRI, November 7, 1993, and JE, TRI, October 20, 1994.

95 The Eiriksson Viking saga is recounted in Ronald Takaki, *A Different Mirror: A History of Multicultural America* (Boston, 1993), 21–22. Letter from Erik Homburger to August Aichhorn, September 7, 1933, AP-SFH, asserting that his biological father had gone to America.

96 K. Erikson, *In Search of Common Ground,* 122, 129.

97 EHE, *Gandhi's Truth: On the Origins of Militant Nonviolence* (New York, 1969), 102, "the child is father." Betty J. Lifton, *Journey of the Adopted Self: A Quest for Wholeness* (New York, 1994), 206, quoting Erikson, "I made myself Erik's son." Harvey videotape, "the freedom in America to become." Understandably, Erikson denied that his new name was "denoting a man's fatherhood of himself" in his statements to the public. See, e.g., EHE, "Further Autobiographic Remarks, August 1977," 3, E-H.

98 Leon Edel, *Writing Lives: Principia Biographia* (New York, 1984), 170, noting that in cases like Ellison and King, name helps to forge a special sense of purpose and responsibility. Caroline Nina Murray, PI, March 11, 1991, on how he could not remain in America as Homburger.

CHAPTER 4

A CROSS-CULTURAL MOSAIC: *CHILDHOOD AND SOCIETY*

1 Letter from EHE to Jean Walker Macfarlane, May 11, 1938, J. W. Macfarlane Docs., AHAP-Akron, on researching less in New Haven and doing clinical work more.

2 Letters from Robert J. Havighurst to J. W. Macfarlane, April 4, 1938; Macfarlane to Molly Putnam, April 29, 1938; Putnam to Macfarlane, May 4, 1938; Macfarlane to Erik Homburger, May 14, 1938 ("the amount you ask"); Erik Homburger to Macfarlane, May 11, 1938. All of the foregoing in J. W. Macfarlane Docs., AHAP-Akron, concern the Rockefeller proposal and the course of negotiations for Homburger-Erikson. See also Lawrence Frank to Macfarlane, November 6, 1938, Lawrence Frank Papers, National Library of Medicine (Container 9).

3 Teresa R. Richardson, *The Century of the Child: The Mental Hygiene Movement and Social Policy in the United States and Canada* (Albany, 1989), 138–45; Ernest R. Hilgard, *Psychology in America: A Historical Survey* (New York, 1987), 543; Jean Loevinger, TRI by LJF, St. Louis, January 12, 1993; Hamilton Cravens, *Before Head Start: The Iowa Station & America's Children* (Chapel Hill, 1993), 197–98, 219–20.

4 JE, TRI by LJF, Cambridge, December 17, 1990, and Harwich, January 15, 1994, on the allure of California and Berkeley public schools. Letters from Erik Homburger to J. W. Macfarlane, August 30, 1938, and Macfarlane to Homburger, September 6, 1938, J. W. Macfarlane Docs., AHAP-Akron, on hiring émigré analysts. Letter from Macfarlane to EHE, October 17, 1938, J. W. Macfarlane Docs., AHAP-Akron, "loss of New England intellectualism." For the attraction of working with normal children and focusing on ego strength, see letter from Erik Homburger to Macfarlane, May 11, 1938, J. W. Macfarlane Docs., AHAP-Akron; JE, TRI, December 17, 1990, March 12, 1991, and May 6, 1991.

5 *Daily Californian* (Berkeley), January 25, 1939, announcing Homburger-Erikson's appointment by the Board of Regents. Jon Erikson, PI by LJF, Harwich, June 14, 1994, on the family trip across the country. Martha Proctor, TRI by LJF, Tiburon, September 13, 1995, on the Baldwins. The campus and general Berkeley setting is described in Robert Nisbet, *Teachers and Scholars: A Memoir of Berkeley in Depression and War* (New Brunswick, N.J., 1992), especially 23–27, 106, 201–206; C. Michael Otten, *University Authority and the Student: The Berkeley Experience* (Berkeley, 1970), 115–16, 126–27, 129 *n.*44; Irvine Stone, ed., *There Was Light: Autobiography of a University. Berkeley: 1868–1968* (New York, 1970), 225, 239–40, 305–8. Marilynn S. Johnson, "War as Watershed: The East Bay and World War II," *Pacific Historical Review* 63 (1994): 315–31, on the nonuniversity community and migration into the area.

6 Troubled Erikson family finances during the early Berkeley years plus new expenses are revealed in letter from Gregory Bateson to George Fielding Eliot, August 11, 1942, Margaret Mead Papers, LC, M32 (including the need to sell the family car); Mary C. Bateson, *Composing a Life* (New York, 1990), 217; and Sue Bloland, TRI, November 8, 1993.

7 Bateson, *Composing a Life*, 218; JE, PI by LJF, Cambridge, May 5, 1991; Jon Erikson, PI by LJF, May 14, 1994, and TI by LJF, August 31, 1996. Sue Bloland, TRI by LJF, NYC, November 8, 1993, July 9, 1994 (on the death of Mary Serson), and November 13, 1996.

8 Letter from EHE to Mark May (n.d. [spring 1939]), Yale IHR, Box 9, Folder 67, "A little teaching." Letter from EHE to Walter Marseille, June 3, 1940, J. W. Macfarlane Docs., AHAP-Akron, quoting Kai ("Daddy, do you want . . ."). Jane Loevinger, TRI by LJF, St. Louis, January 12, 1993; letter from Donald T. Campbell to LJF, July 13, 1993; Daniel Levenson, TRI by William Jacobks, New Haven, February 5, 1991.

9 Letter from J. W. Macfarlane to Robert Havighurst, November 18, 1939, J. W. Macfarlane Docs., AHAP-Akron, "the same dramatic possibilities." Letter from Macfarlane to Alan Gregg, November 18, 1941, J. W. Macfarlane Docs., AHAP-Akron; Macfarlane to Lawrence Frank, March 21, 1939, Lawrence Frank Papers, National Library of Medicine (Container 9). R. J. Havighurst interview, "Erik Homburger Erikson Guidance Study,"

December 20, 1940, General Education Board, Box 375, Folder 3913, Rockefeller Archives; JE, TRI, October 28, 1992.

10 EHE, "Studies in the Interpretation of Play," *Genetic Psychology Monographs* 22, no. 4 (November 1940): 668 *n*.16, "to collect in regular intervals." Loevinger, TRI, January 12, 1993, on Erikson's story for each child. Letter from Loevinger to Donald T. Campbell, July 29, 1993 (copy), on Erikson partially accommodating to the project's methodologies. See also Richardson, *The Century,* 145–46.

11 EHE in "Maturation and Disease as Reported in Play Configurations," Lewin Group, Smith College, December 29, 1940–January 2, 1941, J. W. Macfarlane Docs., AHAP-Akron, "how subjective life space." EHE, "Play Metaphors of Pre-Adolescent Boys and Girls" (n.d.), 1, E-H; letter from Jane Loevinger to Donald T. Campbell, August 9, 1993 (copy); EHE, "Once More the Inner Space: Letter to a Former Student" (1974) in *Women and Analysis: Dialogues on Psychoanalytic Views of Femininity,* edited by Jean Strouse (Boston, 1985), 324; EHE, *Identity: Youth and Crisis* (New York, 1968), 325 *n.3* ("ego strength" as forerunner of the identity concept); M. Blackman, "Inner Space Revisited and Outer Space Reconsidered in the Preadolescent" (n.d. [early 1980s]), 1–3, E-H.

12 Letter from Macfarlane to Robert J. Havighurst, November 12, 1940, J. W. Macfarlane Docs., AHAP-Akron, Erikson "didn't function" and wrote up few case reports. Letter from Macfarlane to Alan Gregg, November 18, 1941, J. W. Macfarlane Docs., AHAP-Akron, "essentially a 'lone wolf,'" "constantly has to be given special privileges," and "a self-seeking and destructive person." See also Havinghurst interview, "Erik Homburger Erikson Guidance Study," December 20, 1940, General Education Board, Box 375, Folder 3913.

13 Letter from EHE to Macfarlane, July 31, 1953, E-H, recalling his displeasure with the institute research and "were already unacceptable to me." Letter from EHE to Maxwell Hahn, January 31, 1955, E-H, "explain significant trends" and "singularly inconclusive results." Letter from Macfarlane to Alan Gregg, November 18, 1941, J. W. Macfarlane Docs., AHAP-Akron, on Erikson seeking half-time work and "a deep personal sigh of relief." Letter from Gregg to Macfarlane, November 21, 1941, J. W. Macfarlane Docs., AHAP-Akron, "My estimate of him."

14 Letter from EHE to Ruth Benedict, March 23, 1944, Ruth Benedict Papers, Box 90, Folder 131, Vassar. See Nathan G. Hale, Jr., *The Rise and Crisis of Psychoanalysis in the United States: Freud and the Americans, 1917–1985* (New York, 1995), 248, on national salary levels in psychoanalysis at the time. Martha Proctor, TRI by LJF, Tiburon, September 13, 1995, on fashionable clothing purchases; Proctor, TI by LJF, August 25, 1996, recalling Orinda in the mid-1940s.

15 Menninger offers to Erikson are noted in letters from Jeanette Lyle to Karl A. Menninger (n.d.), and Karl Menninger to EHE, July 16, 1945, both in KAM. See also JE, TRI, December 17, 1990; Margeret Brenman-Gibson, TRI by LJF, Stockbridge, March 23, 1991; William Gibson, PI by LJF, Stockbridge, December 16, 1992; *TPR* 6, no. 22 (November 2, 1945): 5, and 7, no. 4 (February 15, 1946): 9 (*TPR* was the Menninger staff newsletter).

16 Daniel Benveniste, "Erik H. Erikson in San Francisco" (unpublished ms., 1994), 6–7, 11, on his advance in the San Francisco Psychoanalytic Society. See also EHE, "Preliminary Abstract: *Childhood and Society*" (Orinda, July 1948), W. W. Norton Papers, Columbia; EHE, "Autobiographic Notes on the Identity Crisis," *Daedalus* 99, no. 4 (Fall 1970): 746; letter from Jane Loevinger to Donald T. Campbell, July 27, 1993 (copy); letter from EHE to Anna Freud, March 1949, Anna Freud Papers, LC, "expert on dreams."

17 Letter from EHE to Anna Freud, March 1949, Anna Freud Papers, LC.

18 EHE, TRI by Lerner and Gerzon, May 22, 1971, Reel 1, Tape B, Side A, E-H, on how California colleagues "claim[ed] to be free" in the 1940s but were not. Beulah Parker, TRI by LJF, Point Richmond, October 18, 1994, detailing Erikson's unorthodox analytic techniques from direct experience and noting how Windholz and others attacked his technique. Letter from Donald T. Campbell to LJF, July 13, 1993, on Erikson assign-

ing a Melanie Klein book to his graduate-level seminar. Interestingly, some of the most scathing attacks on Erikson's social emphasis are found in *Rundbriefe* 105 (February 15, 1944): 5, 9; 108 (June 18, 1944): 13–14; 117 (April 20, 1945): 10–12. See also letter from Otto Fenichel to Normal Reider, June 26, 1944, Otto Fenichel Papers, LC.

19 EHE, "Ego Development and Historical Change: Clinical Notes," *Psychoanalytic Study of the Child* 2 (1946): 363, "instinctual energy"; 364, "the mutual complementation"; 395 *n.*15, on Freud's "habitual references"; 360, "what social organization desires," "keeps him alive," "instead of accepting the Oedipus trinity," and "exploring the way in which social organization"; 380, "psychoanalysis came to emphasize" and "only half the story."

20 Ibid., 390, "then we are not dealing" and "child training customs." See also Raymond Dyer, *Her Father's Daughter: The Work of Anna Freud* (New York, London, 1983), 117–18, and EHE, *Identity*, 229–30.

21 EHE, "Ego Development and Historical Change: Clinical Notes," 363, an "awareness of the fact that there is a self-sameness"; 371–72, "to subsume the most powerful."

22 Letter from J. A. Kasanin to EHE, April 28, 1943, E-H (hiring Erikson); Sanford Gifford, PI by LJF, Cambridge, March 24, 1991; Daniel Benveniste, "Siegfried Bernfeld in San Francisco," *American Psychoanalyst* 26 (1992): 13; Stephen Schlein, ed., *A Way of Looking at Things: Selected Papers from 1930–1980. Erik H. Erikson* (New York, 1987), 613; JE, TRI by LJF, January 15, 1994.

23 "Dialogue between Erik Erikson and Joseph Wheelwright," San Francisco Psychoanalytic Society, 1974 (taped and available at the society), recalling the case conference where Erikson replied "so I guess I'll have to speak English." EHE, *Identity*, 17, "lost a sense of personal sameness." EHE, *Childhood and Society* (New York, 1950), 37–38, "their lives no longer hung together." Milton J. E. Senn, ed., *Symposium on the Healthy Personality*, Supplement II (New York, 1950), 16, "a sense of what one is."

24 EHE, *Identity*, 67, "inescapable and immediately clarifying" and "The sense of sameness." Letter from EHE to Andrew J. Weigert, March 27, 1981, E-H, "was suddenly there." Senn, *Symposium on the Healthy Personality*, 70, "a certain intimacy." Schlein, *Way*, 614–17, urging the dropping of diagnostic terms like *psychoneurosis* by wives and community leaders.

25 Erikson's 1945 report "Plans for the Returning Veteran with Symptoms of Instability" was first published in Louis Wirth et al. (eds.), *Community Planning for Peacetime Living* (Stanford, 1945), 116–21, and is reprinted in Schlein, *Way*, 613–17. EHE, TRI by Stewart, January 11, 1968, "I identify with that to some extent."

26 Daniel Burston, *The Legacy of Erich Fromm* (Cambridge, 1991), 4–22, provides useful background on Fromm. Erich Fromm, *Escape from Freedom* (New York, 1941), 206, 254–55, on "identity." "List of the Scientific Papers Read before the San Francisco Psychoanalytic Society from the Time of Its Foundation in March, 1942, through October, 1943" in the Society Archives indicates that on March 1, 1943, Erikson talked about *Escape from Freedom* in a formal meeting.

27 "Dialogue between Erikson and Wheelwright," San Francisco Psychoanalytic Society (tape), 1974; "The Freud-Jung Correspondence: Selected Remarks," San Francisco Psychoanalytic Society (c. 1978), transcript, 39–40; letter from Joseph Wheelwright to EHE, December 21, 1950, E-H. Benveniste, "Erik Erikson," 9. JE, TRI, December 17, 1990. EHE, "Ego Development," 372 *n.*7, evidences Erikson's many uses of Jung. See also EHE, "Preface" (unpublished ms.), June 17, 1977, E-H; letter from J. B. Wheelwright to LJF, May 21, 1992 (dictated to Jane Wheelwright); and Joseph B. Wheelwright, *St. George and the Dandelion: 40 Years of Practice as a Jungian Analyst* (San Francisco, 1982), 7–9, 37–38.

28 Erikson's short 1982 essay on Wheelwright, "My Jungian Friend," in Schlein, *Way*, 713–15, conveys much of the Freud-Jung cross-fertilization evident in their relationship. See also Beulah Parker, TRI by LJF, Point Richmond, October 18, 1994, and JE, TRI, January 14, 1994.

29 Ellen Herman, *The Romance of American Psychology: Political Culture in the Age of Experts* (Berkeley, 1995), and Carlton Mabee, "Margaret Mead and the Behavioral Scientists in World War II: Problems in Responsibility, Truth, and Effectiveness," *Journal of the History of the Behavioral Sciences* 23 (January 1987): 3–13, provide excellent background discussions of the CNM, the CIR, and the OSS during the war. The Margaret Mead Papers at the Library of Congress represent perhaps the best primary source on the interdisciplinary scholarly exchanges that ran through these agencies.

30 Mabee, "Margaret Mead and Behavioral Scientists," 3–13, plus Steven Weiland, "Erikson on America: *Childhood and Society* and National Identity," *American Studies* 23 (Fall 1982): 17; Jerome Bruner, *In Search of Mind: Essays in Autobiography* (New York, 1984), 63; and letter from Karl A. Menninger to EHE, July 16, 1945, KAM.

31 Letters from J. W. Macfarlane to Alan Gregg, November 18, 1941, J. W. Macfarlane Docs., AHAP-Akron, and Alan Gregg to Macfarlane, November 21, 1941, General Education Board, Box 375, Folder 3914, Rockefeller Archives, on Pope's offer to Erikson. Letter from Ruth Benedict to EHE, March 7, 1944, Ruth Benedict Papers, Box 90, Folder 1131, Vassar. Letters from Margaret Mead to EHE, January 17, 1943, November 10, 1944, and May 4, 1945, Mead Papers, LC, B4, exemplify her efforts to involve him.

32 Letter from EHE to Margaret Mead and Gregory Bateson (n.d. [March 27, 1942]), Mead Papers, LC, M32, "more eagerness." Letter from EHE to Ruth Benedict, March 23, 1944, Benedict Papers, Vassar, "I have always wanted." EHE, "Letter from California" (n.d. [1945]), Mead Papers, LC, M32, "to help prevent wars." Letter from EHE to David Lipset, April 16, 1976, comparing himself to Bateson, as quoted in Lipset, *Gregory Bateson: The Legacy of a Scientist* (Englewood Cliffs, N. J., 1980), 172 *n.*; letter from EHE to Margaret Mead and Gregory Bateson, (n.d. [late 1942]), Mead Papers, LC, M32, "an acute case of frigidopedosis."

33 Letter from EHE to Edward Tolman, April 27, 1939, J. W. Macfarlane Docs., AHAP-Akron, "had to stand the scorn of German children" and "I developed nationalistic German tendencies . . . to convince my playmates." Richard Evans, ed., *Dialogue with Erik Erikson* (New York, 1967), 65, "had turned Nazi," attacking "some of my Jewish friends," "to explain this phenomenon to myself," and working on notes of the manuscript. For other Erikson recollections of the paper that began in Vienna and that reflected his German past, see Margaret Brenman-Gibson, "Erik Erikson and the 'Ethics of Survival,' " *Harvard Magazine* 87, *n.*2 (November–December 1984): 60, and letter from EHE to Ruth Benedict, March 23, 1994, Benedict Papers, Box 90, Folder 1131, Vassar.

34 Louise Hoffman, "Psychoanalytic Interpretations of Adolf Hitler and Nazism, 1933–1945: A Prelude to Psychohistory," *Psychohistory Review* 11 (Fall 1982): 68–74, and Hoffman, "From Instinct to Identity: Implications of Changing Psychoanalytic Concepts of Social Life from Freud to Erikson," *Journal of History of Behavioral Sciences* 18 (1982): 138–39, covers this early historiography quite well. See especially Harold D. Laswell, "The Psychology of Hitlerism," *Political Quarterly* 4 (1933): 373–75, and Fromm, *Escape from Freedom.*

35 Committee for National Morale, "Morale in Germany" and "Note on Psychological Offensive against Hitler Personally," as quoted in Louise Hoffman, "Erikson on Hitler: The Origins of Hitler's Imagery and German Youth," *Psychohistory Review* 22 (Fall 1993): 74. Hoffman emphasizes 1942 as Erikson's moment and discusses his three 1942 drafts of his Hitler essay.

36 Schlein, *Way,* 341–45, prints the first of Erikson's reports to the CNM on the "Canadian Project," and 342–43, 345, underscore his theme. It is complemented by Erikson's "Notes on the 'Canadian Project' " (n.d. [early 1942]), Mead Papers, LC, M32, and letter from EHE to Council on Intercultural Relations, February 1943, Mead Papers, LC, M32.

37 Hoffman, "Erikson on Hitler," 77–82, cogently analyzes the sources and revisions for the two unpublished and one published version of Erikson's "Hitler Imagery" essay. In turn,

I have prepared a paragraph-by-paragraph comparison of the 1942 published essay with the 1948 essay and with the versions appearing in both 1950 and 1963 editions of *Childhood and Society.* I can make this comparison available to interested readers.

38 EHE, "Hitler's Imagery and German Youth," *Psychiatry* 5 (November 1942): 483, "subverbal magic design"; 476, "tunes"; 480–81, Hitler as "the adolescent who never even aspired" and "a gang leader"; 486, on how Hitler and followers "relinquished his old self" and proclaimed common doctrine.

39 Letter from Gregory Bateson to Robert C. Tryon, April 15, 1942, Mead Papers, LC, M32. EHE, "Hitler's Imagery and German Youth," 478, on fathers lacking "true inner authority," and 482, on German mothers.

40 Fenichel in *Rundbriefe* 89 (May 15, 1942): 19–20, and 98 (May 7, 1943): 25. See, e.g., William S. Allen, *The Nazi Seizure of Power* (revised ed., New York, 1984), and Richard F. Hamilton, *Who Voted for Hitler?* (Princeton, 1982), for studies going against the class analysis perspective.

41 EHE, "Hitler's Imagery and German Youth," 482–85, on the psychological factors behind lebensraum. This article afforded only cursory incorporation of Erikson's discussion of German "stationary endurance" and the blitz in the context of lebensraum (see, e.g., 489–90). For a fuller discussion of these, see his paper "Comments on Hitler's Speech of September 30, 1942," 16, Mead Papers, LC, M32, especially the portion of that paper included in *Rundbriefe* 98 (May 7, 1943): 24–25.

42 EHE, "Hitler's Imagery and German Youth," 487–88, on the Jew. EHE, *Childhood and Society,* especially 312–14, elaborating on issues of Jewish mobility, identity, and genius. Other psychoanalytic immigrants who shared Erikson's Jewish ambivalence as they described Nazi anti-Semitism are discussed in David J. Fisher, "Toward a Psychoanalytic Understanding of Fascism and Anti-Semitism," *International History of Psychoanalysis* 5 (1992): 221–41.

43 EHE, "Letter from California" (n.d. [1945]), Mead Papers, LC, M32, 3, on the German crisis of "identity" and the split in the German mind; 4, arguing for Nazi Party members not to be categorically disqualified from political participation. EHE, "Comment on Anti-Nazi Propaganda for Council on Intercultural Relations" (n.d. [1945]), Mead Papers, LC, M32, 1, on Germans "who have remained potentially sensitive" and "be put out of action."

44 EHE, "Comments on Anti-Nazi Propaganda," 3, "The very antithesis." Schlein, *Way,* 371, "As far as I can discern"; 373, "Who more than women" and "the matter of reeducation."

45 Schlein, *Way,* 366, "not having been in Germany." Hirsch and Katz, TRI, August 16, 1991, on Erikson's 1946 trip to Haifa and feeling attached to the emerging nation of Israel. See also JE, TRI, December 17, 1990.

46 EHE "Hitler's Imagery and German Youth," 480, and *Childhood and Society,* 294, both deploying the "identify with the *Führer*" phrasing, the latter much more richly.

47 Letter from EHE to Guillermo Delahanty, January 26, 1981, E-H, on "occasional contact" and no "systematic" discussion with Frankfurt School members. EHE, *Childhood and Society,* 372 n.2, on *The Authoritarian Personality.* Project methodology is discussed in Stephen J. Whitfield, *Into the Dark: Hannah Arendt and Totalitarianism* (Philadelphia, 1980), 210. Herman, *Romance,* 58–60, provides good contextual discussion of the Authoritarian Personality project.

48 EHE, "Hitler's Imagery and German Youth," 480, "It frequently happens"—emphasis in original.

49 EHE, *Childhood and Society,* 290–93, on German father-son rapport; 297, on the mother as a "go-between and an in-between"; 295, " 'humanistic' education in Germany."

50 EHE, "Preliminary Abstract: *Childhood and Society.*"

51 Margaret Mead, *And Keep Your Powder Dry: An Anthropologist Looks at America* (New York, 1942); EHE, "Childhood and Tradition in Two American Indian Tribes," *Psychoanalytic Study of the Child* 1 (1945): 348, especially *n.*6, on Mead's portrayal. Rupert

Wilkinson, *The Pursuit of American Character* (New York, 1988), 13–14, provides cogent reflections on Mead's book in the context of early national character studies.

52 Geoffrey Gorer, *The American People: A Study in National Character* (London, 1948), 54, "In few societies"; 56, "encapsulated inside."

53 EHE, "Preliminary Abstract: *Childhood and Society,*" 27–30.

54 EHE, *Childhood and Society,* 245, "can preserve . . . deliberate tentativeness" and "To leave his choices open"; 246, "aristocracy and mobocracy."

55 Ibid., 257, 265, on John Henry; 263–64, "overdefined past," "going places and doing things"; 355, "which was crudely masculine"; 252–53, on travel restrictions of old age and the trailer.

56 Ibid., 248–50, 254, 265, on "Momism" and its roots; 276–78, on family compromises and the traditions of church and political compromises.

57 Ibid., 258, "the stray men"; 214, 216–17, on African-Americans; 274, that white children were "not really intolerant"; 253, on children of immigrants.

58 EHE's psychoanalytic summary of Kenneth for Institute of Personality Assessment, n.d. (1950), 1, E-H.

59 EHE, *Childhood and Society,* 246, "Status expresses"; 247, "jovial friendliness," "seem to lack"; 275, on American "interest groups" and their consequences.

60 George Wilson Pierson, *Tocqueville in America* (Garden City, N.Y., 1959), 468; Cushing Strout, "Tocqueville's Duality: Describing America and Thinking of Europe," *American Quarterly* 21 (Spring 1969): 87–99; Irving M. Zeitlin, *Liberty, Equality, and Revolution in Alexis de Tocqueville* (Boston, 1971), 57–62

61 Schlein, *Way,* 361, "a sweeping synthesis." EHE, "Preliminary Abstract: *Childhood and Society,*" 31. EHE, *Childhood and Society,* 304, 308, "the sons and daughters of all nations"; 242, on American inclusiveness.

62 Robert Nisbet, "Many Tocquevilles," *American Scholar* 46 (Winter 1976–77): 66–67.

63 EHE, *Childhood and Society,* 273 n.13, "invented bigger and better machinery"; 281, on "Bosses" and their effects; 270, "machine ideal of 'functioning' " and "early bowel training"; 254, "standardizing and overadjusting children . . . a mass-produced mask of individuality"; 242, 373–74, on machine society values eradicating America's endearing qualities.

64 EHE, "Preliminary Abstract: *Childhood and Society,*" 25–27.

65 Letter from Mark A. May to Lawrence K. Frank, March 29, 1939, Lawrence Frank Papers, Container 9, National Library of Medicine, Columbia, on the two early essays. EHE, *Childhood and Society,* 96, "mature human living."

66 Mary Catherine Bateson, PI by LJF, Wellfleet, October 22, 1994, on Erikson telling her of the thrill of first reading Benedict's 1928 article. For the Erikson-Kroeber tie and the trip to the Yurok, see Theodora Kroeber, *Alfred Kroeber: A Personal Configuration* (Berkeley, 1970), 115–16; Ward H. Kracke, "A Psychoanalyst in the Field," in *Childhood and Selfhood: Essays on Tradition, Religion, and Modernity in the Psychology of Erik H. Erikson,* edited by Peter Homans (Lewisburg, Pa., 1978), 153; letter from J. W. Macfarlane to Alan Gregg, November 18, 1941, J. W. Macfarlane Docs., AHAP-Akron.

67 Kracke, "A Psychologist in the Field," 149–50, and Regna Darnell, *Edward Sapir: Linguist, Anthropologist, Humanist* (Berkeley, 1990), 395, on early psychoanalytic-anthropological corroboration. EHE, "Childhood and Tradition in Two American Indian Tribes," *Psychoanalytic Study of the Child* 1 (1945), 331, on how the Sioux "roamed the plains" while the Yurok "limited themselves," and EHE, "Observations on the Yurok: Childhood and World Image," *University of California Publications in American Archaeology and Ethnology* 35 (1943): 273, "an extreme localization."

68 EHE, *Childhood and Society,* 138, "strictly institutionalized way," "elastic tradition," and "diverting dangerous instinctual tendencies." EHE, "Ego Development and Historical Change: Clinical Notes," 362, "extensions of the human body." EHE, "Childhood and Tradition in Two American Indian Tribes," 345, on Sioux identification with the buffalo and Yurok identification with the river and the salmon.

69 EHE, "Childhood and Tradition in Two American Indian Tribes," 345, "Machines, far from remaining" and "an unconscious magic attempt." EHE, "Observations on the Yurok," 283, "scientific accounts of children"; 299, "we create isolated places"; iv, "deep estrangement between body and self." EHE, "Observations on Sioux Education," *Journal of Psychology* 7 (1939): 123–24, "hierarchy of centralized bureaucracy," "young American democracy," and "spirit of a hunter democracy." EHE, *Childhood and Society,* 104, "the cheerful ruthlessness of the free-enterprise system" and "Indian problem loses its ancient patina."

70 Kai Erikson, ed., *In Search of Common Ground: Conversations with Erik H. Erikson and Huey P. Newton* (New York, 1973), 54, on becoming more sophisticated about modern America. EHE, "Observations on the Yurok," 299–300 *n.*12, "the remnants of tribal synthesis . . . for the sake," "with race or class replacing tribe," "democratic and national education," and "a new and more universal cultural homogeneity." EHE, *Childhood and Society,* 209, "regions, nations, continents" and "more inclusive identities." EHE, "Environmental Virtues," in *Arts of the Environment,* edited by Gyorgy Kepes (New York, 1972), 73, refers to the Sioux and Yurok self images as "pseudo-speciation."

71 EHE, *Childhood and Society,* 370–73. EHE, "Play, Vision, and Deception," First Godkin Lecture, April 11–12, 1972, 39 (I thank Margaret Brenman-Gibson for this initial draft of the lecture).

72 Letter from EHE to Alfred Kroeber (n.d. [May 18, 1940]), Anthropology Department Papers (Erikson File), University of California, Berkeley, Archives, details Fanny's personal background. EHE, "Observations on the Yurok," 260–62, EHE, *Childhood and Society,* 149–50, and EHE, *Insight and Responsibility: Lectures on the Ethical Implication of Psychoanalytic Insight* (New York, 1964), 55, on Fanny's medical therapeutic techniques and his sense of connectedness to them. See also Kracke, "A Psychologist in the Field," 163–67.

73 EHE, "Observations on the Yurok," 260, "There is a radiant friendliness"; 267, on Fanny's pipe and its significance. EHE, *Childhood and Society,* 146–47, "I could not claim to be her professional equal," "the old woman laughed," and "You big man now."

74 Letter From EHE to Mark A. May (n.d. [1938]), Box 9, Folder 67, YIHR, reviewing criticisms of his work by Macfarlane, Dollard, and others and finding them generally negative. Within *In Search of Common Ground,* 56, Erikson recalls the nature of his contribution and the negativity to it for "idiosyncrasies." See also Géza Róheim, *Psychoanalysis and Anthropology: Culture, Personality, and the Unconscious* (New York, 1950), 270–72, 286–87, and Kracke, "A Psychologist in the Field," 155–56, on how Erikson's portrayal failed to comport with Kardiner's and Róheim's. Fenichel in *Rundbriefe* 59 (July 15, 1939): 16–18, and letter from Clyde Kluckhohn to EHE, March 26, 1944, October 2, 1947, Kluckhohn Papers, Harvard Archives.

75 In "The Unstable World of Benjamin Spock: Social Engineering in a Democratic Culture, 1917–1950," *Journal of American History* 67, no. 3 (December 1980): especially 617–18, historian William Graebner finds that Erikson's perspective was shared by Benjamin Spock and some other thinkers of their generation.

76 EHE, *Childhood and Society,* 368.

77 Ibid., 316 *n.*1; Jane Howard, *Margaret Mead: A Life* (New York, 1984), 278–79; Robert Coles, *Erik H. Erikson: The Growth of His Work* (Boston, 1970), 144; letter from Carleton Mabee to LJF, February 7, 1992, outlining the Benet-Gorer conflict and quoting from his interviews of Benet.

78 EHE, *Childhood and Society,* 316, "What little I know"; 316 *n.*1, on the production of particulars on the film; 340–41, on Erikson's discussion with the translator.

79 EHE, "Preliminary Abstract: *Childhood and Society.*" 33–35. Benveniste, "Erik Erikson in San Francisco," 6–7, on the San Francisco Psychoanalytic Institute presentation. Letters from EHE to Margaret Mead, February 1 and 8, 1949, and Mead to EHE, August 19, 1949, Mead Papers, LC, B4, on the progress of the chapter and reading it to the

Russian Project staff. I was able to review a videotape version of this film in its uncut 1938 format at the Russian and East European Institute of Indiana University. The sources Erikson consulted were listed in his chapter footnotes.

80 EHE, *Childhood and Society,* 324, grandmother "symbolized the primitive trust . . . the peace of mind"; 352–53, "the methods of ancient tools" and "Paradise lost."

81 Ibid., 353, "Wood provided . . . It was the basic material" and the menfolk "are stout, square." EHE, "Preliminary Abstract: *Childhood and Society,*" 33.

82 EHE, *Childhood and Society,* 345–46, expanding Gorer's swaddling hypothesis through "the totality of a culture's configuration" and elaborating on this. See 344 and 347 on Lyenka.

83 Ibid., 353, on the iron and steel imagery symbolized by the wheel, which was essential to the machine; 354, on the Bolshevik machine age of steel and iron, which "is not combustible . . . to master it means . . . steel-like clarity of decision"; 341, "incorruptibility of purpose"; 354, "a planned, meticulously trained elite."

84 EHE, "Preliminary Abstract: *Childhood and Society,*" 33–35.

85 Les K. Adler and Thomas G. Paterson, "Red Fascism: The Merger of Nazi Germany and Soviet Russia in the American Image of Totalitarianism, 1930s–1950s," *American Historical Review* 75 (April 1970): 1046–64, with 1057–60 on Kennan. Ralph Fisher, Jr., TI by LJF, April 1, 1995, on Russian Project staff disagreeing with the "red fascist" construct. EHE, *Childhood and Society,* 355.

86 EHE, *Childhood and Society,* 322–23, "the way stations," "No Luther, no Calvin," "He must learn to protest"; 355, "the temptations Alyosha turns away from"; 357–58, "autonomy, together with unity."

87 Ibid., 357–58. See Weiland, "Erikson on America," 15, for the political implications of Erikson's pleas for American-Russian co-existence.

88 EHE, *Childhood and Society,* 321, on Alyosha's father dying in a "faraway region"; 321–23, on Varvara and her marriage, and Alyosha as "a displaced Pryeshkov" and "finds friends outside of the family."

89 Ibid., 322, "participates rarely"; 350, "literally stalked people . . . wanderer"; 352, creativity through authorship and "tangential to our discussion"; 320, 343, on Alyosha naming himself Maxim Gorky.

90 Ibid., 354, "trained elite of political"; 320, "there is no happy ending"; 355, "the son of a mystic."

91 Ibid., 355.

CHAPTER 5
LIVES IN CYCLE: *CHILDHOOD AND SOCIETY* II

1 EHE, TRI by Robert Stewart, Cambridge, January 11, 1968, recalling dealing with Freud on the superego. EHE, *Childhood and Society* (New York, 1950), 166, on Freud's emphasis on superego-id clash owing to his patient clientele; see also Paul Roazen, *Erik H. Erikson: The Power and Limits of a Vision* (New York, 1976), 109.

2 EHE, *Childhood and Society,* 240–41, 59–60, on Freud reflecting nineteenth-century physics; 239, "The patient of today suffers." EHE, "Talk Given to Freshman Seminar, Spring Term" (n.d. [mid-1960s]), 5, E-H, "identity diffusion in the sense."

3 On the avoidance of Fromm, see Paul Roazen, "Erik Erikson as a Teacher," *Michigan Quarterly Review* (Winter 1992): 19, and letter from EHE to David Riesman (n.d.), DRP, "I have decided to omit all references to Fromm." EHE, *Childhood and Society,* 74–75, clearly drawing on Klein and Balint on mother-child separation without noting them. In EHE, "Studies in the Interpretation of Play," *Genetic Psychology Monographs* 12, no. 4 (November 1940): 570, Klein was castigated for "methodologically irresponsible statements."

4 EHE, "Studies in the Interpretation of Play," 668, "language of play"; 586, "sign level" and hardly an "intermission"; 590, on "repression" and "subverbal experiences." Stephen Schlein, ed., *A Way of Looking at Things: Selected Papers from 1930–1980. Erik*

H. Erikson (New York, 1987), 556–57, "to adapt himself to the verbalized" and "enters the child's world."

5 EHE, *Childhood and Society,* 160, dreams as "the royal road" and play as the way to understand "the infantile ego."EHE, "Preliminary Abstract: *Childhood and Society*" (Orinda, July 1948), W. W. Norton Papers, Columbia, 19–20, comparing children's play to dreams. EHE, *Childhood and Society,* 184, "into synchronization."

6 EHE, *Childhood and Society,* 187, 194–95, 209, 374.

7 EHE, "An Outline of Projected Book *Childhood and Society: Clinical Essays*" (n.d. [mid-1948]), 1, DRP, on the bio-psycho-social approach. EHE, "Preliminary Abstract: *Childhood and Society,*" 7, "everything his business."

8 EHE, *Childhood and Society,* 27, "our first 'specimen'"; 29, Erikson took on Sam while he was in transition between New Haven (Yale) and Berkeley.

9 EHE, "Outline of Projected Book," 1, on the Sam case and how it originated at Yale. EHE, *Childhood and Society,* 25–26, details Erikson's work with Sam.

10 EHE, *Childhood and Society,* 30–31, on the organic aspects of Sam's fits; 27, 31, on loco-motor restrictions; 31, on the issue of ego identity. Maud Mannoni, *The Child, His "Ill-ness" and the Others* (New York, 1970), 34, 40–45, cogently discusses Erikson's failure to address the concerns of Sam's mother.

11 EHE, *Childhood and Society,* 26–27, 31–32.

12 Ibid., 34.

13 Ibid., 34–36. Ellen Herman, *The Romance of American Psychology: Political Culture in the Age of Experts* (Berkeley, 1995), 89, on psychiatric casualties at Guadalcanal.

14 EHE, *Childhood and Society,* 36, "The fever and toxic state"; 36–37, on the marine's background.

15 Ibid., 37–38.

16 Ibid., 39–40.

17 EHE, "Preliminary Abstract: *Childhood and Society,*" 14–15.

18 EHE, *Childhood and Society,* 169, 181.

19 Ibid., 171–72.

20 Ibid., 172–75.

21 Ibid., 174–75, 178–80.

22 Ibid., 180–81; 172, "when they were young enough to perhaps be saved."

23 Sue Bloland, TI by LJF, February 5, 1994, and Bloland, TRI by LJF, NYC, November 8, 1993, on Joan's childbearing experiences and her long-standing views on natural child-birth. JE and EHE, "The Power of the Newborn," *Mademoiselle* 62 (1953): 100–101.

24 JE, TRI, January 15, 1994; Sue Bloland, TRI by LJF, NYC, November 8, 1993.

25 Bloland, TRI by LJF, NYC, November 8, 1993, and May 9, 1995; Bloland, TI by LJF, February 5, 1994; JE, TRI, January 15, 1994; Martha Proctor, TRI by LJF, Tiburon, September 13, 1995; Jon Erikson, PI by LJF, Harwich, June 14, 1994.

26 Robert J. Lifton, "Visit with Erik Erikson, March 23, 1973," RJL-NYPL, 2, telling all three children that Neil had died. Jon Erikson, PI, June 14, 1994, on the lie Erik told him and on sensing his father was not wholly candid. Sue Bloland, TRI, November 8, 1993, and TI, February 5, 1994, on her feelings about Erik's lie and on Kai having been told the truth.

27 Sue Bloland, TRI by LJF, NYC, July 9, 1994, and Jon Erikson, PI by LJF, Harwich, June 14, 1994, on life immediately after Neil's birth. JE, TRI, January 15, 1994, on support-ing Erik's version to her children, on visiting the French hospital, on feeling unable to con-test the decision to institutionalize Neil, and on the places where Neil was moved. Sue Bloland, TRI, November 8, 1993, on Neil undermining the family image, a point sug-gested periodically in JE, TRI, January 15, 1994. Margaret Brenman-Gibson, TI by LJF, January 2, 1993, on the Erikson visits to Neil. JE, TRI by LJF, Harwich, June 10, 1995, showing me dozens of photographs of her normal children and the family of five, finding no photographs of Neil, and with no recollection of ever having photographed Neil.

28 Mary Catherine Bateson, PI by LJF, Wellfleet, October 22, 1994, comparing her mother

Margaret Mead's marriages to Joan's marriage. See also Rosalind Rosenberg, *Beyond Separate Spheres: Intellectual Roots of Modern Feminism* (New York, 1982), 232, on Mead and marriage. Sue Bloland, TRI by LJF, November 8, 1993, and July 9, 1994, and TI, February 5, 1994, and September 18, 1994, provides rich and cogent memories of her parents' marriage in these years. Some sense of the tense marriage and even a possibility of divorce is conveyed in letter from EHE to Anna Freud, March 1949, Anna Freud Papers, LC.

29   Elaine Tyler May, *Homeward Bound: Americans in the Cold War Era* (New York, 1988), 135–61. Voluntary association growth and activities for retarded children and celebrity participation in their behalf is discussed in James W. Trent, *Inventing the Feeble Mind: A History of Mental Retardation in the United States* (Berkeley, 1994), 230–41; Peter L. Tyor and Leland V. Bell, *Caring for the Retarded* (Westport, Conn., 1984), 138, 140, 144–46. Clemens S. Benda, *Mongolism and Cretinism* (New York, 1949), x, reports 1949 data on the pervasiveness of Down Syndrome.

30   For changing research and theories on causes of Down Syndrome, see E. Peter Volpe, "Is Down's Syndrome a Modern Disease?" *Perspectives in Biology and Medicine* 29, no. 3, Part I (Spring 1986): 423, 430–32; R. C. Scheerenberger, *A History of Mental Retardation* (Baltimore, 1983), 221–22; L. T. Hilliard and Brian H. Kirman, *Mental Deficiency* (Boston, 1965), 449, 476. Benda, *Mongolism,* 113–15, elaborated the pituitary-thyroid metabolic disorder.

31   Benda, *Mongolism,* 38, 61, 65, 300–301, exemplified the medical press for institutionalization mixed with the acknowledgment that much could be done for the Down child at home. See also Trent, *Inventing the Feeble Mind,* 237, 241, 266; Tyor and Bell, *Caring for the Retarded,* 137–39; Scheerenberger, *History of Mental Retardation,* 240–41.

32   JE, TRI by LJF, Harwich, January 15, 1994, blaming herself for Neil's birth. David Lane and Brian Stratford, eds., *Current Approaches to Down's Syndrome* (Canton, N.Y., 1985), 33, on 20 percent of Down cases involving the extra chromosome being paternal. Given the extensive writing on modern genetic aspects of Down Syndrome, the Stratford volume is especially helpful to consult. So is Volpe, "Is Down's Syndrome a Modern Disease?"

33   JE, TRI, January 15, 1994, connecting her activities in Orinda and the Austen Riggs Center with her failures with Neil. See also JE, TRI by LJF, Cambridge, March 12 and 28, 1991; Sue Bloland, TI by LJF, February 5, 1994, and October 29, 1997; Bloland, TRI, NYC, May 9, 1995; Mary Catherine Bateson, *Composing a Life* (New York, 1990), 36; Martha Proctor, TI by LJF, August 25, 1996.

34   Sue Bloland, TRI by LJF, NYC, May 9, 1995, and JE, TRI by LJF, Harwich, June 10, 1995, on how the Orinda house arrangements reflected the pattern of family dispersal.

35   Sue Bloland, TRI by LJF, NYC, November 8, 1993, July 9, 1994, and May 9, 1995, in addition to Bloland, TI by LJF, February 5, 1994; Jon Erikson, PI by LJF, Harwich, June 14, 1994; letter from Bloland to LJF, January 19, 1998.

36   JE, TRI, January 15, 1994, on her train trip to visit Neil. Jon Erikson, PI, June 14, 1994, and Sue Bloland, TRI, July 9, 1994, on their grandmother's will. Martha Proctor, TRI by LJF, Tiburon, September 13, 1995, recalling Joan's role in their daughter's abortion; also recalling dinner in Perugia when news of Neil's death arrived. Jon Erikson, PI, June 14, 1994; Bloland, TRI, November 8, 1993, and TI, February 5, 1994; letter from Bloland to LJF, January 9, 1998—all on Neil's burial.

37   William Gibson, *The Cobweb* (New York, 1954), 29, on a copy of *The Idiot* in Reinhart's car. For Joan Erikson's response to this part of *The Cobweb,* see William Gibson, PI by LJF, Stockbridge, December 16, 1992, and Margaret Brenman-Gibson, TI by LJF, January 2, 1993. It is interesting that the character in Dostoyevsky's novel was not an "idiot" in the sense that Neil had been.

38   JE, TRI by LJF, Harwich, January 15, 1994.

39   Schlein, *Way,* 547–68, reprinting "Problems of Infancy and Early Childhood" (1940); 558, "how individuals change"; 549–50, on the fetal development continuing after birth in stages with "the physical and cultural reality"; 561, on conditions in the family. The

relevance of observations of the Sioux and Yurok is brought up in letter from EHE to Alfred Kroeber (n.d. [May 18, 1940]), University of California, Berkeley, Department of Anthropology Records, University of California, Berkeley, Archives, and Richard I. Evans, ed., *Dialogue with Erik Erikson* (New York, 1967), 62–63. Jane Loevinger, TI by LJF, January 12, 1993.

40 In JE-EHE Recognition Reception, Cambridge, November 1991 (tape), Margaret Brenman-Gibson recalled the Menninger Clinic gathering. JE, TRI by LJF, Harwich, January 14, 1994, and June 9, 1995, and JE, TI, March 11, 1995, recalling that Erik increasingly observed their children.

41 EHE, "Concluding Remarks: Infancy and the Rest of Life" (n.d.), E-H, and JE, PI by LJF, Cambridge, June 12, 1993, recalling discovering a play stage. JE, TRI by LJF, Horwich, January 14, 1994, and June 9, 1995 on Erik assuming a wider age range among his patients and on reading Shakespeare with her.

42 Christina Robb, "Partners for Life," *Boston Globe Magazine,* March 22, 1987, 38; JE, TRI, January 15, 1995; JE, PI, June 12, 1993; EHE, "Notes from Harvard Alumni Address, 1977," E-H.

43 EHE, "Notes from Harvard Alumni Address, 1977," E-H, "really ours." JE, TRI, January 15, 1995, describing how different Neil looked and conducted himself from other children, and how she and Erik regarded him. For helpful comparison of the Down Syndrome child to the normal child (which helps to clarify Joan's observations), see Lane and Stratford, *Current Approaches to Down's Syndrome,* 149, 153, 256, 257; Rachael Levy-Shiff et al., "Ego Identity in Mentally Retarded Adolescents," *American Journal of Mental Retardation* 94, no. 5 (1990): 542, 546–47; Hilliard and Kirman, *Mental Deficiency,* 455, 462–63, 475. A. F. Tredgold, *A Textbook of Mental Deficiency,* 7th ed. (Baltimore, 1947), 205, offers interesting commentary on the supposed good temperament of the "Mongoloid" child.

44 Schlein, *Way,* 549, "The result of normal development . . . *monstrum in defectu.*" JE, TRI by LJF, Harwich, January 15, 1994, provided a detailed recall of Neil's qualities as an infant, her feelings while observing him, and general memories of what she and Erik had read about Down Syndrome. Interestingly, Joan's observations were not distant from descriptions of contemporary experts. See, e.g., Benda, *Mongolism,* vii–viii, 32–37, 59, 61, 96–97, 248, 291–92; Tredgold, *Textbook of Mental Deficiency,* 193–207; Barkley Beidleman, "Mongolism," *American Journal of Mental Deficiency* 50 (1945): 35–53.

45 EHE, *Childhood and Society,* 219–22, on trust; 375–77, lauding natural childbirth. These points are echoed in EHE and JE, "The Power of the Newborn," 100–2. Letter from Sue Bloland to LJF, January 19, 1998, on Joan resenting the "idiot" label.

46 EHE, " 'Identity Crisis' in Autobiographic Perspective," *Life History and the Historical Moment* (New York, 1975), 34; EHE, *Childhood and Society,* 60–61; letter from EHE to Harry Wagenheim, November 1, 1982, E-H; letter from EHE to Anna Freud, April 14, 1950, Anna Freud Papers, LC; Raymond Dyer, *Her Father's Daughter: The Work of Anna Freud* (New York, London, 1983), 227–29.

47 J. M. Tanner and Barbel Inhelder, eds., *Discussions in Child Development,* vol. 4 (Geneva, 1956), 143, "the later stages are present in the earlier ones." See also EHE, "On the Sense of Inner Identity," in *Psychoanalytic Psychiatry and Psychology: Clinical and Therapeutic Papers,* edited by Robert P. Knight and Cyrus R. Friedman (New York, 1954), 357, and EHE, TRI by Margaret Brenman-Gibson, Tiburon, April 1, 1983. Milton J. E. Senn, ed., *Symposium on the Healthy Personality,* Supplement II (New York, 1950), 58, on reciprocity and mutuality. Letter from EHE to David R. Matteson, July 30, 1979, E-H, scoring the "search for measurable definitions," which he also does in Evans, *Dialogue with Erik Erikson,* 30. EHE, *Childhood and Society,* 233, and letter from David Riesman to EHE, January 11, 1951, DRP, on the beginning and tentative nature of his formulation.

48 Senn, *Symposium on the Healthy Personality,* 288, "he recognizes that he represents something" and "object relation"; 107, mother "combines sensitive care of the baby's" and

"sense of identity." EHE, *Childhood and Society,* 222, on possession or knowledge without insecurity; 225, "the slow process of becoming a parent." Tanner and Inhelder, *Discussions in Child Development,* vol. 4, 153, "the child's superego is developing."

49 Senn, *Symposium on the Healthy Personality,* 36, 291–92, rejecting "productivity" and "creativity" to capture "a *generative* tendency" and "anything that one produced or created." EHE, *Childhood and Society,* 231, "guiding the next generation," "a parental kind of responsibility," and "stagnation and interpersonal impoverishment." Senn, *Symposium on the Healthy Personality,* 36–37, "still owed him something" and "the pleasure that they could get." EHE, "The Roots of Virtue," in *The Humanist Frame,* edited by Julian Huxley (New York, 1961), 151, "the individual life stages are 'interliving,' cogwheeling" and the "reconstruction of the infant's beginnings." Senn, *Symposium on the Healthy Personality,* 143, "own one and only child."

50 Janet Sayers, *Mothers of Psychoanalysis: Helene Deutsch, Karen Horney, Anna Freud, Melanie Klein* (New York, 1991), 164, on Anna Freud's *The Ego and the Mechanisms of Defense* precedent.

51 Senn, *Symposium on the Healthy Personality,* 58, on identity as the integration of "fragmentary" or "tentative" identities. EHE, *Childhood and Society,* 228, "the inner sameness and continuity." In Senn, *Symposium on the Healthy Personality,* 135, Erikson called this the "sense of ego identity." William Graebner, "The Unstable World of Benjamin Spock: Social Engineering in a Democratic Culture, 1917–1950," *Journal of American History* 67, no. 3 (December 1980): 621, quoting Erikson at the White House conference on a "breakdown of the sense." EHE, *Childhood and Society,* 239, "integrates the infantile ego stages" and "remnants of latent infantile rage"; 228, on settling upon an occupation and falling in love. Senn, *Symposium on the Healthy Personality,* 82, on "passing identity diffusion" lacking pathogenic importance.

52 The continuous pursuit of identity was discussed in EHE, *Childhood and Society,* 228. Senn, *Symposium on the Healthy Personality,* 259, "to derive a sense of identity out of change"; 139, "ready to grasp many chances"; 43, "dominant idea of progress."

53 Senn, *Symposium on the Healthy Personality,* 37, "the individual's ability to accept." Judith S. Modell, *Ruth Benedict: Patterns of a Life* (Philadelphia, 1983), 306, quoting Erikson on "accord with the moral and aesthetic realization" (a 1948 remark descriptive of Benedict in particular and the integrity stage in general). EHE, *Childhood and Society,* 232, "style of integrity," "the seal of his moral paternity," and "death loses its sting." Senn, *Symposium on the Healthy Personality,* 37, "You now become your own parent . . . overcome the sense of dependency." EHE, *Childhood and Society,* 233, "will not fear life if their parents." Senn, *Symposium on the Healthy Personality,* 143–44, "contempt for himself."

54 Senn, *Symposium on the Healthy Personality,* 26, for the chart, including the "social radius" column. EHE, *Childhood and Society,* 238–39, connecting each stage to social institutions. Tanner and Inhelder, *Discussions in Child Development,* vol. 4, 141, "as a series of *encounters.*" EHE, *Childhood and Society,* 222, "represent to the child" and "societal meaning."

55 Senn, *Symposium on the Healthy Personality,* 46–47, quoting Hendrick; 123, "they lack one item: the penis." EHE, *Childhood and Society,* 224, "to modes of 'catching.' "

56 Donald Capps, "Useful Catalyst," *Christian Century* 77 (January 1971): 24, on Erikson's 1946 decision to discontinue articles for clinical journals. Letter from EHE to David Riesman, July 3, 1948, DRP, on moving his overcondensed essays into a coherent outline.

57 Letter from EHE to Ruth Benedict, April 23, 1944, Ruth Benedict Papers, Box 90, Folder 1131, Vassar College, "I still do not . . . a typewriter." "Erik H. Erikson: Biography" (n.d. [1948]), in EHE Academic Personnel File, University of California, Berkeley, on the decision to add six unpublished papers. Letters from EHE to Storer Lunt, August 9, 1940, W. W. Norton Papers, Columbia, "too little time"; July 12, 1948, "I am just about to write a book" and "just for a month or two"; June 1, 1949, on finishing a second draft in July. Letter from EHE to Margaret Mead (n.d. [mid-1949]), Mead Papers, LC, B4, needing to

finish the book as a Berkeley professor. Erikson's advancement to a professorship in the psychology department involved complex variables that shall be addressed in Chapter 6.

58 Robert Coles, *Erik Erikson: The Growth of His Work* (Boston, 1970), 113–14, on the beach house retreat. *Newsweek,* December 12, 1970, 88, on meeting with Wheelwright and others over schnapps. Jon Erikson, PI by LJF, Harwich, June 14, 1994; TI, August 31, 1996, on Erik taking writing to the beach and on Tuesdays by the family pool.

59 Letter from EHE to David Riesman, July 3, 1948, DRP, "Do publishers ever advance" and "and to concentrate." David Riesman, TRI by LJF, Cambridge, March 2, 1991, on the friendship with Erikson rooted in his treatment of Riesman's daughter. JE, TRI by LJF, Cambridge, November 21, 1991; letter from Lois B. Murphy to EHE, n.d., E-H; letter from Carey McWilliams to David Riesman, October 26, 1948, DRP; and Lois B. Murphy, *Gardner Murphy* (Jefferson, N.C., 1990), 168–69, on the initial difficulty getting a publisher for *Childhood and Society.* Donald S. Lamm, TI by LJF, June 23, 1995, on Binger's consultantship status at Norton and his friendship with Lunt.

60 Negotiations between Erikson and Norton are covered in letter from Storer Lunt to EHE, June 22, 1948, W. W. Norton Papers, Columbia; EHE, TRI by Robert Stewart, Cambridge, January 11, 1968; letter from Donald S. Lamm to LJF, October 26, 1995, and Lamm, TI by LJF, August 30, 1994, and April 4, 1995. Letters from Lunt to EHE, November 18, 1949, Norton Papers, outlining the terms of Erikson's contract; EHE to Lunt, May 5, 1950, Norton Papers, "I need money"; Lunt to EHE, May 9, 1950, Norton Papers, sending a $500 advance.

61 Letters from EHE to William Gibson (n.d.), E-H, "never had a mother tongue"; Katherine Barnard to EHE, December 9, 1949, and Storer Lunt to EHE, November 18, 1949, both in W. W. Norton Papers, Columbia; EHE to Lunt, July 6, 1949, Norton Papers, "I expect to have certain details." Joan Erikson's role as editor is discussed in EHE, *Identity: Youth and Crisis* (New York, 1968), 112; Ellen Katz and Ruth Hirsch, TRI by LJF, NYC, August 16, 1991; JE, PI by LJF, Cambridge, August 16, 1990; M. C. Bateson, *Composing,* 83; C. Robb, "Partners," 36. EHE, TRI by Lerner and Gerzon, Reel 1, Tape A, Side B, May 22, 1971, E-H, "It was the transfer of an artistic." Herman, *Romance,* 180, on the Myrdals. JE, *Legacies: Prometheus, Orpheus, Socrates* (New York, 1993), identifying with Pietho.

62 EHE, TRI by Robert Stewart, Cambridge, January 11, 1968, on writing for a widely educated audience and not for psychoanalysts. EHE, "Preliminary Abstract: *Childhood and Society,*" 21–22, on the Irma Dream. JE, TRI by LJF, Harwich, January 15, 1994, on the audience issue and deletion of the Irma Dream essay at roughly the same time the life cycle essay was added as Chapter 7. Letter from David Riesman to EHE, August 18, 1948, DRP, urging inclusion of the Irma Dream essay, and Riesman, TRI by LJF, Cambridge, March 2, 1991. Erikson's Irma Dream essay appeared as "The Dream Specimen of Psychoanalysis," *Journal of the American Academy of Psychoanalysis,* 2 (1954): 5–56.

63 For Erikson's thoughts on his audience, see EHE, "Preliminary Abstract: *Childhood and Society,*" 1; EHE, "Gandhi's Truth: Miscellaneous Papers" (n.d.), E-H; EHE, *Childhood and Society* (revised ed., 1963, 1985), 13, "Afterthoughts 1985." Letter from Storer Lunt to EHE, November 18, 1949, W. W. Norton Papers, Columbia, "a little scattered" and "does hold together nicely."

64 Letter from EHE to Katherine Barnard, April 10, 1950, W. W. Norton Papers, Columbia, "too specific." EHE, "Preliminary Outline: *Childhood and Society,*" 1, "living historical ideas." EHE, "Childhood and Society" blurb for W. W. Norton (1950), "the relationship between childhood training." EHE, *Childhood and Society,* 11, "anxiety in young children, apathy"; 42, on the four clusters arrangement. EHE, "Autobiographic Statement to Freshman Seminar" (n.d. [early 1960s]), E-H, "identity held them."

65 Steven Wieland, "Psychoanalysis without Words: Erik H. Erikson's American Apprenticeship," *Michigan Quarterly Review* (Winter 1992): 13, underscores *Childhood and Society's* varied evidential base. EHE, *Childhood and Society,* 12–13, "a subjective book."

66 EHE, *Childhood and Society,* 11–12, "a psychoanalytic book" and "the ego's roots." EHE, "Abstract of Lectures for the Second and Fourth Days of the Scandinavian Seminar" (n.d. [1952]), E-H, 1–2, "The functioning society."
67 EHE, *Childhood and Society,* 359, "I have nothing."
68 EHE, "Preliminary Abstract: *Childhood and Society,*" introduction, "on the residues within one." Tanner and Inhelder, *Discussions in Child Development,* vol. 3, 17, "configurational level," "the obvious, manifest behavior," and "sides come to some kind."
69 Suzanne R. Kirschner, "The Assenting Echo: Anglo-American Values in Contemporary Psychoanalytic Developmental Psychology," *Social Research* 57, no. 4 (Winter 1990): 848 *n.*57. Rupert Wilkinson, *The Pursuit of American Character* (New York, 1988).
70 EHE, "Autobiographic Notes on the Identity Crisis," *Daedalus* 94 (Fall 1970): 744, "a writing psychoanalyst" and "to repay my debt."
71 EHE, *Childhood and Society* ("Afterthought 1985"), 14, "the first phase." Letter from EHE to David Riesman, July 3, 1948, DRP, "leave childhood behind." Hetty Zock, *A Psychology of Ultimate Concern: Erik H. Erikson's Contribution to the Psychology of Religion* (Amsterdam, 1990), 86, on basic trust in *Childhood and Society* as the basis of Erikson's approach to religion. Kai Erikson, ed., *In Search of Common Ground: Conversations with Erik H. Erikson and Huey P. Newton* (New York, 1973), 54, "my first book was written during the Roosevelt era."
72 Letter from EHE to Katherine Barnard, April 10, 1950, W. W. Norton Papers, Columbia.
73 *Childhood and Society* sales and distribution history from 1950 to 1963 is covered in letters from EHE to Katherine Barnard (n.d. [spring 1951]); Storer Lunt to EHE, March 11, 1955; George P. Brockway to EHE, November 27, 1961 (all in W. W. Norton Papers, Columbia). George P. Brockway, TI by LJF, January 29, 1994; Donald S. Lamm, TI by LJF, August 30, 1994; letter from Lamm to LJF, July 5, 1994.
74 Letters from EHE to Storer Lunt, September 1, 1951, W. W. Norton Papers, Columbia, "no idea how many copies"; EHE to Katherine Barnard, October 1950, W. W. Norton Papers, Columbia, "I don't know." See, e.g., letters from EHE to H. P. Wilson, March 7, 1952, and EHE to Lunt, September 11, 1953, and November 12, 1958, W. W. Norton Papers, Columbia, requesting advance royalty checks. Letter from EHE to Barnard, May 1, 1951, W. W. Norton Papers, Columbia, on the *New York Times* review. EHE, TRI by Robert Stewart, Cambridge, January 11, 1968, "I was simply saying."
75 Letter from David Riesman to EHE, January 11, 1951, and Riesman, TRI by LJF, Cambridge, March 2, 1991; letter from David Rapaport to EHE, October 9, 1950, E-H. Robert Holt in *Journal of Personality* 21, no. 1 (September 1952): 153. Letter from Joseph B. Wheelwright to EHE, December 21, 1950, E-H. Martin Grotjahn in *Psychoanalytic Quarterly* 20, no. 2 (1951): 293. Letter from Robert Knight to EHE and JE, November 15, 1950, E-H. Walter Bromberg in *Mental Hygiene* (October 1951): 644.
76 EHE, *Childhood and Society,* 12–13, "is and must be a subjective book." Robert W. White in *Journal of Abnormal and Social Psychology* 46 (July 1951): 447–48; letter from Gary Kern to EHE, July 27, 1971, E-H; letter from Henry A. Murray to EHE, February 6, 1952, E-H. Letter from Karl A. Menninger to EHE, July 15, 1954, KAM.
77 Esther Menaker, TI by LJF, February 12, 1995, recalled Anna Freud telling her that she disapproved of the book. Letter from Lois Murphy to EHE (n.d. [fall 1976]), E-H, on how Erikson was hurt by Anna Freud's charge that the book was "sociology." Letter from Ernst Kris to Anna Freud, November 1, 1950, Anna Freud Papers, LC. Géza Róheim, *Psychoanalysis and Anthropology* (New York, 1950), 272, 286–88, and Róheim as quoted in Paul Robinson, *The Freudian Left: Wilhelm Reich, Géza Róheim, Herbert Marcuse* (New York, 1969), 144–45. Mable Blake Cohen in *Psychiatry* 14, no. 3 (August 1951): 351; letter from Barrington Moore to McGeorge Bundy, May 22, 1959, Ad Hoc Committee on Human Development, Harvard Archives. Beatrice Whiting in *American Sociological Review* 16, no. 3 (June 1951): 414

78 Elkind in Milton Senn, ed., "Oral History of the Child Development Movement," National Library of Medicine, January 31, 1973; Robert Rubenstein, "Erik Erikson" (n.d. [late 1980s]), 6, San Francisco Psychoanalytic Institute. Abram Kardiner, "Reminiscences," 223, 225, Rare Books and Manuscripts Div., Butler Library, Columbia University (1963).

79 EHE, "Bibliography" (January 1966), Archives of the History of American Psychology, University of Akron, 7, on foreign editions. Nathan Hale, *The Rise and Crisis of Psychoanalysis in the United States: Freud and the Americans, 1917–1985* (New York, 1995), 253, on psychiatric residency program adoptions. Letter from EHE to David and Evelyn Riesman (n.d. [mid-1950s]), DRP, including Rockwell's sketch of Tom Sawyer reading *Childhood and Society.* Donald S. Lamm, TI by LJF, June 23, 1995, on the tripling of sales with paperback publication. Coles, *Erik Erikson,* xi–xiv. Mead in *American Scholar* 30, no. 4 (Autumn 1961): 614–15. Letter from Lamm to LJF, July 5, 1994, contains many cogent insights on changing sales patterns for *Childhood and Society* from the perspective of W. W. Norton and Company.

CHAPTER 6
VOICE AND AUTHENTICITY: THE 1950S

1 Letter from EHE to Henry A. Murray, May 23, 1957, E-H.

2 John Caughey, "A University in Jeopardy," *Harper's Magazine* 201, no. 1206 (November 1950): 68; Joan E. Grold, "A History of the University of California Psychology Department at Berkeley" (unpublished ms., 1961), 32, 44–45; Robert Levine, PI by LJF, Cambridge, March 29, 1991.

3 Grold, "A History," 25–26; Harrison G. Gough, "Along the Way: Recollections of Some Major Contributors to Personality Assessment," *Journal of Personality Assessment* 52, no. 1 (1988): 14–15; Ellen Herman, *The Romance of American Psychology: Political Culture in the Age of Experts* (Berkeley, 1995), 44–46. I have not been able to discover why Tolman came out strongly for Erikson even though Macfarlane was very influential in his psychology department and had a poor view of Erikson. My suspicion is that Sanford's influence on Tolman proved decisive.

4 The Arts and Sciences exploratory committee's report is from E. C. Tolman et al. to A. R. Davis, January 26, 1949, EHE Personnel File, University of California, Berkeley, Archives, Bancroft Library. Berkeley psychology department interest is indicated in letter from Robert C. Tryon to Robert G. Sproul, January 13 and March 1, 1949, EHE Personnel File. Minutes, University of California Budget Committee, February 1, 1949, EHE Personnel File. "Biography," EHE Personnel File, indicating the salary and formal appointment. Letter from Robert P. Knight to EHE, March 23, 1948, Adele Boyd private papers, on Yale's interest in hiring Erikson before the Berkeley offer.

5 EHE–Joseph Wheelwright dialogue (tape), San Francisco, 1974, San Francisco Psychoanalytic Society, on Freud never having been "a full, active professor." Letter from Karl Menninger to EHE, May 12, 1949, KAM, on the Menninger Foundation offer. Letters from Margaret Mead to EHE, February 8, 1949, Mead Papers, LC, B4, recommending Berkeley; EHE to Margaret Mead, February 8, 1949, Mead Papers, LC, B4, "know my weaknesses."; EHE to Anna Freud, March 1949, Anna Freud Papers, LC. "Biography," EHE Personnel File, on the formal appointment and resignation dates at Berkeley.

6 David L. Marsden, "The Cold War and American Education" (Ph.D. diss., University of Kansas, 1975), 248, 275, on the emergence of anticommunism and loyalty oaths. "Editorial Notes: The California Loyalty Oath," *Psychiatry* 15 (1951): 243, reproduces an 1849 California Constitution provision requiring an oath and the May 1949 UC loyalty oath. The course of the actions by the Board of Regents and faculty protests are covered in David P. Gardner, *The California Oath Controversy* (Berkeley, Los Angeles, 1967), especially 10, 27, 116, 154–55, 159; George R. Stewart, *The Year of the Oath: The Fight for Academic*

Freedom at the University of California (Garden City, N.Y., 1950), 40, 138; Nevitt Sanford, "Individual and Social Change in a Community Under Pressure: The Oath Controversy," *Journal of Social Issues* 9, no. 3 (1953): 25–26, 35; Richard M. Fried, *Nightmare in Red: The McCarthy Era in Perspective* (New York, 1990), 105; C. Michael Otten, *University Authority and the Student: The Berkeley Experience* (Berkeley, 1970), 113 *n.9.*

7 Marsden, "Cold War," 279–80; Nancy K. Innis, "Lessons from the Controversy Over the Loyalty Oath at the University of California," *Minerva* 30 (1992): 339–40, 343, 356; Sanford, "Individual and Social Change," 37–38; Stewart, *Year of the Oath,* 39.

8 Donald MacKinnon, "Report of the Special Loyalty Oath Controversy at the University of California" (n.d. [August 31, 1950]), 8–9, IPAR Archives, University of California, Berkeley; letter from Nevitt Sanford to LJF, Berkeley, June 30, 1991; letter from Harrison G. Gough to LJF, Pebble Beach, Calif., February 23, 1993; Innis, "Lessons from the Controversy," 347–48; Donald R. Brown, TRI by LJF, Ann Arbor, November 16, 1992; Grold, "A History," 32.

9 Erikson's discomfort at IPAR is indicated in Donald Brown, TRI by LJF, November 16, 1992, and Francis X. Barron, TI by LJF, February 11, 1993. Nevitt Sanford, TRI by LJF, Berkeley, February 10, 1993, on his discomfort with the psychology department. Letter from Donald T. Campbell to LJF, July 13, 1993, recalling Erikson much prizing his professorship. Letter from EHE to Robert P. Knight, December 29, 1950, Margaret Brenman-Gibson private papers, "academic life has become." Letter from EHE to Anna Freud, February 1, 1951, Anna Freud Papers, LC, "the time has passed."

10 JE, TRI by LJF, Cambridge, May 6, 1991, on fears of losing the Orinda home but on the need, too, to hold firm against the oath. *California Labor School* (Winter 1945): 14, a catalog, lists Erikson teaching "Mental Hygiene Today." Jon Erikson, PI by LJF, Harwich, June 14, 1994, on his high school essay, and letter from Kai Erikson to LJF, January 17, 1998, on his anti-oath activity. Sue Bloland, TRI by LJF, NYC, July 9, 1994, and May 9, 1995, on the Neil issue and on Joan pressuring Erik to hold firm.

11 David Riesman, TRI by LJF, Cambridge, March 2, 1991, elaborated Erikson's reservations, as an immigrant, to speak out against the oath. Letter from EHE to Henry Kellerman, November 30, 1951, E-H, "the psychological spirit of the Constitution." EHE, "Autobiographic Notes on the Identity Crisis," *Daedalus* 99, no. 4 (Fall 1970): 747, "a test of my American identity" and on Korea. "Remarks by Professor Erikson," 1979, 3, Wright Institute, Berkeley, "what had happened in Europe."

12 Innis, "Lessons from the Controversy," 339–40, on Kantorowicz. Sanford, "Individual and Social Change," 28, connecting *The Authoritarian Personality* to the oath. Donald Brown, TRI by LJF, November 11, 1992, on Erikson's seminars. Francis X. Barron, TI by LJF, February 11, 1993, on the Nazi comparison provoking both fear in Erikson and a sense of necessity in opposing the oath.

13 "Editorial Notes: The California Loyalty Oath," 243–45, printed Erikson's full statement against the oath.

14 Ibid., on his students. For Erikson's support of junior faculty, see EHE, "Perspectives on the Life Cycle," Harvard Senior Seminar, Cambridge, October 23, 1985, "Perspectives on the Life Cycle," Harvard Senior Seminar, October 23, 1985, Harriet Harvey videotape; EHE, *Life History and the Historical Moment* (New York, 1975), 42; JE, TRI by LJF, Cambridge, December 17, 1990, and Harwich, January 15, 1994.

15 "Editorial Notes: The California Loyalty Oath," 243–45.

16 "Erik H. Erikson" (n.d. [1950]), for the committee's exoneration of him, and "Biography," EHE Personnel File, for the June 30, 1950, resignation date—both documents are in the University of California, Berkeley, Archives. For Erikson's public explanation for resigning, see EHE, *Life History,* 42, and EHE, Harvey videotape.

17 Letter from Donald W. MacKinnon to Alan Gregg, August 14, 1950, Record Group 1.2, Series 205A, Box 3, Folder 18, Rockefeller Archive Center (emphasis mine and not MacKinnon's). Caughey, "A University in Jeopardy," 73, on some faculty seeing moral

victory with the "new form of contract." Harrison G. Gough, TI by LJF, February 9, 1993, recalling how he and other IPAR staff saw the "new form" as a ruse.

18 Donald R. Brown, TRI by LJF, Ann Arbor, November 16, 1992, recalling that Erikson worked at IPAR in 1950–51. Wallace Hall, TI by LJF, February 10, 1993, reported that he did not find Erikson's name in 1950–51 IPAR proceedings. Letter from MacKinnon to Gregg, August 14, 1950, seeking funds for Sanford and Barron but that Erikson was "to continue his work." Erikson's curriculum vitae for 1959 in his Harvard Personnel File (Harvard Archives) and a subsequent undated vita prepared in the 1970s (E-H) list UC employee status until 1951.

19 Letter from Harrison G. Gough to LJF, Pebble Beach, Calif., February 27, 1993. Nevitt Sanford, TRI by LJF, Berkeley, February 10, 1993. I may be too harsh on Erikson's conduct. I am a "red diaper baby" who sued the University of California to remove its ban on Communist speakers when I was a junior in college. Equivocation in the face of McCarthyism has always been troubling to me personally.

20 Gardner, *California Oath Controversy,* 234–38, 242; *Tolman et al.* vs. *Underhill et al.,* 249 P.2d 280 (1952).

21 Letter from EHE to Karl A. Menninger, February 25, 1951, KAM; letter from David Riesman to EHE, October 26, 1950, DRP; letter from Storer B. Lunt to EHE, September 6, 1951, W. W. Norton Papers, Columbia.

22 Robert J. Lifton, PI by LJF, Bowling Green, Ohio, March 5, 1993, and Robert J. Lifton, TI by LJF, September 3, 1992, on how Erikson never characterized his oath posture as a moment of conscience or talked much about it. Letters from EHE to David Riesman, December 30, 1950, DRP, and EHE to Katherine Barnard, February 1, 1951, W. W. Norton Papers, Columbia. In JE, TRI by LJF, Cambridge, October 28, 1992, Joan explained that Erik discovered a new vocal presence and an inner reservoir of strength as he came out publicly against the loyalty oath, but felt this effort at self-discovery was incomplete—actually left dangling.

23 EHE, "Wholeness and Totality: A Psychiatric Contribution," in *Totalitarianism,* edited by Carl J. Frederich (New York, 1954), 163, "a sense of continuity and sameness" within wholeness; 162, on totality, which, "evokes a *Gestalt*"; 170, "a synthetic identity . . . a totally stereotyped enemy . . . totalitarian conditions"; 171, "wider and firmer identities . . . evolve a new world-image." See Christopher Lasch, *The Culture of Narcissism: American Life in an Age of Diminishing Expectations* (New York, 1991), 167–70, on the cult of authenticity.

24 Letters from EHE to Karl Menninger February 21, 1951, KAM, and Henry W. Brosin to EHE, February 20, 1951, E-H.

25 Lawrence J. Friedman, *Menninger: The Family and the Clinic* (New York, 1990), 212–13; Stephen Schlein, ed., *A Way of Looking at Things: Selected Papers from 1930–1980. Erik H. Erikson* (New York, 1987), 733–34, 737; "Erik Erikson at Austen Riggs," Stockbridge, November 22, 1985, Harvey videotape; JE, TRI by LJF, Cambridge, December 17, 1990; Margaret Brenman-Gibson, TRI by LJF, Stockbridge, March 23, 1991; EHE, "Robert Knight" (unpublished ms., 1969), 2, E-H.

26 Letter from EHE to Anna Freud, February 1, 1951, Anna Freud Papers, LC, on the Pittsburgh professorship. Letter from EHE to Karl Menninger, February 25, 1951, KAM, "My introversion." Donald Brown, TRI by LJF, November 16, 1992, recalling how Erikson asked him about Stockbridge anti-Semitism. Letter from EHE to Robert P. Knight, December 29, 1950, Margaret Brenman-Gibson private papers, on the large house. Schlein, *Way,* 733–34, on Knight's qualities. Brenman-Gibson,TRI by LJF, Stockbridge, March 23, 1991, on Erikson's admiration for Knight's looks and American qualities. Letter from Knight to EHE and JE, November 15, 1950, E-H, "just bursting." Letter from EHE to Riesman, December 31, 1950, DRP, "make excursions from Stockbridge."

27 Erikson's income sources and professional duties are reported in "National Register of

Scientific & Technical Personnel in the Field of Psychology" (n.d. [1957]), E-H, and letter from EHE to Max Levin, June 5, 1957, E-H.

28 EHE at Austen Riggs Center, November 22, 1985, Harvey videotape, "I'm an immigrant." EHE, "Robert Knight," 7–8, E-H, on walking with Knight and Rapaport and hearing their jokes. William Gibson, PI by LJF, Stockbridge, December 16, 1992, on his rapport with Erikson. Letters from Ursula M. Niebuhr to LJF, March 22, 1992, and Mrs. Reinhold Niebuhr to Seward Hiltner, March 18, 1970, Seward Hiltner Papers, Princeton Theological Seminary, on the Erikson relationship. David and Evelyn Riesman, TRI by LJF, Cambridge, March 2, 1991, on friendship with the Eriksons.

29 Aspects of the developing Kai-Erik relationship in the 1950s are covered in letters from EHE to David Riesman, November 13 and 24, 1956; David Riesman to Kai Erikson, May 8, 1953; Kai Erikson to David Riesman (n.d. [1957])—all in DRP. Letter from David Riesman to Wendell Bell, January 8, 1969, DRP, on the difficulty of being seen as Erik Erikson's son. EHE and Kai Erikson, "The Confirmation of the Delinquent," *Chicago Review,* 10 (Winter 1957): 14–23. Letter from Reinhard Bendix to EHE, October 24, 1958, E-H, Erikson's reply on the original letter on how he "would like to work with him."

30 Jon Erikson, PI by LJF, Harwich, June 14, 1994, and TI by LJF, August 31, 1996, reviewing his early life and his relationship with Erik. Letters from EHE to Charles Van Ripper, March 20, 1956, E-H, and EHE to Wendell Johnson, March 30, 1956, E-H, trying to help with Jon's stuttering problem.

31 Letter from Sue Bloland to LJF, January 19, 1998; Bloland, TRI by LJF, NYC, July 9, 1994, and May 9, 1995; Bloland, TI by LJF, September 18, 1994; Margaret Brenman-Gibson, PI by LJF, Cambridge, April 23, 1991. Letter from EHE to Isabel Stevens, September 2, 1952, E-H, on Sue's grade placement in the Putney School.

32 JE, "A Study of the Effect of Replacing Occupational Therapy with a Program of Activities Based on Building 'Ego Interests' in a Psychiatric Patient Group" (unpublished ms., 1952), Rockefeller Bros. Fund Ms., Rockefeller Archives, Tarrytown; JE, TRI by LJF, Cambridge, December 18, 1990, and March 28, 1991, and Harwich, January 15, 1994; JE, *Activity, Recovery, Growth: The Communal Role of Planned Activities* (New York, 1976), 255.

33 JE, "Activity Program," October 1, 1953, Rockefeller Bros. Fund. Letter from JE to Robert P. Knight (n.d. [1952]), Exhibit A-7 in 1952 Annual Report of Medical Director, Austen Riggs Center. JE, *Activity,* 59, 162, 191–92, and 225–26, which deals with the merits of a premodern sort of village over modern suburbia. EHE and JE, "On Generativity and Identity: From a Conversation with Erik and Joan Erikson," *Harvard Education Review* 51, no. 2 (May 1981): 265; JE, TRI by LJF, Cambridge, December 17, 1990, and March 12 and 28, 1991, and Harwich, January 15, 1994; Ess White, TRI by LJF, Stockbridge, March 23, 1991.

34 EHE, *Insight and Responsibility: Lectures on the Ethical Implications of Psychoanalytic Insight* (New York, 1964), 98–99, "true communal recognition." JE, *Activity,* 263, quoting EHE: "the ego's activated adaptability" and "the mutual actualization." EHE, *Young Man Luther: A Study in Psychoanalysis and History* (New York, 1958, 1962), 8, on work and "works."

35 JE, TRI by LJF, Harwich, January 15, 1994, on Erik's sense of why failure with Neil was driving her into activities work, and on their improved marital relationship. Ess White, TRI by LJF, Stockbridge, March 23, 1991, on waltz contests. Margaret Brenman-Gibson, TI by LJF, April 10, 1993, recalling Erik's growing tolerance of Joan's church attendance. Letter from Ursula M. Niebuhr to LJF, March 22, 1992, on teas with the Eriksons. Letter from EHE to Adele Knight, February 21, 1957, E-H, on Joan's throat surgery and its significance.

36 Letter from EHE to "Dear Friends," February 2, 1954, E-H, on the right eye problem. Letters from EHE to Frieda Fromm-Reichmann, March 1, 1954, E-H, and EHE to Richard Sweet, June 3, 1954, E-H, on his stomach surgery. Gerry Pergola, PI by LJF,

Stockbridge, December 15, 1992, and Donald Brown, TRI by LJF, Ann Arbor, November 16, 1992, recalling Erikson's appearance and confidence at Riggs. Margaret Brenman-Gibson, TI by LJF, July 28, 1996, on the swimming incident. Sue Bloland, PI by LJF, NYC, November 13, 1996, on the joy of sweets and comedy television. Myron Sharaf, "Reminiscences of Erik Erikson" (unpublished ms., June 1994), recounts hearing the tomcat joke. Letter from EHE to Seymour L. Handler, February 2, 1977, E-H, recalling his growing appreciation for "hearty laughter."

37 Letter from EHE to Kate Hammond, November 28, 1952, E-H, "escape our magic mountain." Letter from EHE to "Dear Friends," December 12, 1956, E-H, "a place I am very fond of" and "the vitality of large immigrant." Benjamin Spock, TI by LJF, February 23, 1994, on Erikson identifying with the immigrant children, especially the Polish. EHE, *Insight and Responsibility,* 94, on the four-year-old African-American girl.

38 Benjamin Spock, TI by LJF, February 23, 1994, detailing his contacts with Erikson during the 1940s and 1950s. Lynn Z. Bloom, *Doctor Spock: Biography of a Conservative Radical* (Indianapolis, 1972), 172–74, quoting Spock on Erikson at Arsenal conferences. JE, TRI by LJF, Cambridge, December 18, 1990, and November 21, 1991, on the Erikson-Spock relationship. William Graebner, "The Unstable World of Benjamin Spock: Social Engineering in a Democratic Culture, 1917–1950," *Journal of American History* 67, no. 3 (December 1980): 612–29, on the broader vision Spock, Erikson, and others shared. Joanna Erikson, TRI by LJF, Hamden, November 7, 1993, recalling meeting Erik in Pittsburgh.

39 "Psychoanalysis at Riggs" (1982 transcript), 14, and George E. Gifford, Jr., ed., *Psychoanalysis, Psychotherapy and the New England Medical Scene, 1894–1944* (New York, 1978), 274, on the median age of patients. Riggs patient social characteristics and diagnoses are presented in Robert P. Knight and Cyrus R. Friedman, eds., *Psychoanalytic Psychology: Clinical and Theoretical Papers* (New York, 1954), 3–4; Ess White, TRI by LJF, Stockbridge, March 23, 1991. The liberalized open hospital regime is covered in Gifford, *Psychoanalysis . . . in New England,* 276–77. "Riggs: A Winning Fight on 'Nervous Breakdown,' " *Newsweek,* November 30, 1953, 92–95, on the open environment mitigating against severe cases and on the $1,800 monthly fee.

40 In the Harvey videotape, Joan and Erik emphasized their concern with the identity crisis stage and dismissed the psychiatric pathology perspective. This is underscored in Case Conference #7399 (September 12, 1951), 14, Austen Riggs Center; Richard Evans, ed., *Dialogue with Erik Erikson* (New York, 1967), 55; EHE, *The Life Cycle Completed* (New York, 1982), 9; "Interview with Dr. Erikson," Case Conference #1475 (December 1, 3, 4, 1954), E-H. Erikson in "Second Patient Seminar on Work, Play, Activities," August 2, 1955, 3, E-H, "to find out." Paul Roazen, *Erik Erikson: The Power and Limits of a Vision* (New York, 1976), 179, on Winnicott recalling Erikson's clinical approach. See also D. W. Winnicott, *Playing and Reality* (New York, 1971), 47, 81.

41 Review of reports of all case conferences that Erikson attended in the 1950s form the basis for my assessment of Erikson's role. These reports include not only Erikson's comments but evaluations of his observations by others. See especially Case Conference #7653 (September 2, 1955) and #7655 (September 23, 1955). See also #7696 (July 13, 1956), where Erikson rejected Knight's "identity crisis" diagnostic suggestion. Happily, Erikson's psychologist colleague at the time, Eugene Talbot, concurred fully in my assessment (Talbot, TRI by LJF, Stockbridge, December 17, 1992). Richard T. Kramer, TI by LJF, September 23, 1996, on thoughts of "the professor." Kai Erikson has kept several of the case conference doodles.

42 Case Conference #7895 (February 2, 1960), on the twenty-five-year-old man, and #7578 (December 18, 1953), concerning the woman in her late fifties. Case Conference #7479 (August 25, 1952), on the hypochondriac elderly patient.

43 For examples of Erikson's attention to the visual, see Case Conference #7458 (June 11, 1952), #7823 (September 29, 1958) and #7841 (February 20, 1959). Case Conference

#7520 (February 11, 1953), on the supposed cowboy walk. Talbot, TRI by LJF, December 17, 1992, emphasizing Erikson's attention to the visual. Case Conference #7848 (April 3, 1959), on the southern rape complex; #7869 (August 21, 1959), on "a New England conscience"; #7395 (August 17, 1951), on the advertising executive; #7383 (June 25, 1951), on the physician.

44 Case Conference #7429 (February 28, 1952), to "exteriorize"; #7830 (November 5, 1958), on Catholic sense of tradition; #7464 (June 10, 1953), "partly so"; #7861 (July 10, 1959), "with positive and absolute values," and #7824 (October 17, 1958), for a similar perspective; #7382 (June 25, 1981) and #7502 (November 12, 1952), on a Jewish depressive mood.

45 Case Conference #7410 (October 21, 1951) and #7650 (August 22, 1955), exemplifying Erikson's focus on the voice of the patient. Medical confidentiality precludes citing specific examples of intellectuals and their families and the issue of voice.

46 EHE, "Monograph (to be written in 1956/57)," E-H, titled *Varieties of Identity Diffusion,* and listing five Riggs cases on which his book initially was to be built. EHE, "Investigation into the Problems of Late Adolescence," October 1, 1953, 1, Rockefeller Bros. Fund Ms., Rockefeller Archives, North Tarrytown. EHE, *Insight and Responsibility,* 64–65.

47 EHE, *Insight and Responsibility,* 60, and Schlein, *Way,* 533–34. Erikson properly concealed identifying qualities of the patient to assure confidentiality in these published accounts of this case. While I have learned a great deal about the patient from other sources, especially from his patient case file, I am perpetuating this concealment and revealing only what Erikson stated in print owing to Riggs confidentiality requirements.

48 EHE, *Insight and Responsibility,* 57, "a big face sitting"; 65, on faces of God in the Bible; 66, "a wish to break." Discharge Note #7576 (May 2, 1957).

49 EHE, *Insight and Responsibility,* 69–70, 75, connecting Freud on the Medusa to his finding on "the continuous existence of individual identity." A note by Erikson (May 2, 1957) in the seminarian's case file (#7576) at Riggs shows him putting the dream interpretation together.

50 EHE, *Insight and Responsibility,* 67, on how the seminarian's quest for identity paralleled his quest for security in prayer.

51 Schlein, *Way,* 533–34.

52 EHE, *Insight and Responsibility,* 53, on "disciplined subjectivity" and "the two subjectivities join"; 80, contrasting the scientist with the clinician "in the attempt to do"; 75, "the communication between therapist and patient" and "the image of a Medusa."

53 EHE, *Young Man Luther,* 7, and Clyde Kluckhohn in *New York Herald–Tribune Book Review* (November 16, 1958), 4, on the epilogue chapter becoming the core of the book. Letter from EHE to Adele and Robert Knight, February 21, 1957, E-H, "a historic borderline case" and "much light on such religious." Letters from EHE to Ann Faber, August 19, 1959, and EHE to Max Levin, June 5, 1957, both in E-H, on patient and other young reader responses to a book on young Luther.

54 Letter from EHE to Ralph W. Tyler, November 2, 1955, E-H, inquiring about a fellowship year at the Center for Advanced Study at Stanford. EHE, *Young Man Luther,* 7, and letter from EHE to David Riesman, May 23, 1956, on the Foundations Fund support. The letter to Riesman confesses to the appeal of an academic job. William Gibson, PI by LJF, Stockbridge, December 16, 1992, on his increasing interest in writing rather than clinical endeavors.

55 JE, TRI by LJF, Cambridge, December 18, 1990, and Harwich, January 15, 1994, on the initial stop at a southern California beach house and the need to leave the country. Sue Bloland, TI by LJF, August 13, 1995, recalling her father's need to leave the United States to write a full, integrated book. For cogent discussions of the postwar intelligentsia, see David A. Hollinger, "How Wide the Circle of the 'We'? American Intellectuals and the Problem of the Ethnos Since World War II," *American Historical Review* 98, no. 2 (April 1993): 317–18, and Hollinger, "Ethnic Diversity, Cosmopolitanism and the

Emergence of the American Liberal Intelligentsia," *American Quarterly* 27, no. 2 (May 1975): 133–51.

56 Letter from EHE to "Dear Friends," February 22, 1957, E-H, detailing the situation at Ajijic and Jalisco and joking about infidelity. Letter from EHE to Robert and Adele Knight, February 21, 1951, on the local setting. Letter from EHE to Margaret Brenman-Gibson (n.d. [July 1957]), E-H, "in the open air." EHE, *Young Man Luther*, 75, "there are always islands."

57 Letter from EHE to Margaret Mead (n.d. [June 1952]), Mead Papers, LC, B4, on the Luther bibliography. JE, TRI by LJF, Cambridge, December 18, 1990, on stopping at the Berkeley library and on minimal contact with scholars while writing *Young Man Luther*. Letter from EHE to David Rapaport (n.d. [c. 1957]), E-H, on Latin translation and "I had to be" and "all the theoretical implications."

58 For an interesting discussion of Erikson following Murray's approach, see Donald Capps, Walter H. Capps, and M. Gerald Bradford, eds., *Encounter with Erikson: Historical Interpretation and Religious Biography* (Missoula, Mont., 1977), 149–50, 168.

59 EHE, *Young Man Luther*, 15–16.

60 EHE, *Young Man Luther*, 224, "Luther was the herald of the age . . . tried to say what it meant." Letter from EHE to Ann Faber, August 19, 1959, E-H, on the clinician's need to appreciate "relativity." EHE, *Young Man Luther*, 50, "to sift even questionable sources." EHE, "The First Psychoanalyst," *Yale Review* 46 (1956): 61. EHE, *Young Man Luther*, 35, "objective study" and "historical accuracy."

61 EHE, *Young Man Luther*, 37–39, 50, wrestling with the accuracy of the "fit."

62 Ibid.

63 EHE, "To Whomever May Be Good Enough to Concern Themselves with This" (n.d., [September 1953]), Margaret Brenman-Gibson private papers, "the victory of the Renaissance." EHE, *Young Man Luther*, 266, "is continuing in many lands." Letter from EHE to Katherine Barnard, July 1, 1958, W. W. Norton Papers, Columbia, "in contemporary history." Letter from EHE to David Riesman, May 23, 1960, E-H. Peter Heller, "Erikson on Luther," *Psychohistory Review* 22, no. 1 (Fall 1993): 91–93, well underscored the data on Luther that history specialists have mastered indicating that he was hardly a figure of the Renaissance or the modern era, so called.

64 EHE, "On the Sense of Inner Identity," in *Health and Human Relations* (New York, 1953), 124–43, on historic German splits, including "embattled borderlines" and "the provincial and the national." EHE, *Young Man Luther*, 10, on memories of the Holocaust and of Luther's German. Letter from EHE to David Riesman, September 13, 1957, DRP, on meeting and talking with Fromm in Mexico City and Cuernavaca. Sue Bloland, PI by LJF, February 19, 1997, recalls the Cuernavaca visit. Fromm's 1931 essay, "Left Wing Authoritarianism," discussed Luther's troubled youth while *Escape from Freedom* (New York, 1941) underscored Fromm's "from Luther to Hitler" perspective. I am indebted to Daniel Burston, Fromm's biographer, for advising me on several aspects of the Fromm-Erikson connection.

65 EHE, *Insight and Responsibility*, 204, on the fears, anxieties, worries, and dread. EHE, *Young Man Luther*, 46, the leader courting "sickness, failure, or insanity." See also EHE, *Young Man Luther*, 110, 218–19.

66 EHE, *Young Man Luther*, 20, "the resources of tradition." Sigmund Freud, *Moses and Monotheism* (New York, 1955), 139. Hermann Hesse, *Blick ins Chaos: Drei Aufsätze* (Bern, 1920), 184. Bruce Mazlish, "Reflections on the State of Psychohistory," *Psychohistory Review* 5, no. 4 (March 1977): 5, notes Lasswell and compares him to Erikson.

67 EHE, *Young Man Luther*, 34, "inner repose"; 134, "exposed to anarchic manifestations" and require "oversystematized thoughts"; 155, "that alliance of erotic irritability"; 148, "a borderline psychotic" with "prolonged adolescence"; 43, "half-realizes"; 100, "become well enough"; 41, on James's "growth crisis."

68 Letter from EHE to Henry A. Murray, May 23, 1957, E-H, on the fatherly image of

strength and wisdom. EHE, *Young Man Luther,* 124, "of the child's autonomous existence" and "never felt thus generated"; 67, "without being emasculated"; 76–77, less
"Martin than Luther"; 95, on Luther's "father did not mean it" and "creedal explicitness"; 166–68, on the important role of Staupitz and "to experiment with ideas." Lewis
D. Wurgaft, "Erik Erikson: From Luther to Gandhi," *Psychoanalytic Review* 63, no. 2
(1976): 218, and *Young Man Luther,* 210, on Erikson's "liberated craftsman" view of
Luther. Letter from EHE to Henry Murray, May 23, 1957, E-H, quoting Nietzsche.

69 EHE, *Young Man Luther,* 71, "Luther provided new elements"; 72–73, on Luther's
mother "that nobody could speak"; 207–8, "passivity" and "the data of"; 208, "a generosity"; 207–8, "a metabolism."

70 EHE, *Young Man Luther,* 72, "sad isolation." Erikson recalled his mother in EHE, *Life
History,* 31; EHE, "Autobiographic Notes," *Daedalus,* 745; and letter from Erik Homburger to August Aichhorn, September 7, 1933, AP-SFH. EHE, *Young Man Luther,* 10,
"wholeness" and "the bleached bones." EHE, "Autobiographic Notes," *Daedalus,* 743,
on his alienation. Letter from EHE to Rabbi Eugene B. Borowitz, March 8, 1976, E-H,
"my turn toward Christianity." EHE, "Autobiographic Notes on the Identity Crisis,"
The Twentieth-Century Sciences, edited by Gerald Holton (New York, 1972), 16,
"inescapably drawn" and "the Christianity of the Gospels." Ellen Katz and Ruth Hirsch,
TRI by LJF, NYC, August 16, 1991, recalling Erikson's need to visit Israel and his regard
for it as an alternative residence.

71 EHE, *Young Man Luther,* 265, "the guiding voice of infantile"; 206, "let himself go"; 22,
face "the problems of *human existence*"; 191, on Occham; 230–31, on "Here I stand" and
"emphasis on individual conscience."

72 Ibid., 169, "servant of the Word" and "never know"; 47, "The theme of Voice."

73 Ibid., 47, "*his* language"; EHE and JE, "On Generativity and Identity," 260, Luther "created a living language." EHE, *Young Man Luther,* 47, "immense gift for language"; 233,
"a language not intended as poetry," "language was the means," and a "moral energy."
Robert Coles, *Erik H. Erikson: The Growth of His Work* (Boston, 1970), 180, quoting
Erikson "of all things German."

74 EHE, *Young Man Luther,* 122, "a highly compressed store" and "what he had been
unable to say"; 220, "that a thing said less elegantly"; 198, "the voice that means it"; 220,
"craftsmanship."

75 Helmut Wohl, TRI by LJF, Boston, April 24, 1991. EHE to Henry A. Murray, May 23,
1957, E-H, "the voice of young Luther."

76 EHE, *Young Man Luther,* revised typescript (July 10, 1958), 373, Erikson Institute of
Chicago, comparing the southern and northern Renaissance.

77 Ibid., 9, "the dirty work"; 252, "to increase the margin." Evans, *Dialogue with Erik Erikson,* 96, "soul-searching prayer." Letter from EHE to Henry Murray, May 22, 1957, E-
H, "Luther worked through." EHE, *Young Man Luther,* 253, "unconscious deals"; 9, "the
father complex."

78 Steven Wieland, "Becoming a Biographer: Erikson, Luther and the Problem of Professional Identity" in *Contesting the Subject,* edited by William Epstein (West Lafayette,
1991), 203, on Erikson linking liberal Protestantism to psychoanalysis. EHE, *Young
Man Luther,* 265, "we regress in our dreams, too" and "use mechanisms analogous"; 264,
"at their creative best," "back to the earliest individual sources," "alive the common," and
"firmly established."

79 Letter from David Riesman to EHE, December 2, 1957, DRP. In *Young Man Luther,* 17,
Erikson underscored the importance of the analyst facing a face, and added: "Dr.
Staupitz, Martin's spiritual mentor, would know what I have in mind." Gardner Murphy,
"Notes on Erik's Book," April 2, 1958, Gardner and Lois Murphy Papers, AHAP-Akron.

80 Letter from EHE to Gardner Murphy, April 3, 1958, Murphy Papers, AHAP-Akron, noting that a "Yale divinity man" had looked over the manuscript. Actually, it was James Luther
Adams, a Harvard divinity professor; see Adams, TRI by LJF, Cambridge, May 7, 1991,

and JE, TI by LJF, September 30, 1995. Letter from EHE to Storer B. Lunt, February 26, 1958, E-H, listing most of the people he had asked to review the manuscript. Letters from EHE to Margaret Mead, September 13, 1957, Mead Papers, LC, B4, and EHE to David Riesman, September 13, 1957, DRP, "quiet time" and "get a lot off my chest."

81 Letter from Storer B. Lunt to William Langer, August 14, 1958, W. W. Norton Papers, Columbia, "even more profound and exciting." Letter from Lunt to EHE, February 19, 1958, W. W. Norton Papers, Columbia, on the contractual provisions for *Young Man Luther.* Letter from EHE to George P. Brockway, March 18, 1959, E-H, "Can review editors" and reticence over publishing with Norton again. This letter to Brockway plus Brockway to EHE, March 20, 1929, W. W. Norton Papers, Columbia; Brockway, TI by LJF, November 16, 1995, and letters from Donald S. Lamm to LJF, July 5, 1994, and October 26, 1995, detail the sales and promotion problems of *Young Man Luther,* in comparison with Erikson's other books. It was Erikson's only paperback with Norton that did not go to bookstores with a college textbook discount. Still, by the 1964–65 academic year, the paperback edition had sold about ten thousand copies and sales were accelerating.

82 Charles Rycroft, "The Luther Case," *The Observer* (London), December 13, 1959. Talcott Parsons to McGeorge Bundy, June 4, 1959, Ad Hoc Committee on Human Development, Harvard Archives. Osborne's turning the book into a London play is noted in letters from EHE to George Brockway, December 4, 1961, and n.d., both in W. W. Norton Papers, Columbia, and Richard F. Boeke, "The Eight-Fold Path of Erik Erikson," (unpublished ms., n.d.), 7, E-H.

83 Robert K. Webb, TI by LJF, September 30, 1995, on *American Historical Review* policy. G. R. Elton as quoted in William H. Honan, "Ode to Academic Nastiness," *New York Times* (Education Life, Sec. 4A), August 7, 1994. Letter from William Langer to EHE, September 4, 1958, W. W. Norton Papers, Columbia. Donald B. Meyer, "A Review of *Young Man Luther,*" *History & Theory* 1, no. 3 (1961): 291–97. Richard Hofstadter as quoted in EHE, "Psychoanalysis and Ongoing History: Problems of Identity, Hatred and Nonviolence," *American Journal of Psychiatry* (September 1965): 250. James M. Stayer, "The Eclipse of *Young Man Luther,*" *Canadian Journal of History* 19 (August 1984): 169. John Demos, *A Little Commonwealth: Family Life in Plymouth Colony* (New York, 1970), especially 129, 138–39. Letter from Fawn Brodie to EHE, August 24, 1972, E-H; Fawn M. Brodie, *Thomas Jefferson: An Intimate History* (New York: Bantam, 1975), xvi, 62, 116, 121; letter from EHE to Jeanne N. Knutson, October 28, 1977, E-H, on the "excesses." Lecture by Erik Erikson, Santa Barbara, February 19, 1972, E-H, on "psychohistory" disappearing as a label. EHE, "The Jefferson Lecture," Washington D.C., May 1, 1973 (audiotape), also wanting "psychohistory" to disappear.

84 Letter from Reinhold Niebuhr to EHE, April 8, 1958, E-H. Boeke, "The Eight-Fold Path," 6. Roland H. Bainton, "Luther: A Psychoanalytic Portrait," *Yale Review,* 48 (September 1959): 408–9; Bainton, "Psychiatry and History: An Examination of Erikson's 'Young Man Luther,'" *Religion in Life* 40 (1971): 463. EHE, *Young Man Luther,* 64, on Bainton's biography. As the letter from Roland Bainton to EHE, January 6, 1977, E-H, makes clear, disagreement between the two persisted for decades.

85 In his anthology *Psychohistory and Religion: The Case of Young Man Luther* (Philadelphia, 1977), 4, Roger A. Johnson excoriates Erikson for failing to go public with his complaints against his critics because this precluded a sustained public dialogue. EHE, "Notes on Bainton's Review" (n.d.), E-H. Letter from EHE to Edwin G. Boring (editor of *Contemporary Psychology*), August 6, 1959, E-H (unsent), attacking another reviewer for failing to see that his book dealt with postadolescent identity in relationship to ideology. EHE, *Identity: Youth and Crisis* (New York, 1968), 249, on the chancellor of St. Paul's. Letter from EHE to Rabbi Arnold J. Wolf, May 2, 1960, E-H.

86 Letters from EHE to S. I. Apenes, February 28, 1980, E-H, "I was more interested," and EHE to Ann Faber, August 19, 1959, E-H, "the human life cycle."

87 EHE, *Young Man Luther,* 267.

88 Letter from EHE to Julian Huxley, July 14, 1959, E-H. Erikson discusses his World Health Organization connection to Huxley in "The Problem of Ego Identity," *Psychological Issues* 1, no. 1 (1959): 122 *n.*7.

89 For favorable if limited psychoanalytic journal reviews of *Young Man Luther,* see, e.g., Henry Lowenfeld in *International Journal of Psycho-Analysis* 40 (1959): 108–11, and Martin Grotjahn in *Psychoanalytic Quarterly* 29 (1960): 343–46. Letter from EHE to Anna Faber, August 19, 1959, E-H, on Anna Freud's response to *Young Man Luther.* EHE, *Young Man Luther,* 8, acknowledging Sigmund and Anna Freud. Letter from David Rapaport to EHE, February 16, 1957, E-H, "fills me with real excitement."

90 Friedman, *Menninger,* 226–36, on Rapaport's background. Elvira Strasser, TRI by LJF, Stony Brook, August 17, 1990, on her husband, Rapaport. Letters from David Rapaport to Hanna Fenichel, August 19, 1960; Annie Reich to Rapaport, June 12, 1959; Paula Gross to Rapaport, July 2, 1959, Rapaport Papers, LC, concern Rapaport's plan to edit and publish *Rundbriefe,* Otto Fenichel's Marxist-Freudian newsletter. Letter from David Rapaport to EHE, October 9, 1950, E-H, "Dear Erik . . . I wish." Nathan Hale, Jr., *The Rise and Crisis of Psychoanalysis in the United States: Freud and the Americans, 1917–1985* (New York, 1985), 237, maintains that Rapaport always firmly accepted a cultural emphasis in psychoanalytic exploration. JE, TRI by LJF, Cambridge, December 18, 1990, on Rapaport supporting her activities program. Letter from Rapaport to EHE and JE, April 7, 1957, E-H, "made me feel."

91 The ways Erikson benefited Rapaport are noted in the letters from EHE to Ruth S. Eissler, February 2, 1953, E-H; EHE to David Rapaport, December 14, 1953, E-H; EHE to John Benjamin, May 27, 1954, E-H; EHE to Cora DuBois, May 27, 1954, E-H; and Elvira Strasser, TRI by LJF, Stony Brook, August 17, 1991; JE, PI by LJF, Cambridge, July 16, 1990; Ess White, TRI by LJF, Stockbridge, March 23, 1991.

92 "Psychoanalysis at Riggs," American Psychoanalytic Association forum, Boston, 1982 (transcript), 76–77, quoting Erikson "about making order," and 62, "David always put me." Elvira Strasser, TRI by LJF, Stony Brook, August 17, 1991, on Erikson often saying "You know, he tells me." EHE, "Robert Knight," 8, E-H, "my conceptual grandfather." Letter from EHE to "Dear Friends," February 21, 1977, E-H, "passionate demands for." Letter from EHE to David Rapaport (n.d. [c. 1957]), E-H, on how Rapaport helped with *Young Man Luther.* Letter from EHE to Anna Freud, November 1964, Anna Freud Papers, LC, "single-mindedness."

93 EHE, "Outline of Projected Book *Childhood and Society: Clinical Essays*" (1948), 1, DRP; Daniel Benveniste, "Erik H. Erikson in San Francisco" (unpublished ms., 1994), 6; JE, TRI by LJF, Harwich, January 15, 1994 (on deleting the essay from *Childhood and Society*).

94 Letters from Willi Hoffer to EHE, December 6, 1952, E-H; EHE to Willi Hoffer, January 5, 1953, E-H, "my paper gives"; Heinz Hartmann to EHE, August 26, 1952, E-H; EHE to Douglas Noble, September 8, 1955, E-H, tracing through the fate of his article; EHE to David Rapaport, September 8, 1955, E-H, "found little to"; Willi Hoffer to EHE, September 6, 1954, E-H.

95 Letter from Elizabeth Young-Bruehl to LJF, June 29, 1995, and Young-Bruehl, "A History of Freud Biographies," in *Discovering the History of Psychiatry,* edited by Mark S. Michale and Roy Porter (New York, 1994), 160, on Anna Freud's strong objections to the article. Henry A. Murray, TRI by James W. Anderson, Cambridge, May 12, 1981, recalling Erikson telling him of "cutting off all connection." Letter from Robert Knight to EHE, January 7, 1953, E-H, lauding the paper that became the published article.

96 EHE, "The Dream Specimen of Psychoanalysis," in Schlein, *Way,* 246–47, "many in his field," "Like good surveyors," and "psychoanalysis has given"; 251, on the dimensions involved in the manifest dream; 259, "takes the outer world into"; 278, "imbedded in a manifest dream"; 261, "a complicated continuum." EHE, "The Dream Specimen,"

Journal of the American Psychoanalytic Association 2 (1954): 21, "by no means a mere shell" and "the frame of reference."

97 EHE, "Dream Specimen," in Schlein, *Way,* 276, 278, on Freud seeking identity; 262, 274, on generativity. One wonders whether Erikson was trying here (unsuccessfully) to curry favor with Anna Freud. His discussion of Sigmund Freud's personal generativity appears somewhat tenuous since Anna was the last (not the first) of six children.

98 Letter from EHE to Douglas Noble (n.d. [1955]), on letter of Noble to EHE, September 1, 1955, E-H, "objection to my way of dealing with data." EHE, "Freud's 'The Origins of Psycho-Analysis,' " *International Journal of Psycho-Analysis* 36, Part I (1955): 1–2.

99 EHE, "Freud's 'The Origins of Psycho-Analysis,' " 14–15. Bruno Bettelheim, "Freud and the Soul," *New Yorker* (March 1, 1982): 52–93

100 EHE, "Freud's 'The Origins of Psycho-Analysis,' " 15, the science had not "issued from Freud's head," "to his inner motivations," and "to the main currents." The main body of the article (4–14) details this perspective.

101 EHE, *Life History,* 42, "of my childhood." Letters from EHE to Henry A. Murray, May 23, 1957, "complete the immigrant's cycle"; Alexander Mitscherlich to EHE, January 31, 1956; EHE to Mitscherlich, January 26, 1956; Mitscherlich to Frank Fremont-Smith, February 1, 1956—all in E-H. Robert Rubenstein, TRI by LJF, Belvedere, September 13, 1995, on what Hartmann had told Erikson. Karen Brecht, "In the Aftermath of Nazi Germany: Alexander Mitscherlich and Psychoanalysis—Legend and Legacy," *American Imago* 52, no. 3 (Fall 1995): 301, makes clear that the Frankfurt Institute for Social Research co-sponsored with Heidelberg University.

102 Letters from EHE to Frank Fremont-Smith, June 24, 1952, E-H, on his 1952 visit to Germany, and EHE to Mitscherlich, January 26, 1956, "public lectures are difficult." Eugene Talbot, TRI by LJF, Stockbridge, December 17, 1992, recalling Erikson's misgivings about accepting the lecture invitation.

103 Letter from EHE to Austen Riggs staff, May 6, 1956, E-H, "a student of Rapaport's." EHE, "The First Psychoanalyst," *Yale Review* 46 (1956): 40–62, reprints the centennial speech; 40, "Freudian" who "knew Freud"; 41, "a man who had unearthed"; 60, "emotional participation" and "methodological rigor"; 62, "supreme law-giver," "finding a method of healing himself," and "psychological rationale."

104 Letter from EHE to Henry A. Murray, May 23, 1957, E-H.

105 Letters from David Rapaport to L. Frankl, November 5, 1957, David Rapaport Papers, LC; Rapaport to EHE, August 2, 1957, E-H, on Kris; Rapaport to EHE, June 5, 1957, E-H; and Rapaport to Peter H. Wolff, October 18, 1957, Rapaport Papers, LC, articulating the historic-theoretical position he was preparing.

106 EHE, "Identity and the Life Cycle: Selected Papers," *Psychological Issues* 1, no. 1 (1959): 1–3.

107 Ibid., 1, Erikson on "a comprehensive," "less systematic," and "in the history . . ." John E. Gedo, *Conceptual Issues in Psychoanalysis: Essays in History and Method* (Hillsdale, N.J., 1986), 71–72, on the import of Rapaport's introductory essay.

108 EHE, "Identity and the Life Cycle," 11, 16.

109 Ibid., 14–16.

110 Ibid., 16, "over phenomenological." Gedo, *Conceptual Issues,* 77.

111 Suzanne R. Kirschner, "The Assenting Echo: Anglo-American Values in Contemporary Psychoanalytic Developmental Psychology," *Social Research* 57, no. 4 (Winter 1990): 823–24.

112 Jon Erikson, PI by LJF, Harwich, June 14, 1994, recalled this Fiesole visit with his father. EHE, "To Whomever May Be Good Enough to Concern Themselves with This" (n.d. [September 1953]), Margaret Brenman-Gibson private papers, "could formulate." Case Conference #7835 (December 12, 1958), Austen Riggs Center, recalling his arrival in Boston.

113 EHE, *Young Man Luther,* 111, 125. Case Conference #7412 (October 24, 1951), 11, "he had no father to contend," and #7896 (February 6, 1960), an "adopted child."

114 Letter from EHE to Kenneth Keniston, April 24, 1961, E-H, on the death of his mother. Karla Homburger's life from 1935 on is discussed in Esther Ramon, *The Homburger Family from Karlsruhe: A Family Study, 1674–1990* (Jerusalem, 1992), 78; Ruth Hirsch, TRI by LJF, NYC, November 8, 1993, and TI, June 9, 1991; Jon Erikson, PI by LJF, Harwich, June 14, 1994. Letter from EHE to Anna Freud, March 1949, Anna Freud Papers, LC, "She is an."

115 Theodor Homburger's restitution file (480 EK 13 681 Homburger T. Dr. Med.) is within the collections of the Restitution Authority for Württemberg-Baden. It is housed in the Generallandesarchiv Karlsruhe, which supplied me with copies of the core of the file—280 pages covering the 1949–64 period. Tom Segev, *The Seventh Million: The Israelis and the Holocaust* (New York, 1993), chapters 10 to 12, provides good coverage of general restitution proceedings and compensations.

116 Letter from EHE to Kurt von Fritz, December 20, 1976, E-H, on his cousins telling him about Salomonsen and that "I was the illegitimate outcome" and "my struggle for identity." Erikson also offers this account in "Further Autobiographic Remarks: For Friends and Relations Only," August 1977, E-H, and EHE, "Autobiographic Note" (n.d. [c. 1977]), E-H. Erikson notes his response to the Copenhagen letters in an unpublished, undated memorandum (likely mid-1970s), E-H. Sue Bloland, TRI by LJF, NYC, July 6, 1994, on her father telling her, Kai, and Jon that his father was Danish royalty. Betty J. Lifton, PI by LJF, Wellfleet, November 1, 1992, recalled Erikson telling her, too, of Danish royalty.

117 Letter from EHE to Kenneth Keniston, August 24, 1961, E-H.

118 Agnete Kalckar, PI by LJF, Cambridge, June 13, 1993, and TI by LJF, September 19, 1995, on Erikson approaching her husband, Herman Kalckar. When I commenced this project late in 1990, Herman Kalckar was too ill to be interviewed and died the following year. Letter from EHE to William Gibson (n.d. [June 27, 1963?]), E-H., "spoke Danish." I am indebted for a copy of the Kalckar family tree prepared by Herman and Agnete Kalckar's daughter Nina.

119 Agnete Kalckar, PI by LJF, June 13, 1993, and TI, September 19, 1995, on her trip with her husband to Copenhagen to make inquiries for Erikson.

120 Ellen Katz, TRI by LJF, NYC, August 16, 1991, on her trip from Haifa to Copenhagen to meet Svend Abrahamsen at Erikson's urging. Finn Abrahamsen, TRI by LJF, Copenhagen, May 8, 1993, exploring the family archives with me and discussing possible leads he might have given Erikson had he come to Copenhagen. I discovered an enormous amount of material about Erikson's early life by meeting with Finn, but not the identity of Erikson's father. Betty J. Lifton, *Journey of the Adopted Self: A Quest for Wholeness* (New York: 1994), 205, reports a somewhat garbled version of Ellen Katz's trip to Copenhagen based on what Erikson had told her.

121 Letter from David Riesman to McGeorge Bundy, June 2, 1959, Gibson Papers, E-H.

CHAPTER 7
PROFESSOR AND PUBLIC INTELLECTUAL: THE 1960S

1 Gregory D. Summer, "Window on the First New Left: Dwight MacDonald's *Politics* Magazine, 1944–1949" (Ph.D. diss., Indiana University, 1992), 415–16; Maurice Isserman, *If I Had a Hammer: The Death of the Old Left and the Birth of the New Left* (Urbana, Ill., 1993), 109, quoting Reddick. W. T. Lhamon, Jr., *Deliberate Speed: The Origins of a Cultural Style in the American 1950s* (Washington, D.C., London, 1990), especially 135.

2 Kenneth J. Gergen, *The Concept of the Self* (New York, 1971), concerning the roughly 2,000 publications between 1940 and 1970 on the self; Peter Novick, *That Noble Dream: The "Objectivity Question" and the Historical Profession* (Cambridge, Eng., 1988), 372, on the paperback revolution and college reading; Margaret Mead, "The Scholar's Scratch Pad," *American Scholar* 24 (Summer 1955): 378–82. Warren I. Susman interest-

ingly referred to the 1950s rather than the 1960s as the "Age of Erikson" in " 'Personality' and the Making of the Twentieth-Century Culture," *New Directions in American Intellectual History,* edited by John Higham and Paul K. Conklin (Baltimore, 1979), 224.

3 Peter Clecak, *America's Quest for the Ideal Self: Dissent and Fulfillment in the 60s and 70s* (New York, 1983), underscores the quest for authenticity and free selfhood, especially 6–7, 12, 115. Theodor Roszak, *The Making of a Counter Culture: Reflections on the Technocratic Society and Its Youthful Opposition* (New York, 1968).

4 Letter from EHE to David Riesman, May 23, 1956, E-H, "extra-clinical colleagues," and April 3, 1958, E-H, on visiting Winthrop House. Novick, *That Noble Dream,* 329, on Bundy and McCarthyism. Letter from EHE to Karl W. Deutsch, April 1, 1959, E-H, "stay at Riggs." Richard N. Smith, *The Harvard Century: The Making of a University to a Nation* (New York, 1986), 219–24, on the general state of the Harvard campus by 1960.

5 Robert Rubenstein, TRI by LJF, Belvedere, September 13, 1995, recalls how Erikson's clinical work became less central than authorship in the course of the 1950s. Letters from EHE to Anna Freud, November 1964, Anna Freud Papers, LC, "borderline cases, like," and EHE to R. P. Knight, August 8, 1960, E-H, "further developmental . . . closeness to scholars." Eugene Talbot, TRI by LJF, Stockbridge, December 17, 1992, recalling the effect of Rapaport's death on Erikson. JE, TRI by LJF, Cambridge, March 28, 1991 ("It was Erik's move"), and TRI, Harwich, January 15, 1994.

6 Letters from EHE to R. P. Knight, August 8, 1960, E-H; Talcott Parsons to EHE, April 14, 1958, E-H, and April 25, 1959, Parsons Papers, Harvard Archives; David Riesman to EHE, April 8, 1958; and EHE to David and Evelyn Riesman (n.d.), DRP. Letters from Clyde Kluckhohn to EHE, February 5, 1959, and Kluckhohn to EHE, February 18, 1959, both in Kluckhohn Papers, Harvard Archives.

7 Letters from Robert W. White to EHE, March 31, 1958, and March 9, 1959, E-H; White to McGeorge Bundy, June 3, 1959, Ad Hoc Committee on Human Development, Harvard Archives; Michael Maccoby to Marshall Field, June 1, 1959, DRP, on social relations faculty having been adverse to Erikson owing to deficient academic credentials.

8 Smith, *The Harvard Century,* 213, and David Halberstam, *The Best and the Brightest* (New York, 1972), 58, on Bundy's nondepartmental professor appointments and their political significance. McGeorge Bundy, TI by LJF, November 20, 1995, recalled the general course of the appointment. Jerome Bruner, *In Search of Mind: Essays in Autobiography* (New York, 1984), 248, is especially cogent on Bundy's move. Letter from Michael Maccoby to Marshall Field, June 1, 1959, DRP, "to support Erikson" and Bundy's support for the appointment. See also letter from Maccoby to EHE, February 7, 1958, E-H; Riesman, TRI by LJF, Cambridge, March 2, 1991; and letter from Robert W. White to EHE, March 31, 1958, Parsons Papers, Harvard Archives.

9 Kenneth Keniston, "Remembering Erikson at Harvard," *Psychology Today* (June 1983): 29, quoting the psychologist, "Why not Christian Science?" Letters from Barrington Moore to McGeorge Bundy, May 22, 1959, and David C. McClelland to McGeorge Bundy, January 28, 1959, both in Ad Hoc Committee on Human Development, Harvard Archives. Letters from Henry A. Murray to McGeorge Bundy, June 10, 1959, Ad Hoc Committee on Human Development, Harvard Archives; Talcott Parsons to McGeorge Bundy, June 4, 1959, Parsons Papers, Ad Hoc Committee on Human Development, Harvard Archives. Letter from Riesman to McGeorge Bundy, June 2, 1959, DRP.

10 McGeorge Bundy, "Erik Homburger Erikson: Recommendation of the Dean," September 16, 1959, plus letters from EHE to Bundy, April 15, 1960; Bundy to EHE, June 10, 1960; and Bundy to David W. Bailey, June 29, 1960—all in EHE Faculty Personnel File, Harvard Archives. Bundy, TI by LJF, November 20, 1995, recalling the politics of the Erikson appointment.

11 Letters from David Riesman to McGeorge Bundy, June 2, 1959, EHE Faculty Personnel File, Harvard Archives; Michael Maccoby to Marshall Field, June 1, 1959, DRP, on Erik-

son speaking to local undergraduates; EHE to Margaret Mead, July 16, 1959, E-H, "these bright and searching," "bridge the gap," and "develop some kind of teachable."

12 Letter from McGeorge Bundy to George P. Berry, December 17, 1959, EHE Faculty Personnel File, Harvard Archives, on the "Professor of Human Development" title as Erikson's choice and on the medical school appointment. Bundy, TI by LJF, November 20, 1995, on how he did not see that the title linked to Erikson's earlier name change. Letters from Robert W. White to McGeorge Bundy, June 3, 1959, EHE Faculty Personnel File, Harvard Archives, on a somewhat unofficial social relations department appointment; McGeorge Bundy to Paul Buck, December 17, 1959, and Buck to Bundy, December 22, 1959, EHE Faculty Personnel File, Harvard Archives, on the Widener study; EHE to Henry A. Murray (n.d. [1960]), Murray Papers, Harvard Archives, on Bundy's intervention for a Prince House study to which Murray assented. Letters from EHE to Bundy, January 1960, on spring and summer off; EHE to Bundy, January 1960, and Bundy to EHE, February 2 and August 2, 1960—all in EHE Faculty Personnel File, Harvard Archives, on the paper and the course outline.

13 Letter from EHE to Anna Freud, November 1946, Anna Freud Papers, LC.

14 David Riesman, TRI by LJF, Cambridge, March 2 and April 23, 1991; letters from Riesman to EHE, May 20, 1960, and March 13, 1961, DRP. Riesman in "Erik Erikson: The Quest for Identity," *Newsweek,* December 21, 1970, 86. See also David Riesman, "On Discovering and Teaching Sociology," *American Review of Sociology* 14 (1988): 20–21; George Goethals, PI by LJF, Cambridge, March 27, 1991, and Kenneth Keniston, "Remembering Erikson at Harvard," 29.

15 Erikson's physical appearance at Harvard is recalled in Dorothy Zinberg, TRI by LJF, Cambridge, May 1, 1991; Richard Sennett, TRI by LJF, NYC, August 13, 1991; John M. Ross, TRI by LJF, NYC, August 16, 1991 ("breathtaking and mesmerizing"). JE, TRI by LJF, October 28, 1992, on his German accent and appearance. Several of these people recalled the rabbi joke, and it is recorded in Erikson's Sarah Lawrence College lecture, "Inner and Outer Space," April 13, 1964, audiotape, Sarah Lawrence College Library.

16 Letter from EHE to Adele and Robert Knight, August 17, 1964, E-H, on his experience on the Radcliffe Board of Trustees. Zinberg, TRI by LJF, Cambridge, May 1, 1991, on the absence of a departmental affiliation. Letter from C. Sidney Burwell to EHE, March 13, 1962, E-H, on the Cambridge Scientific Club.

17 Erikson's fall 1960 syllabus, "Social Science 139: The Human Life Cycle," in the Harvard Archives. Keniston, "Remembering Erikson at Harvard," 29, "When you write." Pamela Daniels, TRI by LJF, Boston, April 12, 1991.

18 The fall 1960 syllabus, "Social Science 139: The Human Life Cycle," describes course aims. For indications of how Erikson used *Wild Strawberries* in SS 139, see EHE, "Dr. Borg's Life History" (unpublished ms.), February 22, 1984, 1, E-H; EHE, "Reflections on Dr. Borg's Life Cycle: Lecture Notes" (n.d.), E-H; letter from EHE to G. Smith, January 10, 1989, E-H; Pamela Daniels, TRI by LJF, Boston, March 15, 1991; Paul Roazen, "Erik Erikson as a Teacher," *Michigan Quarterly Review* (Winter 1992): 23.

19 SS 139 syllabi for the 1960s (Harvard Archives) plus Richard M. Hunt, "Brief Tribute to Erik Erikson" (unpublished ms.), October 25, 1986, New England Historical Association. Letter from Pamela Daniels to Gordon Fellman, January 20, 1989, Pamela Daniels private papers, listing SS 139 section leaders of the 1960s.

20 Christopher Jencks and David Riesman, *The Academic Revolution* (New York, 1968), 39–40.

21 Kenneth Keniston, TRI by LJF, Cambridge, February 6, 1991; letters from EHE to R. P. Knight, August 8, 1960, and EHE to Keniston (n.d. [April 1960]), E-H; Gordon Fellman, TRI by LJF, February 19, 1991.

22 Pamela Daniels, "Birth of the Amateur" in *Working It Out,* edited by Sara Riddick and Pamela Daniels (New York, 1977), 60–61, 68, on first meeting Erikson and on her editorial assistance. Letters from EHE to Myron L. Belfer, October 23, 1982, E-H, "our

course," and EHE to Lucretta Mowry, February 6, 1979, E-H, "rare combination of conceptual" and "that large class." See also letters from EHE to Jon Erikson, October 31, 1966, E-H, and Pamela Daniels to EHE, January 6, 1972, and April 22, 1974(?), E-H.

23 Pamela Daniels, TRI by LJF, Boston, March 15 and April 12, 1991; Gordon Fellman, TRI by LJF, Cambridge, February 19, 1991; David Riesman, TRI by LJF, Cambridge, March 2, 1991; Roazen, "Erikson as a Teacher," 21–22; Sudhir Kakar, "Erik Erikson in India: A Personal Memoir" (unpublished, Wellfleet Conference, October 1996).

24 Pamela Daniels provided me with copies of course rosters, grades, and special discussion section syllabi for SS 139. They revealed the sometimes fairly autonomous course section and indicated grade inflation. For Erikson's response to a specific episode involving grade inflation, see Sudhir Kakar, TRI by LJF, Boston, April 28, 1994, and Richard Hunt, TRI by LJF, Cambridge, November 22, 1991. The general, nonauthoritative tone of teaching assistant meetings is indicated in Virginia Demos, PI by LJF, Watertown, March 31, 1991; Carol Gilligan, TRI by LJF, Cambridge, April 15, 1991; letter from David Gutmann to EHE, January 14, 1983, E-H.

25 Gordon Fellman, TRI by LJF, February 19, 1991, on the crucifix incident, which is acknowledged in Dorothy Zinberg, TRI by LJF, Cambridge, May 1, 1991. Richard Hunt, TI by LJF, October 15, 1995, recalling Erikson rarely attending Memorial Church and hardly a practicing Christian in the 1960s.

26 Erikson's presence in discussion sections is described in Fellman, TRI by LJF, February 19, 1991; Zinberg, TRI by LJF, May 1, 1991; Virginia Demos, PI by LJF, Watertown, March 31, 1991. Janice Abarbanel lecture notes, SS 133, 1969–70, December 15, 1969, on Erikson castigating his professorial colleagues. SS 133 was changed for bureaucratic reasons from its long-standing SS 139 numbering.

27 Roazen, "Erikson as a Teacher," 23, estimating enrollment of one-quarter of Harvard seniors. Dorothy Zinberg, TRI by LJF, May 1, 1991, reporting her profile of SS 139 students in her capacity as "chief section man." Carol Gilligan, TRI by LJF, Cambridge, April 15, 1991, and Janice Abarbanel, PI by LJF, Washington, D.C., May 4, 1992, on female students being especially appreciative of Erikson. Interestingly, Virginia Demos, PI by LJF, March 31, 1991, and Richard Hunt, TI by LJF, October 15, 1995, reported that SS 139 undergraduates had only a nebulous understanding of Erikson's concept of identity and its place in the life cycle.

28 The Erikson papers in the Houghton Library house a good many of Erikson's SS 139 lecture "maps" and a few tape recordings of his lectures. Jon Erikson, TI by LJF, August 31, 1996. Student and staff reaction to the lectures is illustrated by Peter Wood, TI by LJF, January 25, 1995; Janice Abarbanel, PI by LJF, Washington, D.C., May 4, 1992, and TI by LJF, October 11, 1992; John M. Ross, TRI by LJF, NYC, August 16, 1991; Sudhir Kakar, TRI by LJF, Boston, April 28, 1994; Dorothy Zinberg, TRI by LJF, Cambridge, May 1, 1991; Pamela Daniels, TRI by LJF, Boston, March 15, 1991; George Goethals, PI by LJF, Cambridge, March 27, 1991; Richard Sennett, TRI by LJF, NYC, August 13, 1991.

29 Pamela Daniels, "For Erik's Memorial Service," June 19, 1994, 2, recounting the little boy asking his mother about death. EHE, "Autobiographic Statement to Freshman Seminar" (n.d. [early 1960s]), E-H, "to teach, to learn." Richard Lebeaux in *Introspection in Biography: The Biographer's Quest for Self-Awareness,* edited by Samuel H. Baron and Carl Pletsch (New York, 1985), 242. Mark Gerzon, "Pioneer of the Life Cycle: Erik Erikson" (n.d.), Harriet Harvey private papers, 12–13. Towle in "Erik Erikson: Quest for Identity," *Newsweek,* 85–86. Abarbanel, PI by LJF, Washington, D.C., May 4, 1992. Peter Wood, TI by LJF, January 25, 1995. James Luther Adams, TRI by LJF, Cambridge, May 7, 1991, on the student ovation at the Harvard commencement.

30 The fall 1960 syllabus, "Social Science 139: The Human Life Cycle," in the Harvard Archives.

31 Pamela Daniels provided me with many lists of SS 139 papers, each noting the student,

his or her paper title, and the grade the paper received. She also provided me with summaries of especially interesting student papers that she prepared for Erikson.

32 Richard Hunt, TI by LJF, October 15, 1995, estimating that 25 percent understood the identity concept. Harvard Senior Seminar, "Perspectives on the Life Cycle," October 23, 1985, Harriet Harvey videotape, Erikson recalling the "Are you bragging" remarks made in the Yard that Ess White elaborated (Ess White, PI by LJF, Stockbridge, March 25, 1993). EHE, "The Concept of Identity in Race Relations: Notes and Queries," *Daedalus* 95, no. 1 (Winter 1966): 165, "What do I want."

33 Social Science 139, Fall Term 1963–64 (syllabus), Harvard Archives, using more direct and evocative language. Janice Abarbanel lecture notes, Life Cycle Course 1969–70, November 11, 1969, everything "hangs together." EHE, "Talk Given to Freshman Seminars, Spring Term" (n.d. [mid-1960s]), 2, E-H, "Who am I?" "a voice inside," and "one's inner voice."

34 Peter Stead, *Film and the Working Class: The Feature Film in British and American Society* (London and New York, 1991), 192–94, provides a good analysis of *Saturday Night and Sunday Morning*. Janice Abarbanel lecture notes, Life Cycle Course 1969–70, November 11, 1969, provides copious notes of Erikson's lecture on the film that, to make much sense, must be read against an actual viewing of the film.

35 Gordon Harper, TRI by LJF, Boston, April 22, 1991; letter from Harper to EHE, September 12, 1989 (copy from Harper); Peter Wood, TI by LJF, January 25, 1995; Abarbanel, PI by LJF, May 4, 1992; John Ross, TRI by LJF, August 16, 1991; Nina Holton, TRI by LJF, Lexington, April 30, 1991; Gerzon, "Pioneer of the Life Cycle" (n.d.), 11–12, Harriet Harvey private papers.

36 John Demos, PI by LJF, Watertown, March 31, 1991; EHE seminar for 1964–65 on "Life History and History," E-H, lists all students attending and their papers. George Goethals, PI by LJF, Cambridge, March 27, 1991; e-mail from David G. Winter to LJF, June 9, 1997.

37 Bruce Mazlish, PI by LJF, Cambridge, February 16, 1991; "Interview with John Demos," *The Historian* 55 (Spring 1993): 438; Pamela Daniels, TRI by LJF, Boston, April 12, 1991; Mary Catherine Bateson, PI by LJF, Wellfleet, October 22, 1994; letter from Margaret Brenman-Gibson to EHE, April 24, 1969, Brenman-Gibson private papers; e-mail from David Winter to LJF, June 9, 1997.

38 Letter from EHE to William M. Thompson, July 12, 1976, E-H, "that I have little experience." John Demos, PI by LJF, Watertown, March 31, 1991, on how Erikson never formally presented on Gandhi. Paul Roazen's notes on a session of "Erikson's Seminar" in 1966 (Roazen private papers) were extensive and indicate Erikson's random observations concerning Gandhi, his subject. Richard Sennett, TRI by LJF, NYC, August 13, 1991, on Erikson's disordered mode of presentation close to the unconscious.

39 Letters from EHE to Robert J. Lifton, June 1976, RJL-NYPL, "teaching can advocate too," and Robert J. Lifton to EHE, July 12, 1976, RJL-NYPL.

40 David Riesman, TRI by LJF, Cambridge, March 2, 1991. Margaret Brenman-Gibson, "Erik Erikson and the 'Ethics of Survival,'" *Harvard Magazine* 87, no. 2 (November–December 1984): 62, quoting Kehler. Letter from Pamela Reynolds to EHE, September 26, 1975, E-H, recalling Erikson's encouragement. Wellfleet Conference, October 31, 1992, audiotape, for Gitlin and Herman comments in a session on "Erikson's America." EHE, "On Student Unrest," unpublished brochure (1969), 212, E-H, sympathizing with hippies.

41 The Committee on Correspondence petition issue is discussed in letter from EHE to David Riesman, April 13 and May 23, 1960, E-H, and in letter from Norbert Mintz to EHE, November 6, 19(60), DRP. Gordon Fellman, TRI by LJF, Cambridge, February 19, 1991, on the Bay of Pigs petition. Roazen, "Erikson as a Teacher," 32, and Robert J. Lifton, *The Life of the Self: Toward a New Psychology* (New York: 1976), 155, on anti-Vietnam petitions.

42 EHE, "Postscript" (n.d. [early 1970s]), E-H, 8–9, "storming of administration build-ings" and "faking of pregenital freedom." "Erik Erikson: The Quest for Identity," *Newsweek,* 89, also attacking shallow displays of sexual freedom. Erikson walking out of a Leary lecture in the winter of 1966–67 is reported by several who witnessed it: John M. Ross, TRI by LJF, NYC, August 16, 1991; e-mail from Robert Abzug to LJF, June 1, 1994; Irving Alexander, PI by LJF, Evanston, June 6, 1997.

43 Roger Rosenblatt, *Coming Apart: A Memoir of the Harvard Wars of 1969* (Boston, 1997), provides many insights on Harvard senior faculty and activism in the course of the 1960s. Cogent analyses of Erikson's disposition against bold action are provided in Kai and Joanna Erikson, TRI by LJF, Hamden, November 7, 1993; Evelyn Riesman, TRI by LJF, Cambridge, March 2, 1991; Robert J. Lifton, PI by LJF, Bowling Green (Ohio), March 5, 1993.

44 Letter from EHE to David Shakow, November 16, 1964, David Shakow Papers, AHAP-Akron. The constant stares in Cambridge are noted in JE, TRI by LJF, Harwich, January 15, 1994, and Christina Robb, "Partners for Life," *Boston Globe Magazine,* March 22, 1987, 34.

45 Evelyn Riesman, TRI by LJF, Cambridge, April 23, 1991, on Erikson's continued inse-curity because he had no academic degrees. Dorothy Zinberg, TRI by LJF, Cambridge, May 1, 1991, on Erikson not being invited to social relations department meetings. George Goethals emphasizes Erikson's insecurity in an academic setting and notes the couch incident in "Erik Erikson Symposium," Cambridge Hospital, October 29, 1994 (audiotape). Goethals, PI by LJF, Cambridge, March 27, 1991, on Erikson rejecting Mrs. Pusey and the difficult Erikson-Pusey relationship; see also letter from EHE to Franklin Ford, February 22, 1968, EHE Faculty Personnel File, Harvard Archives.

46 Joan Erikson's activities and doldrums in Cambridge are discussed in JE, TRI by LJF, Harwich, January 14, 1994, and July 5, 1996; Nina Holton, TRI by LJF, Lexington, Mass., April 30, 1991; Ess White, TRI by LJF, Stockbridge, March 23, 1991; Zinberg, TRI by LJF, April 1, 1991; letter from JE to Herman and Agnete Kalckar, March 1, 1962, Kalckar private papers.

47 Letter from Verna C. Johnson to Nathan Pusey, March 13, 1962, EHE Faculty Personnel File, Harvard Archives, is especially instructive on Erikson's self-image as "a writer" first. George Goethals, PI by LJF, Cambridge, March 27, 1991, recalls Erikson fearing death before many writing projects were completed. Letter from EHE to Nathan Pusey, April 27, 1961, EHE Faculty Personnel File, Harvard Archives, "Solitude is a rare privilege." Keniston, "Remembering Erikson at Harvard," 29. Letter from Franklin L. Ford to Nathan M. Pusey, February 7, 1964, EHE Faculty Personnel File, Harvard Archives, on Erikson's two semesters at the Center for Advanced Studies in the Behavioral Sciences. "Memorandum of President Pusey's Conversation with Professor Erik Erikson," February 1, 1962, EHE Faculty Personnel File, Harvard Archives, on the frequent sabbaticals in defi-ance of university policy. Letter from EHE to Pusey, March 16, 1962, EHE Faculty Per-sonnel File, Harvard Archives, on taking the 1962–63 year off. James W. Anderson, "The Life of Robert W. White: A Psychobiographical Exploration" (n.p. [1991]), 24, on Erik-son declining to head a center. Roazen, "Erikson as a Teacher," 20, on Erikson declining to become a training analyst at the Boston Psychoanalytic Institute. Letter from David Ries-man to John Sawyer, October 2, 1969, DRP, on Erikson having arranged to teach only one semester at Harvard and to spend spring semester in Stockbridge; see also letter from EHE to Franklin Ford, February 22, 1968, EHE Faculty Personnel File, Harvard Archives.

48 Ess White, TRI by LJF, Stockbridge, March 23, 1991, and PI, Stockbridge, November 31, 1995; Helmut Wohl, TRI by LJF, Boston, April 24, 1991; "Report of the Medical Director, Austen Riggs Center," July 1, 1960, to June 30, 1961, 1, and July 1, 1967, to June 30, 1968, 6.

49 EHE, *Life History and the Historical Moment* (New York, 1975), 147, "adolescent search"; 117, "that pervasive presence . . . total commitment." EHE, *Gandhi's Truth: On*

the Origins of Militant Nonviolence (New York, 1969), 9–10, 31, on reading Rolland and learning of Gandhi's Ahmadabad trial. EHE Lecture, Social Science 139, December 13, 1965 (tape), E-H, recalling writing on the 1918 strike and later discovering his notes. See also EHE, "Gandhi's Autobiography," *American Scholar* 35, no. 4 (Autumn 1966): 646.

50 Lois Barclay Murphy, *Gardner Murphy: Interpreting, Expanding and Humanizing Psychology* (Jefferson, N.C., 1990), 169, 239–41, 250; Lois B. Murphy, TI by LJF, June 10, 1991; EHE, *Gandhi's Truth,* 13; Kamla Chowdhry, TRI by David Andersen, Cambridge, October 17, 1991; Nina Holton, TRI by LJF, Lexington, Mass., April 30, 1991; Pamela Daniels, TRI by LJF, Boston, April 12, 1991.

51 Letter from Kamla Chowdhry to Gardner Murphy, May 9, 1962, Murphy Papers, AHAP-Akron, on Erik's initial expectations for the Ahmadabad trip. Pamela Daniels, TRI by LJF, Boston, March 15 and April 12, 1991, on Erikson's initial impression of India. EHE, "India: Who Knows?" (n.d.), E-H, on his initial impression of the country and of the political arrests.

52 EHE, *Gandhi's Truth,* 27, "led me to one of his terraces"; 26, "the saintly yet simple old woman." EHE, *Life History,* 146, " 'came back.' " EHE application to American Institute of Indian Studies (n.d. [December 1963]), 1, EHE Faculty Personnel File, Harvard Archives, "the powerful presence" and "dramatic core . . . psychological and cultural as well as." JE, TRI by LJF, Cambridge, December 18, 1990 and May 8, 1991, and Pamela Daniels, TRI by LJF, Boston, April 12, 1991, on Erik's emerging interest in studying the strike. Monier Monier-Williams, *A Sanskrit-English Dictionary* (Delhi, 1963), 130, 1135, on *Satyagraha.* EHE, *Gandhi's Truth,* 198, 411, defining *Satyagraha* in his own way. L. N. Gupta, "Truthforce," *New York Review of Books* 13 no. 6 (October 9, 1969): 60, finding imprecision in Erikson's definition and elaborating an alternative. Richard I. Evans, ed., *Dialogue with Erik Erikson* (New York, 1967), 72, "which I had dimly read about."

53 EHE, "A Note on Our Discussion Following Shiv's Presentation of Tagore's Childhood," Ahmadabad, November 28, 1962, E-H, 1–5.

54 Ibid.

55 EHE, *Gandhi's Truth,* 14.

56 Ibid., 10–11, 161, 403, identifying his "discipline." Letter from EHE to Jon Erikson, September 9, 1964, E-H, "in India there is no reasonably safe travel." EHE, *Gandhi's Truth,* 72, "against the stark facts"; 74, "a haven," "an unconscious transference," "a father or older-brother," and "fatherless child." Sudhir Kakar, PI by LJF, Wellfleet, October 6, 1996, on warning Erikson that he was overidentifying. Parallels between the Ambalal-Gandhi and the Ambalal-Erikson relationships are well discussed in Leonard Gordon's review of *Gandhi's Truth* in the *Journal of Social History* 4, no. 4 (Summer 1971): 423–24, and in J. Michael Lemmon and Charles Strozier, "Empathy and Detachment in the Narratives of Erikson and Mailer," *Psychohistory Review* 10, no. 1 (Fall 1981): 27.

57 EHE, *Life History,* 146, "Middle-Aged Mahatma" and "in my middle years." EHE, *Gandhi's Truth,* 440, "it was time." Sudhir Kakar, TRI by LJF, Boston, April 28, 1994, on being regarded in India as a wise old man. Letter from EHE to Lois and Gardner Murphy (n.d.), Murphy Papers, AHAP-Akron, "strenuous India." Letter from EHE to Jon Erikson, October 31, 1966, E-H, on age. Letter from EHE to Anna Freud, July 16, 1966, Anna Freud Papers, LC, "To the younger." Letter from JE to Margaret Brenman-Gibson, February 14, 1967, Brenman-Gibson private papers, "can't afford."

58 The decision to buy a cottage in Cotuit and the import of that residence for the Eriksons is indicated in JE, TRI by LJF, Harwich, January 15 and October 20, 1994; Joanna Erikson, TRI by LJF, Hamden, November 7, 1993. Letter from EHE to Jon Erikson, October 31, 1966, E-H, "black blue ocean" and "Mom and I" and inviting Jon to visit and see the sounds and colors of the area.

59 Letter from EHE to Kenneth Keniston, April 24, 1961, E-H, on Joan starting her *The Universal Bead* (New York, 1969) and shaping "a crazy and important story." JE, "Eye to Eye," *The Man-Made Object,* edited by Gyorgy Kepes (New York, 1966), 51–52, 59.

60 Letter from EHE to Jon Erikson, September 19, 1964, and October 31, 1966 ("deeply touched by those two kids," Jacqueline "simpe and friendly," the compound "like a swank concentration camp," and several other striking observations about the Kennedys), E-H. Harland Bloland, TI by LJF, December 20, 1995, recalling Jacqueline Kennedy's unannounced visit to Cotuit with Goodwin in the summer of 1966. Helmut Wohl, TRI by LJF, Boston, April 24, 1991, recalled many details about the Eriksons and the Kennedys from his visits to Cotuit, especially Edward Kennedy's consultation on a run for the presidency. Sue Bloland, TRI by LJF, NYC, July 9 and September 9, 1994, on aspects of the Erikson-Kennedy connection. Edward Klein, TI by LJF, November 2 and 9, 1997, provided some detail from his own research on Erikson's possible treatment of the Kennedy children and on Erikson's contact with Goodwin.

61 Letters from EHE to David Riesman, August (1962), DRP, and EHE to Jon Erikson, October 31, 1966, E-H, "getting along fine."

62 Letter from EHE and JE to Gardner and Lois Murphy (n.d.), Murphy Papers, AHAP-Akron, "enjoying grand-parenting." Pamela Daniels, PI by LJF, January 6, 1996, on interviewing, very pregnant, for an SS 139 position. Letter from EHE to Jon Erikson, September 9, 1964, E-H, acknowledging that Joan actually took care of Keith and Christopher. JE, PI by LJF, Harwich, July 5, 1996, on Erik's interest in their drawings and sketches. Joanna Erikson, TRI by LJF, Hamden, November 7, 1993, on Erik taking her sons on walks. Kai Erikson, TI by LJF, January 6, 1996, recalling Erik's rapport with his young sons.

63 Letter from EHE to Jon Erikson, October 31, 1966, E-H, on Kai as "a *good* father" and the "establishments" within the extended Erikson family. Letter from David Riesman to Joseph Gusfield, November 21, 1968, DRP, on Kai as "much less neurotic." Kai Erikson, TRI by LJF, Hamden, November 7, 1993, on how he began to read Erik's publications systematically and was influenced by them in his own writing. Kai Erikson, PI by LJF, January 6, 1996, on his general personal and professional life in the 1960s and how it connected to his father's. Kai T. Erikson, *Wayward Puritans* (New York, 1966), xii, "the counsel he gave." Letter from David Riesman to L. Marquis, June 25, 1969, DRP, on Kai and Joanna after the move to Yale, and suggesting a certain tension there. Joanna Erikson, TRI by LJF, Hamden, November 7, 1993, on the move from Emory to Yale and on summers in Cotuit. Letter from EHE to Jon Erikson, October 31, 1966, E-H, and JE, PI by LJF, Harwich, July 5, 1966, on summers in Cotuit.

64 Letter from EHE to David Riesman, June 24, 1961, DRP, on the wedding near Nice and Harland Bloland "quietly strong" while Sue radiated "pervasive feminine happiness."

65 Sue Bloland, TI by LJF, December 19, 1995, and May 24, 1997, detailing her own and Harland's relationship with her father. Letter from EHE to David Riesman, May 31, 1963, DRP, on his relationship with Harland and how "the intellectual going is rough." See also Jon Erikson, PI by LJF, Harwich, June 14, 1994, and Harland Bloland, TI by LJF, December 20, 1995, on the Erik-Harland relationship.

66 Nina Holton, TRI by LJF, Lexington, April 30, 1991, recalling Joan's views of Jon. Jon Erikson, PI by LJF, Harwich, June 14, 1994, on his stage laborer work and travel and his relationship with his parents. Letter from EHE to Jon Erikson, September 9, 1964, E-H, "To think you have never seen this place."

67 Jon Erikson, PI by LJF, Harwich, June 14, 1994, and TI, August 31, 1996, on the Florence trip and its meaning in the father-son relationship, and on the role of his humorous remarks. Letter from EHE to Jon Erikson, October 31, 1966, E-H, quoting Jon on "seminars" and "Why don't you write a book," while replying that they "sting particularly now."

68 Susan Kolodny, "Notes from a Journal," in *The Doctorate in Mental Health: An Experiment in Mental Health Professional Education*, edited by Robert Wallerstein (Lanham, Md., 1991), 121, on Erik discounting being able to connect writing and artistic activity. Jon Erikson, PI by LJF, Harwich, June 14, 1994, acknowledging the troubled relationship with his parents, especially Erik, in considerable detail. Jon Erikson, TI by LJF,

August 31, 1996, detailing how that relationship made him reticent to visit Cotuit. Margaret Brenman-Gibson, PI by LJF, Cambridge, April 13, 1991, and TI, April 10, 1993, on Jon's relationship with his parents since the 1950s.

69 Letters from EHE to David Riesman (n.d. [early 1961]), and Riesman to EHE, December 29, 1960, DRP, and Riesman, TRI by LJF, Cambridge, March 2, 1991, on the undergraduate audience for EHE, *Childhood and Society* (New York, 1950). Novick, *That Noble Dream*, 372, on the college paperback revolution that commenced in the 1950s. Donald Lamm, TI by LJF, October 31, 1995, explaining Norton's reading of the college market for *Childhood and Society.*

70 George P. Brockway, TI by LJF, January 29, 1994, and November 16, 1995; Donald S. Lamm, TI by LJF, June 24 and August 30, 1994, and June 23 and October 31, 1995; JE, TRI by LJF, Cambridge, November 21, 1991. See also Lewis A. Coser et al., *Books: The Culture and Commerce of Publishing* (New York, 1982), 339, and John Pebble, *A History of Book Publishing in the United States* (New York, 1981), vol. 4, 257–59.

71 Letter from Donald Lamm to LJF, October 26, 1995, detailing *Childhood and Society* paperback sales figures from Norton's records. Letter from Brockway to EHE, May 18, 1965, W. W. Norton Papers, Columbia, "rapidly becoming." Lamm, TI by LJF, June 23, 1995, on Norton's marketing strategy. EHE, TRI by Robert Stewart, Cambridge, January 11, 1968, reporting his thrill over the widespread sales for the paperback edition. Bellah as quoted in "Erik Erikson: The Quest for Identity," *Newsweek,* 84.

72 Letter from EHE to Ruth N. Anshen, November 3, 1965, Ruth N. Anshen Papers, Rare Books and Manuscripts Division, Butler Library, Columbia University. The details of the Cogan negotiations with Norton and Cogan's duties as financial adviser to the Eriksons are provided in Sue Bloland, TI by LJF, NYC, November 12 and December 19, 1995; George Brockway, TI by LJF, November 16, 1995; Robert Wallerstein, PI by LJF, August 13, 1990; and letter from Cogan, Bell & Co. to EHE, August 22, 1977, E-H. Letter from George Brockway to EHE, May 4, 1971, E-H, urging Erikson to decline publication of lectures by university presses and offering $25,000 for Norton to publish Erikson's Godkin Lectures (*Toys and Reasons*). Erikson accepted the offer.

73 Letter from EHE to George Brockway (n.d. [December 1961]), W. W. Norton Papers, Columbia, "I have a copy marked up." EHE, *Childhood and Society:* 1st ed., 75, "original reciprocity," 2nd ed., 79, "original mutuality"; 1st ed., 42, "a clinician's book," 2nd ed., 308, 312, "self restriction" replacing "ego restriction," 308, against restricting observations to patients; 2nd ed., 266, "the dependence of children"; 2nd ed., 60, "fixed character"; 1st ed., 283, "on the basis of a new knowledge and a new identity," 2nd ed., 324, "new technology" and "a more universal identity."

74 EHE, SS 139 lecture of October 20, 1969, Janice Abarbanel lecture notes for 1969–70, on *Childhood and Society* essays as pre-McCarthyite and pre-Hiroshima in the first but not the second edition.

75 EHE, *Insight and Responsibility: Lectures on the Ethical Implications of Psychoanalytic Insight* (New York, 1964), 9, on revising the published lectures at the center. Letter from EHE to Anna Freud, December 12, 1963, Anna Freud Papers, LC.

76 EHE, *Insight and Responsibility,* 9–10, on the book's theme and nature of "insight." Coles as quoted in *Explorations in Psychohistory: The Wellfleet Papers,* edited by Robert J. Lifton and Eric Olson (New York, 1974), 356 *n.*3.

77 EHE, *Insight and Responsibility,* 111–34. Donald Lamm, TI by LJF, October 31, 1995, on the demand for Erikson's life cycle chart and his conditions for reprinting it.

78 EHE, *Insight and Responsibility,* 114, 130–33.

79 Ibid., 112. EHE, "Ontogeny of Ritualization in Man," in *Psychoanalysis—A Generational Psychology: Essays in Honor of Heinz Hartmann,* edited by R. M. Loewenstein et al. (New York, 1966), 601–21, especially 602–3, for the London elaboration of the "Human Strength" essay.

80 EHE, *Insight and Responsibility,* 165–66, 174.

81 Ibid., 220, 221, 243. The text of Erikson's George W. Gay Lecture of May 1962 is in the EHE Faculty Personnel File, Harvard Archives.

82 EHE, *Insight and Responsibility,* 233, 242.

83 Ibid., 226, 238, 242.

84 Letter from Donald Lamm to LJF, October 26, 1995, containing paperback sales figures from W. W. Norton records for *Insight and Responsibility,* and with comparable figures for *Childhood and Society.*

85 JE, TI by LJF, September 30, 1995; Richard Hunt, TI by LJF, October 15, 1995; James Luther Adams, TRI by LJF, Cambridge, May 7, 1991.

86 Paul Tillich, *On the Boundary: An Autobiographical Sketch* (New York, 1966), especially 13, 97. Erikson's address at Tillich's memorial service, reprinted in Stephen Schlein, ed., *A Way of Looking at Things: Selected Papers from 1930–1980. Erik H. Erikson* (New York, 1987), 726–28, best underscores how he read *On the Boundary.* EHE, *Life History,* 30, "I had to succeed."

87 Tillich, *On the Boundary,* 56, on Kierkegaard as "the real founder." Don S. Browning, *Generative Man: Psychoanalytic Perspectives* (Philadelphia, 1973), especially 168–69, puts Tillich well in the context of existential theology and philosophy, linking Erikson to some degree to this tradition. Donald B. Meyer, *The Protestant Search for Political Realism, 1919–1941* (Berkeley, 1961), especially 273–79, is wonderfully clear and complete on Tillich's posture.

88 EHE, *Insight and Responsibility,* 133, "the great Nothingness"; EHE, *Identity,* 293, summarizing the discussion with Tillich on psychoanalysis and Ultimate Concern. Patricia Doyle, *Religion and Sexism: Images of Women in the Jewish and Christian Traditions* (New York, 1974), 31–37, on how Tillich and Erikson were distressed by the elimination of the female element in Ultimate Concern and Tillich substituting the "Motherhood of God." Letter from EHE to John Finley, January 18, 1965, E-H, on SS 139 addressing Tillich's issues. Robert J. Lifton, TI by LJF, February 18, 1996, recalling Tillich telling him of his mixed feelings about Erikson's identity construct.

89 Schlein, *Way,* 728.

90 Ibid., 726–27. Robert J. Lifton, PI by LJF, NYC, April 3, 1991, recalling the "Why both of course" remark. See also Robert J. Lifton at Erikson Memorial Service, Harvard Memorial Church, October 12, 1994 (audiotape) on Erikson's Jew-Gentile religious connection.

91 Schlein, *Way,* 727–28.

92 Ibid., 728, "blend of realism." Richard Hunt, TRI by LJF, Cambridge, November 22, 1991, and PI, October 15, 1995.

93 EHE, "Psychoanalysis and Ongoing History: A Letter" to Professor Roger Fisher, October 1962, E-H, 10, "a natural alliance" and "not acquainted with." EHE, "White House Diary—Postscript," November 19, 1965, E-H, describing his attendance at the Johnson White House reception. While politically liberal, Erikson was not always consistent. In 1978, he voted for California's Proposition 13 to reduce his property taxes even as the measure grossly curtailed public social services.

94 EHE, "White House Diary—Postscript," November 19, 1965, E-H.

95 EHE, "Gandhi's Autobiography: The Leader as a Child," *American Scholar* 35, no. 4 (Autumn 1966): 632–46.

96 EHE, *Gandhi's Truth,* 14, "jot down" and "approximations"; 12, "the kind of worker," "find my way," and "letting subjectivity"; 66–67, on "formulas" and "simply made too great demands." See also letter from EHE to Chadbourne Gilpatrick, September 10, 1964, Rockefeller Archives Center, Research Group 2, Series 200, Box 480, and Sudhir Kakar, PI by LJF, Wellfleet, October 6, 1996, on Erikson's interview approach.

97 Pamela Daniels, TRI by LJF, Boston, April 12, 1991, and EHE, *Gandhi's Truth,* 14, on her role in going over the manuscript. For the Kakar-Erikson relationship, see Sudhir Kakar, TRI by LJF, Boston, April 28, 1994; Kakar, "Erik Erikson in India: A Personal Memoir" (n.p.

[1994]); and letter from EHE to "Dear Colleague," January 19, 1973, E-H. Julie Negrini, PI by LJF, Stockbridge, December 16, 1992. EHE, *Gandhi's Truth*, 14, on Kai's role.

98 Letter from JE to Margaret Brenman-Gibson, February 14, 1967, Margaret Brenman-Gibson private papers, on six weeks of hard work to complete the book. The final typed and edited manuscript of *Identity: Youth and Crisis* (New York, 1968), on deposit at the Erik Erikson Institute in Chicago, reveals much about how Erikson put it together.

99 "Identity: Youth and Crisis" (final prepublication ms.), Erikson Institute, 377, "I am apt." EHE, *Identity*, 10, "it is disquieting"; 11, on Pamela Daniels's role.

100 "Identity: Youth and Crisis," Erikson Institute, with the title page indicating the changed subtitle. EHE, *Identity*, 12, comparing the volume to *Childhood and Society* and *Young Man Luther.*

101 Robert Coles, *Erik H. Erikson: The Growth of His Work* (Boston, 1970), 255, 353, for short acknowledgment of *Identity: Youth and Crisis*. Letter from Donald S. Lamm to LJF, October 26, 1995, and Lamm, TI by LJF, October 31, 1995, reporting promotion and sales figures for *Identity*, and in comparison to Erikson's other books.

102 EHE, *Identity*, 19–20, 22, 87, 324 *n*.20. See also EHE, "The Concept of Identity in Race Relations: Notes and Queries," 147.

103 See EHE, *Identity*, Chapter 5, especially 216–21. Quite helpful here are Hetty Zock, *A Psychology of Ultimate Concern: Erik H. Erikson's Contribution to the Psychology of Religion* (New York, 1990), especially 72, and Donald Capps, "Erikson's Life Cycle Theory: Religious Dimensions" (n.d. [early 1980s]), 13–14, 17, E-H.

104 EHE, "Identity: Youth and Crisis," Erikson Institute, 77, "to dominate the collective mind." EHE, *Identity*, 35–36, on "ideological undernourishment" and "youth have proven more foresighted." EHE, "Letter to the Commission on the Year 2000," American Academy of Arts and Sciences, February 11–12, 1966, 2 (Margaret Mead Papers, LC). The essay was partially republished in the first chapter of *Identity*. For examples of similar Erikson defenses of activist youth at this time, see, e.g., EHE, "On Student Unrest" (unpublished brochure, 1969), 209–210, E-H; Schlein, *Way*, 689–90, 696; Evans, *Dialogue with Erikson,* 34–35.

105 Erikson's 1964 article on gender ("The Inner and the Outer Space") and his 1966 article on race ("The Concept of Identity in Race Relations") were reprinted in *Identity;* the controversies they later sparked shall be treated contextually in subsequent chapters. EHE, *Identity*, 41–42, on "pseudospecies," which "can now spell the end"; 90, "a more *universal identity* . . . all the diversities and dissonances"; 260, "the test of what you produce"; 138, "belief in the species" and "a welcome trust."

106 EHE, *Identity*, 59, on disregarding Jung; 221, on invocation of the "outer world"; 44–45, "patronizing tributes"; 227–28, on "psychoanalytic 'revisionists' "; 44–45, on neo-Freudians.

107 Gardner Murphy, "Notes on Erik's Book," April 2, 1958, Murphy Papers, AHAP-Akron, 2–3, and JE, TRI by LJF, Cambridge, December 18, 1990, on Anna Freud's misgivings over Erikson's writings and how she conveyed these misgivings. Fred Weinstein, "On the Social Function of Intellectuals," in *New Directions in Psychohistory*, edited by Mel Albin (Lexington, Mass., 1980), 11, noting reservations about Erikson within the analytic community. Abram Kardiner, "Reminiscences" (1963), 222–24, on Erikson, Rare Books and Manuscripts Division, Butler Library, Columbia University.

108 Peter Gay, *Freud: A Life for Our Time* (New York, 1988), 555–62, 775–76; Anna Freud to Max Schur, September 17, 1966, Schur Papers, LC. Also see Bullitt's description of the process of collaborating with Freud in Sigmund Freud and William Bullitt, *Thomas Woodrow Wilson: A Psychological Study* (Boston, 1966), v–viii.

109 Letter from EHE to Anna Freud, October 31, 1966, Anna Freud Papers, LC, on how he came to learn of the Freud-Bullitt manuscript. Letter from Max Schur to Anna Freud, October 19, 1966, Schur Papers, LC, on the *Look* article (30, no. 25, December 13, 1966) and Erikson agreeing to review for the *New York Review of Books.*

110 Letters from EHE to Anna Freud, October 31, 1966, Anna Freud Papers, LC, and Max Schur to Anna Freud, October 19, 1966, Schur Papers, LC. Robert Stewart, PI by LJF, February 2, 1996, on Schur and others providing adverse information on Bullitt.

111 Letters from EHE to Anna Freud, October 31, 1966, and Anna Freud to EHE, November 6, 1966, both in Anna Freud Papers, LC.

112 Letter from Max Schur to EHE, November 9, 1966, Schur Papers, LC, replying to the questionnaire with instructions; Schur to Anna Freud, November 9, 1966, Anna Freud Papers, LC, attaching a copy for her of his letter to Erikson; EHE to Schur, December 29, 1966, Schur Papers, LC, and EHE to Anna Freud, December 29, 1966, Anna Freud Papers, with an early draft of the essay. Reviewing the Freud-Bullitt book in the *New York Times,* Robert Stewart (TI by LJF, February 10, 1996) elected not to send a draft of his review to any Freud loyalists.

113 Letter from Max Schur to Anna Freud, September 26, 1969, Schur Papers, LC, noting favorable reception in the analytic community to Erikson's essay: "He did very well on the Bullitt book." *The International Journal of Psycho-Analysis* 48 (1967): 462–68, reprinted Erikson's "The Strange Case of Freud, Bullitt, and Woodrow Wilson," *New York Review of Books* 8, no. 2 (February 9, 1967): 3–5, from which I have quoted. See also letter from EHE to Anna Freud, July 18, 1967, Anna Freud Papers, LC.

114 Paul Roazen, *Erik H. Erikson: The Power and Limits of a Vision* (New York, 1976), 13, 201–203 *n*.44, is to be thanked for detailing the disparities between Erikson's original *New York Review of Books* essay and the essay as it appeared in *Life History and the Historical Moment.* Letter from EHE to Anna Freud, July 18, 1967, Anna Freud Papers, LC, on Miss Freud's private reservations expressed to the *International Journal of Psycho-Analysis.* Robert Stewart, TI by LJF, July 29, 1995, recalls how Miss Freud and Erikson seemed very friendly at the 1971 Vienna meeting. Beatriz Foster, TI by LJF, January 23, 1996, recalling Erikson's pleasure in 1971 at Anna Freud acknowledging his writing. A detailed summary with quotations from the Philadelphia forum is provided in "Panel Report: The Ego and the Mechanisms of Defense," *Journal of the Philadelphia Association of Psychoanalysis* 1 (1973): 35–42.

115 Robert J. Lifton, PI by LJF, NYC, April 3, 1991, "that's my answer." Letter from Robert J. Lifton to EHE, July 19, 1956, RJL-NYPL, establishing contact with Erikson and noting "a coercive form of psychotherapy."

116 Robert J. Lifton, *History and Human Survival* (New York, 1961), 14–15; Robert J. Lifton in Recognition Reception for Erik and Joan Erikson, Cambridge, Mass., November 21, 1991 (tape recording). Robert J. Lifton, PI by LJF, April 3, 1991; Robert J. Lifton and Eric Olson, eds., *Explorations in Psychohistory: The Wellfleet Papers* (New York, 1974), 12.

117 Betty J. Lifton in EHE-JE Recognition Reception, November 21, 1991. See also Betty J. Lifton, *The King of Children* (London, 1989), 302. Kai Erikson, TRI by LJF, Hamden, November 7, 1993. See also Kai Erikson, *Everything in Its Path: Destruction of Community in the Buffalo Creek Flood* (New York, 1976), 168, and Robert J. Lifton and Eric Olson, "The Human Meaning of Total Disaster: The Buffalo Creek Experience," *Psychiatry* 39, no. 1 (February 1976): 16.

118 Letter from Robert J. Lifton to EHE, October 20, 1963, RJL-NYPL, on Erikson first coming up with the idea for the Wellfleet gathering. Robert J. Lifton, PI by LJF, NYC, April 3, 1991, on making Erikson's ideas and presentations the heart of the Wellfleet meeting. See also "Group for the Study of Psychohistorical Progress" (n.d. [February 1966]), E-H, and letter from Robert J. Lifton to EHE, January 2, 1966, E-H.

119 Robert J. Lifton, PI by LJF, NYC, April 3, 1991; Bruce Mazlish, PI by LJF, Cambridge, February 16, 1991; "Group for the Study of Psychohistorical Progress" (n.d. [February 1966]), E-H; Gerald Holton, TRI by LJF, Cambridge, February 15, 1991; Nina Holton, TRI by LJF, Lexington, Mass., April 30, 1991; letter from Robert J. Lifton to EHE, June 17, 1968, RJL-NYPL.

120 Robert J. Lifton, PI by LJF, NYC, April 3, 1991; LJF, "Erik Erikson and Robert Lifton:

The Pattern of a Relationship," *Trauma and Self,* edited by Charles Strozier and Michael Flynn (Lanham, Md., 1996), 138–39.

121 Robert J. Lifton, "From Analysis to Formation: Towards a Shift in Psychological Paradigm," *Journal of the American Academy of Psychoanalysis* 4, no. 1 (1976): 63–94, compared Freud's, Erikson's, and his own images quite clearly, especially 69–71.

122 Ibid., 90–91, "carries Erikson's principle." See also Robert J. Lifton, "Psychohistory," *Partisan Review* 37, no. 1 (1970): 21, 31–32; letter from Margaret Brenman-Gibson to EHE, April 6, 1972 (copy), Margaret Brenman-Gibson private papers, Stockbridge; Robert J. Lifton, "Visit with Erik Erikson in Belvedere, California, March 23, 1973," RJL-NYPL, 6.

123 EHE, "Remarks Made at White House Staff Dinner, June 11, 1969," E-H: Erikson's text, which includes notations on what occurred during the dinner.

124 Sue Bloland, TI by LJF, December 4, 1993, September 18, 1994, and August 13, 1995; Harland Bloland, TI by LJF, December 20, 1995.

125 Schlein, *Way,* 745–47, provides Erikson's "Appleton Chapel Talk" of September 24, 1969.

CHAPTER 8
GLOBAL PROPHET: ERIKSON'S TRUTH

1 EHE, *Gandhi's Truth: On the Origins of Militant Nonviolence* (New York, 1969), 9, "search for the historical presence." EHE in "Letters," *New York Review of Books,* 13, no. 6 (October 9, 1969): 60, on translating *Satyagraha;* this is a response to L. N. Gupta. EHE, "Gandhi's Truth—Miscellaneous Papers" (n.d.), E-H, trying to connect the four phrases. EHE, *Gandhi's Truth,* 91–92, on "authentically," "unfair," "a stranger"; 39–40, on clinical observation. George Goethals, PI by LJF, Cambridge, March 27, 1991, on how Erikson urged him and Zinberg to take over SS 139.

2 EHE application to American Institute of Indian Studies (n.d. [December 1963]), 2, EHE Faculty Personnel File, Harvard Archives.

3 Dean W. Lord, "The Eriksons Return to Harvard," *Harvard Gazette,* October 12, 1984, 4, on Joan studying Indian printing and dyeing. Letter from EHE to Armando Armando, April 2, 1979, E-H, "one of my favorite."

4 Mary Catherine Bateson, *Composing a Life* (New York, 1990), 112; JE, TRI by David Andersen, Cambridge, October 16, 1991.

5 JE, *St. Francis and His Four Ladies* (New York, 1970), 48, 108.

6 JE, *St. Francis,* 129, "our basic bisexuality" and "self-denying asceticism." EHE, *Gandhi's Truth,* 14, "kind of sainthood"; 108, "locomotor restlessness"; 177–78, on Gandhi as "a religious craftsman" and St. Francis as one as well, extending "household" into wider spheres. EHE, "Gandhi's Truth—Miscellaneous Papers" (n.d.), E-H, listing Gandhi's and St. Francis's similar qualities like facing the viceroy and the bishop, embracing untouchables and lepers, etc. JE, *St. Francis,* 127–28, on the "presence" of both men communicating the "infinite in the immediate." EHE, "Psychoanalysis and Ongoing History," *American Journal of Psychiatry* (September 1965): 249, "the stuff parables."

7 JE, "Nothing to Fear: Notes on the Life of Eleanor Roosevelt," *Daedalus* 93 (Spring 1964): especially 799–800.

8 EHE, *Gandhi's Truth,* 230–31, "to continue writing"; 232–43, 252–53, on Gandhi's cruelty to his wife, son, and the girls; 241, "You were right wherever." Carol Gilligan, TRI by LJF, Cambridge, April 15, 1991, on Erikson reading the letter to SS 139.

9 Pamela Daniels, TRI by LJF, Boston, March 15 and April 12, 1991, and TI, February 23, 1996, and Sudhir Kakar, TRI by LJF, Boston, April 28, 1991, recalling Erikson's writing block interval and his need to speak to Gandhi about what he had discovered. EHE, *Life History and the Historical Moment* (New York, 1975), 145, "impulsive need to answer" and "all manner of countertransference."

10 Kamla Chowdhry, TRI by David Andersen, Cambridge, October 17, 1991, that Erikson did not understand the circumstances of Gandhi's purported abuses. Chowdhry noted that India scholar Suzanne Rudolph was unable to find strong substantiating evidence. Sudhir Kakar, TRI by LJF, Boston, April 28, 1991, and PI by LJF, Wellfleet, October 6, 1996, on Kakar's suggestion of a letter to Gandhi. See also Kakar, "Erik Erikson in India: A Personal Memoir" (n.p. [1994]).

11 I am indebted to Robert Coles, *Erik H. Erikson: The Growth of His Work* (Boston, Toronto, 1970), 291, for underscoring the Kierkegaard-Tillich-Buber connection. Buber, "A Letter to Gandhi," in *Pointing the Way: Collected Essays by Martin Buber,* edited by Maurice S. Friedman (New York, 1963), 139–47; 146, "I do not want"; 146–47, "grievous error" and "friends and."

12 No Erikson-related archival correspondence indicates whether he had read Buber's "Letter to Gandhi." I have consulted Erikson's family and many of his friends on the subject. None could remember. Robert J. Lifton, PI by LJF, February 18, 1996, recalled how Buber was very much in the air in Cambridge during the 1960s, how he had been taken by the "Letter," and how Erikson had periodically mentioned Buber's writings and ideas. Gandhi, too, was in the air, especially within the local peace movement. Pamela Daniels, TI by LJF, February 23, 1996, could not document a specific instance of Erikson learning of Buber's "Letter," but believes that he almost certainly came across it.

13 The 1967 *Daedalus* symposium "On the Nature of 'Psycho-Historical' Evidence" is reprinted in EHE, *Life History,* 113–68, see especially 161.

14 Robert J. Lifton, TRI by LJF, Wellfleet, April 24, 1991, recalling the Wellfleet meeting where he advised against including the letter to Gandhi. JE, TRI by LJF, Cambridge, December 18, 1990, and October 16, 1991, also recalls that meeting, how others objected to inclusion of the letter, and why Joan Erikson favored including it. Caroline Murray, PI by LJF, Cambridge, March 11, 1991, on Henry A. Murray seeing the letter as inappropriate.

15 EHE, "Letter to Gandhi," *New York Review of Books* 13, no. 2 (July 31, 1969): 12–22. EHE, *Gandhi's Truth,* 248, "mere avoidance"; 243, "those closest to"; 247, "unilateral coercion"; 248, "on them decisions"; 242–43, "one part of him."

16 EHE, *Gandhi's Truth,* 247, defining "mutuality"; 236, on sexual relations and "mutual consent and artful interplay"; 241–42, "experiment in truth," "I, as a post-Einsteinian," and "the meeting of adult."

17 Ibid., 254, concluding the letter; 397, "It may be just." Philip Pomper, *The Structure of the Mind in History: Five Major Figures in Psychohistory* (New York, 1985), 94, cogently distinguishes Freud from Erikson on the place of the leader.

18 Sudhir Kakar, "The Human Life Cycle: The Traditional Hindu View and the Psychology of Erik Erikson," *Philosophy East and West* 18, no. 3 (1968): 127–36, represents the most comprehensive effort to reconcile and distinguish the two life cycles; see especially 128–30, 135. EHE, *Gandhi's Truth,* 36–38, on *Antevasin, Grhastha,* and *Vanaprastha.*

19 Kakar, "Human Life Cycle," 134, charting a comparison. Subsequently in *The Inner World: A Psycho-Analytic Study of Childhood and Society in India* (Delhi, 1981), and other publications, Kakar continued to affirm the connection between the two life cycles.

20 Sudhir Kakar, TRI by LJF, Boston, April 28, 1991, and PI by LJF, Wellfleet, October 6, 1996, and EHE, *The Life Cycle Completed: A Review* (New York, 1982, 1985), 58, recalling Kakar-Erikson dialogues over the Hindu equivalent of generativity. EHE, *Gandhi's Truth,* 180, 397, linking generativity to the Householder and to "actuality." EHE, "Generativity and the Future," Chautauqua Institute Lecture, August 3, 1978, Chautauqua Institute Library, transcript 4, is also instructive. See also Alan Roland, *In Search of Self in India and Japan: Towards a Cross-Cultural Psychology* (Princeton, 1988), 314, on the hierarchical and dependent nature of Indian childhood.

21 EHE, *Gandhi's Truth,* 38, "impossible to compare" and "which makes them." Sudhir Kakar, PI by LJF, Wellfleet, October 6, 1996.

22 EHE, "On the Nature of Psycho-Historical Evidence: In Search of Gandhi," *Daedalus* 97 (Summer 1968): 721–22, on salt and "the nonsexual." EHE, *Gandhi's Truth*, 427, "Instinct has become." EHE, TRI by Forrest G. Robinson, Cambridge, August 12, 1970, "never learned in Vienna."

23 EHE, *Life History*, 145, "to proceed." EHE, *Gandhi's Truth*, 98–99, "I consider"; 157, "obsessive symptomatology" and "dispositions."

24 EHE, *Gandhi's Truth*, 247, "joined in a universal"; 244–46, "confronts the *inner* enemy," "instrument of enlightenment," "*truth method*," "moral suppression," and "disciplined self-suffering"; 439, "encounters," "militant probing," "not only to think," and "an optimum."

25 Hetty Zock, *A Psychology of Ultimate Concern: Erik H. Erikson's Contribution to the Psychology of Religion* (Amsterdam, 1990), 164, 172, and Richard T. Knowles, *Human Development and Human Possibility: Erikson in the Light of Heidegger* (Landham, Md., 1986), 199, provide very useful discussions of Erikson going beyond traditional psychoanalytic formulations in *Gandhi's Truth*.

26 EHE, *Gandhi's Truth*, 431, recalling Lorenz and the Royal Society meeting and elaborating the meaning of "pseudospeciation"; 400, "mutual differentiations" and "examples of."

27 David A. Hollinger, *Postethnic America: Beyond Multiculturalism* (New York, 1995), 52–57, locates Erikson within the universalistic perspective of Willkie and Steichen. EHE, *Gandhi's Truth*, 433, "*may have*"; 413, "actualizes both." EHE, "The Concept of Identity in Race Relations: Notes and Queries," *Daedalus* 95, no. 1 (Winter 1966): 166, "join their identities." EHE, *Gandhi's Truth*, 433, "For all parts" and "in a sense of widening identity." Kakar, "Human Life Cycle," 130, on the relation of *dharma* to mutuality.

28 Gary Gerstle, "This Land's Not Your Land," *Tikkun* (November-December 1994): 68, and David Hollinger, "How Wide the Circle of the 'We'?: American Intellectuals and the Problem of the Ethnos Since World War II," *American Historical Review* 98, no. 2 (April 1993): 318, are especially helpful on such predecessors of "pseudospeciation" and "universal specieshood." Hans Kohn, *The Mind of Germany: The Education of a Nation* (New York, 1965), 251–52, on *Weltliteratur*.

29 EHE, "Further Autobiographic Remarks: For Friends and Relations Only," August 1977, E-H, "contending and even conflicting." Pamela Daniels, TRI by LJF, Boston, March 15, 1991; John M. Ross, TRI by LJF, NYC, August 16, 1991.

30 Stephen Jay Gould, "A Biological Comment on Erik Erikson's Notion of Pseudospeciation" (n.d.), E-H, 4–5. Gould's final polished version of this essay appeared in the *Yale Review* 73, no. 4 (July 1984): 487–90.

31 EHE, *Gandhi's Truth*, 311, on traditional political leaders in the West and Russia, and how Gandhi "confronted the world." EHE, *Insight and Responsibility: Lectures on the Ethical Implications of Psychoanalytic Insight* (New York, 1964), 239, "reciprocal coercion," "an opportunity," and "*justice which.*" EHE, "Psychoanalysis and Ongoing History," 250, "age old." Richard Evans, ed., *Dialogue with Erik Erikson* (New York, 1967), 74–75, "rock-bottom," "crafty and cunning," and "seeing any contradiction." For Gandhi as partaken in historical actuality or "actualism," see EHE, *Gandhi's Truth*, 411, and an excellent analysis in Lewis D. Wurgaft, "Erik Erikson: From Luther to Gandhi," *Psychoanalytic Review* 63, no. 2 (1976): 221–22.

32 Letter from EHE to Roger Fisher, October 1962, E-H, 29, identifying closely with Gandhi's politics. EHE, "Address, Harvard Chapel," April 30, 1964, E-H, 5–6, "Gandhi would study." EHE, *Gandhi's Truth*, 434, "*engagement*"; 198, "the meeting of bodies" and "solidarity of unarmed bodies"; 435, "*the opponent.*"

33 Letter from EHE to Barbara Epstein, August 26, 1969, E-H, that *Satyagraha* was not passive resistance. Kai Erikson, ed., *In Search of Common Ground: Conversations with Erik H. Erikson and Huey P. Newton* (New York, 1973), 115–16, on Gandhi calling off nonviolent campaigns and "a very self-disciplined." EHE, *Gandhi's Truth*, 375–77, on Jews and combat leading to the potential for *Satyagraha*.

34 Mitchell Ginsberg, TI by LJF, January 4, 1996, and letter from Ginsberg to LJF, Febru-

ary 6, 1996. For Erikson's remarks in group meetings, see "Notes of the Meeting of the HRA-Field Foundation Study Group," July 9, 1969, 7, 9; July 22, 1969, 8; July 30, 1969, 1, 7. This Human Resources Administration group received modest funding from the Field Foundation through its executive director, Lester Dunbar, who periodically participated in discussions. It began meeting toward the end of the winter of 1968–69 and Ginsberg provided me with copies of the minutes of some of its later meetings (the only minutes that he could locate). Erikson began attending in July 1969.

35 EHE, *Life History,* 148, reproducing remarks from the *Daedalus* symposium. EHE, *Gandhi's Truth,* 448, correcting Tagore. EHE, "The Inner and the Outer Space: Reflections on Womanhood," *Daedalus* 92, no. 2 (1964): 582–606. Pamela Daniels, TRI by LJF, Boston, April 12, 1991, observing the impact of India and Gandhi on Erikson's view of "inner space." EHE, *Gandhi's Truth,* 112, "his relation to his mother" and "to unite the feminine." George Goethals reports the SS 139 lecture on Gandhi versus Fanon in his presentation at a Cambridge Hospital symposium on Erikson, October 29, 1994 (tape). EHE, *Gandhi's Truth,* 437, reveals a fuller version of this Fanon-Gandhi contest.

36 "Lecture by Erik Erikson," Santa Barbara, February 19, 1972, E-H, 16, "wanted to get closer" and "search for." EHE, "Gandhi's Autobiography: The Leader as a Child," *American Scholar* 35, no. 4 (Autumn 1966): 632, "I have been trying."

37 EHE, "Gandhi's Autobiography," 632, "a man who." EHE, *Gandhi's Truth,* 402, "feminine imagery" and "prided himself."

38 EHE, "Address, Harvard Chapel," April 30, 1964, E-H, 1, "thinking of Him," "the silent nights," "to visualize that presence," and "we encountered." EHE, *Gandhi's Truth,* 20, "as pervasive."

39 EHE, *Gandhi's Truth,* 395, "what and whom"; 399, "*must* forget." Evans, *Dialogue with Erikson,* 72, on the Golden Rule. EHE, *Gandhi's Truth,* 112, "have to become."

40 EHE, *Gandhi's Truth,* 178, "religious craftsman" and "repaired"; 260, "an economic necessity"; 270, "the skills necessary"; 273, "the symbol of"; 58–59, "spinning, praying"; 260, "to build a community"; 364, Ahmadabad as "a craftsmanlike rehearsal"; 392, "crafty politician."

41 Ibid., 396–97.

42 Ibid., 397, "a man who"; 101, "such men as," "involve the very persons," and "to wrestle." In her insightful study *A Psychology of Ultimate Concern,* Hetty Zock focuses on Erikson's concern with the sense of "I" beginning with *Young Man Luther* and reaching very nearly a culmination in *Gandhi's Truth.* While I agree with her on Erikson's increasing concern with the "I" during the 1950s and 1960s, I am skeptical of a clear "beginning" and "culmination" of this perspective. His journal as a young man evidenced concern with the "I" as did his late-life writings.

43 Norton's promotional campaign and the prizes won are discussed in George Brockway, TI by LJF, January 29, 1994, and Donald Lamm, TI by LJF, June 24, 1994. The prizes are noted in *New York Times,* March 5, 1970; letter from EHE to Peter Blos, November 4, 1974, E-H; *Boston Globe,* March 3, 1970; letter from Edward Darling to EHE, February 18, 1970, E-H. Foreign editions are listed in "Report of the Medical Director, Austen Riggs Center, January 1, 1970–December 31, 1970," 15.

44 Letters from Donald Lamm to LJF, July 5, 1994, and October 26, 1995, report and explain *Gandhi's Truth* sales figures from Norton records. Lamm, TI by LJF, August 30, 1994, and October 31, 1995, and Brockway, TRI by LJF, January 29, 1994, speculating on the drop in sales. Fax from Anabel Gee to LJF, July 30, 1997, reporting Faber and Faber sales figures.

45 Letter from EHE to Peter Blos, November 4, 1974, E-H; Brockway, TI by LJF, November 29, 1994, and Stephen Schlein, ed., *A Way of Looking at Things: Selected Papers from 1930–1980. Erik H. Erikson* (New York, 1987), 741–42, on Erikson's response to prizes and notoriety. Letter from EHE to Gerhard Piel, December 11, 1969, E-H, "with considerable trepidation," "I do not really know," and "more years."

46 Irving Howe, "A Great Man's Greatness," *Harper's Magazine* 240 (April 1970): 105, and Lewis Lipsitz and Herbert Kritzer, "Unconventional Approaches to Conflict Resolution," *Journal of Conflict Resolution* 19 (December, 1975): 724, on *Satyagraha* only working with the British. In K. Erikson, *In Search of Common Ground,* 112, Erikson conceded the point. L. N. Gupta, "Truthforce," *New York Review of Books* 13, no. 6 (October 9, 1969): 60. Floyd Wylie review in *Journal of Asian Studies* 32, no. 3 (May 1973): 526–27. The focus on "the Event" is challenged by Leonard Gordon in *Journal of Social History* 4, no. 4 (Summer 1971): 429, and Wurgaft, "Erik Erikson," 230.

47 Letter from EHE to Kamla Chowdhry and Sudhir Kakar, March 22, 1976, E-H, recalling the attacks on his East-West connections and other hurts he felt from the reviews of India specialists, especially those specialists he knew. Suzanne Rudolph, "Saintly Aggressor," *Contemporary Psychology* 15, no. 8 (August 1970): 484–85.

48 J. L. Masson, "India and the Unconscious: Erik Erikson on Gandhi," *International Journal of Psycho-Analysis* 55, no. 4 (1974): 519, 525. Alan Grey, "Oedipus in Hindu Dreams: Gandhi's Life and Erikson's Concepts," *Contemporary Psychoanalysis* 9, no. 3 (May 1973): 352–53. Letter from Lester Luborsky to EHE, September 10, 1969, George Klein Papers, AHAP-Akron.

49 Letter from G. Morris Carstairs to EHE, September 2, 1971, E-H. Randall Kehler, TI by LJF, February 10, 1996. Robert J. Lifton, "On Spiritual Innovators: Erikson and Gandhi," *Psychiatry and Social Science Review* 6 (1970): 4. Coles, *Erikson,* 399. A more recent reading of *Gandhi's Truth*—Irving Alexander, "Erikson's Gandhi and Erikson—Revisited," *Contemporary Psychology* 41, no. 4 (1996): 311–15—makes exceedingly persuasive suggestions of connections between Erikson's life and his portrayal of Gandhi.

50 Robert Young, *White Mythologies: Writing History and the West* (London, New York, 1990), provides an excellent overview of postcolonial criticism; 14–15, treats Levinas. Hollinger, *Postethnic America,* especially 58–59, offers a cogent critique of the World War II cosmopolitans' embrace of species-centered discourse. Erikson's 1979 keynote address to the International Congress of Psychoanalysts is reported in Alan Roland, "Psychoanalysis in India and Japan: Toward a Comparative Psychoanalysis," *American Journal of Psychoanalysis* 51, no. 1 (1991): 9. Edward W. Said's *Orientalism* (New York, 1978), represents the type of postcolonial critique toward which Erikson may have been heading.

51 Letter from EHE to John Hohenberg, October 17, 1973, E-H, "to retire." Announcement, Harvard University News Office, July 17, 1970, EHE Faculty Personnel File, Harvard Archives, concerning his retirement. Pusey's policy and Erikson's retirement are discussed thoroughly in Richard Hunt, TRI by LJF, Cambridge, November 22, 1991, and David Riesman, TRI by LJF, Cambridge, March 2, 1991.

52 Letter from Donald S. Lamm to LJF, October 26, 1995, listing Erikson's Norton paperback book sales for 1970–71. Letter from George Brockway to EHE, May 4, 1971, E-H, pledging lucrative advances on lectures.

53 EHE at Austen Riggs Center, Stockbridge, November 22, 1985, Harriet Harvey videotape, as "an immigrant." Martha Proctor, TRI by LJF, Tiburon, September 13, 1995, and Peggy Penn, TRI by LJF, NYC, November 8, 1993, on moving back to Stockbridge, buying a house, and dancing. For Erikson's activities at Riggs in the early 1970s, see M. Gerard Fromm, PI by LJF, Stockbridge, March 20, 1992; Eugene Talbot, TRI by LJF, Stockbridge, December 17, 1992; Margaret Brenman-Gibson, TI by LJF, March 14, 1992. Letter from EHE to Peter Heller, March 18, 1971, Peter Heller private papers, on the general routine into which he had settled.

54 EHE, "Memorandum for Friends & Correspondents," September 15, 1970, George Klein Papers, AHAP-Akron, on the internal disorder. Peggy Penn, TRI by LJF, NYC, November 8, 1993, on the nap routine. K. Erikson, *In Search of Common Ground,* 98, "a psychoanalyst." Stephen Graubard, TRI by LJF, Somerville, April 8, 1991, and David Elkind in *New York Times Magazine,* April 5, 1970, 85, on Erikson's manner in the early 1970s. Schlein, *Way,* 712, speaking at the ceremony honoring Blos.

55 *Berkshire Eagle,* June 9, 1972, reports the Brown honorary degree; Yale University Commencement (announcement), June 14, 1971, E-H, announcing an honorary degree;
"Regents of University of California: Degree of Doctor of Law" award to EHE, May 10,
1968, E-H. Letter from EHE to Noel Annan, December 7, 1972, E-H, on the Freud
chair. Letter from David J. McDonnell to EHE, October 17, 1974, E-H, and *APA Mon-
itor* 6, no. 1 (January 1975), on the National Association for Mental Health award. Letter from Richard H. David to EHE, June 1, 1973, E-H, and *Berkshire Eagle,* September
14, 1973, on the Montessori award. *National Academy of Education* (Spring 1969): 11,
32, on election to the National Academy of Education. Letter from EHE to Kurt von
Fritz, March 18, 1974, E-H, "notoriety."

56 JE, TRI by LJF, Harwich, January 15, 1994, recalling the *Times Magazine* photograph.
David Elkind, "Erik Erikson's Eight Ages of Man," *New York Times Magazine,* April 5,
1970, 25–27, 84–85, with Erikson's photograph on the cover. Elkind, "Praise and Imi-
tation," *Saturday Review* 54 (January 1971): especially 51. "Erik Erikson: The Quest for
Identity," *Newsweek,* December 21, 1970, 84, quoting Bellah. Peter Lomax, "The Spiritual Biography of a Psychoanalyst," *New York Times Book Review* (November 22, 1970):
1. Letter from Leonore C. Hauck to EHE, June 7, 1974, E-H, in behalf of Random
House Dictionaries. The 1972 Santa Barbara symposium is reported in *Newsletter:
Group for the Use of Psychology in History* 3, no. 2 (September 1974): 5. Pamela Daniels
to EHE, "Notes on discussion, Godkin Seminar," April 21, 1972, E-H, 4, "I didn't
intend."

57 Dorothy G. Singer, "*Charlotte's Web* and Erikson's Life Cycle," *School Library Journal* 22,
no. 3 (November 1975): 17–19. Letter from EHE to Sudhir Kakar, September 27, 1976,
E-H, reporting the television audience for the Hubley film. Barbara Bowman, PI by LJF,
Chicago, June 30, 1995, on the origins of the name "Erik Erikson Institute." Coles,
Erikson, xvii, "a clinician."

58 Senn Oral History Collection, National Library of Medicine, comment by Sibylle
Escalona, September 6, 1973, on Erikson's attitudes toward being cited and distorted.
Mark Gerzon and Michael Lerner discussion with EHE, Stockbridge, May 22, 1971,
Reel 1, Tape A, Side A, E-H, "Young people." George Goethals, PI by LJF, Cambridge,
March 27, 1991, on the Johnson plaque. EHE, "Memorial for Friends," November 5,
1970, Anna Freud Papers, LC, 81, on the Coles essays and the trade-off between these
essays and coverage by six newsmagazines. For typical rejections of lecture invitations, see
letters from EHE to Gordon F. Derner, July 17, 1970, Derner Papers, AHAP-Akron;
EHE to Peter Heller, March 18, 1971, Peter Heller private papers; EHE written reply on
H. B. M. Murphy to EHE, October 21, 1975, E-H. Erikson's management of publicity
is illustrated by letter from EHE to Traut Felgentreff (n.d. [1973]); Clemens Kalischer,
PI by LJF, Stockbridge, March 27, 1993; Kenneth L. Woodward, "An Identity of Wisdom," *Newsweek,* May 23, 1994, 56. Letter from EHE to Jonathan Black, August 15,
1969, E-H, "I already." George Brockway, TI by LJF, January 29, 1994, and Donald
Lamm, TI by LJF, October 31, 1995, on advance quotations on the life cycle chart.

59 K. Erikson, *In Search of Common Ground,* 12–14; Kai Erikson, TRI by LJF, Hamden,
November 7, 1993, and Kai and Erik Erikson discussion, Hamden, November 24, 1985,
Harriet Harvey videotape; Kai Erikson, TRI by LJF, Hamden, November 7, 1993; Hugh
Pearson, *The Shadow of the Panther: Huey Newton and the Price of Black Power in Amer-
ica* (Reading, Mass., 1994), 209–10, 227.

60 Kai Erikson, TRI by LJF, November 7, 1993, on Erik agreeing to join the Yale seminar.
Michael Lerner–Mark Gerson discussion with EHE, May 2, 1971, Reel 2, Tape A, Side
B, E-H, on Erikson's early failure to see the effects of American racism. Flora M. Rhind,
"Interview of Erik Homburger Erikson," NYC, July 17, 1947, General Education
Board, Rockefeller Archives, Box 375, Folder 3914, recalling Bay Area race relations in
the 1940s. Letter from EHE to "Dear Friends," December 12, 1956, E-H, detailing the
visit to Fisk. EHE and JE, "On Generativity and Identity: From a Conversation with

Erik and Joan Erikson," *Harvard Education Review* 51, no. 2 (May 1981): 258, recalling thoughts of a book on Parks.

61 Erikson's race relations papers were "A Memorandum on Identity and Negro Youth," *Journal of Social Issues* 20 (1964): 29–42, and "The Concept of Identity in Race Relations: Notes and Queries," *Daedalus* 95 (Winter 1966): 145–71. The latter was reprinted as Chapter 8 in *Identity: Youth and Crisis* (New York, 1968). Letter from EHE to Adele and Robert Knight, August 17, 1964, E-H, on meeting with Freedom Summer volunteers. Several Erikson observations on African-American children in Boston's Charleston School, December 1970, are deposited in his papers at the Houghton Library. EHE, *Identity,* 25, on *Invisible Man.* EHE, "Concept of Identity in Race Relations," 164, on the Black Muslims; 162, on "father absence." The visit to Mississippi Head Start schools is covered in Coles, *Erikson,* 410; letter from EHE to Iris Rothman, March 14, 1969, E-H; EHE, "Play and Actuality" presentation at Erikson Institute, Chicago, April 18, 1970, E-H, transcript 19.

62 FBI File No. 157-21288 (Erik Homburger Erikson), secured under Freedom Act Request No. 369,248 and reporting FBI activities plus "black extremist." It is interesting that Erikson's FBI file says nothing about his role during the McCarthy period in refusing to sign a loyalty oath. K. Erikson, *In Search of Common Ground,* especially 10, 121. Kai Erikson, TRI by LJF, Hamden, November 7, 1993. Kai and Erik Erikson, Hamden, November 24, 1985, Harvey videotape. Letter from Kai Erikson to LJF, January 17, 1998.

63 K. Erikson, *In Search of Common Ground,* 54, 60, 84, 90, 121–24.

64 Ibid., 131–32, 138. EHE, "Remarks at Community Learning Center," February 10, 1974, E-H.

65 K. Erikson, *In Search of Common Ground,* 103, "personal" and "impression"; 98, on Gandhi the revolutionary; 79, "to kill that human dignity" and "respond to human love." EHE, "Play, Vision, and Deception," E. L. Godkin Lecture, April 11, 1972, 20, "the law of the land . . . outlaws." EHE, "Remarks at Community Learning Center," February 10, 1974, E-H, "treat me" and "I found."

66 EHE, "Remarks at Community Learning Center," February 10, 1974. Pearson, *Shadow,* 229, on orders to Panther squads; 234, on Newton's capacity to engage very different types of people. Hollinger, *Postethnic America,* 52–57, puts the Erikson-Newton conversations in context of an emerging retribalization. Letter from Kai Erikson to LJF, January 17, 1998, on the publication of an edited transcript by Norton.

67 Letters from EHE to Molly Dougherty, September 22, 1974, E-H; Huey Newton to EHE, September 25, 1977, E-H, and EHE reply to Newton (n.d.), dictated on the original letter.

68 EHE, *Toys and Reasons: Stages in the Ritualization of Experience* (New York, 1977), 12, "invited from retirement." Letter from Pamela Daniels to EHE, March 6, 1972, E-H, on lecture and seminar format and selections for seminar members.

69 EHE, *Toys,* 11, on the lecture topic; 179 *n.*1, on the 1972 American context.

70 For the large crowd attending the lectures and the need to shift locations, see *Boston Globe,* April 12, 1972, and Pamela Daniels, TRI by LJF, Boston, March 15, 1991. James W. Anderson, "The Life of Erik H. Erikson," Course Lecture for Personality and Psychopathology, University of Chicago, May 17, 1989, 7, recalling attending lectures and the seminars with a perspective approximating Daniels's. Letter from George Brockway to EHE, May 4, 1971, E-H, on the Norton advance. EHE, *Toys,* 13, on the dedication to Joan.

71 Letter from EHE to Don K. Price, May 16, 1972, E-H, "It was obvious." Robert Coles in *Washington Post Book Review,* February 20, 1977, N2; Rosemary Dinnage, "Truly Leaping," *Times Literary Supplement,* February 24, 1978, 237.

72 Letter from EHE to Sydney J. Harris, March 26, 1976, E-H, on possible biography projects. EHE, "Play, Vision, and Deception," First Godkin Lecture, April 11, 1972, 7 (Margaret Brenman-Gibson private papers), observing children's play constructions.

73 EHE, *Toys,* 139–45, and "Dynamic Psychology and Education," Wright Institute Symposium, Berkeley, April 20, 1976, 7, E-H, on Einstein. EHE, *Toys,* 43–44, "provides the infantile form." Letter from Pamela Daniels to EHE, April 19, 1972, E-H, 2, quoting Erikson's Godkin seminar remarks on "reach out" and "feel grounded"; 6, on "a symptom" and "leeway." EHE, "Material for *Wellfleet Papers,*" April 19, 1974, E-H, and EHE, "Play, Vision, and Deception," 11, on *Spielraum;* 14–15, on Bruner and Piaget.

74 EHE, *Toys,* 112, on Blake and old man's "reasons" being "blessed by," "a simple integrity," and "old people and children"; 72, on Gandhi's gamesmanship. EHE, "Play and Actuality," Erikson Institute, Chicago, April 18, 1970, E-H, 46, defining "actuality." Letter from Pamela Daniels to EHE, April 21, 1972, E-H, 6, quoting Erikson's seminar remark on the problems of modern life.

75 EHE, "Play, Vision, and Deception," April 11, 1972, 20, on Newton and the Panthers. Letter from Pamela Daniels to EHE, April 17, 1972, E-H, 9 (summary of Godkin seminar), quoting Erikson on the urban neighborhood.

76 EHE, "Play, Vision, and Deception," April 12, 1972, 44, "some women now." Godkin seminar on the "New Woman," April 17, 1972, E-H, 4–5, "we are all bisexual." Letter from Pamela Daniels to EHE, April 17, 1974, 8 (summary of Godkin seminar), on women and the presidency; April 19, 1974, 4 (summary of Godkin seminar), "roles to experiment . . . different for boys." Letter from Pamela Daniels to EHE, April 17, 1974, 11, and especially J. W. Anderson, "Life of Erikson," 7, on the conclusion of the seminar.

77 EHE, *Toys,* 144–45, "makes man lonelier" and "totalistic . . . ideologies." Letter from EHE to Cal —, March 23, 1972, E-H, 9, "mass produced roles."

78 EHE, "Play, Vision, and Deception," April 12, 1972, 39, on Hiroshima. EHE, *Toys,* 164, on My Lai; 116–17, on the Vietnam "colonial war" generally, "technological means," and "loss of imagination."

79 EHE, *Toys,* 11–12, proposing to expand the "Ontogeny" essay, and Part II, "Life Cycle and Ritualization," 67–118, recycles "Ontogeny of Ritualization in Man."

80 Ibid., 90, "sense of 'I' renewed" and "a *separateness*"; 48–49, 91, on the newborn and the mother; 47, "the desired presence"; 149, "an all-human consciousness"; 147–48, on weltanschauung and "a remnant."

81 *New York Times,* December 3, 1972, on the conditions of the NEH selection of Erikson.

82 Letter from EHE to Fawn Brodie, August 9, 1972, E-H, on Stockbridge life and Joan's arthritic hip. For cogent discussions of factors prompting the move to California, see letter from JE to Margaret and William Gibson, March 17, 1973, Margaret Brenman-Gibson private papers; Margaret Brenman-Gibson, PI by LJF, Cambridge, June 15, 1994; Helmut Wohl, TRI by LJF, Boston, April 24, 1991; Robert Wallerstein, PI by LJF, San Francisco, August 13, 1990; M. Gerard Fromm, PI by LJF, Stockbridge, December 18, 1992.

83 Letter from EHE to Otto Will, March 15, 1973, E-H, on buying a house in Tiburon. Letter from Mary Carswell to EHE (n.d. [fall 1974]), E-H, and Carswell, TI by LJF, January 19, 1996, on persuading Erikson to remain on the Riggs Board of Trustees. Letters from EHE to Fawn Brodie, October 12, 1973, E-H, "most difficult" move; EHE to Ruth N. Anshen, May 7, 1973, Anshen Papers, Columbia, "what help." Julie Martino, PI by LJF, Stockbridge, March 20, 1992, and TI, March 20, 1996, testifying to the loss of Erikson's clinical records as one who had packed and mailed them from Stockbridge.

84 Letter from Wallace B. Edgerton to Dumas Malone, December 16, 1971 (copy), E-H, recalling how Erikson decided to lecture on Jefferson.

85 Letters from EHE to Dumas Malone, December 28, 1971, E-H, replying to Malone's offer to help; EHE to Fawn Brodie, August 9, 1972, E-H, "both to the woman"; Fawn Brodie to EHE, August 24, 1972, and September 16, 1973, E-H. See also EHE, "Jefferson Lectures—Notes and Source Material" (n.d.), E-H, and EHE, *Dimensions of a New Identity: The Jefferson Lectures in the Humanities* (New York, 1974), 12, 14, on reservations over psychohistory.

86 Robert J. Lifton, "Visit with Erik Erikson in Belvedere, California, March 23, 1973," 3,

RJL-NYPL, on lecturing from notes with students invited. John and Virginia Demos, PI by LJF, Stockbridge, December 2, 1995, on the Stockbridge trial run.

87 Robert J. Lifton, "Visit with Erikson in Belvedere," 2–3.

88 EHE, *Childhood and Society* (New York, 1950), 368*n*.; EHE, "On Student Unrest" (unpublished brochure, 1969), 210, E-H, with Bellagio remarks. Robert J. Lifton, "Protean Man," *Partisan Review* 35 (1968): 1–27, and Robert J. Lifton, "Protean Man," *Archives of General Psychiatry* 24 (1971): 298–304.

89 Robert J. Lifton, "Visit with Erikson in Belvedere," 15; Robert J. Lifton, PI by LJF, NYC, April 3, 1991.

90 Harland Bloland, TI by LJF, December 20, 1995, on the luncheon that Kennedy hosted. *Washington Post,* May 2, 1973, on the State Department dinner, and May 1, 1973, on pseudospeciation and responding to the *New York Times* reporter.

91 Lois Murphy, *Gardner Murphy: Integrating, Expanding and Humanizing Psychology* (Jefferson, N. C., 1990), 169, on radio broadcasts of the Jefferson Lectures that Erikson gave. EHE, "The Jefferson Lectures," May 1, 1973, tape, E-H, evidencing several jokes.

92 Robert J. Lifton, "Visit with Erikson in Belvedere," 5, "but I don't want to use names." EHE, *Dimensions,* 95, "events in this city . . . the pervasive power"; 110–11, "the sudden shift" and "overadjust[ed] to power" (emphasis Erikson's). See also EHE, *Dimensions,* 93–94.

93 EHE, *Dimensions,* 99–100, "the geopolitical"; 80–81, "How can we really grasp . . . our moral malaise." EHE, "The Jefferson Lectures," May 2, 1973 (tape), E-H, "How can we . . . the Holocaust, Hiroshima, the moon landings." EHE, *Dimensions,* 118, "emphasis from what"; 32–33, "abhors our excesses" and "still looks to America"; 81, "industrial complexes"; 32, "over having transgressed"; 100, "the *inner liberation*"; 81, "to be activated by."

94 EHE, *Dimensions,* 44, linking Gandhi and Jefferson; 73, on "earth . . . bounded by property lines" that must "mean to us."

95 Ibid., 25, "tentatively advocated colonization" and "the status of"; 70–71, discussing Jefferson's letter to Martha.

96 Ibid., 32, "a wider human" and "practical as well as intellectual racism"; 73–74, "the earth belongs," "each child," and "the right to live"; 123, "optimal communal units" and "direct personal"; 72, "odious peculiarities."

97 Ibid., 21, on Jefferson as orator and leader; 95–96, "if given leeway"; 110, "to face the worst"; 71, "the informed love." Pamela Daniels, TRI by LJF, Boston, March 15, 1991, on Erikson whistling the "Star Spangled Banner." In my close examination of the tape recording of his NEH lectures, E-H, I came across the start of a whistle.

98 EHE, *Dimensions,* 40–41, 47–49. For useful background discussion of Jefferson's compilations on Jesus, see Charles B. Sanford, *The Religious Life of Thomas Jefferson* (Charlottesville, Va., 1984), 102–103.

99 EHE, *Dimensions,* 41, depending on Jefferson's *Life and Morals.* . . . Letter from Fawn Brodie to EHE, October 16, 1973, E-H. Steven Wieland, "Jefferson and Erikson, Politics and the Life Cycle," *Biography* 9 (Fall 1986): 298, on Erikson's identity with Jefferson's interest in Jesus' precepts.

100 EHE, *Dimensions,* 98, "age of nuclear"; 97, "the ritualization of warfare"; 96, repression within the self; 31, "no nation with superweaponry." EHE, Jefferson Lectures, May 2, 1973, E-H, "take care of" and "TAKE CARE" and a respectful level of applause; EHE, *Dimensions,* 123, "personal and communal"; 124, on the Hindu "maintenance of the world" and "the only adult meaning."

101 Letter from EHE to Fawn Brodie, October 12, 1973, E-H, "a most difficult summer." EHE, *Dimensions,* 8, on revising the lectures into a book. Letters from EHE to Charles Strozier, July 25, 1974, E-H, on recurrent eye troubles, and EHE to George P. Brockway, March 20, 1974, E-H, on the dust jacket.

102 Letter from EHE to Wallace B. Edgerton, September 24, 1974, E-H. David Gutmann, "Erik Erikson's America," *Commentary* 58, no. 3 (September 1974): 60–64; letter from

EHE to editor, *Commentary* (n.d.), E-H. Edwin M. Yoder, Jr., review in *National Review* 26, no. 35 (August 16, 1974): 936

103 Donald Lamm, TI by LJF, July 1, 1996, on sales figures for *Dimensions*. Letter from John Demos to EHE, October 28, 1973, E-H (emphasis Demos's). Robert Coles review in *American Journal of Orthopsychiatry* (July 1974): 639–40.

104 Robert J. Brugger review in *Journal of American History* 61, no. 4 (March 1975): 1092. Letter from William Sloane Coffin to EHE, July 2, 1973. E-H.

CHAPTER 9
PUBLIC AND PRIVATE MATTERS OF OLD AGE

1 EHE, *Life History and the Historical Moment* (New York, 1975), 10. Letter from EHE to George P. Brockway, December 10, 1976, E-H, on introducing each essay.

2 Letter from EHE to George P. Brockway, December 10, 1976, E-H, "my least successful." Letter from EHE to Kurt von Fritz, December 20, 1976, E-H, culture hero, " as a straw man," and "take pot shots." David Lipset, "The Missing Identity," *The New Leader* 58, no. 15 (July 21, 1975): 25–26.

3 Interviews of Hunt and Elkind in Milton Senn Oral History Collection in Child Development, 1967–75, National Library of Medicine. James O. Phelps, "Observations and Methodological Comments on the Writings of Erik Erikson in Two of His Books" (n.d. [early 1970s]), E-H, 2.

4 Frank E. Manuel, "The Use and Abuse of Psychology in History," *Daedalus* 100, no. 1 (Winter 1971): 199. Letter from Howard Kushner to LJF, December 9, 1992, and Kushner, "Encounters with Erikson," November 9, 1992 (memorandum for LJF). Fred Weinstein and Gerald M. Platt, "The Coming Crisis in Psychohistory," *Journal of Modern History* 47, no. 2 (June 1975): 213. Patrick P. Dunn review in *History of Childhood Quarterly* 3, no. 2 (Fall 1975): 305. "Interview with John Demos," *The Historian* 55 (Spring 1993): 438, 441.

5 Suzanne R. Kirscher, "The Assenting Echo: Anglo-American Values in Contemporary Psychoanalytic Developmental Psychology," *Social Research* 57, no. 4 (Winter 1990): 827, on the three trends in ego/self psychology. John M. Ross and Wayne A. Meyers, eds., *New Concepts in Psychoanalytic Psychotherapy* (Washington, D.C., 1988), 175, citing Kernberg deploying Erikson on "identity diffusion." Paul Roazen, "Transmission: Tausk, Erikson, and Helene Deutsch," *Le Cadre de L'Analyse* (Paris, 1994), 16, on interviewing Winnicott about Erikson. See Geoffrey Cocks, ed., *The Curve of Life: Correspondence of Heinz Kohut, 1923–1981* (Chicago and London, 1994), 24, 136, 224, 239, and Paul H. Ornstein, ed., *The Search for the Self: Selected Writings of Heinz Kohut* (New York, 1978), vol. 1, 443 *n*.11, 471–72 *n*.4, for Kohut's snipes at Erikson. For Erikson's general reaction to these criticisms, see, e.g., EHE, "On the Generational Cycle: An Address," *International Journal of Psycho-Analysis* 61, no. 2 (1980): 216; EHE and JE, "On Generativity and Identity: From a Conversation with Erik and Joan Erikson," *Harvard Education Review* 51, no. 2 (May 1981): 266. For Erikson's distress with Kohut's barbs, see letter from EHE to Peter Homans, December 3, 1979, E-H, "he simply tries," and Margaret Brenman-Gibson, TRI by LJF, Stockbridge, March 23, 1991. Kurt R. Eissler, *Discourse on Hamlet: A Psychoanalytic Inquiry* (New York, 1971), 518, and the response in Erikson's "Eissler's Hamlet" (n.p., n.d.), E-H. The poll is reported in Charles K. Hofling and Robert W. Meyers, "Recent Discoveries in Psychoanalysis," *Archives of General Psychiatry* 26, no. 6 (1972): 521.

6 Erich Fromm, *The Crisis of Psychoanalysis: Essays on Freud, Marx, and Social Psychology* (New York, 1970), 21; see also Fromm and Michael Maccoby, *Social Character in a Mexican Village* (New York, 1990), 20 *n*.27. Tony Smith, "Social Violence and Conservative Social Psychology: The Case of Erik Erikson" (n.d. [1973]), E-H, 8-12, 16, 18, 21–22, and Smith, "Social Violence and Conservative Social Psychology," *Journal of Peace*

Research 13, no. 1 (1976): 5, 7–8. Joel Kovel, "Erik Erikson's Psychohistory," *Social Policy* 4 (March-April 1974): 60–64.

7 Erikson's distressed response from firsthand observation is reported in a letter from Howard Kushner to LJF, December 6, 1992. EHE, "Editor's Preface," *The Challenge of Youth* (New York, 1965), xii, "we must refuse"; EHE, *Insight and Responsibility: Lectures on the Ethical Implications of Psychoanalytic Insight* (New York, 1964), 156, "True *adaptation*." Letters from David Riesman to EHE, May 23, 1963, and EHE to Riesman, May 31, 1963, DRP.

8 Karen Offen, "Defining Feminism: A Comparative Historical Approach" *Signs* 14, no. 11 (Autumn 1988): 122–24, 135–38, 141–42, 148, 155, brilliantly elaborates the Anglo-American versus the continental European contrast in feminism of the early 1970s.

9 Naomi Weisstein, Kinder, Kuche, Kirche *as Scientific Law: Psychology Constructs the Female* (New England Free Press, pamphlet, 1968), reprinted in Anne Koedt, ed., *Radical Feminism* (New York, 1973), 178–97. Weisstein is cogently discussed in Ellen Herman, *The Romance of American Psychology: Political Culture in the Age of Experts* (Berkeley, Los Angeles, 1995), 280–82. Kate Millett, *Sexual Politics* (New York, 1970), 211, 215, 219, 328. Herman, *Romance,* 289, on the "Radical Caucus."

10 Germaine Greer, *The Female Eunuch* (New York, 1971), 88. Elizabeth Janeway, *Man's World, Woman's Place: A Study in Social Mythology* (New York, 1971), 8, 13, 93, 95. Judith Hole and Ellen Levine, *Rebirth of Feminism* (New York, 1971), 178. Phyllis Chesler, *Women and Madness* (New York, 1972, 1989), 76–77. Susan Farber, "Sex Differences in the Development of Intrusive and Incorporative Behaviors" (n.d. [early 1970s]), E-H, presents one of the earliest studies disconfirming Erikson. George Brockway, TI by LJF, January 29, 1994.

11 Letters from EHE to Karolyn Gould, November 22, 1971, E-H, "women writers" and "so angered by," and EHE to editor, *Innovation,* November 2, 1971, "there is much." The EHE reply at the Berkeley forum is written across Sheila Ballantyne to EHE, February 5, 1975, E-H. Letter from EHE to Jean Strouse, October 24, 1972, E-H, and Jean Strouse, ed., *Women and Analysis: Dialogues on Psychoanalytic Views of Femininity* (New York, 1974). The EHE–Robert J. Lifton discussion, November 19, 1970, RJL-NYPL, illustrates how feminist attacks pained Erikson.

12 For good discussions of the shift toward a "culturalist" perspective among feminists, see Alice Echols, *Daring to Be Bad: Radical Feminism in America, 1967–1975* (Minneapolis, 1989), 244, 283; Herman, *Romance,* 391 *n.*78; Linda Kerber, "Separate Spheres, Female Worlds, Woman's Place: The Rhetoric of Women's History," *Journal of American History* 75, no. 1 (June 1988): 14. Nancy Chodorow, "Being and Doing," in *Woman in Sexist Society: Studies in Power and Powerlessness* (New York, 1971), 259–91, and Chodorow, *The Reproduction of Mothering: Psychoanalysis and the Sociology of Gender* (Berkeley, 1978), especially 229 *n.*18, criticizing Erikson.

13 Carol Gilligan, TRI by LJF, Cambridge, April 15, 1991, detailed her relationship to Erikson and how her thinking evolved differently from his for the paper she prepared in the winter of 1975. It became "In a Different Voice: Women's Conceptions of Self and Morality," *Harvard Educational Review* 47, no. 4 (November 1977): especially 481–82, 509, 514–15. Gilligan enlarged this into *In a Different Voice* (Cambridge, 1982), and notes Erikson on 12–13, 17, 98. Gilligan, TRI by LJF, Cambridge, April 15, 1991, and JE, TRI by LJF, Cambridge, December 18, 1990, on Erikson's reactions to the Gilligan attacks. Sue Bloland, TI by LJF, May 24, 1997, discussing her own development with Erikson.

14 EHE, "Autobiographic Notes on the Identity Crisis," *Daedalus* 99, no. 4 (Fall 1970): 736, citing Freud's "An Autobiographic Study" at age sixty-eight; 734, 738, 742, beginning with Vienna training and then dropping back to his earlier years. Letter from EHE to Eugene B. Borowitz, March 8, 1976, E-H, "that autobiography is." Erikson wrote "uncomfortable about" on his copy of a letter by Jürgen von Scheid to EHE (n.d. [1974]), E-H.

15 Letter from EHE to Maria Piers, December 3, 1976, E-H, on the autobiographical essay being intended to shed light on his identity concept. EHE, "Gandhi's Autobiography: The Leader as a Child," *American Scholar* 34, no. 3 (Autumn 1966): 636. EHE, *Young Man Luther: A Study in Psychoanalysis and History* (New York, 1958), 53, "official identity." Graduate student Michael Currey prepared for me a very precise, exacting comparison of the autobiographical essay in its 1970 *Daedalus* form with its form in Gerald Holton, ed., *The Twentieth-Century Sciences* (New York, 1972), 3–21, and with the way it appeared in *Life History and the Historical Moment*. See Currey, "Revision and Self-Revelation: A Comparison of Three Versions of an Autobiographical Essay by Erik Erikson" (n.p. [1993]).

16 EHE, *Life History*, 142, "nobody likes." Letter from EHE to Betty J. Lifton, March 17, 1975, E-H, "what I have wished." All three versions of Erikson's autobiography present the six-stage review of his life.

17 Marshall Berman, TI (taped) by LJF, July 22, 1991, and TRI by LJF, NYC, November 3, 1995.

18 Marshall Berman, TI by LJF, July 2, 1991, and TRI by LJF, November 3, 1995. Marshall Berman, *The Politics of Authenticity: Radical Individualism and the Emergence of Modern Society* (New York, 1970), especially 84, 312–21.

19 John Leonard, "Confessions of a Cultural Commissar: Why One Quits the *New York Times Book Review*," *Esquire* 84, no. 5 (November 1975): 81–83, 187–90, provides cogent comments on his period as editor. Marshall Berman, TI by LJF, July 22, 1991, and PI by LJF, November 3, 1995, on his contact with Leonard and coming to be asked to review *Life History*. See also Henry Gollob, TI by LJF, November 8, 1995, Harrison E. Salisbury, *Without Fear or Favor: The New York Times and Its Times* (New York, 1980), 85–86, and especially Thomas Weyr, "The Making of the *New York Times Book Review*," *Publishers Weekly* (July 31, 1972), 36–49, on Leonard and his proclivities.

20 Weyr, "Making of *NYTBR*," 41, quoting the Brockway letter. Leonard, "Confessions of a Cultural Commissar," 187–90, on pressures he felt as *Book Review* editor. There are abundant sources on the growing critique of the New Left. See, e.g., Irving Howe and Carl Gershman, eds., *Israel, the Arabs, and the Middle East* (New York, 1972), especially 428–30, its reprint of Howe's "The Campus Left and Israel," an op-ed piece from the *New York Times*. Seymour Martin Lipset, "The Socialism of Fools," *New York Times Magazine*, July 3, 1971, 6–7, 26–34. See also the detailed citations of articles in Noam Chomsky's *Peace in the Middle East? Reflections on Justice and Nationhood* (New York, 1974), 153–98.

21 Leonard, "Confessions of a Cultural Commissar," 187–90, on pressures on him within the *Times* leading to his decision to quit. Leonard, PI by LJF, April 28, 1996, noting the Berman controversy was but one of several in which he found himself involved at the time as editor.

22 Marshall Berman, personal notes and draft paragraphs for his *New York Times Book Review* essay, Berman private papers. Berman, TI (taped) by LJF, July 21, 1991, and PI by LJF, NYC, November 3, 1995, on writing and finalizing the review.

23 Berman review in *New York Times Book Review*, March 30, 1975, 1–2.

24 Ibid., 22.

25 Ibid.

26 Margaret Brenman-Gibson, TRI by LJF, Stockbridge, March 31, 1991; Helmut Wohl, TRI by LJF, Boston, April 24, 1991; and Robert J. Lifton, PI by LJF, NYC, April 3, 1991, indicating how close friends felt that much of the Berman critique was valid.

27 John Thornton, PI by LJF, Bloomington, August 18, 1994, on "the Man who Invented" caption upsetting Erikson most. Letters from EHE to Kurt von Fritz, December 20, 1976, E-H, and EHE to Siegfried Unseld, April 23, 1976, E-H, "The review was nasty" and "did raise questions."

28 Letter from EHE to editor, *New York Times Book Review* (n.d. [1975]; unsent), E-H. Letter from EHE to George P. Brockway, May 5, 1975, E-H, on Brockway convincing him

not to send the *Times* letter and on Berman's distressing response to those who published letters defending Erikson. Kai Erikson, TI by LJF, June 29, 1997, on writing to the *Times*. *New York Times Book Review,* May 4, 1975, 56–58, with letters defending Erikson and Berman's response to them.

29 Letters from EHE to Brockway, May 5, 1976, E-H, adding the phrase "which I kept," and May 30, 1976, with even more elaboration for revision.

30 Letters from EHE to Ruth Hirsch, April 1, 1975, E-H, and EHE to Ellen Katz, October 15, 1976, E-H.

31 EHE, "Memorandum," June 1975, Anna Freud Papers, LC, 96.

32 Letter from EHE to "Dear Friend," July 31, 1975, E-H.

33 Erikson's August 1977 general letter in E-H was titled "Further Autobiographic Remarks: For Friends and Relations Only." The undated 1978 version, "Notes on My Parentage," is also in E-H.

34 Fawn Brodie review of *Life History* in *Los Angeles Times Book Review,* April 2, 1975, 10.

35 Letter from Donald S. Lamm to LJF, October 26, 1995, detailed Erikson's book sales figures, taking them from W. W. Norton records, and sought to explain the decline. Useful, too, were George Brockway, TI by LJF, January 29, 1994, and November 16, 1995, and Donald S. Lamm, TI by LJF, October 31, 1995.

36 Letters from Kimberly Wiar to Marshall Berman, April 22, 1975, Marshall Berman private papers; Joel Carmichael to Berman, April 1, 1975 (*Midstream* editor), and Leonard Fein to Berman, April 2, 1975 (*Moment* editor), both in Marshall Berman private papers. Letters from Lionel Trilling to Berman, March 31, 1975, Marshall Berman private papers; Bruce Mazlish to Berman, April 7, 1975, Marshall Berman private papers; Todd Gitlin to Berman, March 30, 1975, Marshall Berman private papers; Jacob A. Arlow to Berman, April 1, 1975, Marshall Berman private papers.

37 Letters from John S. Thornton to editors, *New York Times Book Review,* April 4, 1975, Marshall Berman private papers, and John M. Payne to John Leonard, April 30, 1975, E-H. Mark Gerzon in *NYTBR,* May 4, 1975, E-H; and letters from John M. Ross to *NYTBR,* April 14, 1975, E-H; Ortiz M. Walton to *NYTBR,* April 23, 1975, Marshall Berman private papers; and Martin Kilson to *NYTBR,* March 31, 1975, Marshall Berman private papers.

38 Paul Roazen, "Erik Erikson as a Teacher," *Michigan Quarterly Review* (Winter 1992): 32, recalling his connections to Erikson at Harvard; "I was never." See also letter from Paul Roazen to EHE, June 6, 1965, E-H; Pamela Daniels, TRI by LJF, Boston, March 15, 1991; Gordon Fellman, TRI by LJF, February 19, 1991.

39 Paul Roazen, *Erik H. Erikson: The Power and Limits of a Vision* (New York, 1976), vii–ix ("critical scrutiny" and "what is of enduring"). In 1997, this Roazen book was reissued in paperback by Jason Aronson, Inc. Roazen, "Erikson as a Teacher," 30, "did little" in rewriting his book on Erikson. Roazen, PI by LJF, Cambridge, February 23, 1991, on his responses to the Berman review, including rewriting his book more negatively. Letter from Paul Roazen to Marshall Berman, May 1, 1975, Marshall Berman private papers, on the review essay. Roazen, "Erik H. Erikson's Post-Freudianism" (n.p., n.d.), illustrated Roazen's more positive view of Erikson before the Berman review.

40 Roazen, *Erikson,* 97, "disguising," see also 95; 58, "calculated to"; 165, "Erikson's fundamental outlook"; 49, "remained publicly silent"; see also 44–46, 91, 172–73, on Erikson as architect for social adjustment.

41 Letters from James W. Anderson to EHE, September 29, 1978, E-H; EHE to Nicholas Piediscalzi, October 28, 1977, E-H, "Believe it"; EHE to George P. Brockway, December 10, 1976, E-H, "never consulted" and "quotes so many"; EHE to Kurt von Fritz, December 20, 1976, E-H, "destroying all"; EHE to Maria Piers, October 13, 1976, and May 9, 1977, "the evident lack"—both in E-H. EHE, "Memorandum for the Freud Archives" (n.d. [March 1977]; sent October 1977), E-H; this concerns Roazen's more well known book, *Freud and His Followers* (New York, 1975).

42 Letter from EHE to Peter Blos, November 4, 1974, E-H. Martha Proctor, TRI by LJF,
Tiburon, September 13, 1995, on the Eriksons' two Tiburon houses, which she took me
to visit. Robert J. Lifton, "Visit with Erik Erikson in Belvedere, March 23, 1973," 1,
RJL-NYPL. Letter from Robert S. Wallerstein to LJF, August 5, 1996, detailing the history of Tiburon and describing the Eriksons' two houses, which I later visited.

43 Martha Proctor, TRI by LJF, September 13, 1995, on Joan making the house offer. Sue
Bloland, TI by LJF, December 20, 1995, detailing the course of the Cogan relationship.
A sense of increasing financial worries can also be drawn from the letters from EHE to
Richard Newman, June 7, 1976, E-H, and Cogan, Bell & Company to EHE and JE,
August 22, 1977, E-H; Robert Wallerstein, PI by LJF, San Francisco, August 13, 1990.

44 Letter from EHE to Kurt von Fritz, March 18, 1974, E-H, "to get people." Erikson's correspondence pattern as a celebrity tends to dominate the Houghton Library's Erikson
collection and is typified by EHE to Alan Vaughan, April 4, 1979, EHE to Barbara
Visser, July 7, 1975, and EHE to Rodney G. Triplet, March 20, 1981. Mary Carswell, TI
by LJF, January 19, 1996, on Califano. Jane Howard, *Margaret Mead: A Life* (New York,
1984), 383, quotes Mead.

45 Joan's hip surgery is discussed in the letters from EHE to Noel Annan, January 7, 1974,
E-H, and EHE to Kurt von Fritz, March 18, 1974, E-H; and in John Thornton, PI by
LJF, Bloomington, Ind., August 18, 1994. For Joan's supervision of healthful living, see,
e.g., letter from JE to Margaret Brenman-Gibson, November 11, 1974, Brenman-Gibson
private papers; EHE, TRI by Brenman-Gibson, Tiburon, April 1, 1983, transcript
31–32; Martha Proctor, TRI by LJF, Tiburon, September 13, 1995; Jon Erikson, PI by
LJF, Harwich, June 14, 1994, and TI by LJF, August 31, 1996.

46 Erik's declining hearing is noted in Sue Bloland, TRI by LJF, NYC, July 9, 1994, and
Jean Dietz, "Through the Years of Erik Erikson," *Boston Globe,* November 6, 1980. His
eye difficulties are described in the letters from EHE to Peter Blos, November 4, 1974, E-
H, "influences my mood," and EHE to David D. Van Tassel, October 10, 1975, E-H;
and in John Thornton, PI by LJF, Bloomington, Ind., August 18, 1994. The prostate
surgeries and long-term urinary tract difficulties are noted in letters from EHE to John
Klauber, March 13, 1974, E-H, and EHE to Anna Freud, March 10, 1975, Anna Freud
Papers, LC, 96; and JE, TRI by LJF, Harwich, October 20, 1994; Sue Bloland, TRI by
LJF, NYC, July 9, 1994. Letter from EHE to Norman Birnbaum, January 3, 1976, E-H,
"with me." John Thornton, PI by LJF, Bloomington, Ind., August 18, 1994, reporting
the "I didn't know" remark. Richard T. Kramer, TI by LJF, September 23, 1996, recalling
Erik's "My whole body" remark.

47 Joan's management of Erik's life as well as her own is covered well in Martha Proctor, TRI
by LJF, Tiburon, September 13, 1995; Nina Holton, TRI by LJF, Lexington, April 30,
1991. Their joint research on aging is discussed in the letters from EHE to Milton
Wexler, March 20, 1981, E-H, "rarely travel"; EHE to Carol Hardgrove, November 23,
1981, E-H; and EHE to McGeorge Bundy, December 7, 1978, E-H.

48 Letter from EHE to Mrs. George Curfman, Jr., December 30, 1976, "singularly able,"
"hospitable toward," and "to affirm"; John Thornton, PI by LJF, August 18, 1994; Sue
Bloland, TRI by LJF, NYC, July 9, 1994; Martha Proctor, TRI by LJF, Tiburon, September 13, 1995; Robert Wallerstein, TI by LJF, June 20, 1996.

49 Robert Rubenstein, TRI by LJF, Tiburon, September 13, 1995, recalling the formation
of the group, Erikson's participation, and the water dish incident. See also Beulah Parker,
TRI by LJF, Point Richmond, Calif., October 18, 1994; letters from Robert Rubenstein
to EHE, October 17, 1978, E-H, and EHE to Rubenstein, November 17, 1978, E-H.

50 Robert Wallerstein, PI by LJF, August 13, 1990; letters from R. Wallerstein to LJF,
November 7, 1994, and EHE to Dorothy Burlingham, October 14, 1974, and (n.d.
[1980]), E-H; JE, TRI by LJF, Cambridge, March 28, 1991. Robert Rubenstein, TRI by
LJF, Tiburon, September 13, 1995, cogently comparing Wallerstein's role with Rapaport's.

51 EHE to Kurt von Fritz, October 27, 1979, E-H, "glad when our son." Letter from EHE

to Gordon N. Ray, E-H, on the Guggenheim fellowship. Jon's life in the 1970s and his relationship to his parents is described in Jon Erikson, PI by LJF, Harwich, June 14, 1994, and TI by LJF, August 29 and 31, 1996; letter from EHE to Ruth Hirsch, December 20, 1975, E-H.

52 Letters from EHE to Ellen Katz, October 15, 1976, E-H, and EHE to Ruth Hirsch, December 20, 1975, E-H. Letters from EHE to Kurt von Fritz, December 20, 1976, E-H; EHE to Wallace B. Edgerton, September 24, 1974, E-H; and EHE to Sue Bloland, January 19, 1976, E-H, on the Danforth inquiry. Sue Bloland, TRI by LJF, NYC, July 9, 1994, and letter from Sue Bloland to LJF, January 19, 1998, on her relationship to her parents, especially Erik, at the time of her divorce. Per Bloland, TI by LJF, September 11, 1996, on Erik as grandparent.

53 Letter from David Riesman to Joseph Gusfield, November 21, 1968, DRP, "much less." Margo Jefferson, "After the Flood," *Newsweek,* March 7, 1977, 90–91, "the son." Sue Bloland, TRI by LJF, NYC, July 9, 1994, and Jon Erikson, PI by LJF, Harwich, June 14, 1994, on qualities Kai felt compelled to develop as Erik's son. Letters from Kai Erikson to EHE (n.d. [1974]), E-H, "I obviously," and EHE to Kai Erikson, March 26, 1976, E-H, "Don't you think."

54 Kai and Joanna Erikson, TRI by LJF, Hamden, November 7, 1993, on contacts between their household and the elderly Eriksons' at Cotuit. Letter from EHE to Ruth Hirsch, December 20, 1975, E-H, "sensitive and." James B. Stewart and Norman Rosenberg, PI by LJF, San Francisco, April 19, 1997, on Keith. Letter from Joanna Erikson to LJF, January 16, 1998, on Erik's views concerning Keith and Christopher and the postcards.

55 EHE and Kai Erikson, "Species Divisions among Humans," Wellfleet, 1982, RJL-NYPL, "Do you want." For Kai's case against "pseudo," see letter from Kai Erikson to EHE, September 29, 1982, Kai Erikson private papers. Letter from EHE to Kai Erikson (n.d. [early 1983]), "often unconscious." See also EHE, "Memorandum on 'Pseudo-Speciation'" (n.d. [1982]), E-H. Kai Erikson has maintained a detailed file of the father-son exchange on pseudospeciation and has shared it with me.

56 Letter from EHE to Kai Erikson, December 28, 1978, E-H; EHE and Kai Erikson, "Species Divisions among Humans," Wellfleet, 1982, RJL-NYPL. Letter from EHE to Avner Falk, November 12, 1963, Falk private papers, recognizing that Kai and Jon did not have his religious interests.

57 Nina Holton, TRI by LJF, Lexington, April 30, 1991, on Erikson rambling and difficulty hearing him. Letter from EHE to David Davis (n.d.), written on Davis to EHE, September 25, 1980, E-H, on avoiding speaking engagements. Letter from EHE to Merton Gill, September 18, 1975, E-H, noting his writing difficulties. EHE interview by Richard Stevens, BBC, London, June 3, 1975, E-H, "one could be." Letter from EHE to George C. Rosenwald (n.d.), written on Rosenwald to EHE, November 28, 1973, E-H, that "I have." Letter from EHE to Ruth Hirsch, December 20, 1975, E-H, "I can't stop."

58 Letter from EHE to Ellen Katz, October 15, 1976, E-H, "Without a bit." Letter from EHE to Harry Weinstein, May 25, 1976, E-H, "a sense of being lost." EHE on old-age Wisdom in Stuart F. Spicker et al., eds., *Aging and the Elderly: Humanistic Perspectives in Gerontology* (Atlantic Highlands, 1978), 8. See M. Esther Harding, *The Way of All Women* (New York, 1970), 241, on old-age "Wisdom" by comparison.

59 EHE to "Dear Friends" (form letter to Al Emich), August 9, 1976, E-H, 11, "a certain childlikeness." Letter from EHE to Kurt von Fritz, December 17, 1979, E-H, "in advancing." Letter from EHE to H. H. Thomas, October 28, 1977, E-H, "my adult life." Letter from EHE to Frederick Wyatt, December 5, 1974, E-H, "Say hello." Letter from EHE to Kurt von Fritz, December 20, 1976; and December 17, 1979, E-H, "I am even."

60 EHE and JE, "On Generativity and Identity," 264, and Richard Hunt, TRI by LJF, Cambridge, November 22, 1991, on the origins of Erikson's article. EHE, "Reflections on Dr. Borg's Life Cycle: Lecture Notes" (n.d.), E-H, 1, "most perfect." Letter from David D. Van

Tassel to EHE, December 24, 1975, E-H, and Anne Wyatt-Brown, PI by LJF, Gainesville, April 22, 1995, on the Cleveland presentation and Volkswagen incident.

61 EHE, "Reflections on Dr. Borg's Life Cycle," *Daedalus* 105, no. 2 (Spring 1976): 4, "sunniest summers." EHE, "Reflections . . . Lecture Notes," 8, E-H, "to Find Themselves" and "all Northerners." EHE, "Reflections on Dr. Borg's Life Cycle," 23, "detached yet active." Jerald Wallulis, *The Hermeneutics of Life History: Personal Achievement and History in Gadamer, Habermas, and Erikson* (Evanston, 1990), 122, underscores the personal situatedness of the *Daedalus* essay.

62 Carol Gilligan, *In a Different Voice: Psychological Theory and Women's Development* (Cambridge, 1982), 107, and Gilligan, TRI by LJF, Cambridge, April 15, 1991. Letter from EHE to Robert P. Knight, December 29, 1950, Margaret Brenman-Gibson private papers, on "dreams of getting." Letter from EHE to Kurt von Fritz, June 1, 1979, E-H, on the Lund honorary degree invitation. EHE, "Reflections on Dr. Borg's Life Cycle," 26, "His patients"; 10, "the ethical rule"; 11, on mourning.

63 EHE, "Reflections on Dr. Borg's Life Cycle," 7, "must yet learn"; 14, "to work"; 3, "a pantheistic"; 27, "seems to restart"; 21, "go wrong." In Sanford Gifford, "Interview with Prof. Erikson and His Wife Joan," November 3, 1984 (transcript, Boston Psychoanalytic Society), Side 1, 5, Erikson insisted that Borg was like his first, meticulously procedural and scientific American psychology professor, Edwin Boring, who had experienced psychological disturbance and depression late in life.

64 EHE, "Reflections on Dr. Borg's Life Cycle," 2, 11. See also Wallulis, *Hermeneutics,* 122–23.

65 Letter from EHE to Carol Orr, November 18, 1975, E-H; Agnete Kalckar, PI by LJF, Cambridge, June 13, 1993; letter from EHE to Mark C. Taylor, September 18, 1981, E-H; EHE and JE, "On Generativity and Identity," 260.

66 EHE, "Themes from Kierkegaard's Early Life" (n.d. [1977]), E-H, 1–2, "a deeply committed." For Erikson's decision not to pursue the Kierkegaard study, see letter from Leo Goldberger to LJF, January 8, 1993; Finn Abrahamsen, TRI by LJF, Copenhagen, May 8, 1993; letter from EHE to Carol Orr, November 18, 1975, E-H.

67 EHE, "The Galilean Sayings and the Sense of 'I,' " *Yale Review* 70, no. 3 (April 1981): 357; EHE, TRI by Margaret Brenman-Gibson, Tiburon, April 1, 1983, tape 1, transcript 2.

68 Kai Erikson, TI by LJF, June 29, 1997; Pamela Daniels, TRI by LJF, Boston, April 12, 1991.

69 EHE, "The Galilean Sayings," 321–22, discovering Perrin's book. Letter from EHE to Mrs. George (Hope) Curfman, Jr., December 30, 1976, E-H, "genuine presence." John Thornton, PI by LJF, Bloomington, Ind., August 18, 1994, recalling how Erikson worked with Perrin's volume.

70 EHE, "The 'I' in Religion" (1980) was the earliest full version of what became the *Yale Review* article. The paper was talked through at the annual Wellfleet meeting, August 22, 1980, with the transcript of the presentation and discussion in the RJL-NYPL. The final published essay still represents a rough, uneven presentation. The process of preparing and revising the essay is indicated in EHE, "Reflections" (n.d.), E-H; JE, TRI by LJF, Harwich, January 15, 1994; JE, TRI by David Andersen, Cambridge, October 16, 1991; letter from EHE to Robert J. Lifton, October 13, 1981, RJL-NYPL.

71 EHE, "The 'I' in Religion," Wellfleet, August 22, 1980, RJL-NYPL, transcript 1–7, 19–21. For the flavor of this meeting, I have also listened to the tape recording (RJL-NYPL) and talked with several of the participants.

72 Ibid., 22–23. Language presented a problem for Erikson here since "I" and "eye" worked in English but not in German as *Ich* and *Auge.*

73 Ibid., 48–84, was the heavy discussion part of the session. Robert. J. Lifton, TI by LJF, August 24, 1994, recalling that Erikson appeared unnerved.

74 Kai Erikson, TI by LJF, June 29, 1997, on editing the Galilean essay. The edited draft or

"Kai's version" was EHE, "The Galilean Sayings and the Sense of 'I': Reflections" (n.d.), E-H.

75 EHE, "The Galilean Sayings," 322–23, 339, 347.

76 Ibid., 323, 326, 361. Linkages between Erikson's and the Quaker meaning of the sense of "I" are explored cogently in John S. Dunne, "The Sense of 'I' in Christianity," John A. O'Brien Inaugural Lecture, University of Notre Dame, April 1989 (South Bend, Ind., 1989), 7–8.

77 Ibid., 330, 349–55. Jacques Lacan, *Ecrits* (New York, London, 1977), 2–3, on the "mirror stage."

78 EHE, "The Galilean Sayings," 356, 361. See also EHE, *The Life Cycle Completed: A Review* (New York, 1982), 62; EHE and JE, "On Generativity and Identity," 261. Letter from EHE to Kurt von Fritz, June 1, 1979, E-H.

79 Before Hetty Zock, *A Psychology of Ultimate Concern: Erik H. Erikson's Contribution to the Psychology of Religion* (Amsterdam, 1990), there was little serious discussion of the "Galilean Sayings" article. The Houghton Library's substantial Erikson collection houses few incoming letters that even note the article. EHE, "Some Dimensions of the Sense of 'I,'" September 8, 1981, E-H.

80 EHE, *Dimensions of a New Identity* (New York, 1974), 47–49; EHE, "The Galilean Sayings," 328, 342, 345–47; EHE, "Species Divisions among Humans," Wellfleet, 1982, RJL-NYPL. David Andersen, "Beyond Rumor and Reductionism: A Textual Dialogue with Erik Erikson," *Psychohistory Review* 22, no. 1 (Fall 1993): 51–52, 55–56, provides very cogent commentary on Erikson's portrayal of Jesus' healing powers.

81 Letter from EHE to Mrs. George (Hope) Curfman, Jr., December 30, 1976, E-H. Esther Ramon, *The Homburger Family from Karlsruhe* (Jerusalem, 1992), 149–52, lists Homburgers related to Erikson who were deported to the Gurs concentration camp. Erikson was therefore quite realistic in predicting danger from the Holocaust if he had remained in Germany.

82 EHE, "The First Psychoanalyst," *Yale Review* 70, no. 3 (April 1981): 335, "a lasting sense"; 334–35, "every dimension." Elizabeth Hall, "A Conversation with Erik Erikson," *Psychology Today* (June 1983): 28, "helped to open." Letter from EHE to Mrs. George (Hope) Curfman, Jr., December 30, 1976, E-H, "shining newness" and "one's identity by." Andersen, "Beyond Rumor and Reductionism," especially 64, makes a strong case for Erikson seeing Christianity as evolution from Judaism. However, I do not accept Andersen's compelling argument.

83 Letter from EHE to David Cogan, July 6, 1982, E-H. Helmut Wohl, TRI by LJF, Boston, April 24, 1991. Erikson's increasing difficulty progressing on the Jesus volume is recounted in Sue Bloland, TRI by LJF, NYC, July 9, 1994; Margaret Brenman-Gibson, PI by LJF, Stockbridge, March 20, 1992; David Wilcox, PI by LJF, Cambridge, June 15, 1994.

CHAPTER 10
"THE SHADOW OF NONBEING"

1 EHE, *The Life Cycle Completed: A Review* (New York, 1982), 10; 24, apologizing for republication; 82, "institutional structures and." Donald S. Lamm, TI by LJF, July 1, 1996, reporting sales figures for *Life Cycle Completed* compared with other Erikson volumes. EHE, TRI by Margaret Brenman-Gibson, Tiburon, April 1, 1983, transcript 15, "I have received."

2 EHE, *Life Cycle Completed*, 10–11, on his American career and on Joan; 21, "the reductionist language" and "this century's."

3 Ibid., 96, quoting Collingwood and commenting on it; 103, proposing a massive comparative research project.

4 Ibid., 62, "in our 'middle years'" and "group of mere 'elderlies.'"

5 Ibid., 63, on old-age regression and "mourning not only"; 62, on "faith"; 73, on adolescence; 80, on adulthood and "the shadow of nonbeing"; 64, on the "final psychosexual" and "a *generalization.*"

6 Ibid., 62–63, "the last stage" and "children in viable"; 80, "the times that dream" and "the shadow."

7 Ibid., 45, "*separateness transcended*"; 40, "the human being will"; 45, "the *numinous,* the aura"; 88, "to the *ultimate other*"; 73, "infantile trust" and "mature faith." Steven Weiland, "Aging According to Biography," *The Gerontologist* 29, no. 2 (1989): 192, provides a helpful summary of Erikson's development of this perspective.

8 Joan Erikson shared with me a copy of *The Life Cycle Completed* with Erik's extensive penned corrections and revisions.

9 Letter from EHE to Richard Smoke, April 29, 1983, E-H, and EHE, JE, and Helen Q. Kivnick, *Vital Involvement in Old Age* (New York, 1986), 7–32, on the beginnings of the project that led to the book. Letter from Daniel Benveniste to LJF, June 24, 1991, recalling Kivnick's general role and her positions on Erik's life cycle perspectives. Interestingly, Joan produced an "extended version" of *The Life Cycle Completed* (New York, 1997) after Erik's death.

10 Stephen Schlein, ed., *A Way of Looking at Things: Selected Papers from 1930–1980. Erik H. Erikson* (New York, 1987); Schlein, PI by LJF, Lexington, Mass., March 4, 1991.

11 Schlein, PI by LJF, March 4, 1991; letter from EHE to David Cogan, February 8, 1983, E-H.

12 Letter from EHE to Robert J. Lifton, October 13, 1981, E-H, "you have done." Robert J. Lifton, TRI by LJF, Wellfleet, October 6, 1996, and NYC, April 3, 1991; EHE, "Wellfleet: Lifton" (n.d.), E-H; Robert J. Lifton, "The Doctors of Auschwitz: The Biomedical Vision," *Psychohistory Review* 11, no. 2–3 (Spring 1983): 46. Lifton's 1982 bird cartoon also read "For Erik—wise embodiment of elfhood, elfishness, and elfery" in response to Erikson's reference in *Young Man Luther: A Study in Psychoanalysis and History* (New York, 1958) to "monkhood, monkishness, and monkery."

13 Daniel Benveniste, "Erik H. Erikson in San Francisco" (unpublished ms., 1994), 18, on the Erikson Library. Patricia W. Lunneborg and Vicki M. Wilson, "Would You Major in Psychology Again?," *Teaching of Psychology* 12, no. 1 (February 1985): 15–17, on Erikson citations in psychology textbooks. *Austen Riggs Center News* (Winter 1984): 7–8, on the eightieth birthday celebration. EHE, "Pseudospeciation in the Nuclear Age," RJL-NYPL: his 1984 address to the American Psychiatric Association. JE, TRI by LJF, Cambridge, June 12, 1993, on how the Karlsruhe dedication of an Erikson House impressed Erik only modestly. Jerome Bruner, "The Artist as Analyst," *New York Review of Books* (December 3, 1987), 8. *Center (for Psychosocial Studies) Review* 6, no. 1 (Spring 1992): 3; the audiotape of the November 1991 recognition reception by this center provided the remarks by Mack, Lifton, and Kai Erikson.

14 For the founding of the Erikson Center, see Deane W. Lord, "The Eriksons Return to Harvard," *Harvard Gazette,* October 12, 1984, 4; Margaret Brenman-Gibson, TRI by LJF, Stockbridge, March 23, 1991; Carol Gilligan, TRI by LJF, Cambridge, April 15, 1991; JE at Austen Riggs Center, November 23, 1985, Harriet Harvey videotape. *Harvard Gazette,* October 12, 1984, 4, on the Eriksons returning to teach at the Erikson Center. JE, "55 Trowbridge Street—Financial Timeline" (n.d.), JE private papers, notes the $100,000 loan.

15 David Wilcox, PI by LJF, Cambridge, March 21, 1991, and June 15, 1994, on accompanying Austin to Tiburon. JE's needs and the Austin proposal are also discussed in Margaret Brenman-Gibson, TRI by LJF, Stockbridge, March 23, 1991; Nina Holton, TRI by LJF, Lexington, Mass., April 30, 1991.

16 JE, TRI by LJF, Cambridge, March 28, 1991; John Mack, PI by LJF, Cambridge, June 12, 1993; Julie Martino, TI by LJF, March 20, 1996. *New York Times,* June 18, 1988, C 14, "Living communally." JE, "Timeline for Trowbridge Street Purchase" (1993), and

JE, "55 Trowbridge Street—Financial Timeline" (n.d.) (both in JE private papers), detail the financial dimensions of the house purchase, with specific dollar contributions. "Joint Tenancy Agreement," April 30, 1987, JE private papers, on the conditions of joint ownership. Letter from Dorothy Austin to Donald Lamm, March 21, 1987 (copy), JE private papers, on the Norton bridge loan and other financial aspects of the Trowbridge purchase.

17 *Harvard Crimson,* November 12, 1987, 1, 3, and November 13, 1987, 3, 5, on the Kennedy School scandal implicating the Erikson Center. Context for the scandal is provided in "Harvard's Kennedy School of Government, Facing Criticisms, Examines Its Mission," *Chronicle of Higher Education* 38, no. 25 (February 26, 1992): A20. The internal division and constriction in the Erikson Center promoted by the scandal is discussed in David Wilcox, PI by LJF, Cambridge, March 21, 1991; Lewis D. Wurgaft, PI by LJF, Cambridge, March 1, 1991; Margaret Brenman-Gibson, TRI by LJF, Stockbridge, March 23, 1991; Carol Gilligan, TRI by LJF, Cambridge, April 15, 1991.

18 JE, TRI by LJF, Harwich, January 14 and October 20, 1994, and June 9, 1995; Margaret Brenman-Gibson, TRI by LJF, Stockbridge, March 23, 1991; Martha Proctor, TRI by LJF, Tiburon, September 13, 1995; Per Bloland, TI by LJF, September 11, 1996; Sue Bloland, PI by LJF, NYC, November 13, 1996.

19 Letter from Kai Erikson to LJF, January 17, 1998, and Jon Erikson, PI by LJF, Harwich, June 14, 1994, on seeing materials being thrown away without Erik objecting during the move to Cambridge. For Joan's changed role, see JE, TRI by LJF, Harwich, January 15 and October 20, 1994; Harvard Senior Seminar, "Perspectives on the Life Cycle," October 23, 1985, Harriet Harvey videotape. EHE, *The Life Cycle Completed,* 106. *Twenty Poems from the Hours: Rainer Maria Rilke,* translated by Joan M. Erikson (New York, 1988). Beulah Parker, TRI by LJF, Point Richmond, Calif., October 18, 1994, recalling hearing Erik on "Joan and I." Dorothy Austin recalled Erik's recent dinner table conduct in Erikson Recognition Reception, Cambridge, November 21, 1994 (audiotape).

20 Ruth Hirsch, TI by LJF, June 9, 1991, and Hirsch, TRI by LJF, NYC, November 8, 1993. Sue Bloland, TRI by LJF, NYC, November 8, 1993, and letter from Bloland to LJF, January 19, 1998. Jon Erikson, PI by LJF, Harwich, June 14, 1994.

21 Letter from Daniel Benveniste to LJF, July 24, 1991, on the 1987 visit with Erik, "a great oak." G. Stanley Hall, *Senescence: The Last Half of Life* (New York, 1922), 366. Benjamin Spock, TRI by LJF, Del Mar, February 23, 1994. Letter from EHE to Judy R. Platt, January 16, 1982, E-H, on a cold leading to pneumonia. JE, TI by LJF, October 12, 1993, and Sue Bloland, TRI by LJF, NYC, July 9, 1994, on Erik becoming increasingly inward and asocial.

22 Letter from EHE to Albert J. Solnit, September 1, 1983, E-H, "entirely preoccupied." Daniel Coleman, "Erikson, in His Old Age, Expands His View of Life," *New York Times,* June 14, 1988, C1, "learn to accept." Elizabeth Hall, "A Conversation with Erik Erikson," *Psychology Today* (June 1983), 24, "wonder, joy." Robert J. Lifton, "Talks with Erik Erikson on May 4, 5, 6, 1980, in Tiburon," RJL-NYPL, on making woodcuts and prints. *New York Times,* June 16, 1988, C1, "I can't imagine." Harriet Harvey, PI by LJF, Cambridge, June 16, 1994, recalling Erikson on going to heaven.

23 EHE in Stockbridge, November 24, 1985, Harvey videotape, "for every living creature" and religion providing "something that can be anticipated." EHE, *Childhood and Society* preface to thirty-fifth anniversary edition (New York, 1985), 7, "to experience something." EHE in Stockbridge, November 22, 1985, Harvey videotape, on Niebuhr and "on the border." EHE, "Draft #2 of Baltimore Remarks" (1982), E-H, 10, "a certain freedom."

24 David Wilcox, "Reflections on a Supervision," Cambridge Hospital symposium, October 29, 1994 (unpublished ms.). Wilcox, PI by LJF, Cambridge, March 21, 1991, and June 15, 1994; Wilcox, TI by LJF, June 1, 1994; e-mail from Wilcox to LJF, June 21, 1994.

25 Ibid.

26 Ibid.

27 Helmut Wohl, TRI by LJF, Boston, April 24, 1991; Margaret Brenman-Gibson, TI by LJF, April 23, 1992.

28 EHE, PI by LJF, Cambridge, March 12, 1991.

29 LJF notes on visits to the Erikson home in Cambridge, December 28, 1992, and June 12 and 13, 1993; JE, TRI by LJF, Harwich, January 15, 1994; JE, TI by LJF, June 22, 1996.

30 JE, TI by LJF, August 4, 1992; Margaret Brenman-Gibson, PI by LJF, Stockbridge, March 26, 1993, quoting "Wasn't it beautiful." LJF notes on visit to the Erikson home in Cambridge, June 12, 1993, after a trip to Copenhagen in which the Abrahamsens provided a photograph of Karla.

31 JE, PI by LJF, Cambridge, December 28, 1992, and June 14, 1993; JE, TRI by LJF, Cambridge, November 21, 1991. JE, *Legacies: Prometheus, Orpheus, Socrates* (New York, 1993). "Agreement Terminating Joint Tenancy Agreement," July 1994, JE private papers, on the Trowbridge house, with a $68,153 cash payment to the Eriksons.

32 *Harwich 1996* (Orleans, Mass., 1996), 4, summarizes Harwich history. JE, TRI by LJF, Harwich, January 14, 1994; "On Old Age: A Conversation with Joan Erikson at 92," Davidson Films (interview of August 10, 1995); JE, TI by LJF, June 22, 1996.

33 JE, TRI by LJF, Harwich, January 14, 1994, and June 9, 1995; Sue Bloland, TI by LJF, February 5, 1994; JE, *Poems* (n.p., n.d.), 48, "Cranberry Festival 1993."

34 Sue Bloland, TRI by LJF, NYC, May 9, 1995; JE, TRI by LJF, January 14, 1994, and TI, December 13, 1993.

35 LJF notes on personal visit to Rosewood Manor, Harwich, January 14, 1995, with Joan and Benforado.

36 JE, TRI by LJF, Harwich, October 20, 1994, and June 10, 1995, and PI, Harwich, July 5, 1996. "On Old Age: A Conversation with Joan Erikson at 92," Davidson Films, August 10, 1995; JE, *Poems* (n.p., n.d.), 41, quoting from "Love Song"; Jon Erikson, PI by LJF, Harwich, June 14, 1994.

37 JE, TRI by LJF, October 20, 1994, and PI by LJF, July 5, 1996; "Old Age: A Conversation with Joan Erikson at 92," Davidson Films, August 10, 1995. Letter from Kai Erikson to LJF, January 17, 1998, on both parents requesting cremation.

38 John S. Thornton, PI by LJF, Bloomington, Ind., August 18, 1994; Jon Erikson, PI by LJF, Harwich, June 14, 1994; Sue Bloland, TRI by LJF, NYC, May 15 and July 9, 1994, and TI, August 12, 1994; Ruth Hirsch, PI by LJF, Harwich, June 15, 1994. JE showed me a master list, dated May 31, 1994, consisting of her detailed plans for the service.

39 Jon Erikson, PI by LJF, Harwich, June 14, 1994. Jon referred to photographs in Margaret Brenman-Gibson, "Erik Erikson and the 'Ethics of Survival,' " *Harvard Magazine* 87, no. 2 (November-December 1984): 59–64.

40 James as quoted in Leon Edel, *Writing Lives: Principia Biographia* (New York, 1984), 43–44. Erik H. Erikson Memorial Service, Harwich, June 15, 1994, audiotape, for Thornton.

41 Erikson Memorial Service, June 15, 1994, audiotape.

42 Ibid.

43 Neil J. Smelser, "Erik Erikson as Social Scientist," *Psychoanalysis and Contemporary Thought* 19, no. 2 (1996): 207–24, represents a revised version of a January 1995 presentation at a special San Francisco Psychoanalytic Institute forum on Erikson.

44 See especially Roy Schafer, *A New Language for Psychoanalysis* (New Haven, 1976) and Donald Spence, *Narrative Truth and Historical Truth: Meaning and Interpretation in Psychoanalysis* (New York, 1982).

45 Robert J. Lifton, *The Protean Self: Human Resilience in an Age of Fragmentation* (New York, 1993), especially 1; Kenneth Gergen, *The Saturated Self: Dilemmas of Identity in Contemporary Life* (New York, 1991), 49; Philip Cushman, "Why the Self Is Empty: Toward a Historically Situated Psychology," *American Psychologist* 45, no. 5 (May 1990): 600.

Index

California Supreme Court, 251
Cambridge, Mass., 113, 114, 124, 323–24,
    394, 464–71, 480
    see also Harvard University
Cambridge Hospital, 464, 465, 468
Cambridge Scientific Club, 310
Campbell, Donald, 153
Camus, Albert, 174
"Canadian Project," 167–68
Carstairs, G. Morris, 392
Cartesian dualism, 22, 234, 240
Case Western Reserve University, 445–47
Caste and Class in a Southern Town (Dollard),
    129
Center for Psychological Studies in the Nuclear
    Age, 464
Center for the Psychological Study of Lives,
    325
change:
    identity and, 226–27
    proteanism and, 410, 478
Chesler, Phyllis, 424
Chiang Kai-shek, 245
Chicago, University of, 150, 256, 332
Chicago Review, 256
child analysis, 96–100, 129, 153
    of A. Freud, 56, 59, 62–63, 65, 66, 74–79,
        89–91, 93, 96
    in Boston, 103, 108, 112, 113, 115–19, 122
    EHE's skill in, 59, 60, 65, 95, 113,
        116–18, 129, 135, 202–3, 206
    Jean case and, 205–8, 218, 228, 268
    of Klein, 90
    play therapy in, 71–72, 117–18, 119, 122,
        135, 200–201, 202, 366, 469
childbirth, natural, 136, 208, 220
child development, 135, 262
    epigenetic, 123, 216, 218, 377
    Freudian view of, 123, 129, 131, 136, 216,
        217, 221, 222, 228, 376, 404
    Gesell's work with, 126, 127, 128
    normal, 123, 126, 151, 153–54, 207
Child Development Clinic, 125, 126–27, 155
child development movement, 117, 124–25,
    150
child guidance movement, 117, 150
Childhood and Society (Erikson), 116, 140,
    149, 158, 166–208, 213, 251, 252,
    257, 265, 283, 287, 294, 305, 326,
    351, 410, 416
    atomic bomb and, 188
    audience for, 232, 233, 237, 240–41
    checkerboard charts in, 131
    clinical cases in, 199–208
    combat marine patient, 203–5, 207, 208,
        218, 226, 235

completion of, 229–36
course adoptions of, 237, 239, 240–41
culture and personality movement and,
    135
editing of, 232
on Fanny (Yurok shaman), 189–90
foreign editions of, 233, 237, 240
Gandhi's Truth compared with, 381, 389,
    390, 392
identity crisis in, 161
impact of, 16, 240–41
Insight and Responsibility compared with,
    337, 340, 342
"Legend of Hitler's Childhood" in, 110,
    166–76, 188, 195
"Legend of Maxim Gorky's Youth" in, 44,
    190–98, 247
life cycle model in, 131, 132, 199,
    215–22, 224, 225–29, 233, 234, 238,
    239, 295
limits of critical response to, 239–40
material deleted from, 288
methodological contribution of, 240
1948 outline of, 149, 177–78, 182, 184,
    185, 229, 230, 235
as postcolonial criticism, 186, 191
publication of, 110, 174, 197, 230–33,
    237–41
"Reflections on American Identity" in,
    176–85, 188, 236
reviews of, 237–40
revised paperback edition of (1963), 237,
    240–41, 334–37, 342
royalties from, 231, 237, 255
sales of, 231, 237, 240, 241, 282, 334,
    335, 342, 351, 390, 434
on Sioux and Yurok, 184–91
as social criticism, 240
Spock's views on, 261
unifying themes of, 149, 233–34
unstructured quality of, 188–89, 233
Young Man Luther compared with, 270,
    281–82
child rearing, 136, 177, 187, 363, 379
    of Sioux, 134, 261
Children of Crisis (Coles), 403
"Children's Picture Books" (Erikson), 92
China, 345, 356–57
Chodorow, Nancy, 426
Chomsky, Noam, 430
Chowdhry, Kamla, 326, 349, 371, 417
Christianity, 341, 369
    EHE's interest in, 21, 22, 41–42, 259, 315,
        439, 440, 453–55
    existential aspects of, 41, 42, 344, 345–46,
        448